Enjoy!

Ed Burnett

THE COMPLETE DIRECT MAIL LIST HANDBOOK

Everything You Need to Know about Lists and How to Use Them for Greater Profit

Ed Burnett

PRENTICE HALL
Englewood Cliffs, New Jersey 07632

Prentice-Hall International (UK) Limited, *London*
Prentice-Hall of Australia Pty. Limited, *Sydney*
Prentice-Hall Canada, Inc., *Toronto*
Prentice-Hall Hispanoamericana, S.A., *Mexico*
Prentice-Hall of India Private Limited, *New Delhi*
Prentice-Hall of Japan, Inc., *Tokyo*
Simon & Schuster Asia Pte. Ltd., *Singapore*
Editora Prentice-Hall do Brasil, Ltda., *Rio de Janeiro*

© 1988 *by*

PRENTICE-HALL, Inc.

Englewood Cliffs, NJ

10   9   8   7   6   5   4

Library of Congress Cataloging-in-Publication Data
Burnett, Ed.
   The complete direct mail list handbook: everything you need to
know about lists and how to use them for greater profit / by Ed
Burnett.
      p. cm.
   Includes index.
   ISBN 0-13-159278-5
   1. Mailing lists—Handbooks, manuals, etc. 2. Advertising, Direct
-mail—Handbooks, manuals, etc. 3. Direct marketing—Handbooks,
manuals, etc. I. Title.
HF5863.B87 1988
658.8'4—dc19

ISBN 0-13-159278-5

PRENTICE HALL
BUSINESS & PROFESSIONAL DIVISION
A division of Simon & Schuster
Englewood Cliffs, New Jersey 07632

A Brief
Historical Note

When I started a minuscule direct-mail list business thirty years ago, there were no lasers, there were no zip codes, and third class bulk rates were priced at $10/M (a penny per piece.)

Virtually all list sources for compiled use were printed volumes—directories, rosters, membership rolls, government listings, stockholder listings, trade magazine year books, and "Who's Who" files. All lists for mailing were typed to order on four-part gummed labels and we hoped we could sell a carbon (at no extra cost) before a new source became available. At year end we held a great sale of the piles of carbons for $10/M, and counted every sale as found money.

Friendly list brokers, particularly Arthur Martin Karl of Names Unlimited, Muriel Gilmore of Names in the News, and Lew Kleid of Lewis Kleid, who found we had the largest library of sources for compiled files in the city, plied us with welcome orders. I once tried to first commission, then make a contribution to, Kleid's "favorite charity." Lew declined saying, "You are my favorite charity, Ed." It took me several years to return that favor.

The list business was good to my growing firm, and we moved eastward from Sixth Avenue to Fifth Avenue to Madison Avenue to Park Avenue. Rents then escalated 300 percent, which led us with our sister business in the computerization of lists to our own 22,000 square foot plant in Englewood, New Jersey. After walking to work from Greenwich Village for twenty-seven years I am now a full-fledged reverse commuter.

Along the way I have had some stellar lights in the list business today as partners. First there was Stan Woodruff, now chairman of Computer Directions, then Donn Rappaport and Lisa Price, now owners of American List Council, and for the past ten years, Paul Goldner, president of PAGEX SYSTEMS.

Over the years I have brought a fair part of what is written here to over 5,000 "seminarians" on three continents and have seen one of these seminars turned into the first videotape seen by thousands more. I have had the privilege of adding the fifth character and several thousand business classifications to the Standard Industrial Classification system, initiated the utilization of the fifth digit of zip for selection purposes and created the entire business of list management, which is now the dominant means of bringing mail responsive lists to the market.

This book has been made possible by support given by Paul Goldner of PAGEX who has reviewed all its pages and helped me remove some of the tracks left by segmented gremlins. Without Al Ambrosino at the helm of our list business to relieve me of a good portion of the daily pressures, there never would have been enough time to bring this book to its current state. Special thanks are due to Renee Finkel, secretary and angel, who shepherded over 1,300 sheets of my miserable scribbling which she alone could decipher and convert into something resembling a manuscript. And a deep vote of thanks to my production editor Eve Mossman and copy editor Denise Gannon who so painstakingly reviewed every word and helped me understand the need for extra clarification on about every third page.

A letter in our directory of lists (available for the asking) notes that we have placed over 150,000 list orders to provide over 2,000,000,000 names. I would be derelict if I did not express my gratitude to the thousands of mailers and would-be mailers who have discussed needs, and not lists, and markets, and not lists, and marketing, and not lists, and have thus, along with several consultative clients provided me with a post graduate education in this fascinating field. Without their generous help this book could not be possible.

I also wish to thank the editors of *Direct Marketing and Folio,* and *Industrial Marketing* magazines for permission to adapt articles initially published by them. Plus special thanks to Jack Oldstein. A special vote of thanks goes to Joe Fitz Morris and Ray Schultz, editors of *DM News* who have seen fit to provide me with a forum for a series of articles on the mailing list business over the past years and which are now in part finding their way back into print under the banner of Prentice Hall.

New York-1988

Introduction

This book starts off and ends on the same note—the problems and pitfalls of the direct-response industry. There are good reasons for these problems and pitfalls. If you get no further than the first fifteen pages you will, at the least, be warned that most of the glowing press surrounding how easy it is to profit in direct response is far from a valid picture.

Direct response is a rare business that offers something few other industries can offer—there is something new to learn about it every day. Direct-mail practitioners, even those with years of experience, can be heard saying over and over again, "I wish I had known that last week." Education is a continuing and continuous process. The section on "How to Educate Yourself" offers some help in this regard. However, you cannot learn everything about direct response from books or magazines. You must learn about it by being involved with activities that induce mail responses.

If I had only one minute to talk to new entrants to this field I would stress one aspect in particular, and that is the mathematics of direct response. The number of mailers in America who can with, some certainty, calculate the cost to buy a new customer and the lifetime worth of that customer, is still surprisingly small. This is a field where art and science are melded. The art, of course, is found in the infinities of creativity—copy, format, packages, offers—not to mention the selection of lists.

The science comes from the control of all aspects of costs plus the detailed capture and correlation of data from time, item, amount, source, method of payment, and historical pattern arranged mathematically in cells.

The Primer which is discussed in Chapter 2 puts into a few pages the essential facts you need to know about direct mail. There are fifteen "How To" chapters plus coverage, in some depth, of over thirty five kinds of lists. You will find a good introduction to such relatively esoteric subjects as penetration analysis, dealerization, databases, data banks, merge–purge, and the essential activities of catalog operations, as well as the distinction between teleprospecting and telemarketing.

Finally, the current problems faced by those who own, manage, broker, and rent mailing lists are listed and some predictions are hazarded about the future—a future in which those who utilize what is presented here as a map through the mine fields of this unique business will do better than those who must perforce repeat the same errors of the unwary.

Now I wish you much pleasure, much joy, and much personal fulfillment in your work in the field of direct response.

About the Author

During the course of his thirty-year career in the direct-mail business, Ed Burnett has helped mailers select over 2 billion names. He is president of Ed Burnett Consultants, Inc., a firm specializing in direct-mail consultation, compilation, and management, and he is widely recognized as the pioneer of many of the list-marketing concepts and techniques used throughout the industry today.

Ed Burnett created the business of list management more than twenty-five years ago. Today, well over 70 percent of all mailing lists are in the hands of list managers—many of the major ones were trained originally by the Burnett organization.

Unhappy with the limitations of the conventional four-digit S.I.C. system, Burnett designed and implemented the fifth-digit S.I.C. which is now prominently featured in the directories of every major compiled business list marketer in the field.

Ed Burnett originated the use of fifth-digit zip for sample selection and, in 1963, he wrote the first commercial computer letter (upper case only).

In 1978, MASA named Ed Burnett their "Main of the Year." In 1983 they honored him with the L.U. "Luke" Kaiser Educational Award.

DMA's List Council also honored him in 1983 with an official presentation of the "List Leader" Award at List Day in New York, the first time such an award has been presented by the DMA.

Ed Burnett gives ten seminars a year on the art of mailing list selection and use, and counsels such Fortune 500 clients as Xerox, IBM, and AT&T on direct-response marketing. He is a prolific writer for major trade journals, a frequent keynote speaker at industry functions, and he served as an industry representative on the Technical Advisory Committee to the Postmaster General for three years.

Contents

14   *Database versus Data Bank: A Look at What They Can Do for the List User*   *513*

15   *The How To's of Marketing for Catalog Operations*   *543*

CHAPTER 1

Some Easy Lessons on How to Fail in Direct Mail

The President of the United States has only two problem areas—domestic relations and international relations. A direct marketer, particularly a beginner in the field, must learn to cope with many more problem areas including:

- What product or service to offer
- What cost to pay and what price to sell at
- What appeals to use and what offers to make
- What markets are available and which ones to reach out for
- What use, if any, to make of classifieds, space advertising, cardvertisers, radio, TV, and co-ops
- How to test and when to make rollouts
- How to calculate order margin, breakeven, half life, cost to buy a customer, and lifetime value

Admittedly, this is quite a lineup and we haven't yet broached the esoterics of the cost of money or return on investment, and all those other nice measures that banks and backers for some reason seem to dote on.

This chapter is full of rules—they're here to provide you with guidelines at the start; so you can reap the most benefit from the rest of this book. Use them well.

TWO EASY RULES TO REMEMBER ABOUT DIRECT MAIL

Making a sales call through direct mail at a price tag of 25¢ to 35¢ per unit looks very attractive when compared with the typical person-to-person sales call now costing well over $175.00. But there is mail that works and mail that doesn't, and mail may not be the way to go.

So, *Rule #1* for direct marketers is to determine your objective first, then find out whether direct mail is the best, or only one of the ways to reach that objective. Don't leap into a new marketing venture without a written plan—and a budget.

Rule #2 is to *lean on the experts.* You can find out enough in a few phone calls to knowledgeable specialists to tell whether you are equipped to run a direct-response operation without the help of a consultant. If a large sum is involved, buy the best consultant you can locate. If the world doesn't rest on the result of a given test, you may wish, for cost considerations, to wing it yourself. (However, if it involves direct mail, at least *talk* to experts in the list business. They can improve almost any result you can obtain by yourself by a significant multiplier.) Preferably, do not plan and create the *final* direct-mail package yourself. Do sketch out for the specialist what you wish to say, show, and feature, so your input and feel get into the piece your prospect sees.

Perhaps you should take heart from the fact that over 800,000 establishments (including 300,000 nonprofit operations) do enough direct mail to take out a permit to be allowed to mail at the third-class bulk-discount rate. And it is certainly true that every half hour a new entrepreneur places direct-response ads or enters direct-response pieces into the mailstream for the first time. There are literally thousands of start-ups in this field every year.

BASIC ERRORS OF DIRECT MAIL—AND TIPS
ON AVOIDING THEM

The majority of start-ups are destined to fail primarily because of lack of basic knowledge. This is a field in which a little knowledge is truly dangerous. It is not enough to have a product or service you think a given segment of the market wants or is willing to pay for. In fact, it is reasonably certain that the average person who is intrigued with the great profits to be made by selling direct to consumers or to businesses does not know most of the following facts about this fascinating business:

1. Cold prospecting to outside mailing lists rarely produces enough responses to produce a profit. It is almost always necessary to "buy the customer" at

a loss, and then amortize that loss through additional sales of the same or different products or services. Hence single product sales are hazardous, unless there are good conditions for repeat sales.

2. A "continuous series of one experiment"—one mailing of one offer to one list—is a dangerous way to start. All it tells you is what *that* mailing with *that* offer did when mailed to *that* segment of a particular list.

3. Buying catalogs of merchandise to be drop shipped is a kiss of death. If the owner of the catalog who makes a profit on the printing as well as a profit on the merchandise has not been able to mail the catalog successfully to outside lists, what reason does the unsuspecting buyer have to think this "easy way in" is likely to succeed? (Our firm will not even furnish a list for such a mailing.)

4. In general, it is remarkably difficult with a new catalog or a new solo mail offer to obtain over $600 of gross revenue per 1,000 pieces in the mail. This holds almost irrespective of the average size of the offer. For example, a typical one-day seminar pegged at $150 can probably produce up to three orders per thousand. A typical three-day seminar priced at $500 rarely produces even one order per thousand!

5. Direct mail is a business in which one-tenth of 1 percent may be the difference between profit and loss. *Direct mail is a discipline that features very large differences in very small numbers derived from very large universes.* The difference between three orders per thousand and four orders per thousand is only one order per thousand—one-tenth of a percent. Yet four orders in this example are 33 percent better than three orders. In direct mail, such finite differences are extremely important.

6. Do not think that one or two mailings put you in the direct-mail business. The business of direct mail is to create customers, not sales, and that means making a profit by selling customers something new over and over again.

7. *Don't make the mistake of thinking that direct mail is easy, that anyone can make a go of it.*

   More and more this is a business for pros who know products, markets, media, the mathematics of direct response marketing, the mystique of computers, and back-end control. The beginner needs a good deal of luck, persistence, and a number of helping hands to keep him or her from initial or continuous disaster.

8. *Anything can be sold by direct mail—but only at a cost.*

   There are many desirable products and services sold by direct mail. However, with every increase in postal and mailing costs, the number of products and services that cannot be sold successfully via solo direct mail increases. Many of these products and services can be sold through space, some of them can be merchandised through use of cardvertisers, package inserts, statement stuffers, or co-ops. But their low order margin makes solo direct mail out of the question.

9. *Direct mail is targeted marketing.*

Rifle shot implies hitting the bull's eye. Direct mail might better be considered a shotgun approach to "targeted marketing" in which the attempt is made to hit the several concentric rings of the targeted area, including the bull's-eye. Peripheral areas may be both larger and, in the long run, more profitable than a small identifiable core.

10. *Don't believe you can pick lists as well as a trained professional in the field.*

Given the many offerings of list compilers and list owners and the growing coverage of lists found in SRDS *Lists & Data* we are today creating a whole host of instant list experts who believe they can evaluate offers as well as the so-called experts.

Even professional organizations with years of experience select lists that range 1,000 percent in response from the worst to the best. That's a range of 10 to 1! And if their clients had selected the first 30 lists, that range could easily have been 30 to 1—or 3,000 percent. Don't think you know. Call in the experts. It pays.

11. *Recognize that for all practical purposes there are only two kinds of lists: those that work, and those that don't.*

12. *Don't refuse to mail an older segment that is working just because newer names are not available.*

13. *Don't refuse to mail a list just because it is not precise and complete in every way.* It may well be the best list of its type around.

14. *Don't set up hard and fast rules such as "never mail an inquiry list".* You may be cutting yourself off from some nice neat net profits.

15. *Don't refuse to test a list because the rental price is too high.* Another $10 per thousand may be only 3 percent of the cost in the mail—and you just may be bypassing a list that will increase response by 10 times that.

There are a goodly number of mailers who "shop" for bargain lists— $5 off per thousand—and feel they have beaten the system somewhat. Since lists either work or don't, it follows that a low cost list which fails is a dead loss, while a fair priced list or a higher priced list which succeeds is a bargain.

Mailers who arbitrarily will not try a list priced above a given number of dollars per thousand may be depriving themselves of great response. Price is not the determinant; response is. The name of the game is response—based on the total dollars expended.

16. *Do not take as gospel any rule which stipulates, "Never mail a given list more often than . . ." Instead follow the rule that states, "Mail a list as often as it can be mailed productively".*

    There was a well-known list buyer at a renowned membership fundraising organization who would not mail any list more than once a year. Yet second mailings to his best lists, which were twice as good as average, would have provided him with more members at lower cost than using additional lists. He never did learn—until he was ousted.

THE "TWICE 7" DEADLY SINS OF DIRECT MAIL (PLUS ONE)

When it comes to operations, almost all practitioners of direct mail, start-ups, as well as old line companies, are prone to commit one or more of the Twice 7 (plus one) deadly sins of direct mail. These include both sins of omission and sins of commission, but all of them are deadly. It is not "Thou Shalt Not" as much as "If you do not understand you will end up sinning against yourself." The Twice 7 (plus one) deadly sins of direct mail can be grouped under four headings:

- Sins of origin (Original Sin as it were)
- Sins of control (not quite uncontrollable urges)
- Sins of data usage and reporting (permitting the figures to lie)
- Sins of list use (slothful use of lists).

Sins of Origin

Sin 1: the fallacy of "great expectations"

At least once a month an administrator of a seminar business comes to me and predicts that with my help his or her new seminar will draw ten orders per M (1 percent) at $350 per seminarian. I point out as kindly as I can that if it was possible to prospect for new seminarians and produce $3,500 for every 1,000 pieces in the mail, everyone and his brother would be in the seminar business. These "would-be" entrepreneurs suffer from "Great Expectations." At one direct-mail function, a client of mine, in front of about one hundred mailers, stood up and arrested the interest of the group with this phrase, "Ed, we got a terrible response from one of your lists!" Before he could go on, I had him describe what he was offering, and had him next tell us what he expected. I then predicted he had received about one-fifth of what I noted to him were "Great Expectations."

A new trade magazine was launched in Wisconsin a few years ago with a 10 percent response level. The publisher was ready to scrap the project (which is now very successful) because he had been told not to go on if the response rate was less than 25 percent!

I have seen direct-mail projects die because the initial profit margin, which paid for all incremental costs, plus a reasonable 10 percent profit (and a rather pretty return on investment) was not the 20 percent set as the bogey by the mailer. It is not wise to *expect* too much in direct mail, particularly on untested offers, lists, or packages.

Sin 2: not knowing the "cost to buy" a customer

There are two mathematical concepts in the operation of a direct-response business where the answer "I don't know" is very close to original sin.

In my twenty-eight years in this fascinating business it has been my pleasure to meet and work with a handful of mailers who really know:

1. The cost to buy a customer
2. The lifetime value of that customer

How can any of us make a rational decision as to how much to pay for a new customer without knowing what that customer can be expected to produce from future purchases? How can a rational decision be made as to the number of customers to buy in a given period without knowing the average cost to buy those customers? How can a rational cash flow forecast be made if the number of new customers to be bought at a given cost is not at least approximated?

I am constantly intrigued to find questions like this "Greek" to the majority of mailers. The cost to buy (which some merchandisers are fortunate enough to do at a profit) is reasonably easy to calculate. One method includes all fixed costs per order, and all variable costs based on the cost of promotion. The response produces a given amount of gross profit. That gross profit is checked against all the costs involved in the "costs of goods sold" plus the cost in the mail (or for the promotion or ad) and the difference, per unit, is the cost (or profit) to "buy" that new customer.

Sin 3: not knowing the "lifetime value" of a customer

Lifetime value in simplistic terms (and it is never really simplistic) is an approximation—by each customer cell—of the number of *gross sales* dollars that can be expected over a given period of time, and thus the gross profit dollars that can be realized in that period *after subtracting* the cost of repromotions. (Many mailers make the mistake of calculating the gross dollars and the gross profit dollars, and then fail to take into account the additional cost of the repromotional mailings. You may recall the USPS projected savings from nine-digit zip codes but these so-called "savings" deliberately failed to take into account the discounts necessary to get mailers to add the codes.)

Several important operative words were presented in the preceding paragraph. They are:

> Cells
>
> Gross sales
>
> Period of time
>
> Gross profit

Key among them is *cells*. The value of each customer is dependent on the average of the cell in which he or she is a constituent. Customer cells are defined by six major delineators, expressed in short by the acronym RFU$ISM, which stands for

> Recency—when last ordered
>
> Frequency—how often ordered in a given period
>
> Dollars—total, highest, per time period
>
> Item—what was purchased
>
> Source—from which initial order originated
>
> Method—means of payment

Of these the most important for calculating lifetime value is recency, because as time slips by without an additional sale, so slides down the value of each cell on the file. Using recency only by time slots will produce a reasonably adequate first cut at lifetime value. For a more sophisticated and more precise approximation, each cell must be reviewed in turn for sales over the coming six months, year, two years, and so on.

Sins of Control

Sin 4: ignorance of the half life for direct response

Every promotional effort, which includes every magazine or newspaper ad, every batch of radio or TV ads, every cooperative mailing, every solo mailing, and every catalog mailing has a *half life*—the time (to the day in most cases) in which half of all the responses that will come in have already been received. As this happens very early in the life of the offer, it is a sin of commission not to know this. Thus without this solid base and only part of the facts sound executive decisions cannot be made.

The use of half life for direct-response analysis provides a dramatic breakthrough for mailers who wish to know *early* exactly where they will be, so far as response is concerned, long down the pike. Those who understand and use the principle are back in the mail with continuations, while those who do not are still awaiting the final stragglers of response. There is probably no more striking proof in direct-mail control than to review a group of expired keys to the same offer, all mailed on the same day, and, irrespective of the responses, note that the half life for all of them can be bracketed within *one twenty four-hour period*. Once you have done this for one of your own promotions, irrespective of kind, you too will become one of the "true believers."

Sin 5: thinking like a bookkeeper

A good way to go broke in direct mail is to evaluate each marketing test like a bookkeeper. You must keep in mind that bookkeepers are "bean counters", not marketers, and you must never let their counts, however accurate, obscure the marketing reality disclosed by your test or tests.

Perhaps a few examples of the difference between thinking like a bookkeeper and thinking like a marketer will make this sin very clear.

First, the bookkeeper looks at all costs, including the "sunk" costs of creation, typesetting, art, copy, graphics, photos, layout, and pasteup, while the marketer puts these aside. (You might think of such "sunk" costs as part of research and development, for if no mailing is ever printed or mailed such costs have no possible way to be retrieved through amortization by a successful series of mailings.)

Second, the bookkeeper looks at an initial cost of a test mailing and points out the cost is $500/M, the gross sales only $700/M, the gross profit $400, and hence a loss of $100/M. The marketer looks at the same figures and declares it a great success. How? The marketer figures the cost of the continuation at $310/M, gross sales through selected continuations at $800/M, gross profit $450/M, gross profit per M in the mail $140—and licks his chops over the hundreds of thousands of likely names available. On *Return On Investment*, the difference is even more marked. The bean counter looks at the total dollars required to make the total mailing against the total cost of all goods sold, and "proves" that the return on the use of money is too small to warrant funding the proposal. The marketer doles out the advance money very sparingly, uses the response dollars to keep suppliers happy (as orders are increased for periodic receipt) and makes every dollar work three times as hard as the classic figures produced as gospel by the bookkeeper. The marketer's actual R.O.I. can be, and often is, five times that of the bean counter. Let your bookkeeper do the summing and the counting. You keep on thinking like a marketer.

Sin 6: failing to recognize the important sale

Few in direct response seem to be aware that the important sale is not the first sale but the second. One sale no more makes for a customer than one swallow makes for a summer.

It is odd when you think of it that good catalog customer files produce sales of 3 or 4 or 5 percent when remailed (30 or 40 or 50 orders per thousand new catalogs mailed to them). But 100 percent of the names on those customer files were bought from the mailer at least once prior. That's how they got on the files in the first place.

In newsletter and magazine promotion, the value of a list is not confirmed by the trial (one-time trial buyer) or by the initial conversion (one-time annual subscriber) but by the renewal percentage of that initial first annual subscriber. Then and only then has the publisher or promotion director a reasonably good idea of the worth of the originating list for continuity.

Since few understand the importance of the second order, too few mailers spend enough time, effort, and thought on getting more of their one-time customers to become two and three time buyers. For example, very few premiums are utilized for sale No. 2, when sale No. 1 has been induced in part by just such an added bonus. Too few mailers ask their customers—even their multiple customers—for the favor of being given a name or two of friends who might like to receive the same offer. (Unfortunately, when some of these mailers get such lists of friends of friends they simply mail them like any other prospect list, which is deadly. Instead, they should link the names of customer and friend, which is personalization at a very high and very effective level.)

Some direct-response operators have only product or service which must be sold at a profit to cold prospects, or they will fail. They do not wish to be concerned with the cost to buy a customer, the struggle to amortize that purchase through future sales, and the necessity to get past the initial sale. However, few direct marketers have that luxury. Most of us must pay attention, very close attention, to the production of sales beyond the initial one which converted a prospect or inquirer into a one-time buyer.

Sin 7: overlooking the order margin

Some pundits stipulate that "anything can be sold by mail." I am one of them. But I first add carefully, "at a price." There are many things that are offered by direct response that cannot produce a cost to "buy" the customer that the mailer can afford. Chief among these are low-priced units with high mark ups but with low-order margins. (Order margin is the number of dollars left per unit when the total costs of goods sold and delivered are subtracted from the gross sales dollar for each completed and paid-for sale. *Order margin thus takes into account all costs except promotion* including such often neglected costs as credit, returns, refurbishing, and collection.) Retailers talk about mark-ups—that is, Keystone, or 50 percent—double the manufacturer's selling cost. But direct marketers (except catalog operators) must think of gross order margin. A retailer who sells books at $5 that cost him or her $1 will gloat about the 500 percent mark up. A direct marketer who knows how costs work, will ignore the high gross profit percentage, look at the order margin (something under $4), and recognize that no solo mailing for single sales on such an item can ever pay out.

It is probable that we have already seen the end of solo efforts for products with order margins of under $10, and many with order margins of $15 or $20 are no bargain with today's costs in the mails.

The old wives tale that direct mail needs a mark up of three or four times is, of course, another shibboleth. Many good offers prosper when the gross profit is less than 50 percent but the order margin is $25, $35, or $50. Marketers need to know, understand, and use order margin, and not think like conventional retailers who have been brought up on mark up.

Sins of Data Usage and Reporting

Sin 8: homogenizing variables instead of recognizing their separateness

This sin usually starts with some form of "NINO," which is computer short-hand for "Not In–Not Out." If you do not code for each variable, for each key, or for each type of customer-owned list cell, there is no way reports can be produced for each separate part.

Sometimes this sin originates when owners or operators obtain one overall response rate, and then wonder later on, as the cell counts drastically change, why the one homogenized figure is misleading.

Homogenizing overall response results at, say, 2 percent may bury (and often does) the fact that excellent sales were made to customers, adequate sales to inquiries, above average sales to friends of friends, and disastrous sales to lists used for cold prospecting.

Remember the separate key and keep it holy! Homogenization is excellent for milk for babies. It is a cardinal sin for the reporting of direct-response data.

Sin 9: not knowing whether to code or not to code

If there is any question, you should code. If there is some fear there are too many codes and too much dispersion, opt for every code. It is always possible to recombine codes as long as they exist. There is no way to find out which one of two or three variables most influences response if all three are lumped (or homogenized) under one heading or key.

Probably the worst direct mail is that in which variables (by list or offer) are created, and then the coding is either omitted, not elicited, or in some other way is not captured. All one knows in such a case is the overall response rate, which may, in its homogenized way lose the fact that A is considerably better than B and that both make a laughing stock out of C. (Incidentally, never toss away A until a new "standard" is created that increases response on a split test. And never test B only against C to get a winner, without testing against A the current standard, which just may still be better than both new endeavors.)

What should you do when codes have been omitted or lost in the shuffle? See if you can get *copies* of each list and data on just which offer went where (by state, zip code, or last digit of zip code or Nth number, or alphabetic). Then get your hands on the names and addresses of every response. This type of NINO (Not In–Not Out) leads to RAFO (Research and Find Out) which is both frustrating (because it is so unnecessary) and time consuming as well as costly.

Sin 10: ignoring initial source codes

For some reason, which I cannot really fathom, it is fairly typical to find that a great number of mail-order operators do not retain the initial source code on multiple customers. The order comes in initially, say, on key 127, which is then lost when a new order results from a subsequent offer or a new catalog edition.

Some might ask, "So what? The name is still there, the kind of offer is known, the new catalog is identified." To those who ask "So what?" the kindest answer, and probably the most provocative, is to ask a question in response, namely, "How can we identify which source has produced the kind of customer who becomes a frequent buyer?" And the net result is another case of NINO leading to RAFO— and another costly job to *research and find out.*

As Orwell so knowingly put it, "All animals are equal, but some animals are more equal than others." Similarly, not only are some codes more equal than others, they are also more useful (and therefore more valuable) than others.

Let's take that initial code just discussed, key 127. If we go back and locate this code and connect it to the multiple order, we can, (given counts by key) compare multiple buying production for it against other individual keys, by penetration (percentage of response). However, if the coding structure is generic in nature, for example, 100s are newspapers, 200s are magazines, 300s are direct mail, 400s are inquiries, 500s are friends of friends, 600s are radio, 700s are TV and so on, we can get an answer as to penetration by media by combining the first (generic) digit. Of course, we can get individual data (27/precoded 1) by medium within the media utilized. Wouldn't you like to know which media pays best in multiple customers? Wouldn't you like to know how many new customers you must "buy" by media to develop a new multiple buyer customer? There are different levels of the sin of omission where coding is involved. For everything (including coding) that pertains to a computer, perhaps the law should be, "Think it through first, then think it through again. And don't hurry to jell until you are certain."

Sin 11: living with mathematical competence

All business has as its chief purpose the obtaining and retention of customers. Direct mail sets out to obtain customers without the intervention of other channels of distribution. As such, the obtaining of customers by direct means can be *precisely* measured. *It is the fact that direct response can be accurately measured that distinguishes it from all other marketing.*

However, that measurement means you must at least become acquainted with the simplistic mathematics that are used to compare one result realistically against another. Many of us have some innate fear and insecurity when the subject of simplistic arithmetic comes up. If you are to succeed in direct marketing you must, at the minimum, lose your fear of simple arithmetic relationships.

Actually, all of us can place over our desks a sign reading "Mathematics Spoken Here" because we use mathematics all the time. Up and down are mathematical terms, so are more than, less than, or equal to. You can be overweight or underweight, or some objects can be even weightless. Discussion of day or year, or estimates of time to do a job are purely mathematical abstractions, as are estimates of height or size, or the dimensions of a door, . . . or a car, . . . or a person. (Polls, money, and interest rates have made percentages and fractions such as half a pound or quarter of a dollar into duck soup!)

It is likely that you use mathematical terms like these half-a-dozen times every day. You therefore already speak like a mathematician. Most of the mathematics you will need, at least early in the game, are not any more complex than those you use everyday. So don't fret!

In my years of lecturing I have had the privilege to emphasize the mathematics of direct-mail list usage to no less than 6,000 or 7,000 seminarians, and the videotape of one of these seminars has now carried the same message to another 5,000 or more.

Sadly, less than 1 percent of those who have attended those seminars knew the correct way to select a sample for direct-mail testing. No more than 1 percent knew the confidence level to anticipate, nor what constitutes a significant difference. Very few had been exposed to an introductory course on probability statistics. The "null hypothesis" was an enigma wrapped in a mystery. The number who knew how to read the simplistic charts on sampling, which are easily available to any marketer, was distressingly small.

Sins of List Usage

Sin 12: testing a starter mailer on only one list

If there is any one descriptive phrase in direct marketing which seems appropriate over and over again it is the old adage about "a continuous series of one experiment." Almost every starting mailer (and sadly most books advising them) tends to mail one package conveying one offer to one list as a test. This is to determine the future of this offer in the mail! As most of us know, all this will indicate is what that one offer in that one package accomplished with the names and addresses on only that one list.

It is recognized that response varies (and how!) depending on

Copy—the words used

Package—how those words are clothed

Offer—the proposition

Timing—the time the proposition is received

Market—the List, or Medium, to which the offer, couched in given copy, clothed in a given package, is delivered at a given time

It is therefore evident that one test cell does not constitute an end but rather a beginning toward an end.

If it is better to send a poor mailing to a good list than a good mailing to a poor list (which is usually the case because lists can and do vary by 1000 percent—by 10 to 1!), than the initial test procedure must perforce test a group of lists—five or ten or more—not just the continuous series of one. This means that the best copy that can be devised, the best package that can be designed (or afforded), the best offer with the best creditability that can be initially created, must initially be sent to several lists. Later, tests on variants of the offer, and of the package, and even the copy can be constructed. (Through use of a grid structure, two or more packages, conveying two or more offers to a group of no less than five or ten lists can be used to reduce costs.)

Sin 13: the errand boy syn(sin)drome

All too often a mailer will seek out the best paper, the best typography, the best graphics, and the best layout and deliver the best camera-ready copy (usually at considerable cost) to a good printer. Then the errand boy will be sent out to obtain a list or two.

If anything, the procedure should be reversed. The errand boy should be sent to select the mechanics of the mailing, and *you*, the marketer, should concern yourself with the most important single factor in direct mail—the list. Of course you cannot let the errand boy select a designer, typographer, or printer. Your ego (rightly) gets in the way. After all this is your mailing which concerns your product or service and which you laid out and had printed to your satisfaction. But if your great mailing doesn't get to the right lists, every dollar spent to go to the printer and all of the time spent on minutia is wasted. The list is the market. The choice of the market requires a marketer—not an errand boy.

Sin 14: insufficient list research

It is probable that only the very largest mailers, served by several list brokers and an outside marketing consultant or two do enough list research.

A large mailer using just one broker is seemingly unaware that while the universe of lists tapped by brokers is more or less the same, the knowledge of which lists work for what type of offers is remarkably different. This stands to reason when it is understood that the average list broker does half his volume (from 20,000 lists available) from just *one hundred* lists, and each broker has a somewhat different list of his most used 100 lists. (This fact caused our firm to initiate the whole concept of list management—to move the molecules for the list owner, as it were, on the other 19,900 lists available.)

SRDS (Standard Rate & Data Service for Mailing Lists) is a useful tool for mailers, but its redundancy and deliberate lack of any rating structure makes it somewhat difficult to use for the occasional mailer. There are, for example, some twenty lists of architects, all of which are about the same size and most of which were initiated by no more than two or at most three sources, although the reason for this is far from clear. The user may be excused for asking "Which?" and "Why?"

Even the best list purveyors who are becoming list "consultants" do not have time to do more than brush the surface of the list world. Rarely is a suggestion made for peripheral lists. Rarely do business lists appear on consumer mailing schedules, although businesspeople and professionals are first of all consumers. Even more rarely do consumer lists appear on schedules of business mailers, despite the fact that there are some 7 million American families now known to conduct some type of second business enterprise from their homes. (This might explain why some mixed lists with home and business addresses do quite well for business-type offers.)

Most of us are just too busy and too distracted to do a thorough job. As a result, the list research function can be done exceedingly well, or done on an adequate basis, or not done at all.

Good list research is partially due to the attitude of mailers who will order continuations indicating a test has worked well enough, but not disclose precise results to the supplier. Every bit of input mailers are willing to give suppliers who have the competence to consult on usage with them cannot help but provide more useful grist for more thinking, for more cross-selling, and for more insight into areas to explore. It isn't because the data are not available. A recent study indicates the average list broker serves no more than fifty major clients. It is likely that the average list compiling and merchandising entity serves many more masters but no greater number of major accounts per year.

A knowledgeable list expert can select ten lists for a new offer and have three, four, or five proven winners. The next ten lists may develop two or three proven winners to add to the first group. After that a ratio of 1 winner in 4 or 1 in 5 (if lists exist for the given offer) is more common. (*Reader's Digest* has found it necessary to allocate internal company use for the best twenty lists found so far.)

These ratios indicate a need for most list research and more courageous testing of list concepts, some of which should properly be off the wall. Most importantly there should be more consideration of list suppliers as true consultants who have a need to know exactly what happens to each and every list utilized and every other promotional venture undertaken by the client. If your supplier cannot be treated as such, I would suggest using a supplier who can be treated on the same professional level as your doctor, your lawyer, your business consultant, or your accountant.

Sin 15: lack of individualized handling of mailings to major companies

Sad but true, many industrial marketers mail the same one piece per establishment to billion-dollar companies and to mom-and-pop businesses. A graph of American business by size discloses that of 8.5 million establishments over four and a half million employ less than five people. The top 120,000 companies in the United States (just over 1 percent of establishments) control over 90 percent of *all* commercial activity. For that matter the so-called Fortune 1000 manufacturing companies, about 1/40th of those manufacturing companies making up the top 1 percent of such establishments, control the destinies of 26,000 branch plants (a list, of course), which by themselves employ over 70 percent of the employees in 350,000 plants and produce over 75 percent of the value added to manufacturing in the United States.

Big business buys primarily by committee decisions—decisions made by major executives. A conventional mailing piece is unlikely to pierce the paperwork barrier put up by secretaries and staff assistants. However, a personal letter with a personal appeal, mailed first class and addressed to a top executive by name and title, has a fair chance of getting through.

SHIBBOLETHS IN DIRECT MAIL

In addition to the deadly sins concerning direct mail, there are a number of shibboleths about direct mail that are far from true. They will be examined in four semi-overlapping compartments concerning:

1. Ease of entry
2. Lists and list usage
3. Marketing operations
4. List rental

Ease of Entry

Direct mail is easy to enter; anyone can make a go of it.

This is probably the most damaging shibboleth. The truth is this is a business for pros, who know products, markets, media, the mathematics of marketing, the mystique of computers, and backroom control. The beginner needs a great deal of luck and "*stick-to-it-ivity*," as well as a number of helping hands to keep him or her from initial or continuous disaster.

The purveyors of "How to Make Easy Money in Direct Mail" entice a new batch of hopeful neophytes each year, and with the exception of perhaps two in 1,000, the only ones who profit are the sellers of the service. For years a few catalog houses have sold copies of their mail order catalog to neophytes by telling them all they had to do was find a good list to make a mint. Their pitch includes the time honored, "nothing to stock, nothing to buy in advance, we drop ship for you at 50 percent of the retail price." What the neophyte doesn't know is that the owner of the catalog makes a profit on the sale of the catalogs, plus a profit on the merchandise, and if the owner knew of a list that could pull a profit on the catalog it would be or already has been used by the owner.

Lists and How They Are Used

A fair number of the shibboleths of mailing lists involve misconceptions about lists. Here are a good dozen of the more common fallacies:

I can pick lists as well as any list expert.

Given the many offerings of list compilers and list owners, and the growing importance of lists found in SRDS "Lists and Data," we are today creating a host of "instant" list experts who tend to believe they can evaluate lists for offers as well as the so-called experts.

Let's try and place this shibboleth into context. My organization had the privilege of placing over 400 separate list tests for one attractive membership/fundraising appeal over a period of four years. With all of our so-called knowledge, and despite the fact that only a handful of the 400 lists came from lists within our ken, the range in response from the worst to the best was 1,000 percent (0.5 percent to 5.0 percent)—or a range of 10 to 1! If the client had selected the first fifty lists that range could easily have been 30 to 1—or 3,000 percent. Don't think you know the outcome. Call in the experts. It pays.

My list needs are too small to interest the professional.

That can be indeed true if your needs involve mail order buyers, and you are planning a "heavy" schedule involving test mailing using one list. However, if your need is for a small compiled segment, your only problem is likely to be the minimum charge set by the list owner to handle an individual order. Our organization, for example, compiles all 900 of the SIC classifications plus over 4,400 separate classifications from a current file of 4,700 classified phone directories. If the classification exists in the classifieds we will provide it to your order with phone numbers. Your compiler, in effect, can compile anything you desire, as long as you can afford it. This much is certain: Given sufficient time, energy, and intelligence, there is no list compilation in the United States that cannot be provided.

Interestingly enough, often small, select lists are more easily available to list users directly, rather than through list purveyors. The latter, who offer lists to all, are in such cases obviously too commercial.

Customer files are sacrosanct.

This is truly a crock. First, there isn't a customer file in existence that cannot be improved by augmentation, segmentation, enhancement, analysis, or list management. Second, a good number of customer files suffers from incipient zipitis, hardening of the arteries, multisclerotic duplication, peripheral sterility, unsanitary control, and old blood deficiencies. It is likely that typical customer lists used a few times per year with no regular cleaning procedure have incorrect zip codes of up to 5 percent or more. Many customer lists go back over years and some of the list data have not been qualified (if at all) in years. Even well-known lists from top mail order merchandisers show small percentages of duplication. Think what duplication is involved where modern sophisticated unduplication procedures are hardly even considered. Peripheral thinking—to augment customer lists and cover a targeted market—is somewhat rare in the list world. As a result, many conventional customer files are without the pretty leavening that can be incorporated by unique peripheral thinking.

New lists work better than old lists.

For any given offer there are a number of lists which will work and which will, in effect "pay out" when mailed. For such an offer an old list that works is preferable to a new list that doesn't. Despite this fact of life, mailers often disregard all past usage, to opt only for the new list. New segments of old lists are preferable to older segments of aging lists. However, old lists should not be disregarded completely because of their age.

My mail must go to an individual—not a title.

In the business world, if the name data are current and correct, it is always better to address by name rather than by title. For big business, say, the 100,000 or so companies rated $500,000 and over, it is essential that mail be addressed to the individual executive involved. For a number of functions even in big business where no adequate data exist, it is essential to address mail carefully by title. At the other end of the spectrum where the majority of businesses employ less than five employees, there is one executive who wears all the hats. It is likely only one person reads all business mail. Thus title addressing at this level is quite adequate, particularly if it is at a lower cost than addressing individual names that also tend to age faster than do names of establishments.

Title addressing can be made remarkably explicit by using a bit of creative copy on the envelope or piece. For example:

This message is for the person who purchases carbon paper for the office.

For the executive in charge of materials handling.

Or perhaps you need to print a "laundry list" of the types of executives who might be interested in your offering or catalog.

There is only one source for my lists.

When this shibboleth is voiced it usually indicates the mailer has been brainwashed by a list compiler with only one major list property to promote. If you currently believe this, it will undoubtedly pay you to explore the other possibilities available. In the business list field, you may find added help from magazine subscriber or recipient lists; newly promoted executives; newly formed businesses; trade show registrants; government registers; newspapers, or classified phone books. Whenever you hear "one source" you had better be on your guard. Someone is trying to convince you of something for his or her own good, not yours. (The same is true for large users who swear by and utilize only one broker.)

My list needs are different. No outsider can help me.

That may be a true statement if your needs are so esoteric and finite and small that no one else can afford the time, effort, and energy required to ferret them out. With this exception some, and usually the greatest part, of the list needs of *any* mailer can be handled very nicely by the list brokers and list consultants who know the field. It is odds on that a knowledgeable outside expert can uncover sources never before tried and can extrapolate from your results peripheral markets worth exploring. Again it is odds on that he or she could easily have saved you from some of the disasters *you have* already run in to. At the very worst, the expert will be of no help. At the very best you will open a whole fount of new markets, new data, new lists—and a new way to look at your list needs.

Marginal lists, with or without selectivity, are useless.

For all practical purposes there are only two kinds of lists—those that work and those that don't. But what of the in-between lists—those with marginal response? It should first be understood that any response is an average, that is, if the overall response is 2 percent, there is some 3 percent money in that list, and of course some 1 percent money. The art of list usage is to select the higher responding segments. Thus any list which is marginal should be carefully explored to see if some selection can be exercised to improve the breed. Lists with very low response are losers; marginal lists, especially if they can be segmented, are opportunities.

I must compile and run my own list. No one else can do it as well.

It is both surprising and sad to see intelligent businesspeople continuously reconstructing lists (reinventing the wheel as it were) that the mailing list fraternity has already, in effect, precompiled. I remember well a Texas company laboriously compiling lists of college students, completely unaware of the two major compilers (and two or three minor compilers as well) in this field. There are other companies also laboriously compiling classifications from classifieds. They do this despite the fact that three compilers offer access to some 4,000 classifications totaling 8.5 million records which are continuously being compiled and updated from a complete, current nationwide file of such directories—unduplicated within classification and against other classifications, by phone number.

Before you decide that only you can compile the list you need, first explore the great resources of the list community. In past years most compiled lists were compiled "to order" on special assignment. Today major compilers provide up to 75 million families at home addresses by name, plus 2 million or more farm families as well as over 1 million offices of professionals, 1.5 million institutions, and 6.0 million businesses. All of these are broken down by demographic and psychographic characteristics.

It is safe to say most nonprofessional compiling is wasteful, costly, and time consuming. The average business compiler will supply a list for one-time, two-time, or unlimited use that is already qualified, already zipped, already computerized, and ready for use for far less than the cost to compile one from scratch.

After you buy or rent such a list, your compiler can run the list for you, update it for you, and relieve you of the need to handle the data processing, if you so opt. He or she can produce cards, labels, or sheet lists; sort the file by classification, city size, or alphabetically; provide counts; pick Nth No. or fifth-digit zip code selections; and run two or three carbons with no cost to you to program, handle, and stock.

The chances are if you select your service correctly, your compiler can run your list better than you can at a price you can easily afford. Therefore, there is little merit in the view "no one else can do it for me." (However, be sure that the compiler you select to supply data processing for your lists knows the field. You don't want to pay for his or her education!)

Secrecy increases the value of most mailing lists.

Contrary to the preceding statement, secrecy is a danger signal. There are no secrets in the list business—only people who cloak the obvious in obfuscation. When a list compiler refuses to name his source you should find another compiler. If a mailer refuses to tell you the age of a given list segment, see if you can locate a likely substitute.

The one list concept for which a measure of public "secrecy" seems required is that of fund-raising donors. You may have to rely on your broker for the validity of a list of people who have given $5 or more to a given health fund or to help blindness. In most cases the name of the organization is known but is not used. This convention seems to keep everybody happy. The list is not "commercially" available but the rental income and the exchanges proliferate all the same.

Salespeople make the best list builders for their companies.

In one word this is "bosh." Salespeople are notoriously poor list compilers. They normally hate paperwork, particularly extracurricular paperwork. As in any human endeavor, among a group of salespeople there will be a few superb list builders, a number of adequate ones, but the skew will be to the poor side of the line. Salespeople can be used intelligently to help update a living list but they should not be relied upon to provide the essence of a list.

As far as locating the prospects to call on, a good compiler can provide more complete data than any sales force. I still recall the salesman extolled by his manager for locating every potential plant in his area. I chanced to plot the list built by this paragon, and found his calls clustered at each exit of a super highway. On this list there were no prospects between the exists. It happened that he was covering less than 50 percent of the prospects in the area with over fifty employees.

A list should be perfect and complete in every way. If it has any imperfections it should be returned unpaid.

This shibboleth can perhaps cause more problems for suppliers attempting to help beginners than almost any other. It starts with the misunderstanding that the list owner or the list compiler can and does provide perfect lists. Let me state here for all compilers that every list we build has holes in it big enough to drive a truck through. For example, you know a given restaurant went out of business six months ago and yet here it is on the list. The zip code for this person is 11609, not 11607 and is undeliverable. The list says this is architects, and the record reads Smith Construction Company. I ordered Tropical Fish and received two records from Pump Manufacturers. The same woman is on this list twice at two different zip codes. Horrors!

All of this (and much more) shows up on *any* list. The more you look the more you will find. However, the list user should keep in mind the doughnut— not the hole. A small proportion of incorrect, illogical, unrelated records in a list will have nothing to do with overall results. The effort to get the perfect list (except perhaps in the case of the American Medical Association file of doctors which is available by age and specialty, and which is updated weekly) is rather futile. You learn and make allowances, and you understand that perfect lists are a mirage.

Marketing Operations

Direct mail is rifle-shot marketing.

Whereas rifle shot implies hitting the bull's eye, direct mail might better be considered a shotgun approach to "targeted marketing" in which the attempt is made to hit the bull's eye as well as the several concentric rings of the targeted area. Peripheral areas may be both larger and, in the long run, more profitable than the small center core. As business becomes more and more diversified, direct response must become more target-oriented. A compiler given the assignment to provide 4,000 establishments which make up a given bull's-eye market, will in many cases insist on supplying the most likely 12,000 to 15,000 establishments as a guarantee that the center has been provided in full.

Lists and list segments are self-coding.

This is not true even in cases where lists are coded by classification, profession, or sex, all of which are clearly discernible. For example, a mailing sent to a business can come back from a home. A mailing to a professional may lead to a response from his or her spouse. Testing without precoding the response vehicle is like fishing with unknown bait. You may know you should continue to fish but you will never know how to improve your catch. Coding requires recordkeeping; recordkeeping means paperwork and reports; paperwork and reports means analysis—all of this means work. This much is certain: Without coding and tracking of results there can be no direct-response business of any kind.

Checking of cheshired lists is a waste of time.

Contrary to the above statement, you should inspect the cheshire labels you use for your mailings as a regular rule. What can you find? You order a cross-section, and the list runs all the way from Vermont to Massachusetts. You order fifth-digit zip codes ending in 0 and find only one in six records so zipped. You order the title "Dr." to appear on every record and the label reads "E. Smith." You order names of females and find 35 percent are male. You order names of United States citizens only and find the first twenty pages (880 labels) are Canadian citizens. You order names of businesspeople and their business addresses and find 70 percent of the addresses are three-line only. You asked for an SIC code on your business file and it is omitted.

Have at least some of the list labels you use sent to your office—not to the lettershop. No lettershop can be expected to know what to look for or why. It is true a good lettershop will often catch a list out of your zip range or with foreign addresses, but you alone need to know what you are getting and what you are mailing. That is not the function of your lettershop, and you'll probably be in for a surprise—so look.

Like restaurants, all list brokers are the same.

On the surface this is false, yet many believe each list broker has the same lists, and the same knowledge, and the same overall comprehension of each of the fifteen basic kinds of mail order merchandising. As it happens almost all brokers specialize in such fields as opportunity seekers, culture vultures, magazine subscribers, home repair persons, Catholics, fund raising, business, gardening, and so on. Some brokers now even specialize in nonlist direct response through package inserts, co-ops, stuffers, and cardvertisers. A few years ago a major catalog sales operation used only one broker. I had five list brokers provide twenty suggested lists for this major mailing effort. The owner expected 90 percent to duplicate but only 14 percent of the lists duplicated! Obviously each broker with access, for the most part, to the same lists had a different series of previous experiences to draw upon.

It is only fair to state however that if your needs are for only 50,000 or 100,000 mail order names it is best to work with one broker who will get enough business from you and thus devote time and effort to your account. The choice of a broker is not however only a matter of dart throwing or recalling a name. A bit of careful research, as in all service-minded businesses, is required.

It is better to mail a good mailing piece to a poor list than the reverse.

It stands to reason that the correct answer here is to mail the best possible mailing piece to the best possible mailing list (or lists). However, as lists can and do influence response by a far greater factor than do any of the other four major influences (copy, offer, timing, package) it is likely that a poor mailing to a good list will do better than a good mailing to a poor list. The list is the key to response; it should be the keystone of your mailing effort.

It doesn't pay to review zip codes because the proportion of wrong numbers is too small.

Like most things in direct mail "it depends." If you are renting an outside list, other than a superficial check for validity, a zip code review or analysis is rarely called for. If you are mailing a customer, inquirer, or "friend-of-a-friend" list that you own, it will pay you to review the list as chances are your lists have a wrong zip code factor approaching 4 or 5 percent. Every time you mail such a list you loose $12 to $120 per M in wasted mailing cost. Thus, a periodic review of zips is time and effort well spent. If your list is on tape, you can get a free sampling of your zip code health from one of several specialists in this field.

Marketing is at the top of the totem pole at my computer department.

If marketing is a top priority in your company, yours is one of the rarest of companies because since its inception about 20 years ago computer technology has been the handmaiden of the accountant–financial figure-happy types who control costs and are alarmed by marketing. It is far more likely that marketing, including list and response marketing, is low on that totem pole—so low in fact, that profit-minded and profit-centered entrepreneurs within corporations usually opt to go outside for computer services. By going outside for services they are likely to find computer services ready and willing to provide "effort-key" reports, analysis of half lives and proper attention to updating, segmenting, and usage of the customer file.

List Rental

Overuse of lists destroys their value.

Interestingly, there has never been a shred of evidence for this time-honored saw. Those companies that expend 80 percent of their mailings on their customer file and 20 percent on prospecting may not be augmenting the customer file with enough "new blood." But the repeated use of the customer file, if each mailing pays a profit, does not denigrate the list.

The argument that "my list is so unique, I cannot afford to rent it" does not seem to affect such companies as Kiplinger, Penton, Horchow, Sakowitz, Sunset House, U.S. Sales, Doubleday, Fingerhut, and hundreds of other major mail order merchandisers.

Companies that do rent their lists recognize that they do not own a given name exclusively. Every merge–purge of major mail order lists emphasizes over and over again that a mail order buyer *is* a mail order buyer and he or she can be found on many lists. A small number of list owners have convinced themselves that *rental of their lists would result in loss of business from their mail order customers*. To prove the invalidity of this, all that needs to be done is to split the list and rent only one-half of it while using both halves for customer promotion. Each time we have arranged for such a test, each half of the list has done equally well for the customer. But only the half that has been rented has brought in nice new net extra dollars. With costs as they are now, and the growing need for *augmented* income, list owners have even more reason to take advantage of the list rental market.

With my computer costs, I cannot afford to rent.

This time-worn argument against renting has been provided by cost accountants who divide all the costs of data processing by output, and thus charge list rental with a proportionate share of the whole cost of data processing. Handled this way, a good share of rental income gets buried in overhead burden. (One major publisher, now one of the largest factors in the list rental field, used a fixed cost of over $10/M for cheshire labels for years because of this type of thinking. Modern management now understands incremental costs, and list rental is without a doubt the most profitable segment of the company.)

The easiest way to see the fallacy in such an approach is to consider two companies, each with, say, a $100,000 cost of data processing. One company rents; the other does not. Thus each has the same cost of data processing (about 2 percent to 4 percent of sales in the average company today) to add to overhead. However, the company that rents, using $3/M for incremental costs of production of labels for list rental against a net return of $20/M, adds $25,000 to the bottom line.

Lists that work shouldn't be mailed too often.

One of the best known agencies in the environmental protection field has an iron rule that no list, no matter how successful it is, can be mailed more than once a year. This is a dangerous illusion. If a certain list pays out at 3 percent once a year, and breakeven is, say, at a response of 1.5 percent, it may be that the mailer is depriving the organization of precious, needed income. Tests may and probably will indicate that if this list is mailed twice a year 5.0 percent of sales will develop and possibly 6.7 percent if mailed three times per year. A good list with above average pull can be remailed within a few weeks and pull from 50 percent to 70 percent of sales received from the original mailing.

If the list universe is large enough, and the response attractive enough, it may pay to determine through testing just how often a particular list should be mailed. This can be done by isolating segments of the list and mailing separate controlled segments through marked keys twice, three times, four times, six times, or more per year. The results of such a test should indicate clearly whether or not you can safely mail the same list more often than in the past. It is best to repeat such a test every few years because lists change, tastes change, offers and copy fade, and a list that could be successfully mailed four times a few years ago may only support two efforts a few years later.

For some offers where the universe is rather small, it may be *necessary* to mail a given list several times in a course of a year. For one international newsletter, where the total universe was in the neighborhood of 6,000, monthly mailings aimed at developing a response of about $\frac{1}{2}$ of 1 percent were used. These mailings resulted in opening new subscriptions over the year from 6 percent of the universe available. The only way this was possible was by mailing to every name available each month of the year.

Speaking of response, there is one more shibboleth to put to rest and that is the conventional wisdom, spoken in pontifical tones: "The usual response in direct mail is 2 percent." This is nothing less than errant nonsense. Two percent can be fabulous for one offer and close to disaster for another. Offers can vary by 300 percent; lists can vary by 1000 percent. This underlines the two answers that can be given to any question you would like to raise as to the validity of the pitfalls, sins, and shibboleths of direct mail covered so far. They are:

1. It depends.
2. Test—and find out. (For every mailer who tests too much, there are 999 who do not test enough.)

HOW TO GET BETTER AT DIRECT MAIL—SO AS NOT TO FAIL

This is a field in which education never stops. There is always something new to learn. And the complaint heard most often, even by old timers, is "I wish I had known that yesterday." The best way to learn is to work at one of the top list compiling firms or list management firms, or at one of the top direct response advertising agencies. Next best is to work for one of the major direct response operators. The only reason this is not equated with the first group is that suppliers work with the interests, needs, and problems of a number of mailers, while work for one mailer provides an education in just one way of doing things.

Build a Swipe File

Next, become a packrat and build a "swipe" file of every piece of advertising mail (good, bad and indifferent) and file the pieces either by product classification, or by type (self-mailers, computer spectaculars, windows, teasers, odd sizes, and so on.) This file should include three special lots—consumer catalogs, business-to-business catalogs, and their order forms. It is not enough just to collect. The pieces, the catalogs, the order forms should be carefully studied. See how credit cards, guarantees, 800 ordering, premiums, copy, and display are handled.

Collect List Directories

Become a collector of every directory (most are free) published by list houses. Obtain access to or subscribe to SRDS Mailing Lists Rates & Data. At least scan each issue of the four magazines now flourishing in the field—*DM News, Direct Marketing,* and *Zip,* & *Catalog Age.* The direct mail columns in *Ad Age* are useful, and from time to time direct mail usage is covered by other magazines in the marketing field.

Become a mail order buyer and subscriber. Change your name in some distinctive way and *record* that change and the purchase. Then watch how your "personal" seed gets rented to other mailers.

Participate in Direct Marketing Association Activities

Join the Direct Marketing Association, and if possible register for the annual fall convention of this organization.

Get Exposure to DM Seminars

There are now two VCR Audio Visual Tape seminars. The one published by Ed Burnett Consultants runs for a bit over 4 hours and provides in visual form some of the main subjects covered in this book. It is an ideal course for those who wish to know almost everything they need to know about mailing lists, and the mathematics of their use. Cost is $195. Available in either VHS or BETA. This is a taped version of the Burnett seminar which is given annually at several colleges and universities. Unimail has a training audio visual running about 2 hours for those who wish a primer in the list business, and the work of the broker in the list field. The cost is $300.

With the help of the DMA, a growing number of colleges and universities now offer lecture courses. Those invited to speak at such courses are almost always expert in the phase they discuss. And the cost is quite modest.

Read Books on Direct Marketing

If there is a need to restrict additional reading to just one other book, that should be *Effective Advertising* by John Caples, available through the DMA. This, better than any other source, pounds home the extreme value of testing; in particular split testing.

In time, the library of a dedicate in this field should include the *McGraw-Hill Encyclopedia*, with chapters by fifty experts, edited by Ed Nash; *Direct Mail & Mail Order Handbook* compiled and written by Dick Hodgson, and Jim Kobs' useful set of direct mail case histories in his *Profitable Direct Marketing*. For a complete glossary of terms see the back of this handbook.

For some enjoyable reading in this field, pick up a copy of David Ogilvy's *Confessions of an Advertising Man*. And if you would like to read how the well respected in direct mail got that way, the book of bios called *Mail Order Know-How* by Cecil Hoge may well be your dish.

There are a number of newsletters in the field. Each has its raison d'etre and its adherents. One features late breaking news, another concentrates on catalogs, a third tells who is mailing what, a fourth features postal affairs, while 3 or 4 more cover the field in general. There are in addition several free newsletters and booklets sponsored by list merchandisers, ad agencies, and computer software houses, all with useful data. And the three major associations, Direct Marketing Association, Mail Advertising Service Association, and Third Class Mail Users all see that important data, particularly on rates, costs, and rules are brought to the attention of their members.

CHAPTER 2

A Basic Direct Mail Primer

This chapter provides a brief overview of the size of list markets, including how many pieces are mailed, by how many mailers, and how many different lists are used.

The data on pieces mailed are precise; the data on the size of the markets are quite realistic; data on the number of lists, the value of those lists, and the advertising component of mail received provide reasonably reliable estimates.

This section touches on compiling, but leaves all discussion of segmentation for later in the book. Similarly data on criteria, telecommunications, databases, data banks, list testing, list managers, list brokers, big business, and the great demographic changes of our time are missing here but are covered in some detail in later sections.

Here is a brief description of Direct Mail: Direct mail is a means of promotion delivered exclusively through the U.S. mails on a one-to-one relationship to induce from the individual recipient directly (and usually immediately) response through the phone or the mail. The desired response can be in the form of a transfer of money (for a purchase, subscription, or contribution), or it can be in the form of a request for additional information or a copy of some proferred promotion in the form of a booklet, pledge, or catalog.

EIGHT REASONS WHY DIRECT MAIL IS UNLIKE ANY OTHER FORM OF PROMOTION

Direct mail is unlike any other form of promotion because it is

1. *Measurable*. Unlike most forms of advertising, direct mail always seeks a measurable feedback in the form of response. Mailers lay down a given number of dollars for each 1,000 pieces placed in the mails, and can then measure to one-tenth of 1 percent exactly how many responses this expenditure has produced.

2. *Targetable*. Unlike mass media, direct mail is addressed to a specific individual at a specific address who is known or expected to conform to a given set of unique criteria. No matter the size of the mailing, the targeted audience for each piece is a single individual (or a single establishment).

3. *Infinite*. There is literally no limitation to the infinite possibilities for an individual piece of mail. This includes infinities of size or shape, infinity in the use of words, infinity in the choice of color or formats, infinities in the order and array of individual pieces, infinities in reader involvement, and even an infinity of offers.

4. *Predictable*. Direct mail is the one form of promotion in which all of the factors that influence response can be tested with statistical validity, and thus projections via the future "rollouts" can be made with assurance.

5. *Based on minute differences*. Direct mail is a business of distinct differences in very small numbers derived from very large universes. It is the only form of promotion where a difference of one-tenth of 1 percent can be the difference between success and failure.

6. *Often the only economic choice*. There are thousands of specific markets and audiences where direct mail provides the only economic means available to reach them. This is as true for the church selling raffles to its constituents as it is for a major company offering seminars to business executives with specific interests at given sized companies.

7. *The only means to take the retail store to the customer*. There are over 2 million retail outlets in the United States, plus over 2 million service firms, many of whom also provide goods and services at the retail level. These 4 million plus establishments require the customer to leave home or work and enter the store in order to buy. By means of catalogs (over 5 billion per year) direct mail operators bring the store right into the home or workplace of the prospect. The direct mail specialty store also can be, and

often is, better stocked with more choices and better variety than any single retail outlet.

8. *Both an art form and a science*. The art of direct mail encompasses the copy, the layout, the ambience of the package, and not least, the choice and use of lists. The science comes from the control and capture of every bit of information about every transaction, and the mathematics involved in the cost to buy a customer as well as the lifetime value of that customer.

THE GREAT AMERICAN LOVE AFFAIR WITH ADVERTISING MAIL

The United States Postal Service delivers mail six days of each week to some 87,000,000 households, and some 8,500,000 non–households. Some 44.7 billion pieces—slightly over 30.4 percent of the 147 billion pieces handled in fiscal 1985–86 consisted of advertising mail. About 5.3 billion of this 45 billion—roughly 12 percent—went to non-households—in other words to businesses, institutions, and offices of professionals.

The average household receives about five pieces per week, just a bit over one piece of advertising material by mail—per day. Now let's place that miniscule number in perspective. Through radio, TV, newspapers, self-standing stuffers, magazines, and bus and car cards, the average consumer is bombarded with over 1,000 advertising messages—per day. Just one one-thousandth of that vast advertising clutter comes from direct mail. And the only reason direct mail is singled out is because local newspapers keep alive the absolute lie that the average mailbox is filled with unwanted advertising pieces.

These self same newspapers do *not* mention, by the way, that those self-standing stuffers and folders and advertising supplements which dump out on your rug from each Sunday newspaper in the country by themselves provide more advertising—in number of pieces—than all advertising mail for prospecting put together.

The true fact of the matter is Americans have a love affair with advertising mail. Eighty-five percent of householders state they enjoy receiving mail. (And those who voted include a fair number of householders who are most unhappy to have the postman not deliver anything, even a bill, in their mailbox.)

In smaller cities and towns the visit to the mailbox is an event—newspapers come that way, so do magazines, and news from supermarkets and department stores . . . plus an occasional catalog. How occasional is occasional? Statistics from the USPS prove the average household receives less than one catalog per week, some three or four per month.

The amazing thing about the very small penetration of households made by direct mail is the great effect it has had on retail purchasing.

Sales made via direct response (including solo and cooperative direct mail, and direct response advertising, both in print and electronic, plus telemarketing) now totals some $100 billion dollars—or roughly one-tenth of all retail sales made in the United States. Of this sum a good 50 percent, or 50 billion dollars of retail sales can be traced to response to direct mail. Through this means, America shows its love for direct mail by buying a growing proportion of clothes, food, insurance, books, magazines, newsletters, garden equipment, tools, travel, entertainment, and continuing education directly from printed pieces mailed to their homes and offices.

And don't think Big Business is unaware of this love affair. Mail order retail businesses owned by big business (Quaker Oats, American Can, Unity House, Mobil Oil, General Mills, MCA, and Warner) are showing profits at twice the national average for general merchandise retailers selling conventionally through retail stores.

There is no doubt America has a great love affair with direct mail!

Characteristics of the Direct Marketing Shopper

There is a great deal of consistency among studies about the attitudes and characteristics of in-home shoppers. Some twenty analyses and research reports provide the following profile, which describes the direct response buyers (by mail or by phone) compared to non-in-home shoppers:

- Higher-than-average income
- Higher-than-average level of education
- Higher-than-average occupational status
- Greater use of and access to credit
- More venturesome, risk taking, and more flexible
- More secure and willing to take risks
- More innovative and less conservative
- More likely to plan shopping
- Greater enjoyment of shopping in stores
- More frequent use of in-store shopping
- More worldly in outlook and more sophisticated

- More trusting of business
- Satisfied with non-store shopping experiences

A LOOK AT HOW MAILING LISTS ORIGINATE

Why the Potential Market Size Is Seemingly Endless

Let us look first at five interesting statistics about prospective names for mailing lists:

1. There are approximately 87 million households in America. (The largest name lists can reach 80 to 86 million of these.)

2. There are approximately 240 million individuals in America—approximately 165 million are adults.

3. There are approximately 8.5 million businesses, institutions, and offices of professionals in America. Of these, 6.0 million are businesses, 1.5 million are institutions, and 1 million are offices of professionals. The largest list to date can reach about 8.3 million of these.

4. There are approximately 2.5 million farms left in America. (The largest cleaned list can reach about 2 million of these.)

5. There are approximately 7 million individuals running business operations (often of a sales nature) from their homes. (The largest list to date to reach this hidden market numbers about 1 million.)

To reach these differing prospects, the mailing list business provides approximately 20,000 commercially available lists* with about 2 billion names and/or establishments, which means each adult in America (and many children) and every establishment and farm is on a number of lists.

To emphasize this, I once answered a query for the *New Yorker* magazine on "How does one get off mailing lists?" I noted that one does not get off a mailing list by dying. The name remains. My advice was: "You move to a very small town and you leave no forwarding address, and even then you must be very careful because

- You cannot buy a car or rent a home.
- You cannot get a listed telephone number.

---

*In addition to lists available for rental, it is estimated that there are over 1,000,000 lists in use. Over 790,000 establishments, for example, (about 280,000 nonprofit, and 510,000 "for profit") have third class bulk permits, and each permit implies a list or two or more.

- You cannot register to vote.
- You cannot join a club, church, or enroll in school.
- You cannot open a charge account or use a credit card.
- You cannot subscribe to a magazine or buy a product by mail.
- You cannot give money to a charitable cause.
- You have to just fade away.

While only 25 million American families (about 30 percent) are considered affluent (see page 76), it is believed that at least 50 percent of families buy by mail in a given year. There is a solid core of confirmed mail order buyers, so much so that on almost any given merge–purge, of a group of mail order buyer lists of a given classification and value, the duplication removal ranges from about 8 percent to as high as 26 percent.

Breakdown of Establishments Serving the List Business

In the United States there are:

- 12 major list brokers, plus 100 to 200 minor players
- 6 major list compilers, plus 100 to 200 smaller factors, principally specialists and marketers
- 20 major list managers, plus 100 to 200 smaller firms
- 11,000 computer service bureaus; 1,500 or more of which have upper- and lower-case print capacity, and/or laser printers
- 6,000 lettershops, no two of which offer exactly the same roster of services
- 16,000 advertising agencies, of which about 250 specialize or specifically include direct response
- 4,000 public relations agencies, of which a handful specifically include direct response
- 15,000 publishers including publishers of newspapers, magazines, shoppers, tabloids, and newsletters
- 4,000 house organs
- 35,000 associations
- 1,000,000 mailing lists, of which approximately 20,000 are commercially available

The Changing Nature of Lists

In any given year 18 percent to 20 percent of households change. In other words, from 15 million to 17 million households have new or changed occupants each year.

In business, the change is even more dramatic. The total of all businesses, institutions and offices of professionals stays remarkably stable—within one-half to 1 percent from year to year. However, this apparent stability hides a churning of 30 percent of all nonhouseholds in which 15 percent go "out of business" or are absorbed, or change their names, while 15 percent of new nonhouseholds get their start.

This year

Going out	Continuing in Business
15%	85%

Next year

Gone	Continuing	New
15%	85%	15% New

Following year

Gone	Continuing	New
15%	85%	15% New

Only one in five fledgling new businesses is still around five years later, and some of these die in each subsequent year. Those who fill executive positions have an even shorter average life. Almost half the individual names on a business list will be gone or dead; or will have moved to a new job; or be working elsewhere within a year.

The message is crystal clear. A list even one year old is so burdened by nondeliverables as to be suspect. Lists that are older than that are very expensive (in wasted dollars) indeed.

For a discussion of the changing consumer market see the section on Demographics on page 143. For a discussion of the changing business market see the section on big business on page 306.

How New Lists Are Created

Each year list managers (myself included) proudly offer lists "never rented before," "never available before," or "first time ever rented." Such lists come from new public (or printed) records or from some form of direct response. Such response lists come from

1. Established mailers that finally recognize that a list not rented is an opportunity for profit lost.
2. New mailers who have procured enough names to make a viable list.
3. New data developed to produce:
   a. Inquirers
   b. Catalog inquiries
   c. Requests for printed information
4. New buyers generated from space ads or electronic media or other non-mailing media.

New lists from public (or printed records) include

1. New households
2. New businesses
3. New registrants (auto, telephone, voters)
4. New graduates or students
5. New professionals or professional offices
6. New institutions
7. Newly appointed executives
8. New members
9. New receivers of honors
10. New babies
11. New marriages
12. New credit card holders

The essence of "new lists" is that list creation is a never ending and continuous activity. Lists don't exist, per se, they are created, captured, or nurtured by people who understand their worth. Lists are not necessarily new but additions, changes, and variants of list data are new and always welcome.

Overlays provide another way to "create" new lists. A demographic overlay to a large file like *McCalls* or *Ladies Home Journal* may provide a means to change marginality or submarginality to usefulness. Overlays need not be only demographic. The "questionnaire lists" (see page 218) ask for and obtain data on hobbies, interests, credit cards, direct-mail interest, and usage. These data, when utilized as an overlay to other lists, can provide useful new segments to test. *In general, the cry against the "shortage" of lists is in essence proof that these people are not trying hard enough to locate the names they need.*

Demographers must also be laughing at those who cry that there are not enough lists. Their predictions indicate the total population in the United States will increase by 17 million by 1990 and by 27 million by 1995. Those famous baby boomers are moving from "Yuppie" to "Muppie" (Middle age upwardly-mobile parents of 35 to 44 year olds). From all indications "Muppies" intend to use their increasing discretionary income to live not only well but better. The number of two-wage earner families (along with one-person families) is going to increase, moving millions more into the affluent part of the market (see page 175). Lists, both old and new, will be constantly fueled by these new entrants into family life and into the affluent society which provides a great part of purchases by mail.

HOW MAILING LISTS REACH THEIR POTENTIAL MARKETS

Lists come on the market through three main channels:

1. Companies and individuals whose *major* activity is the list business such as
   a. List brokers
   b. List compilers
   c. List managers
   d. Marketing consultants

2. Companies whose major activity is elsewhere (chiefly mail order companies, publishers, and data processing services) whose list income is *peripheral*.

3. *Printed source materials*—primarily publishers and governments.

Six Types of Available Lists

There are six major types of lists available through the three main market channels:

1. Registration lists
2. Printed sources
3. Originally researched lists
4. Occupant lists
5. Mail-responsive and customer files
6. Compilations

Let's take a closer look at each of these six types of lists.

Registration lists

Telephone directories: The principle directories upon which mailing lists are based are telephone directories, both alphabetic (for consumer lists) and yellow pages (classifieds for business lists). The total number of households with listed phones in 1984 was 57 million. It is now known there are 83 million households with phones. Those missing from the file compiled by R. H. Donnelly are unlisted or unpublished numbers. They turn out to be either one of two kinds, upper-income families who wish to keep their phone numbers private, and in some major cities such as New York City, those families on welfare who are not permitted a listed phone so they pay extra for an unlisted phone.

City directories: For some 2,500 cities and towns, a local person-to-person canvas is made of each household which results in a city directory. The majority of these directories are canvassed and printed by R. L. Polk, which produces a list of some 24 million individuals. The one exceptional bit of demographic information available from such directories is the occupation of those in the households who work. A good number of retired people are also selectable from this source.

Drivers' licenses: The list source with the largest number of names is a file of drivers' licenses. Here, rather than one listing to a family or an establishment, all members in a family with licenses may be found. The total list is probably 160,000,000 or so. A few compilers utilizing records from thirty to thirty-five states have lists of 110 million names. The key data available here are age, including, for some 15 to 20 million, exact date of birth. The primary users of such files are insurance companies.

Voters' registrations: A source that on the surface promises more names than even the driver's license files is voter registrations as this source provides names for those with and without licenses. However, the sources (towns, townships, cities, counties, parties) are so disparate and scattered that, except in specific states, no one apparently has ever attempted to build a universal file. The only known data about a voter's file are that the individual is an adult and what his or her party affiliation is, if any. Some rather sparse data here also tell how often each registrant has voted. For the 1988 Presidential election, a major effort is being launched to compile a massive country-wide file of registered voters.

Printed sources

What people read is a very good indication of their interests and their lifestyle. Thus while there may be a few individuals who read, say, *Rolling Stone* as well as *Foreign Affairs*, readership of such magazines tells a prospective renter a great deal about how they think and what they consider important. Publications provide lists of subscribers, qualified recipients, compiled recipients (by classification), inquiries, giftees, friends of friends, sweepstakes entrants, contestants, advertisers, advertising prospects, editors, columnists, and owners. Announcements in the local papers also provide lists of newly promoted executives, travelers, engaged couples, births, and deaths. And then there are hundreds of printed rosters of clubs and associations, as well as directories covering almost every field of endeavor.

Originally researched lists

Precious few lists are created by research. Hospitals and offices of pediatricians provide data on birth expectancies. The two major compilers of school data (below college level) actually make phone calls each year to the more than 16,000 school districts that have 200 or more enrolled pupils. Both Standard & Poors (S&P) and Dun & Bradstreet (D&B) individually query several tens of thousands of major companies for the data they publish in their directories of big business.

Occupant lists

In addition to name lists, local compilers, now banded together to provide close to national average, provide complete area lists of households (without the name of the resident) that can be addressed to resident or occupant. These lists include all households, including nontelephone homes, noncar-owning homes, and all households of nonlisted phone registrants. Occupant lists, as a rule, are

20 percent larger than comparable name lists. They are initially constructed from phone listings, then augmented by individual review of new neighborhoods plus periodic checking of each household in each carrier route by the USPS. Compilers that have coverage of 90 percent or more of an area in their files may purchase this updating service from the USPS. Almost all occupant files are maintained not only in carrier-route order, but in carrier-walk order, which is the way the individual carrier moves along the route of approximately 350 addresses. As time goes on, more and more occupant lists will feature demographic overlays, including income and number of children.

Occupant files can deliver virtually all of the 87 million households in America but normally 2 percent of them, even on corrected lists, result in nondeliverables due to vacancies.

Mail-responsive and customer files

Most proprietary lists are available peripherally as an adjunct to the main business of each establishment. They come from seven classifications:

1. Companies
2. Customers (or donors or subscribers)
3. Inquiries
4. Warrantees
5. Friends of friends
6. Trade show booth registrations
7. Prospects qualified by sales representatives

Compilations

Compiled lists are discussed in more detail in a later section but in general they fall into one of the following four categories:

1. Consumer
2. Business
3. Educational
4. Special

What happens to the list before it comes on the market? Despite the channel through which the basic list enters or is offered to the list-using market, the following steps, in one way or another, have taken place.

1. The list is converted to or made available on electronic data which can be selected out and printed by a computer.

2. The data are zip coded (for five digits).

3. The data are or can be outputted as printed labels or magnetic tapes (or other magnetic forms).

4. Some lists (and again despite the channel) may be:

    a. Combined (merged–purged) with others.

    b. Utilized as the base of a data bank.

    c. Enhanced by overlaying them with demographic and psychographic data from other sources.

HOW TO CATEGORIZE MAILING LISTS: TWELVE PIGEONHOLES

All lists can be placed in one (or more) of twelve pigeonholes. Lists by source are:

a. Compiled names (compiled from printed source documents)

b. Response-oriented (buyers, inquirers, warrantees, respondents)

c. Originally researched (compiled at the source)

That provides three convenient classifications based on *where the lists come from*.

Each list is primarily distinguishable by address

- At-home addresses
- At-business addresses

That provides two convenient classifications, based on *where the lists go to*.

Each list is primarily found

- *Outside* the company
- *Inside* the company

That provides two convenient classifications based on *the relationship of the list to the owner*.

Thus

$$3 \text{ sources} \times 2 \text{ locations} \times 2 \text{ relationships} = 12 \text{ pigeonholes.}$$

One selection factor that cannot be obtained from a compiled (only) file is that of mail order buyers who are probably one third or more of all families in the United States. If you require a mail order buyer (and there are lists of just the type of mail order buyers you want), it is virtually certain those selective mail order buyer lists will out pull a list compiled for a given set of data. If, however, you wish complete coverage of a classification, say, for example, manufacturers, associations, or law offices, then compiled files alone can satisfy this particular need.

HOW COMPILERS AND COMPILED LISTS VARY

Just as list types and kinds vary, so do compilations of lists. In general, compilations may be said to fall into one of the following major types:

1. Consumers—stratified
2. Consumers—nonstratified
3. Consumers—occupant or resident
4. Businesses—rated, by SIC (with or without executives)
5. Businesses—by classification, nonrated (with or without executives)
6. Specialized—by field of interest

A compiler provides an ordered list of names and addresses, extracted and combined from printed sources, to reach a given market or classification. Note that the compiler does not ordinarily work with original data nor does the compiler do original research. Compilers may research sources, or research to find sources, but the end-product is compiled from printed sources. Dictionaries define compile like this: To put together (data or names) gathered from various sources in an orderly form.

Compilers may work with *internal sources* (company records). But primarily compilers work with *external sources* (printed records).

Internally Compiled List Sources

The main sources for compiling from internal (company) records are

1. Customers (donors, subscribers, recipients)
2. Friends of customers
3. Giftees of customers
4. Warrantees
5. Inquirers
6. Respondents
7. Prospects
8. Sales-force recommendations
9. Targeted, preferred or qualified prospects
10. House organ distribution
11. Influentials—press and other
12. Employees
13. Officers
14. Sales representatives
15. Distribution points
16. Suppliers
17. Stockholders

Externally Compiled List Sources

The main printed sources for compiling from *external* (printed) records—nonresponse-oriented—are:

1. Rosters and membership rolls
2. Directories and registrations of
   a. cars
   b. phones
   c. voters
   d. industries
   e. professionals
   f. householders (city directories)
   g. purchasers
3. Reports

4. Announcements
   a. births
   b. job-related activity
   c. professional activity
   d. social activity
   e. advertisers
5. Overlay material for increased selectability of mailing lists
   a. census tracts
   b. ethnicity
   c. surname
   d. "clusters" (around known homemakers)
   e. professionals
   f. institutions

External compiling itself breaks down into two kinds: (1) Precompiled names and addresses provided to fit a market known to exist, or believed to exist, and (2) compilations to order—or custom compiling to specifications laid down by the customer.

In general, most external compiling operations are moving more and more toward precompiled lists. But the increasing sophistication of list use plus the active merchandising by compilers of multiple-selection factors, are blurring the lines between what is a precompiled list and what is a "custom" prepared list for just one client.

There are at least forty-four kinds of lists available from compilers. Although every list segment can be placed in one of the twelve "pigeonholes," there are many kinds of lists within these types that are distinct entities unto themselves. Thus, it may be useful to differentiate lists within a framework of major kinds that compilers provide. Refer to Tables 2.1 and 2.2 for a more detailed breakdown.

For examples of lists within lists consider the following: Professionals include medical, dental, legal, and architectural. Medical personnel can include veterinarians as well as osteopaths. Lists within MDs can be selected by staff, private practice, specialization, age, and so on. Under engineers, compilers can also provide names (if not from A to Z) from acoustical to welding; including civil, design, electronic, government, management, naval, packaging, and structural.

Table 2.1 lists forty-four different kinds of list by classification, and indicates for each whether it is compiled, or generated (in part for some) by mail order

Table 2.1

Forty-five lists available by category (25 are mail order responsive)

	Business	Consumer	Mail Order	Compiled
Advertisers	x			x
Alumni	x	x		x
Births		x		x
Business Executives	x		x	x
Businesses	x		x	x
Canadians	x	x	x	x
Children		x	x	x
Churches	x		x	x
"Clusters" of Known Homemakers		x		x
Contributors	x	x	x	x
Credit Cards	x	x	x	x
Data Qualified by Field Research, Questionnaires	x	x	x	x
Editors	x			x
Educators	x	x	x	x
Engineers	x	x	x	x
Ethnic Groups	x	x	x	x
Farmers	x		x	x
Financial	x			x
Foreign	x	x	x	x
Government	x	x	x	x
Influencers, Opinion Leaders	x	x		x
Institution Executives	x			x
Institutions (except churches and government)	x		x	x
Insurance	x		x	x
Libraries	x			x
Magazine Subscribers and Recipients	x	x	x	x
Mail Respondents, Businesses	x		x	
Mail Respondents, Consumers	x	x	x	
Medical Disciplines	x	x	x	x
New Businesses	x		x	

(cont.)

Table 2.1 cont.

Forty-five lists available by category (25 are mail order responsive)

	Business	Consumer	Mail Order	Compiled
Newly Established Households		x		x
Newly Promoted Executives	x			x
Occupant		x		x
Owners of Products	x	x	x	x
Professionals-Other	x	x	x	x
Retail Businesses	x			x
Scientists	x	x	x	x
Senior Citizens		x		x
Stratified Lists by Demographic Characteristics		x		x
Students in High School and College	x	x		x
Teenagers		x		x
Trade Show Registrants	x			x
Work-at-Home Operations		x		x
Working Women	x	x	x	x

Table 2.2

Commercially available mailing lists*

Consumer		
Mail order		
Merchandise	14,000	
Books, magazines, newsletters	1,000	
Compiled	500	15,500
Business		
Mail order		
Merchandise	500	
Books, magazines, newsletters	1,500	
Compiled	1,500	4,500
TOTAL		20,000

*(Lists "originally researched" are too few to tabulate here.)

response. In addition, this table denotes whether such classifications cover consumers, only, or business (or businessmen) only, or both. It is of significance that of the forty-four classifications eighteen or close to half include both consumer segments as well as segments originated by or at business.

Table 2.2 provides a rough estimate of the number of Commercially Available Mailing Lists by:

- where the lists come from—compiled, or response oriented
- where the lists go to—home address, or business address
- type of product—published data, or merchandise

The majority of compiled lists are business oriented; the majority of mail responsive lists for merchandise are consumer oriented. However, when it comes to lists of mail responders to publishers, there are more lists of a business nature than consumer.

Fourteen Ways to Compile Lists from Telephone Books

The source used is the initial limitation on a compilation. How the source *is used* is very important. Half-a-dozen compilers can use telephone books for different purposes and come up with distinctly different lists. In fact, two compilers can attempt to compile the same list from telephone directories, and come up with two different lists.

The art of the compiler in discerning lists among raw data is graphically illustrated by the various lists available from phone books, both alphabetic and classified. For in addition to serving as the chief initial source of addresses for virtually all lists, compilers can obtain the following list data from these sources:

1. Reverse directories, in street order, for stratified lists (consumer).
2. Clusters, around selected homes (consumer).
3. New residents—new from one edition of a phone book to the next (consumer).
4. "Old" residents—those unchanged for X years (consumer).
5. Selection on basis of last name, such as Green or Smith (consumer or business), or names of probable Catholic or Jewish persuasion (consumer).
6. Advertisers or boldface print in yellow pages (business).
7. Dual listings (usually home and office) in alpha (business and consumer).
8. Alpha listings for checking addresses (business and consumer).

9. Firms in a given field with phones (business). There are lists where those with phones can be segregated from those without. For example, one-third of registered beauty salons have no phones. The disparity is also great among such classifications as clubs, fraternal orders, labor organizations, and churches. By sorting on phone numbers, lists can also provide one address per phone listing of such classifications as law offices, accounting offices, insurance offices, real estate offices, architectural firms, engineering firms, and doctors' offices.

10. New businesses—new from one edition of a phone book to next (business).

11. "As" that are also "Bs"—or included in "Bs." For example, insurance agencies also listed in real estate; gas stations also listed in garages; or gas stations with carwash advertisements; heating contractors also in air conditioning; coal dealers also supplying fuel oil (business).

12. Boldface and other classified advertisers (business).

13. City size selections—metro area or small town (business and consumer).

14. Phone numbers added to customer files, or compilations, for phone follow-up (business or consumer).

How to Compile Business Lists from Telephone Books

Classifieds are particularly useful for small business classifications that are not otherwise available. However, they are quite far from being a source of "pure" lists. Under the same heading will often be found manufacturers, wholesalers and retailers, plus consultants and anyone else who wishes to pay to have a listing under the given heading.

At times, this can be a plus. "Bottlers" for example, include home offices, branches, local bottlers, some suppliers, and an elusive block of soft drink wholesaler names that are hard to find any other way.

There are, in all probability, several hundred (mostly local) compiling operators that utilize classified phone directories as source material. At least three of these have reasonably complete sets of the 4,700-plus phone books published each year, and they replace the old with the new as they are published and procured. However, compiling from this source is an art that makes a professional compilation easily worth twice as much as a conventional compilation. The classifieds wish to sell listings under every germane classification and although the list compiler seeks to provide an unduplicated list, the telephone company is working assiduously to include every possible duplication. (In the classification of "Insurance" there are two "phone drops" for small insurance companies in Manhattan, with over forty separate listings in addition to duplications between insurance and real estate.) The duplication in classified lists averages between 10 percent and 15 percent. No typist can cope with this duplication but a computer that compares phone numbers can. It is best to find out how your compiler solves the problem of duplication on those lists you find come from classified phone directories.

Three Points to Remember about Using Telephone Books to Prepare Lists

There are three points that should be noted before leaving the topic of phone books. They concern recency, local deliverability, and change in the future.

Phone book lists, both alphabetical and classified (the yellow pages) are the state of the art for almost every major compiled file of names and addresses. These lists are, in turn, utilized by major compilers and data processors to update aging files that may be either compiled or mail-responsive. Therefore, the recency and the deliverability of telephone lists are (or should be) of considerable concern to the list-using fraternity.

Let us first look at the time frame for publication of a typical big city phone directory.

1. It takes the phone company an average of four to six months to canvas an area. (In major cities this canvas goes on for the best part of ten months of every year.)

2. At the end of the canvas it takes the phone company about three months to prepare the book for the printer and get it printed.

3. It usually takes the compilers who work from 4,700 or more directories (whether alphabetic or classified) two months to locate the book.

4. It then takes the converter of the printed page about two months to incorporate the new data into the national file.

5. The data then stay on the file, untouched for a year, until the next directory is available.

6. Meanwhile, back at the telephone company, current data on a monthly, weekly, even daily basis, are available in computerized form.

On a homogenized basis—that is, a cross-section selected from a large number of phone books, the data available from major compilers are no more than 90 percent deliverable.

On a localized basis, it can be better (if the local phone book was just updated) or much worse (if no new local book has been printed in the last ten, twelve, or fourteen months). As the population of America is remarkably peripatetic and 18 percent to 20 percent of U.S. families move *each* year, it is obvious that the dating of the telephone book data has a great deal to do with deliverability locality by locality. Thus, it is important to find out when the phone book was last converted and placed on file if you are going to mail to a market in Syracuse, Birmingham, or Cedar Rapids.

The problem of deliverability underlines the changing world ahead. The telephone companies, after the breakup of AT&T, are the acknowledged owners of both the alphabetic lists and the classified lists they publish. They are in a position to provide current, live data, including "new connects" (new telephone listings) for both households and businesses.

Some of this current data is now being made available. In time, it is likely all phone data will be made available—and this will have a profound effect on the deliverability of a great proportion of all direct mailings made. The firm of Ed Burnett Consultants, Inc. has estimated this will produce a savings to mailers of over $375,000,000 each year.

SIX WAYS OF SELLING BY DIRECT MARKETING

One step—for a single product or service

As the term implies, this is a method that attempts to complete the entire sales transaction in one step. (Some one steps call for extended payments.) This is the form that most direct mail (including catalogs) has tended to take for literally myriads of offers.

Two step

This term describes a methodology in which step one seeks to induce a cold prospect to raise his or her hand by requesting additional information about a product, service, or plan. The information may be contained in a booklet, fulfillment package, or a catalog. Step two then is the attempt to convert these requests or inquiries into sales. It is used frequently in connection with complex and relatively high-ticket concepts and products that require thoughtful consideration, or specialized information, or product demonstration.

Catalog

A catalog is in effect a form of cooperative advertising in which an affinity group of items is offered at one time to a given target group or groups. A catalog, which can be likened to a retail store, takes the store to the buyer through a printed display of merchandise.

Subscription

This is a special form of one-step selling in which an attempt is made to sell an ongoing service for a stipulated period or number of iterations. The most usual form in direct marketing is to acquire both long-term and short-term commitments for magazines, newsletters, and newspapers.

Club

This is a modification of subscription selling in which an offer is made to forward a product under an automatic shipping plan until the customer cancels any more shipments. Payment for one shipment is usually required before the next is shipped; the customer may be committed to take and pay for a given number of shipments before being eligible to cancel.

There are two major versions of club selling: "Positive Option" and "Negative Option." Under the former, the customer is offered a selection (or selections) usually on a monthly basis and only those ordered are shipped. Under the latter, *unless* the customer specifically reports by mail "not to ship," the current offer will be sent. Negative option is primarily utilized in the sales of books and records.

Continuity

This is an offer of a series of items that form a given family or set to be shipped at regular intervals. The number of items may be known or only approximated at the outset. Payment for the latest shipment triggers release of the next in the series. This continues regularly or until the customer cancels. Some book clubs that use this method use a "load-up" means if the second or the second and third units are paid for promptly. "Load-up" features a bulk shipment of the remainder of the books in a given series with payments usually made on an installment basis.

The Thirty-Day Rule

The thirty-day rule is must reading for anyone in the direct-mail field.

The consumer's protection against delays

In the 1970s the FTC established the thirty-day rule which protects the interests of buyers of products and services by mail. Every direct-response operator, irrespective of type, is required to follow the thirty-day rule.

The regulation is only three pages long and should be read by everyone responsible for delivery of products to the consumer. It covers

1. Requirements for the initial solicitation.
2. Requirements for the initial and subsequent notifications of delay.
3. Requirements for internal procedures and recordkeeping.

PROFESSIONALS SERVING THE LIST INDUSTRY AND HOW TO WORK WITH THEM

There are three types of professionals that make their living exclusively from lists. They are the

1. List broker
2. List manager
3. List compiler

In addition, there are three types of professionals that provide special services to lists as well as other aspects of direct mail. They are the

1. Computer service bureau
2. Mailing plant
3. Advertising agency

The next few chapters discuss the work of each of these professionals as well as basic advice on how to work with each one.

CHAPTER 3

How List Brokers and List Managers Operate

LIST BROKERS: SPECIALISTS WHO CATER TO THE MAILERS

What List Brokers Do

List brokers (like brokers in other fields of business) bring together the buyer (the mailer) and the seller (the owner of the list). They are paid a commission, usually 20 percent, which comes to them from the list owner. Despite the fact that the broker is paid by the list owner, the broker owes his loyalty to the mailer. The majority of all mail order buyer list rentals are placed by list brokers. Brokers are (unless in the field as a compiler themselves) of minimum importance in the placement of compiled files.

Brokers seek to represent all lists on the market. There are approximately twenty major list brokers in the United States, and they each manage a file consisting of about 20,000 list cards filed by category. (These card files are now being slowly computerized so the machine can produce universes of lists covering given classifications.) Approximately 50 percent of the income of list brokers comes from only 100 of the 20,000 lists they have. Most brokers serve less than 200 customers and have prospect lists of a few thousand names.

The Missing Ingredient in a Broker's Card File: The List's Track Record

The one precious ingredient missing from the cards put out by list brokers is the track record of the given list as seen by the individual broker. This is the ingredient that makes recommendations of knowing list brokers so helpful and valuable. It is by all odds the one most important fact for the would-be renter to know.

Specialization and Cooperative Mailing Ventures

Brokers tend to specialize because of specialization by mailers. There are brokers known for their acumen and special inside know-how in such fields as gardening, fund raising, gifts, magazines, and clothing; providing financial services, business mail order, insurance, health, do-it-yourself. Brokers may also be known for how to reach culture vultures or opportunity seekers.

As the cost of solo mailings increases we are seeing the growth of cooperative mailings. This has led to broker specialization in other response vehicles, such as package inserts, envelope stuffers, co-op advertising, and cardvertisers.

List brokers have a vested interest in providing the best possible list suggestions to their clients. They lose money on every test and can profit only if the mailer returns for a substantial "continuation" of those lists that tested well.

The Broker's Role as a Marketing Consultant

List brokers tend to become list and marketing consultants to those they work closest with. Those with years of experience can evaluate the likelihood of success, advise on the necessary scope of the test program, provide input for utilization of alternative forms of media, and provide helpful insights into what comparable mailers are doing.

A handful of large brokerage companies can offer to keep track of new mail offers, direct-mail space advertising offers, refunds, premiums, sweepstakes, and write-in offers. They also can provide a constant update on what is new in direct-response lists.

THE "IMPARTIAL" NEGOTIATOR

Because the broker has the confidence of both mailer and list owner, he or she can be very useful in negotiating favorable terms for a rollout through a merge–purge. The broker may be instrumental in arranging for overlaying a customer file by an outside file with desired demographic characteristics.

The more the broker knows about what happens to the mailer's file, offers, and target markets, and the history of what lists and what list types have worked best in the past, the more accurately a meaningful input at the time mailing schedules are being firmed-up can be provided. Brokers can become so knowledgeable about what works and what doesn't that they can help match lists to differences in packages and offers. This type of knowledge is far more useful than that provided by less professional brokers who send broker cards to prospects on what might be termed an "approval basis."

From a list standpoint, the broker is (or should be) completely impartial and live by the lists that work for his or her customers. However, the flux in the list business that affects most list brokers and major list managers, as well as important factors in the merchandising of compiled files, creates opportunities for some favoritism in the selection process.

HOW TO DECIDE BETWEEN SINGLE OR MULTIPLE BROKER USE

If you mail under 200,000 prospect names per year, it is probably best to select one list broker for your needs. This amount of business for a broker (about $2,600 in gross commissions annually) is not enough to get you the support and help you need from two or more brokers. If you mail one million or more pieces you should, by all means, investigate the help that can be given to you by two or more list brokers. Why? Although list brokers work with the same list availabilities, each broker has had different experiences with various lists. The major mailer who restricts business to just one broker might well be depriving himself of some valuable and untouched list sources.

A number of major mailers have decided to go with one exclusive list broker. There is usually a bit of seduction involved as the canny exclusive list broker provides effort-key reports and balance counts to clients, and saves those clients a sizable amount of necessary detail work. This hides the different knowledge a second or third list broker can bring to the table that might well be worth much more than the seductive service offered.

SIZING UP THE MAJOR MAILERS AND BROKERS: SOME REVEALING SURVEY TIDBITS

Standard Rate and Data Service (SRDS) with an assist from Direct Media, Inc., recently published the results of a survey of a cross-section of major mailers and a number of known list brokers. Buried in the figures are some interesting insights into the fascinating business of mailing lists.

In the prior year, the typical broker in this study provided 344 lists for tests and continuations (ninety-seven of them for the first time).

Let's put that quantity—344 separate lists—into context. All well-known list brokers have access to over 20,000 lists. The quantity is just a bit above one-and-one-half percent of 20,000. All this does is give additional credence to a survey I conducted some years ago that indicated the average list broker did 50 percent of his or her business from only one hundred lists (or roughly one-half of one percent of the lists available).

These figures have not changed in the twenty-eight years I have been in this business. They underline the reason for the growth of the list management business that I had the privilege of creating a quarter of a century ago. List managers move the molecules for the lists they represent. Now almost every major list is in the hands of list managers because that is the one way to guarantee obtaining a presence in the process of mailing list selection.

Major brokers obtained lists for an average of forty-one different client mailers within the past twelve months. Let's compare that quantity against a few others. There are over 790,000 mailers with third class bulk permits. There are at least fifteen list compilers and list merchandisers, both business and consumer, who serve 5,000 or more list users per year. They do not average three or four mailers per month but rather 5,000 to 10,000 per year—400 to 800 different mailers per month. If we were privileged to review the records of the thirty-five brokers who participated in this study we would find that on an unduplicated basis the number of clients served would be a far smaller number—possibly one-half or less.

The average list brokers in this study placed an excess of 10 million names per year for their clients. The latest figures indicate that the number of names rented or sold for direct-mail advertising purposes is about 31 billion. The thirty-five brokers in this study apparently accounted for over 350 million names. (There are several major list brokers who, by themselves, provide more than that number of names to clients.) Eighty percent of the list orders placed by the seventy-three mailers interviewed were serviced by list brokers.

This statistic proves the importance of list brokers to users of response-oriented lists. It also underlines the churning within the list-supplying community in the last ten years in which almost all list brokers have become major factors in list management. Some have added compiled operations while many list compilers and list managers, almost perforce, have found it expedient to broker lists for their clients. It is almost as hard today to find a pure list broker, pure list compiler, or pure list manager, as it was for Diogenes, centuries ago, to find an honest man.

Sixty percent of mailers surveyed stated that they "always or frequently" specified particular mailing lists, and over half noted they "always or frequently" made substitutions or additions to the recommendations of their broker (or brokers). This should not be surprising. Mailers know, in many cases to one-tenth of a percent, the response of every list used or tested. They are living in their own individual field and are therefore aware, often long before a new list is placed on the market of new lists both in their market and peripheral to it.

This emphasizes that the mailer must (as the SRDS survey clearly notes) provide a good deal of the management of the list function irrespective of the help offered by the list community.

HOW LIST BROKERS USE ON-LINE SYSTEMS TO LOCATE SEPARATE MAILING LIST CATEGORIES

SRDS (Standard Rate & Data Service) has now placed all data on 20,000 plus lists printed in its Directory of Rates for mailing lists "on line" for computer access through CCX, the list utility. The current service provides the basic facts on each list (quality, pricing, selectivity)—but does not produce a list card to send to the mailer for review. In time, the system will include a means to print out the list cards required by the brokerage fraternity.

Several on-line systems are now available which provide complete data for a list card for 8,000, 10,000, even 12,000 separate lists. Such data is being printed at remote locations. Each of these systems provides selection of list by some 100 separate classifications, as well as by size of purchase, recency of purchase, and other selection factors made available by the owner or list manager of the list.

One of these "locater" lists for such a system is shown in Table 3.1. Note that it is possible to interrogate the system for a specialized type of list such as sweepstakes, ethnic, political or sex within a major classification, such as apparel, or insurance sales. Each list on such a system incorporates the very latest data. In fact, seconds after a change is made in the file the list card selected electronically will incorporate that change. With over 12,000 lists on line updated by a team of six list specialists, a list broker with this system can provide a customized selection for a client in a very short period of time.

LIST MANAGERS: WHY YOU NEED THEM, WHAT THEY DO FOR YOU, AND WHOM YOU SHOULD HIRE

How List Managers and Brokers Differ

As we have seen, the list broker works for the mailer and gets commission from the list owner. The list broker wants the mailers to have successful tests so the mailers come back to order "continuations." (See page 368) The list broker has no vested interest in which list is used or which list "works." His or her role

Table 3.1

Sample online selections for list cards

Code #	Category	Code #	Category
01	General Business	53	Animals/Wildlife
02	Self-Improvement/Motivational	55	Families/Parents, Children, Teens
03	Finance	57	Senior Citizens
04	Tax	58	History
07	Government/Law Enforcement/Military	59	Literature/Fiction–Nonfiction
08	Training/Development/Personnel	60	Art/Antiques/Architecture
09	Professional N.E.C.	61	Collectibles
10	Sales/Marketing/Advertising/Trade Shows	62	Travel and Leisure
		63	Affluent
11	Industrial/Material Handling	65	Men's Reading
12	New-World/National	66	Women's Reading
13	Building/Construction	67	Sexually Oriented
14	Engineering/Architects	69	General Interest Reading
15	Medical/Dental/Nursing/HC Pros	72	Sweepstakes
16	Legal	99	Other
17	Educational/Schools	A2	Stocks/Bonds/Money Market
18	Insurance/Business Only	A3	Real Estate Investments
19	International Trade	A5	Oil/Gas
20	Transportation/Traffic/Shipping	A6	Precious Metals/Gems
21	Communications	A7	Coins and Stamps
29	Women in Business	A8	Other/General Interest Investments
30	Automotive/Motor Sports	B2	Computer Business
31	Aviation and Aerospace	B5	Computer Consumer
32	Science/R&D/Technology	C1	Christian
33	Electronics/Video	C2	Jewish
34	Occult/Science Fiction/Mystery/Astrology	C4	Other (Nonsectarian)
		D1	Conservative/Republicans
35	Puzzles/Contests	D2	Liberal/Democratic
36	Photography	D7	Politically Oriented Issues
37	Tool Buyers	D8	Political—Other
38	Arts/Crafts/Hobbies	E1	Ethnic
39	Cooking/Food & Wine	F1	Performing Arts
41	Health(Drugs/Diet/Physical Fitness)	F3	Music
43	Beauty/Cosmetics	H1	Golf
44	Jewelry	H2	Boating/Water Sports
45	Apparel/Shoes	H3	Camping/Hiking
46	General Merchandise/Gift-type Products	H4	Fishing
		H5	Hunting/Guns/Bowing
47	Stationery—Consumer Only	H6	General—Sports/Recreation Enthusiasts
49	Housewares/Home Furnishings		
50	Gardening/Farming	H7	Sporting Goods/Equipment/Apparel
51	Environment/Ecology	I1	Opportunity Seeker/Making Money
52	Humanitarian/Charities	I8	Saving Money

select lists worthy of being tested for clients. The list broker can only prosper on continuations—not on tests.

The list manager works for the list owner as exclusive merchandiser and sales agent. His or her job is to move the molecules on the list or lists he manages. To do this, the list manager must seek the support of list brokers, list houses, and lettershops, as well as promoting managed list(s) directly to mailers considered likely prospects.

How List Managers Are Paid

The list manager usually is recompensed by a commission of 10 percent of the list rental price on large lists, and 15 to 20 percent of the list rental price on small lists. For this he or she pays for the promotion of the list, logs orders, takes care of the order entry, oversees the production of the tapes or labels (in many cases taking on this role requires paying the processing fee) bills the customer, collects the payments, and remits the net sum due to the list owner. On rentals made directly to users, the list manager customarily claims the brokerage fee as well.

Four Main Classes of List Managers and How They Work

It is interesting to note that 90 percent of all major lists on the market are now in the hands of four classes of list managers:

1. Inside list manager. An owner or publisher who has 500,000 or more names to offer can afford to pay an internal specialist to find increasing markets for his or her lists indirectly through brokers, as well as directly to list users.

2. Independent list manager. An independent list managing firm represents a few select lists owned by others. This type of firm either does no list brokerage, or very little (usually only for clients who place lists with them) and thus can tap the entire capacity of the list brokerage field.

3. List manager–broker. As list management has proliferated, list brokers with their unique knowledge of list sources and list users have moved into the field. More lists are now in the hands of list managers who are also list brokers than any other class of list manager.

4. Exclusive list manager. A few dozen lists are the exclusive properties of a few special list brokers who offer only a split commission to other brokers who seek to use such lists for their clientèle.

A good list manager can generally double the net dollars delivered to the list owner who essays to rent his or her own lists. Thus, the usual 10 or 15 percent list management fee (really list merchandising or list selling fee) becomes inconsequential.

The choice of an outside versus an inside list manager is usually a matter of fees available. A list or group of lists that brings a publisher, say, $50,000 net may have list management sales costs of $10,000 to $12,000. It appears that the owner of this list cannot afford the luxury of an internal department—even a one-person department. However, a firm with list income in the $250,000 (and over) range, may well find it expedient to replace an outside list manager who has several arrows in his or her quiver, with an inside specialist dedicated only to the sales and future of the properties of the given publisher.

List rental income

In a report issued a few years ago by the DMA (Direct Marketing Association) over three-fourths of the membership of the list council of the DMA provided data on the proportion of total company income represented by list rental income. It is likely the proportion is now greater as each year more mailers, even unsophisticated mailers, opt to place their names on the list rental market.

The figures were:

Type of company	Proportion of total company income (%)
For Catalog Houses	6%
Businesses	6
Industrial mailers	6
Financial mailers	6
Publishers	4
Fundraisers	4

To put that 4% to 6% of sales into perspective, over half of rental income drops down intact to the bottom line. Three percent net profit before taxes is equivalent to the usual profit on an additional 50 percent of gross sales! In other words, between half and one-third of *net* profit comes from list rental all by itself.

You have a customer list. Your customers names may be in shoe boxes, batched in manila folders, or stashed away in desk drawers. They may be plated on a disc system or converted to computer, but you have them somewhere, and if they are available in a commercially viable quantity (say, 50,000 or more) you are losing a considerable amount of money if you do not offer them to noncompetitive mailers.

Surprisingly enough, list rental income is not always the only significant benefit to be derived from putting your list on the market. If your names are not already on disc or computer, you can usually find a competent list manager who will pay for the conversion of your names to tape however, the list manager reserves the right to amortize the cost from your net rental income. By having your list on computer you have much more ready access to your own customers. Your best source of new business will always be those customers you've satisfied in the past. In addition, when your list is computerized it's easy to pull off a randomly chosen selection for market–research purposes. If you are a mailer and your list develops a successful track record, you'll be able to exchange with other list owners, thereby enabling you to have access to lists not usually available in the rental marketplace. With the growth of merge–purge operations a list that is not on tape is not in the rental market. However, list rental income is always important and for those owners whose lists are already computerized, it is usually the single most important reason for having the list professionally managed. Let's assume that you've decided to go ahead and put your list on the market. Why would you need an outside manager?

Key Reasons Why You Should Hire an Outside Manager

There are two compelling reasons for hiring a professional list management firm rather than trying to do it yourself. This is true for 98 percent of all list owners. First, a professional (pro) with a solid track record who has spent years developing personal contacts in this highly specialized industry can almost always outsell an in-house operation. It's not enough to know more about your list than anyone else. You have to know the brokers, the agencies, and the mailers who should be renting it. You have to know which mailers are ordering which types of lists, through whom and when. You have to know how to position your list against competitive properties, how to segment it for maximum effectiveness, how, where, and when to promote it. Pros spend years learning this. You can't expect the same performance from your secretary, brother-in-law, or that promising young trainee.

Second, a good list manager can achieve a given level of sales at a lower cost to you than if you do it yourself. The economics of scale apply. When a list manager visits brokers or users of lists on a cross-country trip, at conventions, or trade meetings, he or she can spread selling costs over a number of list properties. Even over the phone, a manager can push more than one list in a single call. The list manager's overhead, which is considerable, is spread across many accounts. Can you hire a full-time salesperson, pay the travel and entertainment bills, and absorb the other selling, production, billing and collection expenses for less than 15 percent of your gross list rental dollars? Probably not. And if you cannot, professional management should make financial sense to you.

Other reasons for hiring an outside list manager

- With a few exceptions, the more knowledgeable and more proficient list managers are to be found on the outside. Inside management only makes sense if the people involved are the equal of outside managers, and since good inside managers tend to gravitate outside, the edge here is with outside expertise.

- Outside costs are predictable. The manager gets a fixed percentage. That fee covers all inside costs, including all promotional costs for advertising, travel, operating booths at trade shows, and WATS lines. Inside costs can easily get out of line, particularly when list volume stays level or dips. The budget is a critical factor for inside management; it is a fixed proportion of total revenues using outside management.

- The threat of loss of an account by an outside manager gives the list owner a great deal of clout he or she does not have with an inside operation. Told to move the molecules faster, the outside manager jumps. This may not be so with the average inside operation. In addition, once established, an inside operation is difficult to dismantle and some costs including people, cannot be saved when a change is indicated.

- Outside list managers usually have better systems for reporting in place.

- The outside list manager touches more bases than the inside manager, and can therefore be aware of more pressure points, including mailers who pay slowly, if at all.

- The outside list manager at the conclusion of what is usually a 1- or 2-year contract period can be fired and a new manager can be appointed who can do a better job. Replacing an inside top list manager is not that easy.

Those lists that call for the use of an outside list manager include:

- *All* lists where economics of scale favor paying part of the costs, not all of costs.

- Virtually any business-to-business list.

- Any new list or new concept.

- Any list where the current staff is already overloaded. (Whenever it is possible to buy outside management either better or less expensively, that is the path to take.)
- Any list where skilled laborpower is not available for inside management.

When to Manage a List from the Inside

From an economic point of view, no list should be managed inside if the costs are greater than the fixed cost involved in hiring an outside manager.

Beyond that there are a number of reasons why some lists should be managed inside.

Reasons for managing a list inside

- Single commitment to the rental, sale, and exchange of the list properties of the company, no diminution of effort to other list properties, no need to prioritize among competing constituencies or list owners.
- Greater knowledge of the lists and their potentials than any outsider could know no matter how experienced.
- Better control, including better control of money; (and no worry as to any intermediary using funds due); fewer misunderstandings in usage and clearance procedures; immediate single-source capacity to negotiate exchanges and large scale usage.
- In the case of a publisher, far better synergism in correlating with the circulation department, and the availability of information in house by a list consultant on circulation as well as total list activities.
- Elimination of any threat to list brokers since the inside manager does not broker any outside lists. (Brokers, given the opportunity, will prefer to work directly with an inside manager than with an outside manager who also seeks additional brokerage business. This once was the advantage of those outside list managers who did no brokering; that breed has disappeared.)

Inside list management makes better-than-average sense for:

- Publishers with large lists.
- Newsletters, where the target markets are specialized.
- Catalog operators who choose to rent mainly through exchanges.
- Large mail order lists that are mature and well known.

Ideally, list management should be a full-time job, either for an internal list manager or for an outside service that is dedicated to the sales and rentals of lists owned by others. Those companies with smaller lists that cannot justify a full-time marketer of mailing lists, usually combine this duty with other duties, such as obtaining outside lists, preparing managerial reports, overseeing the inside computer operations, and so on. The cost of such in-house management (primarily salaries and benefits, as well as sales promotion, advertising, and sales-related travel costs, and company overhead) leaves a given net profit. This needs to be weighed against the fees charged by a list management firm, as well as measured against the gross sales that may be made by using either method.

List Managers Versus the Exclusive Broker Relationship

A number of owners of prestigious lists place their lists with one broker and one broker only on an exclusive basis. Such lists are available to other brokers, on a split-fee basis only. That is, the broker holds 10 percent of the conventional 20 percent list brokerage and offers only the other 10 percent to other indirect sources of list placement. The net result is far fewer rentals of the list to far fewer users. In effect, this is more than satisfactory to the exclusive broker, who partakes of every rental, but it is detrimental to the list owner who receives less than the market can and would offer. List managers (who offer brokers their full 20 percent) have proven many times over that they can easily double the sales of any list marketed half-heartedly. In at least one instance when a cultural file of some note was transferred from an exclusive broker to a knowing list manager, the total rentals of the list increased seven fold and the net to the list owner increased over six fold! This list, as might be expected, has not been returned to "exclusive broker" status.

Here are four of the main functions of list managers:

- They uncover and bring new lists to market, and thus open avenues to rentals and exchanges.
- They provide a professional sales service that the majority of list owners could not otherwise fund.
- They aid in "positioning" the owner's list on the market, and range far wider than the average broker in their efforts to obtain revenue for their list owners.
- They have contacts within list brokerage houses, ad agencies; and they know the mailing community. Thus they can usually outperform inside list management that is run as a part-time operation. Most good list managers

will project double the income through their efforts when compared with an ongoing in-house effort.

This rather impressive set of reasons goes a long way toward explaining why an estimated 90 percent of the lists used by direct marketers are now in the hands of outside list managers. Inclusive of brokers and compilers, who also are list managers, in 1987 there were over 200 such establishments offering lists owned by others.

How to Select a List Manager

All list managers perform the same basic tasks. They bring lists to the marketplace; provide them to likely users; take care of the detail and paperwork attendant to orders, clearances, billings, and collections. All mail order buyer lists utilize the "clearance" procedure, in which a sample mailing piece of the proposed renter is sent to the list owner for review and acceptance ("clearance") or rejection. All provide periodic reports on sales and collections. It should be noted that some pay their list owners very slowly and often under duress. (To hold onto the net sums collected and due the list owner is a proven way to fund a weak financial position.)

There are seven requirements to look for when selecting a list manager:

1. Professional list management competence
2. Satisfied list owner customers
3. Longevity of accounts
4. Adequate staff
5. Computer competence
6. Adequate financial strength
7. Rational promotional plans and expenditures

There should be a "fit" between the needs of the mailer and the place in the market of the list manager. A new mailer with a list of 50,000 or 75,000 names may be lost with a manager who has a dozen lists of 1 million names or more. Some managers are too small. They don't have the reputation, size, or experience to command reasonable attention in the complexity of the list business. One of the easiest businesses to start is list management. All one needs is a small office, a typewriter and letterhead stationery. However, over and above the seven considerations listed earlier, the single most important factor may well be that of "comfort." The list owner needs to feel he or she is being given tender loving care and attention. So if the sum involved runs into many thousands of "nice net neat" dollars—as it usually does—visit the main office of the list manager, meet the people who will work on the account, and make sure the relationship is a comfortable one from the very start.

One caution note: Do not be bamboozled by promises of exceptional dollars. Manager "promises" to gain an account often include a given amount of "hype."

How a List Manager Rents Your List to Others

Most list managers have a stock proposal outlining their services and a generalized marketing game plan.

The styles of the presentations may vary but the substance does not. Managers promote their lists through direct mail and space advertising and pay all the expenses incurred in the process. Managers also point out their extensive personal contacts and their face-to-face sales ability. They will process orders, provide the list owner with sample mailing pieces from prospective customers, bill and collect, and remit monies due to the list owner. They also provide periodic reports on sales and payables. The methodology is fairly standard; you don't buy the means. You buy the firm or the individual who will implement them based on whom you feel will perform all these functions best for you.

How List Managers Promote Sales Activity

The positioning and continuous promotion of a rental list can easily cost a list manager a third of his or her sales commission. (For this reason major list managers set their fees at 15 percent. At 10 percent the one-third for promotion does not go far enough.)

For a new major list, a list manager will do all of the following:

1. Launch the list with a splash at one of the major direct-mail conventions.

2. Provide extra coverage of the list at exhibits at Direct Mail Days and DMA conventions.

3. Include full coverage in the directory of lists published by the manager. (Most such directories are circulated to 5,000 or 10,000 prospects. One or two list managers blanket the list-using universe by distributing 100,000 to 500,000 directories.)

4. Run adequate space schedules in the four major direct-mail magazines. (*DM News, Direct Marketing, Zip,* and *SRDS*)

5. Initiate a separate campaign, including small reminder space in the bulletins of the major local direct-mail and direct-response clubs.

6. Make specific visits to major mailers and major brokers on behalf of the list.

7. Review all in-house information that is likely to point to likely prospects:

    a. If the firm rents outside lists, the lists that work are likely to be successful renters.

    b. Inside customer files are mined for more likely prospects.

    c. Current users are petitioned to use additional segments, or re-use the list over a short time frame at a negotiated discounted price.

    d. If the owner uses merge–purge procedures over a good number of outside rented lists, the proportion of duplication with the house list should provide ammunition to open a few favorable doors, possibly doors only open to exchanges or never available before.

Mailing List Rental Lures

As list segmentation begins to bite into list rental volume, list owners and managers are turning more and more to premiums of one sort or another to get new mailers to use their lists. Whatever has been done to date is certain to increase. Here are a few examples:

- There are a growing number of sweepstakes with substantial prizes created for the benefit of list brokers who arrange to use given lists.

- One company (and possibly more) now offers lists on a net usage basis. If only 60 percent survive a merge–purge, that is the number the owner requests payment for.

- One sweepstakes promoter, who also represents lists, offers a free sweepstakes promotion to any mailer who rents 500,000 or more names.

- One major list manager–compiler offers to affix free labels supplied by his firm. This can represent a small discount on the list rental price but it also serves to build business for the mailing shop which is also maintained by this list merchandiser.

- One magazine has now produced a rate card offering a $15/M discount on full file utilization—the total circulation list of any one of its stable of magazines.

● A number of lists offer 5,000 or 10,000 free names to test. One variant of this is a free test, which if it results in a rollout, will be billed. Failure in this case is free; success is to be paid for.

When to Fire a List Manager

It is time to fire a list manager when:

1. Your net income goes down instead of up.
2. It is obvious the list manager is financing his or her operation with your money.
3. It is no longer comfortable to do business with your list manager.
4. A competitive list manager makes an offer, backed by a guarantee (preferably a check) that you cannot afford to pass up. (This is a nasty practice, but a number of lists each year are "bought" by one manager from another in this way.)
5. You are certain you can do as well, or better, with in-house management.
6. It is clear, through errors and omissions, that you are no longer receiving the care and attention you feel you deserve.

How List Managers Bring New Lists on the Market

List managers are now the major channel through which new lists come on the market. If these new lists are already on magnetic tape, the list manager may not need to do any more than reformat the file, sort it into zip code sequence for third class mailing, and obtain the counts required to initiate a data card. (See page 99.) If the list is not on tape, the list manager will usually work out an arrangement to have the hard-copy list converted to magnetic form, and then have the cost amortized through rentals of the list. Some list managers offer to convert such lists at no charge. It should be noted however that there is no "free lunch," and there is no such thing as a "free conversion." The list owner pays for the conversion either through deductions from the early net sums due him or her for rentals of the list, or in a decreased percentage of the take. A few examples may help here in explaining how these percentages are broken down:

1. List owner pays for conversion or makes available a list already on tape:

List broker	20%
List manager	10%
List processing	10%
Net to owner	60%

2. List manager pays for conversion, with the understanding that he or she will be recompensed from the net sums due the owner from the first rentals. (Some list managers add a fee to the cost of conversion for the cost of money. This is also amortized from early rentals.) In most of these cases the list manager is at risk for the cost of conversion. If sufficient rentals are not achieved to amortize his or her advance, he or she is out the money. (A knowledgeable list manager will rarely advance monies that cannot be amortized several times over through list rental activity):

List broker	20%
List manager	10%
List processing	10%
Amortization	60%
Net to owner after amortization	60%

3. The list manager puts up 50 percent of the conversion cost and is credited with 50 percent of the sum due to the owner. There is no amortization other than the fact that both parties start getting money back on their mutual advances with the first rental. This can take three forms:

Form 1		**Form 2**		**Form 3**	
List broker	20%	List broker	20%	List broker	20%
List manager	10%	List manager	10%	List manager	5%
				Balance to owner	5%
List processing	10%	List processing	10%	List processing	10%
Owner A	30%	Owner A	30%	Owner A	30%
Owner B	30%	Owner B	30%	Owner B	30%
(list manager collects all list brokerage on direct rentals)		(two owners split brokerage on direct rentals)		(two owners split everything including list management fee)	

4. List manager pays for conversion on a nonamortized basis. In such a circumstance the list manager collects 50 percent to 75 percent of the net proceeds after deductions for list brokerage and list processing. It is usual here for the list manager to collect his management fee, as well as all of the brokerage on direct rentals. The initial owner receives his or her share from the first rental.

There are variants beyond those indicated above. One magazine that actually rents its list out over 100 times per year (two times per week!) has reduced the list management fee from an initial 10 percent to 5 percent. Large lists requiring extensive promotion are tending to a 10 percent plus 5 percent set-up fee, where the 5 percent is earmarked expressly for payment of promotion costs.

In past years publishers, in particular, utilized list managers to speed the process of establishing their lists on the market. Then when a given volume of rental income was achieved the publisher's withdrew their lists from list managers in favor of an inside list management operation. Some of these lists have subsequently been turned back to list managers where the total costs, primarily increased trained laborpower costs each year have come to light. A fairly typical internal distribution shows:

List brokerage	15% (some business is direct)
List processing	10%
List rental administration & burden	20%
Net to owner	55%

Against this, the typical outside list manager delivers 60 percent of the gross rental billing, and necessary inside costs may well eat up the 5 percent differential.

Some years ago a small coterie of list managers existed who devoted their entire efforts to promoting their list management properties. They did not offer brokerage of other lists, nor did they double either as a producer or a seller of compiled files. Horrified early on at the temerity of list managers to charge a fee, above brokerage, for list representation, list brokers soon came to an interesting realization: They knew the list owners and they knew the list users, so why not become list managers also, and pick up the extra 10 percent as this author did. They eventually did just this—to the extent that today the largest list management operations are owned by or are run in conjunction with the major list brokers. "Pure" list managers are now virtually extinct and the lines between list broker, list compiler, and list manager are becoming more and more indistinct with each passing year.

CHAPTER 4

How to Deal with the Other Direct-Mail Professionals

HOW COMPUTERS CAN BE USED TO YOUR ADVANTAGE IN DIRECT MAIL LISTINGS

The first fact to keep in mind about a computer is that it is a *tool*. It has no independent intelligence. It *cannot do anything* unless and until a fabulous "computer" called a human instructs it to.

All computers work on what is perhaps, the simplest concept known to man—everything is either on or off, black or white, one or nothing. Four digits, in the basic binary coded decimal system define each of the numbers:

```
0000 = 0
0001 = 1
0010 = 2
0011 = 3
0100 = 4
0101 = 5   (1 + 4)
0110 = 6   (2 + 4)
0111 = 7   (3 + 4)
1000 = 8
1001 = 9   (8 + 1)
```

It is worth a minute to see how this "computer code" is created:

The number one in position 1 = 1

The number one in position 2 = 2

The number one in position 3 = 4

The number one in position 4 = 8

As the machine can understand *only* 1 or 0 (black or white, on or off) and not the arabic numbers we deal with all the time, all instructions to a computer involve 1's or 0's only.

The computer is a *very* dumb beast, which operates very quickly in billionths of a second. It has three parts: input, computation or work, and output. It can perform only three basic functions:

1. It can add and subtract. (To multiply, it simply adds, very quickly. To divide, it simply subtracts, very quickly.)

2. It can compare two values and decide if these two values (numerical or alphabetical, or alpha numerical) are equal, or if the first is greater (or less) than the second. This is the essence of two functions of great interest to marketers:

    a. The ability to merge (and compare) two or more sets of values and purge out or identify probable duplicates.

    b. The ability to sort a file in any given array from highest to lowest or vice versa.

3. It can store and retrieve, thus list data can be stored on tape or disc and then updated, changed, or retrieved.

With only these three functions—add (and subtract), compare, and store, the computer can process data by:

1. *Classifying*. From a list point of view, this means selecting data so they are meaningful to the user.

2. *Sorting*. This function arranges data into a predetermined sequence for more meaningful or more useful processing. Random data can be sorted by a desired field such as zip code, sales volume, SIC, make and model of a car, or value of a home.

3. *Calculating*. For list data this arithmetic capacity is used to provide counts by segment, as well as particular analyses, merge–purge allocations, and effort-key analyses.

4. *Summarizing*. Direct response is continually looking at summaries for average size of order, dollars spent per new order, and lifetime value of a cell of customers.

5. *Storing*. All types of list data require storage that keeps the processed data for future reference.

There are five acronyms that are useful to keep in mind when using or analyzing computer data. They are

KISS

GIGO

DIDO

NINO

RAFO

KISS—Keep It Simple, Stupid. Nothing that human beings have ever created can make errors so quickly and so disastrously as a computer. In business the very dumb but very energetic person must be approached with care. No human being is as dumb as a computer, and no human being can do as much damage in so short a time.

GIGO—Garbage In, Garbage Out. This is a phrase we heard a great deal about some years ago. It is now coming more to the fore as mailers and their service bureaus attempt to merge–purge groups of lists with all different kinds of purposes and different levels of discipline.

DIDO—Duplication In, Duplication Out. Unless you can identify and tag duplicate records, your list is destined to suffer from a chronic case of "duplicatitus."

NINO—Not In, Not Out. This is undoubtedly the most important phrase in the computer lexicon. If you don't put it in, you cannot get it out. If you bury two or three separate kinds of businesses under one code, there is no way you can break out one of the segments later on. Remember NINO, and keep it sacred!

RAFO—Research and Find Out. This is a very expensive way to make up for not putting the data on file in the first place. This author will never forget a compilation of a million records where it was judged unnecessary to include county codes. A major mailer, who worked by counties, would not use the list without county code selectivity. It costs twenty times as much to add these codes after the fact than it would have cost to place them on the file as part of the initial list building operation.

A little over a generation ago, lists were typed from hard-copy sources. Today it is difficult to think of doing anything with lists without involving the computer. Just listing all the ways a computer is involved in direct mail and direct response provides the outline for another book.

For mailing lists, a computer

- Selects by all of the various criteria coded into lists.
- Sorts into various required sequences.
- Updates with adds, kills, and changes.
- Qualifies for five-digit and carrier-route discounts.
- Tags and thus adds selected new data from an outside source.
- Overlays to provide demographic enhancement.
- Builds files with data bank characteristics for multiple use and access.
- Counts data by segment or field.
- Merges two or most lists together into one stream.
- Corrects zip codes.
- Purges and eliminates unwanted records.
- Identifies data that belong together in some new way.
- Reports on all forms of direct-response activity and marketing.
- Causes conversions as the need for electronic data handling becomes evident.
- Makes possible rentals to outside list users.
- Transforms data from one mode to another—as tape to floppy disc.

For direct-mail control, computers are used for

- Customer identification, classification, and use
- Order entry
- Inventory control
- Literature fulfillment and product fulfillment
- Sheet listings and "crutch" files
- Transaction runs
- Sequence numbering
- Effort-key reports
- Historical reporting
- Analysis by zip code, carrier route, cluster
- Catalog analysis by page, item, spread, issue

For terminal access, computers provide

- On-line data by unit, price, projection, availability, specials, sales
- "Sales prompts" by item
- List ordering by machine
- Add-on selling through telemarketing and teleprospecting

For printing, computers are utilized in the production of

- Computer spectaculars
- Computer letters (match fill and complete)
- Computer sales data on invoices
- Laser letters
- Word processing
- List output
- Labels, tapes, cards, and sheet lists
- Direct addressing, including dual-print stations

For internal controls, computers are utilized for

- Accounting records (AR/AP/inventory/payroll)
- Job control—utilization of assets other than people, versus standards
- Employment productivity—utilization of people versus standards

And computers, in the wrong hands, can be dangerous. See page 651.

HOW TO WORK WITH A COMPUTER SERVICE BUREAU

In 1965, a compilation of every record that dealt with data processing in every classified directory in the United States had slightly less than 1,000 records. Ten years later this list totalled 12,000 records. By 1985, the total number had grown to over 60,000,* with over 8,000 establishments offering software service; 17,300 establishments offering service bureau functions; 12,000 establishments offering computer parts and supplies and repair services. There are a large number

---

*The balance (1987) consists of over 22,000 computer stores.

of service bureaus (estimated at 10,000) that handle list work connected with computers. A large number, at this time, are major factors in the list business and in the direct-mail business. Some of them are now getting into the list brokerage business. In other words, service bureaus have come into the direct-mail field through the fulfillment business by means of the computer.

As a list merchandiser, I often stipulate I am "alive and well and living in a computer." Although not quite accurate, the phrase does indicate how pervasive the computer has become in the direct-mail business. Mailers are dependent on their computer service bureaus for maintenance of house lists, as well as for merging and purging those lists against all rental lists utilized for mailings. This is a critical relationship—one that must be carefully nurtured.

Choosing the Best Service Bureau for Your Needs: Some Guidelines

The choice of an outside computer service bureau and a computer merge–purge specialist, (which may or may not be a single-source choice) is one of the most critical decisions faced by a direct-mail operator. It is good to start this section with some advice on how to select a service bureau.

First, it is best to place cost of service in a secondary position. Comparing the "laundry list" of charges by two or three computer service bureaus may help weed out those that are extremely high-priced and those who are outrageously low. (These low-cost bureaus must make up the difference by what the trade calls "creative billing." Some are almost as good at this as lawyers are.) Price alone will not in any way indicate which bureau (high or low) has the capacity to do the jobs needed, much less the capacity to work within the time restraints required.

Computer service bureaus interact with mailers (both customers, and non-customers), brokers, list managers, and service bureaus. A service bureau under review should be willing to give you two short lists, as references: one of current list customers, and one of former list customers. It is best to start with the latter, and attempt to get answers from the person who was in direct contact with the computer service. Why did this customer leave? What complaints did he or she have? Where did the business move to? What change (if any) has occurred in the service? Customers should be asked how they came to select this particular service. What changes (if any) would they like to see? What kind of cooperation are they getting?

Perhaps the most useful information will come from interviews with other service bureaus. They know the competence of their peers, as well as which ones can handle a business merge, which ones have enough "bodies," which ones have the best programming staffs, and which ones can handle large jobs expeditiously. This type of valuable corroborative data can be elicited. Each service bureau called knows that the getting in a word or two on the competence of the service bureau is a good opportunity. (See also data on merge–purge on page 485).

The next and possibly least step is to make a few calls to major list brokers, major list compilers, and managers. They will add some insight into the industry and provide another measure of how the industry views a given vendor.

Once the number of vendors you've considered has been narrowed down to two or three, a request can be made for a laundry list of costs for service. If any particular cost seems out of line it is likely that this can be easily negotiated once the service recognizes some "give" may be required to obtain the account.

The last step should be a shop visit by *those who will be involved* in working with the service bureau. It is not enough for a principal or treasurer to make this visit if that is the last time he or she will have any contact with the service bureau— other than to sign a check. The mail list people, marketers, and inside computer folks who will be involved should meet with the bureau, to stop, look, listen, glean, and determine which group they have the most trust in and the greatest feeling of cooperation and support from.

Care should be taken to ensure that, irrespective of what happens, the company owns, controls exclusively, and has daily access to its own list data. A security reel, after each update, should be made a mandatory part of the contract.

The laundry list should spell out, as best as possible, pricing on a scheduled basis, as well as the adders that are inevitable on a demand basis. It is a good idea to review the list every six months to see if it is fair to both supplier and client.

In addition, the basic work to be performed should be stipulated with as much detail as can be furnished conveniently. This data should include quantities, updates, rental use, house use, merge–purge requirements, and the timing of reports. The more information placed on paper, so both parties know what is involved, the more likelihood that both sides will be pleased with the operation.

How to Periodically Review How Well Your Service Bureau Performs

In this section on computers, a sizable list of tasks are given that your computer service (in house or out) will be called upon to do. These tasks involve selection, printing, updating, provision of counts, and such esoterica as stop counts, merging, unduping, match codes, stat tabs, sequence numbering, sorting or arraying by alpha or size or SIC. If the service bureau is not familiar with list forms, preparation of the mail for carrier-route sequencing, or is not clear on what is required to make canape changes in an update routine, that service bureau is not an expert in list work and you (or they) will have extra costs. The rule here is a *very* simple one: Do *not* teach your service bureau the list business.

Investigate, if you can, how the service bureau you are considering works.

Does it force-fit all activities to its chosen system, or is it flexible enough to handle unusual assignments. When (if ever?) does it say "no" instead of "yes." (The number of service bureaus in the list business who never say "no" can be counted on the fingers of one hand.)

Does the service bureau have adequate programs to do a bag analysis (based on size and weight of piece and quantity being mailed) to determine the optimum minimum quantity for carrier presort qualified which will reduce bag utilization? [Providing the greatest number of bag tags (slides) often is not economic for the mailer.]

Is the service bureau able to furnish labels, computer forms, and bag tags in bag and bundle sequence rather than zip code sequence? For larger mailings, can it provide all such data in bulk mail center sequence for best movement at the fulfillment shop?

Does the service bureau have a good reputation for its merge–purge system? Does it differentiate between a merge–purge for a consumer list and one for a business list? Are the costs about the same for either? (If so, watch out! No business merge–purge can be done correctly in a single "pass" as is normal for consumer merge–purges.) Do the merge–purge reports include duplication counts, allocation counts, samples of matched (duplicate) pairs, and effort-key counts for every requested split?

Does the service bureau know its way around the dozens of different forms of floppy discs? Is its price for conversion to floppy discs part of that laundry list of costs that was supplied? Does it convert to floppy discs in house or go outside? (There is nothing wrong with going outside—you just may prefer to do that yourself.) Does the service provide a user-friendly operational program with each floppy disc?

CCX: The Computer List Utility

Approximately 4 or 5 percent of all mail carrying advertising is addressed by the computers of CCX, Inc. On its computers are over one billion records for several dozen clients, including R.H. Donnelley, D&B, R.L. Polk, Data Base America, American Management Association, and many mailing lists for magazines. All of these files, under controlled conditions, can be accessed by dedicated terminals or PCs. Selection of any criteria is available on each file by the user and there is no intervention by human programmers. All three DataBase America files—namely All-Business (8.3 million), Big Business executives (5.0 million), and Consumer (86+ million)—are resident in Conway Arkansas on CCX computers. They provide CCX with its largest single list client.

Virtually all the data are stored online. Tapes are utilized almost exclusively to accept input from customers and to provide output on the client's format on tape. All processing is run from a huge "disc farm." Over 140 list owners, compilers, brokers, list managers (including a number of major list wholesalers) are connected to CCX by terminals via a nationwide network.

Counts for several of the major files processed by CCX are now available on line, with any configuration available within three to five seconds. Thus counts, even esoteric ones, can be researched for an owner, broker, or list manager while the client is on the phone. The client no longer needs to be told the count will be run overnight and phoned in the next day. There is, of course, a price to be paid for such "quick counts."

At the very cutting edge of technology is the CCX system in place for MCI, the giant communications company. MCI has created a combined data bank utilizing input from major compilers embracing almost every nonhousehold establishment available on compiled mailing lists, including Data Base America. These data, by classification (SIC), size, and geography can be ordered by any of the U.S. offices of MCI through individual PCs. The stored data are selected at CCX and printed on "call report" forms, as well as provided on tape cassettes. Data from the call reports, including information on long distance utilization, are key-stroked at the local offices and the updated cassettes are returned monthly to CCX for systemwide updating and reports. Over 6 million companies are being called, some several times a year, by a force of over 500 telephone salespersons.

MCI is adding data about American businesses and American businesspeople to its already voluminous data bank. As the data grow, CCX is prepared to increase the master file from 256 characters to 512 characters. Local branches, through their PCs, can produce area reports, city reports, SIC reports, and individual sales representative reports. The system stores data by establishment of first time called, last time called (which delineates how long the account has been serviced), and all requests for callbacks. All callbacks with all pertinent information are printed and returned to the branch (and the individual salesperson) in a timely fashion irrespective of the time between posting the call and responding to it. This is believed to be the most advanced utilization extant of PCs and computerized access to a large dynamic and growing proprietary data bank.

Computer Letters and Computer "Spectaculars"

For at least the last ten years, pundits have predicted the coming death of the computer letter. During that time computer letters, computer forms, computer spectaculars, ink-jet addressing, Western Union letters, laser letters, and that great USPS bargain, E-COM Service (now defunct) have increased in quantity.

It is fair to say that as long as human beings value their own names and their own activities that computerized, personalized pieces will be a continuing and increasing part of the mail flow. The concept that people will in time become blasé about personalization has been effectively refuted. Some early efforts with meaningless "name drops" through the letter were self-defeating. But like testing, for every mailer who has been hurt by too much personalization, there are a great number of mailers who could have done better with some or better personalization.

The future is clear. Personalization will increase, not decrease, and it will be more and more tied to what is known either demographically or psychographically about the individual prospect or customer. Thus a review of a service bureau requires checking into its competence in the handling of personalized data. Can it normalize addresses, provide upper- and lowercase handling, and genderize a list for personal solicitations? If not, you may have to look elsewhere. However, the firm that handles your mailing list should have the option to utilize specialists in computer letter and laser letter production, where required.

Computerized (Ink Jet) Addressing

Ink-jet addressing offers some immediate advantages, and points the way to greater personalization of mailing packages, particularly catalogs, in the future.

One immediate advantage is a dramatic increase in the proportion of coded orders received. With double-jet heads, this system provides mailers for the first time the ability to print the *same* code on the order form *and* on the mailing label in the same pass. Some ink-jet systems can even code multiple order forms, also in the same pass. In addition, the computer can print up to six additional lines of data as the codes are imprinted. This copy is limited only by the imagination of the marketer. The message can announce a new product, offer a special discount, refer recipients to certain pages. Such data can be generic for everyone or for given classes of recipients. (For example, one message can be used for regular customers, a "last chance" warning message of termination can be used for dormant accounts, and one, two, or three different messages can be used for prospects. All these messages can be merged into the same zip code string for postage discounts). However, the wave of the future is in the capacity of the computer to personalize each message according to the recency or frequency of purchase or the items purchased! This type of personalization on the label, overleaf, or overwrap is only a prelude to the personalizing of individual pages in a catalog (just as the consumer order-entry systems now provide individual "prompts" for each and every item or group of items called up on the screen).

The use of ink-jet addressing replaces cheshire labeling or pressure-sensitive labeling. While the latter provides a means to have the recipient peel off the label and apply it to the order form, only some buyers will do this by mail. Those that do not, have lost the code so essential for tracking. With ink-jet addressing the code is made a permanent part of the order form and is available on all mail orders. If either the catalog or the form is on hand the code is easily retrieved for telephone orders.

Preparation of the tape for ink-jet addressing must conform to the program utilized to control the print imaging. While a bit different than for cheshire production, most service bureaus performing merge–purge can provide the tape in the required format. It is no more difficult than the required preparation of tapes for other electronic addressing such as the production of computer letters or Western Union's electronic letters. The overall costs for ink-jet addressing are slightly higher than for cheshire labeling—but the return on investment, in the form of increased data from coded returns, is well worth the modest differential.

Provision of data for ink-jet addressing handling requires some special "know how." Does your service bureau have this special knowledge? Do they have any problem providing a label-image tape?

Where the printer or the mailing service is to be sent a tape for computer or ink-jet addressing of a carrier routed business file, it is important to check to see if seven lines can be accommodated: two lines for the key and the carrier-route identification and up to five for the address at the branch or division. Such addresses make up as high as 20 percent of major merge–purge business lists. Where the service can only handle six lines, a line is simply "dropped." This deals a deadly blow to business–catalog deliverability. Where the creator of the tape is knowledgeable and informed of this problem it may be possible to format the key data to fit on the company name line, and thus provide a six-line label for addressing. If something like this is not done, there is trouble ahead for the mailer, the printer, and probably for the merge–purge service, even though the latter may be innocent.

Credit screened lists (see page 511) are another highly specialized form of computer handling. While the steps involved are not difficult, the way they need to be made and the sequence of handling them can have a great deal to do with the tab you will get for that handling. Is this the first one the service bureau has ever seen? Does the service bureau know the formats required for each of the major credit bureaus?

Computer Technology

Computer technology has spawned many new products for the direct response field—including astrocharts (individual horoscopes based on date and time of birth), bio-rhythm charts (based on personalized psychological data), personnel charts (based on scoring of individualized answers to banks of questions) . . . as well as books, particularly those individualized for a given child or family. While outside the usual purview of a service bureau specializing in list work, it is likely that such a bureau is more likely to have the programming talent and computer competence to handle such esoterica than a conventional business-oriented service bureau.

Specialized Handling

There are however a few forms of list handling that require specialized handling—subscription fulfillment for a paid magazine (or one converting or attempting to convert to paid) and the various club continuity plans, both negative and positive option, where control of dollars is intrinsically bound into the computerized system. Here the service bureau must provide "caging" for control of cash and checks and refunds, and be intimately involved in all aspects of consumer service, including the handling of complaints (real and imagined) that such services inevitably generate. (Do not, in other words, teach your service bureau subscription fulfillment, or continuity series control!)

GUIDELINES FOR TRANSFERRING DATA ON COMPUTER TAPES

The Direct Marketing Computer Association (now a council within the Direct Marketing Association) has formulated a set of guidelines for *transfer* of list data for use on computers. The major guidelines are discussed below.

In the absence of other specifications, the tape standard is 9-track, 1600 BPI (bits per inch) in IBM (EPCDIC) standard code. [For large files, the packing can be 6250 BPI. An alternative code is ASCII (American Standard)].

Tapes must be clearly labeled by an external physical label. Old labels should be removed when the tape is reused. This label should contain the following essential information: mailer, list name, tape attributes, reel ID, record quantity, job name, key code, list description, originating job number, service bureau source, and creation date. The file header label should be a "road map" describing the layout of the data file.

List data should be in files of sequential, fixed-length records. Fields should be consistent across all records of the file. All coded information is interpreted.

A "dump" (listing, character-by-character) of the first 200 or so records should be included with the file layout and the tape reel. It should include both the printed characters and the hexidecimal values, to allow the receiver to compare the tape layout with the actual data generated on the file.

Detailed record counts for selected data fields should be included to assist in the confirmation process.

Each tape shipment should be accompanied by a shipping and packing slip. In addition to the record data this slip should include the contact name and phone number at both the sending and the receiving address.

Where there is a need to check off and confirm given data, counts and codes should be carefully provided. (In addition the receiver should have on hand, in advance, a list of all inputs with their keys and anticipated counts, along with an order expressing exactly what the job entails and precisely when the job is to be completed and shipped. (See page 666 for tape billing and control.)

HOW TO WORK WITH A MAILING PLANT*

What makes the mail house (lettershop) so important is that today the average package in the mail costs between $350 and $400/M. These costs can be broken down into percentages where: 30 percent is spent for postage, 15 percent for lists, 50 percent for printing, and 5 percent for mailing service.

The 5 percent for mailing services for your package is where everything you've worked on for months is concentrated. One mistake here, or not getting it out on time, can make the difference between success or failure. Mailing is neither glamorous, exciting, nor sexy—but it is important. It is the one DM area that most people know the least about. Not to use professional service means living dangerously. Hopefully, you will take it as seriously as we in the industry do.

This section discusses the mailing process in general and specifically addresses the following issues:

1. How to select a mailing service.
2. What the mailing service can do for you.
3. What you can do for the mailing service.
4. Checklist of do's and don'ts for trouble-free mailings.

Tips on Selecting a Mailing Service That's Right for You

Let's start with three easy preliminaries:

1. Look in the yellow pages of the telephone book under the heading of Direct-Mail Advertising or Services or Lettershops.

*Based on a contribution by Lee Epstein, president of Mailmen, Inc.

2. A better way is to get a copy of the MASA Roster, the trade association for mailing service organizations, and select two or three shops in your neighborhood. Members of MASA are recognized as the preferential and reliable shops around the country.

3. The best way is to find out from others in our industry who they use and why they like them. Then call three or four shops and write to them, or call to stop in and discuss your requirements and their services.

Mailing shops, like anything else in life, come in all different sizes, shapes, personalities, and services. A good shop will tell you right off whether what they do is what you need. After you have met with a few shop representatives and narrowed down your choices, you should know the following:

- The size of their shop
- Their equipment
- Their services
- Their facilities

Get a list of their customers that you can check for references. You may also have gotten an idea of their pricing. *Warning:* Price should not be the only basis for selecting a shop. I believe quality of service is more important. They may not go together. Your job is to make sure that all you are spending on copy, art, layout, printing, and list rentals will result in a successful fulfillment.

Now you are ready for the plant visit. Here you will see the plant and meet the people who run it. You should find out the following:

- Is the shop clean, neat, and orderly?
- Are the people friendly, interested, and helpful?
- Does the shop appear to be working in a smooth and orderly fashion?
- Who will be servicing you—the salesperson and/or the customer representative?
- Are their reporting forms in order?
- Do they have adequate facilities for receiving and storing your material?
- What are their postage advance policies?
- How do they handle overage materials?
- Do they charge for pickups and deliveries?

If you follow the suggestions above your chances for smooth, problem-free mailing are excellent. It's also important that you listen to the people running the plant for any cost saving ideas they may have on format, postal regulations and rates.

What the Mail Shop Can Do for You

A good mail shop will save you money *and* keep you from getting grey hair and high blood pressure. Let's take a look at some of the following operations and procedures that a mail shop should perform for you:

1. If you are using a personalized continuous computer form, the mailing list should be able to burst and fold, slit, nest, and interstack.

2. If you use self-affixing labels the mail shop should be able to label your outer envelope, outer form, self-mailer or catalog—anything from a cut label to 1-2-3-4-5 across, EDP, or computer printouts. They should also be able to:

- Piggyback affix
- Tip affix
- Stamp affix
- Key
- Imprint
- Credit card affix

If they have computer printers, they should have:

- Impact
- Ink-jet, or
- Laser

They should also be able to handle either rolls or flat stock.

Machine inserting equipment is manufactured by Bell and Howell, Pitney Bowes, or Phillipsburg which can take both paper and poly from the smallest envelope to 9 × 12 inches. Inserters do not only insert, they can also:

- Nest
- Tip affix

- Double and triple pass for multiple inserts
- Key
- Meter
- Imprint
- Affix
- Insert pencils, swatches, foil packs, and so on
- Handle end-fold pieces and accordian folded pieces.

Internal Procedures that should be performed by your mailing plant include the following:

1. Issue receiving reports as components and/or labels are received.
2. Take out mailing permits and make sure that your postage advance is on deposit.
3. Keep you informed of job progress and developing problems.
4. Make up mailing receipts, issue mailing reports showing:
   a. Date of mailing
   b. Quantity mailed by key
   c. Postage spent
   d. Cumulative costs to date
5. Issue overage reports and request disposition.
6. Invoice on a timely basis and attach the 3602s as proof of mailing and postage spent.
7. At the start of the job, give clients specific instructions on how to carton, pack, and skid incoming material including contents.

What You as the Mailer Can Do for the Mailing House—Communicate!

1. When placing your order, be specific as to quantity, mail dates, home delivery date, delivery dates of components, and vendors. List keys, quantities, and names of list and list brokers.
2. *Talk* to the mailing house before you go to press on sizes of components in relation to outer envelope. (Space is needed for inserts in envelopes!) And be certain to cover the following:
   a. Permit indicia number and return address
   b. Legend ACR return and forwarding

    c. Sortation levels—three tiers

    d. Label position on order card

3. Communicate changes in schedule as they occur, and put the changes in writing.

4. Visit the shop when the job is to begin.

5. Approve inserting samples for sequencing and facing before production starts.

A well run lettershop uses forms for keeping the client informed. Check to see what forms your shop will make available to you, including:

1. Advance postage request form

2. Material receiving guideline

3. Insurance form

4. Preload detail

5. List receipt form

6. Material receipt form

7. Mailing receipt form

8. Overage receipt form

9. Job difficulty report (internal procedure for billing reconciliation)

Checklist of Do's & Don'ts for Trouble-Free Mailings

This list will help you save money and ensure on-time mailings by eliminating or minimizing difficulties in production:

1. *Do* take advantage of the expertise of your mailing house personnel. Show them your proposed formats *before you go to press*. You'll be surprised at the suggestions they can make that will save you time and money.

2. *Do* allow at least $\frac{1}{2}$ inch clearance right and left *after* inserting the components into the envelope.

3. *Do* tell your envelope manufacturer to cut back the glue on the flap behind the stamp area when you are using a live postage stamp for your mailing.

4. *Do not* accordion fold an insert unless the mailing service is using the Pitney Bowes inserter, or if they have a friction-feed attachment for the Bell & Howell inserter.

Figure 4.1a

FOR ZONE RATED MAIL USE PS FORM 3605

U.S. POSTAL SERVICE
STATEMENT OF MAILING WITH PERMIT IMPRINTS

MAILER: Complete all items by typewriter, pen or indelible pencil. Prepare in duplicate if receipt is desired. Check for instructions from your postmaster regarding box labeled "RCA Offices."

PERMIT NO.

NUMBER OF

SACKS	TRAYS	OTHER CONTAINERS
371		118

POST OFFICE: *Melrose Park IL*

DATE: 5/21/85

RECEIPT NO.

CHECK APPLICABLE BOX
- ☐ 1st Class single piece rate
- ☐ Presorted 1st Class rate
- ☐ International
- ☐ 1st Class Carrier Route
- ☐ 2nd—Newspapers and magazines entered at Transient rate.
- ☐ 3rd—Circulars and other printed matter.
- ☐ 3rd-Carrier Route Presort
- ☐ 3rd—Merchandise less than 16 ozs.
- ☒ 3rd—Books or catalogs or 24 pages or more, seeds, etc., less than 16 ozs.
- ☐ 4th Library rate
- ☐ Special 4th rate
- ☐ Presorted Special 4th Class

NAME AND ADDRESS OF PERMIT HOLDER (Include ZIP Code)
Ed Burnett Consultants
99 West Sheffield Avenue
Englewood NJ 07631

TELEPHONE NO.

☐ Check if non-profit under 623, DMM.*

NAME AND ADDRESS OF INDIVIDUAL OR ORGANIZATION FOR WHICH MAILING IS PREPARED (If other than permit holder)
Leslie P. Lee
4600 W Roosevelt Rd
Hillside IL 61162

WEIGHT OF A SINGLE PIECE: 4.01 oz.

RCA Offices:

	TOTAL IN MAILING		RATE CHARGEABLE		TOTAL POSTAGE
	PIECES	POUNDS	AT ☐ PIECE ☒ POUND ¢ $		
	297,82	7465			

PRESORT COMPUTATION (If applicable)

			RATE/PIECE	POSTAGE	
1. PIECE RATE POSTAGE CHARGE	NO. PIECES 297,782		4.2 ¢	1250 84	
			RATE/POUND	POSTAGE	
2. POUND RATE POSTAGE CHARGE	NO. POUNDS 7465		.384	2836 70	
3. PRESORT	NO. QUALIFYING PIECES			RATE REDUCTION POSTAGE	
					4087 54

NET POSTAGE (1 or 2 minus 3)

*The signature of a nonprofit mailer certifies that: (1) The mailing does not violate section 623.5 DMM and (2) Only the mailer's matter is being mailed; and (3) This is not a cooperative mailing with other persons or organizations that are not entitled to special bulk mailing privileges; and (4) This mailing has not been undertaken by the mailer on behalf of or produced for another person or organization that is not entitled to special bulk mailing privileges.

SIGNATURE OF PERMIT HOLDER OR AGENT (Both principal and agent are liable for any postage deficiency incurred)

TELEPHONE NO.

PS Form
Jan. 1981

90

Figure 4.1b

FOR USE OF POSTAL SERVICE ONLY

WEIGHING SECTION—COMPLETE APPLICABLE PART BELOW

PERMIT NO. 118

☐ (Check here if company permit)

STATION OR UNIT

NAME OF PERMIT HOLDER

FINANCE NO. | ZIP CODE

RCA OFFICES ONLY

RECEIVED AND WEIGHED

DATE | TIME ☐ A.M. ☐ P.M.

☐ LETTER SIZE—All mail normally processed through letter cases.
☒ FLAT SIZE—All mail normally processed through flat cases.
☐ PARCELS—Not normally distributed in letter or flat cases.

NUMBER OF

CLASS 3 | WEIGHT OF A SINGLE PIECE 1.01

SACKS 311 | TRAYS | OTHER CONTAINERS

NUMBER OF

RATE CHARGEABLE

PIECES IN A POUND 3† | TOTAL PIECES | TOTAL POUNDS 7465

FOR PIECES QUALIFYING FOR PRESORT RATE

☐ PIECE ☐ POUND | AT | TOTAL POSTAGE $

PRESORT COMPUTATION (if applicable)

	NO. PIECES	RATE/PIECE	POSTAGE
1. PIECE RATE POSTAGE CHARGE			
2. POUND RATE POSTAGE CHARGE	NO. POUNDS 7465	RATE/POUND 3.5	POSTAGE 2836.10
3. PRESORT	NO. QUALIFYING PIECES	RATE REDUCTION	POSTAGE

WEIGHT OF PIECES (lbs.)

LESS TARE (lbs.)

NET WEIGH (lbs.)

FOR TOTAL MAILING

TOTAL WEIGHT (lbs.)

LESS TARE (lbs.)

NET TOTAL WT. (lbs.)

NET POSTAGE (1 or 2 minus 3)

SIGNATURE OF WEIGHER

I CERTIFY that the matter mailed has been inspected, the statement of mailing on the reverse of this form has been verified, and the annual mailing fee has been paid.

PC 211-82

☆ U.S. GOVERNMENT PRINTING OFFICE: 1982—377—186/5029

FINANCIAL DOCUMENT—FORWARD TO FINANCE OFFICER

5. *Do not* make your order form stock too flimsy if you are going to label it. The minimum stock should be at least .006 inch thick. For business reply cards the minimum thickness the USPS will accept is .007 inch.

6. *Do* let your mailing house key the order cards or reply envelopes while labeling. This will save you many on-press keying and inventory control headaches.

7. *Do* merge all your lists to produce one list in zip code sequence. This will enable the mailer to make more direct sacks and will speed your mail to the recipients with a minimum of delay and rehandling by the postal service.

8. *Do* provide your mailing shop with computerized bag slides to accompany the carrier, five-digit and residue labels. Also, have your computer service bureau do a bag analysis to determine the optimum minimum quantity for carrier presort qualified to reduce bag utilization.

9. *Do* get with the state of the art and furnish your labels and/or computer forms to the mailing house in bag and bundle sequence rather than zip code sequence. For larger mailings, you should be in bulk mail center sequence.

Form 3602: Certification of Mailing by the USPS

The first thing to look for is the presence of the form itself, signed by the USPS, attached to your bill for services by the mailing plant or fulfillment shop. Accepting a bill for mailing service without a 3602 provides you with no proof of the number of pieces mailed nor any proof of the date the mail was delivered to the post office.

The two sides to this form are shown in Figure 4.1 (a and b). One side is filled in by the mailer or his or her agent and it includes all the data except the time of day. The significant data on the certification side of the form are

1. Weight of a single piece
2. Total number of pieces and total number of sacks
3. Total pounds in the mailing
4. Rate per piece × the rate/piece
5. Rate per pound × the rate/pound
6. Total postage dollars for piece rate

Figure 4.2

```
***  *******************        BAYONNE NJ         07002   BLOOMFIELD NJ       07003   BOONTON NJ          005
* TIER 1 - CARRIER RTE TAGS*    3C FLATS CARRIER ROUTES    3C FLATS CARRIER ROUTES    3C FLATS CARRIER ROUTE 0501
*******************             MAILING SER.NEWARK NJ 07102 MAILING SER.NEWARK NJ 07102 MAILING SER.NEWARK NJ 07102

CALDWELL NJ        07006        CALDWELL NJ        07006   CALDWELL NJ         07006   CLIFFSIDE PK NJ     07010
3C FLATS CARRIER ROUTES         3C FLATS CARRIER ROUTES    3C FLATS CARRIER ROUTES    3C FLATS CARRIER ROUTE 1003
MAILING SER.NEWARK NJ 07102     MAILING SER.NEWARK NJ 07102 MAILING SER.NEWARK NJ 07102 MAILING SER.NEWARK NJ 07102

CLIFFSIDE PK NJ    07010        CLIFFSIDE PK NJ    07010   CLIFFSIDE PK NJ     07010   CLIFFSIDE PK NJ     07010
3C FLATS CARRIER ROUTE 1005     3C FLATS CARRIER ROUTE 1006 3C FLATS CARRIER ROUTE 1006 3C FLATS CARRIER ROUTE 1011
MAILING SER.NEWARK NJ 07102     MAILING SER.NEWARK NJ 07102 MAILING SER.NEWARK NJ 07102 MAILING SER.NEWARK NJ 07102

CLIFFSIDE PK NJ    07010        CLIFFSIDE PK NJ    07010   CLIFFSIDE PK NJ     07010   CLIFFSIDE PK NJ     07010
3C FLATS CARRIER ROUTE 1012     3C FLATS CARRIER ROUTE 1012 3C FLATS CARRIER ROUTE 1013 3C FLATS CARRIER ROUTE 1013
MAILING SER.NEWARK NJ 07102     MAILING SER.NEWARK NJ 07102 MAILING SER.NEWARK NJ 07102 MAILING SER.NEWARK NJ 07102

CLIFFSIDE PK NJ    07010        CLIFFSIDE PK NJ    07010   CLIFTON NJ          07013   CRANFORD NJ         07016
3C FLATS CARRIER ROUTE 1015     3C FLATS CARRIER ROUTE 1015 3C FLATS CARRIER ROUTES    3C FLATS CARRIER ROUTE 0603
MAILING SER.NEWARK NJ 07102     MAILING SER.NEWARK NJ 07102 MAILING SER.NEWARK NJ 07102 MAILING SER.NEWARK NJ 07102

CRANFORD NJ        07016        CRANFORD NJ        07016   EAST ORANGE NJ      07018   EDGEWATER NJ        07020
3C FLATS CARRIER ROUTES         3C FLATS CARRIER ROUTES    3C FLATS CARRIER ROUTE 1806 3C FLATS CARRIER ROUTES
MAILING SER.NEWARK NJ 07102     MAILING SER.NEWARK NJ 07102 MAILING SER.NEWARK NJ 07102 MAILING SER.NEWARK NJ 07102

ESSEX FELLS NJ     07021        ESSEX FELLS NJ     07021   FANWOOD NJ          07023   FORT LEE NJ         07024
3C FLATS CARRIER ROUTE 1        3C FLATS CARRIER ROUTES    3C FLATS CARRIER ROUTES    3C FLATS CARRIER ROUTE 2407
MAILING SER.NEWARK NJ 07102     MAILING SER.NEWARK NJ 07102 MAILING SER.NEWARK NJ 07102 MAILING SER.NEWARK NJ 07102

FORT LEE NJ        07024        FORT LEE NJ        07024   FORT LEE NJ         07024   FORT LEE NJ         07024
3C FLATS CARRIER ROUTE 2407     3C FLATS CARRIER ROUTE 2409 3C FLATS CARRIER ROUTE 2410 3C FLATS CARRIER ROUTE 2411
MAILING SER.NEWARK NJ 07102     MAILING SER.NEWARK NJ 07102 MAILING SER.NEWARK NJ 07102 MAILING SER.NEWARK NJ 07102
```

93

7. Total postage dollars for pound rate

8. Total of postage dollars, piece rate, pound rate combined

9. Time of receiving and weighing

10. Certification stamp of the receiving post office and the date stamp

11. Signature of the certifying postal official

If a given mailing requires two or more "drops" on different days, the total count of the names should be checked against the total of the pieces on the certifications. (The quantity on the certifications is expected to show a slight "undercount" due to loss in addressing and inserting.) Any substantial differential should be probed at once while the circumstances of the mailing are still fresh in your mind.

Figure 4-1a is a completed copy of one side of Form 3602, utilized to certify a given mailing by a given mailer on a given day of a specific number of pieces of a given class of mail.

Figure 4-1b is the other side of Form 3602. This side includes the all-important date stamp and signature of a postal official certifying "that the matter mailed has been inspected, the statement of mailing on the reverse side of this form has been verified, and the annual mailing fee has been paid."

Third class bulk mail including all such mail carrier-route sorted is delivered to the USPS in bags. Each bag is identified as to T/or (the type of service) as well as the destination and the originating post office. These tags or slides, now computer produced, are inserted, individually into a receiving slot on a metal clasp closing each bag. Bags must be "made up" based on weight and size and number. Bag tags must be printed in just the order required by each individual mailing. Figure 4.2 is a reproduction of computer-generated bag tags.

The mail using industry has standardized a 5 × 8 inch card which provides all pertinent information about a single list on one side. The reverse side is often utilized to provide state counts. The latter are particularly useful to mailers who wish to reach regional markets.

This section shows reproductions of three list cards:

1. A compiled file—Standard & Poors directors at home addresses (see Figure 4.3).

2. An association file—The American Chemical Association (see Figure 4.4).

3. A consumer mail response file—AT&T 800 Directory requestors and buyers (see Figure 4.5).

Figure 4.3

A Typical Compiled Business List Card

ORDER FROM YOUR FAVORITE BROKER OR:

eb

ED BURNETT CONSULTANTS, INC.

99 W. SHEFFIELD AVE., ENGLEWOOD, N.J. 07631   (201) 871-1100   (800) 223-7777

LIST COMPILATION
LIST MANAGEMENT
MAIL LIST COUNSEL

1986   Standard & Poor's

Date: 3/86

BOARD OF DIRECTORS AT HOME ADDRESS
63,595 $ 50/M

Source: Directory

Addressing:

4-up Cheshire	N/C
Pres. Sensitive	$ 7.50/M
Magnetic Tape	$20.00
(non-refundable)	
3x5 Cards	$25.00/M
Sheet Listing	$15.00/M

This 1986 compilation will put you in contact with the
Lee Iacocca's of America. Reach the core of affluence
and power in America, and reach them at their home.

Excellent prospects for hi-ticket offers, business
publications, fund raising, etc.

Geographic Selection available, as well as ....

Selections:

# of Boards	$ 5/M
Age	$ 5/M
State Key Code	$ 2.50/M
State, SCF	N/C

# of Boards:		Age	
1	....	Under 40	 4,520
2	....	40 - 50	 17,795
3	....	51 - 60	 23,880
4	....	Over 60	 24,523
5	....	Unknown	 518
6	....		

(Left column values: 1: 26,379; 2: 13,556; 3: 8,571; 4: 5,731; 5: 3,414; 6: 5,944)

Figure 4.4

An Association File

THE **AMERICAN CHEMICAL SOCIETY**

161,000 @ $ 75/M

PROFILE: The American Chemical Society mailing list consists of members of the Society and non-member paid subscribers to ACS publications.

This top-level audience is comprised of corporate and operating management, R&D and other highly trained professionals active in the chemical field. They are involved in all facets of chemistry and its applications.

Productive prospects for informational media - books - magazines - seminars - newsletters - symposiums - instruments - products, materials and services used in the chemistry field.

* Sample mailing piece and list rental agreement required.
* List rental reciprocity is required by ACS.
* Not available for telephone solicitation.
* Once approved mailing piece must be re-cleared if changed.

DATE: June 1987

SOURCE: Direct Mail

SELECTIONS:
Chemical Interest	$ 5/M
Job Function	$ 5/M
Publication	$ 5/M
State,SCF,Zip	$ 5/M

ADDRESSING:
4-Up Cheshire	N/C
4-Up P/S	$ 7.50/M
Keycode	$ 2/M
Tape	$ 20.00

($50. refundable deposit)

MINIMUM ORDER:
4,000 names

SEE SEPARATE DATA CARDS
FOR CANADA AND
INTERNATIONAL

JOB FUNCTION

INDUSTRIAL

Corporate Management (50)	15,023
Technical Management (51)	14,020
Production (53)	5,410
Supervisor (54)	7,724
Plant Maintenance(55)	766
Process Control (56)	4,019
Quality Control (57)	9,457
Engineering (58)	7,302
Engineering Design (59)	3,279
Chemists (60)	21,247
Process R&D (61)	13,968
Product R&D (62)	19,455
Analytical Research (63)	14,385
Basic Research (64)	23,697
Technical Service (65)	11,592
Marketing/Sales (66)	3,752
Advertising (67)	3,713
Purchasing (68)	1,490
Development (69)	3,235
Government (70)	10,063
Govt. Regulating Functions (71)	1,319

ACADEMIC

Graduate Students (72)	5,954
Undergrad. Students (73)	120
Post Doctoral Research (74)	1,013
Research Professors (75)	4,102
Secondary Teachers (76)	676
Universities/Colleges (77)	2,946
University Administrators (78)	1,117
Professors (79)	37,411

CONSULTANTS

Consultants/Professors (80)	3,898
Consulting Chemists (81)	1,229
Consulting Engineers (82)	776

LABORATORIES

Clinical Labs. (83)	469
Independent Labs. (84)	1,082

OTHER

Public Utilities/Transport. (85)	1,527
Retail/Wholesale (86)	684

SEE OTHER SIDE FOR MORE DEMOGRAPHIC INFORMATION

Figure 4.4

(cont.)

CHEMICAL SPECIALTY/INTEREST

Agricultural/Food/Pesticide Soils/Fertilizers (R)	7,719
Analytical (L)	18,813
Biochemistry (B)	9,230
Cellulose, Paper & Textiles (C)	1,295
Chemical Education, Information & Computers (F)	8,481
Energy (M)	5,439
Environmental (E)	7,426
Health & Safety (Q)	2,466
Industrial & Engineering (W)	6,410
Inorganic (P)	7,050
Marketing & Economics (T)	1,540
Macromolecular Science & Technology (2)	12,180
Medicinal (D)	5,867
Organic (K)	18,634
Physical/Colloid & Surface (S)	9,956

PUBLICATIONS

Accounts of Chemical Research (01)	4,303
Analytical Chemistry (02)	21,853
Biochemistry (03)	3,609
Chemical & Engineering News (04,31)	131,728
Chemical Reviews (05)	2,175
Chemtech (06)	8,666
Environmental Science & Technology (09)	10,598
Industrial & Engineering Chemistry Journals (10,11,12)	2,500
Inorganic Chemistry (13)	2,273
Jrnl. of the American Chemical Society (14)	8,035
Jrnl. of Agricultural & Food Chemistry (17)	1,868
Jrnl. of Chemical Information & Computer Sciences (18)	1,712
Jrnl. of Chemical & Engineering Data (19)	520
Jrnl. (The) of Organic Chemistry (20)	6,251
Jrnl. of Physical Chemistry (21)	2,099
Jrnl. of Medicinal Chemistry (27)	2,449
Langmuir (30)	684
Macromolecules (25)	1,455
Organometallics (28)	1,953

The callouts point out salient facts such as:

- Total size of list (exact figures should *not* be used; round them off).
- Demographic profile
- Rental price per M
- Minimum order
- Source
- Specifics concerning
    Type of addressing
    State, SCF, zip code selections
    Key coding
    Tape charge

Figure 4.5

A Consumer Mail Response File

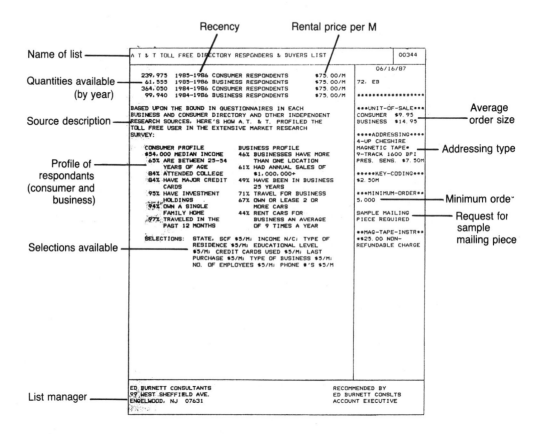

Elements of a List Card

The elements of consumer mail response cards include:

- Name of the list
- Total number of names available
- Selections and quantities available
- Price per M
- Availabilities by:
    Age on the file (hotlines)
    Sex
    Size of order
    Frequency of purchase
- Suggested Markets
- Updating and cleaning (if any or last date when performed)
- Add costs for:
    Titling
    Key coding
    Zip code selection
    State selection
    Pressure sensitive labels
    Tape reel (nonreturnable) charge
    Floppy disc
- Minimum order size
- Average order size or range (in dollars)
- Inquiries and requests (if included)
- Users (if any)

The elements of a compiled business list card include:

- Name of the list
- Quantity
- Source

- Selections available:
  If by individual:
    Name
    Title
    Sex
  If by establishment or company:
    SIC
    Number of employees
    Sales volume
- Price:
    Add for
    Title
    Key code
    SIC selection
    Employment strength or sales volume
    Zip code or state selection
    Pressure-sensitive labels/tape reel/floppy disc
- Minimum order size
- Updating or cleaning

If there are major segments say, individual magazines within a master un-duplicated file, or individual list rental, package insert and billing stuffer availabilities for a major direct-mail operation they should each be given a separate card. Each list card should be updated at least twice a year.

The most precious knowledge about a list concerns who has used it for what offers and how successful each such utilization has been. These data are never given on a list card, although some data about users who have continued is beginning to be released by knowledgeable list managers well aware of the sales value of such information. In any case, some information on use is available—and this should be searched out on any response list.

List cards can be placed very quickly in two piles: those to be considered (because of sex, price, or availability of new current names) and those that do not meet this initial screen. Then, and then only, does it pay (for a given offer) to review the given data, although it may be sparse. The changes in data from year to year or possibly from quarter to quarter, on hot lines provide a trail on activity. Sometimes sex selection is noted, other times it is not. Some business lists have mixed four-line addresses for establishments and three-line addresses probably for home addresses, and may or may not disclose this.

ADVERTISING AGENCIES

Role of the Advertising Agency in Direct Mail

Until about 1950, when there was only a handful of promotion-minded advertising agencies, barely any direct mail was produced or controlled by advertising agencies. None was being handled by major agencies. They found direct mail much too difficult, much too wearing, and much too easily monitored as to actual results to have anything to do with it. In the intervening years, fledgling direct-mail promotion agencies have blossomed into major factors, and with almost no exceptions have been purchased by major *AAAA* advertising agencies who now recognize the need to have direct-mail expertise as part of their promotional armaments.

Direct Response: A Separate Function in Today's Advertising Agencies

Every major advertising agency has found it either expedient or essential to purchase or develop a direct-response arm. One agency, Young and Rubicam, which has three separate direct-response agencies, reportedly now bills the equivalent of $250,000,000 in what most advertising agencies up to recent years have considered "collateral" (nuisance) services. The development of a special council of advertising agencies by the Direct Marketing Association is more proof that the agency thrust in response has come of age.

Not a day now goes by without the announcement of another direct-response client by one or another of the top twenty agencies. To give you an idea of the commitment to this growing field is the fact that media buying for direct response is now a separate responsibility in some agencies from the conventional media department. This is a development certain to grow as advertising agencies learn that account executives cannot be both good service representatives and knowledgeable media buyers for their clients at the same time. This practice, still utilized by most agencies in or entering the field, is a good demonstration of the "errand boy" approach, in which the best copy is written, the best offer is created, the best paper and graphics and printing are employed, and then the "errand boy" is sent out to rent some lists.

The better agencies are further along in the study of the costs of new customer acquisition and lifetime value than their clients. They also are fueling many of the innovative means to learn how better to segment lists, particularly the files their customers have, than their customers do.

Trained In-House Personnel Versus Outside Specialists: A Question of Expertise

Because of their rather sudden and forceful emergence in the direct-response market, the direct-response agencies, particularly those in New York City where most are located, are having a stressful time attracting and then holding trained, knowledgeable people who know what to do with a direct-response program. This has led to unconscionable, high-cost raiding of young, bright people who are being pushed too far and too fast for the good of either the agency or its clients. Few of them are capable, at their best, of being the marketing director of the companies they service, and that is what account management requires. As an end concomitant of this, the training of agency direct-mail professionals is lagging light years behind the elegant in-house training programs for general advertising.

Where this shift is leading to is quite clear. As only the direct-response agency with full service in research, media, public relations, and sales promotion can embrace every part of an integrated direct-response program—from classified phone book listings to data-bank management, the control of major direct-mail programs is more and more going to flow into the hands of the major ad agencies with demonstrable track records. Payment for these services will of necessity be on a fee basis rather than the conventional basis (15 percent agency commission). Only in this way will the agency be compensated properly for its investment in account management.

Because of the need to appear to be the master of all levels of promotion, ad agencies are surprisingly loath to utilize on a regular, planned basis, the expertise of specialists in direct-mail lists, statistical analysis, unusual media, specialized printed formats, list management, and marketing consultation. It is becoming clear to agency management that their growing operations cannot possibly attract the best talent in all aspects of direct response. A move to involve such outside experts in their planning operations is now beginning to emerge for these agencies. As agencies mature in this field, we can expect to find more of them embracing such expertise for the ultimate benefit of their client relationships.

List Availability

From a list marketing point of view, advertising agencies are both an opportunity and a problem. It is an opportunity because more and more of the major accounts are being serviced by them and thus they represent a growing market. It is a problem because all too often the agency is more concerned with the more lucrative space or electronic media placements and permits this to color their marketing advice. The movement, however, is all in one direction toward increasing professionalism on the part of the agencies and a growing realization by them that list professionals, list brokers, list compilers, and list managers, can offer valid help on almost any account.

Lists of advertising agencies provide many ways to reach this market:

- The 4As (American Association of Advertising Agencies) provides 400 of the largest and strongest companies in the country at some 600 offices.

- SRDS "accredited" agencies lists approximately 3600 agencies automatically given space discounts for ad placements by publishers.

- Ad agencies by number of employees:

100 or more employees	300 agencies
50 or more employees	600 agencies
20 or more employees	1800 agencies

- Ad agencies with net worth
  ratings of $500,000 or more   250.

- Ad agencies listed in classified yellow pages with phone numbers:
  In metropolitan areas   11,000 agencies
  Countrywide   22,000 agencies

- Ad agencies (independent or as division of larger agencies) specializing in direct mail advertising   1,000 (estimated).

Most compilers and list managers welcome advertising agency requests, and almost universally provide AAs with the same 15 percent agency discount available to them by other media. List brokers, who have at best a 20 percent commission on list placements, ordinarily do not commission ad agencies, but rather invite them to add their commission to the full rental price. It should be noted that most agencies bill for direct-mail services on a fee basis. The standard 15 percent commission for media does not provide for the large range of services involved in taking a direct-mail project from concept to mailing and analysis.

CHAPTER 5

How to Rent a List: From the Viewpoints of the Owner and the User

This chapter tells you what's involved in renting a list from two sides of the business. The first part is written from the perspective of the *list owner;* the second part covers the viewpoint of the list user. Much of the data of prime importance to one side of the list transaction is also important to the other. So, regardless of your particular interest, I suggest you look at the perspectives of both sides.

PART I: RENTING A LIST FROM THE OWNER'S VIEWPOINT

LIST RENTAL INCOME

One of this nation's most successful inside list managers publicly stated, "A mailing list as a profit-producing asset is almost too good to be true." What other aspect of your business or any other business brings down 55 to 60 percent of gross sales as pure profit to the bottom line? Like a record that produces music each time it is played, a mailing list produces profit each time it is rented but the names are not depleted. Usually all the costs attributable to the development of the list have been borne or amortized for another in-house utilization, so the lists are in effect cost-free.

While list rental income does affect the value of a name (those companies

105

that rent their names get added income from this source, those who do not rent do not get such added income) it is not usual to incorporate list rental income into lifetime evaluations. If the sum is a large one, it should be properly included. There have been a few mail order fortunes made by companies able to produce great quantities of new names very inexpensively in which the rental contribution has been a great consideration. But these are rare. Some magazines do show a considerable portion of net profit from list rental. *Inc.* Magazine reportedly obtains $3,500,000 net per year from its 450,000 subscribers. That means each name provides $8.00 of net rental income. Several trade magazines have peripheral net income from list rentals running from $1.00 per name per year to $2.00 per name. One of these is DM News where rentals provide over forty "turns" per year of the entire list.

WHAT TO CONSIDER BEFORE RENTING YOUR LIST

Three Ways to Determine the Value of Your List

If you are planning to rent or exchange your proprietary list there are several points to take into consideration. To begin with, the more selectivity, efficiency and control you can provide, the greater value of your names to the renter. There are three sectors to cover here: *segmentation availability, production flexibility,* and *output modes.*

1. List segmentation based on list elements. On a customer file this covers the gamut of "RF$USISM" (see page 333). On an inquiry list this includes type of product and recency. On a compiled file, access to the list elements is the key.

2. List production. Here you, your service bureau, or your list manager must be able to provide statistically reliable segments as requested:

- Geographical—by state, metro area, county, city, three-digit zip code and five-digit zip code.
- Sampling—by nth number, or fifth-digit of zip code, or fourth and fifth digit of zip code.
- Continuations—when a mailer tests your list and comes back for more he or she normally will wish to exclude all records used on the test sample lot. Only if you can do this can your renter be assured of the best level of

response. You'll want your renter to succeed so he or she will return for yet another and usually larger, "continuation."

- Flexibility to meet customer requirements—Among the requests a renter may be asked to fulfill, other than time, which is often the controlling factor, are:

  a. Stop counts
  b. Adding of codes
  c. Adding of a second line of titling
  d. Moving post office box number to a different line
  e. Selecting one criteria within another
  f. Selecting an SIC among four, both primary and secondary
  g. Utilizing Boolean logic to select executive one, two, or three
  h. Selecting names for the same company on different flights in order to bypass mailroom glut

- Balances—It is important to be able to supply to a renter, particularly one who has come back for a continuation, how many names with the same criteria are available to him or her.

3. Output modes. Historically we first moved the pieces to a lettershop where lists were produced by typewriter, either directly onto the piece, or on sets of gummed label sheets which were then stripped, moistened, and applied. In the early half of this century, lists were principally converted to files of metal plates. Later a portion of them was typed on stencil cards. The material was then moved to the shops where addresses were either stamped on or transferred by direct addressing. Occasionally the plates or cards were used to produce a "one-up" label in whatever sequence the list was maintained. The early computers, prior to the early 1960s, were punch-card operated. The machines interpreted holes punched in the cards and produced addresses on sheets or envelopes through impact printers. With the advent of magnetic tape, lists were converted (by various forms of keystroking) to tape which provided electronic data processing thus eliminating slow, cumbersome, and costly mechanical means. (It should be noted that now there are still many lists still on plates, IBM cards, or only now being converted to cards for holographic or purple ditto transfer. There are still sets of gummed labels, as well as would-be lists still on hard copy in the form of responses, orders, inquiries, and warrantees. Lists in these forms have virtually no place today in the rental marketplace.)

The Four Major Computer List Outputs and How They Work

In some cases, output (the way a list can be delivered) is dictated by the mechanical or electronic form in which it is stored and accessed. For example, most unit card systems (Xerox, Scriptomatic, Pitney Bowes) can output one-up labels (north/south) and not the conventional four- or five-across labels produced by a computer.

The major outputs of lists from computers today are:

1. Cheshire labels—usually four across, in zip code sequence

2. Pressure-sensitive labels

3. Magnetic tape—now usually 9-track, 1650 (or 6250) BPI, and what is called IBM or EBCDIC mode

4. Specialized outputs

Cheshire labels

Cheshire labels are sent to the mailer or mail house to be affixed by one of several makes of cheshire affixing machines. These machines first chop one line horizontally, then guillotine vertically between the four labels, apply glue to the underside, and affix the labels individually, in sequence, to the individual piece or envelope. These machines operate at speeds of up to 16,000 to 20,000 addresses per hour. For those unfamiliar with cheshire (and label production in general) the first fact to know is that the width of the printing area of a standard computer is 132 characters. This limits the width of the largest line on commercially produced labels to:

- Thirty characters for labels printed four across. (4 × 30 = 120, leaving twelve spaces between the four labels.) This is the standard for almost all business lists, and most mail order response lists.

- Twenty-four characters for labels printed five across. (5 × 24 = 120, leaving twelve spaces between the five labels.) This is the character width by all occupant lists and many runs for demographic consumer files.

A four-across Cheshire label is shown in Figure 5.1.

Note that the sequence runs horizontally left to right, with label No. 5 coming under label No. 1 to start the second horizontal row. (Where you need to make a four-way split of a list, this can be done by using paper already prepunched with one centered hole between one label and the one immediately below it, and then

Figure 5.1

Layout of a four-across computer printout (for cheshire or pressure-sensitive labels)

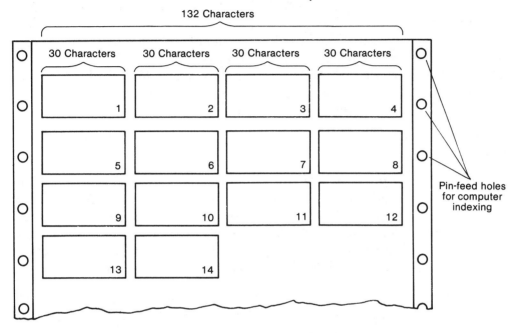

guillotining the run into four vertical strips. This provides an exact 1-for-4 split of the file.)

Pressure-sensitive labels

These are pregummed labels, adhering to a backing sheet which are printed by computer just as cheshire labels are.

Pressure-sensitive labels can be peeled off individually, and adhered permanently to a mailing piece or envelope by pressure. They are used for small runs or for mailings where the glossy appearance (as opposed to the dull surface of standard cheshire) is desired. Or the cheshire affixing machine can chop through and affix the backing sheet (with the pressure-sensitive label attached). The recipient of this format can be invited to peel off the mailing label and press it down in the area indicated (usually on an order or return form). A variant of this is the "piggy back" pressure-sensitive label which carries an impression of the address on the backing slip. Thus when the label is peeled off and applied elsewhere, the original address data still remain on the piece.

Magnetic tape

Virtually all lists shipped on tape are on 9-track tape, and "packed" either 1600 or 6250 BPI in an IBM mode known as EBCDIC. Almost all such lists use fixed fields for each addressing or selection element on the tape. No tape should be shipped without a careful description of tape record length and count, and the tape reel should be accompanied by a tape layout as well as a tape dump. (The layout specifies where to find each element or field of the record on the tape; the tape "dump," as it's name implies, is a character-by-character printout of a few hundred records for verification of the tape layout.)

Specialized outputs

Heat transfer labels. Labels printed by computer with an inverted carbon which produces a carbonized mirror image of the address on the underside of a cheshire label. This carbon image is "transferred" by heat and pressure to the face of the mailing piece. (This is a print-image, albeit a rather weak or fuzzy one, not a label.) The process also produces a set of one-up labels with the original imprint on the face which can be utilized for a second identical addressing.

Heat sealing labels. A special ultra-thin stock, addressed as a cheshire, which is affixed to an envelope or piece by heat that "welds" the label into the paper face of the mailing.

One-up labels. There are also occasional calls for one-up labels, where each record is in a vertical string with a pin-feed hole in the center of the strip. These are made for both cheshire labels and for pressure-sensitive labels.

Printronic label. A label with a preprinted border and lines that can be printed in cheshire format by a computer. Some mailers find this form increases responsiveness.

There are also several other outputs that may be required—some of which may be for nonmailing purposes:

Sheet listing. Data printed by a computer in columnar form on lined or unlined cheshire size stock, line for line rather than in three- or four-line label format. Data can be selected, sequence numbered, printed in one line or more as required. When a mailing is to be followed up with a phone call, the sheet list, double spaced for posting space, is usually preferred over a carbon copy of the labels (cheshire without a phone number for mailing; the sheet list with a phone number for follow-up.) Two sets of cheshire can be utilized but this means both will include the phone number. If this is utilized the telephone number can be reversed which converts it, to the unpracticed eye, into another long key line.)

3 by 5 Cards. All data that can be printed on a single line of a sheet list can be printed (on multiple lines) on a 3 by 5 card.

Card output is preferred by many telephone callers since cards can be annotated, shuffled, filed in tickler sequence, and passed from one operator to another. Cards are usually printed "one-up" or "two up" . . . and such pinfeed forms are expensive. As computer printers get "hiccups" printing multiple lines on output formats one-up or two-up, printing of 3 by 5 card copies are also more expensive than sheet listings or cheshire addressing. (Some users request output on 5 by 8 cards, or $8\frac{1}{2}'' \times 11''$ sheets. Where this cannot be accommodated by the computer, pressure-sensitive labels can be run off and applied to the form. Market research is probably the major user of this type of output.)

IBM cards. IBM punch cards can be created (one at a time) by a computer. The holes can then be "interpreted" and the list data printed across the top of the card. Occupant mailers find this format ideal for USPS updating of their carrier route files.

Floppy discs. More and more names and addresses are now being made available on the horde of different forms and formats of floppy discs for word processing. A few list purveyors now offer to provide lists in this form. Ed Burnett Consultants is one of the leaders in this business, providing not only the list on floppies for DOS handling, but for the same price a floppy disc program to make it easy for the customer to address labels or envelopes or letterheads and to store, change, sort and clean the mailing list provided.

Three common forms of list output are illustrated here:

IV-E-1 Figure 5.2 is from a four-across set of cheshire labels. The records here are four-line, covering individuals by name (or title) at their company addresses. Consumer lists are almost always three-line addresses.

IV-E-1 Figure 5.3 is a typical *telemarketing card,* showing classification, sales, employment, and a ten-digit phone number. Note that it takes eight lines to print all these data on a 3 × 5 inch card.

IV-E-1 Figure 5.4 is a typical *sheet listing* with all data available on a 3 × 5 inch card printed in three horizontal lines across the full width of the $14\frac{3}{4}$ inch wide computer sheet (shown here in reduced size). Note the headings at the top covering each element of information.

Figure 5.2

Reproduction of a 4-across Cheshire label run (4-line business addresses)

```
                    PP14                                      PP14
D WHITELEY                           JOHN CRAVENS
NORTHEASTERN INS CO HARTFORD         R G DICKINSON & CO
400 LOCUST ST.                       200 DES MOINES BLDG
DES MOINES         IA   50309        DES MOINES       IA   50309


                    PP14                                      PP14
JEFFREY LEE SIMPSON                  DEAN STROMER
MID SEVEN TRANSPORTATION CO.         KLEMME COOPERATIVE GRAIN CO.
2323 DELAWARE AVE.                   122 W. MAIN ST.
DES MOINES         IA   50317        KLEMME           IA   50449


                    PP14                                      PP14
SUSAN BRADY                          PHILIP R BRANDT
WARTBURG COLLEGE                     GARNAVILLO MILL, INC.
222 9TH ST NW                        MAIN & OAK STS.
WAVERLY            IA   50677        GARNAVILLO       IA   52049


                    PP14                                      PP14
EDWIN L INGRAHAM                     ETHLYN COWLES
LIFE INVESTORS INS CO OF AMER        CITIZENS MUTUAL TEL CO
4333 EDGEWOOD RD. N. E.              114 W JEFFERSON
CEDAR RAPIDS       IA   52499        BLOOMFIELD       IA   52537


                    PP14                                      PP14
FREDERICK D FUESSEL                  DAVID A CHRISTENSEN
DAVENPORT ELECTRIC CONTRACT CO       DAVENPORT MACHINE & FOUNDRY CO
529 PERSHING AVE., BOX 4229          1628 W. 4TH ST.
DAVENPORT          IA   52808        DAVENPORT        IA   52808


                    PP14                                      PP14
DEAN M ANDERSON                      ALFRED GRETZINGER
ANDERSON BROTHERS REFRIG SVC         PRECISE TOOL & DIE CO INC
12450 W. COLFAX PL.                  12720 LISBON RD
BUTLER             WI   53007        BUTLER           WI   53007


                    PP14                                      PP14
JAMES KAUFMANN                       GEORGE BEHN
LANSON IND                           REIMERS PHOTO MATERIALS CO.
6700 IND LOOP                        300 E. BAY ST.
GREENDALE          WI   53129        MILWAUKEE        WI   53207


                    PP14                                      PP14
ELEANOR PROM                         ROLLYN KARAS
POHLMAN STUDIOS, INC.                S. J. BROWN, INC
527 N. 27TH ST.                      2200 N. 31ST ST.
MILWAUKEE          WI   53208        MILWAUKEE        WI   53208


                    PP14                                      PP14
JEANETTE BERBAUM                     RUTH CRAWFORD
BERBAUM MILLWORK INC.                CONTRACTORS SUPPLY CO.
3403 W. KIEHNAU AVE.                 6101 N. TEUTONIA AVE.
MILWAUKEE          WI   53209        MILWAUKEE        WI   53209
```

Figure 5.2 (cont.)

PP14

RICHARD L GOODSON
THRIFT DISCOUNT BROKERAGE
INC
1014 MIDLAND FIN BLDG
DES MOINES   IA   50309

PP14

MARY CAMPBELL
CAMPBELL INDUSTRIES INC.
3201 DEAN AVE.
DES MOINES   IA   50317

PP14

JOHN B SIMPSON
CREST PAK INC.
1515 N. 15TH
HUMBOLDT   IA   50548

PP14

JOLEEN MERTEN
CITIZENS FIRST NATIONAL BANK
5TH & LAKE
STORM LAKE   IA   50588

PP14

ARTHUR ALBERS
BENTON COUNTY ELEC COOP ASSOC
1006 W. 4TH ST.
VINTON   IA   52349

PP14

H KILIPER
COLLINS DEFENSE COMMUNICATIONS
855 35TH ST. N. E.
CEDAR RAPIDS   IA   52498

PP14

LYNN HOWARD
MOHASKA STATE BANK
124 S 1ST ST
OSKLAOOSA   IA   52577

PP14

CHARLES W BURKE
MCCARTHY IMPROVEMENT COMPANY
4321 E. 60TH ST.
DAVENPORT   IA   52807

PP14

D H SHAW
IOWA-ILLINOIS GAS&ELEC CO
206 E 2ND ST
DAVENPORT   IA   52808

PP14

JAMES E O'HARA
MUELLER LUMBER CO.
501 W. SECOND ST.
DAVENPORT   IA   52808

PP14

ROBERT L BERGMAN
NASHOTAH MOULDING CO., INC.
528 INDUSTRIAL DR.
HARTLAND   WI   53029

PP14

THOMAS P LARSON
ROCK RIVER TEL CO
136 UNION ST
JOHNSON CRK   WI   53038

PP14

B R SHERMAN
ST FRANCIS S & L ASSN
3545 S KINNICKINNIC AVE
MILWAUKEE   WI   53207

PP14

R A PIETSCH
A. J. PIETSCH CO.
3535 W. STATE ST.
MILWAUKEE   WI   53208

PP14

THOMAS H BENTLEY III
BENTLEY & SON, INC.
3031 WEST MILL RD.
MILWAUKEE   WI   53209

PP14

JOHN GRAF
BENZ OIL INC
2724 W HAMPTON AVE
MILWAUKEE   WI   53209

PP14

RICHARD W STAR
ENGMAN-TAYLOR COMPANY, INC.
2830 W. STARK ST.
MILWAUKEE   WI   53209

PP14

EVELYN JORGENSEN
JORGENSEN CONVEYORS, INC.
3806 W. DOUGLAS AVE.
MILWAUKEE   WI   53209

Figure 5.3

3 × 5 telemarketing card

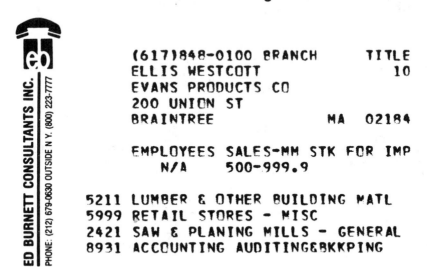

ED BURNETT CONSULTANTS INC.

PHONE: (212) 679-0630 OUTSIDE N.Y. (800) 223-7777

```
(617)848-0100 BRANCH      TITLE
ELLIS WESTCOTT               10
EVANS PRODUCTS CO
200 UNION ST
BRAINTREE              MA   02184

EMPLOYEES SALES-MM STK FOR IMP
   N/A       500-999.9

5211 LUMBER & OTHER BUILDING MATL
5999 RETAIL STORES - MISC
2421 SAW & PLANING MILLS - GENERAL
8931 ACCOUNTING AUDITING&BKKPING
```

DATE	SALES REP	COMMENTS

Figure 5.4
Sheet Listing–Horizontal

COMPANY... / NAME...	ADDRESS... / DEPARTMENT...	CITY...	SEX	TITLES..	ST ZIP..	TELEPHONE... / H/B	SIC1 SIC2 / INT SIC3 SIC4	SALES STK	EMPLOYEES FORTUNE
CENTRAL FED SAVINGS BANK / CARLOS A DEL VALLE	66 COLL Y TOSTE ST	ARECIBO	M	92	PR 00613	809-878-1360 H	6120	7	0
BAYAMON FED SVGS LN ASSN PR / A LOPEZ JIMENEZ	BAYAMON CTR CORNER RD 167	BAYAMON	X	7106	PU 00619	6122	8 0	6
BAYAMON FED S & L ASSN / A HIRSH	P O BOX 60-1435	BAYAMON	X	91	PR 00619	809-785-2557 H	6120	7	0
CAGUAS FED S & L ASSN OF PR / LORENZO MUNOZ FRANCO	BOX 7199	CAGUAS	M	84	PR 00626	809-746-1916 H	6120	7	0
PONCE FED SAVINGS BANK FSB / MANUEL TEXIDO	VILLA & CONCORDIA STS	PONCE	M	90	PR 00731	809-844-8100 H	6120	7	0
FIRST FED SAVINGS BANK / MARIANO J MIER	1519 PONCE DE LEON AVE 23	SANTURCE	X	84	PR 00910	809-721-6200 H	6120	7	0
BANCO DE SANTANDER PR / BENITA CANTALAPIEDRA	168 MUNOZ RIVERA AVE	HATO REY	F	R4	PR 00919	809-759-7070 H	6020	9	0
BANCO CENTRAL CORP / ANGEL B BOTTEY	AVE PONCE DE LEON 221 BX BV	HATO REY	U	92	PR 00936	809-753-2500 H	6020	9	0
BANCO POPULAR DE PUERTO RICO / A NEIL MONTILLA	GPO BOX G	SAN JUAN	M	9090	PR 00935	809-765-9800 H	6020 8931	9	0
BANCO DE PONCE / ALBERTO M PARACCHINI	GPO BOX 3108	SAN JUAN	M	7184	PR 00936	809-754-9400 H	6020 8931	9	0
CHICOPEE SAVINGS BANK / E H CHARTRAND	70 CENTER ST	CHICOPEE	X	84	MA 01014	413-594-6692 H	6120 6020	6	0
COMMUNITY SAVINGS BANK / DOUGLAS A GUYETT	200 MAIN ST	HOLYOKE	M	9116	MA 01040	413-536-7220 H	6020 6120	7	0
NORTHAMPTON INST FOR SVGS / DAVID W SHEARER	109 MAIN ST.	NORTHAMPTON	M	9081	MA 01060	413-584-0997 H	6022 6020 6120	6	4

HOW TO HANDLE TEST SAMPLINGS

The list owner normally pays the costs of providing reasonably adequate test samples from a large list or a large list universe (say 1,000,000 or more). This can be handled most expeditiously by establishing test sample lots:

1. Such test samples should be drawn off periodically say, once a quarter, to avoid obsolescence.
2. Such test samples should be of sufficient size to provide unduplicated test samples—a unique lot of 50,000 should do nicely.
3. The sample lots can be selected on the basis of last digit of the zip code. In this way access to the main file without duplicating one record on the *current* test sample file is assured.

If your data processing service can tag every record of every order, and can report differing rental usage of each record in your file, that is preferable to fifth-digit-of-zip code select. But the number of services that do tag every rental record is very, very small.

TIPS ON PROCESSING RENTAL LISTS

Data on which records from which excerpt have been used for a given test must be kept for a period of at least six months. Only in this way (or through skipping the entire segment or fifth-digit zip select) can continuations be made that are guaranteed to be unduplicated.

Each list utilization should include those records that have been inserted by the list owner or at the instigation of the owner as his dummies. Dummies or "seeds" are names which prove to the mailer that a given mailing or segment has been delivered to the USPS. Records should be kept that record the utilization, mailer, broker, format, method and date of shipment, and cost of shipping. These records should be maintained at least for two years.

If the list owner does not have a copy of the rental file, which is often the case where the list is generated from the order file, a security reel copy should be made at each update and returned to the list owner. This guarantees continuity in case some catastrophe overcomes the list processor. Almost all good list processing shops keep two or more generations on file so security can be maintained at the processing shop level barring disasters.

The list rental company should be able to provide any type of label extant, including one-up pressure-sensitive labels, 3 × 5 inch cards, sheet listings, duplicate sets of cheshire or sheet lists, (with sheet eject between breaks if required); utilize stop counts, Nth number selection, fifth-digit selection; and sort data by name or city (as well as by such demographic data as SIC, number of employees); and provide counts by state, three-digit SCF, and five-digit zip code; and asterisk coding for end of zips and end of sectional centers should be optional. Be sure the shop can handle tapes for ink-jet addressing, provide extracts for credit checking, and modify lists if a need exists for upper- and lowercase mailing. While not a necessity, it may be a comfort to find the house is also sophisticated enough to provide list data ready for automatic typesetting. It is important *not* to have to teach the list processor the list business. When the list is to be updated it is the list processor's responsibility to provide the list for mailing or research with a unique identifying number (usually a sequence number tagged to the file at the time of production) so that "kills" can be handled expeditiously, inexpensively, and most importantly, correctly through keystroking of only a few digits instead of a long match code.

Where a third class mailing (with sequence numbers) has been made with "address correction," the processing shop should be able to identify all returns, and mail them third class bulk again as half of them will not come back the second time and ostensibly are still deliverable. If desired, the shop should then mail the returns by first class to attempt to obtain the new address, if existent. It must be kept in mind that the USPS employs 780,000 people in 36,000 separate post offices, and the activity from post office to post office, in fact from postal clerk to postal clerk, is subject to a fair amount of variation.

When an update of the mailing list is made, the processing shop should provide a transaction run, which shows what each record handled was and what it is now. This permits checking of the accuracy and completeness of the update procedure.

For small lists, the ideal means to keep it pristine is to supply a copy to the owner on a duplicate sheet listing (usually alphabetic) as a "crutch file." All changes and kills to be handled in the next update must then be recorded, preferably in colored ink, on a copy of the crutch file. Adds need to be separate and should, preferably, be provided on forms with adequate size boxes for each character and each digit.

HOW TO DETERMINE AN ACCEPTABLE LIST SIZE FOR RENTING

Although there is a rental market even for small lists, the costs of promotion, processing, billing, and collecting make it reasonable to have a list of at least 25,000 names. Lists smaller than this leave the renter no place to go even if a test succeeds.

Interestingly enough a mail order buyer list of 30,000, 50,000, or 70,000 names, virtually identical to one or more lists already on the market, is a rentable commodity because only a small portion of the names will be duplicates. But a compiled list of the same size may not be rentable as there may be some lists well established on the marketplace with virtually the identical names.

If a list is small it is usually nonproductive to offer small splits by specialty. (One manager recently took a book buyer's list of 60,000 names and offered thirty-four separate segments. The list barely covered the costs to market it.) The rule is quite simple: Each segment should be large enough by itself to be worth testing for a possible continuation.

A compiled file will have a better chance on the market if it fulfills all or most of the following criteria:

1. Covers the complete universe (coverage for one city, state, or section of the country usually cannot succeed).

2. Is current so that deliverability of 90 to 92 percent can be guaranteed.

3. Is on tape with accurate zip codes.

4. Is part of a larger file with greater coverage.

5. Has a "track record" (usage) that conveys credibility.

6. Has built in selection factors of interest to mailers that include:

    a. Businesses classified by size of establishment, name of executive, sales volume, phone number.

    b. Consumers classified by income, age, education, number of children, car ownership, buying habits, change of address, telephone number.

Know the List Market (Don't Reinvent the Wheel)

Before investing in compiling a given list or classification or a group of classifications, make certain you know all the lists already on the market. All too often a newcomer to the list business will offer a list manager or compiler a "new" list, only to find his or her effort wasted. A typical example is the entrepreneur who laboriously collated and computerized a list of 500,000 college students, only to find that *Newsweek* and *Time* magazines each sponsors two large compilations annually, which provide access to over 5 million students by name at college or university addresses. As these two lists are available for rental, there was no way his "part" of the market could compete.

All too often someone offers a classification taken from classifieds laboriously prepared from 4,000 yellow page directories. What these would-be compilers fail to see is that two or three nationwide compilers, each with all 4,700 classified telephone books, now make updated countrywide lists of almost every classification available. (Now, every last classified listing in every last classified (yellow pages) directory on an updated basis, is available.)

THE FINE ART OF LIST PRICING AND PRICE CHANGING

If we look first at compiled files, the prices per M for a minimum quantity have been something like this over the last 30 years:

Prior to 1955	$15/M
From 1956 to 1965	20/M
From 1966 to 1972	25/M
From 1973 to 1979	30/M
From 1980 to 1982	35/M
From 1983 to 1984	40/M
1985	50/M

The years between 1973 and 1979 were a period of great tumult and change and the price of a classified list or a compiled business list stayed unchanged. In the years since 1979, prices have increased by two-thirds. The average price of a compiled file today, based on total volume and not the price for a minimum quantity, is about $30, or 60 percent of the $50/M asked for a minimum quantity.

It is difficult to determine the "average" for mail order buyer lists. These lists were in the $35/M range when compiled files were $15 to $20/M. A somewhat similar differential has held up to the present time where the average business magazine file commands $60 to $70/M, while low-level product buyer lists go at $50/M, and high-level product lists are priced at $70 to $85/M. A few list owners, notably Horchow, decided the right price is $100/M. And there are now specialized lists in the market, including credit approved names, that rent for over $150/M, while "new connects" on a current basis can bring even more.

How to Set a Fair Price for Your Mailing Lists

In essence, pricing must be set between the cost to produce the product or service and what the market will bear.

To determine the ideal sum to charge for a new list it is best to confer with list managers and list brokers. They will take into account the type of list, the quantity, the growth potential, the segmentation available, and the competition. They will also provide a very narrow range for consideration. The reason this range will be narrow is that lists tend to fit patterns for pricing, and these patterns are part of the general knowledge of the list community.

Pricing will cover:

- The basic minimum and rental price per thousand names on cheshire labels or on tape.

- Address for different formats.

- Address for segmentation which can be for selection by:

Consumer Compiled	Mail Order Buyer	Business File
Income	Recency	SIC
Age	Frequency	Number of employees
Education	Dollars	
Number of children	Source	

- Availability and cost of telephone numbers.

- Merge–purge minimum quantity and percentage guarantee.

- Quantity discounts (if any).

Each of the major types of lists have different price ranges. Figures here are given for test quantities of 5,000 to 10,000:

Consumer compiled names and addresses	$30 to $50
Business compiled names and addresses	$35 to $60
Mail order buyers—(not just respondents or inquiries)	$50 to $100
Occupant or resident names	$15 to $25

Pricing is usually set to aggrandize the greatest number of dollars from the rental market. There are small specialized lists priced as high as $300/M. There are very large lists where a million names can be rented for $15/M. They represent two ends of a scale affected by what is called the *elasticity of demand*. In the case of the very high-priced list, it is felt that changing the price, even a lot, will not increase the number of uses. In other words, there is no elasticity of demand here. So for the few rentals expected, a high price is exacted.

The low-priced list probability indicates a very high elasticity. At $30/M or even $25/M, the ultimate customer might prefer to go to a competitive list. The more competitive, the greater the relationship between price and quantity and rental income. No list exists in a vacuum.

Consider the "Turns" Your List Will Generate

To aggrandize dollars, pricing must take into account the number of "turns" that list rental will generate. A list of 60,000 names which "turns" five times at $60/M produces 300 times $60/M or a gross sale of $18,000. That same list may turn eight times at $50/M (8 × 60 = 480,000 names at $50/M = $24,000). Pricing can help "make" a list, or it can hinder its growth, or reduce the net income to the list owner to a figure where rental does not seem worth even the small effort required. One caution here. Do not have too high expectations or listen to the largest siren sing about the net sums involved. Only a small number of lists produce a phenomenal number of turns and hence phenomenal dollars of profit.

Look at the List's Position in the Marketplace

Pricing should (but rarely does) take into account the need to "position" a list in the marketplace. Promotion has more to do with positioning than price, but the current price for the current position is important if the list is to be positioned to capture a fair share of the available market. Positioning involves knowledge of the market, of the promotion in the market, and of the acceptance in the market. But most of all, it involves knowing what to do to get the attention of brokers, compilers, managers, and the major users of that particular type of list.

Pricing, to aggrandize the most rental dollars from a given list is an art, not a science. You can get a considerable helping hand if you will utilize the following seven rules.

Seven List Rental Pricing Rules to Follow

1. If you hire a list manager, let him or her set the price of your list. The list manager is in touch with the market and knows what price should aggrandize the greatest income return for your list.

2. Tabulate the prices of those lists nearest in nature to your own—the same or similar classification, the same or similar price lines.

3. Ask three or four list brokers who are handling or are about to be petitioned to handle your list. They are in the middle of the market between list owner and list user, and have a good "feel" of what is possible.

4. Don't bother asking one of the trade associations. Pricing is not their province.

5. If you are going to raise a price, don't do it in small steps. Change the price at once. A list increased in price from $60 to $70 can lose almost 20 percent of its former volume before the dimunition affects the bottom line.

6. If you have a number of lists, utilize selective pricing rather than identical pricing. In George Orwell's* words, "All animals are equal, but some animals are more equal than others."

7. The right time to increase a list price is when mailers are seeking to rent your names more times than you feel comfortable about. In general, a price increase at such a time will not reduce the demand.

HOW TO PROMOTE YOUR OWN MAIL LISTS

If you as a mailer wish to test the waters of list rental by your own efforts, you should do the following:

1. Collect a dozen different list cards from as many list owners and brokers and managers.

2. Call up several list managers and brokers and have them check your "feeling" for the price of your list.

3. Create a list card for your list, making certain you provide the prospective user with all the information needed to make a decision about your list. If this is the first time your names have been made available, be sure you emphasize this fact. Mailers for good reasons like new lists.

4. Send a copy of your card to every list broker you find listed in source directories or in SRDS Lists and Data.

5. Send a copy of your card to SRDS with a letter specifying that you are the exclusive owner of the names. Have them offer your list to "All Brokers."

6. Send a copy of your list card, with a letter, to those mailers you know have the same demographics and the same lifestyle interests indicated by your list.

Then sit back and wait—without great expectations. For it takes weeks, sometimes months, for data on lists to filter down from list brokers to prospective users, and then for the latter to have an opening for a test of your file.

* Animal Farm

If your list is large enough, and promises enough return to the company, an internal list manager may then be delegated to do all the other things necessary to place your list before all logical users. (You can, of course, initially opt to place your names with a list manager to give adequate promotion to your file.)

Let us look at these other considerations:

1. Your list can be possibly featured in a list catalog or directory. The major promoters in this market issue 200,000, 300,000, or 400,000 full scale directories per year.

2. A budget can be set for sales promotion and advertising to cover (1) showings at major trade shows, (2) a special mail campaign to cover every indirect source of list business (list brokers, list compilers, list managers, advertising agencies, PR agencies, direct-mail advertising and mail fulfillment shops, mail-minded data processing shops), (3) space ads in the trade press plus reinforcement ads in selected areas of SRDS.

TWO MISCONCEPTIONS ABOUT "BARGAINS"— FREE TESTING AND LIST EXCHANGES

As more and more lists come onto the market and more and more firms are attracted to the rental and sale and management of the lists of others, the offers of "free" lists and bargain price test quantities tend to proliferate. The list is just a modest part of the cost of mailing a test. A typical 5,000 test has an in-the-mail cost of approximately $1,500. If the list is free, that cost may reduce by $50/M to $1,250. The logic is simple—keep your eye on the doughnut which will cost $1,250 or $1,500—not on the hole which might save $250.

There is nothing wrong with a "free" test except that it's not free. If the "free" list appears to have a fair chance of being a worthwhile test in the first place, and a large merge–purge against a sizable customer base is in prospect, such a list can be keyed into the merge–purge and then mailed or not mailed, depending on the penetration shown through a merge–purge allocation segment against the customer base.

One expert in direct mail repeatedly announces that the lower cost for an exchange list will be a significant factor in the cost per sale from the exchanged list. This simply perpetuates one of the shibboleths of direct mail that "exchanges save money." There are two "sales" to an exchange: A receives a list from B without paying for it. However B also receives a list from A without paying for it so the exchange is the same as if both purchased the list of the other at the same price. To handle an exchange transaction properly, the imputed cost of the list obtained on an exchange must be added to the cost per M of that list in the mail. In other words, there is no free lunch in the exchange world. What is gained on one side is lost on the other.

ARRANGING AND CONTROLLING EXCHANGES

As exchanges are arranged at the same price on both sides (zero cost and zero income), the best way to arrange them initially is at an agreed upon and mutually acceptable fee per thousand names. The exchange, arranged to permit access to lists not otherwise available on a rental basis, then becomes a monetary transaction. It is far easier to adjust a monetary transaction by mailing a check then it is to keep track of who owes whom how many names from what period. Inevitably, even the most successful exchanges between two good companies gets out of balance. By placing a monetary value on the names, this average or underage can be adjusted amicably without leaving a festering umbilical of "you still owe me's." (On exchanges, it is best to determine up front what is to transpire if one user and not the other wishes to mail additional names. Ideally the right to continue, for a given rental price per thousand, protects both sides.)

CAN A LIST BE RENTED TOO OFTEN?

On at least three occasions my firm has worked with a list owner who was worried about the effect of "over renting" on his own sales to his customer file. In each case we finally resorted to the only method available to prove that list owner's fears right or wrong: We split the customer file in two equal parts (increasing, as it happened, the cost of updating due to recombining and then resplitting the two sections). One half was left on the list market (total rentals went down dramatically because successful full run continuations could only be about half as large as before), the other half was not rented. The result? Sales by the client to his own list were virtually the same for the two halves. The only true difference was that half of the list left on the market brought in comfortable list rental income while the other half brought in no rental income at all. A list like *Inc.* magazine is now renting over one hundred times per year; *Business Week* was last turning over forty times. One well known trade publisher in the technology field is showing an average of thirty turns, with bellwether magazine lists exceeding this.

The real key to this question is that a list owner has no exclusive lock on a given group of names. The list owner's customers more than likely can be found by a competent list sleuth on fifteen or twenty lists. If some foundations would like to fund a "nice-to-know" study, I would like the task of seeing just how many lists can be found that those thirty-five percent or more of us are on that buy by mail. The answer would seem to be that *your* list cannot be rented too often by you.

HOW TO READ A LIST PURCHASE ORDER

A proper list order will provide quick answers to the following questions:

1. Who sent the order (company, ad agency, list broker, list compiler, list manager)?
2. Who is the mailer?
3. What list is desired?
4. On what form or format is it to be delivered?
5. When is it due (and is the due date reasonable)? Do you have time to check credit?
6. What key coding if any is requested?
7. What is the offer? For Mail Order Lists, is a sample mailing piece included for "List Clearance"?
8. What selection is desired? Are there any problems with producing the selection as desired? More importantly, with your knowledge of the list, does this selection make sense for the offer?
9. What price is stipulated? If the price is incorrect, *this* is the time to catch it and report the need to change pricing to the indirect source or to the mailer. If you accept an order marked $40/M and do *not* turn it down unless changed to, say, your established $50 price, you have a contract that any businessperson would note is valid at the price posted.
10. What quantity is ordered? Can this quantity be delivered?
11. What is the mail date? On a large order it is incumbent upon you to provide "protection" against a competitive offer. So you need to post the mail date and the user to your rental usage control.
12. What are the shipping instructions? Are they clear? Are they suitable? If UPS is marked but the mailer wants delivery in a few days, find out if he or the broker will pay for expedited delivery—or you will find it difficult to get paid for what the mailer considers an "extra charge."

13. What are the special instructions? Any reader of this book is aware of all of the special requirements that mailers order (and are prepared to pay for). These can be as simple as a fifth-digit zip code select or omission of prior orders (sometimes 2 years old!).

14. Has all information been put in writing? That is what the list purchase order attempts to do from the mailer's end. If you find a need to have the instructions, time, price, or methodology changed, be certain to convey this cordially to the order writer but insist he or she either sign a copy of such changes that you have initiated, or a change-order (which can affect just one item among many if that is all that is involved) and send a copy to you for your files.

15. Are all terms placed in writing? Your terms, which may include one time rental only with payment due within 60 days of receipt or 30 days of mail date, whichever is closer should always be in writing.

INSERTS: FOUR ESSENTIAL CHECKPOINTS

If you rent your list, you may also wish to rent "space" in your bills, your prospect mailings, and in your packages.

The physical constraints for each of these forms is given in some detail in the section on Alternative Media (see page 597.) They are of primary importance, both to the "mailer" and to you as the producer.

There are a number of points to consider which fall under the following headings:

1. Scheduling
2. Receiving
3. Checking
4. Completion and billing

Scheduling

The total number of pieces that can be accommodated is determined by the maximum number of outside pieces that will be accepted multiplied by the probable total number to be mailed for each type of carrier for each near month.

(Longterm commitments may be made but they should be understood to be provisional.)

A visual schedule by month-by-carrier-by-insert should be established. All data for each inset should be kept at hand. These data include:

- Insert order
- Contact: name, address and phone number with name of phone contact
- Copy of the insert
- Quantity
- Program involved
- Date started
- Number inserted to date
- Estimated completion date

A job ticket should be created for each insert for each program, and all receiving data should be posted to the *outside* of this job ticket.

It is imperative that this schedule include every house piece or bounce back. The time of insertion is particularly important if dated or timely material needs to be inserted.

It is politic to keep open parts of cells (which will tend to delay completion dates for regulars a bit) for tests. Tests are the lifeblood of future inserts and even when there is no immediate opportunity for a continuation, they should be scheduled.

Receiving

Each shipment of inserts should be acknowledged, and the quantity (if given) and the weight and the time of receipt should be posted to the individual job ticket envelope.

If there is any apparent discrepancy between what has been ordered and what has been received (in number, appearance, or size) this should be reported to the mailers contact person as quickly as possible.

You need to specify the way in which inserts are to arrive—boxed, cartoned, or on a skid. The count should be clearly marked on each segment, and the day it is expected that delivery will be made should be specified.

Receiving should return one sample to indicate receipt. If more than one code is involved a sample should be sent off for each code so the client knows what has been received as well as what has not been received.

Checking

At least once a week or more often if large quantities are involved, supervisory employees should extract a sample from the line just before it is to go into the mailstream to determine if the scheduled pieces, and only the scheduled pieces, are being inserted. If there is any discrepancy every effort should be made to determine where the central system fell down, and how it can be improved.

Some years ago while consulting for the National Technical Information Service (NTIS) of the U.S. Department of Commerce, which at the time was placing 2,500 orders from private businesses in the mail each day, I convinced all hands that no package should go out without a bounce back from the NTIS offering all of the serials and services available from this unique repository of U.S. government research data. On my review three months later, not one package carried a bounce back—and no one knew why.

Completion and Billing

When the quantity of inserts ordered or the entire print run furnished (if that is within 10 or 15 percent of the ordered quantity), has been inserted, an invoice should be rendered covering the following details:

- Client name
- Description of piece
- Program
- Date insertion started
- Date insertion completed
- Quantity inserted
- Balance (if any) on hand and disposition if this is known
- Price per M for insertion

This invoice should be stapled to a copy of the piece. The description is insurance in case the sample piece is misplaced.

The paperwork flow in handling inserts involves:

- Scheduling
- Receiving
- Establishment of job tickets
- Checking recap
- Billing
- Collecting
- Reporting

PART II: RENTING A LIST FROM THE USER'S VIEWPOINT

This section looks at the operation from the "desk" of the list user. The data here, somewhat overlapping the preceding information on renting from the viewpoint of the owner are divided into four parts:

1. Rentals in general (irrespective of the kind of list to be used)
2. Compiled lists
3. Mail order lists
4. Hints on how to rent in general

HOW TO ORDER A MAILING LIST

Prepare a Detailed Description of What's to Be Tested

Write out a full description of the product or service to be tested. Then in an ad hoc manner, list the kinds of lists which are likely to provide the type of affinity groups that might be expected to need or like your offer.

Make sure you are on the same wavelength with your list source and have communicated exactly what you need or have decided between you and the list source on which way to go.

Be Specific About What You Want

It is important at this point to "tell all" to your list supplier and indicate as best you can the classifications, sizes, areas, thoroughness of coverage, professional or other special qualifications, ownership, recency, updating, and data on who uses these lists. The more you bring to the table in the form of a "want" list, the better able your list professional will be to solve your list needs.

Take insurance, for example. Do you want all agencies, or just those that provide life insurance? If nonlife insurance agencies are desired, do you wish to drop those with ties to large companies, or do you wish to select only those with three or more lines? Does the user understand the difference between an agency (a company) and an agent (a person licensed to sell one or more forms of insurance)? Is it clear that a list compiled from classifieds may or may not be one-per-phone, but will definitely include adjustors, agencies, agents, branch offices, brokers, company home offices, general agents, real estate agents handling insurance, services to insurance agencies, and special agents? Is it clear they also cannot be selected or omitted? Does this invalidate using this "insurance world" approach? Is the list to cover a city, a zip code area, a metro market, a group of counties, a fifty-mile radius, or a group of states? Is a second copy in zip code sequence desirable or necessary? Are titles significant? Is rating involved? Can the fulfillment shop handle one-up as well as four-across cheshire labeling? How much time is available?

Keep Track of Sources and Dates for Each Order

Make certain you know the source and the date of every compilation you order. There are no secrets in this business but there are some secretive people supplying lists. (If you need donor names you may find it necessary to test a number of lists on faith because the field itself is secretive). In the compiled field, if your list source will not or cannot tell you the source of data for his or her compilation, check with those who can and do.

Be very careful if any list supplier, or for that matter, any list user, tells you, "there is only one way to reach that market." What works for one mailer may fail for another. Some offers must have an individual name, some not. Some suppliers work with computer letters, others do not. Some mailers who believe business mail order lists make it unnecessary to test business lists by classification and rating are missing the best part of their market. Note the many approaches or concepts embraced by those who compile and ask for each one: "Is there gold in this approach, for my offer?"

The use of lists is a bit like dentistry; you really don't know how well you have been served at the time the service has been provided. This is at best a buried art and far, far from a science. So there is one good note to follow in this field: When you locate a careful, logical, knowing list purveyor who is tuned in to your needs, latch on! Such purveyors are few and far between.

Decide How the Names Are to Be Used

The next consideration is to determine "How are these names to be used?" This determines what form the list data should take: tape, cheshire labels, pressure-sensitive labels, sheet listing, or 3 by 5 cards. (If tape is used, it is essential to identify the reel and provide a tape dump and a layout, as well as the tape specifications to be utilized.)

The answer here also determines the "order" or "sequence" in which the data are to be delivered: zip code (if not otherwise noted), alphabetic (by name), alphabetic/geographic (alphabetic by name within city within state), SIC, array by size, array by zip code, array by phone number or carrier-route streams, or any variant you may require.

You should also determine at this time whether duplicate copies are required and in what form and sequence (for example, a set of pressure-sensitive labels in zip code sequence for mailing, and a set of 3 by 5 cards, perhaps in alphabetical order for checking or for telephone calling).

Include Key Codes on All Samples

Be sure the data transmitted to mailer, printer, and list supplier contain the key code for the segment. If you are using more than a test sample of a list, break it down into smaller test segments each with its own separate key code. (see the section on Testing on page 329.)

Key codes can vary from an eight- or ten-digit generic code to a single numeral or alpha character. Keys can be alpha only, numeral only, or both alpha and numeric. By use of a tabular lookup, codes of single or two-digit codes (designed to make it easier to order) can be translated by the computer to the more useful generic codes.

Determine When the Names Are Needed

The final determination is to decide When the names are needed. If needed for a merge–purge, the answer may well be five or six weeks prior to the anticipated mail date. If names are needed for labels for an immediate mailing, two weeks before the mail date is usually ample time. Most data processing centers can deliver in time if the list arrives a week ahead of the mail date. It does not do any good to have a list arrive at the last minute. Such a list will not "make" the merge–purge and if used, will need to be mailed unduplicated and by label or ink-jet addressing. Asking a data processing plant to put everything aside for one late list is unfair to the plant and unfair to your program, and in some cases, if it is done at all, it may be rushed and prepared incorrectly. Be prepared however if a number of lists are being utilized from a number of different owners that one or two will almost always arrive later than you like.

Four Ways to Reduce Headaches When Ordering Lists

When you order lists:

1. Be sure each list is identified as follows:
   a. Your company name
   b. Your order number
   c. The name and phone number of your contact
   d. List description
   e. Counts (round off to the nearest 100 or 1000—exact numbers are ridiculous)
   f. List key
   g. Tape specifications (if tape is used)
2. Give similar instruction to printers and envelope suppliers with a "signed-off" proof and a list of all segments of the planned mailing, including a control list of all lists and all list codes.
3. Instruct the printer and mailer to provide daily reports of lists received so you will have time to get after the few lists that will inevitably lag.
4. Provide a firm date for the mailing, and avoid such meaningless terms as "Rush," "ASAP," "Mail on Receipt," or the like. Be specific and provide enough *time* for your suppliers to fulfill your orders in a correct and timely manner.

WHAT TO ASK BEFORE RENTING AN OUTSIDE LIST

There are a number of questions to answer about any outside list that is being considered for rental. Where the answer is not forthcoming from the list purveyor,, find another source. There are *no* secrets in the list business (except for, perhaps, the translucent wrappings surrounding certain fundraising lists). Every question should be readily answered.

1. How old is the list? In the case of a mail order list or a magazine list this question refers to the desired segment such as the latest ninety-day buyers. In the case of a compiled file, generally, the newer the list, the higher the deliverability. Where households and establishments change at 20 percent per year, a file not updated within the last year poses a delivery problem.

2. What is the source of the list? If the list is compiled the answer should identify specifically the source or sources utilized. If the list is based on mail order, the source, (mail, space ads, co-ops, cardvertisers, radio, TV, "Take-one") should be given. If it is a magazine, the source of the name needs to be determined (solo mail, agent mail, paid-in service, and so on).

3. What selections are available? You may want to review the section on Criteria of Lists (see page 143) before proceeding with this section. In addition to the regular demographic and psychographic selections, the user may need to know if local or regional areas can be pulled. On large data banks of executives it may be a good idea to determine if one individual can be selected per address.

4. What is the minimum order charge? Most read this, incorrectly, as the minimum number of names that will be produced. In actuality it is the minimum amount the owner seeks to charge for any pull of up to a given number of names. A minimum order reading 5,000 names at $50 means that a pull of only 3,000 names will be billed at the minimum charge of $250.

Where such a billing is in the offing, the mailer may prefer to take the extra (free) 2,000 names in some nearby area. Where the quantity is likely to come up light it is best to work out with the list owner or representatives of the list owner, how best to handle the need. Many good list managers in such cases will make two pulls and give the customer the opportunity to add names to those originally requested for a modest extra charge. The use of a large data bank that provides a large number of unduplicated records per local area may be indicated.

HOW TO RENT OR BUY COMPILED LISTS

Unlike mail order lists for which there are track records, most compilations must be obtained primarily on faith. The comparative value of two compiled lists is not easy to discern, and lists of various compilers sound very much alike (see also page 485).

The worth of your list is based on the worth of the compiler. The list you get depends on:

- Your specific needs and how well you have communicated these to your compiler.

- How much he or she knows about marketing products and services.

- The range and currency of his or her source material.

- How good his or her knowledge and utilization of these sources are.

- The extent computerization is used by the compiler to solve modern marketing needs.

If your list need is quite small, a few hundred or 1,000 names, you may need to shop around a bit to find the rare compiler who believes that each order is an opportunity—no matter how small. The interesting thing about this attitude is that the minimum set by the list compiler assures the compiler of a fair profit even on the smallest lists.

Tips on Finding a Compiling Service to Suit Your Needs

Here are a few suggestions to help you locate the best compiling services for your needs:

1. Assign one person in your firm or operation to become your local list "expert." Have him or her investigate the various capabilities and specializations of list brokers, list compilers, and list managers. Ask people in the field for their opinions about the compiled files you are interested in.

2. Collect data on all compilers who offer lists in your field. Start with SRDS. Then request catalog and data from three or four of these sources which seem to serve your field. It is better to collect data ahead of time so you will not find yourself searching for a compiler at the last minute.

3. Request names of nearby customers or customers in or peripheral to your field that are serviced by the compiler. Call them and compare notes.

4. Write up a set of specifications for a given compiled list and send it off to several list compilers serving that field. You may be surprised to learn that some compilers review such requests and decide that they are too small to bother with. You may receive only one or two answers to five inquiries. This tells you something about the way they value an opportunity to do business with you.

Specifications for a business list can cover such details as:

- SIC—What are the classifications of the business? It may be your offer is not viable with retailers, churches, or doctors, and if the list is selectable by SIC such unwanted classifications can be omitted.

- Percentage of individual names—Are names to be with or without titles? Do you want a percentage of titles only?

- What proportion of the file has apparently come through the purchasing office rather than from the individual buyer? If this is properly tagged, you may wish to select on that fact and suppress such names.

- What is the availability of "ship to" addresses as opposed to "bill to" addresses? "Bill to" addresses are usually accounts payable departments and thus not a logical locus for a mailing requiring a decision by an end user.

- What is the general distribution by size? You may wish to have small firms on your list and not the Fortune 1,000 companies. Whatever size company you desire, when you review a circulation statement of a magazine, it is always important to check the size of these firms. Few publishers, except those covering small vertical markets, can afford to select companies for distribution with less than fifty employees.

Specifications for a compiled household list can cover such details as:

- Family income
- Age of head of household
- Family size
- Length of residence
- Multiple adults
- Children by age groups
- Make, model, year, number of cars
- Value of home
- Single family vs. multiple dwelling unit
- Sex of head of household
- Carrier route coding
- Addition of "or resident" to name file
- Counts prior to printing
- Telephone number

To determine which of two or three occupant lists to rent, it is best to put price aside until the quality of the respective files can be determined. Counts may provide the answer. If two owners, given the same geographical areas (usually 5-digit, 3-digit, or state) came up with numbers within a handful of each other, the prospective renter is then quite certain that each has updated their files recently with the USPS. (The USPS, if given 90 percent or more of any specified area, will, for a fee, supply all the missing addresses.)

How to Make Regional List Selections

Almost all retail and local service mailings are confined geographically to a city zone or trading area. There is one major rule to keep in mind for regional mailings: *The smaller the size of the universe to be covered, the larger the list concept must be*. Stockbrokers, insurance agents, department stores, repair shops, and franchisees of all sorts obtain their business locally. Thus the lists they use must conform, first and foremost, to the geographical area that encompasses their market. What this means for most programs is the utilization of a major list concept that can provide a reasonable number of names or establishments. For business, this means tapping one of the large data banks of executives, or one of the major files supplying virtually every business, institutional, and professional establishment. For consumers, if neither demographics nor names are essential, a local occupant list can be used. For name use, one of the several files incorporating telephone number, make of car, or driver's license data will be required.

In general, list brokers are not usually willing to provide local "pulls." They are all too aware that this may be, and often is, a one-time request with no continuation in prospect. But major compilers who run dozens of orders on a given file per week can and will handle such requests. Their minimum charges are such that they can and do profit on small orders. It is important on such small orders to check minimums. As this book goes to press one major business compiler has a minimum for its handful of nonexclusive resellers of $650, which is a fee that most small mailers correctly feel makes any order for one or two thousand names excessively costly.

You should not infer from the above statements that mail order buying lists are ruled out entirely for regional use. For membership and fundraising for local and regional cultural institutions, it is essential to tap lists of people who have indicated by purchase, membership, or support that they are good prospects for the next cultural offer. The numbers available even from large lists of local areas can be small but they are valuable and much more responsive than the much larger compiled lists of affluent families. Every effort may have to be made to tap them.

Relatively small local mailings, as opposed to countrywide mailings, tend to be ordered on pressure-sensitive labels that can be applied and mailed by the renter. In a fair proportion of cases, a duplicate copy of the names mailed to is ordered for checking and follow-up. Where this listing has phone numbers, it permits phoning prospects that have already been mailed to. One type of regional marketing that very often utilizes the mail-and-phone approach is seminars. Seminars given over a period of time in multiple cities may be reduced to local mailings for each locality. (See also the sections on "Dealerization." page 464 and "Lists for Seminars" page 317.)

Name versus Title Addressing for Business Mailings

How should a business mailing be addressed? This question comes up at every business list meeting or seminar. The answer is simple: If you can mail to a name, and it is the correct name, that is the way to go. If you also have with that name the correct title of the person, then the right answer is to mail to that name with that title.

If you have a title that is doubtful but the name is correct, mail to the name. If a title is called for substitute the doubtful title with the title of your choice.

If you have a name that is doubtful but the title is correct, it is probably best to mail it as is. If the person is no longer there the job title will still be there. Through the title you may reach the new holder of that job.

If the name is absent it is far better to address by title only rather than pulling a possibly incorrect name.

Large business compilers (who do not have names on their files) have compiled research on the name versus title addressing question and have proved title addressing is best. Publication lists, which are almost always available by name and title, take the opposite view.

It comes down to this: When the supplier can provide only the name and address of the company, the cost to match this against other files and pick up a specific name to attach to it may be much too costly—so title addressing is often the best solution.

Title addressing

As the United States moves more and more into a service-oriented economy, the thrust of the United States economy from producer-oriented (manufacturing, mining, construction, agriculture) to a service-oriented economy (wholesaling, retailing, finance, real estate) emphasizes the approaching need for even greater segmentation of business lists. The move to services is fueled by small and very small businesses. Well over 80 percent of service establishments have four or less employees. This may explain why title addressing does so well in reaching the decision makers among services. There is one person in the majority of small business who wears all the hats and receives all the mail, irrespective of what title is given. Title addressing, however, is not the best way to mail to Big Business.

CHECKLIST FOR RENTING MAIL RESPONSE LISTS

George Kaufman once quipped, "One man's Mede is another man's Persian." That expresses to some extent the variation that exists in the ways lists are maintained by list owners. The capture of data for a mail order operation has one primary purpose: to expedite the entry and delivery of an order. So there may be (and usually is) relatively poor data discipline in the coding and keystroking of the data. (See how this impinges on the problems of business merge–purge on page 495.)

It is a good idea to get some idea of the following characteristics on rented lists of consumer or business mail order buyer lists:

1. If inquiries and customers are combined, can buyers be selected?
2. What offer is involved, and how was the offer made? (Space ad buyers respond differently than direct-mail buyers.)
3. How "pure" will a selection by offer be?
4. What date stamping is on the file? Can data be selected by recency?
5. What selection is available by size of order? (Is the data for one order, multiple orders, or orders over a period?)
6. What selection is available by sex?
7. What geographic selection is available?
8. Do you wish three-line address, or four-line address? Is this selectable?
9. What is the availability of repeat buyers (two or more times from the same company or person) or multiple buyers (more than one *item* from the same company or person)?
10. How often is the cycle updated? When is the next update scheduled for?
11. What is the size of list including counts for dated segments?

Whether a list consists of consumer mail order buyers or business mail orders, it is always a very good idea to look at a copy of the promotion piece. This gives you a good indication of the kind of buyers you can expect to find on the list.

Perhaps the most important characteristic is to find out who has been using the list consistently. List brokers and list managers have one precious pearl of knowledge that hardly ever surfaces on list cards: The knowledge of who has used a given list and which of these have come back for continuations.

Finally, *see* and *analyze* what you receive in the form of lists. This is the one best way to avoid costly surprises. Most mailers using rental lists, whether the names are on labels or tapes, never see the names sent to them. Where labels are utilized, it is far better to have the labels shipped to you and not to your fulfillment house. Be sure to look at them and see exactly what was sent to you:

1. Did you get four-line business addresses or three-line consumer names?
2. Did you get the geographical area requested?
3. Did you get female or male names as desired?
4. Is the correct key on each label?
5. Was the sample selected by fifth-digit zip?
6. Is the proper title on the label?
7. Are there any major errors, such as duplicated addresses, or blanks?
8. Is the total count in line with what you ordered?
9. Is the state count given, and is the selection spread well enough apart?
10. Is the list in strict zip code sequence?

When tapes are used, your service bureau can be directed, as part of its job, to provide sample runs. Or in ordering lists where it is common to request a tape dump, which usually includes the first 200 or so records, you may request a copy of the dump to be sent to you. It is as important to review list data prior to its entry into a merge–purge as it is to review the results of that operation.

HOW TO SECURE LIST CLEARANCE

List clearance is the permission given by a list owner to a company that wishes to mail to the names owned by the list owner. This is for mail responsive lists only; most compiled lists required no clearance.

The procedure is fairly simple. The would-be mailer furnishes a sample of his or her piece (or a mock-up clearly indicating what it will look like) directly to the broker, list manager, or list owner. The owner then agrees or denies permission. If permission is granted, an order, which may have accompanied the sample, is entered, a due date for delivery is transmitted, and a mailing date clearance (if one is required) is also transmitted.

The closer the products sold by the list owner are to those the mailer is also offering, the more likely it is that a request for clearance will be rejected. But the absolute worst that can happen is to get a "no" from the list owner. Because list owners, like the rest of us, like money, it is often surprising which lists can be obtained. Each list owner has his or her own rules as to who can and cannot rent. Some list owners are much more concerned about product overlap than others. The rule is simple: You will never know unless you try.

Quite often a list that cannot be rented because of the competitive factor will be available on an exchange basis. If a sample is turned down for rental it is good practice to see if the owner would like to exchange some of his or her good names for some of yours.

Sample Mailing Piece

On virtually all compiled files there are no requests for sample mailing pieces.* However, most mail order lists require that a sample piece (or at least enough information about the offer) must be presented so the list owner can judge whether permission should be granted or not. List owners have the right to refuse a list to a prospective renter—it is their list and only those offers they "clear" can be mailed over their list. Clearance permits the list owner to protect his or her list against offers considered too competitive, or possibly, soon to be considered too competitive. (If you rent your list, or plan to, you will wish to preserve this right.)

Order early—or be prepared to wait

Most compilers today can quickly prepare all but the most complicated orders. It should be understood that the compiler handles many orders daily and is prepared to provide quick service. This is not so for the average service bureau for mail order lists and subscription lists. Whatever promises are made it is considered prudent planning to add two weeks to your delivery date, which means it is important to order early.

WHEN TO USE A LIST BANK

A list bank is *not* a data bank. It is a bank that contains data about lists that have already been tested and proven to have high response levels. These lists are stored "in the bank" for future use. As more and more mailers utilize merge–purge means to eliminate duplication from lists, the concept of a bank of proven names is bound to increase.

Lists in the list bank can and often are arrayed according to expectation of

---

*Some new list entrants, such as new homeowners, new connects, and credit approved names do require a sample mailing piece for clearance.

response based on prior performance. Thus when a cut off is made for a given quantity, only the first and best group of proven names are referred to.

New lists do *not* belong in a list bank. They must be tested conventionally and prove to be at a high-response level before they can be considered for entry into your list bank.

Like any bank, deposits (new list segments and new counts) and withdrawals (usage by time by segment) must be carefully noted on the control cards utilized.

NEGOTIATING LIST RENTAL PRICES

Some years ago, the Federal Trade Commission (FTC) discovered that all list brokers in New York City were observing a commission scale based on 20 percent of the gross rental (or sale) price of the list. This sounded to the FTC like a perfect case of price-fixing and collusion. FTC agents charged into New York City to nail these perfidious mailing list malefactors. Luckily, someone directed them to my office first, where in a few minutes, I explained that the 20 percent commission was observed, but only for modest mailings. I further explained that hardly any company renting one million or more mail order names from a given list broker was paying the full 20 percent, and that those renting in the tens of millions could and were paying no more than 10 percent. The average commission earned by major brokers was probably closer to 14 percent than it was to 20 percent.

Shortly before that, a modest customer for compiled lists, but who was on the way to being a 10 million mailer of response names, offered my firm all of his rental business at 10 percent. I suggested he go back to his two brokers and promise each of them 5 million names but only at 10 percent, which he did. Not long ago, a major business press publisher was told that much deeper discounts than the $2\frac{1}{2}$ percent his firm was then getting were available. This man, not one to dilly dally, stopped a 4 million piece mailing in its tracks until his list buyers agreed that all future list rentals would be at 10 percent commission and credits would be on hand for the mailing already addressed and ready to go into the mail. His abrupt decision saved his company $50,000 over the next nine months.

One of the top general mail order houses of yesteryear attempted, not without success, to arrange a 20 percent net name payment on large mail order lists. In other words, an agreement was reached to pay for only one of five names received irrespective of the number mailed. For the AT&T "800" directory (see "A Psychographic Case History, page 220) where each name that exceeded a minimum-family income level screen was to be mailed four times for the same project, negotiations were undertaken with every one of the 173 response lists originally selected. A few list owners insisted on full payment for each use. They received what amounted to token orders on a program that initially required over 2 million names. Those who made what we felt were more rational decisions were allotted much larger participations. The net saving to the customer, overall, was over 40 percent of the one-time price.

At least one list owner has decided to go the last mile and offers his list on a net basis—that is, payment is to be made only for names taken into a merge–purge which are actually mailed. This mailer is of the opinion that his list will net greater rental income from more and larger list orders by this ploy.

One form of list use where negotiation would seem to be called for is for credit-checked mailings. It is quite usual for not over 20 percent of good mail order lists to survive a given credit level—not because the names do not qualify but because 50 percent or more of the names are not on file with the credit bureau and therefore are returned with "no credit" information. If only those names that pass the credit check are to be mailed, the user would seem to have a legitimate request for some accommodation on names paid for.

This points out that negotiation on price is an ongoing practice in the list business. The question is not whether to negotiate or not on large utilization, but rather *how* to negotiate. The most that can happen is to receive "no" for an answer. However, the number of "yes" answers is increasing to one degree or another with each passing season. (Negotiation on price on compiled files is really a way of life. Almost every major compiler of names—consumer or business, standard telephone, car registration, or special classifications, publishes or acknowledges a scale of quantity discounts. Such discounts are even available to merchandisers of lists on a cumulative basis for resale to multiple customers.)

CHAPTER 6

Criteria: The Key Factors in the Art of List Selection

This chapter has been split into seven parts because of the primary importance of *criteria* in the selection of lists and list segments.

Part I provides an overview on how to select lists, giving the four main criteria for selectability, namely:

1. Demographics—population characteristics

2. Psychographics—lifestyle characteristics

3. Mail order characteristics—relation of name to list owner

4. Physical characteristics—mechanical characteristics

Part II concentrates on what is included within the term *demographics* and covers ten myths about demographic implications.

Part III studies the impact of geography on mailing list use and response.

Part IV shows the enormous influence of affluence on success in direct mail.

Part V demonstrates how age impacts on mailing list availabilities and usage.

Part VI studies ethnic lists as they affect the mailing list business.

Part VII provides a guide to psychographic (lifestyle) list selection.

PART I: FOUR MAIN CRITERIA IN SELECTING LISTS

Criteria determine the ways one list varies from another, as well as the ways one list segment within a list varies from another segment in that same list. Thus criteria are the *essence* of selectability and thus the *essence* of what makes one list segment produce a different response. Location of the right raisins in the rice pudding of lists is the art of list selection.

Criteria can be and often are selected as single entities, lists of say, $50 buyers, new moves, or those who buy by American Express. However, as mailers begin to delve into the wealth of options open to them, more and more selections are based on one criterion within another, for example, $50 buyers who have made a mail order purchase charged on the American Express card in the last six months.

Some mailers that order lists by multiple criteria tend to forget that each "cut" of a criteria by the part represented by another criteria reduces the size of the list segment available. After two or three "cuts" a list selected in this way may be too small to warrant using or testing.

To illustrate this point consider the following:

In zip code XXXXX there are	10,500 homes
Of these homes 63 percent have family incomes of over $25,000 leaving	6,600 homes
Households headed by females are 15.5 percent and are to be eliminated which leaves	5,600 homes
Those owning two or more cars are 28 percent which leaves	1,600 homes
Of these 22 percent have purchased a car in 1984 or 1985 which leaves	350 homes

In this case, by selecting one criterion within another, only 350 names within a universe of 10,500 are utilized.

We will now look more closely at the main criteria for selectability.

Demographic

The major *demographic* criteria for a consumer list (data on who the individuals are and where they live) are:

- Individual data:
    Income (usually family income)
    Age (usually of head of household, if for a family)
    Education (usually for head of household, if for a family)
    Family size
    Age and sex of children
- Household data:
    Type of dwelling (single family or multifamily)
    Length of residence
    Value of home
    Geographic location
- Telephone/car registration
    93 percent of families have a telephone
    70 percent of families have a *listed* phone number
    23 percent of families have an *unlisted* phone number
    7 percent of families do not have a phone
    70 percent of families have a car in an available list

Psychographic

The major psychographic characteristics (what people do, how they live, and their lifestyles) are disclosed by:

- What books and publications they buy (and read)
- What products they buy
- What they *do* with their leisure time
- What organizations or clubs they join
- What charities or groups they support
- What political party they register for
- What petitions they are willing to sign

Three Factors That Influence the Capacity and Willingness to Buy

Demographics and psychographics, but particularly the latter, are remarkably impacted by three influences that must not be overlooked:

The first is literacy. An adult functional illiterate cannot read a road sign, menu, or headline. Sad to note, 25 percent of *adults* in America are functional illiterates and another 35 percent are completely illiterate. This leaves 60 million of 130 million or 135 million adults who *can* read and comprehend a newspaper, magazine, book, or direct-mail offer.

The second major influence is discretionary income (see also page 176). Twenty-five million of the 87,000,000 families in America live well enough (above the costs of living and of taxes) to have extra income that they can spend by choice and not by necessity. While a number of direct-mail response offers are deliberately aimed at those without discretionary income, the majority of solo direct mail (including catalog mailings) is aimed at those who have income over which they have discretion as to how they spend it and for what.

The third major influence is a tendency or willingness to buy by mail. To paraphrase Gertrude Stein, a mail order buyer is a mail order buyer is a mail order buyer much like a rose is a rose is a rose. There are now over 2 billion names of mail response customers commercially available. If we assume that the average size of a purchase from prospecting mailings is in the $30 range, then new transactions (first-time orders on a list from direct-mail prospecting, much of it among mail order buyers found on other lists) total over 500 million transactions. Customer mailings, where the average order may be closer to $60, will add 600 million transactions to this. A billion or more transactions produce over $40 to $45 billion of gross sales from direct mail. This billion or more transactions come from a total universe which numbers only 230 million people of which roughly 130 million are adults. These adults reside in 87 million households and work in about 10.5 million establishments including over 2.5 million farms.

If the $40 billion of direct-mail sales were spread equally over each individual, then the average individual (both adult and child) would buy approximately $200 through direct response in the course of a year. However, surveys indicate that not over 40 percent of adults (or families) will buy anything by mail. If that is true then the universe of buyers from direct mail is limited to 40 percent of the 130 million adults (about 52 million) who in essence are likely to live in 40 percent of the 87 million households (about 34 million). Using these figures, the average known mail order buyer spends an average of $700 per year on mail offers. Based on these figures each family that buys by mail order is then responsible for an average of $1,200 per year of mail order purchases.

There is a great deal of redundancy on lists because the average mail order buyer can be found on a number of mail order buyer lists. The closer the lists are psychographically (as to what is purchased and at what price) the greater the likelihood of interlist duplication. Mailers who use multiple lists go through a merge–purge process to eliminate such duplication.

Such duplication is particularly apparent in cultural lists—lists of buyers that are lovers of books, magazines, theatre, opera, art, interior decor, and music. A merge–purge of half a million names from, say ten such lists will disclose and eliminate 25 percent of the records inputted and will provide a list of unique, unduplicated names and addresses for one-per-individual or one-per-family mailings.

Thus far this discussion has provided the key data defining demographic criteria and psychographic criteria, as well as the three major "outside" influences. Without any doubt these outside influences will also influence response rates.

Mail Order Characteristics

The third major set of criteria are mail order characteristics. In other words in what ways a given segment in a list of mail order buyers varies from another segment or, what is more true in practice, in what ways a given segment selected on the basis of multiple criteria varies from another segment also selected on the basis of multiple criteria.

RF$USISM

A mnemonic to aid recall of mail order characteristics is RF$USISM. This stands for: *R*ecency *F*requency *D*ollars *I*tem *S*ource *M*ethod of payment. There are a number of cells or "cuts" within each one of these.

Recency measures the last order placed on the file for a given customer, donor, or subscriber. Recency can be measured by the last week, last month, last quarter, the last six months, or the current year.

Frequency is how often the customer has purchased (from the company on whose list his or her name is found). Frequency includes: one-time buyers only, two-time buyers, or more than two-time buyers. It should be noted there is a difference between a one-time buyer from last week and a buyer who has not bought since a first buy $2\frac{1}{2}$ years ago.

$US stands for dollars. However there are different kinds of dollar data and they provide different data to understand and test. There are variances in size, in consistency, as well as highest dollar amount in a given order, and cumulative dollars:

- Size of orders may vary in amounts ranging from $1, $5, $10, $25, $50, $100, and over $100.

- Highest dollar may be based on the latest order, earliest order, or first order.

- Cumulative dollars may convert a recent buyer who spends only $5 into a regular customer who has spent more than X amount of dollars over the last two or three years.

- A review of purchases by period (quarterly, semiannually, annually) will disclose those who buy regularly, semiregularly, sporadically, every two or three periods, and so on. Each pattern discloses a different type (and cell) of buyer as far as the mail order company is concerned.

I stands for item or the products or services that have been purchased. It is common to code a large number of different items generically into group classifications, perhaps ten to twenty in number. In this way statistical analysis is possible, along with selection of buyers of one product who might then be good prospects for an allied product.

S stands for source. There is a distinct difference between customers who buy from space ads or electronic media and customers who buy through direct mail. Similarly a buyer from one list may be different than a buyer from another list. It is imperative to code every effort and attempt to record every order by its source, and never to lose the initial code.

M stands for method of payment. A person who pays by cash is different from one who pays by check. They both differ from a person who pays by money order or credit card. There are also differences in response, which can sometimes be subtle or significant, between those who pay by travel and entertainment (T&E) cards (Amex/Diners Club) and bank cards (Visa & Mastercard). There can be a difference in response between buyers who use T&E cards and mail in their orders as opposed to a group that phones in their orders.

Physical Characteristics

The fourth basic type of criteria is physical. Lists can vary physically by such factors as:

1. List data as a whole
2. Deliverability
3. Selectability
4. Format
5. Means of reproduction
6. Accessibility

We will now explore these variances in greater detail.

List data as a whole—vary in size and completeness.

Size: Perhaps the first fact needed about a given list is the number of names it contains. Lists available for rental range from a few hundred names to tens of millions. Other factors (age, source, reputation of owner, accessibility, means of reproduction, for starters) being equal (and they rarely are) the list with the greater quantity will be preferred. Tests are made to locate lists that can be continued at a profit. Lists that are small may not be considered for test purposes because there is "no place to go" if a test is successful.

Completeness or coverage (the proportion of the universe available for the classification or type): In compiled files the element of completeness has particular importance. For example, there are at least twenty lists available of architects and architectural services. Most of them contain about the same number of establishments or professionals. A list half the size of these complete files will have little chance in the list marketplace. (A list of architects who buy by mail should not be expected to include all architects. Those who buy by mail from one supplier represent a special segment of the universe of architects available from compilers.)

Sometimes, however, the smaller list may embrace a greater portion of the known universe than a larger list. For example, an industrial magazine file of recipients, averaging, say, 1.7 records per plant may be matched with a compiled list consisting of the same number of records. The compiled list, if representative of one record per plant, will cover a higher proportion of the totality.

Deliverability

1. Cleanliness of the list—the methodology and timing of the cleaning and purging process.

2. Duplication factor—the proportion of names that are duplicated.

3. Updating cycle—when the list was last updated and when it will next be updated.

4. Feedback for updating—the gathering of data on expected lack of deliverability.

5. Zip code status—the proportion of good zip codes; utilization of zip code cleaning passes.

Note on Currency: Some mail order lists have value even though they are many years old. (Members of a Humphrey Bogart book-buying fan club, for example, might well outpull other lists several years after the death of the star and the operation of the club.) In any case it is important to find out when the data were put on file and when they were last mailed and cleaned.

The deliverability of compiled files is inversely proportioned to their currency. The latest compilation (providing the source is current) will have the greatest deliverability. In this field two questions should be asked about any list being considered: (1) What is the source? and (2) When was the data updated or cleaned?

There are *no* secrets in the list business. If a compiler will not or cannot give you a reasonable answer to these two questions, the best thing to do is find another compiler to deal with.

At the present time most telephone registrants are being compiled by converting data from both alphabetical and classified published listings. As noted on page 53, these data are aged before they can be obtained. Meanwhile, back at the phone companies up-to-date data are continuously available. Thus a list coming from a phone company tape, which is now slowly beginning to happen, is far more current than data converted from printed phone books.

Selectability

1. Individuals
2. Company names
3. Titles
4. Codes for titles

Format

1. Layout of data and discipline followed
2. Fixed versus variable length fields
3. Sequence in which the list is maintained
4. Sortation fields (if any)
5. Sequencing of crutch files (if any)

Means of Reproduction

1. Cheshire
2. Tape
3. Other
4. Cost factors of reproduction

Accessibility

1. Time requirements (on demand or scheduled)

2. Approval process

3. Who has access

4. When maintained

Physical Constraints

The aspect of deliverability is dependent on the currency of the file. However, the accuracy with which the data have been placed on tape and the accuracy of the zip codes, have a good deal to do with deliverability as well. Two lists compiled from the same source at the same time in which currency is not a factor can be far apart in deliverability because of the difference in the "physical" handling of conversion and zipping.

It is more than likely that the average list in America has a zip-error percentage of 4 to 5 percent. Every last zip error results in undeliverability by third class mail.

Some years ago the method of reproduction had a great deal to do with how the list was judged by the list-using community. Lists on plates or cards, or particularly lists on thirty three-up labels (requiring moisture to adhere) were used but somewhat reluctantly. Now with costs dictating the necessity for merge–purging of duplicates prior to mailing, lists for rental must be on tape and be available on tape. Availability of tapes is a restraint because some list owners will provide labels for rental but not on tape even for computer letters or merge–purge.

On almost every merge–purge consisting of more than five lists, one or two will almost inevitably show up days (sometimes weeks) after the merge–purge final date for acceptance of data has passed. Because a list is on the market does not guarantee its owner or computer service access in the time frame desired.

One major provider of business lists is notorious in this regard. It is rare for this company's list to come in until all other lists, compiled, magazine subscribers, and mail order buyers alike, have been on hand for several weeks. Because this firm has data very difficult to obtain from any other source, mailers continue to order—and hope.

Foreign lists, even Canadian lists, pose a problem of accessibility. Occasionally a desired list withholds its data from the market for a period of time for its own use. (The two compilers serving *Time* and *Newsweek* magazines, for example, are ordered to halt their services several months each year so that outside offers to college students cannot be mailed.) Also occasionally, a list is unavailable due to some upset at the company or a serious glitch in the computer servicing the list. Usually in such cases there is a reasonable alternative solution.

Some lists are available only if the owner or his *dedicated* service bureau does the addressing and mailing. Once a common practice, this is now reduced to only a handful of particularly valuable files. Where the need for such specific names is so great, the mailer must "heel" and send his or her pieces for mailing.

Almost all mail order buyer lists of all kinds have no phone numbers. In addition many owners will not permit outsiders adding phone numbers for tele-prospecting, or in the case of subscription renewals, telemarketing sales.

With the tremendous growth of word processors and P.C. users the market for lists to be placed on floppy discs is growing apace. Until recently the problems inherent in providing data on floppy discs has deterred compilers from providing their data in this form. The establishment of the DOS operating system for most floppy disc operations has now changed this. The Burnett operation now not only provides data on floppy discs at moderate extra costs for the conversion, but for the same price includes a program (also on a floppy disc) that permits the list user to sort, or copy, data and provide it in hard copy form on sheets, cards, envelopes, or pieces.

CHECKLIST OF DIRECT-RESPONSE LIST CATEGORIES

All direct-response lists can be categorized by relation to the list owner, as well as how the names come onto the list.

In relation to the list owner the segments are:

1. *"Actives" or active buyers.* Those who have made a recent purchase (usually within the last year or eighteen months).

2. *Multibuyer.* Those who have made more than one purchase.

3. *Former buyer.* Those who have made a purchase at some former time, prior to the period designated "active."

4. *Hot-line list.* The most recent names added to a list, usually limited to the last three months.

5. *House lists.* Lists maintained of customers, inquiries, friends of friends, and so on.

6. $10, $25, $50, $100 buyers. Buyers who have made at least one purchase of a given dollar range.

7. *Inquiries.* Those who have inquired for additional data or requested a booklet or a catalog.

8. *Gift buyers*. Those who have purchased products or services and had them sent to others.

In relation to how the names come onto the list the segments are:

1. *Premium buyers*. Those who were influenced to purchase a product or service by the offer of a similar product or service made up of an essential part of the offer.

2. *Cash buyers, credit card buyers*. Buyers who paid for their orders with cash or credit cards.

3. *Catalog buyers or space ads, TV, or radio buyers*. This is the source of the order.

4. *Giftees*. Those given gifts of products or services by others. (Also known as gift buyers.)

PART II: HOW DEMOGRAPHICS AFFECT MAILING LISTS

Demography and mailing lists are so intimately entwined that it is literally impossible to speak of one without the other. From a consumer mailing list point of view the major demographic aspects are:

- Income
- Age
- Sex
- Family size
- Type of residence
- Education

In the sections on demographics that follow, some of the myths of demography are shattered (a bit), while there are some separate sections on:
- Affluence (Discretionary Income)
- Influence of Women on Direct Mail Response
- How to Learn More about Your Neighborhood
- Baby Boomers
- Age Criteria

- The Senior Market
- Working Women

TEN MYTHS ABOUT DEMOGRAPHY*

Myth One: We are in the midst of a new baby boom. It is true that the number of babies now born each year is near the high level of the late 1950s. However, births are now up because the number of potential parents is up. The babies born today come from parents who were the "baby boomers" born in the 1950s.

The average number of children born to women of child bearing age today is only about half of what it was during the 1950s. This rate hovers near record lows. Once the members of the baby-boom generation pass into middle age, they will be replaced by the "baby bust" generation born during the 1960s and 1970s. Births will then fall rapidly, leading to a new baby bust shortly before the turn of the century.

Myth Two: The family is extinct. Actually the family is changing, not dying. According to the census bureau there were fewer married couples with children in 1980 than there were in 1970, even though the total number of households increased 26 percent in that decade. But the family lives on even though people marry later, have fewer children, and divorce more than in the past. Over 90 percent of all Americans marry, and two children per family is still the most popular number.

However, the nuclear family is becoming a vanishing species. Only 19 percent of American families consist of married couples with children in which the woman is at home on a full-time basis.

Myth Three: The typical family numbers four people. The average American family unit is now 3.25—down from 3.58 in 1970. By 1990 we will hit 3.0. So if there is a typical American family it has three members, not four.

Myth Four: America is a nation of "grey beards." If anything, we are a nation of young adults. Because of the baby boom over one-third of all Americans are now between the ages of twenty and thirty-five. There are however, more people over sixty-five than teenagers for the first time. But we will not be a nation of elders until well into the next century when our young, baby-boomer adults turn old and gray.

Myth Five: Less than half of all women work. This is not true. Fifty-two percent of American women now work outside the home. More remarkable than this is the participation of women with preschool children in the labor force. They make up 50 percent of the workforce compared with only 30 percent in 1970. This has helped demolish the myth that a woman's place is in the home.

(Based on a series of articles by Bryant Robey as reported in *American Demographics*.)

Myth Six: All singles are young and swinging. This is far from the truth. Over half of the 19 million American adults who live alone are aged fifty-five or older. Only 27 percent are younger than thirty-five. But this homogenizes the figures for the sexes. Women make up over 60 percent of single-person households. More than six million women aged sixty-five or older live alone but fewer than 1.5 million men live alone. Childless married couples tend to be home-oriented and 60 percent of these couples are fifty-five or older.

Myth Seven: Families headed by women are always single-parent families. There are nine million families headed by women, but over three million of them have no children. They do not fit the image of a woman alone with young children struggling to make ends meet.

Myth Eight: Americans are moving back to the city. Actually the nation's cities stopped gaining residents in 1970. Baby boomers will be replaced by the baby busters, of whom there will be fewer. It may appear then that young adults are fleeing the cities but this may simply be due to a decline in the numbers of young people.

Myth Nine: The sunbelt is growing at the expense of the frostbelt. This was true for many areas in the 1970s, and those people who migrated from the north to warmer areas were not replaced by more births. However by the 1980s the frostbelt was beginning to hold its own, and the industrial bases in the north are better spread than those in the south.

Myth Ten: Americans are becoming wealthier. Less than one-third of families in America have any discretionary income to spend after paying for living expenses and taxes. The gap between richer and poorer is widening. In 1970, 36 percent of households had a family income of less than $15,000 (as measured in 1981 dollars). This figure climbed to 40 percent in the early 1980s.

Incomes are split among family lines. On average, people who live alone and women who head families, are "under water," while two-income married couple families are on top.

HOW WOMEN INFLUENCE DIRECT MAIL RESPONSE

There are some classifications in direct response, notably automotive, home repair, insurance, opportunity seekers, sports, and business magazines and newsletters that have men as their primary audience. But when responses to direct mail are dissected by sex, it is the female of the species who is much more important than the male. Women buy for the home, women buy for the children, women buy gifts the family gives, women buy for the garden, women buy cosmetics, jewelry, stockings, and clothing for themselves and, to the surprise of many, women buy the majority of clothing and gifts and jewelry for men. So "cherchez la femme" is the watchword in the mail.

But with the changing status of women, in which today most women work outside the home and only a minority of adult women are homebodies only, the status of women as consumers in their own right—particularly of financial services is changing marketing in America, particularly marketing by mail.

In 1960 only a bit over 50 percent of American women 14 years and older had some form of income. By 1982 that proportion was nearly 9 out of 10, and the total number with income was 82.5 million. The same proportion of women now have a checking account. And the proportion of these accounts now in a women's name only rather than jointly, has increased in 10 years from 15 percent to almost 30 percent.

The growth of the two-earner family has impacted every level of society. Married women are four times more likely than single women who maintain families to have a family income of $30,000 or more. Six in ten women who are the sole parent and wage earner in a household have family incomes of less than $15,000.

Earnings

Women still have to reach equality with men as far as earnings are concerned. In 1982, women working in full-time jobs earned 65 percent of the salary men earned for the same job. This is the same proportion found in 1967.

In fact, earnings for women lag behind that of men at every level of education. A female college graduate working full time in 1982 earned just about $300 per year more than a man working full time who did not even graduate from high school.

Financial Assets

The number of adult women owning stock rose 44 percent between 1981 and 1983, while the number of male stockholders grew only about 22 percent. (The total is now about even, but the women's total includes widows who inherited stock from their husbands.) The typical first-time investor of the early 1980s was female, 34 years of age, married, and working in a clerical or sales job.

Women are buying a greater share of life insurance. In 1972 adult women's insurance policies represented about 12 percent of the total amount of ordinary life insurance bought that year. In 1982 women's purchases were almost double that, or 23 percent.

Education of women by median income (25 years or older)
(dollars adjusted for inflation)

Educational level	1963	1970	1982	1985
8 years	$1,200	$1,800	$4,700	$5,100
High school	2,300	3,400	7,000	7,800
1 to 3 years of college	2,300	3,700	8,600	10,300
4 years of college (graduate)	3,400	5,400	11,700	13,600
1 or more years post graduate	4,000	7,900	16,800	19,700
Post graduate income in relation to grade school	3.4 times	4.4 times	3.5 times	3.9 times
Post graduate income in relation to high school or equivalence	1.7 times	1.6 times	2.4 times	2.6 times

There is a very strong relationship which has existed for over twenty years between educational attainment and income. Women with one or more years of post graduate study have a median income 3.5 times greater than women who did not go to high school, and 2.4 times those that graduated from high school. Part of the large differential in earning power is explained by the fact that women with more schooling are more likely to hold full-time jobs. When those over twenty-

Figure 6.1

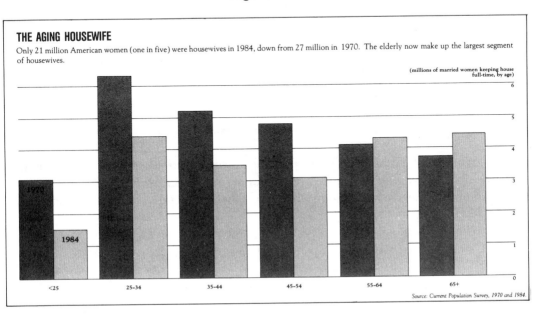

THE AGING HOUSEWIFE

Only 21 million American women (one in five) were housewives in 1984, down from 27 million in 1970. The elderly now make up the largest segment of housewives.

(millions of married women keeping house full-time, by age)

Source: Current Population Survey, 1970 and 1984.

Figure 6.2

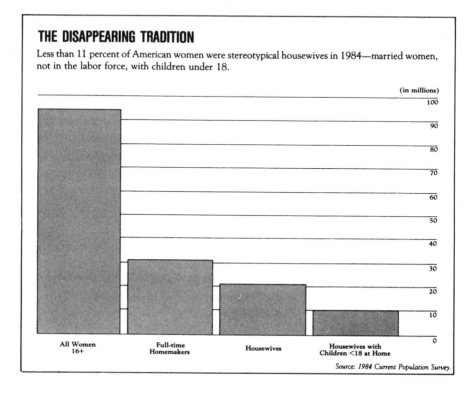

THE DISAPPEARING TRADITION

Less than 11 percent of American women were stereotypical housewives in 1984—married women, not in the labor force, with children under 18.

(in millions)

All Women 16+	Full-time Homemakers	Housewives	Housewives with Children <18 at Home	

Source: 1984 Current Population Survey.

five years of age with full-time jobs only are compared, those with five years of college had a median income in 1982 of $21,500, or more than twice that of women with eight years of schooling. Figures 6.1 and 6.2 illustrate the decline of women as full-time homemakers.

Economic Hardship

Women who maintain families on their own are more likely to face economic hardship than women in other types of family relationships. Families maintained by women are nearly five times as likely to be below the poverty line than married-couple families.

There is a significant economic difference between white women, black women, and women of Spanish origin for females fifteen years of age and older: 13 percent of white women are below the poverty line, 39 percent of black women are below the poverty line, and 31 percent of women of Spanish origin are below the poverty line.

Divorced Women

Divorced women report the highest individual income for women of any marital status, in all probability because they are more likely to work full time. In 1985, the median income for married women was $6,000; while the median income for divorced women was almost twice as high at $11,700. Three out of four divorced women were in the workforce.

Working Women*

Forty years ago, only one of four wives was in the workforce. Today, well over half of all wives are employed outside the home. (There are many millions more, uncounted as of yet, working from their homes for themselves or for outside companies.)

The more education a woman has, the more likely she will be employed. This means that on a literary basis only, working women can read and understand more about the business world than the woman who stays at home. (At high levels of income, most woman do *not* work outside the home—only the man does this. These women are however, more highly educated on the average, than either women in the workforce or women who are part of families not in the affluent class.)

In the years ahead, the proportion of working women will continue to increase but at a slower pace than in the past simply because so many women are already employed.

The data tape of the 1986 "Current Population Survey" by the census bureau contains detailed information on the characteristics of households in which there is a working wife. This tape shows 54.6 percent of all husband-headed households had a working wife. The distribution is highly influenced by age as shown below:

Age group	Approximate percentage of working wives (percent)
Under 34 years	65 (percent)
35–44 years	69 (percent)
45–54 years	62 (percent)
55–64 years	38 (percent)
65–69 years	11 (percent)
70 and over	4 (percent)

(Based on information from *American Demography* magazine and the United States Census).

Women, according to Rena Bartos, senior vice president of J. Walter Thompson (one of the world's largest advertising agencies), can be broadly categorized into 4 groups with estimated proportions.

	Group (percentage)
1. Working Women	
a. Those who want or have a career.	22%
b. Those to whom their work is just "a job."	37
2. Homemaker	
a. Those who plan to work outside the home in the future (as they do their proportion shrinks).	13
b. Those who plan to stay at home full time.	28

Each of these groups has a distinct psychographic profile, and the women in each profile hold unique attitudes about themselves, their work, their children, and their family. This definitely affects their buying behavior. Members of each profile can and do think like members in the other three buying groups.

Career-minded women have a strong interest in style, are loyal to certain brands and are more likely to have checking accounts, credit cards, and investments. They are the most likely to own cars, and are among the best customers for travel. They are more in the affluent group compared to homemakers, or they aspire to be in it. Therefore they are more likely to be direct-response customers.

"Just-a-job" women tend to fall at two ends of the age spectrum: under twenty-five and over fifty. They are least likely to be loyal to certain brands; they are very concerned about money; more responsive to promotions (including sweeps) and new products; and are impulse buyers. They are however unlikely to have investments.

"Plan-to-work" women mostly have young children. They are most concerned about the economy, reject conformity, consider themselves stubborn, use financial services like the career woman they plan to emulate, and take an active role in shared decisions about major purchases.

"Stay-at-home" women are cautious shoppers, mildly concerned with style, and admit they can be persuaded by direct mail offers.

As more and more young women have entered the workforce, the average age of working women has tended to be younger. By 1982, 49 percent of all working women was between the ages of eighteen and thirty-four. These are the young women from the baby boomers of the 1960s which have dramatically impacted the twenty-five to thirty-four year age group. (Over the next twenty years, the average age of working women is destined to climb.)

By 1986, 55 percent of all working women were married, 16 percent were divorced or widowed, 4 percent separated, leaving 25 percent who were single.

Mothers with children play a significant role in the workforce. Fifty percent of women with children under 6 years of age are working, while nearly 65 percent of women with children between the ages of six and seventeen are working. The 52 percent of women working contrasts with only 12 percent in 1950.

Seven million wives earn more than their husbands and this number is growing rapidly. Two million are the only providers for their families, while 5 million have husbands who earn less than they do.

The Bureau of Labor Statistics states that the number of women entrepreneurs in 1982 was 2,900,000, and there are probably one million more of them in America today. If all of that million had phones (and the great majority do) that would be $12\frac{1}{2}$ percent penetration of all establishments in America. By far the largest type of woman-owned small business in the nation is beauty shops, with over 55,000. Most woman-owned businesses are service oriented (45 percent) or retail (30 percent) and are solely held. The entrance of large numbers of women into well paying professional jobs will provide an increasing pool of trained women decision makers who well may become entrepreneurs in the future. In the decade of the 70s, the number of women engineers increased 100 percent, the number of female lawyers and judges 377 percent, women doctors 84 percent, and women bank officials and financial managers, 256 percent.

List sources for working women are of two basic types: lists of given classifications of working women, and lists selected primarily on a psychographic basis that promise access to working women. Examples of the first type are:

- Women executives at major companies—about 30,000, roughly 5 percent of total executives of the largest U.S. companies.

- Women with Kehoe Plans—over 1 million women who have established a retirement plan in their own names.

- Working Woman magazine—several hundred thousand female subscribers who identify themselves and their particular needs as working women.

- Women professionals—there are several lists of women professionals by discipline.

- Women educators—list people can reach several million teachers in the United States, both at school and at home addresses.

- Women in government—hard to uncover, but some list data are available.

- Nurses—over 1 million can be found on each of at least three lists. In addition, there are several magazines that service the nursing field.

- Who's Who data—provides data on females in various lines of endeavors.
- Entrepreneurs—beauty parlors, women's ready-to-wear stores, boutiques are normally headed by a woman.

To reach working women through aspects of lifestyle (what they read, what they buy, what they belong to, what they support) leads to such list sources as:

- Women subscribers to nonhousehold magazines such as *Psychology Today, MS, New York, NY Review of Books,* and so on.
- Women buyers of business logs and time management programs. Women participants at business, marketing, or finance seminars.
- Women book buyers and newsletter buyers on business subjects.
- Members of business associations (for example, the Direct Marketing Association covers a field where women are far more successful than in most other fields of endeavor).
- Women heads of households who own cars.
- Women pilots.

PART III: THE IMPACT OF GEOGRAPHY

CLUSTERING

Clustering is a technique now being used to provide a program, based on demographic similarities, to select from lists those records in zip code areas believed to be most likely to work for a given type of offer. List owners or list managers with large consumer lists can apply such a program to their house lists to help generate more rental revenue. Mailers can use the program in otherwise marginal lists to "lift" response into the black.

There are two types of clustering available. The first splits all zip codes into some forty predetermined groups based on demographic data provided by the United States Census Bureau. The data include city size, population density, housing characteristics, mobility, income, size of family, ethnicity, and social status. The names given to each group indicate the broad brushstroke approach: "emigrant minorities," "back country," "bohemia mix," and "upper mobile." Users of this technique are advised to keep in mind that what is involved is that each zip code is far from homogenous, and grouping of zip codes simply compounds this lack of homogeneity.

The system has its place but for serious analysis it is too gross for comfort.

Clusters

If one were to chart geographical selection on a cluster basis, it might for the country, look like this inverted pyramid:

Number of Divisions		Number of Families
1	Country as a Whole	87,000,000 Families; 75,000,000 by Name
9	Sections of the Country; East, North, Central States	7,000,000 to 15,000,000 families
50	Major Metropolitan Areas	500,000 to 12,000,000 families
100	Minor Metropolitan Areas	3,000,000 to 15,000,000 families
250	3-Digit Zip Code Areas	50,000 to 400,000 families
900	Counties	500 to 500,000 families
3,100		10,000 to 15,000 families
35,000	5-Digit Zip Code Areas	
7,500	Census Tracts (Metropolitan Areas Only)	
160,000 USPS and 240,000 Pseudo	Carrier Routes	700 to 1,500 families
400,000	Subblocks (or EDs)	200 to 450 families
3,000,000	Near Neighbors	100 to 175 families
40,000,000	Next-Door Neighbors	10 to 40 families
87,000,000	Individual Homes	2 to 4 families
		1 family

163

The advantage is that it can be applied to almost any list where the list owner will permit selection by zip code. Mailers use the argument that unless zip code selection is made available, they will not again rent lists that have tested marginally or below the line.

The second form of clustering might be termed "variable clustering" or perhaps better still "custom clustering." This form utilizes a regression analysis of mailing results (or of the customer base) to provide a statistical insight into which of the factors among many are significant to both positive and negative response. This methodology provides data down to the subblock and enumeration district (far smaller districts than a census tract and far smaller yet than a zip code.) That limits its usefulness to those concerns with lists large enough to justify the high costs of subblock coding and use. (For reasons not too clear, "customer clustering" which is enamoured with the detailed data available at the subblock level, has not shown to date much interest in providing its analysis at the carrier-route level. Although it is true carrier routes vary, they do not vary in any given six month period. All lists, not just the few large ones, are available by carrier route. The cluster methodology may be a growing wave for a few but if it is ever to be available to the next level of mailing size this writer believes it will need to bow down to the need to work at the carrier-route level to become part of the wave of the future for direct-mail use.)

REGIONAL SELECTIONS

Almost all retail and local service mailings are confined, geographically, to a city zone or trading area. There is one major rule to keep in mind for regional mailings: the smaller the size of the universe to be covered, the larger the list concept must be. Stockbrokers, insurance agents, department stores, repair shops, and franchisees of all sorts obtain their business locally—and thus the lists they use, first and foremost, must conform to the geographical area that encompasses their market. What this means for most programs is the utilization of a major list concept that can provide a reasonable number of names or establishments. For business, this means tapping one of the large databanks of executives, or one of the major files supplying virtually every business, institution, and professional establishment. For consumers, if neither demographics nor names are essential, a local occupant list can be used; for name use one of the several files incorporating telephone, car, and driver's license data will be required.

In general, list brokers are not usually willing to provide local pulls. They are all too aware that this may be, and often is, a onetime request, with no continuation in prospect. But major compilers, who run dozens of orders on a given file per week, can and will handle such requests. And their minimum charges are such that they can and do profit on small orders. It is important on such small orders to check minimums. As this is written one major business compiler has a minimum for its handful of nonexclusive resellers of $650, which is a fee that many small mailers, correctly, feel makes any order for one or two thousand names excessively costly.

CARRIER ROUTES: THE WAVE OF THE FUTURE
FOR GEOGRAPHICAL SELECTION

Although the United States Census Bureau provides data for virtually all 400,000 enumeration districts and subblocks, only a few major consumer compilers make selection available based on these data. (A few large customer files have been coded for subblocks by one of the majors—but on a commercial basis, only a few lists provide such list data to users.) Thus for all practical purposes the wave of the present and the wave of the future for geographical selection is the carrier route. To the 160,000 carrier routes established by the USPS (to coincide with the routes followed by the several hundred thousand letter carriers) major list compilers now have added comparable geographical segments to cover all rural routes, star routes, and noncity delivery points which totals 240,000 additional discrete "clusters" of households.

It is true that relatively few lists are carrier-route coded today, but the discount given by the USPS for carrier-route coding and sorting has made it virtually mandatory, in order to save postage dollars, for every merge–purged list and every major mailer to provide carrier-route coding of the mailing tapes. A mailing list service that cannot carrier-route code a list today is a dying breed. The record speaks for itself. As noted on page 620 more than half of all "for profit" third class bulk mailings are now mailed at carrier-route discount rates. Thus it is fair to say that any mailer who places his or her list in the mailstream and has coded that list for carrier routing, will be able to determine the counts for each carrier route and the penetration by carrier route. This virtually universal access to carrier-route data (and the extremely limited availability of the somewhat finer breakdowns by enumeration districts and subblocks) indicates that the future for analysis of response and the selectivity for future mailings will be governed by carrier-route coding.

It is interesting to note that both carrier routes and enumeration districts and even census tracts provide much more detailed segmentation than zip codes.

This is not to say that penetration by zip code segmentation does not have its place, but as more and more data become available for carrier routes there will more than likely be a trend away from zip code marketing for response to carrier route marketing.

Several companies now attempt to provide analysis of clusters of zip codes rather than individual zip codes. They do this by dividing the country into forty categories of zip codes, averaging 900 zip codes per cluster. Using one of these systems the mailer pulls only given zip codes from rental lists and mails the entire zip code. By carrier-route analysis, there may be only two routes, which on a penetration basis, justify such selection. It is perfectly feasible for entire zip codes to be included in cluster grouping where not one name will be taken on the basis of carrier route results. But for certain size lists, where 400,000 pieces of real estate to analyze is a chore which cannot pay dividends, then zip code clusters may be ideal.

R.H. Donnelley, R.L. Polk, Data Base America, and Metromail, which have finite and virtually exclusive data on enumeration districts and subblocks, are beginning to swing over to carrier-route demographics. Each one is providing vastly increased amounts of data on each cluster of 350 households that make up a carrier route. They have also arranged to provide these data in updated fashion every six months when the USPS publishes a new carrier-route coding tape (CRIS). They too are committed to carrier-route marketing as part of the wave of the future.

This discussion is focused only on geography. Relatively few practitioners of direct marketing are fully aware of the great effect geographical location has on response. One test made by this office for a publisher of a desk calendar book involved use of 60,000 records of T&E credit card holders.

One might think such a list, of people who can charge a $12.50 workbook to their businesses, would be reasonably homogeneous, irrespective of the state they live in. But of 12 states, eight were failures, four were successes, and the four successful states did well enough to pay for the states that did not do well. That is just on the basis of testing 5,000 per state in 12 states.

I have noted to clients many times that if they wish to pick a group of states and then let me pick another group I can almost invariably arrange to come out 20 percent above or 20 percent below their response.

A direct response ad (irrespective of offer) placed countrywide in say *Parade* magazine on a milline basis will show a three-to-one difference in response across the country. That is 300 percent, almost exclusively from geography.

But states are a very gross way of picking lists on a geographic basis. (In effect they are too gross for comfort). There are 50 states. That can be broken down into:

900 three-digit SCF's
3,000 counties
35,000 five-digit zip codes
160,000 carrier routes
400,000 sub-blocks

and knowledgeable list people can, by utilizing much finer geographical divisions, almost make wine out of water as far as response is concerned.

Direct mail can follow population into Texas, Florida, and California, can provide new residents and new businesses in John Naisbitt's 10 cities* of great opportunity, can target to those families and those businesses with the best potential for response.

Currently there are two Spanish language classified phone directories in the country—one for Miami, the other for New York City. The next one to surface will be in California—and that means that comparable attention is likely to follow in Texas border cities. (Note how this dovetails with the 10 cities of opportunity, above.) Direct mail is the key means to locate the listing base, and then find the distribution base of Spanish-speaking businesses and families. And, since Spanish-speaking Americans will in a few years be a larger minority than American blacks, all this means is another growing opportunity for the target marketing capacities of direct mail through lists of ethnics found in the main on geographical lines.

As population moves out of cities to towns, out of towns to rural areas, direct mail can follow, and continue to reach people with given interests virtually wherever they have located.

Movement of people changes localities. Some gain, some lose. Direct mail is not tied to the fortunes of one city or one locality—and can target its offering to clusters of booming times adjacent to a nearby city in the throes of economic collapse.

The greater the proliferation of lifestyles, the greater the segmentation in the market, the more certain it is that direct marketing will be a- or the- central communication channel to reach such segmented markets.

Most of us in direct marketing, if given a moment to reflect, are comfortable (almost) with the market (U.S. and to a small degree, Canada) we know; and we tend to fear the unknown. Foreign direct marketing is, except for a few global ad agencies, and a few far-sighted firms who have searched out competence overseas, a "terra incognita" (unknown territory) and we tend to avoid it as we would a plague.

---

*Albuquerque, Denver, Tampa, Austin, San Antonio, Phoenix, Tucson, Salt Lake City, San Diego and San Jose.

Certainly foreign markets are a magnificent challenge to those who seek to find the raisins in the rice pudding of segmented markets, not only in the U.S., but also in the Western world and the growing Third World as well. We give plaudits to marketers who succeed in the disparate markets that constitute the United States. The time will come when such plaudits can only be earned through success in the much more complex web of markets that make up the world market.

PART IV: THE IMPORTANCE OF DISCRETIONARY INCOME AND HOW TO REACH THE AFFLUENT BY DIRECT MAIL

Discretionary income is the number of dollars you have left *after taxes,* and after the payment of all necessary expenditures. Parts of the data presented here were developed through a joint study by the Consumer Research Center of the Conference Board, and the United States Bureau of the Census.

It almost goes without saying that where one lives and how one lives changes the dividing line between those families with discretionary income and those without. A family of four with an income of $20,000 in a small town, for example, is more likely to have discretionary income, than a family of three with the same income in most large cities.

The Census Bureau and the Conference Board first calculate the *average* amount of money required to maintain a given comfortable standard of living, based on age, city size, and type of residence. Households with expendable incomes that exceed the average of their group by 30 percent or more were considered to have discretionary income.

Let's look at some total figures for the United States as a whole:

1. In 1980, 25 million families, or about 31 percent of the nation's households, were in the discretionary income class. (It is interesting to note that the percentage usually accepted for mail order buyers in the United States is 31 to 35 percent.)

2. The total income available for discretionary spending was almost $200,000,000. That is $7,600 per family, on average, for the 25,000,000 families.

3. On a per-capita basis, discretionary income (homogenized as it were for the average per family) was just $2,700. The 25,000,000 families "above the line" total near $200 billion—$7,600 each. The 57,400,000 families "below the line" do not have any income that can be called discretionary.

Distribution of families (in millions) by family annual income ranges for 1980 is as follows:

- eleven percent of families (9 million) have incomes of $40,000 or more.
- 56 percent have less than $20,000 gross income.
- the average family income for 1980 was $21,000. It is over $22,000 today.

	Income by ranges	Number of families (in millions)	Percentages
Non affluents	Under $15,000	34.9	42.3
	$15,000 to $19,999	11.0	13.3
	$20,000 to $24,999	10.0	12.2
Affluents			
	$25,000 to $29,999	7.8	9.4
	$30,000 to $34,999	5.8	7.1
	$35,000 to $39,999	3.9	4.8
	$40,000 to $49,999	4.5	5.5
	$50,000 to $74,999	3.5	4.1
	$75,000 or more	1.0	1.3
	Total	82,400	100%

Note: The Census Bureau utilized a total household count of 82 million households. The USPS has 87 million household deliveries.

This makes rather clear the answer Willy Sutton gave when he was asked, why did he confine his robberies to banks, which was, "That's where the money is." And the majority of consumer mailers go "where the money is"—to the affluents—with discretionary income to expend.

Where will the money be by 1990? During the decade of the 1970s total real personal income grew at an annual real rate of about 3.3 percent, while the money available for discretionary spending rose at an expanded pace of 3.8 percent. Thus discretionary income increased about 20 percent more quickly than the growth of real personal income.

By 1990, it is anticipated that discretionary income, as measured in 1980 dollars, will be around $325 billion for an increase of somewhat over 66 percent. It is anticipated real personal income will grow again, at an annual rate of 3.3 percent, but spendable discretionary income will grow at an appreciably more rapid pace of 5.3 percent. The rich will get richer, even more quickly, and there will be more of them. As a guess, the 25 million "above the line" in 1980, will increase to 39 million by 1990. If that figure is in the ballpark, each affluent family in that group will have $11,500 of annual discretionary income (in 1980 dollars) in the year 1990.

Much has been mentioned of the division in this century between the growing class of "haves"—those families in the middle class that are moving up, and the growing class of "have nots"—former middle class families that have failed to keep up with the pace. There is a definite division between families in the middle class that for years went unrecognized. Certainly, the figures following on the growth of discretionary income amply demonstrate the movement upwards from middle class to upper mobile.

Howard Ruff writes the "Financial War Room," which he terms "The Early Warning System for America's Middle Class." Howard Ruff states:

> *This decade will be a grim battle for financial survival for the middle class. . . . America has malaria—with recurring bouts of* chills *(rescession) and* fever *(inflation) every four to six years. Because of ignorance, the middle class will shrink. You can become richer or poorer. You cannot stand pat.*

Marketing in the 1980s, from a demographic basis, will be much different from marketing in the 1970s. For example, in the 1970s, total households grew by 25 percent, but households headed by persons under thirty-five (the baby boomers) grew by more than 50 percent although their incomes are still modest. At the same time, homes headed by persons thirty-five to fifty-four (when income runs between 25 percent and 33 percent above the average for the country) increased by less than 10 percent. Such peak-earning families will increase by at least one-third in the 1980s— or more than three times as fast as the 1970s. Despite the problems of the economy, this change will fuel the growth of those with discretionary income to spend. This will result in an increasing market for what might be termed "luxury spending." Direct marketers are certainly poised and ready to take advantage of this "movable feast."

About 11 percent of the nation's homes have annual incomes of $40,000 and above. These 9 million or so families have about 65 percent of all discretionary income.

The Bi-Modal Family Household Universe

For some time demographics have been foretelling the development in which the rich get richer, the poor get poorer, and the so-called middle class begins to merge with the underclass. Such a tendency has been in progress for over 20 years in America—but with increasing inequality since the late 1970s. One can look at income, only—or at wealth. The disparity of wealth is particularly startling:

Number of families	Percentage of population	Percentage share of total income	Percentage share of total net worth
1,740,000	Top 2	14	28
6,960,000	Next 8	19	29
8,700,000	Top 10	33	57
34,800,000	Next 40	43	38
43,500,000	Bottom 50	28	5

While the top 10 percent of families in America receive a third of all income, they have close to 57 percent of all the wealth (net worth) in America. The bottom 90 percent split 2/3 of the income, and have only a bit over 40 percent of net worth. Note that half of America owns 95 percent of net worth; the other half has just 5 percent. From a direct mail point of view it is probably more important to remove ownership of homes and real estate from the net worth figures. When this is done the top 2 percent own 54 percent of all net financial assets, the top 10 percent own 86 percent. The "middle 40 percent" have the balance, 14 percent, while the bottom 50 percent actually have zero or negative financial assets.

From figures available from the Conference Board where affluence is measured as income 30 percent above the cost of living and taxes, just 25,000,000 families qualify—leaving 62,000,000 below the affluence line.

While insurance is purchased by millions who are not affluent, it is clear that the market for financial offers for all practical purposes is with the 25,000,000 affluent families, and primarily to the upper third of these, who control almost 60 percent of the wealth of America (and over 85 percent if home ownership and real estate are removed.)

Downward Pressure on Middle America

Changes in income of middle income families over the past decade have been pervasively downward—due to high unemployment coupled with displacement (by more productive and/or less costly foreign labor) and by the feminization of the work force. From 1976 through 1985 the number of middle income jobs (in the $15,000 to $25,000 range) for year-long full-time male workers decreased by 15 percent. In a period in which total male employment increased by 7,400,000 jobs, 400,000 middle income jobs for males disappeared. There were obviously large gains in the lower levels of the earnings distribution.

Leslie Thurow, soon to become the Dean of the Sloan School of Management of M.I.T., points out that the growth of productivity in such countries as West Germany and Japan is 3 to 5 times the rate in the United States. The nation's huge balance of trade deficit (about $170 billion in 1986) is a particularly visible symbol of a much more competitive international economy.

It takes one million full time year-round employees in U.S. manufacturing to produce $42 billion dollars worth of goods. (The average factory worker in other words is worth $42,000 of saleable production.) Hence, says Thurow, the trade deficit of some four times that amount has squeezed more than four million workers out of manufacturing—and forced them to take other jobs. The main effect of foreign competition has been to increase the variation in earnings within each affected occupation or industry and to push American male workers farther down the earnings ladder. From a direct mail point of view such displaced workers produce a diminution in family income, and tend to pull down middle class families nearer to the "just getting by" majority of American families.

Age

On an age basis, the most important group is the broad range from forty to sixty four years of age that accounts for 39 percent of all homes and over half of spendable discretionary income.

"Young" homes, those headed by people under thirty years of age—have little discretionary income on a relative basis. Although that age group accounts for another 20 percent of all homes, it has only 10 percent of all discretionary resources at its disposal.

As more and more direct marketers are finding out, the over-65 age group market consists of 20 percent of all households and is not to be sneezed at. It accounts for 17 percent of all spendable discretionary income.

I turn to *American Demographics* for some amplification on the over-65 age group in America:

> *We know that the percentage of the population over 65 is increasing and will continue to increase, but we may not be aware of some of the changes in that composition.*

> *Since 1940 the number of widowers over 65 has decreased by 10 percent, and the number of widows has increased by 80 percent. The fundamental factors continue—in the first marriage the wife is about two years younger than her husband and has a seven-year longer life expectancy. But this fact may change because if the present trends continue children born today will have a 50 percent chance of divorcing. Eighty percent of divorced men will remarry women seven or eight years younger but these women will still have a seven-year greater life expectancy.*

Working Women

Do working women make a difference? You can bet on it. Approximately 32 percent of all households have a working wife. That second income accounts for more than 45 percent of those families with discretionary income. This means there are 11.5 million families in the middle class with husbands and wives who work. (There are, however, 20 million more families where both husband and wife work but even with their combined income they do not have any discretionary income.)

Bankers might not be surprised, but most of us might be, by the fact that the average discretionary income is a good deal higher when only the husband works rather than when both spouses have paychecks. In the very high earning bracket, relatively few wives work outside the home.

Education

Educators have proclaimed for decades that education pays. The discretionary dollar can be considered a well educated dollar. Less than 35 percent of the heads of households have had at least some exposure to college but they account for 60 percent of total discretionary spending power. Is a higher education degree an indication of those who have discretionary income? The answer points to "yes." Less than 19 percent of all households are headed by persons who have earned a college degree but they control over 43 percent of total discretionary power. And the higher the degree, the higher the discretionary income as shown below.

	Share of discretionary income
15.6% have some college education	16.8%
10.2 have a college degree	21.0%
8.2% have graduate education	22.4%
TOTAL	60.2%

Occupation

In keeping with the importance of education, well-educated professionals and managers have a disproportionate share of discretionary income at their disposal. Professionals and managers make up 23.6 percent of households but have half (49.8 percent) of the discretionary income.

Where the Affluent Live

Basically, discretionary income follows population but it is substantially higher in suburban communities than in central cities. These differences are more pronounced in major metropolitan areas than in smaller areas.

Only two-thirds of Americans live in their own homes. The other third rent. Owners are more affluent and more of them have discretionary income. Owner-occupied families make up 85.8 percent of all families with discretionary income. Renters provide the 14.2 percent balance. On average, the family that owns a home has 40 percent more discretionary income than the family that rents. But per capita, the difference is minimal because the average family that rents is smaller.

From a list point of view, it is relatively easy to omit multiple dwellings and thereby eliminate a high proportion of renters. Some data are now available on owner-occupied single family homes but for the most part, except for California, such data are not easily available on commercially available mailing lists. This however is due to change.

Race

Only a bit better than 1/7th of all black and nonwhite families, and families of Spanish origin have been able to touch the "American Dream" and enter a world of discretionary income to spend as they desire. One-third of white families have crossed this divide.

Number of Persons per Household

The nuclear family in America, which consists of father, mother, and two children, is an endangered species. Less than 15 percent of households are so populated.

One person households now account for 23 percent of households and their number is growing. Their average income ($11,000) is half or less that of multi-person families. Per capita, their income is more than two-person families; about equal to three-person families; and considerably more than larger-sized families. The great majority of such one-person households (80 percent) have some discretionary income, but their share of 13 percent is obviously smaller than for larger families.

Family Structure

The current population reports of the Census Bureau contain some interesting data on family structure:

> *The trend toward unmarried couples is leveling off. There was a big increase in the number of such arrangements between 1970 and 1982 but no increase in 1983 (1,900,000 couples). During the thirteen years, however, the composition of the households changed. The percentage of unmarried couples with children under fifteen dropped from 37 percent to 28 percent. In 1970, 30 percent of the couples had one member under forty-five compared with 80 percent in 1983.*

> *The changing composition of unmarried couples reflects the increasing number of young people who do not get married. Among men 20–24 the "never married" group has increased from 56 percent in 1970 to 73 percent and for "never married" women this has increased from 36 percent to 56 percent. In the next age bracket, 25–29, the "never married" men went from 19 percent to 38 percent and women from 11 percent to 25 percent. In the age group 30–34 men went from 9 percent to 20 percent and women from 6 percent to 13 percent.*

The Importance of Two Wage Earners in a Family

For the top 10 percent of families by income, it is rather rare for there to be two wage earners. But most families, to enter the ranks of affluence require two wage earners, and for the most part, two full-time wage earners. This is mainly because the average female worker earns just 52 percent of what the average male worker makes. The full-time female worker makes just 65 percent of what her male counterpart makes. In fact, as an increasing number of families obtain the earning power of two full-time workers, the households that do not will tend to fall farther and farther behind economically.

With 31 percent of families headed by women, this nation is also seeing the "feminization of poverty." Women and children account for over 75 percent of those living in poverty; half the poverty population live in families headed by females with no husband present. To escape from poverty a single female must have a job paying substantially above the average.

What is becoming increasingly clear is that the two-earner family is becoming the norm. In 1984, 11,000,000 families (of 28,000,000 reporting two incomes) had two full-time workers.

How to Reach the Affluent Via Direct Mail

It is certainly comforting to know how affluent a society we have, and that at least for the years between 1985–1990, the number of families that will be able to spend as affluents, will increase. The question now is; *How can they be reached?*

The first thing we need to do is to take notice of all of the basic list concepts, which in one way or another, offer access to affluents. Such concepts include compiled lists and response lists:

		Address	
		Home	Business
I.	**List Concepts—Compiled**		
A.	Clusters	x	
B.	Stratification	x	
C.	Original field research	x	
D.	Business executives	x	x
E.	Professionals	x	x
F.	Institutional executives	x	x
G.	Owners of special products	x	
H.	Membership	x	x
I.	Trade show registrants		x
J.	Seminar attendees		x
II.	**List Concepts—Response**		
A.	Magazine subscribers and recipients	x	x
B.	Travel and entertainment credit cards	x	x
C.	Contributors	x	x
D.	Investments	x	x
E.	Travel	x	x
F.	Mail order buyers (by classification)	x	

Sources of names

If we are to use any of these lists effectively, we must know the sources of the names, how these names get on a list, where each type is available, and the strengths and weaknesses of each type. This section concentrates on discussions of each of the types of lists. We will first discuss those that are *mainly compiled*.

Clusters: This type of list is compiled on the concept that one's neighbors have reasonably comparable tastes, incomes, education, and so on. The cluster approach requires the name of an individual and a home address about which a great deal is known or can be surmised. The cluster is a small group of names of from five to fifteen that are chosen to provide names of all nearby neighbors of the known individual. All such names come from major metropolitan areas. This concept makes it possible to cluster around any starting home point, including the customers of a given mail order merchandiser. At the time such a list is compiled a breakdown between apartment house dwellers and owners and occupants of single-family dwellings can be made.

The key list built on this concept is one made up of the members of boards of directors at-home addresses *and their neighbors*.

This list contains close to 2 million names and it is the largest list of affluents available. Research indicates that the median income is well over $50,000. This is one list which is available to give you the names of members of the boards of General Motors, IBM, AT&T, DuPont, Exxon, and many more, along with the names of their next-door neighbors and other families that reside within the same census tract subblocks.

Stratified lists: The major stratified list compilers, R.H. Donnelly, R.L. Polk, Data Base America and Metromail, can each provide 75 million or more of the 87 million households in America. (Someday, one of these "majors" is going to obtain enough data from "occupant" compilers, who cover virtually every household in America, to provide a list to match, on a household basis, the 87 million households known to be deliverable by the USPS.) These lists are initially based on telephone registrants, car owner registrations, and city directories.

By overlaying these "listings" with United States census data and with the number, brand, type, and value of cars, and also by applying these data to 340,000 enumeration districts or subblocks, these compilers are able to ascertain income levels that are surprisingly accurate from poverty level all the way up to affluent. These data are available for all of the 160,000 carrier routes.

By adding outside lists to their files, primarily of drivers' registrations, and mail order buyers, each of these firms offers data by age, education, family size, home type and value, and an increasingly better approximation of individual family income. The Census Bureau shows that 9 million families have incomes of $40,000 or more. These lists come close to providing almost complete coverage of this level of affluence. These compilers also can provide the home phone number for over 80 percent of these homes.

One thing is certain; No matter what other method is used to select people of affluence, their names and addresses will be found, for the most part, within the overall coverage of affluence provided by the stratified approach.

In effect, stratification is a gross form of clustering. The range of clustering would descend as follows:

- State

- Metropolitan area

- City

- 3-digit zip code

- 5-digit zip code—1,000 to 10,000 families

- Census tract—800 to 900 families

- Carrier route—300 to 350 families

- Enumeration district or subblock—140 to 180 families

- Individual street block—40 to 50 families

- Cluster of neighbors—5 to 15 families

- Next door neighbors—1 or 2 families

Field and original research: The major list source that is field researched is a file of 1,500 city directories; the data published in these directories come from actual house-to-house canvases. From these sources, lists by occupation, one of the "indicators" of affluence, can be obtained at home addresses.

New moves, credit checks (particularly on insurance buyers), phoning of school districts, checking of basic business data on companies and executives by both Standard & Poors and Dun & Bradstreet, are examples of original research.

Questionnaires can provide some psychographic insight into families of presumed affluence, by determining what products and services are used, purchased, or owned, as well as the hobbies and interests of householders. If such data are to be used to identify affluents, they need to be handled with care, as all of us have a tendency to appear bigger and better and more knowing than we really are when answering a questionnaire.

Business and professional executives: Compiling on the basis of professional and business status is limited by the kind of data available, and the obvious lack of certainty that a given group compiled on this basis is indeed earning a stated income. The method, however, is reasonably adequate and provides a heavy concentration of desired individuals. Most of those who do not actually meet the criteria may come close.

Here are examples of some of the lists available: Doctors in private practice ages forty-five to sixty-five (median income known to be over $100,000,000); other professionals—architects, accountants, dentists, veterinarians, optometrists, and so on; two large classifications of professional names are available for education and engineering; at-home addresses (over 60,000) and business addresses (over 100,000) of members of boards of directors.

Executives: Lists for executives include many types such as: million and half-million dollar club executives; users or prospects for data processing; rated businesses by size; business professionals by type—stock brokers, advertising executives, bank officials, presidents of smaller firms, and so on; business professionals by function—sales executives, public relations executives, controllers, chief engineers, and so on; specialized business classes—airline pilots, home economists, research executives, data processing experts, and so on; Who's Who compilations by business classifications; and magazine subscribers and recipients by classification.

Virtually every major publisher now makes access available to an unduplicated list of subscribers—selectable usually by function as well as by size and type of business. There are now eight or ten data banks in which multiple lists from multiple owners have been merged–purged to provide access to 7 million to 10 million executives. To cover only big business, Standard & Poors covers top executives at their home offices of this country's largest companies, with data as to sales, number of employers, classification, exports, imports, stock exchanges listing, and telephone number. One compiler, Ed Burnett has incorporated this file by contract into a data bank that reaches 5,000,000 executives in big businesses in America.

Compiled business firms, and compilations of executives and professionals by classification at business address almost always make the business phone number available.

Some idea of the wealth of available data can be illustrated by the several lists of doctors available. They include the American Medical Association's (AMA) virtually 100 percent coverage and 100 percent deliverable list; a list of doctors at-home addresses, which are actually all listed in alphabetic phone banks; a list of doctors in private practice, all of which are listed in classified books; a list of doctors by discipline from directory sources; and half dozen files of doctors who buy given products and services by mail. In addition, the medical list, recently placed on the market, covers almost the entire spectrum with data provided by the individual practitioner himself.

Institutional executives: As the economy turns more and more toward a service basis, the trained professional in institutions is becoming more and more important. Lists of institutions are easy to locate. Lists of executives in these fields are somewhat more difficult to find. Among the available lists of individuals are: hospital directors, foundation executives, church leaders, school superintendents, fund raisers, club leaders, fraternal directors and elected government officials.

Owners of special products: This concept selects individual ownership of special products as likely to show a high correlation with upper income. Some consideration must also be given to family status and age. These include owners of expensive imported and domestic cars, airplanes, boats with ship-to-shore radios, co-op and condominium apartments, and all types of investments, including stocks, bonds, real estate, mutual funds, and insider stockholders. The explosion in the computer field has led to a proliferation of lists of owners of minicomputers and even more microcomputers.

Membership: Very often what a person joins or contributes to provides a good profile of his or her economic and cultural attainments. Lists in this category include: yacht club members, country club members, business school graduates, alumni fund supporters, college alumni (publications regarding these individuals are often sporadic and commercial data are often outdated); college students (two large compilers, Market Compilation of Los Angeles and Market Development of St. Louis, each produce lists of over 3.5 million student names—about 60 percent of the present college student population. Addresses are available at both home and school; parents of students who go to high-tuition schools also can be selected); passport holders, and association affiliations.

Trade show registrants: A way to reach business executives who travel to stay up-to-date in their chosen speciality, is to tap trade show registrations. Among the classifications on the market are: engineering, advertising, manufacturing, financial and computer.

Seminar attendees: With the increase in continuing education, particularly at the management level, a number of lists of "seminarians," those who have taken seminars in all forms of management and personal advancement and understanding training, are available.

Response lists: This group is made up of lists of people who have bought something by mail. Although their purchase was made by mail it does not necessarily mean that the response was generated by direct mail. In some cases it is possible to obtain names of only those people who have responded to a direct-mail offer. Studies have shown that people who have a history of responding to a direct-mail solicitation are more likely to respond to another one than are those who have responded to a solicitation in other media. The range of products purchased by mail is quite broad. (It is now possible to overlay demographic data on large mail order lists using zip code areas and sectional centers as a base.)

Mail order lists are divided into two broad categories: buyers of consumer products and buyers of business products. However, more and more consumer items are being sold to businesspeople. Credit card holders can also be classified as mail order buyers as many of these lists are being used by their owners to sell a wide variety of products by mail.

Not all of the lists made up of people who have purchased consumer items by mail are "people of means" however. When the object is to ferret out this type of person, the type of product purchased and the average size of the order are usually a good tip-off as to the individual's ability to buy. Typically, "people of means" are found among owners of credit cards, contributors to charitable causes, and mail order buyers of high-ticket items such as watches, jewelry, cameras, travel, food and kindred items, cultural products, sports equipment, products for the home, and so on.

Some marketers with a good instinct for marketing psychology can frequently derive a great deal of information about buyers by the kinds of products bought.

Among the commercial companies, the major airlines have probably done most to add to their files data based on computer logic (frequent travelers, for example) and identification of specialized interest groups (sports enthusiasts, influentials) from market research surveys.

It should be noted that there are aberrations in mail order lists. Lists of mail order bargain hunters may work; buyers of spicy books or magazines may work; buyers of low-price merchandise may qualify as buyers of the better things in life. The range of possibilities is quite broad. The selection of such lists is more an art than a science.

The listing above best indicates that one-track list thinking for mail proposition may be severely limiting. Good list testing implies testing *by* concepts as well as *within* concepts.

In a country where at least four lists of mail order buyers total 25 million names or more, it is likely that five out of ten families buy something by mail each year. As incomes increase, discretionary money tends to increase, and the number of families with discretionary money also tends to increase.

A special note about magazines: Where there is a need to locate affluents with specialized interests (say in art, antiques, collectibles, or classic cars), magazine subscriber lists often offer targeted opportunities. Readers of art books and interior design may be ideal for offers of connoisseur prints. Readers of financial journals may be good prospects for investment plans. The proliferation of magazines spanning the computer field offer opportunities to reach those affluent enough to participate in the new wave of consumer "appliances."

Magazines also provide a useful channel when there is a need to reach young people with means (now commonly referred to yuppies). Magazines such as *Playboy, Psychology Today, MS., New York, Working Woman, Esquire, Gentlemen's Quarterly*, and *"W"* reach, in good part, a younger breed of people who have some of that valuable discretionary income to spend.

Although not exhaustive, this section covered all the major ways to tap those with discretionary income through commercially available mailing lists. People of means can be reached in many ways. In a way, we are looking at a grid that has income as the key and is broken down demographically by age and family status and location, and psychographically by hobbies, interests, occupation, membership and ownership. The grid is further overlaid by reading habits, education, and lifestyles—an entire host of lists criss-cross the upper spectrum of America.

FIND/SVP—The Information Clearinghouse

The preceding pages have covered two aspects of the market for affluents:

1. The makeup of the market of those with discretionary income.
2. How to reach affluent citizens through commercially available mailing lists.

Now with the help of FIND/SVP, the Information Clearinghouse, some new data are available on this subject that are rather near and dear to the hearts of direct marketers.

FIND utilizes a cutoff point of $40,000 and above of household income in 1980 as its definition of affluence. On this basis, the number of families in the affluent range increased from 6.2 million households in 1970 to 8.9 million in 1980. FIND's forecast, which parallels that of the United States Bureau of the Census, is that this number will increase to 16.6 million in the 1980s. Such affluent households represented 9.5 percent of all households in the United States in 1970, 10.8 percent in 1980, and are expected to represent 16.8 percent of affluent households by 1990.

The share of aggregate household income held by the top 20 percent of families has remained surprisingly constant. For the last decade this percentage has accounted for between 41 and 42 percent of total household income each year. (The other 80 percent of households share less than 60 percent of the total sum available.)

Half of all affluent families have household incomes between $40,000 and $50,000. They are affluent without being considered "rich." The other half, have incomes over $50,000 and split up most of the 42 percent of total family income logged by the affluent group as a whole.

Among the other major conclusions reached by FIND were the following:

- About one-fourth of all affluent heads of household fall into each of the following three age brackets: 35–44, 45–54, 55–64.

- Three-quarters of all affluent households consist of married couples in which there are no children under the age of six.

- One-half of all affluent households consist of married couples in which both adults work outside the home.

- At least two-thirds of all affluent households do not have any one individual whose total income exceeds or equals $40,000. (That is, affluence is created by the combined efforts of two or more household members.)

- One-half of all heads of affluent households completed college, and 60 percent are employed in professional or managerial positions.

- Over one-half of all affluent households are located in the suburbs, one-fourth in inner cities, and about one-fifth in nonurban areas.

The five largest affluent metropolitan markets are:

New York City	15% of all affluent households
Los Angeles	10% of all affluent households
Chicago	7% of all affluent households
San Francisco	6% of all affluent households
Washington	5% of all affluent households

Forty-three percent of families with incomes of over $40,000 are located in these five markets.

In many ways, affluents are ideal targets for direct-mail marketing. They are literate, educated, and are far more likely to get their information from printed materials, unlike their less-affluent neighbors. They watch on the average 25 percent less television than the average American household. Magazines are generally their media of choice.

Direct marketers will be pleased with the next finding of FIND:

The affluent spend their money to achieve two goals—convenience and increased quality of life. Convenience involves saving time and avoiding drudgery. Increasing the quality of life involves surrounding oneself with high quality possessions, expanding one's leisure and entertainment activities, cultivating the mind and body, and doing good.

FIND then looked at trends in purchasing by affluents, and concluded that affluents were moving in the following directions:

1. Away from quantity and toward quality (fewer but better possessions).
2. Away from tradition in such matters as living arrangements and the roles of men and women but toward formality in terms of lifestyles.
3. Away from conspicuous consumption toward the consumption of goods and services that are meaningful to the individual rather than impressive to the group.
4. Away from the ideas of consumption, abundance, and waste and toward ideas of doing with less, scarcity, and conservation (which will lead to the purchases of more services and fewer goods).

In what might be considered advice to direct marketers, the demographic experts at FIND/SVP offer this gem on the sale of products that can only be purchased by the affluent.

At some point in an exclusive product's lifecycle, it may be appropriate to change the marketing and pricing strategy from an emphasis on the product's exclusivity to an emphasis on some other quality, such as its ability to raise the quality of life of the purchaser, regardless of how many purchasers there are. Advertising can still suggest exclusivity, but exclusivity can no longer be the main theme, and a price adjustment may be needed to fully exploit the lower portion of the affluent market as that portion gradually becomes a "mass" rather than "class" market.

FIND/SVP reports that affluent discretionary income is expended in the following approximate proportions:

Home	35%
Automobiles	35%
Travel and entertainment	21%
Clothing, personal care items, and services	9%
	100%

As FIND/SVP notes, the rich, no matter how they are defined, are few in number:

- *The "almost rich."* In 1981 the IRS estimated that there were 1.8 million individuals with gross assets of $500,000 or more. Within this group, the average net worth was $903,000.

- *The "middling rich."* In 1981 U.S. Trust estimated that there were 638,000 individuals with a net worth of $1,000,000. In 1981 the IRS received 655,000 returns showing an adjusted gross income of $100,000 or more.

- *The "very rich."* A combination of U.S. Trust and IRS data suggests that there are about 40,000 individuals with a net worth of $5,000,000 or more. In 1981 the IRS received 5,300 returns showing an adjusted gross income of $1,000,000 or more.

- *The "inconceivably rich."* The cut off for inclusion on the 1983 Forbes four hundred listing of America's richest individuals was $125,000,000 in net worth. Forbes found fifteen billionaires, whose combined net worth totaled $20 billion.

Locating Millionaires

An IRS study of great wealth indicates the number of millionaires has more than doubled in the last fifteen years from 180,000 to over 400,000. Over 4.4 million individuals have gross assets of at least $300,000.

From a mailing list point of view, millionaires are a very special form of "raisins in the rice pudding" of all individuals or families, with, say, $40,000 or more gross income. They can be provided on mailing lists only if they are included as part of a group of affluents that are selected on some other basis than those certain to have incomes of $1,000,000 or more. It is no problem to tap a Forbes article or Fortune 1,000 presidents and chairpeople of boards to locate small clusters, but a long list of millionaires has so far eluded every compiler who has tried. Some lists are described as millionaires, and they do include great wealth, but none will guarantee any sizable proportion of the 400,000 millionaires among us known only to the IRS.

How to Learn More About Your "Neighborhood"

If you run a local retail, service, or professional business, you may find a great deal of local information about just your area in the 1980 "Neighborhood" data report by the United States Census Bureau. Approximately 1,300 cities, countries, and townships participated in the program. To find out if your community participated, all you have to do is contact your local city or county planning agency, or call the nearest census bureau regional office. The neighborhood reports includes data about:

Population

- Age
- Family composition
- Income
- Poverty status
- Employment status

Housing

- Median value (or rent)
- Persons per room
- Type of heating equipment
- Bathrooms
- Year the house was built
- Vacancies
- Year of original occupancy

Ethnicity

- Spanish-speaking families
- Black families
- Nativity and place of birth of individuals
- Language spoken at home

In addition, a nine-page narrative profile is provided for each neighborhood which highlights some of the data provided in the data tables. These narratives cover such topics as marital status, educational attainment, income, poverty status, ethnicity, and the characteristics of the neighborhood's housing. Other topics include school enrollment, mortgage data, occupation, educational attainment, and even data on dropouts and unemployment training needs.

To help define the geographic limits of each defined neighborhood, the census makes photographic reproductions of individual map sheets available.

These data are very valuable to school boards, economic development organizations, and churches, as well as to social service agencies that provide assistance to the elderly and handicapped, and those agencies that require information on day care and employment needs.

PART V: HOW AGE INFLUENCES DIRECT MAIL

People living at the same time might be considered as sharing a common heritage and a common set of basic knowledge about what has happened in the recent past. This is reasonably true for people of the same age, education, and inclinations. However, people who live at the same time are *not* all of the same age, and their memories on how they have lived are remarkably different. The median age of all Americans in 1985 was thirty-one years of age, half of those under the age of thirty-one were less than fifteen years of age. In addition, as noted on page 145, one-third of Americans are functional illiterates. As a further example, here are some data on the proportion of Americans who do not share what many over sixty years of age include as part of a common heritage·

- 94% of the American population cannot recollect World War I.
- 92% do not remember when women couldn't vote.
- 86% do not remember the stock market crash of 1929.
- 74% are unable to remember the great depression.
- 68% have no recollection of World War II.
- 65% cannot remember life before the Korean War.
- 53% are not able to remember the first Sputnik.
- 44% do not remember the assassination of President Kennedy.
- 32% are unable to remember when man first walked on the moon.

AGE OF THE MARKET—AN IMPORTANT DEMOGRAPHIC FACTOR*

Few, if any, of the 20,000 or so lists that are available in the consumer market can tell us the age of an adult. A direct marketer who sells insurance in the United States seeks to reach people over fifty years of age. Few lists are made up completely of people over fifty. A direct mail marketer of children's books must reach households with a preschool child in order to be effective. Few lists carry this piece of information for selection.

There are products that must reach the right person at the right place. The right offer must be made for the product at the right time. Very often, the right person equates with the right age for that product or service.

For nearly every product category there is a basic audience age. For example, in marketing, a standard auto club package achieved best results when it's directed at an audience forty-five to sixty-eight years of age and the primary audience is found to be from fifty to sixty-five years of age.

Age marketing is a good example of the classic 20/80 principle—20 percent of your products' consumers purchase 80 percent of your product.

DSI has tagged age data to one hundred seventy five mail order lists that total over a billion mail order names owned by its customers. Because of its emphasis on age marketing, DSI has determined basic and primary audience ages for thirty categories of products and services sold through the mail. (See the chart on the next page.) The ages of those people most likely to respond to a direct mail offer are listed within each category. Where children's ages are targeted, the offer can be directed to their parents.

In building its vast age files, DSI has been able to capture 100 million birth dates of children and adults. This list makes celebrating 400,000 individual birthdays per day possible! For marketers who wish to select by zip code clusters, the DSI basic list includes both Prism and Acorn designators.

(There are now four or five classification programs that split the 36,000 five-digit zip codes of America into forty or fifty "clusters" of some "similarity." Two of these are "Prism" and "Acorn." R.H. Donnelley, R.L. Polk, and Data Base America have further refined this procedure to provide "cluster type selection" by enumeration district, or subblock, or by carrier route in which the size of the "cells" of households are on the order of a few hundred, instead of the 4,000 family "average" for zip codes in America.)

---

*Based on an interview with Marvin Monsky, President of Demographic Systems, Inc.

Primary Product Age Group

Offer	Basic Audience Age	Primary Audience Age
Auto Parts and Accessories	16–35	18–26
Auto Magazines	16–27	16–20
Auto Clubs	45–68	50–65
Book Clubs—Continuity	26–37	29–34
Cosmetics—Jewelry	16–26	16–22
Collectibles	45–62	50–58
Children's Offers		
Infant	Under 2	Under 2
Pre-School	3–5	3–5
Grade School	6–12	6–12
High School	13–18	13–18
College	19–23	19–23
Electronics	35–48	39–44
Financial	48–59	50–55
Fundraising	50 +	65–71
Insurance		
Birthday/Life	24–55	32–41
Accident and Health	50 +	52–68
AD&D	65 +	65–71
Income Protection	45–65	50–62
College Endowment	27–35	30–33
Land	27–40	30–36
Merchandise		
Gift	45–67	50–65
Credit	26–42	28–39
Magazines		
Women/Shelter	31–54	33–45
Romantic	24–34	25–33
Men/Adult	30/40/50/60	
Senior Citizens	50 +	54–63
Photo Developing	24–36	28–34
Record Clubs	14–29	16–22
School Education	18–24	18–23
Recipe Cards—Books	19–29	19–29
Travel	50 +	55–68

Source: DSI

TARGETING TEENS*

Teenagers are a diminishing part of the American population but their influence is growing. Their changing role within the American family has given them power beyond their numbers. Not only do they help to determine what their families buy but a significant number of them work and most of their income is discretionary. Estimates of teen spending power range from $30 billion to over $40 billion a year.

The teenage population has been gaining in affluence as much as it has been diminishing in size. In 1985, there were 25.6 million people aged thirteen to nineteen (figure 6.3) in the United States. This figure is down by over four million since the teenage peak in 1976—a drop of 14 percent.

Figure 6.3

Teenage Rollercoaster

The number of Americans aged 13 to 19 peaked in the mid-seventies and will decline through the early 1990s.

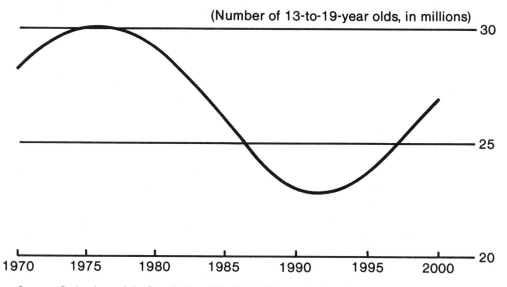

(Number of 13-to-19-year olds, in millions)

Source: Projections of the Population of the United States, by Age, Sex and Race: 1983 to 2080, Current Population Reports, Series P-25, No. 952, U.S. Bureau of the Census.

*Adapted from *American Demographics* magazine.

Only 74 percent of ten-to-seventeen-year olds lived with both parents in 1983. Fully 20 percent lived with only their mother and less than 3 percent lived with only their father.

A preference for getting an education and for living independently has replaced early marriage for many teens. In 1970, nearly one-third of nineteen-year old women had married; in 1985 only 13 percent had married. Among teens aged eighteen and nineteen, 37 percent were in college while the rest worked full time, joined the military, kept house, or "hung out" on the streets.

Most young adults continue to live at home. Despite the change in the economy, more young adults aged eighteen to twenty-four now live at home than young adults in the same age bracket did fifteen or twenty-five years ago. A fairly consistent proportion of young adults aged twenty-five to thirty-four have been found to live at home since 1960. The following tables shows these proportions in more detail.

Age	1960	1970	1980	1983	1985
18–24	41%	46%	49%	54%	54%
25–35	9%	8%	8%	11%	10%

In the 1970s there were so many teenagers that competition was fierce for after-school jobs. Today, "help wanted" signs are posted in fast-food restaurants and other businesses that depend on young people for labor.

Jobs may hurt teenagers academically if they do not keep up on their studies but working puts money in their pockets. The 1983 Rand Youth Poll estimated that girls aged sixteen to nineteen had a weekly income of $55; earnings accounted for $33 of this amount, and allowance for $22. Teenage boys aged sixteen to nineteen had weekly incomes averaging $54; $32 from earnings and $22 from allowance.

Working mothers have necessitated a need for teenagers to become more independent. Teens must now find their own ride home after school, make their own snacks, and in many cases shop for food and begin preparing dinner.

Brand loyalty is formed early among teenage shoppers, according to the findings of a 1980 study sponsored by *Seventeen* magazine and conducted by Yankelovich, Skelly, and White. In a survey of women between the ages of twenty and thirty-four, at least 30 percent said they made a brand decision as a teenager and continued to use the brand at the time of the survey.

Teenagers watch less TV than adults at an average of 23 hours a week compared with 30 a week for adults. The good news for most publishers is that teenagers are reading again. In 1974, students surveyed by the NASSP said they read less than one book a month, including reading assigned at school. Students today say they read, on the average, two books a month for their own enjoyment and start a third before the end of the month. Reading was the second most mentioned hobby in the 1983 Rand Youth Poll, but the next to last hobby mentioned in the NASSP survey of 1974.

For their personal lives, teenagers predict college degrees, prosperous careers, stable marriages, and an average of 2.4 children. Because of their greater independence, teenagers today are better informed about their choices and about the world in general.

BABY BOOMERS

This generation now has one known common thread. All of its members, approximately 78 million adults were born between 1946 and 1964. Forty percent of all families in America are headed by baby boomers. (Because the number of baby boomers are much larger than prior generations, they are destined to be larger than those that follow. The peak year for baby-boomer births—was 1957 when there were 4.3 million births—the highest in history and likely to remain so.)

Most of the older baby boomers (now aged thirty to thirty-nine) live settled lives, while many of the younger ones (aged twenty-one to twenty-nine) are still looking for spouses, housing, and satisfying jobs.

By a freak of timing, the 42 million older baby boomers gained an advantage in the housing market that the 36 million younger ones missed. Sixty percent of thirty to thirty-nine-year olds own a home; only 31 percent of twenty to twenty-nine-year olds do, partly because over a quarter of them still live at home with their parents.

The average monthly mortgage payment for baby boomers who bought homes before 1980 is less than $450. For those who bought homes in 1985 or 1986, the average monthly payment is $800. The relative affluence of the older baby boomers will separate them from the younger ones for many many years.

Although this is the best educated generation in American history, half of the baby boomers never went to college, and only slightly over half of those that went to college were graduated. One in eight did not graduate from high school.

Before 1946, there were more males than females in America. Since then there have been progressively more females. By the year 2,000 there will be 7 million more females than males. The concept that a woman would be supported by a man all her life has lost its meaning. A substantial fraction of women have to support themselves.

In 1960, one out of every four children was the first-born child. Now the ratio is one out of two children. By 1990, the average American family will consist of only 3 people: husband, wife, and one child.

This will be the age of the growth of the entrepreneur, due to a glut of middle managers, most of whom cannot possibly make it to the upper ranks of management.

The Educated Baby Boomer*

The following table shows the median income of baby boomers based on education levels:

Level of Education	Number of Households (34,001,000)	Median Household Incomes ($21,300)
Less than High School	4,253,000	$11,900
High School Graduate	12,325,000	19,200
Some College	7,990,000	22,700
College Graduate	5,178,000	28,100
Graduate School*	4,255,000	32,300

*Note that those with graduate school training have a median income 2.7 times greater than those who did not finish high school.

"YUPPIES"

Yuppies is an acronym that stands for "young urban (and supposedly upwardly moving) professionals." Those who seek to market to this group will probably be surprised to learn that they account for only 5 percent of the baby boomers and they have gotten a great deal more press than their numbers seemingly deserve. In most cases it takes two incomes to be a Yuppie. Almost 75 percent of Yuppie households (with a household income of $40,000 or more) consist of married

*Based on information from *American Demographics* magazine.

couples. But only 8 percent of married baby-boomer couples qualify for Yuppie status. Eighty-one percent of Yuppie householders are college graduates. However, four out of five college-educated baby boomers have not made it to Yuppie status. Because people like to buy products and services that make them feel more affluent than they are, the Yuppie image has a much greater influence on marketing than its numbers suggest. Mail Marketers will find Yuppies are more likely than almost any other segment of the market to utilize travel and entertainment credit cards.

"BOOMER-INSPIRED" HOUSING

Ryan Homes, the fourth largest homebuilder in America installed computerized control centers in 8,000 new homes in 1985. This is a small electronic box manufactured by the General Electric Company that plugs into a television set. By using a handheld remote clicker and a TV screen, the new residents can reset up to one hundred lights, appliances, furnaces, and air conditioners on a daily schedule.

These buildings were designed to attract only the market Ryan Homes wanted—baby boomers between the ages of twenty-seven and thirty-five who were college educated. The rationale behind this was that these people were generally familiar with electronics. Both husband and wife worked so they were willing to pay to guard their leisure time. If a device could make their daily routine easier then they would want it, just as they wanted a garage door opener and modern appliances. This is a good example of a product that has been designed to attract a given segment of the market—not the just marrieds, not the elderly, but the young alert couple on the way up, at an age when the latest electronic marvels are just precisely the added feature to make the sale. This is marrying demographic thinking with a product offer.

SENIOR CITIZENS—A SPECIAL STATUS IN AMERICA

The over-fifty-five age bracket falls into a market that can be broken down into two age groups. Each of these age groups can be further broken down into married couples (living together) and singles (divorced, widowed, never married). The following table shows how age has a great deal to do with this distribution.

Age Group	Total	Married Couples	Single
55–61	10,256,000	6,715,000	3,541,000
62–64	4,201,000	2,413,000	1,788,000
65 and over	19,880,000	8,007,000	11,783,000

The 11,783 Singles over 65	Widowed	Never Married	Divorced
2,448 males	1,399,000	501,000	347,000
9,335 females	7,655,000	829,000	625,000

The distribution of family income by age and marital status indicates how well off our senior citizens are. This really should not be so surprising. The American executive or businessperson tends to increase his or her income over the years, and by age fifty-five has, in general, reached his or her highest income plateau.

Family total income, by age can be categorized as follows:

		Married Couples	
Age Group	Median Income All Households	Median Income	$30,000 Family Income or More (Percent)
55–61	$23,400	$29,180	48%
62–64	$17,650	$23,300	34
65 and over	$11,470	$16,310	19

Twenty-four percent of units based on age (a married couple living together or an unmarried person) aged sixty-five and over live with other family members; 75 percent live by themselves. In the 1980 census, the younger relative is considered the householder and the family that consists of those both below and above sixty-five years of age is classified as "families under 65."

Note that 48 percent of units aged fifty-five to sixty-one have a family (or individual) income of over $30,000. This means that almost one-third of *all* households with family incomes of over $30,000 are in this fifty-five-to-sixty-one age group. The rest of America shows only about a 14 percent level of this affluence.

Data published by the Conference Board Consumer Research Center based on a report funded by CBS emphasizes the relative wealth of the aged among us. Americans over fifty years old comprise an $800,000,000 market with far greater (discretionary) buying power than younger households. Over-50 age bracket households account for 42 percent of the nation's consumer demand, compared with 32 percent from households in the 35–50 age bracket and 25 percent from those under 35, according to Fabian Linden, executive director of the Conference Board and the study's author. Further, over-50 age bracket households control one-half of the nation's discretionary income, with average household incomes that are 20 percent higher than the national average. Other factors that make older Americans "a promising market for luxury goods . . . quality merchandise," says Linden, are fairly steady incomes plus tapering basic needs and freedom from mortgage payments.

THE MYTH ABOUT THE ELDERLY POOR

One of the best myths of the day is that the elderly are more poor than the rest of America. The scandalous truth about poverty is that the poor are disproportionately young not old.

The median age of the American population is thirty-one. The median age of the poor is only twenty-three. Amazing as it sounds, the median net worth of families with members younger than twenty-five is only $5 (Federal Reserve Bulletin, 1984). For families headed by a fifty-five-to-sixty-nine-year old, their median net worth is $56,000.

Poor people aged sixty-five and older total 3.7 million but there are 13.3 million poor children, or one out of every five children.

One fact the lobbyists for the American Association of Retired Persons use in their propaganda campaign for the "elderly poor" is that the median income of the elderly households of $11,800 in 1983 was only 56 percent of the $20,900 median income of all households at the same time. On a per capita basis, however, the median income of the elderly rises to 71 percent of the per capita median for all Americans because elderly households are smaller than the average for the country. According to the Census Bureau, after taxes, the average per capita income of the elderly is 13 percent greater than the after-tax income of the average American.

Earning capacity from fifty-five-to-sixty-four-years of age is on average considerably higher than for those aged twenty-five to thirty-four. (The salad years for earnings for most are between the ages of thirty-five and fifty-five which is about 15 percent above the median income for those aged fifty-five to sixty-four.) Advertisers, both conventional and direct mail, are well aware of the importance of our relatively affluent senior citizens—and their offers and copy to this group are exceptionally well targeted. Here are a few examples:

HOW ADVERTISERS USE VARIED COPY/CONCEPTS IN TARGETING MATURE MARKET CONSUMERS

If you're 65 or over, spend a year in the country.

That is the headline for Eastern Airlines as they operate a special year-round (except for certain peak periods) pass program for adults aged 65 and over. Full page ads use photos of active seniors in tourist spots. A discount coupon is also included, to be taken to your travel agent or Eastern Airlines. Other airlines have similar senior citizen discounts and clubs.

It pays to be early for dinner at Love's.

Love's Barbecue restaurants use one-quarter of a page to bring senior citizens to their 3–6 P.M. dinner "specials." This creates more business at a normally slow time.

The drinks are on us.

McDonald's restaurants promote their "Golden Arches Club" for persons aged fifty-five and over. Members receive a free regular size soft or hot drink with any purchase. Using one-quarter of a page ads in *Senior Voice, Anchorage,* and so on, the campaign is an ongoing program.

Senior citizens are special at Jack LaLanne's.

Senior citizens are actively into physical fitness and LaLanne health spas know senior citizens are more likely to use their spas during the day while others are at work or in school. They offer, in subhead copy "six months for $120, plus six months free!" to those aged sixty-two or over. Ad size is three columns by eight inches, and the ads run in all Senior Publishers Group (SPG) publications in southern California. Campaigns have already been renewed based on response to the initial advertisements.

For people 55 or over! From the Sears family of companies . . .
MATURE OUTLOOK
A new organization created especially for you!

Sears Roebuck/Allstate uses half-tabloid size page ads in many newspapers (and full pages in magazines) for its new senior target marketing program. Ads incude membership applications, "800" telephone numbers (in very bold type), expository text, plus a "menu" list of benefits for the $7.50 membership fee.

Let us show you how very special seniors are to us.

Marineland introduces its September senior citizen discount program for adults aged 60 "or better" in 50-column-inch ads in southern California newspapers. The offer is for a half-price admission during September which produces business at a time when most others are at work or in school.

If you're 60 or older, Wichita State Bank could be saving you money.
60+ Banking.

Wichita State Bank offers checking, Social Security direct deposit, bank-by-mail, and notary service as listed benefits—all for free. The ad is presented in a boldly bordered coupon and it contains mailing information.

Fiscal fitness for people over 60

North Carolina National Bank presents its NCNB 60-Plus Club in full, two-color magazine page size ads. The target program offers prepaid dues of $10 (by the bank) in the North Carolina Senior Citizens Association in addition to other special and free services.

Blue Shield's Coronet Senior
A Medicare supplement plan with extra benefits helps You Keep Dollars
in Your Pocket.

This is the headline of full page ads with large coupons run by Blue Shield of California.

If you think Medicare will cover your health bill, you're only 44
percent right.

Blue Cross of California dramatically illustrates this message with a half-torn dollar bill shaped into a coupon to request information. An "800" telephone number is also prominently featured for call-in requests.

SELLING HEALTH CARE TO THE ELDERLY*

In the five years between 1978 and 1983, health insurance benefit payments in the United States increased by 100 percent—from $48,000,000,000 to $100,000,000,000—while the number of civilians protected by one or more forms of private health insurance increased by an average of 3 percent. Those covered totaled over 192 million, or 82 percent of the civilian noninstitutional population.

Over 176 million people under age sixty-five—representing 86 percent of this age group—were covered, while nearly 16 million people over age sixty-five—representing 60 percent of the older population—held private health insurance policies to supplement benefits available through Medicare.

This vast market is served by over 800 private insurance companies that include a total of ninety loosely federated but individually run Blue Cross/Blue Shield plans.

In 1965 national health expenditures constituted 6 percent of the gross national product (GNP). This proportion has continued to increase over the years, reaching close to 11 percent in 1983–84. According to projections made by the Health Care Financing Administration (355 billion in 1983 at an average of $1,460 per capita) expenses for health care reached $465 billion in 1985 and are destined to reach $756,000,000,000 by 1990. Per capita figures in 1985 were $1,882, or 30 percent more than in 1983. By 1990 per capita expenditures are projected to be $2,982. At that point the United States may be looking at a total health cost of over 15 percent of its gross national product.

Private insurance companies provide almost one-half of all health insurance benefit payments while Blue Cross/Blue Shield and other plans provide the balance.

Somewhat like the services available for direct mail, the coverages available are somewhat similar, but no two are truly identical. This includes the sixty-seven Blue Cross plans available countrywide in 1984 which with joint operation, provide ninety separate Blue Cross/Blue Shield plans.

There is a number of competing forms of coverage from several different types of insurers, including group plans, individual plans, hospital and medical

---

*Statistics are taken from the Source Book of Health Insurance Data

service plans, and a relatively recent development loosely defined under the term Health Maintenance Organizations (HMOs). So rife is the competition for this vast market that a number of Blue Cross/Blue Shield Plans have now started HMOs of their own! Another important development, as the costs of health care escalate, is a move by major companies for their group coverage toward self insurance. Some of these self-insured plans are administrated by labor unions, fraternal societies, communities, or by rural and consumer health cooperatives.

Two Direct-Response Health Care Markets

From a direct-response point of view "health care" consists of two substantial markets:

1. Group plans
2. Individual coverage

The literal welter of offers provides one of the most complicated problems of education and communication ever seen in a mass market.
The offers involved are:

- Hospital expenses
- Surgical expenses
- Physicians expenses
- Major Medical expenses
- Disability income (shortterm and longterm)
- Dental expenses

These are affected by:

- Age
- Pre-existing conditions
- Exemptions
- Choice of physician
- Transferability
- Deductibles

- Percent of coverage
- Replacement and inclusion of Medicare

HMOs provide comprehensive health care services for their members for a fixed periodic payment. In such plans, a group of physicians, surgeons, dentists, or optometrists furnish care to subscribers as specified in the contract. From mid-1971 to January 1985, the number of operational HMOs increased from 33 to 377 and the number of subscribers increased from 3.6 million to 16.7 million. Careful surveys indicate that the care and attention given by these groups, where the choice of a professional is limited, is equal to that provided under Blue Cross/Blue Shield where the choice is up to the individual.

Approximately 60 percent of all expenditures for health care are made for those aged twenty to sixty-five. This leaves 40 percent for those over age sixty-five. Many over age sixty-five who sign up with a carrier for health care do not know that they are *not* only supplementing Medicare but are also cutting themselves off from the Medicare rolls—as the governmental sums involved are paid to the insurer instead. This is only one of the "benefits" that some policies, and a good deal of advertising, do not mention.

How to Sell Health Care by Direct Mail

Most selling in this field is accomplished by eliciting a lead, and then utilizing mail, phone, staff, and agents to initiate a conversion to a sale. Some direct sales are initiated through full page newspaper ads that are now more and more augmented by multipaged self-standing stuffers which attempt to provide a complete rationale for an immediate choice.

Because this is insurance, all states (and many localities) have numerous restrictions on what can and cannot be said about the policies so competitive copy claims tend to produce a blur in the eyes of the reader.

With 40 percent of health care dollars for adults already being spent on those over age sixty-five, those not yet covered by Medicare supplements (about two out of every five people) and those just turning sixty-five years old are now being bombarded with alternatives. This has fueled the increase in the collection and utilization of driver license files—the chief source of data on exact date of birth of adults in the list business.

The age group of sixty-five and sixty-nine, by definition, is healthier than those between the ages of seventy and seventy-five. Those 70-to-75 year olds, in turn, have fewer health maintenance costs than for the group over age seventy-five. Thus it is no surprise to find insurers making special offers to senior citizens who reach 64½ years of age, and again at the age of sixty-five. The intensity of these offers decrease as the seniors age beyond sixty-six to sixty-nine. Typical Blue Cross/Blue Shield plans, many of which have annual "open enrollment" periods where restrictions are relaxed for those over age sixty-five, show an average age of seventy-five or seventy-six for their Medicare supplement coverage. (This age–cost dependence causes carriers to seek out and offer additional products to their customer base.) With costs on the increase, the premiums or charges for such extended coverage has more than doubled in the last few years. Today the premium is in the $40 to $45 range per month—no longer an insignficant cost. In the long run almost all over age sixty-five, except the indigent, will find it almost mandatory to enroll.

The insurance field requires the utilization of a full range of direct-mail services, including rental of lists, creative advertising and fulfillment packages, a trained telemarketing staff, and complete database management. It is not uncommon to find impressive insurance companies serving the health field that have barely tested offers; have never merged–purged rental lists against their customer base which, in turn, produces all kinds of confusion; cannot establish the cost of a lead; and do not have a clue as to the proportion of qualified versus unqualified leads and costs of phone follow-ups. They can, however, provide brilliant reports on the costs of care and the actuarial prognostication of costs per age contingent.

If they are to succeed in the over age sixty-five market, which includes Blue Cross/Blue Shield plans that may seem preeminently positioned to serve this market, such insurers must, out of necessity, add commitment to expertise and learn to control and make every aspect of their difficult marketing operation more cost efficient.

A fair proportion of health care coverage is written by insurance agents, sometimes by default when the carrier either turns over the lead without trying (or trying very hard) to convert it. Here too competition is pervasive where an agency can be offered $250, $200, $175, $100, and $50 for what, on the surface, appears to be the same type of closing. As the agent who goes out to see the individual receives 50 percent or less of the commission, the size of the commission can have a major bearing on which offer is advanced. Many leads provided for one carrier can be easily switched by the agent to another in a face-to-face interview.

Tracking leads provided by carriers to agencies seems to have an exceptionally low priority. It just may be one of the greatest "name drains" in America. (Agents are pleased to service health care inquiries for the opportunity to sell other insurance products.)

The telephone is now beginning to come into its own in this field. Starting usually with a few retired registered agent field workers, carriers are finding telephone inquiries are a golden opportunity to reach customers and prospects on an individualized basis. Where open enrollment has been marketed, WATS lines have provided the ideal means to handle inquiries and requests. It also has been but a small but important step to utilize outgoing telemarketing to lure lapsed customers back into the fold. As most insurance carrier databases are financially controlled, the fact that a policy has lapsed or is in danger of lapsing becomes known universally.

From a list point of view, the health care field includes carriers, professionals, adjunct services, and, of course, both business and consumer prospect bases.

HOME HEALTH CARE AND THE AGING MARKET

Perhaps the two most important developments in health care in recent time have been the great increase in cost and effectiveness of hospital care and the tremendous expansion in home health care.

Home care now includes and supplies dialysis treatment, physical therapy, wheelchairs, whirlpool baths, food fed during sleep, and special clothing for adults. The home care market can be measured in billions of dollars and is fueled by a simple demographic fact: The elderly population is both increasing and growing older. Census figures for 1985 project by the year 2000, Americans aged sixty-five and older will comprise 13 percent of the population while those aged eighty-five and over will increase from 2.7 million to 4.9 million.

As the field of home care is fragmentated, turbulent and uncertain, the commercially available lists of those needing special equipment, services, and drugs are sparse, hard to find, and not rented for offers that the list owners feel may be competitive.

LIST SOURCES FOR SENIOR CITIZENS

Because of its growing importance, the senior market is served by a number of list sources. Following are some examples.

R. H. Donnelley, R. L. Polk, Data Base America, and Metromail all provide names from their huge files of householders who are senior citizens. They can identify those enumeration districts and subblocks and/or carrier routes where the median age, as given by the census, is high. They then also can provide those households within these districts and subblocks where the telephone number has not changed in up to sixteen years. By selecting names on these two criteria, a reasonable approximation of those over age fifty-five, sixty, or even sixty-five can be made. Some of the names furnished will, however, inevitably be "less aged" than desired.

The great advantage of these lists is that they provide coverage of all areas, and they can be selected by income as well as age. When coverage of a small geographic area is imperative, these sources provide a good universe to select from.

R. L. Polk canvases 24 million families individually to produce its roster of 1500 city directories. One of the categories they provide is a list of retired people.

Herbert Dunhill, creator of the "Golden 50's" list, and a specialist in this market, has created a large file of householders by age, fueled in part by access to retired data.

Several insurance companies make their prospect files available. When the owner has recently mailed and "cleaned" a given state, such lists are both deliverable and useful. However, users must check that these lists are updated because an insurance company may not be licensed to do business in a certain state and the data can be very dirty indeed.

Over 50 is a magazine that is gaining influence in the senior market. The major magazine in the field, however, is *Modern Maturity,* which is published by the American Association of Retired Persons. It has a fantastic circulation of over 10 million adults aged, for the most part, fifty-five or over.

Senior members of boards of directors can be selected by age. (It is likely that the neighbors of members of boards are also over age fifty-five just as the members themselves are.) Doctors also can be selected by age through either the Medec or AMA files.

There are now over 10,000 clubs for senior citizens. These clubs account for a disproportionate share of travel, particularly bus travel.

Some health-oriented mail responsive classifications have ample list resources, such as all forms of diet and reducing programs, including books and drugs, vitamins and supplements, health magazines, and the names of health club members.

There also are selected lists for individual sports, including tennis, golf and racquetball, and skiing, as well as such esoteric fields as sports medicine, which can include doctors involved in sports medicine.

According to the Department of Labor, approximately 6.1 million persons were *active* in the health field in 1984. They included:

484,000	Physicians
127,000	Dentists
153,000	Dental assistants
69,000	Dental hygenists
44,000	Dietitians
1,409,000	Registered nurses
782,000	Practical nurses
1,218,000	Nursing aides, orderlies, and attendants
149,000	Pharmacists
83,000	Psychologists
110,000	Radiological technologists
202,000	Therapists (occupational, physical, respiratory, and speech)
31,000	Optometrists
8,000	Oculists

The above statistics would make available, in list form:

300,000	Offices of physicians
125,000	Offices of dentists
8,000	Offices of osteopaths
22,000	Offices of chiropractors
9,000	Offices of podiatrists

as well as

6,000	Medical laboratories
10,000	Dental laboratories
48,000	Pharmacies
8,000	Hospitals
20,000	Nursing homes
41,000	Outpatient care facilities
3,000	Alcohol and drug rehabilitation centers
2,000	Oxygen therapy
12,000	Hospital equipment suppliers

and

8,000	Gymnasiums
21,000	Health clubs
2,000	Massage centers
11,000	Health food stores
4,000	Recreation centers
5,000	Youth centers

The health field is served by lists made up of:

1,000	Insurance companies
165,000	Insurance agencies and brokerages
300	Biological products manufacturers
400	Medical, chemical and botantical product makers
1,000	Pharmaceutical preparation manufacturers
600	Soap and detergent manufacturers
1,500	Cleaning specialty manufacturers

3,000	Rubber and plastic producers
500	Pressure and blown glassware manufacturers
500	Industrial gas manufacturers
200	Synthetic rubber producers
500	Makers of work clothing
500	Special furniture producers
1,000	Producers of paper products
1,000	Control instrument manufacturers
600	Makers of optical instrument and lenses
3,000	Surgical, medical, and dental instrumentation
1,600	Orthopedic, prothesis, and surgical appliance manufacturers
700	Dental equipment and supplies manufacturers
1,000	Opthalmic goods manufacturers

PART VI: ETHNIC LISTS AND LIST SOURCES

Few Americans can trace their ancestry back more than two or three generations. But most Americans, as becomes members of what was once called "the melting pot," can trace their ancestors by ethnic origin.

Let's take a look at the "ancestry" of the population of the United States, with the help of the 1980 census. This census was the first to collect ethnic data on persons regardless of the number of generations removed from the country of origin. (Ethnic data collected in previous censuses came from questions on the country of birth of persons and their parents, and identified ethnicity only for foreign born or native persons of foreign or mixed parentage.)

Eighty-three percent of the U.S. population answered the questions on ancestry. Six percent of the balance wrote in (on a self-identification form) "American" or "United States." Fifty-two percent reported a single specific country or area of origin. Thirty-one percent provided a multiple response.

THE MOST COMMON ANCESTRY GROUPS
REPORTED BY AMERICANS

Here is what we Americans reported about our origins: English and German were the most frequently reported ethnic groups. About 50 million persons reported being solely or partly of English ancestry; 49 million reported being German or part-German.

Figures for the most frequently reported ethnic groups (single and multiple) were:

Ethnic group	Population
English	50 million
German	49 million
Irish	40 million
Afro–American	21 million
French	13 million
Italian	12 million
Scottish	10 million
Mexican	8 million
American–Indian	7 million
Dutch	6 million

Of the large European ethnic groups, Irish, French, Scottish, Dutch, and Welsh were distributed fairly evenly by geographic region. Other groups were more concentrated. For example, more than one-half of the nation's Italians lived in the northeast (33 percent in only two states); while more than 50 percent of the Norwegians lived in the north-central area (32 percent in only two states).

California, the largest state in the United States, ranked first in population size for a number of European ancestry groups including English, German, Irish, French, Scottish, Dutch, Swedish, Danish, and Portuguese. New York, the traditional port of entry for many immigrant groups, had the largest number of persons reported for Italian, Polish, Russian, and Hungarian ancestry. Other states ranking first were Minnesota for Norwegians; Illinois for Czechs; and Pennsylvania for Welsh.

Similar to European groups, some of the non-European groups had high proportions (50 percent or more) residing in one state. New York, for example, contains more than 70 percent of the population of Barbadians, Dominicans, and Guyanese that reside in the United States, as well as high proportions of Trinidadians, Tobagonians, Haitians, and Jamaicans. More than 60 percent of Bahamians are in Florida. California, interestingly enough, has almost three-fourths of all Salvadorans, as well as high proportions of Guatemalans and Nicaraguans.

The following table indicates that New York and California contain the greatest number of ethnic groups.

Ancestry	State	Population (percent)
Armenians	Massachusetts and California	over 50%
Belgians	Michigan and Wisconsin	32
Canadians	Massachusetts and California	30
Czechs	Illinois and Texas	24
Danish	California and Utah	25
English	California and Texas	16
French	California and Louisiana	17
German	California and Pennsylvania	16
Greek	New York and California	28
Hungarian	New York and Ohio	27
Irish	California and New York	17
Italian	New York and New Jersey	33
Polish	New York and Illinois	25
Russian	New York and California	37
Swedish	California and Minnesota	25

MARKETING FUNDAMENTALISM IN THE "BIBLE BELT"

With the growth of fundamentalism in America, certain states located in what is referred to as the "Bible belt" have proved particularly responsive to Christian-oriented offers of books, records, cassettes, 8-track tapes, Tracts, and Bibles. These states are West Virginia, North Carolina, South Carolina, Georgia, Alabama, Tennessee, Kentucky, Iowa, Missouri, Kansas, Nebraska, Louisiana, Arkansas, Oklahoma, and Texas.

Public Office and Ancestry

There is one form of marketing that is particularly interested in ancestry and ethnicity. It is the "marketing" of candidates for public office. On a national scale, immigrants who came to America in the twentieth century, their children, and grandchildren, together with the descendents of African slaves, have become the majority of the country's population. These groups also have more young people than the great-great-grandchildren and other descendents of the Anglo-Saxons who came to the New World Prior to 1900.

The distribution of delegates to the 1984 Democratic National Convention is some measure of this population and ethnic origin shift. Polls indicate that about 36 percent of all Democratic delegates in San Francisco were white Protestants. This compares with almost 75 percent of the delegates to the Republican National

Convention in 1984. The Democrats, proportionately, also had six times as many Blacks, virtually all Protestant, and three times as many of the Jewish faith as did the Republicans.

It is becoming increasingly clear to students of voting habits that where one stands politically in the United States depends in good part on when and where his or her ancestors arrived and the ethnic bloodline.

HOW TO REACH ETHNIC FAMILIES THROUGH COMMERCIALLY AVAILABLE MAILING LISTS

All the ethnic data previously discussed came from the census of 1980. Interestingly enough, by law, no data can be collected by the census on religious belief or affiliation. Religious lists therefore are based either on surnames (Sweeney, Schwartze, Esposito) or on membership or support.

Major compilers can identify 15 million Catholic families, 2.5 million Jewish families, 6 million Spanish families (on basis the of surname). Through census data 7 million families are assumed to be black because of their location in areas where the black population predominates.

This type of data, which is available from R.H. Donnelley, R.L. Polk, Data Base America, and Metromail, provides data from the census overlay to permit selection of Catholic, Jewish, Irish, Spanish, Italian, and Black families by individual family income, as well as by sex of head of household, type of household (single-family home, or multiple-dwelling) length of residence, ownership of automobile and so on. A host of median data on such factors as age of head of household, family size, education level, and home valuation can also be provided.

The availability of valid individual incomes on ethnic pulls from these large lists makes testing possible for the value of the ethnic selection as well as the influence on response of differing income segments. There is no difficulty in stratifying Catholic, Irish, Italian, Jewish, Spanish, or Black families by income level. The spread of such incomes is somewhat restricted for Spanish-speaking or Black families.

Perhaps the best student of ethnic derivation by surname (or, ancestry, if you will) is the social scientist, Dr. Loretta Poggio, who has developed a computer program that takes into account variants in the same surname depending on the location (by state) of the family. Her program has been overlaid on a number of lists with high success for the larger ethnic groups and with some success for smaller ethnic groups such as Poles or Lithuanians.

One way to reach ethnic groups is to tap what they read. There are magazines for Blacks (*Ebony, Essence*), as well as magazines for various religious denominations, and local papers for ethnic concentrations in large cities. A number of magazines exist for Reformed, Conservative, and Orthodox Jews. There also are major journals that reach the Spanish-speaking market.

Donor lists are often a good indicator of ethnic origin. There are numerous lists of Catholic and Jewish donors, fewer lists for Indians and other minorities. Some lists for Black organizations provide a concentration of more affluent Black families. There are also certain mail order offers that produce names essentially of one persuasion, particularly covering the Catholic market.

It is likely, despite the availability of donor lists, magazine lists, and mail order lists, that the major source for ethnic selection is based on surname lookup. The maxim, birds of a feather flock together, is particularly true of ethnic distribution. Recent Russian immigrants can be found mainly within a few blocks of the boardwalk in Brighton Beach in Brooklyn; New York City has the second largest Dominican population in the world. Cubans are beginning to populate a fair part of Miami. Spanish-speaking Americans will soon outnumber native-born Blacks. From an overall view the "melting pot" concept might be applied but the reality is a proliferation of ethnic lifestyles that are as great or perhaps greater than the proliferation of lifestyles over the past generation in America. Thus for most mailers who have yet to tap the ethnic diversity of America, a challenge now faces them to learn more about how this "other population," about one in four of us, lives.

SIZING UP THE HISPANIC MARKET: A LOOK AT THE SOUTHERN CALIFORNIA AREA

There are substantial data now on file to indicate that within a few years the Spanish-speaking population will be the largest minority in the United States— surpassing Black families for the first time.

This section gives information about Spanish-speaking families in Los Angeles and Southern California. It is relevant for the entire crescent from across the southwest and up the eastern coast to New York.

Over 80 percent of the female heads of household (ages twenty-one to fifty-four) were born *outside* the United States. On average they have been part of the U.S. ethnic mix for a period of twelve years. Two-thirds of them have children between the ages of 5–17 years.

Over 70 percent of these children speak Spanish. Approximately 52 percent of them are bilingual. They are without doubt the group of youngsters in America who have advanced verbal skills in two languages which is something very few other American educated children can claim.

Income, as might be expected, rises with the length of time Spanish-speaking immigrants are in the United States. Almost 90 percent of those making $10,000 to $19,900 speak mostly Spanish or only Spanish. Half of those families with incomes of $20,000 or more speak as much Spanish as they do English. (The average income is $16,000—or $5,000 below the average for the country, as a whole.) Thirty percent of Spanish-speaking families now earn $20,000 or more.

Overall, the Spanish-speaking population in the United States reports a low educational level. Only 35 percent have a high school education. One-third of the householders own their own homes.

Only half of those households have a savings account, one-third have a checking account, one-fifth have a credit card. These proportions are markedly lower for low-income families. Despite that, in half the households someone has taken an air flight within the last year, and most have radios and TVs. One-fifth of these families purchased a new car in the last two years. One in ten bought a truck.

The Hispanic population grew six times faster than the general population between 1970 and 1980. The figures by origin are as follows:

Total	Non-Spanish	+11%
Total	Spanish Origin	+61
	Mexican origin	+93
	Puerto Rican origin	+41
	Cuban origin	+47
	Other Spanish origin	+19

In an article for the magazine Madison Avenue, Antonio Guernier suggests the Hispanic population, now estimated at 19 million (with 5 million undetected alone) could reach 30 million in 1990 and 44 million by the year 2000.

Hispanic populations by state show

State	Population (%)
California	19%
Texas	21
New York	9
Florida	9
Illinois	6
Arizona	16
Colorado	12

Eighty-seven percent of Spanish-speaking families concentrate in metro areas compared with 74 percent of the general population. The Hispanic median age is seven years *younger* than non-Hispanics—twenty-three years for the Hispanic and thirty years for the non-Hispanic. By 1990 this differential is projected to be twelve years, and by 2000 a fifteen-year gap is indicated.

From a direct-mail point of view there would seem to be several points of interest here:

1. The increasing size of this market is a challenge in itself. If Hispanics make up 44 million of the 250 million people in the United States by the year 2000 that will be 18 percent of American families. This is more than *all* other minorities combined.

2. Affluence for the Spanish-speaking market is "manana." Only a very small proportion of the Spanish-speaking market has reached the plateau of affluence.

3. The youthfulness of this market requires rethinking about product and service offers.

4. The longer Hispanics are in America the higher their English literacy and the higher the proportion of use of the English language. Like all other immigrants to our shores they will become more and more assimilated in the years to come.

5. Most mailers can disregard the Spanish market for now and permit selection by income, age, and psychographics to identify the fringes of this population that are open to offers of interest to the population in general. The operative word here is "now." Special attention will be required in no more than five or ten years from now.

6. Special efforts to reach this market will begin to proliferate locally in Los Angeles, New York, New Mexico, and so on. Today 60 percent of Hispanic adults in southern California speak Spanish only. Surprisingly little mail is directed to these families in their native language. This limits the effectiveness of direct-mail and newspaper advertising printed in English only.

PART VII: PSYCHOGRAPHICS: A LIFESTYLE GUIDE TO LIST SELECTION

The essence of psychographics

. . . is selection on the basis of what actions people take, what they do, not what they say they do.

It is what people read
   what people join
   what people buy
   what games or hobbies they play
   what they support
   what they are willing to sign

Psychographics, the latest buzzword of avant-garde advertising agencies and advertising research, is the so-called science of reaching people not by the demographics of *where* they live but rather by their lifestyles—*how* they live.

HOW DEMOGRAPHICS AND PSYCHOGRAPHICS DIFFER

Demographics might be called the socio-science of the *measurable externals* of a life pattern among which are age, income, occupation, value of home, location, duration of residence, head of household, and size of family. Psychographics might be called the socio-science of the *internals* of a life pattern which produce measurable behavior patterns, and measurable expenditures of time, energy, and money. For example, education level is demographic. The use that education is put to is psychographic. The occupation of a person is demographic; the hobbies and leisure activity of a person are psychographic. The income of a person is demographic, the way a person spends disposable income is psychographic.

When a list is selected based on the home addresses of boards of directors and their next door neighbors, that is demographic selection. It is based on the fact that neighbors of people making $50,000 or more per year are likely to have comparable incomes. When *TIME* magazine sends a special letter to a former home of a moved subscriber (because it works) the thinking here is psychographic. The new owner of a given type of home is likely to lead the same type of lifestyle as the subscriber who just left. However, the new owner may have a comparable income but a different lifestyle, which explains why the neighbors of subscribers to a metro magazine like *Atlantic Monthly* are not good prospects for that magazine.

The real story of our time is the somewhat fantastic proliferation of lifestyles—particularly the youthquake among the young and well-to-do which is creating a whole series of minimarkets.

Sociologists call the present time the "age of alternatives—a time of doing your own thing." We now have multiple overlapping markets of highly varied, differentiated affluent, educated adults who are demanding, demonstrative, articulate, multifaceted, with a considerable cynicism toward traditional advertising and marketing.

There are over 100 million licensed drivers in America; more people are awake at midnight in the United States than anywhere else on earth, maybe more than all the rest of the world put together. We are educating millions more in college than we can employ in managerial positions, which may be one good reason that multiple careers are now socially acceptable. Multiple careers affect both sexes and over half of all married women work outside their homes.

What seems to be emerging from all this is what Alvin Toffler cogently calls "Future Shock"—the dizzying disorientation brought on by the premature arrival of the future. Toffler said, "Most travelers have the comforting knowledge that the culture they left behind will be there to return to. The victim of future shock does not. This well may be the most important disease of tomorrow."

A prominent advertising critic, writing in *Advertising Age,* predicts "advertising will be profoundly reshaped over the next few years. The mass market will become obsolete. Advancement in communications will make it possible to communicate instantaneously with almost anyone anywhere at any time by voice, sight, or written message."

A buyer is a buyer is a buyer

To a mailer, the fact that a man or woman buys a book, record, magazine, or pays for a cruise or a product is far more important than that man's or woman's income, occupation, age, number of children, location of home, or any other demographic pigeonhole into which that buyer can be placed. A buyer is a buyer is a buyer, and what he or she has already bought tells us more about what else he or she is likely to buy than all the demographic statistics available per tract, block, or enumeration district.

It is no chance result that in every case a good list of mail order buyers will outpull a good list compiled demographically by a sizable margin. It is better for major mailers to concentrate on mail order buyers when they go into the marketplace, and to pay the modest modern costs of unduping to increase the efficiency of each piece mailed.

A book buyer will buy more books or a record buyer will buy more records until all the shelves are stocked. Such a buyer, if the need arises, will deprive himself or herself of some element of comfort or reduce his or her apparent scale of living in order to have the discretionary income available to indulge in his or her way of life—the psychographic pattern as it were.

It is now possible, only through direct mail, to narrow in on proven book buyers as a class, and book buyers who have already bought books by mail. While book buyers come in assorted sizes, they also come in assorted flavors and colors, each of which can be identified and tested individually. There are psychiatric book buyers; history book buyers; buyers of novels; buyers of biographies, mysteries, or mystic arts. Books for readers of science can be academic, popular, erudite, or recondite, and they can be in social science, biological science, physical science, or in science fiction. There's also an audience for cookbooks, floral books, how-to books, poetry books, short stories, plays, adventure, discovery, sexology, psychology, child care, personal health and grooming, and encyclopedias and "Who's Who's" in a dozen different fields. There is a whole group of readers who buy what the trade calls "hardware" books—books bought essentially to be seen on library tables and not necessarily to be opened or read. What advertiser discussing the psychographics of mass media A, B, or C as markets for given types of books can narrow cast as the expert user of mailing lists does?

The buyer of records such as rock, country, western, blue grass, revival, dixieland, children's musicals, or the mass-merchandised nostalgic records advertised on TV, is not the same kind of cat as the so-called "long hair" who goes for Bach. The buyer of Bach records may have little in common with the classical buyer who finds the classics started with Moog and not mood, and finds Bartok and Stravinsky old hat and worships strange new gods (to some ears) with names like Beno, Boulez, Mimaroglu, Stockhausen, and Varese.

Some record collections feature words and music, some feature only sounds and not music. Stereo buyers eschew monaural while "four-trackers" believe stereo is passé. The compact-disc buyer may only nod at the cassette buyer, and both will sniff at "old fashioned" records. Once again, only through direct mail can marketers make any such approach as to what the lifestyle differences are—the psychographics in this case of taste (and equipment) in the enjoyment of music.

Using Past Performance as a Measure of Future Behavior

B.F. Skinner in *Beyond Freedom and Dignity* is the exponent of the theme that man is what he does not what he thinks. Although there is acrimonious debate over this subject, no one in direct mail is likely to argue with the main thrust of Skinner's position because a giver or donor demonstrates his or her position by the gifts or donations he or she makes. The remarkable proliferation of mailings made to donors of one cause by other causes is due to the fact that those who have acted as a donor for one cause are more likely to give to another cause than are people who "should" show an interest. Direct mail is playing straight psychographics in its fundraising role.

A grower seeks out buyers of plants and seeds; a vitamin producer seeks out those who wish greater vitality; the school seeks out those who evidence an interest in self education; the gourmet food packer seeks out those who cherish a better diet; the insurance company seeks out differentiated psychographic markets (like new physicians, men and women on their way up in business, women who work, newly formed households or businesses, or retirees). The seller of desert or coastal sand looks for a lifestyle ready for investment now and retirement somewhat later.

In mail order terms, thinking psychographically can also be interpreted as thinking peripherally because individual lifestyles or psychographics can best be pictured as a bundle of more or less common characteristics and not as a single isolated strand. Thus the mailer with a cultural item to sell is able to tap different strands in the more or less common bundle of cultural activities by testing lists of buyers of many different facets of culture. Students of the current growing cultural market calculate that there are 6 million to 7 million family groups (within the 87 million households in the United States) which make up the so-called "cultural market." From a direct-mail point of view, such a market is made up of people who have demonstrated their cultural bent by one of the following lifestyle acts.

- Buyers of books (and peripherally, buyers of gourmet foods):
  Wines
  Expensive gifts
  Records
  Music
  Magazines
  Journals
  Services
  Art
  Vanity press

- Tickets or subscriptions to:
  Concerts
  Art shows
  Lectures
  Theatre
  Films
  Reading

- Donations to:
  Museums
  Historical societies
  Colleges and universities
  Art preservation

- Graduates of:
  College
  University

Art and drama school
Professional or graduate school
Teachers college

- Current Student in:
  College
  Adult education

- Membership in:
  Art societies
  Record clubs
  Amateur music societies
  Museums
  Book clubs

Lists Mirror Lifestyles

It is clear that each element within this cultural complex can be reached through given mailing lists which in effect mirror the lifestyles of those who have made some overt act that has landed them on specific lists of like-minded people.

Students of direct mail have been students of psychographic patterns for years, before the "need to probe beneath the surface of human motivation" was publicized by advertising–market researchers. Some of the great mail order successes of our day have been built around service to an isolated group with a definite specialized interest—from health to model cars to Americana to rocks to baby toys to patterns to roses to wines to Astrology charts to insurance for those over 50 . . . and hundreds upon hundreds more.

These careful mailers know that the best prospect list for a special-interest mailing is a list that parallels as closely as possible their customer files. Those mailers who use merge–purge to identify duplication are well aware of the correlation between multiple buyers and higher response.

The recent proliferation of lifestyles and the growing power of TV have made the road for general interest magazines such as *Life, Look, Saturday Evening Post,* an exceedingly rocky one. However these times have hastened the development of special interest publications like *Psychology Today, New York Magazine, Smithsonian, New York Review of Books, Weight Watchers, Playboy,* and *Mad.* These magazines, in turn, have produced lists that are particularly attractive to special-interest mailers.

In an advertisement directed to media buyers, *National Geographic* asked this psychographic question: "How classy is your mass?" The usual run of direct-mail users don't have to attempt to qualify the class of their mass. They know it by the solid evidence of a purchase denoting a definite internal participation in a given class of lifestyle.

Those relatively-few very-large mail companies with lists based on sales of a plethora of products either have learned or are learning that what they really have is a group of different products. Each in effect catering to a different lifestyle group. Sears utilizes over 170 different cells when selecting customers to receive specific catalogs and flyers. They tailor the list to fit the offer psychographically by selecting segments based on recency, frequency and dollars, item, and correlations between items.

The ancients recognized differing lifestyles in the phrase, "One man's meat is another man's poison." If the Ancients were writing that phrase today, they might say, "One man's medium is another man's tedium." That is why direct mail is the great psychographic medium today. It seeks out only those people who are preconditioned by their lifestyles, to accord harmoniously with the message of the mailer. Direct mail selects individuals with known life patterns.

The success of direct mail is based on its ability to locate known mail order buyers who are ready and able to buy. Because of their predilection they are ready to buy a specific product or service that fits their psychographic or lifestyle needs.

USING QUESTIONNAIRES TO OBTAIN DIRECT MAIL PSYCHOGRAPHICS AND DEMOGRAPHICS

A relatively new list phenomenon has been the creation of very large consumer lists that are based on long involved questionnaires as to hobbies, interests and even brands.

Such questionnaires are being used increasingly to elicit valuable list data—both psychographic and demographic.

There are now four lists of over 5,000,000 consumers based on mailed-in answers to questionnaires. The first of these, and to date the largest, the "The Lifestyle Selector," delivers its long series of questions as part of warrantee cards packed in with millions of products bought at retail by consumers. About 18 percent of those who "register" their warrantee by mailing it in furnish data as to hobbies, interests, reading, mail order purchase, even frequency of flying—along with a complete demographic profile.

One of the four, named appropriately enough "The Behavior Bank" asks consumers to indicate their brand usage in coffee, pet food, cereals, milk, coffee lightener, and saltines as well as floor wax, pantyhose, denture cleanser, laxatives, cigarettes, detergents, athletes foot control, and, as if that were not enough, the questionnaire goes into credit cards, mail-order buying, hobbies, and occupations.

For every classification, "The Behavior Bank" has a sponsor who offers a coupon of small value to those already committed to his brand. But those who denote using a competitive brand are offered a sizable coupon inducement to switch. The mailer of the survey gets a cut for each coupon provided. R.H. Donnelley is using almost every flight of its successful Carol Wright co-op to add additional names to its list of several million consumers who answer a questionnaire as to tasks, interests, and lifestyles. Each consumer who answers is rewarded with a small gift. "The Blair List" is similarly constructed. Owners of such "desirables" as VCRs, PC-type-computers (by brand), microwave ovens, and disc phonographs, are denoted on such lists.

From a direct-mail point of view, these lists also offer large numbers of self-styled golfers, campers, gardeners, boat lovers, and so on. To make them work for direct-mail offers, it is usually necessary to combine two or three classifications (for example, hobby, age, and credit card use) which reduces the quantities quite drastically. In any case, large use of this list concept must be undertaken with care.

One or two of these "questionnaire lists" offers to code mailer's lists with the demographics reflected on the "Questionnaire file." It is probable such an overlay should only be done when tests of segments of the Q list itself provide sufficient response to qualify as a major list source.

Trade magazines make certain recipients qualify for circulation by screening answers to a questionnaire that is made a part of the subscription or qualification form. Some valued professional magazines require filling out a detailed questionnaire as the only way to ensure continuation of service. One medical publication has physicians mark their medical specialties on a list containing seventy-six disciplines, as well as providing data on type of practice, hours worked, number of prescriptions written per day, hospital accreditation, board-certification, continuing education in last twelve months, ownership of a computer and video equipment, exact date of birth, and year graduated from medical school. And if this is not detailed enough, the doctor is asked to check off forty-seven different types of prescription drugs by use! Ninety-nine percent of the doctors responded, as the one way to obtain a very valuable desk bible on every drug and its use and cautions.

Some catalogs, particularly in technical fields, tend to become "product bibles" and are saved from year to year. A few of these, infer by means of a "renewal" questionnaire that those who take the time to answer questions about equipment use, product need, and purchasing habits will be assured of receiving the next edition.

Response to such questionnaires is surprisingly high—each filled-in questionnaire provides a wealth of data for future selection and use.

A PSYCHOGRAPHIC CASE HISTORY

After divestiture, AT&T was left primarily with the long lines (interregion, interstate) telephone business, including $7,000,000,000 of revenue for 3.5 billion calls on inbound WATS lines. There are now 275,000 installed WATS lines. In 1985, AT&T first published two directories listing 75,000 of these. One was for consumers; the other for business. (A large number of WATS lines are for individual company use only.)

The distribution of these books was designed to do three things: (1) increase WATS usage by both consumers and business, (2) make a modest profit from advertisers who wished to promote their WATS service, and at the same time, (3) help reduce the staggering load of free information calls for 800 WATS numbers logged each day. These calls now are running at the rate of 300,000 per day, or close to 100 million free calls per year.

The need to attract advertisers to this new form of classified information had a great deal to do with the kind of distribution required. Rather early on it became clear that attempting to sell the books directly to two audiences—the consumer and business—was bound to fail. Even if books could be sold at under $10.00 through conventional mailing means, there was no guarantee that such sales would provide a pattern that would attract advertising revenue. Without a guaranteed base, the chance for any kind of advertising was remote. Sales after the fact simply added additional circulation at no extra cost to the advertisers.

By means of focus interviews with prospective advertisers, the guaranteed distribution of the business book (approximately 315,000 copies) took shape rather quickly. There were small groups of classifications that needed to be covered irrespective of size, such as travel agencies, PR agencies, ad agencies, and beyond that larger businesses carefully selected by SIC and by number of employees. Four major sources were tapped: the Standard & Poor's composite of big business, National Advertisers, Dun & Bradstreet's file by SIC and employee strength, and the Burnett Data Base America master business file covering 8 million companies, institutions and offices of professionals. Every establishment with over fifty employees received at least one book; larger firms received two. The executive titles were selected on the basis of research on WATS-line usage. The several inputs were put through a careful merge–purge clearing process (see page 485) and tapes and labels were prepared.

For the consumer book, target mailings of 1 million free copies (plus a sizable number of added copies through sales) were established. The question then became how to best select from 87 million families in America the 1 million most attractive to AT&T as prospective WATS users, and for the same reason the 1 million most attractive to advertisers. The following specific requirements were then set:

1. Credit card holders

2. Buyers by direct mail in the last six months

3. Each purchase to have been made from mail order companies offering free "800" inbound service

4. Each purchase (actually almost every purchase) to be made by telephone and charged on a credit card

5. Ninety percent of all buyers selected (from ninety-four separate lists over twenty-three separate product and service classifications) to have sufficient income to pass a screen of $35,000 and over. (The average family income selected in this way was over $56,000.)

There were a few more complications on this assignment.

1. There were three promotional mailings, one prior to delivery of the directory and two after delivery. Hence rentals were negotiated with each list owner for a four-time use.

Prior to the massive merge–purge, it was necessary to negotiate a price for four mailings. The first was a prepublication letter announcing the coming of the "800" directory, the second was the mailing of the directories, carrier-route coded for the $15\frac{1}{2}$ ounce consumer book, but via parcel post for the much heavier business edition. The third and fourth mailings were instituted to stimulate more use of the books as well as to obtain some relevant information through research for the 1986 edition. With over 170 lists to negotiate with over 145 list owners and managers, the acquisition phase proved to be the most protracted and difficult part of the entire assignment.

2. Those who received the 1985 directory were given an opportunity by mail to place their name on the list to get the 1986 directory. (These names identified for list source by keys were compared to the totals mailed for each list and the lists showing the highest proportion of interest in the 800 directory were continued for the next edition.)

3. A large number of names across the whole spectrum of the mail order lists had to be provided with telephone numbers for pre-publication and post-publication research use.

4. An initial small number of recipients who requested a copy were given preference.

There were two other complications. First, each state was to receive its proportionate share of distribution, based on total population. (This might have been somewhat easier if the distribution was based on the proportion of affluents, rather than on total population.) The second was the need to meet the guarantee of 1 million names with no more than a few thousand, at most, over that total. To match these requirements it was necessary to arrange for the initial utilization of over 2 million mail order buyers. In the merge–purge of over 13.5 million records, several hundred thousand multiple WATS line buyers were utilized, and the result was a file of just over 1,050,000 which was pared down on a state-by-state quota basis to 1,015,000.

There were some interesting side effects. To have a WATS number listed at no charge in the directories, a company had to approve this by phone or in writing. Several hundred WATS owners called when the book was published to make certain they would be included in the 1986 edition. A good number of prospective advertisers who stayed out of the first edition called to reserve space in the next.

AT&T, finding itself with a new viable annual directory, has provided lists of new WATS lines by classification. These newest entrants to toll-free calling will each get an opportunity to advertise next to their listing. In addition, AT&T has located a large number of WATS users not available when the book was closed for 1986. There are also plans to increase, perhaps dramatically, the sale of the 1987 directories. One idea, whose time has not yet come, is to have the 800 service provide the requested information, and then through call forwarding offer a copy of the directory for sale. One problem with this unique concept available to AT&T only, is that no one can predict with any accuracy how many books might be sold. The figure of 3 million does not seem inappropriate.

For the coming edition, a stat-tab or unmailable match-code identification of each consumer recipient was saved as a possible suppress file . In addition, 170,000 requests for the new edition and 40,000 or more purchasers were run against the stat-tab file to provide input for a penetration analysis (see page 443), which was then used to refine even further the selection by list source for the new edition.

Each of the buyers of the prior edition is being offered an opportunity to buy the new edition. Each of those who utilized the directory, and requested through the mail that a copy of the directory be sent will be on the current distribution list. These requests will be an input to the next merge–purge with one special difference: They will survive by serving, in effect, as an AT&T customer file. This file of buyers and requestors is now available for rental through Ed Burnett Consultants. It is the first list ever disseminated for mailing by AT&T.

BUSINESS LIST PSYCHOGRAPHICS

Business lists also have psychographic characteristics. There are 9* million establishments (not including farmers) in the United States that pay social security for the proprietor or self-employed, as well as employees. At the upper end of this "pyramid" of establishments is the so-called *Fortune 1,000*. These are the 1,000 largest industrial companies in the country. These 1,000 companies, which control the destinies of 5 percent of manufacturing establishments but employ over 70 percent of all industrial employees and produce over 75 percent of the value added to production, are quite unlike the 170,000 manufacturing plants with ten employees or less.

Factors that somewhat affect how and what businesses buy by mail psychographically (and demographically) are:

1. Size (Number of employees)
2. Home office or branch
3. Classification
4. Mail order responsiveness
5. City size/Geographical location
6. Business-oriented membership
7. Promotional mindedness
8. Type of distribution
9. Lifespan
10. Make or buy decision
11. Influence of research
12. Influence of government

*The IRS stipulates, based on their tax returns, there are 15 to 16 million establishments. The balance for the most part is individuals, mainly in sales, working independently out of their homes with no listing in the classified phone directories. Those with listed business phones total 8 million.

In addition to demographic and psychographic criteria of mailing lists, there are market qualifications to consider.

1. Size of the list
2. Size of the universe the list can be obtained from
3. Accessibility of the given market
4. Rarity of the given market or market segment
5. Completeness of coverage
6. Seasonality factors
7. Peripheral market coverage (if any)
8. Changing status of the market
9. Age of market
10. Qualification of name
    a. Preferred, acceptable, undesirable
    b. Proof of buying influence
    c. Periodic sales for qualification
    d. Selection factors utilized

Value depends on size. A list of 3,000 is not usually worth one-half of a list of 6,000. This size factor is dependent on accessibility, rarity, cost to reproduce, and the total size of the market or market segment aimed at. Lists with greater quantities will always be preferred. Tests are made to locate lists that can be continued at a profit. Lists that are small may not be considered for test purposes because there is "no place to go."

Sometimes the smaller list may embrace a greater portion of the known universe than a larger list. For example, an industrial magazine file of recipients, averaging, say, 1.7 records per plant, may be matched with a compiled list consisting of the same number of records. The compiled list, if representative of one record per plant, will cover a higher proportion of the totality.

The direct mailer must also consider a list's physical characteristics—factors relating to coverage and deliverability.

1. Size of the list
2. Age of names on the list
3. Cleanliness of the list

4. Duplication factor
5. Updating cycle and technique
6. Feedback for update
7. Zip code status
8. Titles
9. Individuals versus company names
10. Format and discipline
11. Method of reproduction
12. Cost factors in selecting, handling, and reproduction
13. Sequencing of file
14. Sequencing of crutch files (if any)
15. Selectivity (if any) and how handled

CHAPTER 7

Specialized Types of Lists and How They Work

PART I: INSIDE LISTS (INSIDE COMPANY OR ESTABLISHMENT)

HOT-LINE LISTS

The term *Hot Line* refers to the most recent names available from a list, either response oriented, or compiled. They can be any of the following:

1. New names in the current week or month
2. New names in the last three months
3. New names in the last six months
4. Latest names added to the file

Some mailers that use the advice given in the section on Testing to make certain that the newest names are utilized by the owner two or three times before releasing them for rental, have hot lines that should be initially called "just released" rather than "just received." These names qualify as the most current and selectable from a file placed on the market.*

---

*Some names of newly connected phone registrants are only available 60 to 90 days later to give the registrants time to decide whether to have their names offered for rental or not.

Recency is a remarkably important factor in direct mail. Many offers can make only the latest names work and no others. In fact, if the latest desired names of a list do not work out well, that is tantamount to predicting that no other segment of the list will be worth testing. Interestingly enough, many mailers tied into mailing only at programmed times use monthly hot-line lists. However, they mail a good portion of them three or six months later. The right way to mail hot-line names, when feasible, is as fast as they come on the market and can be delivered to you.

GIFT LISTS

Many consumer catalogs are able to capture the name of the giver of a gift as well as the names of the giftee, which is similar to tying together the name of a friend with the name of the customer who provides the name and address of a good prospect. Simply mailing a catalog at least acknowledges the availability of the new name. A far more subtle but effective form of merchandising is to mail the giver a form listing the name and address (and the gift) that he or she ordered and had sent last year. Such a form also includes space for a greeting to accompany each gift as well as a data column for when the gifts are to be sent. In a large operation the storage of such connected data must be computerized. Smaller operators can file these "lists" and use them prior to the holiday season.

WARRANTEES

Warrantees are mailed in by buyers at retail for tools, electronic equipment, (VCRs, TVs, and microwave ovens in particular) photographic equipment, lawn mowers, boats, snowmobiles, motorcycles—in other words, almost everything we use that moves or has moving parts.

Warrantee cards become mailing lists of "buyers of X or Y." With warrantee cards the specific item is denoted by its code number and is captured and can be utilized as a selection factor.

With the advice and help of mailing list managers, most warrantee cards now include basic demographic data including age, income, source of purchase, sex, and occasionally, family size and function.

The Lifestyle Selector list of several millions of respondents started out with, and still mainly consists of, names from photographic warrantee cards. The difference is this warrantee list compared with others is that it includes a sixty-question questionnaire that is answered in full by 15 percent of those who provide their own stamp and envelope to register their warrantees.

Warrantee names are not usually mail order buyers. But they do "respond" by direct mail. Thus they single themselves out from those who do not send in their warrantees by this response action. This may explain why these relatively low-level lists tend to work somewhat better than compiled files for selected mail-response offers.

TRADE SHOW LISTS

Although it is a good idea to look at the labels of any rental list, it is usually imperative that you inspect a sample of any list of trade show registrants.

Trade shows attract students, salespeople, the press, foreigners—all logical attendants but not perhaps the ones you want. Check what selections are available. Some show lists can be selected by business classification; others by functional title.

In addition, trade show lists often exhibit poor data-capture discipline with missing zip codes, wrong zips, and much duplication. Look. Study. Take Care!

FRIEND GET A FRIEND—CUSTOMER GET A CUSTOMER

Names that are elicited from satisfied customers are doubly important because

1. They can be virtually cost-free.
2. They are most often the most valuable names, other than the customer file, that can be obtained.

Many companies request their customers fill in a form with the name or names of those they believe wish to receive like offers. However, not one in one hundred offers to thank the recommender in any way, and most only mail offers to the names they receive without tying together the name of the recommender with their friends.

At this point, if data are available, it would be helpful to review the following:

1. What it costs to buy a request such as a catalog request.
2. What it costs, in promotional cost, to obtain a new customer.

Let's make a few cost assumptions here. Catalog requests (other than those elicited through the catalog itself) cost $2 each and they convert at 10 percent or a cost of $20. A new customer-by-mail requires the expenditure of $30 in promotion cost. (Thus if the cost in the mail is $300 and the response averages 1 percent or 10 per 1000, a sum of $30 has been expended for each new customer added.)

The assumption above indicates catalog requests are converted to customer status at a total cost *lower* than that required to buy new customers through direct mail. This arithmetic shows that the operator should "buy" as many catalog requests as possible (as long as the total cost of initial conversion is lower than that same cost per direct sale by direct mail).

That brings us back to "friend-of-a-friend" names. If conventional catalog requests produce one new customer per ten requests received, then friend-of-a-friend requests will produce a minimum of one new customer in five, more likely one in four. If we use one in five names as an example, such names are worth at least *twice* as much as conventional names.

Here we now have a name that is twice as valuable as one conventionally elicited and which has basically cost close to nothing to buy. Although the value is great, the numbers tend to be small because there is *no* reward to the recommenders (other than a nice feeling) for their valuable gifts. To change this into a bounteous flow, the promise of some small useful gift (often something in the catalog or an ink-on-paper-booklet) does wonders. Once the value of the name has been established, a gift providing a good part of this value can be considered.

There is, however, one important caveat about friend-of-a-friend mailings. Simply mailing the requested material to the friend will not elicit a high response. That highly anticipated response can only be elicited if the name of the referrer is clearly delineated as part of the mailing package. This personal touch is what gives life and lift to the concept of "friend get a friend."

MAGAZINE LISTS

Twenty-five years ago a list broker might have been hard pressed to offer five or ten rental files from known magazines. Fifteen years ago this list manager published a directory of individual magazine lists only, with ninety-seven titles. Today, it is difficult to find more than five or ten well known magazines, both consumer and business, that are not on the list rental market. The reasons are not difficult to discern. Magazine files that are current and deliverable but most of all "targeted" to specific markets make very attractive rental lists to mail order merchants, and the net rental dollars these magazine files generate without impeding or impinging on the basic operation of the publications are a welcome form of peripheral income. Certainly no other commercial activity of a magazine can substantiate a net profit nearly as high as list rentals.

A Look at What's Available

Magazine circulations tend to parallel the very markets sought by mail merchandisers. There are magazines for automobiles, hobbies, sports, leisure, travel, politics, education, science, science fiction, and every segment of business, institutions, and professionals covered by the SIC system (see page 322). There are magazines for plumbers, bankers, realtors, travel agents, freight forwarders, executive recruiters as well as for 200 kinds of manufacturers and over 50 types of wholesalers. Magazines cover humor, public affairs, sex (dressed and undressed), parenting, decoration, flowers, over-the-road vehicles, museums, zoos and so on. If enough U.S. citizens are engaged in a specific or specialized activity, there is almost certainly a magazine serving their specialized needs. There are over 400 consumer magazines that accept advertising and over 4,000 business and industrial journals. In addition, there are over 7,500 newsletters—each of them finely targeted to a specific audience (in some cases even more finely targeted than a magazine because newsletters tend to have smaller and more sharply defined audiences than magazines serving the same areas of interest). Another source of printed data, also targeted toward specific interests is the 4,000 internal house organs produced primarily by major companies for their employees. A few hundred of these major companies produce an external house organ mainly for the edification of their stockholders.

Although some rentals are obtained from newsletters and some rare rentals for special offers (usually of public intent) are obtained from house organ lists, it is the magazine files that mailers turn to for lists prequalified as to readership, income, and specialized interest.

Reaching New Sources

Business-to-business mailers have access to a number of different list sources:

1. Compiled files of establishments by SIC
2. Compiled files of executives by function
3. Mail order buyer lists
4. Magazine files

It is a relatively rare successful business-to-business offer that finds no magazine worthy of a continuation.

On the consumer side, magazines may provide the one best avenue to reach a given market. For example, to reach affluent young people, structured lists by income rarely provide adequate coverage of heads of families under the age of thirty-five. However, readers of *Psychology Today, Playboy, MS, New York, Village Voice, Ski,* and selected automotive and sports titles provide an excellent concentration of them.

To reach the upper eschelons of the affluent market (with the added boon that all of a magazine's lists are known to be readers and subscribers by mail) mailers may include such magazines as *Architectural Digest, Forbes, Town and Country,* and *Vogue* on their list schedules.

To reach those businesspeople most likely to embrace the new, many list schedules include *Inc., Venture, Boardroom Reports,* and selected segments of *Business Week.* However, knowing that a magazine covers an area of interest is not sufficient for the direct-mail expert as each magazine publishes data (usually a wealth of data) about the market it serves and how the list it offers is constructed.

The Audit Bureau of Circulation

Most consumer magazines are audited by the Audit Bureau of Circulation (ABC) every twelve months. Although media buyers look at such esoteric data as grace period, print order, and back starts, the direct mailer is primarily interested in the answer to three questions: (1) how do recipients become listed on the file? (2) how much do they pay in relation to the full subscription charge? and (3) when do their subscriptions start? Selection is almost always available on the basis of recency, and many mailers who use consumer magazines (usually to sell other consumer magazines) find only the latest names are worthy of use. Names sold by direct mail (and not by DM agents) are preferable, when selectable. "Mail order sold" includes DM agent sold when these sold by direct mail are not selectable.

There are three large mailers who create their own co-op offer of multiple magazines at discount prices. The best known of these is Publishers Clearing House (PCH). PCH pays all the expenses of its huge mailings. Through PCH, the average buyer subscribes to four or five magazines. The publication receives a small fraction of the sales income received by PCH (in the 10 percent range) plus a tape of the new subscribers. Names sold in this way are less desirable for direct-mail offers than those sold by solo direct mail.

Lower in quality for direct-mail use are "field-sold" subscribers as they are not mail order buyers. They are subscribers who were acquired by magazine agents going door-to-door to obtain bulk orders for multiple magazines. Some of these magazines are "add-ons" produced by the blandisments of the sales agent and as six, seven, or eight magazines begin coming at one time, readership of any given title can be quite small. Field-sold bulk orders are usually billed and collected over a somewhat extended period.

Renewals

One class of subscribers that can prove quite valuable to mailers is the renewed subscriber, particularly if the subscription was originally generated by direct mail. The best class of these subscribers consists of those who have renewed more than once. These subscribers have paid full price for the publication for at least two consecutive years. They are confirmed readers of the magazine—and confirmed mail order buyers—because renewals are virtually all created through direct mail.

"Grace" service—to a group of former subscribers or trial subscribers who have not renewed—should be omitted. A good proportion, 50 percent or more of these, depending on the magazine, will not renew. It is fair to say they are less interested in the editorial approach of the magazine than those who have just subscribed or resubscribed. Grace service can continue for three months beyond the end of a paid-for subscription or trial and still count in the rate base. Graced subscriptions are not desirable as far as direct response use is concerned.

Print media subscribers are, after direct-mail subscribers and renewals (conversions, renewals, and renewals of renewals) the next best bet for direct response. Most print buyers (and for that matter most direct-mail subscribers) come from other magazines. They are, in effect, already doubly screened for readership and interest.

Exchanges for lists in the magazine world are often made page for page rather than name for name. If exchange-created names will be used for direct mail, it is a good idea to find out which magazines were involved in the exchange, and how well their subscriber base correlates with the magazine file that is rented.

"Intro" subscribers in good part accepted at half price, may sound like a poor bet but the factor of recency is so powerful that these often make up the majority of the only segment some magazine promoters can use.

"Blow-ins" are part of the hot line. They are now coming online at a discounted rate but it is obvious that someone reading the magazine was prompted to enter a new subscription (or attempted, usually successfully) to add to a current subscription at a discount price.

Agent-sold subscriptions almost always have a lower renewal rate but if they are current they will also be part of the latest hot-line adds. Therefore, they will be more responsive to new offers than the more solid subscriber base. However, field-sold new adds should be omitted if possible . . . as they tend to be less desirable names for mail promoters.

When a new subscriber is given the choice of paying on credit or with cash in advance, a large proportion of credit "buyers" fail to pay the bill. Until the magazine stops service, such non-pays, or "offs" receive the magazine. Their demographics have not changed because they have not paid but the proportion of offs is some measure of the pull of the magazine. From a direct-mail point of view, offs are live, recent, new, and show up in quantity in the hot lines offered by almost all publishers.

Only the most sophisticated magazine list purveyors will make available some of the ABC characteristics noted here, however when they are available, selection by them can improve response.

Most consumer magazine files offer the following minimum selection:

1. Sex
2. Geography
3. Recency
4. Inquiries versus buyers

When possible, those selections should be augmented with:

1. Direct mail versus print acquisition
2. Renewal history
3. Source data

At the very least, an analysis of ABC statements will indicate which magazines are most likely to prove productive. Finding out who has used the magazine list successfully, and which part of it was most successful (as indicated by continuations) is even more valuable. However, these data are not always easy to come by.

Price and Order Considerations

Magazines that start out controlled—that is, free and then attempt to convert all or most recipients to paying customers, need to go through an entire set of cost variables. What is the order margin? What part of the subscription price does it cost to fulfill—that is to establish, interfile, control, and bill a name, collect the subscription price; and print and mail the publication for the given term? How long must a subscriber be held to recover the promotional investment to obtain the conversion? What is the anticipated renewal rate for Year 2? For Year 3? How good is the cash flow? (This determines how long at a given cost per order the publisher can continue to invest in "buying" subscribers.)

Let's see how this works out in an example.

- Subscription price is $15.00 for service for a year
- Mailing cost $300/M
- Fulfillment cost $6/Subscription (Printing, Control, Mailing)
- Order margin $15.00 less $6.00 = $9.00 per subscription
- Average response   1.8%-or 18 new orders per 1000 pieces mailed

- Eighteen orders per
  M(mailed) × $15.00 per order   = $270.00
- Cost in the mail, per M   = $300.00
- Loss per 1000 pieces mailed   = $ 30.00
- Loss to acquire new customer   = 18 at cost of $30.00
    = $ 1.67 per new subscriber

Actually this, for purchase of a new subscriber, is only part of the story, because the cost of fulfillment, $6 per subscriber per year in this example must be added to the minus $1.67 per subscriber, so the actual loss per new subscriber is $7.67, not $1.67.

Where a conversion from a free or controlled subscription is made to a paid one, this is not adding a new name to the list—and the cost of fulfillment is already being borne for the controlled name.

If the publisher seeks to get 10,000 conversions in a year, the publisher will be required to advance (at 18 orders per 1000 conversion pieces in the mail at $300/M) the cost of mailing of 555,000 pieces—for a total of out-of-pocket of $166,000. *Wrong*. Although it is true that eighteen conversions per 1000 mailings to obtain 10,000 paid subscribers will require 555,000 pieces, and 555 × $300/M = $166,000, the prudent publisher will not advance $166,000, but more likely one-tenth of this, or $16,600. This same sum will then be used as a revolving investment ten times over the course of the year. The example here shows that each mailing will return almost the total sum advanced, so the publisher will have the use of this same investment over and over again.

With only one possible exception—*The National Geographic* which has a fantastically high renewal rate of over 90 percent—every paid-for publication in America "buys" its subscribers at a loss.

The publisher of a 100 percent paid-for publication has, in some respects, a much harder row to hoe on a continuous basis than the publisher attempting to convert from controlled to paid. The former must produce enough new adds each period to replace those who fail to renew. For the average successful paid publication that means from 30 to 40 percent (over 50 percent in the case of a home handyman type magazine) of the total circulation must be replaced each year just to keep circulation at the same quantity. To increase circulation means "buying" more new subscribers on top of such replacements. And since all such new subscribers are purchased at a cost, this is a never ending form of investment that a paid-for publisher is involved in. (For that matter so is the cost of replacing losses per year by magazines with controlled or qualified circulation.)

From a mailing point of view, it is this very fact that 30, 40, 50 percent of the circulation of a magazine is new and different each year that makes magazine lists so attractive. This is particularly true if only the latest names added turn out to be responsive enough to justify continuing use.

Magazine Hot Lines

Hot lines mean the most recent subscribers added to the files. In the case of a magazine, this is a continuous process and new names are added monthly. Typically, another magazine using this attractive list segment will mail once or twice a year as part of a major mailing program. Thus, the average "new adds" will typically be anywhere from two months to six months old. In fact, if only those added in, say, the last four months are ordered, a fair amount of bona fide "new adds" will never be accessed. The right way to use hot-line lists is on a regular monthly basis, in which the latest names are mailed just as fast as they are added to the magazine file being used. You "buy" recency as a selection factor on hot-line lists and they should be mailed as soon as they become available.

You might now ask: why would anyone keep on mailing when the dollars returned are less than the dollars expended? Good question. It has a good answer. Let us look ahead a few years and make a few more assumptions:

1. 50 percent of the first year subscribers can be induced to subscribe for a second year.

2. 80 percent of those who subscribed for two years in succession will subscribe for the next year.

3. 90 percent of those who have subscribed for three years or more will subscribe for the following year.

You are now looking at a scenario that every paid circulation publisher in America constantly looks at. If a new subscriber is worth X amount of dollars today, that same subscriber may be worth three times that much a few years from now. It is evident that the publisher who must buy new subscribers at a cost can come out "whole," if he or she can afford to wait several years to amortize acquisition cost.

Case Example: How to Amortize the Cost to Buy a New Subscriber

Let us now look at an example of how a magazine publisher amortizes the cost to buy a new subscriber. Let us assume that a solo mail campaign for a major magazine with an annual subscription price of $17.50 brings in new subscribers at a cost of $30.00. (This hypothetical example calls for 1 percent or 10 subscribers per 1,000 pieces mailed, with a promotional cost in the mail of $300/M.) The ten new subscribers produce $175.00. Thus there is a loss of $125 per 1,000 pieces in the mail, or a cost to buy a $17.50 subscription at an investment of $12.50. This would indicate it would have been far less expensive to "give away" subscriptions except that only those readers who have paid for a new subscription can be expected to pay for a renewal.

The mathematics of that $12.50 loss per subscriber works out like this:

50% of the new subscribers will renew at $17.50	$ 8.75
80% of those on the rolls at the end of one year will renew again	7.00
90% of those on the rolls at the end of two years will renew again.	6.30
	$22.05

This looks as though the pay out is halfway through the second year of the renewal series but that calculation takes into account the cost of promotion only. In this example, to print and mail the magazine for a year costs $4.50. So the loss was not $12.50 for the first year subscriber but was actually $4.50 more, or $17.00.

In the next year, the fulfillment was down to 50 percent or $2.25 per subscriber so the sum to make up for is now $19.25. Eighty percent of that 50 percent equals $1.80 more, or a total of $21.05 to amortize. Thus it is not until the subscriber has renewed *three* times that the cost of promotion, plus the cost of fulfillment, has been amortized.

Let us look at another side of renewals—what they tell us about the magazine and its readership. If three paid circulation magazines in a publisher's stable show renewal rates of 40, 70, and 90 percent and you have been given the responsibility to fire two people, one from each of two of the three magazines, who would you fire and why? Interestingly enough, the three widely differing renewal rates give a good insight into what must be done.

The magazine with a renewal rate of 40 percent indicates a definite problem with the editorial contents. The magazine cannot deliver what the promotion promises. (This may be due to promotions that promise too much but it is more likely to be a weakness of the product produced. That sounds as though a new editor would be the practical approach to take.)

The magazine with a 90 percent renewal rate suffers from poor promotion. It is reaching and holding the "hard core" that becomes the bedrock of a successful periodical but the promotion is not expanding enough to locate new subscribers some of whom could possibly become part of an expanded hard core later on. You may want to fire the promotion director or the person who limits the budget—who just may happen to be the publisher!

The magazine with a 70 percent renewal rate is doing very nicely. It is holding 90 percent of its hard core and attracting 40, 45, 50 percent of its new subscribers to renew.

When the entire file of one consumer magazine provides a fruitful market for either another magazine or a direct-mail effort, the same or similar mailing tends to produce the same results a year later. There are two reasons for this. The mailing hits a likely chord in the renewal portion of the magazine and it is also exposed to a sufficiently high proportion of new subscribers who are the more likely to buy. When a retest fails to hit a desired response rate six months later, the rationale indicates that not enough change has taken place in the list. Only if results are extraordinary, can the active list be utilized two or more times in the course of a year.

NEWSPAPER LISTS

Newspapers are the source of several unique lists:

- Lists of engaged couples can be found in small town newspapers as well as reports of the marriages that follow.

- Some ghoulish investigators pick up death notices.

- Business newspapers provide excellent data on newly promoted executives. The *Wall Street Journal* is particularly useful for keeping in touch with executive changes in big business.

- Legal notices are a specialized source. When there are theatrical and real estate syndications, the names and addresses of all participants must be published as a legal notice. Some major city dailies cover arrival of out-of-town buyers. Candidates for local offices can be found here in political seasons as well as award winners in various fields.

The major use of a newspaper's list for direct-response prospecting is to provide a means to deliver the welter of self-standing stuffers to subscribers. The majority of home-delivered daily newspapers in the United States now provides "total market coverage" which is obtained by mailing via third class occupant mail to that share of the market not serviced on the home-delivery rolls.

It is little known that preprinted self-standing stuffers (all for prospecting) have exceeded all direct mail with advertising (for prospecting) put together. Self-standing stuffers are now approaching 60 billion pieces per year. Direct-mail prospecting with advertising now totals 30 billion pieces. This competitive picture may have aroused the American Newspaper Publishers Association (ANPA) to claim bitterly that there are preferential rates for third class bulk mailings (the chief class of mailing used for carrying advertising).

Freestanding advertising purportedly represents over 15 percent of all newspaper advertising revenues—$3.2 billion of $20.6 billion. Newspaper revenues from newspaper inserts have grown every year for the last decade. Newspapers distribute 80 percent of cents-off coupons. Direct mail obtains only 4 percent.

More and more daily newspapers are now offering demographic selectivity by delivery zones. These do not, for the most part, approach the pointillistic demographics available through direct mail but rather delineate markets that are less appealing and can be eliminated by zonal selection. One Los Angeles newspaper now provides over one hundred zones to select from.

Split tests of self-standing stuffers can be developed with the help of a knowledgeable printer who can print two or four versions of the stuffer and distribute each equally throughout the newspaper circulation.

CABLE TV LISTS

Five "Cablese" Terms and What They Mean

It is helpful in discussing Cable TV to understand these "cablese" list terms:

1. Franchise territory
2. Homes passed
3. Homes wired
4. Customer files
5. Add-on sales

The *franchise territory* is the area usually designated by zip code and city or county limits, in which the operator has an exclusive franchise to provide service.

The *homes passed* area, within the franchised territory, includes all homes passed by cable wires that are installed. This may not, and usually does not, cover the entire franchised area. Certain locations such as hills, an area across a major highway or bridge, or an area of poverty may be missed because it is deemed uneconomic to lay wires there. Homes passed are denoted by beginning and ending street numbers street by street.

Homes wired are within homes passed by wires but may not, and usually are not, equal to them. There may be vacant apartment buildings on the street, vacant lots or turbulent buildings, or some geographical anomaly.

The customer files include current customers for regular cable operator service, as well as expires. The add-ons are those that pay, both currently or in the past, for such for-pay services as HBO or for-pay special programs.

The lists of customers, expires, and add-ons are maintained very carefully by each system and customers pay the cost for the service. However, the essential lists of homes passed that can be obtained from outside sources are generally in poor condition irrespective of the system.

In cities, the chief lack is a source of data for the number and designation of apartments in multiple-dwelling units. As this book was going to press, not one system in one hundred has this data in its homes-passed lists.

How Cable Operators Can Obtain List Help

More cable operators are turning to the list rental market for some peripheral income and are thus becoming list purveyors themselves. Cable operators need list help as well as overlay data to build data banks from their homes-passed lists for future segmented marketing.

For the smaller cable systems requiring access to 2,000 or less names, the ideal methodology seems to be to furnish each operator with a set of pressure-sensitive mailing labels for *every* dwelling unit in areas delineated by three-digit and five-digit zip codes in street and number order. (For lists of this size there is no economic way to select occupant data by street number, although if carrier routes are known, every occupant mailer in the country can select on that basis.) These pressure-sensitive labels can be titled "Occupant," "Resident," "Cable TV Patron," or something similar for every dwelling unit including every apartment coded by its appropriate letter or number. These lists can be carrier-route coded and thus can be sorted back to the carrier. The franchisee can remove subscribers as well as areas not served, and have a complete mailing list of prospects as a result.

Sad but true, many smaller cable companies can only provide records on hard copy. For any data processing to proceed, such data must first be converted to magnetic tape. Some systems are magnetic in form but are on diskettes which are not easily made to be compatible with magnetic tape. Some systems can only provide list data in print image format (which is useless for merge–purge purposes); some are in non-EBCDIC mode. Some are still on 7-track drives for Honeywell or Univac. Variants abound!

For larger franchises, more data are needed. The methodology required involves provision or creation of a locater file defining geographic parameters, plus utilization of an occupant file (the only way to get a total list of households in the homes-passed area), plus the use of one of the major telephone–auto lists or driver-license lists to add demographic data to each home passed. (One interesting note here is that the names of individuals living in apartments do not have apartment numbers on them, so using two lists for overlays may provide all apartment numbers and some individuals at apartments but no data to tie the two together.)

In this way larger franchises can obtain

1. Complete and current lists of homes passed.
2. Such demographics as age, income, probability of children, which can then be added to 50 or 60 percent of all records, including customers and expires, as well as all prospects.
3. Every business office, institution, and office of a professional can also be identified and logged on the completed file, if desired.
4. Mail order buying characteristics by matching the cable customer list with major lists of publications which primarily determine interest in sports and cultural activities.

Data-Base Coverage

Much is made of the term *data bank*. If ever there was an industry that needed data-base coverage of its market area, it is Cable TV. The cable operator has a defined market (homes passed), a specific mix of customers and prospects (based on demographic factors) and a need to reach specialized groups within a defined area for special promotions. It is clear to many in the list fraternity that the cable TV field needs list people to clean up cable lists, expand coverage, and provide the means to address three major problems of Cable TV everywhere: (1) "churn" as customers subscribe, then quit, then re-subscribe, then quit again, (2) sophisticated access to groups by demographics, and (3) complete access to all households within their franchise.

Once the homes-passed file has been corrected for its missing households and apartments, a pass can be made against one of the major name files with individual demographic data by household as well as median data for segments, such as zip codes and carrier routes. (Such lists have data on subblocks and enumeration districts but these cannot be matched against the cable list). Major data that can be attached to a fair sized portion of the individual households, with medians at least for the balance, are:

- An individual family income
- Length of residence
- Sex of head of household (as given by the phone book)
- Ten-digit local phone number
- Ownership of a registered car
- Additional group data on:

    Median age of head of household
    Number of children under eighteen per one hundred families
    Value of the home
    Proportion of home ownership
    Median level of education

Once such data are tagged, the operator can group characteristics to reach "golden age" groups, families with children, families by income and so on. The operator will then be in position to target certain designed offers to reach identified segments.

Add-on services, such as movies and Sports channels for pay have their own type of churning and as far as list use is concerned, are because of size of little interest locally. Nationwide interest is another matter, and such lists are either coming on the market or plans are being developed to do this.

There has been tremendous debate over the privacy of Cable TV subscriber files. From a mailing list point of view, the whole issue is moot. The lists are not that useful or important. Even lists from large local markets are finding modest play when they tiptoe into the rental market. There are now over 6,000 systems! By dint of a federal law, in good part promulgated with the help of the Direct Marketing Association, Cable TV subscribers must be informed of "potential commercial disclosure" and given the option of "negative check-off" before their names can be released when files are made available for rental.

LIST FORMS AND USES

Originally Researched Lists

For some time the only lists of importance that could claim to be originally researched (on which each record has been individually checked) were the lists of big business compiled by Dun & Bradstreet and Standard and Poors. About 15 years ago, MDR, which made its mark initially in the educational field, produced a school file for which every one of the 16,000 school districts in the United States with 200 pupils or more was individually surveyed. (Dun & Bradstreet which purchased MDR in 1985 is continuing this practice. QED, the other major compiler of school lists also bases its data on interviews made with each school district each year. QED provides its originally researched lists for inclusion in a national list exclusively to Data Base America.)

Dun & Bradstreet has individually researched doctors at business addresses for which names, addresses, and phone numbers have all been verified. To this list it has recently added relatively complete lists of insurance agents and real estate agents, as well as a list of the so-called "cottage industry," individuals running businesses from their homes. These additions may be temporary, as D&B notes that updating, a costly procedure where each name must be reverified, will depend on how well these lists are accepted by the market.

The Medec list (see page 297) is based on annual questionnaires. City directories (see page 289) are based on scheduled recanvassing of all households in a given area. A new list of government officials in which all relevant address data even to room number comes from phone interviews has also been placed on the market. (U.S. Government names without room numbers may not be deliverable.)

Small, Specialized Lists

Most list owners and compilers have established minimum charges based on a test sample of 5,000 names. (Fewer names can be obtained but the minimum charge may make the price per name somewhat prohibitive.) There is a considerable number of list needs that call for smaller quantities, for example, Fortune 500, the 550 members of Congress, 600 banks with foreign desks, 200 restaurant and motel chains, and many more. By dint of a bit of "shopping," it is usually possible to get list suppliers to "break" their minimums for such a small quantity. Or you may get two or three sets of labels at the minimum charge.

However, there are small specialized lists that are too esoteric for precompiling by the list compiling and list wholesaling fraternity. This includes registrants at a given special meeting, signers of a given petition, people who attend art auctions of a given kind, or owners of a given breed. For a given mailer these small specialized "on target" lists are truly golden but they must be acquired by the mailer or publication that needs them. They cannot be provided at an economically justifiable cost by a list professional.

Third Party Endorsement Lists and Syndications

In its usual guise without an endorser, solo mail is a two-way street between the mailer and the customer. In third party endorsement, the mailer provides the pieces that have been "personalized" with the endorsement of the list owner who then circularizes the list. The third party here is the endorser whose list is being used.

In most instances, orders go to the originator of the mailing (either directly or more usually second-hand through the list owner) and the originator fulfills the orders. Almost all third party endorsement mailings are fulfilled by drop shipments. The list owner never has to take in inventory (although he or she will find him- or herself in the middle on return goods.)

The process of providing both product and offering literature through stuffers for gasoline card statements, utility billings, or expensive four-color creative pieces for third-party endorsed direct mail is called *syndication*. The creator syndicates pieces (and then personalizes each use) for mailing by multiple list owners. It is not unusual for the creator to make provisions to handle the "paper" created by offering credit terms on large-size purchases.

It is important at the outset to provide a written stipulation as to the ownership of the names. Do they belong to the mailer, who has sent the offer over his or her own list, or do they belong to the entrepreneur who has made the goods available and arranged for drop shipping them as orders are received? One good way to solve this is to permit both companies to use the names generated—but only for their own offers. If the list is to come on the market through one company and not the other, an agreed-upon split on revenues can resolve any questions that may come up later.

Unless expressly and explicitly specified, such names do *not* belong to the fulfillment bureau that is charged with the task of capturing the order data and shipping the goods. The same is true of lists created by product refunds or premium redemptions. Such lists are not owned by the fulfillment house. It is true some lists do come on the market through such services when a fallingout occurs with the principal. If such lists are to be considered, it is good practice to make certain the initial owner of the names is authorizing use. Someone who offers names obtained through efforts by a major company should be able to substantiate the right to offer them. Where this right is not available, lists tentatively offered by fulfillment companies tend to fade away.

International Lists

The majority of list sources available to U.S. mailers that seek international coverage are the 500 multinational mail response and magazine subscriber files with overseas segments. In general, these lists are available through U.S. list brokers, some of which are on an exchange basis only. The fact they are from English-speaking sources indicates that English can be used acceptably.

Gower Publishing Co., Ltd. publishes a relatively comprehensive catalog of compiled businesses and mail order respondents for Great Britain. In addition, this catalog also lists a number of listings for continental Europe. The firm of Market Location Ltd. is a specialist in developing leads for businesses in England. Counterparts for industrial pharmaceutical and professional and academic lists can be found in most European countries.

In the United States the chief specialist for direct mailing overseas is Dillon and Agnew, with offices in New York and on the continent. This firm offers its years of experience in the creation, printing, and mailing of offers to each foreign country.

Books, magazines, financial services, cassettes, tapes, seminars, and educational products tend to cross international borders with few hitches, but typical mail order products run into classic customs hurdles and costs. Insurance and fundraising also require careful individual handling for each country.

How to Reach Influentials in America: Twelve Main Areas of Classification

One hope of many public-relations personnel is that a list of influential people will become available for distribution of major speeches, news of acceptance awards, special appointments, and important events concerning top executives of their firms.

It so happens no such list exists—nor should it exist—because each company seeks to go out to different constituencies at different times. Thus a good list of influentials is one that is compiled to order, constituency by constituency.

Lists compiled to order reduce the suppliers to those few who have the sources and the will to take on this type of specialized compiling.

It should be noted that sources are ordinarily quite conventional. The use to which they are put and the range of requirements make work in this field a far cry from running a few thousand names and addresses from a precompiled data bank.

A well honed "influentials" list can have only two or three inputs, or two or three dozen, depending on the constituencies to cover and the importance of the need.

These constituencies are usually encompassed within the following basic classifications:

- Politics
- Labor
- Education
- Professionals
- Business
- Finance
- Engineering
- Science
- Social Services
- Clergy
- Farming
- Media

A source book available through Ed Burnett Consultants contains over 200 sources that can be tapped. (Copies are available by writing PR Desk Burnett, 99 West Sheffield Avenue, Englewood, N.J. 07631.) Some idea of the vast coverage available through the source book follows.

Politics and Government	
Congress	550
Congressional staff	1,500
State legislators	7,500
State and county chairpeople	6,000
Armed forces installations	400
Planning commissions	5,000
Labor	
National and international unions	180
Labor press	200
Labor leaders	1,000

Education
Senior colleges	2,000
Junior colleges	1,000
Business managers of colleges	1,500
Superintendents of school boards (by largest number of pupils)	4,000
Special librarians	11,000
Training directors	23,000
Professors at college (by 200 disciplines)	647,500

Professionals

Medical

Doctors (by thirty-five specialties)
Dentists (by six specialties)
Hospital administrators (by number of beds)
Out-patient care (by Discipline)

Legal Services
Major firms	10,000
ABA committee members	3,500

Accounting and Bookkeeping (as well as architects, management consultants, public relations firms, advertising agencies)
Firms
One person offices
Participants and partners at firms

Engineering

There are over 1,000,000 engineers available within forty disciplines including
Aerospace
Automotive
Chemical
Plastic
Civil
Design
Mechanical
Electronic
Nuclear

Business

For classifications see "of S.I.C.," page 322
Selection by
    number of employees
    sales volume
    area

classification
executives by name and twenty-three functional titles
Fortune 1st 500 industrials
Fortune 2nd 500 industrials
Fortune (6 × 50) 300 top nonindustrials, also top 1000
S&P second 1,000 industrials, second 1,000 nonindustrials
35,000 top women executives at major companies
National advertisers
Subscribers to major magazines
Industrial laboratories
Computer operations
Companies with foreign investment
Exporters and importers

Finance
Same SIC selection as business
Same size, employees, area and classification
 with executives
Banks
Savings and loans
Credit unions
Insurance
Real estate
Stock and bond brokers
Bankers involved in foreign trade
Financial analysts
Trade-show managers

Science
There are over 1,500,000 scientists and
 technocrats as well as several million people trained
 in computer use. Lists are available by
 specialization, including
 Physicists
 Mathematicians
 Chemists
 Biologists
 Operations Research
 Geophysicists
 Think tanks
 Government grantees

Social services
Associations
Chambers of commerce
Foundations
Fraternal orders
Youth organizations

Drug and alcohol remedial programs
Poverty law programs

Church and clergy
  Churches with edifices—180,000 churches
   including forty sects
  Catholic hierarchy
  Jewish synagogues and centers
  Protestant leadership

Farming
  Selection is available by
   Cultivated acres
   Type of crop
   State and county areas
   County agents

Media
  Radio
  TV
  Newspapers
  Magazines
  Newsletters
  House organs

There are two New York City services: Media Distribution and Public Relations Aids which update lists of every editor, writer, and broadcaster for every medium on a *daily* basis. Where selectivity by subject matter, use of pictures, and names of the executives in charge is of prime importance for a public relations release no commercial compiler can match their coverage.

Matched City Pairs

Airlines are particularly interested in lists that link travelers in a given city with a prospective need to go to some other city on their routes. For example, if a home office and several branch plants are served by a given airline, the executives who can be located at these locations might qualify as above-average prospects. The development of large executive data banks for the first time offers a source for this particular need.

One major realtor who had to fill a new large building used this concept in reverse. He had this compiler produce a list of companies with branches in Manhattan and home offices outside the state. His mailings led to a major home office change by a company enabled through a major rental agreement to identify its new headquarters as the XYZ Building.

A somewhat less esoteric use of matched city pairs is to identify two cities of comparable population, manufacturing, and geography, and utilize two different forms of promotion in theme, or one common form of promotion in both, plus a support program in just one. Compilers are occasionally called upon to provide lists by area (and by classification) to satisfy such marketing and research needs.

The "Great Name Drain"

It is likely that every company, even those engaged in direct response, suffers from the "Great Name Drain." Retailers, with few exceptions, do not know the names of customers unless they appear in their billing records. Most retailers who accept payment by credit cards fail to capture—and later use—names and addresses of this group of affluent buyers. For example, one company purchased 38,000 leads for a $4,500 machine by direct mail, and could find only 6,000 leads when a remailing was proposed. A major merchandiser of communications gear generates 150,000 technical inquiries to its engineering department and provides name data on less than 4 percent of these inquiries. One major magazine without being aware of it, is currently renting its own expires out to magazine agencies who then get paid almost the full value for renewals that the magazine itself could pick up for less than 10 percent.

One manufacturer gets its purchase order confirmations from purchasing agents (who are not decision makers on technical purchases) and discards the name of the party ordering—in many cases this is the very decision maker who belongs on the permanent customer rolls.

At one of the top fifty companies in the country, this author was surprised to find a thorough penetration analysis (share of market) on hand for every two, three, or four-digit SIC—but only for rentals. The following conversation with the marketing director took place:

"Great, remarkable! Now let's look at sales."

"We don't keep records on sales."

"What proportion of placements are now sales and not rentals?"

(Reluctantly) "About 11 percent."

"Is that cumulative or current?"

(Very low voice) "Cumulative."

"What is the current proportion?"

(Very faintly) "33 percent."

A major mail order operator keeps the "bill to" address (which is often only an accounts payable department) on file and disregards the valuable information on new sites offered by an analysis of the "ship to" records.

Some mail order operators who offer gift handling at holiday periods carefully maintain the giver and toss away the names of the donees, all of whom have been adequately "sampled" with wares paid for by the giver.

Few companies pick up names and addresses of those customers interested enough to write in on their own stationery to complain, comment, or seek some help. These "white mail" names are often the most valuable names a mail order operator can receive. Similarly, few companies register the names and addresses of individuals considered worthy of a written reply.

I can show you a dozen companies who file written quotations, usually for multiple units or some special order, and who have never extracted names and addresses from these above-average prospects to add to their mailing lists. In addition, a fair proportion of all inquiries considered worthy of service, in the form of a packet of information or a booklet, are discarded.

Not too long ago, tens of thousands of entrants to a major sweepstakes offer of an original Rockwell print were trashed after the winner had been selected by the company that judged the contest. A great number of warrantees, carefully filled-in with name data and product information, end up as useless bales of paper because they were not converted to magnetic tape.

It seems as though the Great Name Drain is an American tradition. Even today, when more and more business people realize how valuable names and addresses are, this drain continues. Hardly any one in business (or out for that matter) will fail to pick up a dime on the street—but large numbers of businesses let thousands upon thousands of dimes, quarters, and dollars simply drain away by not using the names and addresses they receive.

Retail name drain

Murray Raphael, who lectures on the Great Name Drain to retailers on three continents, uses this true story in almost every speech he gives.

An owner of a local supermarket called Murray for lunch. He was depressed by his sales figures which were $30,000 short of breaking even nearly every week. His first anniversary was coming up, and unless he could get his numbers up he would have to go out of business. Murray asked him what kind of promotion he was doing and the answer was

"Oh, the usual newspaper pages and some circulars to all homes in the trading area—about 75,000 tabloids a shot."

"Do you have a list?"

"Naw, what's a list?"

"Don't you keep a list of your customers?"

"No."

"Do you let your good customers cash checks and pay by check?"

"Of course!"

"How do you know who's okay?"

"I have this shoebox full of cards and we check them."

"What's on the cards?"

"Names"

"And addresses?"

"Of course!"

"That's a list, man."

"Oh."

Mailings to that list quickly changed the store from unprofitable to profitable. The shoebox full of unused names and addresses of the store's best customers typifies the Great Name Drain going on all around us.

Despite the fact that almost everyone in retailing is aware that customers are the mainstay of business and people who come in to shop or to buy are the lifeblood of the business, few retailers attempt to obtain a name and address in the store. For one of the giants in the computer business I once calculated that it would cost over $12 in promotional costs to get a neighbor to visit a new computer store. Then I calculated the staff could not "afford" the $.15 it might take to obtain the name and address.

Retailers might well take a lesson from Tandy Corporation, whose store managers are measured, in part, on the percentage of addresses that are illegible, incomplete, or that prove to be wrong addresses. To ensure better compilation of all names, the clerk—not the customer—must fill in the sales slip information. (Even with this system, about one-fourth of addresses are still incorrect.) The major error in gathering this information turns out to be the zip code. One-third of all customers either do not know or incorrectly report their own zip codes. (Tandy Corporation corrects this by adding zip codes after the customer's name and address are converted to their mailing list.)

PART II SPECIALIZED MAIL ORDER RESPONSE LISTS

CULTURAL LISTS

Although there is a considerable correlation between affluence and cultural interest, affluence alone is not enough. For example, to booksellers a $12,000 postgraduate student who buys books is a better bet than an executive who makes $50,000 a year but has not bought a new book since college. The main emphasis should be on "proof" of cultural interest such as

- Buyers of books, records, tapes
- Readers of magazines
- Buyers of tickets to
    theatre
    opera
    dance
    symphony
    avant garde movies
- Members of
    museums
    cultural associations
- Supporters of
    zoos
    museums
    endangered cultural activities

There are many peripheral lists that indicate cultural interest, most of which can be grouped under travel, specialty mail order buyers, and selected sports. A list of these follows.

- Travelers
    Passport holders
    VAT buyers (value-added taxation on overseas imports)
    World cruise buyers
- Specialty mail order buyers
    Art
    Sculpture

> Fountains
> Gourmet food
> Wine
> Interior decor
> Designer clothing

A number of magazines are designed to serve the cultural scene. Among them are

> *Architectural Digest*
>
> *Arizona Highways*
>
> *Bon Appetit*
>
> *"W"*
>
> *Travel/Leisure*
>
> *Town and Country*
>
> *Vanity Fair*
>
> *New Yorker*
>
> *New York Review of Books*
>
> *Smithsonian*
>
> *American Museum of Natural History*

As a devotee of opera is an ideal prospect for dance, theatre, arts fairs, or museum appeals, the lists of buyers and supporters for a number of cultural activities in several major cities have been merged, and this unduplicated list is made available to each participant as an "insider." The list may also be rented to approved "outside" renters. Where the function is local and such a list is available it should be the primary list utilized.

Virtually all cultural operations print a report on their activities. These reports include the names (but not the addresses) of trustees, donors, benefactors, and officers. These names can be compiled and then checked (laboriously!) against local phone books for local addresses to build a list of prospective major donors. In any such endeavor the list of foundations that provide funds for cultural activities should be included.

There is a correlation between engaging in specific sports and cultural outlook. While not a perfect correlation, those people who read *Tennis* magazine or one of the squash journals are certain to be more interested in cultural affairs than those who follow bowling or baseball. Golfers who belong to private clubs and have their handicaps provided by computer are more likely to support a cultural event than readers of golf magazines.

HOW TO SELECT LISTS FOR FUNDRAISING

There are four major constituencies approached by fundraisers: contributors, and 3 classes of prospects (foundations, businesses, people). Foundations are always addressed to the institutional office (the business office). For business contributions, businesses are almost always addressed to business offices. For people contributions, individuals are almost always addressed at home addresses.

In marketing terms, donors (contributors) are the equivalent of customers for a direct-mail operation or subscribers for a newsletter or magazine. For all three, including fundraising, response is the name of the game, and direct mail is just one of the players.

This discussion will omit data on foundations and business fundraising and concentrate on the use of direct-mail lists for fundraising from the general public.

There are two basic factors implicit in any fundraising operation: An appeal to a given *psychographic profile* (how the individual sees and reacts to life, and to some extent what that lifestyle is) and *discretionary income* (dollars that can be expended as the individual sees fit, beyond what he or she perceives to be the necessities of life).

Some fundraising, for given objectives, must operate for the most part within a distinctly limited province. A college seeking to build a new football stadium needs to obtain most of such support from current donors, alumni, and season ticket holders as well as support from businesses in the locality.

Some fundraising, with ethnic requirements, must operate primarily within that ethnic group, just as political fundraising must tap its own segment on the political spectrum from conservative right to liberal left.

It should be clear that until the objectives of the fundraising operation—and the constraints within which it must function—are known, any discussion of lists and list sources would be specious. This is, interestingly enough, no different for a commercial venture where any discussion of lists before markets or lists before needs is putting the well known cart before the well known horse.

Before one starts, at least the following must be known:

1. Objective
2. Probable market segments
   a. Internal
   b. External

     (1) Psychographic factors
     (2) Affluence factors
     (3) Constraints and limitations
        (a) Religion
        (b) Color
        (c) Locality
        (d) Other

3. Type of donation required
4. Size of donation (or range of size of donation) desired
5. Area to be covered
6. Budget
7. Anticipated yield per 1,000 mailed.

Fundraising, and the specific lists that pertain to them, can usually be categorized within ten major classifications:

    Education
    Cultural
      Arts
      Civic, local
      Civic, National/International
    Religious and Ethnic
      Minorities
      Religions
    Civic and Political
      Local
      National
      International
      Governmental
      Armed Forces
    Energy
    Recreation
    Children

Animals

Health

    Disease

    Handicapped

    Hospitals

    Sight

Disaster

    Violent

    Endemic

    Population

There are cross currents in any such arbitrary listing. New York donors to a Catholic library may not be very responsive to a new wing of a city library. Donors to liberal black causes may provide a blank for a new opera house. People who give for some immediate disaster may not be responsive to a similar endemic appeal.

This much is certain about donors. A person who has donated to a cause very close to *your* heart is more likely to give to you, than a nondonor. If he or she has donated more than a few dollars to such a cause, you are even better off.

If he or she has donated to that comparable cause recently, you are still better off. Note this follows the rules for all direct marketing: buyers (donors) are better than prospects. Large buyers (donors) are usually better than smaller ones. Multiple buyers (donors) are better than solitary ones. Recent buyers (donors) are better than lapsed buyers. The recency, frequency, and dollar syndrome—one of the master keys to successful commercial direct marketing—turns out to be the master key to *successful* fund raising. The working of the customer (subscriber, donor) base lies at the heart of all direct marketing efficiency.

Those donor lists that are commercially available for rental by another fund raising operation are offered by list brokers on conventional 5″ × 8″ list cards. Data include name, source, size of donation, quantity, age of each offered segment, price per thousand, minimum order required, and any extras for tapes, pressure-sensitive labels, or selection by state or three-digit zip code area. As specialization is the order of the day, it is not surprising to find two or three of the top thirty list brokers in the United States are particularly knowledgeable in this area.

One or two of these specialists have access to donor lists not always found on the market. Listen well to what they say and what they recommend. The broker who knows fundraising files has that precious ingredient that a tyro or a newcomer to this field cannot possibly have—knowledge of how given lists have worked for nonprofits.

Reversing the coin, almost any list broker, and most list compilers, interested in your problem can provide lists that reach people with ability to give—those people of means with discretionary income. Mailers of all kinds—insurance companies, stock brokers, stock services, gourmet foods, class magazines, cameras, jewelry, books, credit cards, travel, sports, all the so-called offers of the "better things of life"—have a definite interest in reaching upper-income people. It is understandable, thus, that a not inconsiderable portion of the dollars expended in building, maintaining, and merchandising mailing lists is spent on supplying different ways to reach the affluents—affluents who have the highest portion of discretionary purchasing power and the greatest ability to "give."

Fundraising might be described as the search for discretionary money. In general, the greater the income, the larger this discretionary money becomes. (At the upper end of this scale, indications are that more available money does not mean a higher *proportion* of giving.)

Other than mail-response lists (donors), most lists of affluents originate as a result of *registration, membership, ownership,* or *occupation.* Registration includes phones, cars, voting, education, homes, farms, boats, passports, warrantees, births, weddings, and even trade show viewers.

Membership generally indicates an institutional cast—associations, fraternities, clubs, alumni, foundations, charities, trustees. (Donors to certain organizations become "members" by the act of giving or subscribing.)

Ownership includes such diverse items as cars, boats, cameras, stocks, airplanes, art, and co-op apartments.

Occupation can generally be split into business and professional classifications: bakers and candlestick makers; doctors and dentists; management consultants and advertising agents; teachers and administrators; financial analysts and stock brokers; airline pilots, data-processing programmers. Functions of business occupations are usually also grouped here—members of boards of directors or executives in sales, production, engineering finance, purchasing.

These four sources of orgination develop into a whole series of lists. If you wish to use any of these lists effectively, you must know the sources of names, how these names get on a list, where each type is available, and the strengths and weaknesses of each type.

Much fundraising starts out with exaggerated expectations. It is a hard lesson to learn that most cold prospecting for funds will not initially produce enough dollars in return to pay the cost of the mailing. This means if you have a cost in the mail, nonprofit, of say $125 per thousand (covering postage, list rental, printing, envelopes, and fulfillment for mailing third class bulk, or third class bulk carrier presort), a return of $100 in donations may be an extremely favorable response. This is because within three months, secondary mailings to the few who have responded will provide enough additional dollars to make the program "profitable."

Fundraising is much like most other direct marketing—the original "order" or "donation" may have to be bought at a cost. The true art of fundraising lies in the working of the donor file.

Too many fundraising mailings consist of a "continuous series of one experiment." The mailer learns only what one appeal does when mailed to one list. As it is better to mail a poor mailing to a good list than a good mailing piece to a poor list, (because of all factors that influence response, the list has the greatest impact) it stands to reason that fundraising offers should at the very least test different list concepts and different lists within such concepts.

What this comes down to is that list selection and use is obviously an art and not a science. It should be clear after you use the best graphics, the greatest photos, the most persuasive copy, and the best package that the right answer is not to send out the errand boy to locate a mailing list. Study, learn, and lean on those who have made lists their life work.

Fundraisers that use the mails commit the same sins and fall into the same pitfalls as all other users of this media (see the section on sins and pitfalls on page 5). Typically they have expectations that are too high; are prone to gauge results on a single mailing to a single constituency; believe that direct-mail fundraising is easy (all you need is a letter and a list); fail to code results; and thus move in the dark, and have little idea of the factors that influence response.

Four Lessons to Learn about Fundraising

There are four hard lessons that perhaps every fundraising effort needs to come to terms with. Lesson One is the need to create a budget. One of the most difficult roles in fundraising is to obtain a given budget to fit a given objective. While used with relative rarity, one way to solve this is to establish the budget for fundraising as a portion (or percentage) of the expenditures by the institution for educational activities. When fundraising is thought of in this way it plays an important role in what educational activities will be entered into by the institution.

Measurement is based on the number of dollars received against the number of dollars expended. It is relatively rare to breakeven on this basis on fundraising appeals to prospect lists. The usual report for annual fund drives usually shows a *cost* to buy a new contributer. This cost, if modest, can be easily amortized in the next fundraising effort as the new donors know the charitable operation and are already favorably inclined to have the organization continue with the work it is doing.

Lesson Two is the need to recognize atypical donations and eliminate them from future projections. It is usual in reviewing test data for a fundraising offer to examine

1. Number of dollars of response per thousand pieces mailed.
2. Number of donations received per thousand pieces mailed.

Utilizing such data to evaluate whether or not to continue with a given source or list the number of responses is a safer criteria than the number of dollars. It is not uncommon for a fundraising appeal to elicit twenty donations of from $5 to $15, and one donation of $100 or $200. The latter increases the total dollars received markedly but there is no guarantee that in a future continuation other donations of this size will be realized.

Lesson Three is that owners of lists of donors *rarely* ask them for further contributions *often enough*. Donors like to receive mail from the social services they support. For every one fund raiser who is concerned about mailing to donors too often, there are ninety-nine that do not mail the donor list often enough.

It is a hard lesson for list owners to learn that donors are not the exclusive property of any one fundraising or charitable institution. The average donor can be found on a number of other donor lists and these organizations repeatedly ask the donor for help.

Lesson Four is that *any* donor file is not homogenous. It consists of current, old, former, and deceased donors, in effect, cells of donors with distinctly different characteristics. There is a need to differentiate between them and to learn to cultivate them differently.

POLITICS VERSUS POLISTICS (POLITICS PLUS LISTS = POLISTICS)

There is probably no other phase of human endeavor so dominated by list thinking and list usage as the field of politics. From lists of voters to lists of poll watchers; lists of donors to lists of politicians; lists of ethnic groups to lists of columnists; lists of drivers to lists of phone operators—all the way to lists of home party givers and their yield, a list of party goers—everyone in politics has a little (or a big) list.

If there is one recent change in politics it is in the size of national mailing lists of both donors and fundraising prospects and prospective voters. Files for the Reagan administration consist of donors to President Reagan, donors to Republican senators and donors to Republican congresspeople. Twenty-four hours after President Reagan added a five-minute "I am running" to his campaign address on the state of the Union, a flight of 2,200,000 pieces for fundraising was in the mail with the expectation that 40 percent would be delivered the next morning and that 10 percent would produce new donations to the Republican presidential cause.

Those using very large files have now bypassed word processors and their floppy discs in favor of very fast laser sheet printers that can print two complete letters in less than one second. Only the recent availability of these high-speed computerized photo printers makes possible sending out 200,000 letters over an evening to take advantage of some fast-breaking news or local announcement.

Five Major Inputs for Soliciting Prospective Voters

It is no real surprise to find that behind the Reagan donor file stands one of the most sophisticated and complete data banks of prospective voters ever assembled. It has a total of over 80 million families that was constructed by combining and unduplicating several of the five major lists utilized to construct a name and address file of any size.

These major inputs and their approximate total counts include:

1. All registered and listed telephone subscribers (approximately 57 million)
2. All commercially available registered automobiles (approximately 57 million)
3. All registered voters (one of the more "iffy" lists—but consisting of tens of millions)
4. All commercially available registered drivers in twenty states (approximately 80 million)
5. All recently compiled adult residents in city directories (approximately 45 million)

Phone registrants and car registrants are available, and together they provide access to over 71 million of this country's 87 million families. Drivers' licenses provide multiple adult names per family for approximately half the states. City directories, most of them canvassed on a 12- or 18-month basis, offer house-to-house data for virtually half of America except the five largest cities. One of 1,500 independent canvassers and publishers in this field produces 26 million of these names.

Political Name Banks

With the advent of modern high-speed computers it is no longer difficult (although it is a bit time consuming) to merge–identify such lists and provide access to multiple prospective voters at tens of millions of residences. Such a name bank provides individual data as to age (even date of birth) number of family members, age and names of children; other adults living in a household; number, age, make, model and value of cars; value of home; and a rather sophisticated individual income. Length of residence, type of dwelling, and inferences of educational level can also be reviewed, along with ethnic background.

Voter Records

Missing from most of these name banks are the pearls of greatest worth in the field of polistics—namely those of last year's voters—and data on their party affiliation and their voting habits. The reason for this is not hard to find. Voter records are kept by city, county, water district, zip code, election district, and other units, and on any "system" from signed registration cards to stencils to magnetic tape. In many states there is no good single list available and almost any list of voters of any size consists of former voters, deceased voters, voters who have relocated, and blank areas where no names are available at all. In states where each county keeps rolls of voters, Republicans in charge in one county, Democrats in charge in another, this reduces the chances for one candidate or the other to amass *all* records. (In New York City the roll of registered voters is kept up to date on magnetic tape by the Board of Elections. Any person proving a political need for the data may, for a few dollars per thousand names, get an extract on sheets, labels, or tapes with all data selectable by party affiliation, election district, even assembly district.)

You might ask, If all these other names are so accessible, why is so much effort exerted by politicians at every level to obtain actual voting lists? This is because more than 50 percent of Americans who are eligible to vote fail to do so even for a presidential election. The candidate who can accumulate all those names most likely to vote (former voters, first time registrants—a list in itself) can win an election from a competitive campaigner who must try to reach those who will actually vote by some form of costly overkill through mass list sources.

In a primary campaign, where perhaps 10, 12, or 15 percent of those eligible to vote do vote (and almost always the same faithful 10, 12, 15 percent) the odds against mass circulation are infinitely greater. However, these campaigns are more localized and each captain or campaign manager is nearer the political source of the voter registration list so that such names are usually known. They can if all else fails, be copied from local voter's rolls which historically are open to anyone with a given need to know.

One thing is certain: If there were any simple way to amass voter registration lists on a national basis, the major consumer list compilers would have long ago had these data dripping from their files with identification by party affiliation and psychographic history of voting no less meaningful than the recency, frequency, dollars, item, source and method of payment data made available by major mail order merchandisers.

Richard Vigurie established what might be called the "iron law" of getting elected in America. He declared that if candidate A uses direct mail intelligently and candidate B does not use direct mail intelligently then irrespective of the relative merits of the two, candidate A will win in 85 percent of cases (100 percent if Vigurie runs the direct-mail campaign). Vigurie is the principal fundraiser for the Republicans and for specific conservative Republican candidates. Roger Craver serves the Democratic National Party and selected liberal Democratic candidates. Vigurie maintains one of the largest complexes of lists of conservative donors in America. Craver has found it more expedient to tap the resources of the list community to locate people by psychographics (by what they do and what they support) of a liberal persuasion.

Qualities of a Political Donor

The first of many qualities of a donor is *empathy*—a sympathy with the program, procedure, or politics that are espoused. The second quality is having a history of giving. Someone who has given to a particular persuasion in the past, particularly in the recent past, is more likely to give to another similar request. The third quality is an ability, through disposable income, to write a check. Fourth is a desire to participate, even in some minor way, in the political process. There is no good way to estimate the total number of Americans who vote with their money instead of their minds, but the total is in the millions.

Once a potential donor has been moved from a prospect to the ultimate status in polistics of a donor, the ubiquitous computer maintains records by size of donation, date of donation, type of appeal, and number of contributions. Such files can be so sophisticated that donors can be differentiated from those who loan money to the campaign and those who "give" money. These in turn can be split between those to whom the loans have been repaid and those who having been repaid return the sum as a contribution. Every Democratic candidate is busy cultivating the best contributors in their donor files in order to get committed givers to contribute even more. They are just as adept at working individual cells by dollars, frequency, and recency, as the most advanced practitioners of other forms of direct marketing.

There are a few special rules that apply only to political donor lists. In the short run every person who has given over $200 must be disclosed to the Federal Election Board. Donor records must be kept for review. The top list of donors must be personally addressed, which often means the messy job of extracting data for conversion to floppy discs and later returning any historically changed data on the discs back to the master donor tape.

Key Lists for Political Parties

Certain lists are as attractive to political parties as honey is to flies. Such lists include:

- Congresspeople
- Congressional staff
- State legislators
- Political commentators
- Business columnists
- Presidents of major corporations
- County party Chairpersons and treasurers
- Political consultants, fundraisers, and campaign directors
- Governors and mayors
- Foundation presidents
- Registered voters
- Newly registered voters

One entry missing from this brief list of lists is the prestigious file of doctors from the American Medical Association (AMA). The AMA has never condoned the use of its list for either politics or fundraising. To countermand this, ubiquitous creators of lists have made three rather impressive substitutes available so doctors can be tapped. They are all doctors in private practice (as indicated by classified phone listings). All doctors so titled on the 71 million file at home addresses, of householders, and by discipline 250,000 doctors from published rosters by specialty. The 425,000 of Medec is also available for political mailings.

One of the most unusual lists in polistics consists of the invitees to a presidential inauguration. That involves very "touchy" standards of selection and allocation. These standards depend on the event and closeness that the invitees (staff, Supreme Court, Cabinet, major government administrators, governors, mayors, judges, business executives and so on) have to the President. The logistics of who gets to go to what is a nightmare when one considers the work involved in compiling invitations, envelopes, tickets, directions, even notes on dress. And then every name must be cross-checked and then rechecked.

The list of those the president thanks is a bountiful "Who's Who" of the president's own political persuasion.

The Power of Presidential Mailings

Occasionally a given mailing attains a life of its own. For example, during the Eisenhower run for the presidency, the chief Republican copywriter floated ten different appeals. The letter, in which Ike stipulated that if he was elected he would go to Korea, pulled ten times as many dollars as any of the others. That pledge became the centerpiece of the campaign.

When Nixon, another Republican, was in office he signed a letter to Republican voters in a western state favoring the reelection of a harassed Republican incumbent senator. Approximately 160,000 computer-generated and computer-signed letters were sent out on White House stationery. The Democrats in the state were furious to find that these mass-produced form letters were being framed and hung in living rooms all through the state. Some very "wise" politician decided to counteract this move, and had certain editors of the local press print the full letter on the front pages of their newspapers. They specifically directed attention to the computer-generated style of the letter. This move failed however when, on the entire front pages of the opposition presses a letter from the President of the United States was printed requesting the return of one of his faithful Senators! Most people saw that letter and never examined why that particular letter was front and center on the front page of their favorite newspaper!

Making the Most of Ethnic Backgrounds

Polistics makes more use of ethnic codes and overlays them more than almost any other specialized form of direct marketing. The census provides data as to the proportion of Blacks, Spanish, and Whites by market, county, zip code, census tract, even down to the small bit of geography known as a subblock or enumeration district. A fair proportion of Jewish and Catholic households are reasonably well defined by reference to surname tables. For example O'Reilly is Irish; Luciano is Italian and so on. Further refining by surname is done by a few specialists to identify Scandinavians, Germans, Italians, Japanese, and Indians. Once such prospective voters can be identified it is a simple matter to write letters designed to appeal to their supposed ethnic biases.

How Telephone Listings Can Help Secure Votes

Possibly since Alexander Graham Bell called, "Come here." to Watson, the telephone has figured heavily in political campaigns. At first used only near the end of a local campaign to "get out the vote" (including lining up those who needed transportation to and from the polls) phoning from lists is now just as much a part of the political scene as addressing and stuffing envelopes.

Ed Koch, the mayor of New York City, had one of his very few political defeats when he attempted to "steal" the Liberal line in a New York election district. The Liberal Party added phone numbers to the list of all registered liberals and proceeded to call each name at least five times in one week. That particular group of voters got the message and Koch was buried by the votes of outraged party members.

Today, any worthy campaign manager makes the obtaining of phone numbers, particularly of regulars or converts a "must." Lists are pulled for phoning based on income, ethnic background, donation, or interest. It should be noted however that all names phoned must first be gathered on some list. Major campaigns build in phone registrant data with the complete phone number carefully included in every record. Prospects found particularly on voting records as well as those found in city directories, car registration lists, or driver registration lists are matched against a countrywide list of all phone registrants for just one main purpose—to add phone numbers to the records.

The telephone is the main communication form used to gather supporters and hold fundraising dinners for candidates. Those supporters who open their homes to campaigners and candidates are actively marshalled by one group of phone campaigners, while the invited "guests" are called from lists culled for interest, propinquity, and possible donor status. Former Vice President Walter Mondale had a team operating in this field. His staff reported obtaining $1,500,000 in donations from a group of these parties in the state of Iowa alone.

Current office holders treasure lists of constituents, particularly those they can reach through bulk postage rates which may or may not be paid by their office or their party. Almost every Congressperson (or at least every Congressperson who wishes to be reelected) has a newsletter printed in large type that tells constituents what is being done for (or to) them in the halls of Congress. More assiduous Congresspeople have special lists of special friends (as we all do) and friendly newspeople as well as "small-fry" politicos with whom they keep in touch. Political parties, at every level, have their lists of members and influentials on their particular political scene. No worthy politician would ever subscribe to Lord Koko's declaration that "I've got a little list, and they'll none of them be missed."

Expediting the Mail—Compliments of the United States Post Office

The United States Postal Service is enjoined from political action but it does offer one special service to all politicians of whatever persuasion, creed, or party: Delivery of any mail that a candidate or manager declares is political in nature is expedited during a campaign. Normal mail, which can take eight days to travel fifteen blocks in a big city, can be delivered city or countrywide the very next morning even if it is brought to the post office late at night. Political mail, even flimsy flyers, once addressed and placed in the mailstream leads a charmed life and gets better delivery than costly express mail. It is in your best interest to let your postmaster know in advance what you want mailed so that your bags, trays, or boxes are given priority by special postal agents.

Suppliers of lists to politicians have learned, through hard and costly experience, to ask for and receive compensation for lists on a cash with order basis before providing the labels or tapes. It would be foolhardy to break this rule. Once a campaign is over, the organization disappears, the candidate melts back into the wood work or charges off to a state capital or Washington D. C., and there is no one left to answer a phone call.

Key Questions to Ask About Political Listings

Politicos deserve more from list suppliers than they now generally receive because the candidate or the candidate's manager does not know what data to ask for to evaluate a list coordinator or supplier. The questions are few and if answers are not satisfactory it is better to find another service or source. Ask your list source:

1. What is the source of the names I will be using?
2. When were they compiled?
3. When (if at any time) have they been updated?
4. What guarantee of delivery can I count on?
5. What proportion of duplication should I expect?
6. What is the cost of each list segment? Of each phone list?
7. What are the qualifications of the list supplier?

8. What other political campaigns has the supplier been involved with?

9. Whom can I talk with at similar other campaigns?

SWEEPSTAKES LISTS

Ever since some direct-mail genius invented a means for all entrants, those who buy (or say yes) as well as those who do not buy (or say no), to participate in a drawing of chance, sweepstakes—or sweeps—have been with us. There is a psychology that "feels" the chance to win is increased by a "yes" vote, which increases response, often by more than enough to offset the extra cost of the prizes. We will have sweeps as long as men and women love a chance to win prizes.

From a list standpoint a sweeps entrant (particularly one who responds "no," which is the preeminant vote) is a good prospect for other sweeps. However it is important to know the source of the "no entrants" because although sweeps *do* work, they do not necessarily expand the marketing universe for any given offer. The sweeps will not create new markets; they can generate better response from targeted markets that are "right" for the offer.

If sweeps names are to be used they should be used early after acquisition. Somewhat like TV ad buyers and premium redemptions' lists, sweeps "direct respondents" as a list source tends to tail off on response for offers quite early in their life.

The Effect of "Sweeps"

In the section on Rules for Testing there is a brief analysis of the five factors in direct mail that can cause response to vary. Second to the variances caused by list and list-segment selection, the factor with the greatest impact on response is the offer. This impact can be so large so as to affect the lists mailed by "creaming" them of a fair percentage of names used. There are two such offers in particular that can have this affect on the list and thus to some extent on the list owner. They are all forms of "yes-no" offers or sweeps where the entrant is given a chance to win one of hundreds or thousands of attractive prizes with or without purchase. The typical type of offer invites the prospect to get involved by positioning a token of some sort in either a "yes" slot or a "no" slot with either answer being eligible for the prize drawings for all entrants.

Historically, sweeps have proven to be an exceptional method to increase direct-mail response dramatically. (Not all sweepstakes are successful. If the universe mailed to is too small to support the prize structure offered, or the product offered is not considered worthwhile, sweeps can be a disaster.) Some of this increase probably comes from a feeling by consumers that their chances to win are improved if they elect to buy (and thus vote "yes").

It is not unusual for a well designed sweeps direct-mail package, particularly the computer-printed spectaculars that address customers "personally" to obtain bona fide answers from 10 percent or more of each list used. The majority of these responses are always cards marked or identified as "no" entrants. These "no" names are then converted to a magnetic tape for list rental by list managers who know they provide a good revenue source. In fact, for some offers such "No"s respond better than do the "Yes"s. "No" names are interested in obtaining something for nothing; they read direct mail; respond exceptionally well to other sweepstake, puzzle, and contest offers; do well on opportunity offers; buy nonlife insurance through the mail; and are above-average prospects for charms, good-luck jewelry, and household items.

From the mailer's point of view, a sweepstakes can provide a substantial list that can produce significant revenue. From the list owner's point of view, rental of his or her list for a sweeps offer may be detrimental—one offer can siphon off an additional 10, 15, or 20 percent of a solid list of mail order buyers and the price of this list rental may not, when the facts are known, be very attractive. When a sweeps has been able to carve out a large enough portion of a large list in one such pull, that segment of names can easily be identified by the list owner as being sweeps "no" entrants from list X. This is not usually done as the sweeps designation can be used to cover names from all lists used but there is the danger this may occur.

Some years ago, a new cultural magazine with elegant, bona fides and adequate financing was launched with a sweepstakes. The magazine subsequently failed, but the list of "no's", that were extracted by the sweeps appeal from the top magazine lists became a popular list for mailers who would ordinarily be unwelcome in the cultural community. As a further example, I once happened to create a mailing offering a credit card good for the first hotel room on the moon just prior to the successful effort by the United States to land a man on that bleak satellite. The main list used consisted of credit card holders. All respondents (a quite amazing 18 percent) were then re-offered as "holders of two or more credit cards." This offer was logical, legitimate, even fun for me but not to the one list owner who found he had received $50,000 in list rental and now found 180,000 of his customers available for rental on a competitor's list.

The builders of large lists of respondents with multiple interests obtain data on brand usage, computer interest, and cable interest as well as ownership of dogs, cats, video recorders, computers, and so on. What might happen if they were able to construct a question to get valid answers as to which magazines were read? Considering that respondents to questions total multi-millions, how far-fetched would it be to offer names of these claiming readership of magazines not on the rental market such as the *New Yorker* and *National Geographic?*

OPPORTUNITY SEEKERS—THE ENTREPRENEURS

Opportunity seekers cover a remarkably wide range of propositions—from work-at-home possibilities to franchises costing tens of thousands of dollars. It is necessary to review the actual offers and advertisements utilized to build any list being considered for rental. The "get rich" scheme is or can be a far cry from an offer related to writing ability.

There are a number of lists of would be salesmen and saleswomen for shoes, Christmas cards, automotive specialties and so on. Some of these lists, through the Stroh organization, are organized each year into a single, large list. A growing number of lists are appearing that consist of multilevel inquirers—those who wish to sell products through the efforts of others.

At the low end of the scale are the scams that take money from the unaware and unsuspecting through pyramid clubs, addressing at home, or the sale of mailings offering a sale of mailings. Such lists do work for some offers as there is always an audience for those who hope to get rich quick.

One of the cruelest opportunity-seeker offers is to set up an entrepreneur in the mail-order field with his or her own preprinted catalog. The buyer is not experienced enough to understand that he or she cannot buy the syndicated catalogs (at a profit to the producer) and make mailings for drop shipment which will even recover the additional cost of the postage and lists. It should be evident (but is not) that if the purveyor of the merchandise (at least 50 percent off list) and of the catalogs could make a profit the opportunity seeker would be mailing the catalogs for his or her own account. The better list merchandisers refuse to rent names to these innocent entrepreneurs in an attempt to stop them from throwing more good money away.

Franchise operators, particularly those for franchises requiring a substantial cash investment, usually find it necessary to utilize space ads such as in *The Wall Street Journal* and the *New York Times,* as well as mailings to obtain qualified and interested investors. For an automotive product, it is usual to go to the Automotive Aftermarket (gas stations, garages, carwashes, parking lots, trailers, campers, and allied lists of off-road vehicles, motorcycles, and boats). For a fast-food operation, where the investment may be well up in six figures, the lists that are used tend to consist of professionals, business executives, and affluent consumers.

As in all forms of response, the value of the inquirer and the proportion of conversion dictate what can be paid for each lead. It is not uncommon in the opportunity-seeker field to pay several dollars for a low-cost lead (which may come from classified advertising) and then spend 5 or 10 dollars or more, in an attempt to convert that lead to customer status. (See "Two Step" marketing, page 453.)

GARDENING AND HORTICULTURAL LISTS

It may come as a bit of a surprise that the most popular outdoor leisure time activity in America is not jogging, golf, tennis, even fishing—it is gardening. Eighty percent of American households (as reported by Gallup) work on their lawns or gardens. A national gardening survey called "Gardens for All," which was conducted by the National Association for Gardeners, found 63 percent of Americans were involved in lawn care, almost 50 percent in flower gardening, while 40 percent tended indoor houseplants. Forty percent of households had a vegetable garden, which means a lot of city folk are cultivating a small plot for the table. Other surveys indicate that the average household that grows vegetables spent an average of $32 on gardening materials in 1984. The yield was stupendous—some 13.5 billion pounds of vegetables were grown on these small plots in 1984 with an estimated retail value of over $12 billion!

Interestingly enough, the more affluent a household, the more likely it is to garden. (The less affluent own a smaller proportion of homes than average, and many such households do not have a lawn or any space for a garden.) The lists tend to be upscale. College-educated gardeners spend more than their less-educated neighbors. According to "Gardens for All" households with over $40,000 of income account for fully one-third of total lawn and garden purchases. They are more interested in quality and freshness than in price. (Households with over $40,000 represent some 9 percent of all households.)

Gardeners tend to live in the suburbs. Over one-third of all gardeners, including most of those who are more affluent and better educated, live in suburban and rural areas. As a consequence the lists of mail-order buyers available tend to be even more suburban and more upscale than gardeners in general.

Lists are available for buyers of lawn care, both countrywide and local, seeds, plants, flowers, and trees. Individual growers provide lists of buyers of roses, dahlias, tulips, even orchids. In the list world a few list brokers specialize to some extent on horticultural lists, and knowing mailers tend to use the services of these specialized experts.

This is a market in which peripheral list thinking does not work. Known mail order buyers of seeds, plants, or trees is the only targeted market to reach.

LIFE INSURANCE COMPANY LISTS

Lists are available for insurance companies by type, including names of their executives, as well as for insurance agencies and brokers, plus some relatively inadequate data on agents by names, including newly appointed or commissioned agents.

Householders are available by age, income, size of family, education level, age of children, and value of home.

A number of insurance companies make lists available of applications ("apps" as they are called) as well as customers for special forms of insurance such as health, cancer, and major medical.

Virtually an entire industry has been created to utilize various list sources to produce current inquiries which are then sold to insurance companies, general agents, insurance agencies, and agents. Almost all major insurance companies have programs in effect whereby their agents can participate in some form of cooperative mailings of pieces produced and approved by the company. When the companies have been slow to offer automated direct-mail selling to their agents, forward-thinking general agents who have jurisdiction over an area and a large group of agents are initiating mail campaigns themselves.

A considerable volume of direct mail is generated to sell life insurance policies to American consumers. There are even five or six companies that sell insurance only through the mail, sending over 100 million pieces through the USPS. Collected in Table 7.1 are the major facts about life insurance in the United States.

Table 7.1
Fact sheet on the life insurance market

Companies	
Number of life insurance companies	2100
New companies (average per year)	100
Discontinued operations (per year)	70
Employees—Head Offices	
Life insurance	532,000
Health insurance	153,000
Other home office personnel	548,000
Total home office	1,233,000
Agents and brokers	519,000
Total employees	1,752,000

Table 7.1
(cont.)

Average Amounts of Life Insurance in Force
Per family	$58,700
Per insured family	$68,300

Ownership of Life Insurance by Households
All households	81%
All families	85%
Household income (twenty-five thousand dollars and above)	92%
Not retired	83%
Retired	75%

Ownership of Life Insurance by Occupation

	All types (percent)	Individual Purchases (percent)	
		Male	Female
Managers	88%	61%	46%
Professional/technical	88	54	45
Sales	74	51	50
Administrative support	71	48	43
Service workers	80	53	45
Skilled and Semi-skilled	83	58	42
Unskilled labor	69	50	37
Retired	71	53	48

Purchase of Ordinary Life Insurance (by year, 75% whole life, 25% term)

	Dollars (in billions)	Number of Policies (in millions)
1978	$283	14.0
1979	329	14.2
1980	386	14.8
1981	482	15.8
1982	585	15.6
1983	753	17.2
1984	820	17.7
1985	900	18.1

This is a market that is growing
1. As more children are born.
2. As more families cross over into affluence.
3. As more coverage is extended through groups.

LEISURE ACTIVITIES

There are now four major consumer lists based on questionnaires in which the respondent ticks off up to sixty different hobbies and interests. In all cases, the filled-in forms come in by mail to qualify as a "mail response."

The numbers are huge—in the millions. For example, this mechanism produces the largest number of "tennis players" on any list in America. This can be more than eight or ten times the size of actual mail order buyers or subscribers to tennis magazines. However a good portion of those who off-handedly tick off tennis as one of their hobbies are not necessarily ideal prospects for tennis gear by mail.

Some answers can also be misleading. Initially 85 percent of those checking off squash were women. That doesn't fit too well with the knowledge that over 95 percent of squash players are male. A phone follow-up revealed that most of the women were ticking-off an interest in squash, the vegetable.

The lists of interests offered for ticking-off can and do change. In recent years one of the four lists has added Cable TV, home computers, science, technology as well as Bible reading and recreational reading. (The latest, in 1987, offers an opportunity to be self-styled "frequent flyers.") Given an opportunity, 8 percent of those answering through warrantees, tick-off the option to have their names removed from the rental base.

There is no doubt however that lists that provide lifestyle knowledge about individuals is a viable concept. With each update, counts increase and make the size of multiple selects all that more valuable.

INDIVIDUAL PRODUCT LIST RENTALS
AND HIGH-PRICED RENTAL LISTS

There was a large number of raised eyebrows when *Horchow*, a high level mail order catalog operator, decided to raise its rental price a few years ago to $100/M, about 20 to 40 percent above the costs for lists then considered of roughly equal value to renters. The first $150/M list caused far less commotion (and much less rental income). Now one company, Norm Thompson, is offering to rent buyers of individual products (where the totals run from 500 to about 40,000) for an imposing $300/M. *Pricing* is the art of selecting the proper price (for a given set of reasons) between the cost to produce the goods or service and the amount the public is willing to pay. It is probable that at $300/M (which changes the average direct-mail package from between $300 & $400/M to some $525 to $625/M) is not intended to aggrandize the most dollars. (That might actually happen at $10 or

$15/M above the basic cost of the list as the loyalty is to Thompson, not to a renter of its lists.) Rather this price casts an aura over the list, a cachet of excellence as it were, and provides some additional revenue each rare time a renter does wish to have the selection made.

When the rental price for a given list goes out of sight, that is the time to spend extra efforts to locate other sources. In the case of individual products, these efforts can include both solo mailers as well as other catalog houses which may be able and willing to select by product code.

PART III: PERIPHERAL LIST THINKING

CREATIVE WAYS OF MAKING NEW LISTS FROM OLD

This section might be termed "how to make new lists from old, or two lists from one." Peripheral list thinking is just one more example of the creativity of list people.

Lists of college students at home addresses as well as campus addresses are available. Those at home addresses can include students who commute or students who live at their colleges. By using the home address and addressing the envelope to "The Parents Of" a list of parents of students in college can be created.

If the addresses of doctors, dentists, lawyers, or other professionals are at-home addresses, pieces can be addressed to their spouses.

It is difficult to reach secretaries by name in large businesses but there are extensive lists of business executives by name and title. To reach the secretaries of these executives, address all correspondence to the secretary to Mr. or Ms. so and so—and a new list of hundreds of thousands of names will be at hand.

A form of peripheral list thinking involves tapping customers to provide the names of those they believe would like to receive given offers. This means of adding the names of non-buyers to lists provides another responsive group called friends of friends.

How to Find New Businesses by Comparing
Old and New Telephone Directories

Business lists are available by classification and size. From certain business lists new businesses such as those just starting out, can be carved out. One method used for years has been to compare the former yellow pages classified directory listings with the new directory, which is the procedure still used to update classified files today. Those "new" businesses found in the most recent directories total approximately 900,000 per year. While not exactly "new" when you locate them, since a year or more elapses between printings, these business lists are offered monthly as "businesses in motion." They are selectable by classification and available with phone numbers. For some offers, it has proven desirable that some time has gone by since the formation of these "new" establishments.

One company has placed contract workers in the offices of the registrars of records in major cities to report all new listings for both business and households. This produces a list of approximately 300,000 new business listings, most of which have not yet been published in the upcoming classified phone directory. One or two companies are making available daily changes. One company providing flood insurance is starting to market data not on householders who have recently moved but actually those who are about to move.

Lists of approximately 10 million new households per year, served up at the rate of 800,000 or so per month, are available from updating procedures that maintain the name lists compiled mainly from alphabetic telephone books. Approximately 3 million or more of these new listings are reported annually through clerical listing at the offices of registrars, and those data, like the business segment, are available before publication in the next alphabetic phone directory.

The breakup of the Bell system into twenty-two separate operating companies, grouped into seven geographical regional systems, is now beginning to impinge on the production and utilization of the names and addresses of listed telephone registrants. In mid-1985, one company, Illinois Bell, offered both alphabetic listings as well as its classified customers. The region it belongs to, Ameritech, has now brought the records of the states of Ohio, Wisconsin, and Indiana to the market. For the first time this availability provided access to *current* data. Ameritech new businesses and "new connects" for households are now accessible on quarterly or monthly, increments. Over the next few years, as other phone companies market their current names, access to these data will increase deliverability of every compiled list of householders and businesses in America by a full ten percent. Once all of the current phone data are in place, these current addresses will serve as the basic overlay to correct outdated lists of all kinds.

Three Unique Alphabetic Telephone Lists

The alphabetic telephone list as compiled now will have greater deliverability once current data are provided by the phone companies. It is also the source for a number of other lists created by peripheral thinking. The firm of Ed Burnett Consultants taps every title attached to the name of a registrant published in the alphabetic phone books to produce three unique lists:

1. Doctors listed in alphabetic directories—about 320,000. This is not quite doctors' at-home addresses since addresses and phone numbers in major cities are often at professional offices. There are also some PhDs on the list, as well as a handful of "selfstyled" doctors. Over 85 percent are legitimate MDs. But this list responds better for offers of a personal nature such as travel than lists of doctors found through the classifieds or the AMA.

2. Pastors at-home addresses—about 350,000. This compilation picks up every Reverend and Reverend Doctor (some of them even "self-styled"). It embraces all faiths and is not selectable by denomination. It is by far the largest list of its kind.

3. Armed forces officers at-home addresses—about 325,000. This compilation tends to pick up large clusters of officers selectable for noncoms, as well as lieutenants, and higher-ranking officers that live in or near major armed forces installations. Care must be taken in using the list, as an entire unit can be relocated at any time. It is a unique and useful way to reach a market that is almost inaccessible.

Companies Doing Business in Multiple Classifications

In the SIC system there are about 14 million individual listings under classified phone book listings. These listings boil down to about 8 million unduplicated establishments. This means that there are some 1.6 SIC listings for each unduplicated establishment. In fact, barring professional classifications of doctors, dentists, lawyers, engineers, and accountants, on the average duplication is greater than two listings per establishment. Thus it is possible to pull lists that are both As and Bs; bowling alleys with restaurants, grocery stores that also vend gasoline, insurance agencies that provide pension planning, hotels with bars, and so on.

Neighbors and Near Neighbors of Known Addresses

An unusual list based on peripheral thinking is "members of boards of directors and their near neighbors." Without much doubt this is the largest list (1,900,000 names) of true affluents ever compiled. Members of the board at-home addresses are published each year by Standard & Poors. The telephone list is compiled and updated each year and is maintained in numerical order by street within a zip code. Working with Ed Burnett Consultants once or twice a year Data Base America utilizes a merge-identification run to match the S&P data to the file. They then use these targeted names as locaters for nearby neighbors.

A variant of the "members of boards" cluster is to provide all names in an enumeration district or a subblock where one or more targeted names are found. This provides a cluster of approximately 140 to 200 names around each such name.

How *Time* Magazine Successfully Reaches Prospective Subscribers

Time magazine successfully mails to new residents of homes recently vacated by *Time* subscribers. The reason for this is that *Time* has found new householders will be enough like those who have moved out to make them good prospects for subscriptions to *Time* magazine. On this basis it is likely the next door neighbors of *Time* subscribers that have similar interests and outlooks may be logical candidates for subscribing. This method will not work for magazines that cater to more specialized interests. Differences in lifestyles, but not economics, among neighbors who live next door to a person who reads magazines of special interest, foil all attempts to seek new subscribers from new moves into houses of former subscribers or from the neighbors of that household.

As noted in the section on affluents, there are many peripheral ways to reach this moneyed group in the list world. (See page 176.)

A number of campaigns have found that consumer offers can be mailed successfully to executives' business addresses, thus converting business lists into a special form of consumer outreach. The opposite approach, in which mailers deliberately mail business offers to individuals at their homes, also is becoming more appealing.

The creation of a new path for business mailings is fueled by the fact that more and more individuals are conducting businesses from their homes. The great increase in computer use at home, either for personal use or, more often, for business reasons, is another reason why mailings for supplies, aids, books, services, and newsletters tend to do better when mailed to targeted householders than many would expect.

BUSINESS EXECUTIVES AS CONSUMERS: DON'T IGNORE THE HUMAN FACTOR

A few years ago the Hewlett Packard Company (HP) offered a handheld engineering computer/calculator which sold for $475—a price much too low to justify selling it right along with other HP products by personal sales representatives.

Direct mail was the channel chosen to sell this product. Two distinctly different packages were designed and tested. The first package was aimed at the engineering market, and it was a no-nonsense dollars-and-cents, factual description of what this new computer could do, how much time it could save, and how valuable it could be in dozens of different engineering and architectural applications. The second package looked similar to other packages offered by consumer mail order companies. It had four-color pictures, a large pull-out folder that provided a picture of the full size unit—all the stops of a direct-response pitch. It seemed likely that the factual, no-nonsense package aimed at the engineers would, without question, win out. Right? Nonsense! The four-color folder direct-mail approach won by a substantial margin.

The business logic is clear. The engineer, architect, or entrepreneur is a human being first and a businessperson second. He or she may not respond to consumer offers as a consumer but rather as a businessperson. However, he or she *is* a consumer. Thus, it stands to reason that certain consumer offers should make test mailings to businesspeople. Business executives total about 20 million or about 10 percent of the total population but more important, they represent almost 20 percent of the wage earners and a much higher proportion than that of the affluent society.

This knowledge has led to the development of a number of lists of business-people and professionals at-home addresses. Business magazines, in particular, seek out lists of known businesspeople at their home address; it is no longer surprising to find that over 50 percent of magazine circulations are sent to home addresses rather than business addresses.

Peripheral Thinking for Educators

A good deal of peripheral thinking is getting mailings to individual classroom educators when the names of the educators are not known. The data on schools and school districts, as well as the number of pupils per school and school district, the grades educators teach, and the number of dollars spent for books and educational material per student are well known. But the names of teachers, by grade, is problematic. Some mailers solve this by addressing mailings to each grade such as fourth or fifth grade teachers or by title such as art teacher or music teacher, at each grade known to be included in the curriculum at each school.

Customers Options to Remove Their Names from Mailings

There are three options customers can choose among to remove their names from mailings:

1. Since 1971 the Direct Marketing Association has been the pioneer in providing a nationwide consumer assistance service that enables individuals to get off *or* on a large number of lists. This service is called the "Mail Preference Service"

and it operates on the premise that no mailer wishes to waste his or her costly offers on recipients who are not potentially willing recipients. Interestingly enough, when given the opportunity to remove or add their name many more individuals opt to *add* their names to mailing lists than to request removal of their names through this service. The reaction to this well promoted service is another indication that only a very small percentage of American consumers wish to stop mail from coming to their homes. This voluntary service for the benefit of the industry has been of special value in reducing the pressures made by consumer groups and Congress to take over the policing of mailing lists. (Some enterprising mailers have surmised that the list of those wishing to be removed from lists is an above-average list. They reason these people must read their mail as they have responded twice to the DMA by mail and have used their own postage.)

2. Almost all major companies that are notified by a recipient that additional mailings are not desired will remove the name from the customer file. This is done as a sign of good business.

In this light, a mail recipient who finds certain mailings to be salacious or sexually offensive in nature can have the USPS make certain that no other such mailings are received from that company. There is a criminal charge involved here, so name removal is virtually assured. However, if you report, as some of us might like to do, that those long forms from the IRS are "sexually offensive" you'll be advised by the USPS that government mailings are not covered by the act.

3. The third form of removal involves the rental of customer names. Many major direct-mail companies (including for example Fingerhut and American Express) periodically write to their customers and provide them with the option to have their names removed from future outside mailings. The copy used to provide this option is very important. It would be possible to draft a message that would result in a large number of people asking for removal. In actuality, only one-tenth of 1 percent (1 person per 1000) opts for such name removal. Here is the copy that Fingerhut uses:

> *We make our customer list of names and addresses available to carefully screened companies and organizations whose products and activities might be of interest to you. If you would prefer not to receive such mailings, please write your mailing address and customer number on a piece of paper and mail it to "Mail Service, Fingerhut Corporation."*

As telephone lists come on the market, the phone companies are careful to first give registrants an opportunity to have their names removed from the rental market. Chesapeake and Potomac does this for example for all "new connects."

From a list point of view the "Mail Preference Service" tape comes into play when it is utilized as a suppress mechanism or in some case an add mechanism at the time of a merge–purge. Some merge–purge services automatically include this in their work. Others include it when they are ordered to by the mailer or agency responsible for the ultimate names that will be mailed. It is a good idea to check your data processing source on this use. The actual loss on a conventional merge–purge is minimal. (Recently the DMA has established a telephone preference service to give consumers a partial answer to removal of their names from lists with telephone numbers.)

At the individual company level, the request for name removal is simply a "kill" at the time of the next customer list update. The rental suppression request calls for tagging of a group of records so they will be skipped. If rental records are run from a separate file from the customer record file, these tagged records are simply omitted in the creation of the rental tape.

CHAPTER 8

Compiled Lists for Consumer and Business Marketing

PART I: CONSUMER LISTS—KEY SOURCES OF CONSUMER COMPILING

The total number of compiled lists in America is close to astronomical. A minimum of 50 million compiled files exist because we are *all* compilers of lists. Families compile Christmas card lists and almost everyone has a personal telephone list. However, only a very small percentage of professionally compiled lists, perhaps 20 thousand, are available commercially as mailing lists.

Thirty years ago almost all such lists were compiled "to order"—a book of names in a given classification was accessed for typing. Now lists are precompiled and the data are accessed by a computer by individual precoded criteria.

Despite the sophistication of modern selection techniques, compilations are made, converted, and selected by human beings. In most compilations there are holes (missing data) large enough to drive a truck through. For example, a local drugstore may not be on a certain file due to any number of reasons: It may have been missing on the source, it may have been mispunched, or it may have the wrong zip code. Whatever the reason, the compiler needs understanding and compassion from those who use compiled lists.

THE "BIG FOUR" COMPILERS OF CONSUMER NAMES AND HOW THEY OPERATE

Until 1986 the only service that compiled names from alphabetic telephone books was R.H. Donnelley. Donnelley sold a copy of this file to Metromail. Metromail, until 1985, sold a copy of those ten or twelve states that no longer permit rental of car registrations to R.L. Polk. R.L. Polk, which is the major and until very recently, the only company that obtains car registration data, provides a copy of all car registration data (except for new cars) to R.H. Donnelley. R.L. Polk adds approximately 26 million individually canvassed records from its city directories to its basic lists. Each of the "Big Four" provides about 75 million names from 87 million households: 57 million also contain phone numbers. Data Bank America marries one of the major age-base files plus the 20,000,000 behavioral records to one of the three major compiled files—incorporating over 200 million records in a vast merge-identification to produce a list in which the majority of the household records, for the first time, are confirmed by a second source.

How Lists Are Stratified

Each of the "Big Four" consumer list compilers *stratifies* (breaks into small demographic blocks) by overlaying phone, car, and city directory lists with census data. These major compilers go beyond the 25,000 census tracts published by the United States Census Bureau which cover every metropolitan market and over 70 percent of the population, by providing data also by enumeration districts and subblocks. Each of these defines the small geographic area given out to an individual census canvasser.

There are over 400,000 such "bits of real estate" that can be selected, each of which provides data in the form of medians for a reasonably homogenous block of about 125 to 200 families.

In addition, these lists are all coded for carrier-route discount—covering the 160,000 USPS carrier routes, plus an additional 240,000 pseudoroute groupings by delivery points. These codes break the entire country into small geographic segments of similar households.

Special extracts can be made from these huge files of all households to locate doctors' at-home addresses (actually doctors' addresses listed in alphabetic rather than classified phone directories), pastors' at-home addresses, armed forces officers' at-home addresses, and a list of all families (the affluents) with, say, incomes of $40,000 and over.

One selection factor these giants are now beginning to add in part to their files is mail order respondents or in some cases, mail order buyers by type of product purchased. The only major demographic factor not as yet included is credit rating, and this is destined shortly to follow. The purchase of Executive Sources Age Base list by the credit arm of TRW is proof of this.

Two Types of List Compilations—and How to Select the Right One for Your Needs

Two separate types of data are available on the major lists of compiled consumer names. The first set of data is on an individual basis for each household, the second set is on the stratified basis of medians.

The *individual data* available on each household are:

1. Single family residences versus multiple dwellings (on all)
2. Sex of the head of the household (on all)
3. Number of years of residence (up to 16 years based on data of 57 million listed, connected, and published telephone listings) (on all)
4. Ethnicity (by surname selection for major groupings) (on most)
5. Number, make, model, year, and value of car or cars based on data of 57 million registered automobiles in 40 states (on those incorporating registrations)
6. Exact age (in many cases) of the head of the household
7. Number of children in the family by age groups (for a majority of families with children)
8. Size of family (and other adult members beyond the head of household) for most households
9. Family income (available on all four lists)
10. Individual purchase or mail response data.

Family income deserves further explanation. The most important fact about a household on a compiled list is income. Data are provided in increments of income of $1,000 up to $75,000 a year.

Data up to $40,000, which covers about 60 million of this country's 87 million families, are surprisingly accurate. An income of more than $40,000 a year can indicate the availability of discretionary (disposable) income but actual individual family data for the "upper echelons" are blurred.

Stratified data available for those small groups or clusters of families in each subblock or enumeration district provide a median for several valuable demographic categories including:

1. Family income, which is used along with car ownership, value of home, geographic location, age of head of household and other factors to establish the *individual* income for each family.

2. Home value

3. Percentage of ownership of home

4. Age of head of household

5. Education (last grade completed of head of household)

6. Inventory of major household appliances

These categories can also include over fifty other bits of demographic data most of which are not worth pursuing by the average direct marketer.

It is worth repeating that the data available on this side of the ledger are stratified—that is, data are provided in medians *not* individually (except the individual family income derived in part from the median income for the subblock).

The significance of these two listings is that each item of information can be used as a selection factor. For example, by selecting male-headed households with a median age in the range of 30- to 45-year olds that live in single-family houses where a new phone has been connected in the last two years, the chances of reaching young parents with young children is remarkably increased over the average of the data.

By selecting groups of males or females who in the previous decennial census had a median age of 50 years or older, and who have lived at the same address with the same phone number for fifteen or sixteen years, the chances of reaching senior citizens is quite high. This selection also can add in an overlay by family income which, for the most part, is not available on other golden age lists.

In a similar manner income levels can be tested; the relation of income to make of car can be determined; the variance between single-family dwellings and multiple-dwelling units can be ascertained. As I have often said at my seminars, the difference among those who use selection factors instead of simply copying or using phone book listings, is as great as the difference between wine and water.

Medians—Key to List Stratification

The key to stratification is understanding the use of medians. A median is halfway from the beginning to the end. Thus a census tract or subblock median income of $19,000 means that half the people in that tract make more than $19,000 while half make less. Some tracts have wide spreads; others have small spreads. The art in using medians consists of testing in substantial volume to determine which factors influence orders and which do not. Then tracts and subblocks with comparable demographic characteristics are selected. This is a form of marketing that lends itself primarily to clients who have needs for large lists or for thorough coverage of smaller areas.

DEALING WITH COMPILING LIMITATIONS

Because of the wealth of available data it may appear that any list you desire is available commercially. That is incorrect. There are some requests (probably on the order of one per one hundred) that skilled compilers cannot provide. But it is true that any list can be obtained if enough time, energy, and money is devoted to it.

Some List Requests Not Yet Available Commercially

A list of bona fide millionaires. It is this author's opinion that any such list is suspect. Although it is true that one of the financial giants could provide a list from its customer base, this just does not happen.

A list of paramedics. This list can be compiled but the cost has so far deterred all who have checked into this field.

A list of executives within telephone companies who determine policy.

A verified list of chief executives and chief financial executives of top companies that is 99 percent deliverable. A list that is 90 percent deliverable in this field is considered exceptional.

A list of large company executives responsible for renting outside space.

The owners of given franchises which have been purchased for $250,000 and over.

Adequate lists of government employees including the armed forces.

50,000 major users, by classification, of Air Cargo.

In addition there are many small, extremely valuable, and often esoteric lists that only the list user can obtain because these lists may be too specialized or too small or difficult to compile to attract a commercial compiler. Such lists include registrants at seminars and continuing education classes, signer of petitions, and guests at political or fundraising dinners or functions.

Specialized and Unusual Lists That Are Available for Rental

The list community is remarkably efficient however in bringing highly specialized lists to light. For example, rental is available today for:

20,000 women who own businesses, plus 50,000 additional minority business owners

The 10,000 largest receivers of mail in the United States.

6,000 special officers at major businesses involved in equal opportunity

35,000 women who have executive positions with the largest 100,000 corporations

7,500 newsletters and 4,000 company house organs

Every social service organization with nonprofit status

35,000 doctors who have computers in their offices

200,000 individuals who state they plan to buy a VCR

50,000 buyers for off-the-road vehicles

26,000 yacht owners

35,000 owners of Corvettes manufactured in 1975 or earlier

400,000 inquirers for data on solar heating

250 retailers offering drafting equipment

Every new telephone connection (both business and consumer) installed in a number of states

Subscribers to over 500 highly selective learned associations

Families with two or more children aged eighteen and under by name and birth date

SELECTIVE NEIGHBOR LISTS

The major massive lists of household names and addresses are maintained by street name in even and odd numerical order. Computer programs given any starting number and street, can reach and select records of neighbors on either side of a household as well as across the street.

In all probability, the best known and most used "neighbors" list in America is the list of "members of boards of directors and their neighbors" created by Ed Burnett Consultants. This list is based on the 70,000 members of boards of directors' at-home addresses and is published and updated annually by Standard & Poors, a list source represented by the Burnett organization. It is almost certain this list of approximately 1 million families is the highest-income list of affluents available.

This list is then augmented by adding *all* households in the client's enumeration districts or subblocks in which the board members live. For example, if two or three board members are found in one large high rise apartment in New York, the program takes all residents of that building. In a similar manner, any subblock in which a board member lives is included in an extension of the basic file. This extended file numbers almost 2 million—certainly close to the top 2 million families by income of the 87 million households in America.

A program that can identify a board member or his or her next-door neighbor can identify the next-door neighbors from any group of known addresses. (It is not necessary or even helpful to know the name on the record used as a locator.) Thus given a list of owners of a given make and model of car, air conditioner, furnace, or boat, it is now practicable to write to their next door neighbors or to call them. (In the majority of cases the phone number is also available.)

Once identified and selected, each household can be reviewed by such individual characteristics as dwelling unit, sex of head of household, length of residence, family income, and age. Or data can be developed on neighborhood characteristics based on median income, number of children, as well as specific data on number, make, and model of automobiles.

Directories that provide lists of residents in street order are published for over 1,500 cities. R.L. Polk alone publishes approximately 1,000 lists of individual data that include the occupational status of 26 million families. When a plumber, or a sales manager for siding, or screen, porch, garage, cable, or solar energy wishes to know the name of a next door neighbor before a doorbell is rung, these directories can be invaluable. Few directories, other than those published by R.L. Polk are available on tape for mailing purposes.

In addition there are a large number of "reverse" phone directories published. These directories have conventional alphabetic lists of phone registrants and then sort the data by street and number. This provides names and telephone numbers for each published phone number by neighbor. (As noted earlier, phone lists are far from being complete rosters of households. There are over 83 million families with phones but only 57 million of them are published, and several million of the 57 million have no local address thus rendering them unmailable. In this regard, it is important to note that the total number of households with televisions is 85 million or within 2 million or so of the grand total of households in America.)

Before census data were added to phone and car registration lists, and before the USPS began offering discounts for third class mail sorted by carrier route, the concept of "neighbor select" was used very little even though it was highly valuable. With access to the 400,000 bits of real estate for subblocks (each containing a cluster of 140 or more households) and to approximately 160,000 actual carrier routes as well as approximately 240,000 pseudoroutes (each with a cluster of about 350 households), the need to develop finer selectivity (for example, by the block face, nine-digit zip code or the next-door neighbors of "neighbor select") has tended to be a form of "overkill" in which the data obtained or obtainable are too detailed for statistical analysis.

OCCUPANT LISTS

Two companies in the United States, Advo and Harte Hanks, dominate the list field. They are owners of a number of local fulfillment or lettershops that emphasize occupant mail. Advo reportedly delivers 1 billion occupant pieces to the USPS. In 1984 Harte Hanks was responsible for mailing 2 billion pieces, all but a small portion addressed from its proprietary occupant files. These two companies claim that between them they control about 33 percent of all occupant mail that contains advertising.

An occupant list, like any other list used for mailing, is only as good as its updating process. New developments, apartment complexes, or areas can only get on file through regular and ritualistic on-the-ground surveillance. Thus while all occupant lists are ostensibly equal, some are more complete than others. There are about 200 compilers of occupant files in the United States. Thus, there is usually more than one source for a given area, state, or group of states.

Occupant files cover all but a minute part of the 87 million household addresses in the United States. The largest files compiled from printed records total approximately 75 million households. These occupant files reach 82 million households or 14 percent (on average) more households than the largest name files. Even when occupant lists are updated that day or week by the USPS they have a nondelivery factor that averages about 2 percent. Many people ask, "Why?" The answer lies in vacancies: about 2 percent of households are vacant at any given time.

TWO MAIN LISTINGS FOUND BY MOTOR VEHICLE RECORDS

Driver License Lists

The chief source of data on exact date of birth of adults comes from files of registered drivers compiled state by state.

In addition to age, these lists include data on those who must wear glasses in order to drive a car. Some lists also include data on weight. Since it is likely several members of a family drive, these lists, like voters registration files, provide an average of more than one individual to a household.

Driver's licenses are issued or renewed, for the most part, for periods of three years although some states now favor four years, and at least one state renews licenses by using birth dates as the renewal dates every five years. Thus a file of new data as obtained from the state registries is normally 33 percent undeliverable. Even after some overlays with more current available telephone or auto registration data, the deliverability of driver license files is somewhat suspect.

Driver license files are used in two major ways in the building of lists: (1) as a means to augment files, and (2) as the major component of nationwide files of people at-home addresses.

Automotive Registration Lists

With the exception of about six state lists also purchased by others, the only compiler of auto registration lists in the country is R.L. Polk. Thirty-four states make their lists available through Polk with no restrictions. Sixteen states restrict availability of their lists to car-related offers only. Eight to ten states (the number shifts from year to year) have completely removed their registration lists from the market. A copy of car data compiled by R.L. Polk is sold to R.H. Donnelley Company each year.

Most automobile registration lists are issued to R.L. Polk in the spring: each state list is then used for only one year as the data continuously deteriorate during the time lapse between updates. By merging data on make, model, year, number, and value of cars with the telephone list, both R.L. Polk and R.H. Donnelley are able to produce data of surprising accuracy for individual family incomes, of up to about a $40,000 income level. (Data above that income level are mostly based on guesswork.)

Fifty-five percent of names of people who own cars can also be found on the telephone file. Therefore, a majority, say, of owners of Chrysler Le Barons can be reached by phone as well as by mail. (A good number of those names on the car file where no matching telephone number can be found indicates that these people rent cars and usually have an above-average income.)

The states where R.H. Donnelley, R.L. Polk, and Data Base America could not provide car registration lists in 1986 were Alaska, Arkansas, Connecticut, Hawaii, Indiana, Kansas, Nevada, New Jersey, New Mexico, Oklahoma, Oregon, Pennsylvania, South Dakota, Virginia, Washington, and Wyoming. In those states, the legislators have passed laws forbidding the release of the names of such registrants on the basis of invasion of privacy.

Some other list selections available through vehicle registrations include:

- Truck registrations
- Motorcycle registrations

- Motorized home registrations
- Two-car families
- Buyers in last twelve months of cars (U.S., foreign, or both) valued at $12,000 and over
- Rolls Royce registrations
- Station wagon registrations
- Mini-wagon registrations
- All Xs, Ys, and Zs for Years One, Two, Three, or Four (or One through Four)
- New car buyers by brand

CONSUMER LISTS FOR BUSINESS MAIL

Business lists are used by many mailers because business is a profitable market for some consumer offers. The concept that a businessperson, professional, or executive is first a human being (and therefore a consumer) is proved every day. This concept is also true of business mailings to business because copy, art, and offers, created with the consumer mentality in mind, often outpull straight "nuts and bolts" packages—even to supposedly square minded engineers. However, to date, very little has been done to send business mailings to consumers at their homes. More will certainly be done for three primary reasons:

1. There are certain business offers of general appeal that have a fair likelihood of reaching a part of their markets at home addresses.

2. There is a growing proportion of households today where one or more members are running a for-profit enterprise out of their homes. In 1980 the United States Census Bureau found 2.2 million households in this category and probably missed as many more. The fact that 8.2 million enterprises with business phones provide, according to the I.R.S., over 15 million tax paying enterprises may be proof of the proliferation of "business at home." Two lists are now on the market that offer $1/2$ a million of such households, with more to come.

3. The proliferation of home computers means millions more of those employed outside the home will establish their offices in their homes.

There is no doubt by list compilers that there are millions of "at-home" business operations.

The following list of kinds of business offers that may do well when mailed to at-home addresses are advocated by many list marketers.

- Business services
- Credit cards
- Office and workplace products, supplies, and equipment
- Business gifts
- Professional guidance
- Books, magazines, newsletters, seminars, cassettes

PART II: BUSINESS LISTS—COMPILED AND MAIL ORDER

There are two ways to compile a business mailing list: You can (1) compile your own list from internal company records, external printed sources, or external lists precompiled or assembled by others, or (2) you can hire an outside service to compile a list for you from internal company records, external printed sources, or external lists precompiled or assembled by others.

Your best bet is to engage an outside list expert to build a business list. The operative words here are "list expert." He or she may be a compiler, consultant, list broker, or an advertising agency executive. The title is not important—the expert knowledge of all of the various list sources is. (The three major sources of business list data by classification—Dun & Bradstreet, Data Base America by Ed Burnett Consultants, and the file compiled from classifieds by American Business Lists, are discussed in the section on Business Compilers on page 283).

Despite the fact that an outside service should be used, there are small highly desirable list components that only the client can acquire or locate. These should be pursued by the client.

TWELVE MAIN SOURCES OF BUSINESS LISTS

The list expert has all of the following business list sources at his or her command. Some of these are excellent sources; others are not. Some are worth using or testing; others are not. It pays to get expert help.

1. Directories

Business and classification These directories report on businesses by industry, market, state, or community, and usually include names, addresses, personnel (by name and title), and some demographic data, which can include the size of company, number of employees, telephone number, and products sold or professions employed. There are over 5000 such directories published in America and at least 500 new ones are started each year.

Telephone book classifications There are 4750 separate local classified directories published in America that have formerly been compiled by several major compilers into a universe consisting of virtually all businesses, institutions, and offices of professionals. This universe includes over 13 million individual records, about 7.5 million independent establishments, and over 3500 separate classifications. Today, only one firm utilizes the classifieds (or Yellow Pages) in this way.

City There are several thousand city and local directories, many of which provide the only or main source of occupational data with at-home addresses. R.L. Polk canvasses and publishes data on 26 million households on cycles ranging from 12 months to 36 months.

Rosters These include membership rolls of affinity groupings such as associations, societies, clubs, industry leaders, and so on.

2. Trade show registrants

Trade show registrants are of two types—those who register at individual booths at a given show, with a specific interest in a particular product or source, or, more likely, those who register for the trade show itself, a listing of whom is later published by the trade show manager, coded according to such functions as sales, engineering, finance, design, plus a means to select or omit students, librarians and the like.

3. Attendance rosters

Some of the best small lists available are of attendants of meetings, seminars, or shows. If a meeting is worth attending for you or one of your people, it stands to reason the list of all attendees can be a valuable list source.

4. Magazine publishers

There are over 1500 industrial magazines that cover one hundred classifications. Most of the publishers now rent names of their subscribers or recipients.

5. Newsletter publishers

There are approximately 8000 newsletters circulated in America. All but a small number serve individual specialized business markets. Those which make their lists available for mailing usually work on an exchange only policy.

6. Multiple magazines master files

Virtually every publisher of three or more magazines offers an unduplicated master file of all recipients. Among the major list sources here are: McGraw-Hill, Thomas, Chilton, Penton, Industrial, CMP, and Technical.

7. Business public data banks

There are several lists of names ranging from 7 million to 10 million of executives that are compiled by combining and unduplicating various compiled lists, mail order buyers, and magazine recipient files:

- *MDA* by Mal Dunn Associates, which includes all McGraw-Hill and Standard & Poors data.

- *The American Register* by Dun & Bradstreet which includes the D&B list of major businesses.

- *List Technology* which are primarily mail order lists and magazine lists in technical markets. (See Data Banks, page 578 for a list of privately owned data banks.)

- A new master file of business executives is now available through Data Base America. It features all data from Standard & Poors, and includes numerous compiled files.

8. Dun & Bradstreet

In addition to providing about 70 million of this country's 8 million business establishments, D&B also makes names available of: million-dollar company executives; 8 million business owners and major executive files; doctors, lawyers, and insurance agents individually qualified by telephone research; 750,000 businesses run from homes; and over 1 million businesses qualified by phone research.

9. Standard & Poors

This is the key directory to major manufacturers, which lists most of the 45,000 largest companies in America with 250,000 executives by name and title. This is the major component of Ed Burnett Consultants' universe of major business executives. S&P also makes members of major boards of directors' at-home addresses available which is the key input to the Burnett list of members of boards and their neighbors' at-home addresses.

10. Business mail order buyers

There are over 600 known mail order businesses that sell to other businesses by mail, primarily by catalog. They can be selected by classification.

11. Compiled business mail order buyers

Direct media has combined a number of business mail order lists into a data bank of known mail order buyers. The list totals 2.5 million and is selectable by SIC classification.

12. Specialized sources

While there are multiple sources for almost every classification, there are specialists (both compilers and publishers) who have established themselves as primary sources for given classifications, including: libraries; schools and school teachers; colleges and college teachers; banks, savings and loans and credit unions; stock and bond brokers; dentists; lawyers; nurses; hospitals; and advertisers found in magazines.

Specialized Medical Lists: Seven Sources

One list classification with specialized sources is doctors, or MDs. Relatively few people in the list field are aware that there are at least 7 different sources for names of doctors.

1. The primary list in this field, without a doubt, is the AMA (American Medical Association). This list includes every doctor in America, including retirees, and is the only source for all medical students, residents, and interns. Data on each MD includes specialty (and secondary specialty), area of patient care, age, and medical school attended. The list totals over 400,000. The crux of this list is total coverage and access to MDs by specialty. This is the one MD list that requires clearance from and payment of a royalty to the AMA for each use. The list has no phone numbers. The list is amazingly current. Each of some eleven contractors that run this file must update it *weekly*.

2. The next most used list is a file of all doctors in private practice listed in classified phone directories. This list includes 190,000 physicians at 140,000 separate offices. It makes selection of one per office possible as well as doctors serving in group practices. It includes a fair amount of data on specialty. It also includes a phone number for every record. This list is as good as the phone books and the compiler who works with them.

3. D&B provides a list of verified names, addresses, and phone numbers of over 100,000 physicians in private practice. The updating cycle in this file has not as yet been determined.

4. In the file of 57 million registered household telephones there are names and at-home addresses of 320,000 doctors. (In major cities, doctors tend to list only their business phones in alphabetic directories.) Research indicates that about 85 percent of these listings are of MDs, over half of them are at-home addresses. They have a phone number but no data as to specialty. This is the largest list primarily offering doctors at-home addresses. It tends to outpull either the classifieds or the AMA file for such offers as travel that are best directed to the home.

5. There are several files of doctors in private practice (some include dentists and other professionals) who buy items for their offices by direct mail. Such lists usually contain names of from 20,000 to about 60,000 people. They do not include specialty nor phone numbers.

6. The AMA will not permit its file to be used for any fund raising or political mailings and it turns down many other mailings that might not bother most list owners. To provide access to lists of doctors by specialty, a large list is now generated from individual rosters of specialists. The usual availability is about two-thirds of the AMA file, which turns out to be close to the total on the AMA file for in-patient care. No royalty or clearance (other than reasonable taste) is required. There are no phone numbers.

7. The newcomer on the block is the "Medec" list which is that rarity—an originally researched list—that covers every doctor in practice, by specialty, age, treatment processes, and ownership of VCRs and computers among other things. This company provides a copy of its volume on key drugs to doctors who answer a long questionnaire. Because this "Bible" of drug availability and use is so valuable over 99 percent of active physicians are willing to fill out the questionnaire to make sure they get their desk copy. This list offers virtually 100 percent coverage of the market once covered exclusively by the AMA. No royalty payment is required. Phone numbers are not included.

Executive Lists

Newly appointed executives are another specialized subsection of Business List sources: There are a number of sources for obtaining names including daily monitoring of the "New York Times" and the "Wall Street Journal." Both D&B and S&P can provide names of executives new this year to their tomes of lists on big business. Monitoring of business magazines and internal business house organs produces names not found in the national newspapers.

With the coming of the phone company lists, current data on newly connected companies, institutions, and offices of professionals will be universally available in time.

HOW BUSINESS MAGAZINES PROVIDE CONTROLLED SOURCES FOR NEW LISTINGS

From a renewal point of view, the business press is very much like the consumer books. A paid circulation book in a field will require leavening of 30 percent or more new subscribers in order to maintain its advertising rate base, which is measured by its circulation. Where the book provides a qualified circulation (each recipient has, for the most part, requested the service by mail or for some publications, the recipient must qualify by actively being in the field) the turnover per year can run from 20 to 40 percent.

A controlled circulation publication in which the publisher chooses the establishments that will be served, may have a changeover during the course of a year of 15 to 30 percent of its recipients.

Given a choice between two magazines covering the same market, one with paid circulation, the other controlled, the paid circulation list will be selected as the better bet for mail order solicitations. But a good controlled circulation list, and particularly a good mail qualified request circulation list may provide higher response. Recipients of controlled circulation magazines have high incomes, occupy high positions, and they are almost always part of those who individually, and through their businesses, have adequate discretionary income. Most of them have been in this affluent influential position for years. Because these lists are mailed and cleaned monthly, they are exceptionally deliverable, even within the confines of big business where the lack of room number or department number is enough to cause some compiled mailings to be trashed. These executives are middle- and uppermanagement executives and owners who can and do pay their bills promptly.

Business Magazine Mailing List Classifications

There are mailing lists by classification of trade or industrial journals in virtually every SIC class. This means that the mailer can find hundreds of availabilities in every type of contracting, marketing, transportation, communications, utilities, wholesaling, retailing, banking, insurance, real estate, institutions, professional listings, chain stores, and services, including governmental services.

Most of the sources are audited by the Business Press Association (BPA) and audited books provide detailed and accurate counts by:

1. SIC classification
2. finetuned title of the readers
3. geographic location

Many magazines report on such useful facts as the consumption of given materials (for example, metals), and uses (for example, the types of computers installed).

Those vertical publications that cover one classification (say, plumbers or interior designers) and have circulations approaching the universe of such establishments range from the largest entities to the smallest—much like a compiled file from the classified phone books. However, most horizontal books (in engineering, or metalworking, for example) tend to concentrate on providing lists of multiple executives in the largest establishments—primarily those with fifty or more employees. Knowing only the name of the magazine is not enough. It is essential to review the BPA statement, and check out how close you can come to just the precise segment you desire.

Care must be taken, if you desire only one or two names per establishment, to make certain the magazine can produce names that way; otherwise you may receive forty or fifty names of executives at one location. One way to avoid this is to select names by title or titles.

Major industrial publishers now make an unduplicated file available from a combination of the recipients of all of their magazines. Thus one can obtain purchasing agents, say, by name or sales managers, or traffic managers, across ten, fifteen, or twenty magazines (for even greater coverage either geographically or by function, see the section on Data Banks on page 513).

Three Differences between Compiled Files and Magazine Files

The basic differences between a compiled file (usually based in part on all records from a complete set of approximately 4,700 classified phone directories) and a magazine file in the same basic classification are three-fold. First, the compiled file, in almost every case, provides more complete coverage of the classification universe. Second, the compiled file is normally sorted down to only one record per establishment. Third, except for professionals and other special lists (including those provided by D&B) the compiled file is a list mainly of establishments, while almost all business magazine files consist of the names of executives at their establishments.

What Business Magazine List Users Should Know about BPA Statements

There are two audit certification services for magazine circulation lists: Audit Bureau of Circulation (ABC) for consumer magazines, and Business Publications Audit (BPA). List people rarely look at an ABC statement although they should. There is a distinct difference in the caliber and response value of a subscription sold by direct mail and one sold by field sales. But *anyone* thinking of using a business magazine list should first study the BPA statement carefully.

The BPA statement first describes the field covered, and then details those executives by function and classification that are qualified to receive the publication.

The circulation statement then goes on to break down the readership into counts by number and percentage as follows:

1. Four digit SIC—provision for selecting by classification.
2. Size of the company (by number of employees)—a means of selecting establishments with a given number of employees.
3. Job function—a means of omitting specific functions, say, administrative or purchasing functions from an engineering book.
4. Geography—both state counts and major geographical area counts are given.

A typical BPA audited magazine that serves a selected classification in engineering will include the following breakdown by functional titles:

1. Company management—corporate officials, vice presidents, general managers, owners, and partners.
2. Plant management—managers, superintendents, supervisors, and production managers.
3. Engineering (engineers by type)—industrials, plant, methods used, and specialized engineers serving a given field.
4. Purchasing—purchasing directors, agents, and buyers.
5. Distribution—storage, warehousing and distribution (if included), traffic manager, warehouse manager, storekeeper, inventory managers.
6. Auxilliary Distribution—sales, marketing, and other personnel.
7. Free advertising—ad agencies, complimentary copies.

Many of these magazines can select by actual titles rather than group titles such as plant management. If your need is for names of traffic managers only you may not wish to take every executive coded for distribution from a given book. (When your need is this finite, it is probably better to turn to one of the data banks with established, master unduplicated files from multiple magazines by major business publications, or to one of the public data banks that include inputs from such publishers.)

Magazine files make it possible to zero in on job functions and titles with great specificity. One real problem is that the complexity of business tends to proliferate specific titles. Not too long ago for one client who wanted to reach executives who had decisionmaking power, by name and title in order to rent outside warehouse space, we provided a list that included over 500 separate titles. This indicates that selection of proper titles and functions for a given mailing is not a simple matter. Functions and titles are not necessarily the same thing. In the Standard & Poors data base of major companies, there are tens of thousands of executives with multiple titles (so much so that the average number of titles or functions per executive is over 1.5). There are presidents and treasurers; executive vice presidents and sales directors; chief operating officers and secretaries. The counts for this file provide a good idea of the complexity of American big business. Titles by function (such as sales, advertising, finance, production, research, international trade) total 160,000, and then there are 140,000 vice presidents (other than executive VPs, corporate VPs, and senior VPs) which have no other designation. For many mailings such addresses to only vice presidents never get mailed, but they represent close to one-half of VPs available through one of the great publishers of executives by name and title.

HOW PUBLISHERS USE "BINGO CARDS" TO MEASURE AUDIENCE RESPONSE

Many publishers of industrial and trade books provide a "bingo card" as a means to indicate the responsiveness of their audiences. This card is "ticked off" by the reader and mailed postage-free to the fulfillment arm of the magazine.

As there is no outlay of postage expenses by the reader, and all the reader has to do to request information is place an X or a checkmark next to a number on the card (there is no limit as to the number of Xs to be placed, which means some users simply place an X next to every listing) the response here tends to come from groups of students, information collectors, and those simply casually interested.

The magazine counts each X—not each person, and every X is transmitted back to an advertiser to fulfill his or her offer of further information. In general, bingo card list names are the most basic form used to generate response and are the least likely inquirers to convert into buyers.

General advertising that offers free booklets will generate a good portion of casual inquiries. However, these individuals must take the time and trouble to clip the coupon and pay for postage to mail it in. (Test after test indicates that if such offers are qualified by the need to include 25¢, 50¢, or $1, the number of casual inquiries is reduced substantially. Catalog operators now call for a payment of $1, $2, even $5 for a sample catalog, usually with the promise to rebate the qualification sum against the first order.)

To prove that there is always something new under the sun, A.C. Neilsen is now offering an electronic version of the traditional bingo card. Readers can directly dial an 800 number into a Neilsen computer, and then key in individual coded requests on touchtone phones. (Those without touchtone phones can dial in to a Neilsen operator.) These "instant requests" are batched and forwarded to advertisers daily. Response time by this means is trimmed down by several weeks.

Why Big Business Is Big in the List Business

In the business field and the business-list field, the Fortune 1000 companies, the largest industrial companies on the basis of gross sales for the given year, have an aura about them that attracts mailers of virtually every type vying for every dollar. And this aura, coming as it does from the word for gold, well becomes this prized 1000. These companies control the destinies of approximately 25,000 branch plants and subsidiaries (about 6 percent of the approximately 425,000 manufacturing establishments in the United States) and produce over 75 percent of the value added to production in the United States. They also employ over 70 percent of the millions of people that work in manufacturing. Ten years ago, the Fortune 1000 branch plants only totaled about 14,000—not the 25,000 today. In recent years one hundred of the companies that were once members of the Fortune 500 have been absorbed by larger companies. Each year fifty to one hundred Fortune 1000 companies are removed from this category because of mergers, acquisitions, divestitures, or changes in sales volume. At the top of the Fortune 1000 are 900 companies with sales of one billion dollars or more; at the lower end are "modest" companies with sales of about $500,000,000 and that employ 10,000 or more people (based on 1986 figures).

Most mailers to big (Very) businesses utilize the Fortune 500 Manufacturing Companies, or the Fortune 1000 Manufacturers, and occasionally, the so-called Fortune 300 consisting of the fifty largest retailers, banks, construction firms, insurance companies, transportation companies, and utilities. Perhaps the most likely reason most list users use these industrial lists is habit, convenience, and the offerings of list compilers eager to provide these "fashionable" lists.

Few marketers seem to be aware that there are 1800 manufacturers who fall below the Fortune 1000 list but who all have sales volumes of over $300,000,000. There also are now 8000 manufacturing firms with sales of $50,000,000 and over, which was the cut-off figure for "making" the Fortune 1000 a few years ago.

A Better Way to Look at Big Businesses

Those that measure big business by the Fortune 1000 list also fail, for the most part, to recognize that nonmanufacturing giants abound in the United States. For example, there are 1000 nonmanufacturing firms with sales volumes of over $1,000,000,000 compared with 900 manufacturers. At the $100,000,000 and over level, there are *twice* as many nonmanufacturing companies as manufacturing firms (5600 compared with 2800).

Thus a mailer who orders and is delivered the Fortune 500 list may be surprised to learn this list does not include banks, airlines, utilities, mining firms, wholesalers and consists of manufacturers only. In addition the mailer might find it advisable to mail not only to the Fortune 500 manufacturers but also to the 5,000 major companies in the United States, all of which have sales of $200,000,000 or more, or to the home offices of the 8500 companies that have sales of $100,000,000 or more.

Mailers can order the largest 1,000, 2,000, 3,000, 5,000, 10,000, or 20,000 companies and they can specify classification, as well as geography.

For mailers who look at big business in terms of number of employees, the employee table indicates that about 50,000 companies have one hundred or more employees. (The comparable figure for sales—the largest 50,000—is $10,000,000 and more.) Another 30,000 firms have fifty to one hundred employees. At the upper end of the list there are over 6,600 firms who have over 1,000 employees.

How to Mail to Big Business

The very size of a big business should give pause to the average mailer who usually elects to send one piece of mail per company to the president, treasurer, or chairperson of the Fortune 1000. If each of these companies are equal to ten, twenty, or one hundred smaller firms, then it might stand to reason that a *series* of letters is required, or that a *group* of executives must be reached, rather than only one executive. The care and feeding of big business is an art known only to a few top sales promotion agencies, and learned at great cost over many campaigns. Big business is not like business in general—and should not be approached as such.

How to Avoid Mailing Duplications to Big Businesses

Mail to individuals by name and title. Mail first class. Make your offer as businesslike as possible. There are a number of duplications in conventional major business sources that a sound computer program can identify and wring out. Let us start with *internal* duplication in any of the major sources—duplication you get by using a major directory *as is*. By sorting through phone numbers, two or more companies with different names that share the same phone number at the same address can be identified and eliminated. A good merge–purge program will reduce the average directory in this way by 5 percent. A subsequent pass examining individuals within companies, including board members serving on multiple boards, can be expected to remove another 2 percent of duplication of individual executives.

Those with "slide-rule" minds can see that the savings at say, $300 to $500/M in the mail, are more than the cost of the list if unduplicated files are used in place of the conventional sources that are unduplicated.

Using Executives by Name and Title: A Look at What's Available

The availability of executives by name and functional title from such a composite file, is shown in Table 8.1.

Note that coding for special vice presidents permits identification of three levels of executive direction within some major companies namely, executive vice presidents, manufacturing vice presidents, and senior vice presidents. Also note that owners of noncorporate businesses are a larger part of Big Business than most observers are aware. (Good practice in ordering list data for presidents by size is to order presidents and primary owners—one per company—to cover firms not headed by a president.) The total number of titles available is greater than the total number of executives because even in big business executives wear two or more hats (such as secretary-treasurer, president and chairperson, sales manager and advertising manager). Similarly there are some major companies with more than one president so the names of presidents of the largest 1,000 firms may total 1,050 or 1,075 and still be quite correct. (For stand-patters who believe 1,000 firms should have 1,000 presidents, list compilers utilize a program to limit the pull to one president per firm.)

Factors to Select for Your Mailings to Big Businesses

The thrust of the preceding section is that data are available that make controlled mailings to big businesses possible by a number of useful business

Table 8.1

Executives by name—available by functional file unduplicated from big business master file

Title	Title Total	Number of Companies
President	141,000	132,000
Owner-primary	8,000	6,500
Owner-secondary	3,000	1,500
Chairperson of the board	29,000	25,000
Treasurer	47,000	42,000
Chief financial officer	49,000	33,000
Comptroller	17,000	16,000
Executive vice president	33,000	22,000
Senior vice president	24,000	500
International director	1,800	1,500
Secretary	40,000	38,000
Vice president	137,000	59,000
Manager	175,000	50,000
Sales manager	44,000	33,000
Advertising manager	13,000	9,000
Purchasing director	30,000	28,000
Data processing manager	6,000	5,000
Director of manufacturing	17,000	13,000
Director	200,000	85,000

demographic characteristics. Here are twelve factors you can use on your next mailing to big businesses:

1. Sales volume
2. Number of employees
3. Primary SIC. (two-, three-, or four-digit)
4. Secondary SICs (usually up to three)
5. Fortune 500, Fortune 1000, Fortune 1300, Fortune branch plants
6. Any addition you desire to pull from Fortune lists
7. One, two or three executives per company
8. Executives available by twenty-six functional titles
9. Primary owners as well as subordinate owners
10. Directors' at-business addresses as well as at-home addresses (with selections by age and board)

11. Geographic by state, metropolitan area, three-digit zip codes, and five-digit zip codes

12. One executive per company by any title of up to thirty characters

Big business in America is covered in some detail by two large financial publishing empires: Dun & Bradstreet and Standard & Poors. D&B data are available through the company's own network of company sales representatives. Ed Burnett Consultants Inc. is the list manager for S&P and the S&P data are available through both S&P and the Burnett network of independent list wholesalers.

Selection by company is usually made by classification (SIC) and by size (employee strength or sales volume). Where local geography is involved, it is often necessary to open the parameters of size and/or classification to obtain a given number of establishments. (Compilers find it necessary to tell clients and prospects everywhere, "We cannot provide more than exists.") These files cover the home offices of every firm with sales of $5,000,000 and over in the United States, plus a great proportion of those with sales in the range of from $1,000,000 to $5,000,000. For example, on the S&P file there are over 1,500 companies listed with sales of $1 billion and over. Over 4,000 of these companies have sales of $200,000,000 and over. There also are over 100,000 executives available with approximately twenty-five major business titles within companies with sales of over $75,000,000. Adding unduplicated coverage from banks, industrials, stock brokerages, savings and loans, all national advertisers, all major advertising agencies, and qualified retail, utility and insurance companies, this big business file totals 710,000 key executives at the top 217,000 companies in America.

Broken out by major SIC group, the counts are as follows:

SIC		Firms	Executives
1–9	Agriculture, Forestry, and Fisheries	730	3,370
10–14	Mining	1,820	10,800
15–17	Contract Construction	3,210	15,010
20–39	Manufacturing	110,470	371,550
40–49	Transportation, Communication and Utilities	7,460	36,830
50–51	Wholesaling	7,250	37,480
52–59	Retailing	14,040	50,960
60–69	Finance, Insurance, and Real Estate	68,690	170,360
70–79	Services for Businesses	9,400	49,050
80–99	Services by Professionals and Governmental Agencies	1,330	8,150

THE GROWTH OF BUSINESS GROUPS AND THEIR IMPACT ON MAILING LISTS

One of the phenomena of our time has been the development of charter air traffic, particularly the great growth of "group" travel.

Human beings are highly society-minded animals that join in groups, clusters, affinities, and associations. Virtually every activity of modern day life involves some form of "belonging" to a communal lifestyle from group practice to the barber shop quartette, secret groups to political action activists, Helen Hokinson Garden Club chairpeople to specialists in such disparate disciplines as physics, hairdressing, coin collecting, actuarial science, real estate, educational business administration, legal reporting, production and fullfillment of direct mail.

Having once been a member or a participant ensures being counted in some groups or lifestyles (if the records are good enough)—for example, alumni associations, former servicemen, retired school teachers or employees and former elected officialdom.

From a mailing list point of view, there is no single, simple means to cover groups essentially because of the great disparity and dispersion among groups. But with the growing importance of the group as a purchaser of travel, insurance, and investment services; publications; premiums; gifts; education and art, and the list-compiling fraternity (another group, if you will) has responded by making several hundred lists in this field available.

Three Ways to Classify Taxable Group Organizations

In the United States today, there are approximately 11 million entities (companies, individuals, and institutions) that report social security taxes to the United States government. These are roughly divided as follows:

1. Self-employed
Farmers	3,000,000
Professionals	1,500,000
Business	1,000,000

2. Institutions   1,000,000
3. Business (other than self-employed individuals)   4,500,000

Thus, the outer limits of "group activity" (as registered by some form of tax roll) is about 4.5 million plus, perhaps, another 1 million groups (clubs, fraternal orders, associations, foundations, governmental and political bodies and the like) that have no reason to be found on tax rolls.

Some idea of the range of these groups can be demonstrated simply by going through the alphabetic finder of a major city classified directory. Here, for example are some of the applicable classifications gleaned from the letter "A" in the Manhattan yellow pages:

Abstracters

Accountants

Actuaries

Adjusters

Advertising agencies

Advertising—direct mail

Airports

Amusement parks

Animal hospitals

Antiques

Apartment houses

Architects

Armories

Art schools

Artists

Assayers

Association management

Associations

Astrologers

Athletic organizations

Automobiles—antique and classic

Two Key Areas Available for Group Mail Order

For convenience and categorization, groups available for mail order solicitation can be grouped under two major headings, with a great deal of interchange between them: services and businesses.

Some idea of the size of groups, within *services*, all of which are individually available as markets for mail are given in the following five lists:

General services

Educational services

Governmental services

Cultural services

Recreational services

Under the second major heading for groups and *businesses*, we find all nine major SIC classifications of business principally by:

Agricultural

Professional

Financial

Retail

Business in general

Services in General	
Associations	35,000
Fraternal orders	
with phones	15,000
with and without phones	45,000
Social service with phones	110,000
Labor organizations	
with phones	14,000
with and without phones	60,000
Charitable organizations	
registered in New York	4,000
probable country total	50,000
Foundations	29,000
Women's clubs	50,000
Burial services	5,000
Community centers	5,000
Chambers of commerce	10,000
Hospitals	10,000
Nursing homes	20,000
Political organizations	2,000
Educational Services	
Private high schools	1,500
Catholic high schools	2,000

(*continued*)

Catholic elementary schools	10,000
Public and private colleges	3,400
School districts	16,000
High schools	28,000
Nurses' training schools	1,800
Public libraries	6,000
University computer centers	1,200
University research centers	2,200
Alumni associations	10,000
Religious orders, convents, retreats	7,500
Day nurseries	51,000
College stores	2,500
Fraternities and sororities	
on campus	3,000
honorary	7,000
Head-start groups	6,000
Technical, vocational, and business schools	3,000
Correspondence schools	500
Business education seminars	1,500
Dormitories at colleges	2,000
Governmental Services	
City departments in major cities	12,500
Volunteer fire departments	20,000
Counties	3,000
Cities with populations over 10,000	2,300
Airports	500
4-H clubs	1,000
Military establishments	1,000
Civil defense groups	1,000
Prisons	2,500
Dispensaries and clinics	41,500
Foreign governments	
embassies, ministries, United Nations	250
consulates	3,000
Public school bus companies	1,000
Cultural Services	
Historical societies	1,500
Museums	3,000
Art schools	500
Cable and wire TV systems	6,000
Churches	250,000
Recreational Services	
Marinas	1,500
Summer camps	3,500
Dancing schools	1,500
Dancing studios	4,000
Golf clubs	7,000

Yacht clubs	1,000
Bridge clubs	3,000
Tennis clubs	2,000
Fishing and sporting clubs	3,000
Boy Scout and Girl Scout councils	2,000
Boys clubs	4,000
Educational TV stations	1,100
Arenas and stadiums	3,900
Automobile clubs	1,000
Entertainment bureaus	1,000
Health and reducing clubs	15,500
Riding academies and stables	400
Kennels	2,500
Airports	7,000
Ballrooms	1,000
Bowling alleys	7,000
Billiard and pool parlors	2,000
State and national parks	500
Cabanas and beach clubs	1,000
Hobby centers and model car centers	7,000
Race tracks	500
State and county fairs	2,000

Agricultural

Farmers' cooperatives	10,000
Farmers registered for farm labor	Unknown
Class I and Class II farmers	300,000
Grain elevators	7,000

Professionals

Law firms	10,000
Medical groups	6,000
Accounting firms	30,000
Architectural firms	11,000
Engineering firms	12,000

Financial

Credit unions	23,000
Mutual funds	400
Stock and bond brokers	6,000
Financial analysts	12,000
Real estate copartnerships	Unknown
Realtor associations, local	500
Real estate management firms	500
Credit rating bureaus	4,000

Retail

Shopping centers	6,000
Bookstores (most with lending libraries)	15,000
Department stores with charge accounts	2,500

(*continued*)

Business

Agriculture, forestry, and fishery establishments with over ten employees	5,000
Mining establishments with over ten employees	6,000
Contractors establishments with over ten employees	50,000
Manufacturers with over ten employees	140,000
Utilities, transport, and communications establishments with over ten employees	25,000
Wholesale establishments with over ten employees	60,000
Retail establishments with over ten employees	130,000
Financial establishments with over ten employees	4,000
Business Service establishments with over ten employees	30,000

Some Specialized Business Groupings

Computer services with time sharing	500
Industrial laboratories	8,000
Private business libraries	5,000
Publications	15,000
Recreational departments of businesses	60,000

Individual Owners

Yacht owners	11,000
Plane owners	
business	40,000
personal	30,000
Owners of cars by brands	120,000
Computer user councils	100
Cooperative apartments	20,000
Real estate	
Credit card organizations	Unknown
Investment clubs	5,000
Consumer co-ops	1,000
Trailer owners	250,000 +
Trailer park operators	15,000
Wake-up call services	500

There also are some groupings that tend to be based primarily on ownership, particularly articles of a status-type nature.

FINANCIAL LISTS

The aim of most financial mailers and teleprospectors is to generate an inquiry from a person qualified essentially by income with discretionary dollars available for investment. But the players in this field are changing rather radically. Not long ago it was unheard of for a bank to utilize the mail to build deposits. Money funds and credit cards changed that, probably forever. Now banks, credit unions, insurance companies, stock brokers, finance companies, mortgage companies, investment trusts, tax shelters, and credit card companies are all in the financial market, competing essentially for a share of the same dollars from the same targeted market. As a result, the same names are appearing on lists that are used again and again by one or another of these players.

Three Types of Financial Lists Used Most Often

The lists most predominantly used are:

1. Known owners of stocks and bonds, divided mainly by subscriptions to stock and bond reporting services and tip services.
2. People of means, identified by profession, business, and affluence.
3. Readers of financial and high-level business magazines, including *Forbes, Barron's, The Wall Street Journal, Fortune, Business Week, Inc., CFO,* business sections of *Time, Newsweek* and *U.S. News.*

The Importance of Prospecting

A fair amount of prospecting is done from names compiled by major business publishers such as Dun & Bradstreet and Standard & Poors. The major data banks of executives also are tapped, for this purpose, along with the master business files of D&B or Data Base America. Names are available from Ed Burnett Consultants, Inc., D&B, and S&P, along with phone numbers which makes them particularly attractive to services that sell leads to financial mailers. There is a substantial market in such names and several list purveyors concentrate their marketing in this area. Affluent householders report they are on the receiving end of a stream of phone calls, (two or three per week is not unusual) and most of these calls are becoming shorter and sharper. However, prospecting by this means must be useful overall or it would not continue. There is not an insurance agent in the top 10 percent of sales who does not make his or her daily allotment of cold calls or follow-up calls after prospect mailings.

For area coverage, large business files (D&B, MDA, Data Base America) are tapped by zip code. Home address files are tapped by income, type of residence, length of residence, and other demographic data from the basic files compiled by Donnelley, Polk, Data Base America, or Metromail.

Why Credit Screens Are Often Helpful

A number of financial mailings involve a credit screen. The usual pattern after a merge–purge is to provide an extract (a set of match codes for all consumers on the file), per orders of the credit bureaus involved, which after a few weeks is returned in three lots: approved (for the stringency of credit required), not approved, (either for negative information on the file or failure to meet the credit conditions laid down), and a third and much larger part marked no information. It is surprising to most mailers who run such checks how small the proportion which survive such credit screens. The percentage of approvals on lists that might otherwise be assumed by their very nature to be credit worthy is rarely over 20 percent. (The main reason is the preponderance of nonmatches where no information is available.) In the last few years credit approved names, unmatched against other files, have been offered to the financial world. They have been eagerly accepted at high costs per thousand.

Once the marked extracts are returned, the computer house must run them against the original file of all names presented to select the complete, approved mailable records. Only these records may be mailed, unless some dispensation has been given by the credit bureaus. The cost per name in comparison to normal rentals is extremely high. Because of this comparison a good deal of negotiation ensues among list owners to get as close as possible to a net name basis. One means of reducing the cost per name is to send a *credit approved* financial offer say, for a $15,000 automatic line of credit, to the approved names, and utilize a standard long form *application for credit* which will be a part of the offer to those names that do not show adverse data.

Several of the lifestyle questionnaire lists attempt to get information on future needs of respondents, and this information finds its way into the data bank of names that work for financial offers.

The range of mail order buyers is remarkable—from selling of a $10 book to invitations to seminars on making money in real estate, to highly selected lists of people who appear to be good prospects for paying $50,000 or more for a given bond or offer.

Twenty years ago the actual stockholders of some major companies were available for rental, usually through surreptitious channels. Now the only lists of known stockholders are such lists as "insiders" who traffic in their own stock as reported through public announcements by the SEC., or lists of those who have answered questions on stock ownership. The United States government also publishes lists of pension funds by size as well as approved plan investors. There also are several sound sources for executives in charge of pension funds, profit-sharing funds, and investment trusts.

Banks can be classified by asset size as well as deposits. An average of ten executives by name and title for the 14,000 commercial banks, as well as their branch office managers are available by name. Savings and loan associations, credit unions, mortgage bankers, insurance companies, real estate companies, financial advisors, title guarantees, trusts, Small Business Investment Corps. (SBICs) and stock and bond brokers are all similarly available. There is even a rather good list available of bankers by name (under 1,000) who are involved in international transactions.

RETAILING: WHY CUSTOMER IDENTIFICATION IS CRITICAL TO SUCCESS

The one classification in America that most needs to answer the question, "Do you know where your customers are?" is retailing. The number of retailers is phenomenal (over 2 million with phone numbers; the number with a mailable customer file is probably on the order of a few thousand).

One important truth in retailing (either face-to-face or direct-response) is that the one best list is a list of current customers. Most establishments that sell items across the counter either have no interest in obtaining, or find it too troublesome to obtain, names and addresses of their buyers. (Tandy Corporation, which attempts to log the name and address of every customer, uses the success of this list gathering function as one means of measuring the effectiveness of the store manager.) Where the retail outlet has its own credit card, the growth of the list is controlled by the importance given to the acquisition of new charge accounts by management, as indicated by the quotas set, and the inducements provided for new applications.

Where a list exists, the retailer is in a position to invite customers and listed prospects to special sales or "preferred customer-only" evenings prior to a sale period open to the general public.

One of the better ways to get store customers to leave their names and addresses is to offer a prize drawing. Store visitors are invited to fill in a form and drop it into a fish bowl. This type of name-building offer works particularly well if the gift is featured, by means of a sign in the front window. J.R. Tobacco, which still has a modest stock of high-priced pre-Castro Cuban cigars uses a box of these cigars as the prize for drawings in each of its stores.

The one time retailers think of mailing is when new stores are opened. Names, usually from stratified lists, can be selected by income and a few other demographics within the zip code where the store is located. Stores designed to serve an uppercrust market can select names by income and location in order to attract the affluent residents within a given number of miles (or length of time of travel) to visit the store.

Retail malls that provide cooperative advertising vehicles for tenant stores such as mall advertisements, almost universally seek to reach the highest-income families in the immediate trading area of the mall. (Some tenant stores that recognize this, make special arrangements with the publisher of the cooperative to utilize such lists for solo mailings.)

Tabulations of fall and Christmas catalogs received through the mails indicate that local retail store catalogs comprise the most numerous single category of catalogs received by consumers. As store traffic builders, these catalogs may be successful; as creators of direct mail sales they seem to be primarily designed for failure. Their product line reflects the general line of the stores that originate them, and the nuances of direct response (guarantees, separate order form, emphasis on WATS and credit cards, and copy designed to provide credibility) are more often missing than not.

Credit cards issued by others (American Express, Diners Club, Visa, MasterCard) are now accepted at hundreds of thousands of retail outlets. Credit cards imprint the name of the holder (without an address) on the charge form. In most cases no attempt is made by the store to request the local address in order to add the name to the mailing list. Some of the nation's most pretigious retail stores accept tens of thousands of charges, particularly from American Express, and have no idea later of how to reach these valuable store customers. Most such stores have their own charge cards, but have provided no way to invite outside charge customers to apply for their inside "preferred customer" charge privilege.

Sears Roebuck and Company (Sears), which has over 66 million customers on its books, has launched its own universal charge card, called "Discover." It is very likely that Sears will have the staying power to position this new credit card as a major player in the financing of retail purchases.

EDUCATIONAL LISTS

College Educators

Two organizations, Educational Directory and College Marketing, each compile the names of approximately 500,000 college educators by discipline at their college and university addresses. Besides providing listings for over 200 different types of professors, selection is available for presidents, deans, professional schools, extension directors, placement directors, purchasing directors, business managers, book store managers, and alumni directors, as well as all libraries.

Both services also list book buyers by discipline and learned associations. Among the more esoteric availabilities are buyers of books on network design, solar energy, ultrasonics, ceramics, puppetry, Beowulf, black studies, sociology of women, neural sciences, quantum mechanics, and labor economics.

Library Lists

There are two major classifications of libraries; public and private and/or special. Public libraries can be selected by number of purchase dollars available per year for book funds. The public sector includes public libraries, high school libraries, and college libraries. The private sector includes specialized collections such as science, business, law, medicine, and religious collections. There are also lists of librarians by name, including members of the Special Libraries Association.

HOW TO ACQUIRE LIST DATA FOR SEMINARS AND CONTINUING EDUCATION PROGRAMS

One important market for lists and peripheral list thinking is adult education, particularly when provided in the form of seminars and continuing education by field of interest. There are seminars in almost every field of human endeavor from equal employment to how to write or speak, personnel and the law, accounting for the nonfinancial executive, as well as specialized seminars in technology, research, real estate, finance, production, investment in China, sports medicine, FTC rules, how to work with the government, and even zip codes.

Lists taken from seminar participants are aimed at one specific goal: to identify and reach people with a predilection to know more about a specialized subject. This makes targeted direct mail the major, and in most cases the only, economic means available to reach these people.

Eight Tips for Testing Mailing Lists for Seminar Operators

From a list standpoint, seminar operators should:

1. Recognize Geographical Concerns when Mailing for Seminar. The lower the cost of the seminar and the shorter the period, the more localized attendance will be. For a one-day seminar that costs $200 or less, the major city in which the seminar is located will produce the majority of the responses. The metro area surrounding it will produce the greatest part of the balance and the state beyond the metro area will produce a modest number. States on either side of the major city will produce only a minor amount of responses. This emphasizes the need to mail in depth, locally, and with decreasing quantities over distance.

To get some idea of the importance of geography in this field, maintain counts by three-digit zip codes for all mail sent. Then tabulate the participants to seminars by zip code and the percentage of responses by each three-digit zip. If you have never done this before, you may be in for an awakening.

This local "syndrome" is the reason why a seminar can do quite well in major markets, when the universe of those with a "need to know" is large enough to tap, and then fall by the wayside in some secondary markets. The lack of a sufficient universe in and around given cities is the reason givers of seminar are forced to reach out to nearby states.

2. Work with list experts to determine if the universe of names available locally is large enough to support a seminar offer. If not expand the market, coverage, phone calling, or expand the range of the seminar. List people cannot provide more names than the universe available.

3. Learn to test for price. The demand curve for most seminars is *not* elastic. (Price reduction will not increase response proportionally.) Raising prices will probably not affect response at all.

4. Every list used to elicit response for educational programs should be rented with phone numbers when available. Follow ups should be made by telephone on *every* number—and every list that can be followed up can be made better by mail-then-phone, than by mail alone.

5. Be prepared on multiple data, multiple city programs, which are becoming the standard in the industry, to kill a losing date or city. Most buyers can be switched or rescheduled. The seminar operator does not do any good for his or her speakers or his or her own operation by running a seminar with only a few attendees.

6. Never throw out the old standard unless and until a new one proves better. In the seminar field although mailing pieces do "wear out," long after the originator becomes tired of a given piece, prospects will have hardly even noticed. Never toss away the old before a new one proves the winner in a split test. Don't guess. Test and find out. Don't test B against C to get a new standard winning offer. A, the current standard, may be better than both. When testing, keep in mind last year's results may not hold. Test anew and find out.

7. Offer cassettes for each program. Current sales of cassettes surprise many old-line givers of seminar. Cassettes should be priced high, but well below the cost of the seminar they cover. (They must, however, be "audited" and "edited" for commercial use. The raw recording of the give and take of a seminar includes interruptions and dull spots which must be edited out.) In most cases the cassette buyer is not a likely prospect for the seminar itself.

8. Capture all data on every inquiry, phone call, and registrant. The more known about every name, the more specific and individualized the approach can be to each specialized cell of customers and prospects. Do not be afraid to ask for demographic data on job functions, titles, jobs, age groups, education levels, and outside interests. Participants write about their favorite subject—their selves.

SALES FORCE AS COMPILERS

Some sales managers have the naive belief that their salespeople in the field know all the prospects and all the projects in their territory where their goods and services can be sold. If you do not believe this, you should have your sales force send in a complete prospect listing, say, of every establishment in a local three-digit zip code. (Sectional Center Facility (SCF) with 50 employees or over— hopefully in either zip order or alphabetical by name of company. Then invite a list compiler to provide you with a sheet list for these same SCFs). The compiled list will be larger, probably two or three times larger, and there will be names on the sheet list that have *never* appeared on a sales report even from salespeople with ten years of knowledge of a territory. Salespeople make very poor list compilers. Compilers know more about the location of establishments than you can expect or hope salespeople to know. Let list compilers compile your prospect lists—let salespeople sell!

Several major companies, particularly in the office machine field, use their sales forces to review mailing lists, customer records, lead listings, and recommended prospect files on a periodic basis. Given no directive, salespeople (except for a few who are exceptionally market-minded) will sit on their hands and do nothing. The kind of list help that local salespeople *may* provide may be (and usually is) a far cry from the type of list help they *could* provide. However, keep in mind that this is not their job; they are trained to sell not fill out paperwork and they may not have ways available to keep up to date with executive changes, much less project shifts. If there has been a switch, shift, or substitution of representatives, the cleaning and list help available may be minuscule at best.

Salespeople *can* check and qualify list data furnished by the home office, and they can add qualified names to the list, if they understand the following:

1. The importance of names and addresses to the company, and the data that can be tagged to them.

2. The importance of such names to themselves for future sales.

3. What happens to misaddressed mail.

4. How to use the forms *you supply* to make changes, kills, and adds as painless as possible.

However, you should anticipate resistance from salespeople. Salespeople are notorious for balking home office directives concerning names, addresses, and follow-ups on list updating.

HOW THE UNITED STATES GOVERNMENT USES MAILING LISTS FOR COMMERCIAL PURPOSES

There are a number of typical "commercial" uses of mailing lists by the federal government, including mailings to sell subscriptions of departmental series and notification of new offerings by governmental agencies.

There also are some unusual government uses. The FBI uses commercial mailing lists to help track down wanted criminals. For example, if a name on the FBI wanted list is known to frequent barbershops, the FBI will place a photograph and description, plus an announcement of a reward in barbershops in five or six states. Mailing lists are occasionally used to help dispose of surplus federal property. Doctors and pharmacists on lists have been mailed data on unusual drugs or specimens. Lists used for presidential balls and receptions and inaugurals include commercially purchased segments.

An IRS "Hit List" for Tax Violators?

There is one on-going use by the federal government that has aroused the animus of the entire list-using and providing community—that is, the rental by the IRS of commercial mailing lists to match against those who make (or should make) federal income tax returns to identify citizens who have not filed. This was the only use to be made of such data.

The IRS attempted to rent names from each of the major compilers of householders in the United States, but was turned down. A Washington-based list purveyor supplied a 2 million name test for four states, which is still being evaluated. Problems related to the discipline of the list data obtained and the quality of the addresses on the IRS list and its internal computer matching capabilities apparently adversely affected the program. The latest word on this is that more tests will be necessary to validate this use.

Sources of Government Lists

Few people outside the list field have any idea of the pervasiveness of the government in providing the essence of mailing lists. All car registration data as well as driver license records come from government sources, as do all voters' registrations. And all data on titles, mortgages, and new homeowners come from local (usually county) recent filings.

Most lists of professionals, and many lists of business specialists, come from government sources (for example, lists of doctors, dentists, lawyers, insurance agents, real estate brokers, plumbers, electricians, accountants, CPAs, actuaries). Businesses must be registered with the state. Some states, notably California, make lists available by classification.

In addition, the United States government licenses ham operators, two-way radio-, telephone-, and radio-operators, TV and cable TV stations, and controls and lists holders of pension funds and IRAs, as well as 10K and 10Q reports from publicly held big-business firms.

The United States government is also the source for a surprising variety of other lists such as:

Subscriptions to Commerce Business Daily

Overseas employees of the state department

Deposit account customers of NTIS (National Technical Information Service)

Government-sponsored book buyers and pamphlet buyers

Armed forces camps and armed forces personnel

U.S. high schools

United States government purchasing officers and directors

Doctors that are licensed to distribute narcotics (this list exists but has been released to only one list compiler)

Companies subject to toxic waste and waste water controls

Government employees

Government contractors

Largest recipients of direct mail

Establishments with own nine-digit zip code

Toxic waste disposal areas

Post offices

Approved chemicals for human consumption

Government approved slaughterhouses

Overseas requests for product information

American companies with interests abroad, by country

Most favored nations

Then there are several master lists within the government which are not available for any non-governmental purpose, including

Passport holders

IRS taxpayers

Social Security numbers

SIC: TOOL FOR REACHING INDUSTRIAL MARKETS

SIC is the three-letter designation for "Standard Industrial Classification."

This government-sponsored (Department of Commerce, Bureau of Census) classification system provides a four-digit number to identify the function of the entire field of economic activity covering every business, professional, and institutional employer or self-employed person in the United States.

The SIC system, thus, is a convenient means to "pigeon-hole" every name and address by kind of activity, and retrieve selected names by close to 1,000 different four-digit numerical "handles."

In the SIC system the first *two* digits are used to define the ten major fields of endeavor.

1–9	Agriculture, Forestry and Fisheries
10–14	Mining
15–17	Contracting
20–39	Manufacturing
40–47	Transportation
48–49	Communication and Public Utilities
50–51	Wholesaling
52–59	Retailing
60–65	Finance
70–95	Services

The 70XX to 95XX Services grouping includes the following specialized kinds of services:

70–72	Services, Personal
73	Services, Business
75	Services, Automotive
76	Services, Repair
78	Services, Entertainment
80	Services, Medical
81	Services, Legal
82	Services, Educational
86	Services, Institutional
89	Services, Other Professional
90–94	Services, Governmental

In the same way, the Finance codes can be broken out:

60–61	Banking
62	Stock Brokers
63–64	Insurance
65	Real Estate and Allied

A good introduction to the significance of the third and fourth digits of SIC is provided by examining the "Food and Kindred Products Manufacturers" codes. In the SIC system, all twenty manufacturing classes are coded from 2000 through 3999. All food manufacturers start with the digits "20"—and, thus, the breakdowns within food range within the codes 2000 through 2099.

> The 201s cover meat.
> The 202s cover dairy products.
> The 203s cover canned foods.
> The 204s cover grain and cereal products.
> The 205s cover baked products.
> The 206s cover sugars.
> The 207s cover confectionery.
> The 208s cover liquids and flavorings.
> The 209s cover all other miscellaneous foods.

Within the 202's (dairy products) the fourth digit provides a means to identify the major activity of each such plant:

202/1	Creamery butter
202/2	Natural cheese
202/3	Condensed and evaporated milk
202/4	Ice cream and frozen desserts
202/5	Special dairy products
202/6	Fluid milk

Under the SIC system, selection can be made by two digits, three digits, and four digits. (The system actually extends to seven digits, but for list purposes, government-assigned codes are available by four digits only.)

To trace a given commodity vertically requires utilization of the appropriate codes within each major field. For example, one can trace cheese as follows:

0132	Dairy farms (agricultural production)
2022	Natural cheese (Manufacturing)
4221	Farm products warehousing (transportation)
5043	Dairy products wholesale (wholesaling)
5451	Dairy products stores (retail)

. . . Cheese also is sold in grocery stores (5411), general stores (5393), restaurants (5812), hotels (7014), golf clubs (7947).

The major data available on most SIC tape files are:

SIC Classification of Establishment

Headquarters vs. Branch

Corporate vs. Non-Corporate Form of Operation

City Size in Which Establishment is Located

Geographic Locations (State, County, Metro Area, 3-Digit SCF Zip Code, 5-Digit Zip Code)

Number of Employees

Advertising in Yellow Pages (if Yellow Pages Based)

Key Executive of Establishment

While most classifications are straightforward, out of necessity there are some unusual combinations or exclusions. Printing, publishing, and industries that serve the printing trades are a major class of manufacturing. But news services are listed under service industries; textile printing and finishing are listed under textiles while printing ink is found in chemical manufacturing.

SIC is in effect a means to provide a pigeonhole for each classification whether of business, institutions, or offices of professionals.

That is a highly desirable objective. The rub is there are over 4,000 different classifications in the land, and the SIC system, even after a highly promoted revision of the 1972 classifications in 1987, provides only 1,050 pigeonholes into which to force fit these 4,000 classifications.

In essence the SIC system has been established as a means to identify manufacturing industries, at the expense of everything else—which includes most of us—in contracting, transportation, communication, utilities, wholesaling, retailing, finance, and services.

For example:

	Approximate number of 1972 codes	Approximate number of 1987 codes	Estimated number of establishments	Ratio establishments per code
Manufacturing	450	460	475,000	1,000
All Other	450	510	8,550,000	17,000

This chart goes a long way to explain why the firm of Ed Burnett Consultants, as long as twenty years ago, devised a fifth digit for business compilations to break down categories that we knew to be too general.

In effect each fifth digit SIC, as it has come to be called, (there are now 4,600) is an indication of a lack of definition provided by the SIC System.

Four-digit code "1711" is still assigned to "Plumbing, Heating and Air Conditioning Contractors," but I doubt that if you needed a plumber, that an air conditioning expert would do you much good. And you may decide not to mail to 110,000 such 1711 contractors to reach the 32,000 air conditioning contractors in America. (Sad to realize most users of SIC were forced to such waste by the inadequacies of the coding available.)

Among the complaints of marketers who use SIC, and wish it were more useful to help profile their customers, and segment business lists for testing, are the following:

One code for 10 kinds of engineering services

One code for 15 kinds of professional equipment

One code for 30 kinds of industrial supplies

One code for all types of restaurants

N.E.C. is possibly the most prominent classification within the SIC System; it stands for "Not Elsewhere Classified" and is therefore a catch-all for variants that the SIC system does not know what to do with—even in manufacturing.

N.E.C. includes   10 percent of all food manufacturing
15 percent of all chemical manufacturing
10 percent of all fabricated metal manufacturing

In addition N.E.C. includes
10 percent of all wholesalers, and
over 50 percent of all machinery and machine shop producers

There is a tug of war between marketers who want more sharply defined classifications, and the U.S. Department of Commerce statisticians who want consistent data, collected in the same way, over long periods of time. It is obvious marketers have once again lost, and the statisticians have won. Sad! This is a perfect example of the most important acronym ever developed for data processing—"NINO." That stands for "Not In–Not Out." For if the government established subclasses, marketers could get what they want. And by simply recombining data for subclasses back to the desired four-digit SIC, the statisticians could get commensurate data to compare with the past. But that is too clear, too logical, too helpful. So the 1987 revision is just a *cosmetic change* that cannot possibly cope with all the new materials, all the new producers, all the new fragmentation, all the new retailers and wholesalers who will continue to be "buried" or "lost" under N.E.C.

The result? Business list compilers, utilizing the fifth digit of SIC are doing their best to fill this obvious void. And what is so disheartening is that the USDC had from 1972 to work on this problem, and provide a useful system for the world as it is now—not as it was in 1957 when SIC was in its infancy.

Let me provide just one concrete example of what this is forcing list purveyors to do. The current SIC provides just twenty-four four-digit SIC pigeonholes for Business Services. The Data Base America file, the most thorough breakout of business yet constructed, has no less than *260* separate classifications, or over *ten* times as many as the Government believes adequate for this magnificent proliferating economy.

Without fifth-digit SIC there would be no way to isolate such important business services (all with 6,000 to 20,000 establishments in America), as:

- Letter Shops & Addressing Services
- Commercial Photographers
- Secretarial Services
- Copying & Duplicating Services
- Word Processing Services
- Janitorial Services
- House Cleaning Services
- Snow Removal Services
- Sand Blasting
- Employment Agencies
- Executive Recruiting
- Temporary Help Services
- Computer Consultants
- Public Relations Consultants
- Marketing Consultants
- Security Patrol Services
- Industrial Equipment Rental
- Contractors Equipment, Rental
- TV Dealers/Rentals
- Rental Yards
- Photo Finishing (Retail)

- Appraisers
- Auctioneers
- Interior Decorators
- Telephone Answering Services

This just covers twenty-five separate business classifications not available through the government's SIC system. And there are no fewer than *200* additional business services that the government would prefer to have American business consider as "Not Elsewhere Classified."

Is there any question why most of us using this SIC system believe the government coding is a disgrace?

Development of a Business (not Government) Sponsored Code

To meet the future needs of business marketers to reach desired SIC segments, the two main compilers of business lists, Dun & Bradstreet and Data Base America, under the aegis of the Direct Marketing Association, are in 1987–1988 cooperating in the creation of a six-digit SIC classification system—which will expand the current U.S. Department of Commerce Four-Digit SIC System to some 6000 separate business classifications. (D&B actually is expanding this to eight digits and an anticipated 15,000 separate classifications.)

The Direct Marketing Association plans to publish this expanded classification system. Data Base America and Ed Burnett Consultants plan to incorporate the six-digit code (and some 6500 classifications) into printed catalogs at that time.

The six-digit system is "hierarchical" that is each six-digit code is embraced within a five-digit code, which in turn is contained in the government standard four-digit code.

A sample of this might be as follows:

Code	Classification
76-	Repair service
7699	Miscellaneous repair service
7699X	Scientific equipment repair
7999XA	Medical equipment repair
B	Optical equipment repair
C	Photographic equipment repair
D	Scales, repair

MULTIPLE SICs FOR BIG BUSINESSES

The two major publishers of big-business lists (D&B and S&P) provide primary SICs (the major line of business at an establishment) as well as secondary SICs. Those compilers with access to the S&P data can select establishments by SIC for primary lines only, or primary plus secondary lines. (The latter pull is usually about 10 percent larger than a pull by primary lines only, and in most cases secondary lines are included unless instructions are given to omit them.)

Where a list is to be presented as a sheet listing and sorted by SIC, it is usually best to select on a primary basis only. If secondary lines are to be included in such runs, it is necessary to move the desired SIC to the primary position before printing.

A fair part of multiple SICs for manufacturers includes codings for wholesale classifications as well. Many manufacturing establishments do wholesaling from the same establishment.

SICs are coded by human beings, which means some human error is likely to creep into every SIC classification. The chance for errors is far greater for large plants with multiple SICs because every secondary SIC is an attempt to cover miscellaneous production in plants that have one main product line.

The very large files of establishments (D&B and Data Base America), which are based in part on classified listings, provide upwards of 14 million SICs in files totalling about 8 million establishments. This means that several million records reflect multiple types of operations, each with its own SIC. (While the SICs are multiple, the output is an unduplicated file of establishments.) Both the D&B file and the Data Base America file provide designators for primary as well as secondary SICs for establishments conducting more than one kind of business activity.

CHAPTER 9

How to Test Mailing Lists

Good lists are the lifeblood of successful direct mail. Shakespeare may have been thinking of mailers when he had Sir John Falstaff state, "I would to God thou and I knew where a commodity of good names were to be bought."

"I've got a little list" can be said by everyone of us because everyone compiles lists of friends for sending Christmas cards to, as well as lists of preferred restaurants, frequently-called telephone numbers, items to buy at the store, of birthdays of children and grandchildren, and wanted books or records plus much more.

Prospecting for new respondents is an artistic endeavor insofar as selection of lists is concerned. It is a scientific endeavor insofar as measurement of response is concerned.

Accurate measurement of response is absolutely essential because this is a field unique among all fields of marketing. The difference between success and failure may well be determined by something as small as one or two-tenths of 1 percent. Prospecting, in direct mail, comes down to relatively large differences (1/10 versus 2/10 = 100 percent) in very small numbers of responses, derived from relatively large universes.

The total universes that can be sampled contain approximately 8 million of the known 10 million nonhouseholds, and 75 million householders by name of the 87 million households serviced by the USPS.

Lists exist for more than 4,600 separate classifications of business. There are over 20,000 lists commercially available for people at households, with a total count of over 2 billion names. These figures indicate that the average householder in America can be found on twenty-five different lists. Confirmed mail order buyers—perhaps one-third of the nation—can be found on two or three times that number.

This chapter discusses the rules of testing and carefully explores the factors that cause responses to vary. It further explains in detail how to select test samples so that the resultant response will have statistical validity. In addition, this chapter contains useful rules to determine order margin and the "value" of a name. The former is the key to initial profit or loss; the latter is the key to ultimate success or failure in the operation of a direct-mail business.

WE ARE ALL MATHEMATICIANS

Do you think of yourself as mathematically inclined? If you don't perhaps you should revise your thinking because you use mathematics all the time in everyday life. The following list shows how you just naturally use mathematics in different forms.

Time You tell time, ask about the time, set time, lose time, try to save or make up time.

Size In Clothing, Housing, Animals, Children, Cars, Toys, and so on all can be measured by size.

Weight As are its counterparts, underweight, overweight, and weightless.

Length You judge length by the inch, foot, yard, kilometer, or mile. You also use this mathematical concept quite casually when you discuss blocks, streets, or aisles.

Up and down You are on familiar terms with stock market reports, escalators, multistory buildings, attics, mezzanines, elevators, and stairs.

Weather While all we usually do is talk about the weather, terms such as temperature, wind velocity, amount of rain or snow, barometric pressure—and even more currently centigrade instead of fahrenheit are all mathematical concepts.

Stop and think for a moment how often you use descriptive phrases—mathematical to the core—such as "near or far," "close by," "almost," "heavy or light," "large or small," "lengthy or brief," "under or over," "now or later," "first or last," along with "seasonal," "higher or lower," "faster or slower."

Fairly often you bump into mathematical reminders expressed in figures such as "overdraft," "bank balance," "sales tax," "social security," "first class postage." You also can even casually play around with fractions used in everyday life such as "half fare," "third off," "quarter" (of a dollar), or "four out of five."

Ralph Waldo Emerson wrote, "Nothing astonishes people so much as common sense and plain dealing."

GETTING STARTED: WHY TEST?

Testing should be designed with two results in mind:

1. *Determine which activities will produce more profit and do more.*
2. *Determine which activities will produce less profit and do less (or nothing).*

Just as you find these statements about testing easy to grasp, the mathematics of testing that frightens some people and baffles others, when looked at closely, is not much more than the application of common sense. Don't get lost. You already think, talk, plan, and act like a mathematician in everyday life and you will have no difficulty understanding and applying all the rules of testing covered here.

There is never an end to testing. Nothing stands still—people, tastes, competitors, and lifestyles constantly change, and offers, campaigns, marketing concepts must adapt to meet these changing challenges. The overall rule of testing is: *You will test and retest and then retest—and never stop testing.* For in the field of direct *response* (and response is the name of the game, and direct mail is just one of the players) every mailing, every insertion, and every phone campaign should be part of a learning cycle. Testing must be a continuous process—not added to the mix now and again. If testing is not made a regular part of your program, you will lose much more than the cost of testing in misdirected promotion.

Don't be concerned about doing too much testing or paying too much for testing. For every direct response campaign that is tested "to death," and for which a good deal of money was spent there are one hundred campaigns where money has just been poured down the drain that proper testing could have saved.

Let us now discuss testing in detail. Remember that the figures themselves do not count; it is what is done with the figures that counts.

SEVEN WAYS TO IMPROVE THE BOTTOM LINE
WHEN PROSPECTING

Much of direct-mail testing relates to prospecting. There are seven basic ways in which to improve the bottom line when prospecting. Three of these are due to "increases." Four of them are operational as "decreases."

1. Increase the response per thousand mailed.
2. Increase the average size of the order.
3. Increase the order margin (gross profit per order) by increasing the price.
4. Decrease credit loss and collection costs.
5. Decrease the cost to mail.
6. Decrease the cost of goods sold.
7. Decrease the cost of fulfillment.

Two simple rules can be formulated from a careful examination of these methods.

1. *Never cease to attempt to* increase *the total dollars from a given effort through obtaining greater response, higher average order size, or increased order margin.*
2. *Never cease to attempt to* reduce *the costs of doing business as long as the customer is well and honestly served.*

THE IMPORTANCE OF INCREASING THE RESPONSE RATE

At the point where costs have been shaved and the order margin fairly well set, direct mailing then focuses on the ways and means to increase the response rate. A small increase in the response rate can translate into a remarkably high increase in profit and return on your investment. Let us look at an example:

Item A—total costs, exclusive of promotional costs	$ 8/unit
Selling price	$ 30/unit
Order margin	$ 22
Cost in the mail	$220/M
Average response—1.0% (10 orders per M)	
Average order size—1.3 units per order	

An increase of two orders per M	
mailed (2/10 of 1%) adds	$ 57/M
An increase from 1.3 units per	
order to 1.4 units per order	
which adds	$ 22/M
A decrease in unit cost from $8 to $7 per unit	
which adds	$ 13/M
A decrease in cost to mail of $10 saves	$ 10/M

Here, an increase of only two orders per M (from 1.3M to 1.5M) is greater than the combined additions from the other indicated changes. It is usually far easier to determine a means to increase the number of orders, at any point, than it is to obtain comparable bottom-line improvement by working on factors that affect gross profit on a per-order basis. (We are not talking about the variable worth of different types of new customers here. We are looking at the raw cost of adding a customer to the rolls.)

KEY FACTORS THAT CAUSE RESPONSE TO VARY

Because increasing the response rate is critical, this section discusses the next step you should take: Look at the factors that cause response to vary. Figure 9.1 shows these five factors; **copy, package, timing, offer, and market or list.**

Each is important, but the degree of importance varies.

Once a good piece of **copy** has been written, it is difficult to write different copy that will increase response by more than 10 to 15 percent.

Once a good **package** has been designed and polished, it is difficult to produce a competing package that will increase response by more than 10 to 15 percent.

Once a tested pattern of **timing** is set (unless the product or service is seasonal, and mailing to meet certain holidays is crucial), it is difficult to create a different pattern that will increase response by more than 10 to 15 percent. (See Figure 9.2.)

Mailers who have started late, print late but who are willing to mail 300,000 or 400,000 untested catalogs are asking for disaster. (If the cost to continue is less than the probable return of the added investment, it is at the least, reasonable to proceed. The added downside risk should, however, be well understood.)

A change of one word in a headline can dramatically influence response. The addition of a brochure or a "lift" letter to a package can dramatically influence response. Mailing of a pre-Christmas offer to customers as early as July or August can dramatically influence response. But once good copy is placed in a well-tested package and mailed at the right time, then, and then only, can the increases

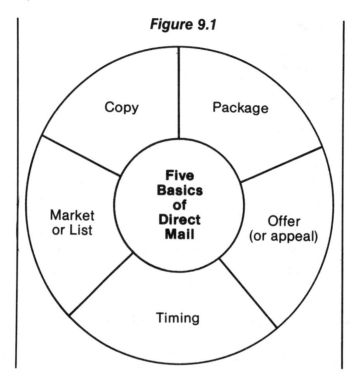

Figure 9.1

explained earlier be in the ballpark. A 10 percent increase in response from 1.0 to 1.1 percent, for example, can be significant and have a definitive influence on profitability.

Once a good standard **offer** has been set, it is possible to devise a variant that will increase response by 100, 200, or 300 percent instead of 10 or 20 percent.

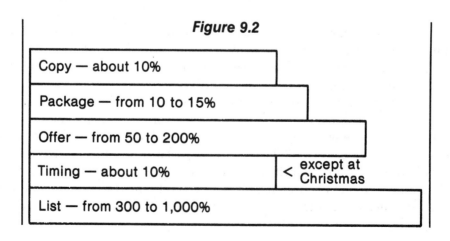

Figure 9.2

Adding credit to a cash-only offer or selecting a good premium can result in these high percentages. Adding involvement on the part of the recipient such as "yes-no" tokens to full-fledged sweepstakes, can increase response significantly. A simple change in the apparent value "Buy three books for $10" to "Buy two books for $9.95 and get the book of your choice *free*," works wonders. So offers can and do vary remarkably.

Even more interesting, however, is how the **market** or list affects response. If the same offer is clothed in the same package, couched in the same words, and mailed at the same time to twenty lists chosen by a tyro, the variance between the best and worst will be thirty to one (3,000 percent)! If chosen by a knowledgeable list expert, the variance between the best and worst (depending in part on knowledge, luck, and what list concepts are being investigated) will be somewhere between six to one and ten to one (600 to 1,000 percent)!

Christmas Testing: A Matter of Timing

There are some mailings which because of the high value of the items and the nature of the gift lend themselves particularly well to Christmas mailings. The problem is how can you test for Christmas mailings when Christmas is months away?

Experts use three methods: one very conservative, one with some risk, and one very risky, depending on what is being offered and the time of the year.

If you need to be certain that an offer is worth a substantial mailing at Christmas time but time does not allow for a pre-Christmas test, you should set up a full-fledged Christmas list, package, and offer test *without* any large blocks of names. The results of the years test are stored, and on or about June 5th, work starts on a large rollout plus new tests. At this time a pre-Christmas offer mailed as early as August also should be implemented.

Such testing can suffer from a distinct downturn from Christmas present to Christmas to come. However, in general, if the program is destined primarily for Christmas, this usually does not overly affect the operation.

If the mailer starts early enough, it is at least possible to inject a small test schedule as early as the first week of September, and still get back in the mails with a rollout by the first week of November. Every day in such a schedule is tight and excellent cooperation is needed among mailers, printers, list suppliers, and mailing shops. If the program is important enough, the September offer can go out by first class mail. This will speed up the time required to read the half life on response; and then order list continuations in time to mail in the last week or two of October. If the product already has a September–November mail-drop listing, the relation between the two months is valuable as a "correction" factor that determines how the September drop might have done if it were mailed closer to Christmas. Without this knowledge, the mailer cannot do any better than adding a bit—10 or 15 percent—to the September test results as some idea of what Christmas might bring. For customer files, even earlier mailings (not only tests) are put in the mails with Christmas goods as early as July. Without some historical data it is not worthwhile testing new lists for possible Christmas rollout in July. It may work but it is more likely to do nothing or possibly even kill lists that could do well later in the season.

Six Rules to Consider When Planning a Mail Campaign

Using the preceding information on how the offer and the market can affect response, several rules in planning a direct mail campaign can be formulated:

1. *Always split every mailing in a meaningful way. At the very least, test a group of lists in any test mailing.*

2. *Never be guilty of committing a "continuous series of one experiment" in which one offer is made at one time to one list.* All you will ever know is the response that one offer at that time received from that one list. Too many one-time mailers are guilty of this syndrome.

3. *Concentrate tests first on markets (lists) and then on offers.* To broaden the size of the data bank of names for future successful continuations, spread market tests from directly affiliated product lines to concepts that offer some promise in allied lines.

4. *Do not set a price for the market.* As price is the single most influential variable in an offer, let the market determine the right price for you by split testing.

5. *In split testing, test prices both above and below where you think the market will determine the right price to be.* If it is a low-cost impulse item, test price lining as well (for example, test for $9.95 instead of $10.00; deluxe edition for $12.95 instead of $12.50).

6. *Recognize the fact that it is better to send a poor mailing to a good list than a good mailing to a poor list.*

Keeping in mind the five factors that cause response to vary, let's see what it pays to test and what it doesn't pay to test.

All elements that have a minimal effect on response should be eliminated. Elements such as color or stock of envelope, number of pictures in a spread, minor copy changes, third class indicia versus third class precanceled stamps, dated or undated mailings, unless offer with expiration, number of stamps, who signs the letters, unless the person is a celebrity or acknowledged authority should *not* be tested.

Be prepared to test, and in time to retest, the following:

1. *Markets:*
   a. list concepts
   b. prospects by type
   c. customers by cell

2. *Offers:*
   a. cash versus credit
   b. addition of credit cards
   c. addition of WATS ordering
   d. addition of a premium or premiums
   e. sweepstakes
   f. upgraded unit or units
   g. "hard" versus "soft" offers
   h. price lining
   i. stipulation of perceived value
   j. split price to let market decide
   k. involvement devices
   l. lift letter (which invites recipient to open and read, whether ordering or not)

3. *Copy:*
   a. headlines
   b. long versus short

4. *Packages:*
   a. large versus small
   b. self-mailer versus letter and envelope
   c. teaser on envelope
   d. four-color versus black and white (when appropriate)
   e. first class versus third class
   f. stock (primarily on catalogs)
   g. business envelopes

New Product Tests

Following is a hierarchy of lists based on response arranged in descending order

1. Most current customers
2. Next most current customers
3. Live customers from prior periods
4. Most current requests and inquiries
5. Next most current requests and inquiries
6. Buyers of the same type of products
7. Buyers of similar types of products
8. Affinity groups with similar tastes
9. Compiled specialists in or near the field of speciality

Hierarchies such as the one above emerge only when a mailer has a good handle on response by cell from his or her customer file, and can roughly approximate the probabilities of outside lists based on how close they approximate the interests shown by the customer base.

New products should be tested against the highest-response group. If this test does not provide adequate results it is a virtual certainty that other segments will produce even less response and a higher cost to buy a customer for the new product. Once you have a customer file, new products that are complementary to your product line should be first tested on the customer list only. (If the product is removed from the type of item connected with your name, you may as well try the customer file for one of the multiple tests required to learn what the overall market can tell you.)

HOW TO SELECT A SAMPLE FOR TESTING

Let's assume you want to test three lists: The first consists of 50,000 names, the second consists of 100,000 names, and the third consists of 500,000 names. Let us also assume, for purposes of this discussion that you can obtain the perfect Nth number sample of each of these lists. Furthermore, let's assume that the three keys you are mailing will have no other variance, except the list. There will be an identical mailing piece going to each of the three lists, thus providing a test of one list against another.

Many mailers use a "magic number" for the quantity of names they utilize to test a list. The problem with using a magic quantity all the time, as George Kaufman put it is "One man's mede is another man's persian." The magic number for one mailer can be completely misleading for another. The key is in the number of responses—not the size of the list. Only with enough responses for statistical reliability will you be able to order your continuations with confidence.

So, how do you go about testing these three files? Do you take a percentage of each list? Do you take a few thousand names off a 25,000 list, a large number off the 100,000 list, and an even larger number off the 500,000 list, to get better results? Do you take the same number off each list irrespective of the list size? Or do you take an entirely different approach?

The three different selection methods noted above are illustrated in the following chart. Note that 5 percent across the board is comparable to 10 percent across the board, that the modification pair show increasing quantities to test based on the universe to be tested, while the final pair utilize the same size sample irrespective of the size of the list.

	List A	List B	List C
Universe	50,000	500,000	1,000,000
5% sample	2,500	25,000	50,000
10% sample	5,000	50,000	100,000
Modification	5,000	10,000	20,000
Modification	10,000	25,000	50,000
Identical	5,000	5,000	5,000
Identical	15,000	15,000	15,000

You probably will have selected one of the above choices. If you have not selected one, it may be because you are not sure which choice is correct. If some people select one method, others select a second, and still others select a third method or take their own approach, this indicates there is some confusion as to what constitutes a valid test sample and which approach is correct. In other words, someone is probably right but then the others are probably wrong. It is safe to say that in list testing in general, most people are wrong most of the time. As an example, if we have made one hundred identical tests of 1,000 each, of a list consisting of 100,000 names, this means that we have one hundred keys of 1,000

Figure 9.3

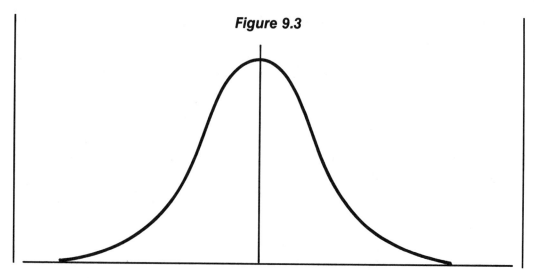

each. If the average response to the particular offer we have made is 2 percent, this means that on the complete 100,000 names mailed we have received twenty per M, or a total of $100 \times 20 = 2,000$.

The question now before the house is, Did each of the one hundred tests come in at 2 percent? As you visualize this example, you may balk at the idea that every one of the 100 tests came in exactly at 2 percent. You may have assumed that some of them came in at under 2 percent, some of them came in at more than 2 percent, and that some of them must have come in at just 2 percent. That is exactly what happens.

The distribution, irrespective of the list that is used, the offer that is made, or the package put into the mail, will show that some come in below average, some come in about average, and some come in above average as shown in the Standard Distribution Curve in Figure 9.3.

In the example it is likely that one of those test one thousands came in with a response as low as 0.5 or 0.3, and that one or maybe a few of them, came in as high as 3.0 or 4.0. However, most of them, as you can see by looking at the curve probably came in between 1.5 and 2.5. Statisticians can tell you that approximately two-thirds of responses will come within the shoulders of this curve. You can handicap any test that you make by checking it against the general expectancy this chart describes. Keep in mind, on *any* test of 1000 identical lots from one list the curve will show the bell-like structure shown in Figure 9.3. Perhaps it will help to visualize this if we post these figures to a repeat of the bell curve:

Figure 9.3 (cont.)

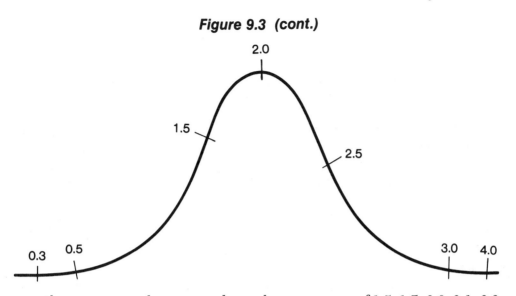

The postings on this curve indicate that any answer of 1.5, 1.7, 2.0, 2.1, 2.3, or 2.5 is valid. This explains why, when you make a test the first time and get an answer of 1.8 for instance, and then make a continuation, the continuation comes in at 1.6 or perhaps 2.0, which sounds different from the first sample. All of these answers are still within the realm of statistical probability. In other words, your first test results of 1.8 only indicated that you were likely to come in between 1.4 and about 2.2, and therefore any continuation that falls within that range is to be expected. It is possible to get a highly skewed or erratic answer from a small sample of a whole as shown in the curve.

For example, there is one chance in a one hundred that you'll get an answer as low as 0.3, even though the average for the hundred tests came out at 2.0. This testing indicates that you need to obtain enough responses to have statistical validity. In fact, that is the rule of the game. It is not the size of the list that dictates the size of the sample; it is the size of the response.

SIX GUIDELINES FOR ACHIEVING AN ACCEPTABLE CONFIDENCE LEVEL

The art of testing is to select a sample size that provides reasonable confidence so that the results of the test are reasonably projectable and within acceptable limits. This is called the *confidence level,* and it is achieved by observing the following guidelines:

1. *The size of the sample required for a test is determined by two factors*
   a. The number of responses necessary to achieve breakeven. (If breakeven is not reached, the list will not lead to a continuation.)
   b. A sample that is sufficient to produce enough responses for statistical validity.
2. *In direct mail testing, breakeven may be—and more often than not is—at a loss. Few direct-mail tests actually show a profit.*

A typical magazine will offer a six-month trial offer at half price, say $3 and set its breakeven response at something like 2 percent. Any list that produces twenty orders per M or more is considered a success. Twenty orders at $3 each equals $60. The Mailing costs total, say, $180. Therefore, the loss on each order at breakeven is $6 ($180 − $60 = $120 ÷ 20 orders = − $6.00 per order).

The loss is actually somewhat greater because the publisher must fulfill the subscription for six months, which costs another $3 for every order. The actual loss to place the new short-term subscriber on the books is more like $9 each than $6 each.

The return on this type of investment lies in the proportion of initial renewals, possibly 50 percent the first year, and the number of years of renewal at full price thereafter. A typical catalog operator that sells products to business may set breakeven at 4 to 7 orders per M, with an acceptable net loss per order in the $10 to $30 range. Expectations are made to pay off this cost of acquisition through additional sales in a period of six to fifteen months.

3. *As a rule of thumb, the average direct-mail offer requires forty to fifty responses for statistical validity.* Thus, if breakeven is, say, ten orders per M (1 percent), the sample size required to obtain fifty responses at 1 percent return is 5,000. (Ten orders per M × 5,000 = 50 orders.) If breakeven is five orders per thousand (0.5 percent) the sample size required to obtain 50 responses is 10,000.

The necessity for adequate responses for statistical validity is shown in the following table:

If the number of responses is:	Then chances are 95 out of 100 that the return on the identical mailing to the same quantity selected the same way from the same list will be between
1	0 and 3
5	0.5 and 9
10	4 and 17
20	10 and 29
50	35 and 65
100	80 and 120

4. *The larger the number of responses, the higher the confidence level.* In similar fashion, the larger the sample, the higher the confidence level will be. Make no mistake though, it is the number of *responses* that governs. A test of 10,000 that produces three orders per thousand—a total of thirty—is nowhere near as good an indicator of the future as a test of 5,000 that produces fifty responses. With too few responses, a few missed keys or the loss of only one or two orders may seriously affect the response rate.

5. *Doubling the size of the sample does not double the level of confidence.* It does, however, increase it by about 50 percent. Doubling the number of valid tests produces more useful information than doubling the size of valid tests.

As testing is essentially a means of finding out which factors influence response, it is generally better to get an adequate indication from ten tests of 5,000 (if that satisfies sample size selection) than to be 50 percent more certain of results by starting with five tests of 10,000 each.

In the selection of the lists to test, it is a good idea to keep in mind the list demographics and psychographics compatible with the given corporate strategy. Lists that produce one-time buyers, excessive no-pays, excessive returns, or result in nonqualified subscribers may look very attractive on the front end or test mode, and very unattractive when the back-end costs are factored in.

6. *The measure of success is profit not only response.* Keep in mind however that obtaining sufficient responses for validity is the initial requirement of a test program.

These guidelines can be further summarized in to the following rules:

1. The size of the list has nothing to do with the size of the sample.

2. All test samples should be of the same size.

3. If a desired list is so small that the test sample will utilize a fair portion of the list, rather than test, take the entire list.

4. Do not set arbitrary limits on the size a list must be to make it worthy of testing. Two lists of 50,000 that produce responses of ten responses per thousand are far more profitable than one list of 100,000 that produces seven responses per thousand.

5. When two lists of similar nature are available and you have only one test cell open, select the list with the larger number. If the test is successful, the continuation will be larger and more likely more profitable.

We need to backtrack now and look at two somewhat difficult concepts: *order margin* and *value of a name*. Without the first, the response necessary to produce a mailing at breakeven cannot be determined. Without the second, how much you can afford to pay to add a given new customer to the rolls cannot be determined.

DETERMINING ORDER MARGIN

To understand the meaning of order margin, the costs that must be borne by a mailing must be broken down into two categories:

1. Promotional costs Printing, envelopes, list rental or production, premium if any, postal charges, and all aspects of fulfillment to get the package addressed and into the mailstream. These costs are *variable* costs, independent of any fixed charges.

2. All other costs Product, transportation, picking, packing, shipping, collecting, returns and allowances, refurbishing, bad debts, logging, computerization, and overhead. These costs can be considered *fixed* costs per unit sold.

Order margin is the differential between net response, after returns and allowances, and "all other costs," all costs except promotion. Note that this is not "mark up." In direct mail you must think "order margin" and not "gross profit" or "mark up."

Examples showing this difference follow:

Product: Book

Selling price	$7.50
All costs except promotion	1.50
Mark up	400%
Order margin	$6.00

On a mark-up basis this margin appears to be a bonanza. But despite the high mark up, this offer has no chance in direct mail because the order margin is too small.

Product: gift item

Selling price	$55.00
All costs except promotion	27.50
Mark up	100%
Order margin	$27.50

Here the mark up (simple keystone) would seem to be much too small but the order margin is large enough to warrant testing through direct mail.

Once the order margin is known or approximated, and the cost of promotion is known, determining breakeven response is very simple. On the gift item just noted, for example, let us assume the cost in the mail (all promotional costs) is $350 per thousand. Then $350/M (promotional costs) ÷ $27 (order margin) produces breakeven (for promotional cost) at 13 orders per thousand.

WHY MARKETING-WISE BOOKKEEPING IS ESSENTIAL

You must be creative and exclude certain costs from the preliminary analysis when you read the results of a test mode. Let's look at two examples here: one for a bookkeeper, the other for a direct-mail marketer. The bookkeeper's profit and loss statement (P&L) shown below is simple, straightforward, and frustrating.

1. Cost to create (from paste-up through camera-ready copy)	$10,000
2. Cost to print and mail 50,000 pieces at $500 per thousand	25,000
3. Total promotional costs to amortize (1) and (2)	$35,000
4. Net sales (after returns)	$60,000
5. Less all costs of goods sold	−35,000
6. Gross profit except for promotional costs (4) minus (5)	$25,000
7. Profit (loss) on mailing (3) minus (6)	($10,000)

Your bookkeeper may see that after a continuation mailing, with better response through selection, some part of this so-called "loss" will be recovered but don't count on it! The net result is the program will die and with it, so does opportunity.

The "creative" P&L of the direct-mail practitioner bears almost no relationship to that of the bookkeeper.

1. Cost to create	In abeyance
2. Cost to print and mail 50,000 pieces, at cost anticipated for continuation of 500,000 pieces ($300/M)	$15,000
3. Total promotional costs to amortize (1) plus (2)	$15,000
4. Net sales (after returns)	$60,000
5. Less all costs of goods sold	35,000
6. Gross profit except for promotional costs (4) minus (5)	$25,000
7. Profit (loss) on mailing (3) minus (6)	$10,000

The sun is now suddenly shining and there is money to be banked. While it's true the overall program is $10,000 under water, the "real" costs are $35,000, and the real gross profit is $25,000. But what a different outlook!

A continuation mailing of 500,000 will produce a profit of $200 per thousand (for an out-of-pocket expenditure of $300 per thousand) a nice R.O.I. that translates into a welcome profit of $90,000. In the bookkeeper's P&L, this profit would have been lost along with the $10,000 spent to get the program to the printer.

Note that the costs for the initial 50,000 piece mailing ($25,000 of promotional cost plus $35,000 for product and all related costs) are recovered in the test mode. The actual investment at this point is the original $10,000 to create and prepare the promotional package.

To mail a 500,000 continuation at $300 per thousand costs $150,000. Costs for products and all related costs to service this mailout are roughly $350,000. The total anticipated outlay is $500,000. So don't think like a bookkeeper; think like a marketer!

How to Self-Finance a Program

The gross profit on the continuation mailing discussed in the previous section is $200 per thousand pieces in the mail. The indicated R.O.I. on this basis, over, say, a three-month period is 16 or 17 percent. But by paying for lists, fulfillment, and printing forty-five to sixty days from the mail date, and buying inventory only a bit faster than actually needed to fulfill orders, this R.O.I. can run well over 50 percent.

This type of leverage is attractive to direct-mail entrepreneurs who quickly learn to parlay a single actual investment into repeated mailings in which the same sum is used over and over again to produce multiple profits from the same offer.

If a bookkeeper is shown a budget calling for, say, a 2 million name list mailing at $300 per thousand, plus attendant costs of an equal sum, the bookkeeper comes up with a cash flow need of about $1,200,000 ($600,000 for the mailing, $600,000 for attendant costs).

The entrepreneur, on the other hand, plans five flights of 400,000 each, and calls for part of the $120,000 (400,000 × $300/M for promotion) and for part of the attendant costs of $120,000. With test data in hand, the entrepreneur seeks an initial investment of less than $100,000. Thereafter, the program produces an R.O.I. of 40 to 50 percent and is self-financing.

Three Ways to Handle Costs of Initial Test Programs

If you want to be in direct mail, you must not think, test, or fund like a bookkeeper! Instead, you must follow these basic rules on how to handle the mathematics on initial tests of new programs:

1. *Disregard the cost to create and produce camera-ready copy.* This is a research cost that only can be recovered if the program from that point on is successful enough to warrant financing it. This cost involves copy, revision, layout, art, photos, typography, paste-up, proofreading, and final approval for printing.

You may ask "Isn't this a cost?" It is, of course, but consider what would happen if you went through all these steps and then did not print and mail. What then? Surely in the long run the mailing program will need to absorb (at so much per thousand pieces mailed) these start-up costs. But if you think of them, in relation to testing for viability, as sunk (expended) research costs, you will be able to read test results much more meaningfully.

2. *Calculate all such start-up tests as though a large mailing, which will follow if the test is successful, were being done.* Otherwise the costs of short runs, both in printing and lists, may adversely affect your ability to recognize the future status of the program.

3. *Calculate breakeven—not breakeven plus a percentage for profit.* Many programs that are profitable are killed at the start because of some arbitrary bogey or profit that must be met to make funding possible for continuation.

HOW TO SUCCESSFULLY BUDGET YOUR TEST MAILINGS

As testing is and must be a way of life in the field of direct response, it is essential to budget a share of the total promotional expenditures for new tests that can be tests of new media, or tests of new mediums within a given media or tests of offers and always and forever, tests to beat the current "control." Good solid management of a direct response operation will allocate at least 10 to 15 percent of promotional cost to controlled testing.

The proportion of a mailing program dedicated to testing varies with the needs of the mailer. Initially, the entire program consists of tests. For a reasonably successful offer, of any ten thoughtfully selected test lists, two, three, or four will be worthy of continuations, two or three will be marginal and two or three will be losers. A subsequent group of ten new lists may do as well, but for every mailing program there comes a time when the ratio of winners drops from one in three to one in four, or one in five, which indicates a need to reexamine the entire spectrum.

It is not unusual for the early continuation mailings to be not much larger than the total mailings launched on new tests. But, as the data bank of reliable names increases, and larger continuations are possible, the proportion of the budget required for new tests is reduced. For an offer in this halcyon period when total quantities per flight are increasing, the test budget can drop to 10 percent of the total mailing quantity, or even slightly less. However, as noted in the section on testing, there is never an end to the need to test.

It is good practice, particularly on continuing campaigns, to reserve one or two open test cells each mailing period for the new or unusual list that looks particularly "right." If such cells are not available with their own unique codes, there may be little flexibility as the mailing program develops.

Special Costs That May Get Overlooked in the Testing Process

Testing provides a tried and true means to limit risk by utilizing relatively small quantities to determine whether or not to authorize the expenditure of much greater sums for expansion. The availability of the testing mode is thus particularly attractive to all current and would-be direct marketers. But some attendant costs to testing that must be understood and not overlooked include the following:

1. The test must be adequate for its purpose. In other words it must provide adequate data upon which to base the next step—whether it be to kill the offer, revise it, or continue it. If the test is continued, the way to do so must be determined.

This text has previously warned against a continuous series of one experiment. At a minimum, testing requires obtaining response from at least five to ten lists, in which all other factors that influence response are kept identical. If the program to be tested is important, initial tests, through a grid test must include a spread of prices, as well as two or more packages. The idea that there is a free lunch in testing via direct mail is a dangerous delusion.

2. New or original testing requires new or original costs to create and develop an advertisement or a mailing. Such costs are expended costs if the program is never run, and can only be amortized through profits produced by successful market expansion if the test results project a likely success. These costs should be budgeted separately. They can, in relation to a modest test schedule in space ads or in the mail, be surprisingly large and frightening for first-time entrepreneurs. They are best thought of as the equivalent of research and development for a manufacturer.

3. The very word "test" conveys a need to budget the excess costs included in short runs. This includes almost all facets of production from printing and purchasing envelopes to fulfillment, as well as the test costs of space such as when tests are based on regional rather than national editions and one-time rates rather than multiple insertion discounted rates.

4. The very nature of tests, requires a greater application of time, dedication, and management than on-going programs do. There is a distinct element of wear and tear on all people concerned in launching a new program or new product. This is usually underestimated by those overseeing the operation.

FIVE WAYS TO DETERMINE THE VALUE OF A NAME

Value of a name is essential in testing to help determine how much you can afford to pay to buy a customer. (If the value is very small or nothing at all, or if there is no other use for the name, then the acquisition of the customer must be accomplished at a profit.) For test purposes, the mail order entrepreneur is *most* interested in lifetime value. To state it another way, he or she is most concerned with the profit possibilities inherent in the ownership of that name to be derived from future mailing offers. An example should be helpful:

A catalog operator determines that a block of new customers in the current year will produce *an average* of $100 of gross sales in the next year; $60 of gross sales in the next following year; and $30 of gross sales in the year after that. Thus, the "generation" of new customers over the next three years will develop $190 of gross sales.

At a 40 percent mark up, this produces a gross profit (disregarding the cost to promote) of about $76. In the first year after acquisition about $40 of this $76 can be anticipated.

This enables the operator to budget so many lost dollars for new customer acquisition at $5, $10, $15, or $20 each to obtain growth. A cost of $20 is reasonably certain to be amortized in six months. At a cost of $5 or $10, this mailer can afford to buy every new customer he or she can reach. At a cost of $40, possibly to be amortized within a year, the cash flow requirements to buy customers may force a reduction in acquisition.

Most operators that buy customers at a loss must make continuous decisions along these lines: "Do I lose more money in building the customer base, or do I cut down on prospecting and make more profit?" For many this is a never-ending series of never-ending changing decisions.

How do you calculate the value of a name? To the inexperienced, the answer to this question is quite simple: Any accountant should be able to come up with a valid answer based on simple addition of the following cost factors:

- Cost to acquire
- Cost to convert
- Overhead factor
- Capitalization of assets

To the list analyst, this is one of the most difficult questions to answer, not because he or she lacks knowledge, but because these factors encompass only a small part of the answer.

While every list analyst uses his or her own special formula, most either empirically or subjectively use five other interrelated sets of facts to come up with an answer. These are:

1. Relation of the list to the owner
2. Market qualification
3. Mechanical considerations
4. Use considerations
5. Rentability prospects and policies

Let's take a brief look at each one.

Relation of the List to the Owner

1. What kind of a name do we have?
   a. customer (or subscriber or donor)
   b. former customer
   c. prospect—preferred, acceptable
   d. friend of customer
   e. giftee of customer
   f. stockholder
   g. employee
   h. supplier
2. What is the primary purpose of the list?
   a. direct mail
   b. corporate business
   c. recordkeeping
   d. mixed

Assume for a moment that the name on the list is that of a customer (for a magazine, read subscriber or recipient; for a fundraising operation, read donor or supporter; for a membership operation, read member or associate). The casual observer might be content with the fairly simple relationships between costs to acquire and number on the file. Multiplying one by the other gives a nice, neat, encapsulated answer. The casual observer is certain to be dead wrong.

This simple assumption has one small flaw: A customer is a customer. In reality a customer may be elegant, good, sporadic, recent, new, one-time, multiple-time, former, previous, duplicated, or a nondeliverable customer, or even dead.

The list analyst must know the following:

1. History
    a. recency
    b. frequency
    c. dollars
    d. items purchased (if available)
2. Cost to acquire
3. Reason for the cost to acquire
4. Current flow of new customers
5. Mail order orientation
6. Mail responsiveness (measured by secondary product or service sale)
7. Probable lifetime expectancy

Lifetime Value

The *lifetime value* of a customer who has purchased for the first time is the *present* value of the contribution to profit to be derived in the future from additional sales. This definition takes into account the fact that dollars *now* are more valuable than dollars to be produced in the future. Usually this discounting of future dollars involves the deduction of a cost of money (current or anticipated) year by year to such anticipated dollar contributions. On a very conservative scale, this deduction for interest can be increased to further reduce the value of a contribution hoped for in the future.

We have in this book utilized gross or total figures (not corrected for the cost of money) when showing sales from one year to another. For a *rough* idea of the value of the customer this refinement is not *required*. If the initial cost to "buy" a new cell of customers is five dollars each and historically one quarter of these can be counted upon to provide $22 of gross profit within the next nine months, it is clear that well before a year has gone by the cost to buy these customers will have been amortized by their additional purchases.

The question still remains however as to the ultimate (lifetime) value. And for that we need to extend the calculation over a period of years.

Let us assume 1,000 new sales *today* at a cost to buy of $5.00 each. We know we must amortize this "cost to buy" through contributions to profit to be made from future sales. The size of that "cost to buy" influences how many new customers we can afford to buy—but it does not influence the calculation to determine the Life Time Value. In effect cost to buy is an investment. Life Time Value determines just how valuable that investment will be (or has been).

Calculation of Lifetime Value Extended Over 4 Years

No. of first time customers	Anticipated Sales				
	In First Year 1,000	Second Year 1,000	Third Year 1,000	Fourth Year 1,000	
Purchases	400	310	160	85	
Contribution to Profit per Purchase	$20	$24	$25	$20	
Total Contribution to Profit by the Cell of "First Time Customers"	$8,000	$7,440	$4,000	$1,700	$21,140
Reduced by Present Value of Money (10% per year per year)	$7,270	$6,200	$3,080	$1,210	$17,760

In this example each new customer will produce a net contribution to profit over a period of four years of $17.76. In all likelihood not over 50 percent of the initial 1,000 customers over this four year span will have purchased again. But their purchases, cumulated, indicate that *on average* it has been very worthwhile to buy all 1,000 initially. In this scenario, the initial cost to buy the entire 1,000 has been amortized in the first year they were on the file. Note also that the contribution per customer (on average!) from the cell decreases each year:

1st Year	7.27 or	41%	of $17.76
2nd Year	6.20 or	35%	of $17.76
3rd Year	3.08 or	17%	of $17.76
4th Year	1.21 or	7%	of $17.76

Note also that the proportion of orders from the 1,000 customers in each ensuing year reduces rather dramatically:

Initially	**1,000**	=	**100%**
First Year	400	=	40%
Second Year	310	=	31%
Third Year	160	=	16%
Fourth Year	85	=	9%

Since names come on the customer file in different time frames, this means that there is a *different* Lifetime Value for each cell of names added to the file at the same time. And if these have come from different sources (say direct mail *vs.* space) then those new to the file at that time by each source must be tracked as an individual cell. Only by creating a lifetime value for every such cell on your file can you create a realistic lifetime value for the customer file as a whole.

Where you have historical records of sales (and profits) for several years it is best to use such data in your lifetime value calculation. What to do if this is your first year? First make certain you have a real good grasp of all costs which must be taken into account. Next provide a realistic contribution per new order. Then set up three separate scenarios, high–medium–low, for number of purchases (*not* number of customers—for while some will not buy, some will buy more than once in a given year):

	Year 1	Year 2	Year 3	Year 4
High	40%	25%	18%	10%
Medium	25%	17%	12%	8%
Low	15%	10%	9%	6%

After the first full year, you will be able to adjust the percentage for Year 1—and modify Year 2. After the second year, you will have reasonably adequate data for Year 2 and can then adjust for Year 3. How far do you carry out this projection? Until the anticipated next-year sales have a minimal effect on the cumulative total value established through the prior year. For example, if in the sixth year on the chart on page 352 the number of sales from this cell drops to 20 the addition for that year to the cumulative contribution per initial customer created will be just 40¢.

The data above does not take into account rental income for the new names acquired. Rental income, once the list has reached commercial size, can be most attractive. And the net sum from rentals applies to *all* current names added to the file. A few figures here may be helpful.

Assume a rental price of $70/M for a mail order buyer list.

Assume a net profit after all costs of $35/M.

Assume a 10 time "turn" per year (which means every name on the list at the beginning of the year is rented out and paid for 10 times). Then we have 3.5¢/name × 10 rentals per name = 35¢ per name per year. After four years we will be able to add $1.40 for net profit. If that were added to the $17.76 accumulated per new customer through new sales over four years it would represent 8 percent. Certainly not to be sneezed at—but that would represent

40 rentals of each name over the four year period. Perhaps you can think of rental income as a bit of lagniappe which makes your life time calculation just a bit more secure.

In a speech this author gave on the conversion of lists, I asked an audience interested in the future of the computer letter, which is one more variable in the pattern we are looking at to consider a few special acronyms.

The acronyms were:

KISS
GIGO
DIDO
NINO
RAFO

While expressed principally for computers, the principles hold irrespective of the mechanics of the mailing list.

These five terms have an interesting ring. Let's see what each of these computer terms means.

How many of you have heard of KISS? It is one of the prime lessons to learn when using a computer. It means, "Keep It Simple, Stupid!"

GIGO means, "Garbage In Garbage Out." No matter how good you, or your computer systems people are, if you don't put in the right data, you are not going to get the right data out.

DIDO means "Duplication In Duplication Out." We must learn how to get rid of duplication.

NINO is the most important acronym in direct marketing. It means "Not In Not Out." You cannot use any data you may have, or may have had, if you have not placed it on tape in the first place. The best time to start is now. For example, if you wish to establish a buying history, you must enter what you now know and then add transactions as they are created.

RAFO means "Research and Find Out." For example, a buying history probably can be constructed from previous transactions—Item purchases may be available from ledger cards; or list data may be buried in branches, sales offices, or dead storage. It is likely that many of you are letting go of one or more segments of data that would produce good list data or augment the value of lists already in being.

RAFO can change the value of a name or a list. A list of customers varies as to recency, frequency, average and highest dollars sold, items bought, number of times customers were unsuccessfully mailed to, and cost to promote and keep on the list. As all markets change the list may improve, retrogress, or stay the same.

The list may increase in size and/or die at the same time. No simple formula is going to provide an easy, simple answer.

A customer file can be 100 percent mail-oriented; or mostly or partly mail-oriented; or not mail-order oriented at all. If it is 100 percent mail-oriented it can be virtually useless for any other product other than the one the list was built upon. For example, a list of bona fide mail order liquor buyers that can be often multiple, and regular, reordering customers, are by and large not good mail order prospects for outside use. Even related products by mail do not do overly well on such a list despite the fact the average unit of sale is near the $100 level and cash is paid in advance.

Note that the cost to acquire can be either plus or minus. This depends on who is doing the counting and which costs are included. These costs, whatever they are, do affect the value of a name. It may pay off to buy a customer name at an initial loss if in the long run, that name can add demonstrably to net profit in the future. The list analyst wants to know the actual cost of acquisition and the reasons for this cost.

Market Qualifications

Market qualifications are so varied that it would be easy to write a book on them alone. The following items need to be considered:

1. Size of the list
2. Size of the universe the list can be obtained from
3. Accessibility of given market
4. Rarity of the given market or market segment
5. Completeness of coverage
6. Seasonability factors
7. Peripheral market coverage (if any)
8. Changing status of market
9. Age of market
10. Cost to reproduce list data
11. Qualification of name
    a. preferred, acceptable, undesirable
    b. proof-of-buying influence

    c. periodic sales force qualification

    d. selection factors used

Value of the list partly depends on size. A list of 3,000 names is usually not worth one-half of a list of 6,000 names. The size factor is dependent on accessibility, rarity, cost to reproduce, and the total size of the market or market segment aimed at. The kind and validity of source data also enter this equation.

Some lists gain in value or rentability with peripheral coverage, others lose. A list selected to remove all peripheral markets may be too fine to be commercially viable. A list like the Ohio Envelope compilation of mail-responsive insurance agents is greatly augmented in value by the removal of all agencies with ties to large companies that are not likely to be masters of their own purchasing. Names that have been qualified by size, buying influence, or buying criteria are likely to be more valuable than those added without such qualifications.

Mechanical Considerations

Here is a list of fourteen mechanical factors for consideration:

1. Size of the list

2. Age of names on the list

3. Cleanliness of list

4. Duplication factor

5. Updating cycle and technique

6. Feedback for update

7. Zip code status

8. Titles/individuals/companies only

9. Format and discipline

10. Method of reproduction

11. Cost factors in handling and reproduction

12. Sequencing of file

13. Sequencing of crutch files (if any)

14. Selectivity, if any, and how handled

It is far easier to list these simple mechanical factors than to cost them out. Most list owners do not know the duplication factor in their lists; most probably are unaware of the normal cleaning lag even where a fair system to update exists. Most lists have no date of origination on them. Most cleaning procedures do not include date-stamping each record. Thus a list can waste away if it is not given tender loving care to grow and produce.

Use Considerations

Factors to be considered in this category are:

1. Scheduled use
2. Demand use
3. Who controls use
4. Selectivity
5. Cost of selections
6. Need for multiple files to obviate selection but build in duplication
7. Need for crutch files (hard-copy lookups)
   a. cost to maintain
   b. space to maintain
   c. difficulty to maintain

While usage does not necessarily reflect value (a company can be using a good list once a year, and a poor one once a month), in general terms the value placed on the list is measured by the owner. The fact the list exists at all establishes some value. The use that is made of the list simply helps measure this value. The type and accuracy of the coding and the mechanics of selection, determine the value of selectivity. A plated file, requiring high selectivity, is probably segmented to obviate run costs, and has an extra factor of duplication built in almost out of necessity. A computer file on magnetic tape may require a crutch file on sheets or cards in some other order. Thus to make the list work, a subsidiary file may be required. The need for such a file may relate to the value inherent in the name.

Rentability Prospects and Policies

If the policy of the company is "no rentals, no exchanges," valuation based on rental value is nil. If the policy is to open a given list for exchanges only, this establishes a rentability value. It should be understood that it makes no difference whether lists are exchanged at no charge with another owner, or lists are exchanged at full rental value with another owner. In both cases, the answer is the same: The net value of the dollars exchanged at the same price is zero. If the policy is to open the lists for rental, then a valuation based on rental income or prospective rental income, is certainly part of the value of a name.

Rentability is affected by quantity, type, mail-order orientation, and competitive lists. To a larger extent than is commonly recognized, rentability is also affected by two other factors: (1) The track record of the list because this record is bruited around by the major mailers in the field with remarkable rapidity; and (2) the merchandising done on or for the given list.

Like most concepts studied in direct mail, the value of a name "depends." The preceding paragraphs give an idea of most of the factors that should be considered when such a valuation is attempted. A good intuitive view probably covers the high spots here by osmosis as it were.

CHAPTER 10

The Major "How To's" of Direct Response

The various rules set forth here are all designed for one purpose: To provide useful guidelines on the "how-to's" of direct mail. These rules cover the basic operations of how to mail; when to mail; how to continue mailing; how to order; and how to record.

Knowing how to select a list and how to choose a sample is not enough. Neither is knowing how to prospect. You must become a master of the approach to prospecting; to the correct operation of the prospecting function; and last but not least, to the proper handling of the end result of prospecting—the development of a customer file. The crux of these "how to's" involves operations, and that is the subject of this section on the rules of testing.

HOW TO TRACK RESPONSES AND READ RESULTS

How to Calculate the Half Life of Mailing Returns

Half life is a mathematical measuring stick for early calculation of mailing returns. When you were two years old, you were slightly more than half as tall as you are now. Your height half life was reached with great rapidity, and it took you the next fifteen to twenty years to reach your full height. By the age of two your adult size could be determined.

On the basis of the half-life theory a farmer can predict the average yield a cornfield will produce a few weeks after corn breaks through the surface.

Half life in carbon dating (the actual or relative age of archaeological finds) is based on the fact that half the radioactive carbon 14, an isotope of carbon which occurs naturally, decays to Nitrogen 14 in a precise period of time—5,760 years to be exact. To most of us, this relation of radioactive carbon (14) to regular carbon (12) is the half life we are most familiar with.

But there also are valuable half lifes buried in your mailing return rates, which if used properly, can be as valuable to the direct-mail specialist as carbon dating half life is to the archaeologist.

Every mailing list has a half life (a time when half the responses which will ultimately come in have been recorded). This half life is specific, virtually certain, and occurs within a very brief period of time after returns began arriving.

For the mail order specialist, half life determines the success or failure of a mailing; the success or failure of a given key; the success or failure of a given copy, offer, or list test. With experience success or failure can be predicted within a few days (if first class) or a few weeks (if third class) of receipt of the first responses.

Historically, the curve of response to a mailing dropped on the same day shows a swiftly rising response at the beginning of the period, followed by a slow descent per day, week, or month, followed by a long, long tail end of responses. It is not unusual for a given mailing of some size to produce some responses every week for a series of months. But such responses on the tail end of the mailing are always sporadic, small, and rather inconsequential in the evaluation overall of the offer.

Plotting Responses with Curves

Without an expiration date say, as on a seminar, plottings of response will produce one of three curves as shown in Figure 10.1.

When responses stutter that is almost always a sure sign that the results will be dismal. When responses come in quickly and stay high, it is apparent that particular test is doing exceptionally well. The normal curve requires early analysis to determine whether or not to continue with that key.

As the normal curve is virtually invariable, it stands to reason that establishing the half life in number of responses will enable decision making weeks or months before the receipt of the final responses. (See Figure 10.2.)

Successful tests should be expanded—that is, lead to continuations as soon as possible, because conditions are dynamic and constantly change. The longer

Figure 10.1

The three types of curves created by plotting response by day to *any* direct response offer.

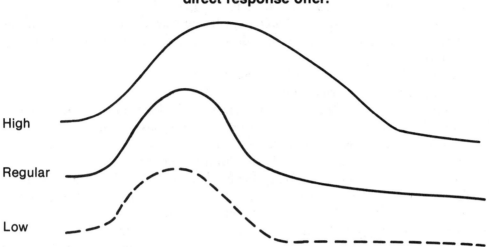

High

Regular

Low

the period of time between an initial test and the subsequent continuation, the greater the possibility that results will be affected by this "change in timing." The mailer who uses half life reduces this time lag dramatically and gains a tremendous advantage over the mailer who waits for the last dribbling orders on the tail end of a test.

Figure 10.2

Marking the half-life on a typical response distribution by days

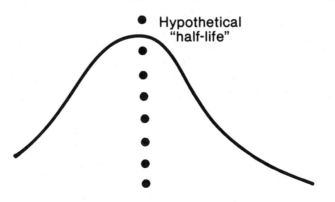

Hypothetical
"half-life"

Six Steps for Determining Half Life

How does a mailer determine the half life on his or her mailings? To determine the half life on your mailings, here are a few simple rules to follow:

1. *Drop all mailings on the same day.* If you stagger mailings, you will lay one curve over another, as shown in Figure 10-3 and destroy the validity of any given half-life.

2. *Record responses for each key every day.*

3. *Be sure your recordkeeping includes:*

Cumulative responses at the end of each day by key and total. (Cumulative figures can be processed weekly, if desired, once responses begin to dwindle.)

Records for each day, even if there is no response for a given key on a given day. Every day is significant even those with no response.

Some easy visual means (a pair of ruled lines will do) to identify responses for Tuesdays. (Tuesdays, which usually include responses for Saturday, Sunday, and Monday, are normally significantly higher than the other days in the week.) When response on a given Tuesday is lower than the preceding Tuesday, response has undoubtedly "peaked," and the curve of response from that point on will generally be downward. (In past years business reply envelopes and business reply cards arrived daily, including Mondays. Today, many major post offices hold such mail over the weekend until Tuesday.)

Posting for a given key for a period of three months or six months if the offer shows there will be life after three months.

4. *Include the following information:*

Mailing description or number.

Key number.

Description of the variable involved (such as list name or copy test A).

Date of drop. (If this varies by key or test, it is important to date each such segment.)

Total quantity ordered.

Total quantity mailed equals the universe (100 percent) against which responses are calculated. Note that this hardly ever is the same as the total quantity ordered. For example, the quantity ordered will be 10,000; the actual number mailed may be 8,200. This difference can make a significant change in the true response percentage.

Estimated or actual cost of the mailing package in the mail per thousand.

The response rate you require to consider continuing that given test. (This is your breakeven percentage.) This is your predetermined guide to the number of responses and/or the number of dollars you are looking for.

To measure half life correctly, you must obtain *daily* counts of orders and

Figure 10.3

Staggered mailings destroy half-life calculations

Staggered mailings destroy
"half-life" calculations

inquiries by individual key. Once a key begins to respond, these counts must be given and blanks must be noted for each key. Blanks are significant for indicating the tail end of a given offer . . . or the start of a "stuttering" key.

Don't be confused by extremely early orders. Be careful. Half-life count begins with the first day of response, *not* with the day of drop. A few orders may arrive with surprising speed because the offer has been seen at the printer or the fulfillment shop. These orders should be disregarded. The half-life count begins when the mainstream of the order flow arrives and it continues day-by-day.

The best way to speed up the measurement of half life is to implement an "800" number. (Mailing first class, of course, has a shorter half life than mailing third class bulk.) Response by telephone will develop its own pattern, which in most cases, will anticipate results that will come in later by mail. In all cases, where both phone and mail responses are involved, it is essential to review each separately.

5. *Bind one copy of each mailing with its number and samples of each variable mailed, plus the daily and cumulative results into a book, so you cannot easily take it out.* You will find this book invaluable when the time comes to review mailings, mailing results, and the calculation of half life.

6. *Track and compare response periods.* If you have such records for prior mailings, draw a bold red line beneath the day's posting for each key, which cumulatively includes 50 percent of the total responses.

If your particular offer, package, mailing list, and timing follow visual patterns, you will find these red lines virtually parallel on a whole series of tests. If you have mailed first class, these marks are made nine days from the date of the first posted response, not from day dropped. Out of twenty red marks, not more than one or two will be outside the range of eight days (nine minus one) to ten days (nine plus one).

How Third Class Bulk Mail Deliveries Vary

If you have mailed third-class bulk (most bets are now off if you have mailed third-class piece-rate due to the vagaries of post office handling), the variation between the red marks will be plus or minus half a week. That is, if most such marks are at the end of the third week from the date of the first posted response, not from day dropped, then out of twenty red marks, not more than one or two will be outside the range of two and one-half weeks (three weeks minus one-half of a week) to three and one-half weeks (three weeks plus one-half of a week). For half weeks, combine Monday–Tuesday and Wednesday–Thursday–Friday.

It should be noted the "half lifes" shown in Figure 10.4, are average, or typical. *Your* half life as denoted by the fact the red marks across different keys mailed at the same time may be just six days, or just two weeks. What you will find, which may be mind boggling, is that such half lifes will all be within *twenty-four* hours of each other. Once you have checked half lifes on a series of tests which have been concluded, you will be a believer for life!

Test after test, including the continuing tests monitored by the Third Class Mail Association, the average delivery is made within a period of eleven days. This means that delivery time will range from two or three days to about twenty-two days and the average time is eleven days. This spread is consistent with the half-life determination found in third class mail.

The data shown in Figure 10.4 apply exclusively to "solo" or one-time mailings. Series of mailings have their own unique curves that cannot be measured in the testing stage. The number and frequency of mailings in a series is definitely an art—not a science. Charting half lives, however, can prove useful in determining the number and frequency of such typical efforts as collection and renewal series.

If you have mailed a catalog, variation among the red marks will tend to center around the fifth or sixth week. But the evidence here indicates that response, particularly length of response, varies for reasons the merchandise was bought (impulse buying versus a solid reason for buying, for example); class of customer (business houses react slower and continue to produce long after consumer mailings have tailed off); and time of year (at times a Christmas catalog does not just fall off but simply becomes stone cold dead in the marketplace). An offer involving sweepstakes or credit can also produce a different pattern of response than one that does not involve participation or charge privileges.

In addition, half life on a catalog is usually not as important as half life on an individual offer. In the case of the catalog, the whole mailing is usually committed, and the half life simply advises management of where they are now and where they will likely be some time later. On an individual product or service offer, the half life is one of the ways management can proceed with confidence based on only part of the facts.

Figure 10.4

A simulation of results to 4 keys mailed at the same time. Note that half the responses, irrespective of the total number finally received, are received in the same time period.

A half-life determination

	Key 1	Key 2	Key 3	Key 4	
Daily posting	X	X	X	X	
of responses,	X	X	X	X	
plus weekly	X	X	X	X	
cumulations	X	X	X	X	Plus or minus
	X	X	X	X	24 hours!
Half of responses	50	70	45	35	
	X	X	X		
	X	X	X		
	X	X		X	
	X	X	X		
	X	X			
		X	X	X	
		X			
		X			
100% of responses	100	140	90	70	

Note: Do *not* measure from day of drop. What you are measuring here is response rate from the first day of response.

How Expiration Date Affects the Response Curve

When there is an expiration date for an offer, the response curve is changed from the typical pattern shown in Figure 10.5 to a double-humped camel, which looks like Figure 10.6.

It is not unusual for a sizable proportion of the total responses to come in one, two, or three days prior to the expiration date. (A seminar is a good example: as high as 10 percent of those attending have made up their minds to attend in

Figure 10.5

Figure 10.6

the last forty-eight to seventy-two hours and there are always a number of "walk ins" at the door of those who have decided to attend at the last minute.)

While the basic curve itself is inherent, the actual slope of the curve and the bulge at the end must be researched for each type of offer.

There are some seminar responses, for example, in which the response curve is remarkably flat at the beginning with one, two, or three responses coming in each day sometimes for weeks at a time. This is followed by a flurry as the expiration period arrives. Such a curve looks like, Figure 10.7.

How to Test Two or More Variables Simultaneously

If you need to test two or more packages, say a self-mailer versus an enclosed piece, or a computer letter versus a "Dear Friend" letter, and at the same time test two or more offers over a series of lists, learn to use grid testing as shown in Figure 10.8.

Let's suppose you require, say, 4,000 names per cell to obtain thirty or forty responses so that you have reasonable confidence that continuations of that cell will do about as well. To provide enough names in the above grid to test each cell would require twenty cells of 4,000 each, or 80,000 names. This may well be more than the total sum you can allocate to this test.

If you now place 1,000 names (and not 4,000) in each cell and read results from the horizontal and vertical totals only, you will note that each list has 4,000 names (and the same chance for response as all other lists). Package A will have 10,000 in the mail compared with 10,000 for Package B.

Combining responses by offer will result in Offer 1 having 10,000 in the mail against 10,000 for Offer 2. Thus in one grid test you can find out which package is best, which offer is best, and which lists (if any) are worth continuations. This is the one way that several variables can be tested simultaneously at a reasonable cost.

The next time you hear that only one variable can be tested at a time, bring out your trusty grid. (*Caution:* you *cannot* read results *within cells* with any safety. Your internal response is too small for statistical validity. If you use grid testing,

Figure 10.7

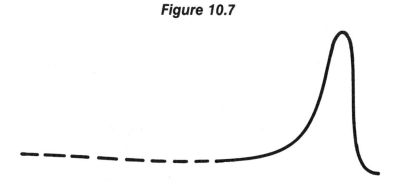

you must record all responses within the grid to be able to read results with any confidence.)

A variation of Murphy's law states, "If it can happen, it will." This statement runs rampant in the direct-mail business. In too many tests, a bug, error, omission, or wrong key seems to slip in. It pays to go over all segments of a grid test to be certain no gremlin has slipped in to invalidate some or all of the test results. Careful design of a grid test is the first requisite. Following that, careful admin-

Figure 10.8

Layout of a grid to test simultaneously two packages, two offers, and, in this case, five different lists. The grid can be expanded, within reason, to handle additional variables.

	Package A		Package B		
	Offer 1	Offer 2	Offer 1	Offer 2	Total
List AA	X	X	X	X	4X
BB	X	X	X	X	4X
CC	X	X	X	X	4X
DD	X	X	X	X	4X
EE	X	X	X	X	4X
	5X	5X	5X	5X	

10X   10X

10X   10X

istrative supervision particularly at the mailing shop is necessary to make certain that design is followed explicitly.

NINE BASIC RULES FOR MAKING CONTINUATIONS

Following are the basic rules for making continuations:

1. *If time permits, do not jump from a test to the entire balance of a large list. Instead, take an increased proportion of the list.*

2. *If you have tested 5,000 with reasonable success, try a continuation of 25,000 selected on the same basis.* If the 25,000 does almost as well as the earlier test, increase the size of the next continuation.

3. *If possible, use a continuation to learn more about the segmentation in a list.*

If a cross-section of the list works, it is certain that part of the list will be better than the average, and part will be not as good. Thus if you have successfully tested a cross-section of a large list that has a number of selectable segments available, your continuation should ascertain the variance available within such segments as most recent, most frequent, credit card buyers, largest dollar buyers as well as location.

Since the leverage represented by additional points of response is so desirable, it may be that more profits can be generated by mailing a segment than by mailing a continuation of the cross-section, which may include an entire group of names destined to produce a loss. Every response ratio is made up of two components: those above the average response and those below. Test to improve the average.

4. *If your continuation is nothing more than another cross-section of the list originally tested, split the continuation into several Nth number samples and key each lot.* Note the results of the tests in Figure 10.9.

If your results are consistent, as in continuation under List A in the figure, and the variance from the mean is quite small, you can take another and larger bite for your next continuation with confidence. But if the results of the individual keys run all over the lot, as shown in continuation under List B in the figure by the wide swings from the mean, any large continuation may produce trouble for you. You are alerted to proceed with caution.

5. *It usually does not pay to make a retest of lists that test marginally or slightly submarginally.* Wishful thinking will not make them cross the line, and usually all a retest does is confirm the results of the first test. If you can improve the results by using a better selection procedure, that is a different story.

Figure 10.9

Review of variance from the mean—if continuations are keyed for segments rather than mailed under a single key.

	List A		List B	
If as one key:				
Original test	5,000-2.0%		5,000-2.0%	
Continuation	25,000-2.0%		25,000-2.0%	
		Variance from mean		**Variance from mean**
If each segment keyed separately:	5,000-1.9%	0.1	5,000-1.4%	0.6
	5,000-2.1%	0.1	5,000-3.1%	1.1
	5,000-2.0%	—	5,000-1.8%	0.2
	5,000-1.8%	0.2	5,000-2.1%	0.1
	5,000-2.2%	0.2	5,000-1.6%	0.4
		0.1		0.5

6. *If a large rollout is planned without intermediate continuations, get expert advice on the downside risk.* If the results of your early tests are particularly strong (confirmed by the results from several lists—not only one!), and there is some worry that you will lose the market to a competitor during the continuation period, a rollout may be called for. But be cautious—rollouts to large numbers can prove disastrous.

7. *If results are surprisingly high rerun the same names.* If the results of some list tests on a solo mailing are so far above breakeven that a repeat mailing to the same names even with a drop-off of 40 percent, will be better than most other lists, you should schedule a repeat mailing at the same time as the scheduled considerable continuation. This will determine whether the entire list can be perhaps used twice within a relatively short time frame.

8. *Pick up and run all new names added to a list following a successful test with a separate key.* If new similar names are available for a recently tested list and scheduled for continuation, determine if their number justifies testing them or taking them as a block. The latter is preferable if the initial results were particularly strong. Recency is one of the most important factors influencing response.

9. *If a program has a considerable history, and test and continuation results are beginning to fade, take care!* Such results are a warning to cut back and not

try for an extensive rollout. Every package and offer has its own life curve, and the fadeout can be faster than the initial growth.

A great deal of money is lost every year in direct mail by practitioners who attempt to "milk" a mailing with one last large rollout. A decrease in income is still better than a disaster. Look for the danger signals. They are always there when you go back to look.

HOW TO MAKE THE MOST OF REPEAT USAGE OF LISTS

Like every other facet of direct marketing all questions on this not too well understood topic can be answered by two time-tested answers—one, "it depends" and two, "test and find out." For it should be clear that reutilization of the same list segment is different for customer files than for prospect files, and the use of the latter is influenced by the universe available, the seasonality of the offer, the drop-off percentage involved, and, like it or not, the predilections of those spending the money for the mail. In addition, the economics of reuse can be and often are different for business to business mailers than for business to consumer mailers.

Nine Rules to Remember about Reusing Lists

Loss in direct mail can come from doing something that costs more than it should. Or it can result (on paper at least) from not taking advantage of some opportunity guaranteed to succeed. It is this last that characterizes the use of most direct response customer files. Only the very rare direct mail operator segregates each cell in his customer file and records results of all mailings (plus cumulative totals) to determine how often he can mail each such identified group. There are a few rules here:

1. *No matter how often you are mailing your customer file, it is fairly certain you are not mailing it often enough.*

2. *Any aging cell in a customer file selectable by date of last order should be mailed as long as it produces more orders and more dollars per thousand pieces than the best of prospect lists.* (This of course is also true for an inquiry list. Such files should be retired only when outside lists do better.) There are instances where buyers who have not come back in six, seven, or eight years still outperform cold prospect lists. One well-known business-to-business mailer has increased his customer mailings from six times per year to twelve times per year. He finds cells four years old—now mailed twelve times—continue to outperform the same number of cold prospects by over 50 percent.

3. *If you expire your customers after a given period—say two or three years—*

do not throw them away. Rather mail them with an age key until the response drops below that which you can obtain from good prospect files.

4. *If your recent expires, in general, do not outpull conventional cold lists, it is likely this is a reflection on the way these customers were originally attracted. That should disturb! You need to RAFO. (Research and Find Out.)*

5. When prospecting for new customers either at home or business, if the universe is large, and solo or catalog mail is being measured, *it is always better to mail to fresh names (of the same characteristics within the same list) than to mail a second time to the same names.*

6. *As a corollary of this, for business mailings it is better to mail most offers to one executive or title per establishment, rather than multiple pieces to the same establishment.* It is true that multiple mailings to companies will produce more responses *per* company—but not per 1,000 pieces mailed. This, of course, may not be true where a major investment in time or money for a large company is involved, and the purchase is controlled not by an individual, but by a committee.

7. *If the response rate the first time is so high (that a drop-off of 35 percent will still provide a very attractive response rate) then at the same time a continuation is made a retest should also be made of the names initially mailed.* The fact this retest using the same mailing piece (but a different key) may come just a month or two after the initial mailing should not deter. The rationale here is the desirability of determining the total response from a given list from two identical mailings as early as possible—and then, where economic, budgeting for both mailings.

8. *If the universe that can provide at least the breakeven response required proves to be quite small, it is time to retrench, possibly retreat, or even retire.* When initial tests over sufficient lists do not begin to develop a "bank" of names to continue with, it is time for a change, possibly a drastic one.

9. *If there is just one universe to be mailed, and multiple mailings are called for, every effort should be made to vary the package, the offer, and the copy.* For with a fixed list, the one factor that varies most in response—the market—has been eliminated. Some years ago for a well-known international newsletter, a specialized prospect list of just 6,000 names was laboriously compiled. This miniscule universe was mailed twelve times a year, with new subscribers developing each month at the rate of one-half of one percent—or 6 percent per year—after twelve mailings. We even went so far as to include the first page of the last issue as one variant of the package.

Conventional wisdom seems to be to return to marginally successful lists on an annual basis. In the case of magazine recipient files this means that some 30 to 35 percent of the file consists of new names not mailed the year before. If a file has greater turnover, such as the 50 percent new subs attracted each year to the average home handyman magazine, it may be possible to mail more frequently. There is just one way to find out for certain on your offer . . . and that is to mail part of such a list once per year, part twice, part three times, and so on, and find out. Few mailers have the patience to do this. It is obviously much easier to follow some rote method, such as "once a year," than to research and find out whether a different schedule might produce better results. For a number of years one of the major societies in the natural history field had a list-buying "expert" who would not use any list, no matter how responsive it proved, more than once per year. Data was placed in front of him which showed that even with a 50 percent drop-off after six months (highly unlikely) one or two bellwether lists would outperform all other lists available to him. He looked at data (somewhat modified for illustration's sake) like this:

	Annual mailings	Second mailing 4 months later
A List	4.5%	2.7%
B List	4.4%	2.6%
Best of others	2.2%	1.5%

If "A" list and "B" list were mailed twice, total response would be 7.2 percent, or an average of 3.6 percent per mailing. The second mailings of A and B are higher than the "best of others" and well above the breakeven response needed of 1.8 percent. Moreover, the total of "A" list and "B" list is virtually equal to all other lists able to reach breakeven. Thus mailing A and B twice is bound to net more members, more donors, and ultimately more dollars per thousand pieces mailed. The answer was still "no"—another example of a well-known management maxim that is "Don't confuse me with the facts, my mind is already made up."

Measuring Response Fall-off on Repeat Mailings

One special type of multiple mailing to the same list is made possible by merge-purging in which the duplicates (multibuyers) are identified and put aside while the "unique—one per household" file is initially mailed. Some mailers make it a practice to mail multibuyers (all with two or more duplicated records) a second time for each offer shortly after the original "one per" list is mailed. There are several considerations here, the first being one of ethics—for unless the mailer has made rental arrangements for a second use with the list owners he may not have the right to a second use. The second is that automatically mailing duplicates (because they are considered the most likely buyers) may not be economic—and such a repeat mailing should be subjected to proof for each offer or group of offers. The same of course is true of "hotlines," particularly for mailers who can make only the most recent names of a list work. As a rule of thumb, if a response fall-off the second time of thirty or thirty-five percent will not be acceptable, don't remail. But even with such a rule, it is best at least once or twice to test such a remail policy. It is always good practice to try and keep those who use statistics a bit on the honest side.

While not exactly on target, there is some elegant data from those who have offered product for sale to oil company credit cards. If sales to those who have used their card for gasoline purchases in the last six months are treated as 100 percent, a typical "fall-off" steps down as follows:

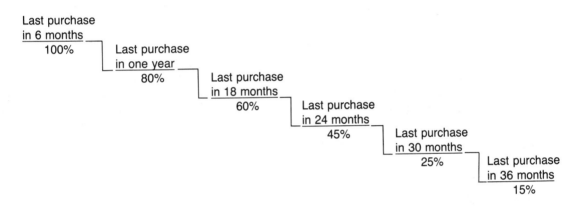

What this indicates is that the more current the credit card customer, the more likely that customer will be to buy other wares on that oil company credit card. (What this says for the use of gift product to reactivate old unused credit cards, can be left for another time.) The percentages for repeat mailings to the same list will of course be different. But the chart, step by step, will look very much the same.

It might well be asked, "Doesn't time have something to do with the efficiency of a repeat solo mailing?" And the answer is, "Of course." But any identical repeat mailing made to the same list within a month or two (before any substantial change in the list) will show a drop-off, depending on the offer, of from 25 to 50 percent—with 30 to 35 percent usual for most. It is not unusual for this drop-off to be 20 percent when the same list segment is exposed to a repeat mailing six months later. It might be well to note that the first mailing "creams off" that small percentage of recipients who see the piece in the first place and who are most inclined to buy immediately. Such immediate buyers may be just a few tenths of one percent of all names mailed. (That is one of the wonders of direct response—that success or failure can be measured by something as small as 1/10th of 1 percent—for measurement is of very large differences in very small numbers from very large universes.) Buyers the first time through are obviously unresponsive when the repeat mailing is received. So the second-time response, typically, is lower, usually considerably lower.

Business versus Consumer Repeat Mailings

At the outset I noted that mailers to business tend to look at repeat mailings differently than do mailers to consumers. For one thing, in business the universe is much more likely to be somewhat limited, all architects for example, or only the small proportion of establishment with fifty or more employees. (The latter is the natural market for example of the majority of all industrial magazines.) For another, the size of the initial sale, and hence the order margin to be gained from such an initial sale, is usually greater by a factor of 5, 10, 15, or 20 for sales to business than for sales to consumers. Thirdly, the business mailer can usually count upon a longer relationship once a prospect changes to a suspect, then to an inquirer, and finally to a customer. Finally, while both types of mailers usually buy new customers at a loss, the time required to amortize this cost to buy is probably less on the business side than on the consumer side.

Despite these generic differences, successful business mailers are just as careful to avoid inadvertent repeat mailings as are mailers to consumers. Merge-purge, originally conducted only for consumer offers is now S.O.P. for major business mailers (even though the cost for an efficient unduplication is two or more times as costly per thousand records handled.)

Most business mailings are by (or to) classifications. Mailings to schools and school districts tend to peak in July and August, and again in January to coincide with educational purchasing operations. And those who mail to them take no chances with repeat mailings to this attractive market in other months. Mailers to large files within one classification, such as insurance agencies, churches, real estate agencies, trucking companies, or contractors seldom utilize multiple mailings; rather the procedure is to course through each universe, before starting all over again. In essence both types of mailers learn rather early to be aware of the economics (in reverse) of repeat mailings.

That leaves us with some utilizations of repeat mailings that are made on a pattern basis. Major producers of business and industrial equipment follow the time-tried method pioneered by NCR and Rand to mail a series of letters about a single piece of equipment to any prospect qualified by the sales force. These companies have found that only in this way can they impart their complete complicated sales story for an expensive unit. There are mailers making complex offers to consumers for investments, homesites, insurance, or franchises where one or two mailings do not produce the results obtainable with a longer series. And where would publishers be if renewal notices were dropped after the first mailing? So as we started, on this subject, we end. It depends!

Multilist Continuation

If you plan a large schedule, use a grid list for basic testing and then select what you believe to be the best package with the best offer and use this package for individual list tests. This will reduce costs for split mailings. The relation this selection has to other variables tested in your grid can be eventually applied to these individual tests.

Figure 10.10

A grid structure for continuations following prior tests of a large sampling of different lists involves selection of best single package and offer for most keys, while providing a continuation of grid testing for an additional group of lists.

| | Large Schedule Grid Testing | | | | |
| | Package A Offer | | Package B Offer | | |
Lists	1	2	1	2	Total
AA	x	x	x	x	4x
BB	x	x	x	x	4x
CC	x	x	x	x	4x
DD	x	x	x	x	4x
EE	x	x	x	x	4x
FF		4x			
GG		4x			
HH		4x			
JJ		4x			
KK		4x			
LL		4x			
Total		4x			

HOW TO ESTABLISH TEST SAMPLE LOTS

If you are a list owner and pay the costs of providing reasonably adequate test samples from a large list or a large list universe, you may find it beneficial to establish test sample lots. The following are some guidelines for establishing test sample lots:

1. Test sample lots should be drawn off periodically, say, once per quarter, to obviate obsolescence.

2. Test sample lots should be sufficient in size to provide unduplicated test samples for all similar offers.

3. It is a good idea to draw off samples of different sizes, to make modest continuations possible without referring to the main file. For a frequently tested list in the 300,000 to 500,000 range, we recommend unduplicated sample lots be drawn of 50,000 and 25,000. A user who moves from 5,000 to 20,000 can easily be accommodated within the first two blocks without referring to the main file.

4. These test sample lots should be selected on the basis of the last two digits of the zip code. Each quarterly selection should be based on different groups of two-digit zip code groups. In this way, access to the main file without duplicating one record on the current test sample file is assured.

Here are statistical data based on analyses of large files of small beauty shops and schools based on last digit of zip code, and all big businesses rated $500,000 and over:

Table 10.1

Proportion of establishments by last digit of zip code

Last digit of zip code	Beauty shops (percentage)	Schools (percentage)	Big businesses (percentage)	Average (percentage)
1	17%	16%	19.5	18.0
2	10	10	12.0	11.0
3	9	9	9.0	9.0
4	9	9	9.5	9.0
5	8	9	9.0	9.0
6	9	9	9.0	9.0
7	9	8	8.0	8.5
8	7	8	6.5	7.0
9	6	6	5.0	6.0
0	12	13	12.5	12.5

HOW TO MAKE ZIP CODES WORK FOR YOU ON LIST TESTS

If a client asks this author's office, "What is the best method to select a test sample from a large list?" our answer is *not* the time-honored Nth number sample. We advise the use of the last digit of zip codes or the last two digits of zip codes. Reasons for this follow.

1. Nth number samples (every 100th, 125th, or 150th name) are one of the most talked about but least used methods of test selection.

If the computer service does not have an Nth number selection capability, a new program must be provided, tested, and debugged.

Computer services often find it easier to "take the first so many of" as the first two hundred in a state, or the first three hundred in a three-digit SCF.

The Nth number sample while statistically ideal, is too much trouble.

The average user cannot determine by inspection if the test sample has been drawn on an Nth-number basis or not. As a result Nth-number tests are easily fudged.

2. In most cases Nth-number samples *cannot* be skipped on continuations.

Unless the computer service has a sophisticated program that tags each record used for a test, there is almost no way that Nth-number test quantities or prior continuations can be identified. If the computer cannot identify such records, it cannot skip them.

Very few mailers involve themselves in such sophisticated programming.

Most, if not virtually all, continuations must, by their very nature, incorporate duplication of records already run before.

If a list is updated between uses in any way, such as the removal or addition of only one record, this will kill any possibility of guaranteeing to skip the prior test sample.

3. The use of last digit of zip codes or last two digits of zip codes is safe, sure, economical, and simple.

If you run all or most of your records ending in a given digit or pair of digits for your test, you can make certain of skipping the test simply by omitting such digits in your continuation.

If you wish to see what a second mailing to the *same* records will do, select records with the same last digit or last two digits. While it may be true that a few names may now be on file due to an update, a 10 or 20 percent increase or decrease in the file will not obviate the validity of such a test. (Proof on request happens to be for the same reason that nixies have *nothing* to do with the success or failure of a rented mail order list. You may wish to argue this one also.)

(Assume that your breakeven is 1 percent—and you use a rented list known to be no more than 90 percent deliverable. Now assume that you test this list and receive five orders per M in the mail. Adding 10 percent to this (as if the list were 100 percent deliverable) increases the five to five and one-half—far from the required 10. On another rental list the test comes in at thirteen orders per M. Had the list been 100 percent deliverable, your result would have been fourteen orders per M. You continue, disregarding the "nixie" factor. Please note, the "nixie" factor does matter on customer files!)

Using the last digit of zip codes gives a reasonable cross section of any file. As Table 10.2 indicates, the last two digits of zip codes in business lists and service lists (this also will hold true for consumer lists as well) range from 6 percent on a typical file to 16 percent. Seven of the last ten numbers of zip codes are within a small fraction of covering an even 10 percent of the list.

Where a 1 for 10, 1 for 15, or a 1 for 20 selection will not provide sufficient sampling through the whole list, use of last two digits of zip codes will guarantee sufficient sample size. If a list of beauty shops has 100,000 records and a test of 3,000 is desired, taking a single last digit of zip, say no 2 (which is found on 10% of all zipped records) will provide some 10,000 records countrywide. By stopping at 3,000, roughly one third of the country will be sampled. To produce a statistically valid sample all through the country of 3,000 from this same list, simply pull all records with the 4th digit 0 and the final digit 2 (3.04 percent on Table 10.2) (3.04 percent of 100,000 = 3040 records).

Table 10.2

Proportion of establishments by last two digits of zip code

Last two digits of zip code	Beauty shops (percentage)	Schools (percentage)	Average (percentage)
01	9.41%	7.61%	8.01%
02	3.04	2.10	2.57
03	2.08	2.22	2.15
04	2.07	2.19	2.13
05	2.07	2.24	2.16
06	2.43	1.95	2.19
07	1.08	1.51	1.29
08	1.07	1.30	1.19
09	1.62	1.16	1.39
10	2.10	1.96	2.03
11	1.07	1.59	1.33
12		1.38	
13	1.23	1.68	1.46

Table 10.2 (cont.)

Proportion of establishments by last two digits of zip code

Last two digits of zip code	Beauty shops (percentage)	Schools (percentage)	Average (percentage)
18	1.30	1.01	1.16
19	1.10	.90	1.00
20	2.20	2.05	2.13
22	1.22	1.25	1.24
25	1.10		
26	1.14	1.08	1.11
27	.84	.91	.73
28	.71	.93	.82
29	.61	.80	.72
30	1.63	1.78	1.71
31	1.06	1.14	1.10
32		1.12	
33	.80	1.04	.92
34	1.09	.88	.99
35	.96	1.08	1.02
36	.80	.90	.85
38	.75	.86	.81
39	.60	.73	.67
40	1.07	1.87	1.47
45	.75		
47	.64		
49	.53		
50	1.42	1.55	1.49
51	.71	.96	.84
53	.70	.84	.77
54		1.05	
56	.60	.84	.72
57	.60	.82	.71
58	.46		
59	.13		
60	.16	1.67	.92
62	.73		
66	.73		
67	.63		
68		.66	
69	.50	.63	.57
71		.69	
72		.69	
73		.63	
74	.47	.63	.55

Table 10.2 (cont.)

Proportion of establishments by last two digits of zip code

Last two digits of zip code	Beauty shops (percentage)	Schools (percentage)	Average (percentage)
75	.41	.53	.47
77	.52	.66	.59
79		.47	
80	.74	.84	.78
81		.53	
82	.11	.49	.30
83	.44	.53	.49
85	.23	.45	.34
89	.10	.29	.19
95	.21	.28	.25
96	.16	.17	.17
98		.13	

Note: Zip Codes are comprised of five Digits: The first three digits describe the sectional center and the last two digits are assigned to individual post offices and/or neighborhood areas within cities. Note that the use of 01 (for virtually every zip area) makes two-digit zip "01" by itself the equivalent of any last digit zip. (01 = 8%, last digit zip 2 through 0 range from 6% to 12%). As is logical, 02, 03, 04, 05, 06 are next largest, and are indeed the only two-digit numbers other than those ending in zero with 2 percent or more of the records. There is a strong correlation between the business file and the professional file which were zipped by two different organizations. The variance, except for 18 small two-digit zips that appear in one list and not the other, are in the neighborhood of ±10 to 15%. Over 95% of the records in each list can be compared directly by 2 digit zip.

It is easy to record usage by last digit of zip codes, as well as easy for the list owner to comply with such selection and omission.

Even the problem of leaving records unused in a file can be solved. Let us assume you have tested zip code records ending in 2 with a 5,000 sample lot, and the list has 200,000 names on it. From Table 10-2, zip codes ending in 2 equal 10 percent of the file, or 20,000. You can call up the balance of these records ending in 2 either by stipulating "start at 5 digit XXXXX," or by stipulating, if this is the case, "skip the first 5,000 zip code records ending in 2 and take the balance."

HOW TO AVOID DUPLICATION ON CONTINUATIONS

By renting each list (up to ten lists) with a different last digit of zip codes, it is possible to easily rent 50,000 to 100,000 names that are guaranteed *not* to include duplicates. By using even and odd configurations on the fourth digit of zip codes in conjunction with the fifth digit of zip codes, twenty lists can be rented with not more than a minuscule possibility of duplication as the following table shows.

XXX (EVEN) Fifth		Fifth (ODD) XXX	
2	0	0	1
4	1	1	3
6	2	2	5
8	3	3	7
0	4	4	9
	5	5	
	6	6	
	7	7	
	8	8	
	9	9	

It is interesting to ascertain the possible level of duplication on, say, five lists of 5,000 names each chosen with a spread from five different computer installations. These names come from fifty different states and are found in 400,000 carrier routes, or in 400,000 enumeration districts or subblocks. Unless some discipline has been exercised to select each list from a confined area, say, one state, the chances of duplication are certain to be less than 1 percent. If a merge–purge is used it would simply add costs without providing any savings to offset these costs.

Where names are run at the same time as the house file, and the quantities of house plus rented names exceed, say, 250,000, a merge–purge is indicated. Incidentally, do *not* follow the advice of some so-called experts who recommend that rental lists be selected specifically to be different from the house list. The more closely outside lists match the house demographic and psychographic profiles, which usually show an above-average penetration of the house file, the better such lists are for prospecting by the owner of the house file.

OPERATIONAL FACTORS FOR TEST MAILINGS

1. *Never retire a successful package, which is called your "control," until you have a new package that shows a significant difference when tested adequately, head to head.* Occasionally, but rarely, two packages may be outstanding, each one for a different part of a market. Testing to find such packages must be limited to large mailers that have large market possibilities.

2. *Never test new package A versus new package B and disregard the control.* *Many times the control will win against both and you will only be picking the better of two losers.*

3. *Never change any significant element in the control without testing to see what that change will do.* If you add items, change a price, drop or add a piece, or change the terms you no longer have the same control.

4. *Get to new fresh lists, particularly from new sources, early.* New lists tend to work best when they are first placed on the market.

5. *Always have a "contestant package" in the wings that you hope will beat your current control.* Each mailing and offer has a life, which given time, will develop from introduction to continuation to rollout to extended reach. At some time, however, it is certain to show a drop off in response. Long before this time, you need to have a test contestant to reintroduce to the market.

6. *If you do not as yet have a control, create one with your first tests.* At the very least you can place a good offer in the mail that is written in simple English and clothed in a neat and appropriate package. Thereafter, try to beat this at every opportunity.

7. *Disregard any supplier who claims to be the only source for your particular market.* Very likely this is a supplier who wishes to force fit your offer to his or her proprietary file. There are always alternatives.

8. *There are no secrets in the list business.* The offer of a "secret" list is a danger signal. There are no secret lists—only secretive individuals who wish to obfuscate the availability of lists. When a list compiler refuses to name his or her source, find another compiler. If a mailer refuses to tell you the age of a given list segment, see if you can locate a likely substitute.

9. *On every flight of lists, type up a pressure-sensitive label with your name and address and cover up one name on one (or two) of the cheshire lists with its proper zip code.* In this way you will get a good check on the mailing shop and learn when to expect response. If a merge–purge is involved, make certain your own name is included. If necessary, make this an addition as part of your instructions.

DRY TESTING

Occasionally, a mail response operator wishes to test the market for a new concept or product before committing for production or taking stock into inventory. This is referred to as dry testing and it is a practice usually frowned upon by legitimate direct-mail users.

There is, however, no more wrong with this kind of dry testing, if done properly, than with multiple price offers or other offers to test market acceptance for the same product. Where the product is not available at the moment, each order received must be impounded. If the money has been deposited, it must be sequestered, and before the end of the thirty days from receipt each buyer must be notified when or if the product will be available. If it is certain the product will not be available months before delivery can be made, then the money must be returned with a note of thanks. If at some future time you plan to sell other products to these trusting souls it will pay to explain the "test" nature of the offer.

AVAILABILITY MAY DETERMINE MAILINGS

Some mailers are so bound by scheduling and rituals that they cannot adjust to variants that might dramatically increase response. Two or three magazine circulation directors who can only make the most current names of a number of good lists work for them insist on mailing such names once or twice a year despite the fact such names are available monthly. They would find it far more profitable to schedule these names on a monthly basis. Once such a schedule is in place, the big problem of mailing more than once or twice a year will become a simple control problem.

WHY ROLL-OUTS DO NOT DO AS WELL AS TESTS

For years rollouts tended, almost universally, to log in at response rates somewhat lower than test results. This is not because the list purveyor has loaded the list with the best available names (by age, or size of order, or credit card, or change of address.) It is likely, from a statistical point of view, that regression of continuing bites of a given list tends toward the mean figure. The lists that are continued are not those that are average or below average, but always the ones that do best. These tests may well be above the mean response that would have been recorded if the entire list, rather than a test segment had been run. Thus the rollout tends to move toward that mean figure which has a good likelihood of being lower within statistical probability, than initial test results. Similarly, the smaller the sample, the smaller the number of responses will be, and the greater the likelihood of such a dropoff.

SMALL LISTS

Many mailers set a rule not to test lists of less than a certain amount. They reason that it does not pay to test below a given size because the continuation will be too small. Mailers with this rule may well be shortchanging their companies. If given the opportunity to rent two lists of 25,000, each of which will produce 1.1 percent or one list of 50,000 which will produce 0.9 percent, the mailer who will not test any list that is smaller than 50,000 will be throwing away money.

This is not to say that very small but very attractive lists should not be tested. There is no reason to test 5,000 names from a list that has a total of only 10,000. But if the demographics and the psychographics are particularly appealing then the small list should be placed in its entirety on the schedule. It is not unusual for such choice small bits to produce three or four times the required breakeven. A handful of them can be far more productive than a single much larger list.

A FEW COMMON SENSE RULES

1. Recognize that for all practical purposes there are only two kinds of lists: those that work and those that don't.

2. Don't refuse to mail an older segment that is working just because newer names are not available.

3. Don't refuse to mail a list just because it is not precise and complete in every way. It may well be the best list of its type around.

4. Don't set up hard and fast rules such as "never mail an inquiry list." You may be cutting yourself off from some nice neat net profits.

5. Don't refuse to test a list because the rental price is too high. Another $10 per thousand may be only 3 percent of the cost in the mail, and you may be bypassing a list that will increase response by ten times.

There are a good number of mailers who "shop" for bargain lists—$5 off per thousand—and feel they have somehow beaten the system. As lists either work or don't, it follows that a low-cost list that fails is a dead loss while a fair-priced list or a higher-priced list that succeeds is a bargain.

Mailers who arbitrarily will not try a list priced above a given number of dollars per thousand may be depriving themselves of great response. Price is not the determinant; response is. The name of the game is response based on the total dollars expended.

SOME STATISTICAL HELP

Table 10.3 lists data for mailing response at a 95 percent confidence level. That 95 percent confidence level means that 95 times out of 100 the results obtained the first time will be repeated within a statistically valid range the next time. While some mailers insist on a 99 percent confidence level, they must mail much greater quantities to get that assurance. Those who use a 90 percent confidence level mail fewer pieces by far, but leave the fact open that one out of every ten times the results will go awry. (At 95 percent, that chance drops to one in twenty.) Most statistically minded mailers use the 95 percent figure, which also is recommended by this author.

On page 342 a recommendation was given that stated fifty *responses* provide a reasonable confidence level. Let us see how this figure works out on the 95 percent level shown in Table 10.3.

If we know the number of responses we are seeking (in this case 50) we need to create a scenario in which the number of responses per thousand is set. Let us assume that our breakeven is seven orders per thousand. Seven per thousand is 30 percent less than ten orders per 1000. So we need to utilize a sample size that will produce ten orders per M $\pm$ 30 percent—with a 95 percent confidence level.

Starting with the far left column of percent of response in the table, we move down to 1.0 percent and then go across to .30. The figure given is 4220. This is the minimum sized sample we should use. If this figure is rounded off to a sample size of 5,000, and we get a 1.0 percent response, we now know that 95 out of 100 times a *similar* sample from the *same* list will produce 1.0 $\pm$ .3 or between seven and thirteen orders per thousand. Table 10-3 can be used to establish the needed sample size given the anticipated percentage response and the variation, plus *or* minus, which can be lived with.

Now let's use the table to determine if two results show a significant difference. If there is not a *statistically* significant difference, the two responses are considered the same even if the two figures appear to be far apart.

Response to an offer—by List—Tests of 5000 each

- List A–1.1%
- List B–1.4%
- List C–1.7%

On the surface, List C would seem to be best. But is it significantly better than Lists A and B? Are Lists B and C really both better than A? To find this out, we again refer to the table.

Table 10-3

Test sample table for mailing response levels and a 95 percent confidence level

Percent Response	.02	.04	.06	.08	.10	.12	Limits of Error .14	.16	.18	.20	.30	.40	.50	.60	.70
.1	95944.	23986.	10660.	5996.	3838.	2665.	1958.	1499.	1184.	959.	426.	240.	154.	107.	78.
.2	191696.	47924.	21300.	11981.	7668.	5325.	3912.	2995.	2367.	1917.	852.	479.	307.	213.	156.
.3	287256.	71814.	31917.	17953.	11490.	7979.	5862.	4488.	3546.	2873.	1277.	718.	460.	319.	234.
.4	382623.	95656.	42514.	23914.	15305.	10628.	7809.	5978.	4724.	3826.	1701.	957.	612.	425.	312.
.5	477799.	119450.	53089.	29862.	19112.	13272.	9751.	7466.	5899.	4778.	2124.	1194.	764.	531.	390.
.6	572783.	143196.	63643.	35799.	22911.	15911.	11689.	8950.	7071.	5728.	2546.	1432.	916.	636.	468.
.7	667574.	166894.	74175.	41723.	26703.	18544.	13624.	10431.	8242.	6676.	2967.	1669.	1068.	742.	545.
.8	762173.	190543.	84686.	47636.	30487.	21171.	15555.	11909.	9410.	7622.	3387.	1905.	1219.	847.	622.
.9	856581.	214145.	95176.	53536.	34263.	23794.	17481.	13384.	10575.	8566.	3807.	2141.	1371.	952.	699.
1.0	950796.	237699.	105644.	59425.	38032.	26411.	19404.	14856.	11738.	9508.	4226.	2377.	1521.	1056.	776.
1.1	1044819.	261205.	116091.	65301.	41793.	29023.	21323.	16325.	12899.	10448.	4644.	2612.	1672.	1161.	853.
1.2	1138650.	284663.	126517.	71166.	45546.	31629.	23238.	17791.	14057.	11387.	5061.	2847.	1822.	1265.	930.
1.3	1232289.	308072.	136921.	77018.	49292.	34230.	25149.	19255.	15213.	12323.	5477.	3081.	1972.	1369.	1006.
1.4	1325736.	331434.	147304.	82859.	53029.	36826.	27056.	20715.	16367.	13257.	5892.	3314.	2121.	1473.	1082.
1.5	1418991.	354748.	157666.	88687.	56760.	39416.	28959.	22172.	17518.	14190.	6307.	3547.	2270.	1577.	1158.
1.6	1512054.	378013.	168006.	94503.	60482.	42001.	30858.	23626.	18667.	15121.	6720.	3780.	2419.	1680.	1234.
1.7	1604924.	401231.	178325.	100308.	64197.	44581.	32754.	25077.	19814.	16049.	7133.	4012.	2568.	1783.	1310.
1.8	1697603.	424401.	188623.	106100.	67904.	47156.	34645.	26525.	20958.	16976.	7545.	4244.	2716.	1886.	1388.
1.9	1790090.	447522.	198899.	111881.	71604.	49725.	36532.	27970.	22100.	17901.	7956.	4475.	2864.	1989.	1461.
2.0	1882384.	470596.	209154.	117649.	75295.	52288.	38416.	29412.	23239.	18824.	8366.	4706.	3012.	2092.	1537.
2.1	1974486.	493622.	219887.	123405.	78979.	54847.	40296.	30851.	24376.	19745.	8775.	4936.	3159.	2194.	1612.
2.2	2066397.	516599.	229600.	129150.	82656.	57400.	42171.	32287.	25511.	20664.	9184.	5166.	3306.	2296.	1687
2.3	2158115.	539529.	239791.	134882.	86325.	59948.	44043.	33721.	26643.	21581.	9592.	5395.	3453.	2398.	1762.
2.4	2249641.	562410.	249960.	140603.	89986.	62490.	45911.	35151.	27773.	22496.	9998.	5624.	3599.	2500.	1836.
2.5	2340975.	585244.	260108.	146311.	93639.	65027.	47775.	36578.	28901.	23410.	10404.	5852.	3746.	2601.	1911.
2.6	2432117.	608029.	270235.	152007.	97285.	67559.	49635.	38002.	30026.	24321.	10809.	6080.	3891.	2702.	1985.
2.7	2523067.	630767.	280341.	157692.	100923.	70085.	51491.	39423.	31149.	25231.	11214.	6303.	4037.	2803.	2060.
2.8	2623825.	653456.	290425.	163364.	104553.	72606.	53343.	40841.	32269.	26138.	11617.	6535.	4182.	2904.	2134.
2.9	2704390.	676098.	300488.	169024.	108176.	75122.	55192.	42256.	33388.	27044.	12020.	6761.	4327.	3005.	2208.

3.0	2794764.	698691.	310529.	174673.	111791.	77632.	57036.	43668.	34503.	27948.	12421.	6987.	4472.	3105.	2281.
3.1	2884946.	721236.	320550.	180309.	115398.	80137.	58876.	45077.	35617.	28849.	12822.	7212.	4616.	3205.	2355.
3.2	2974935.	743734.	330548.	185933.	118997.	82637.	60713.	46433.	36728.	29749.	13222.	7437.	4760.	3305.	2429.
3.3	3064732.	766183.	340526.	191546.	122589.	85131.	62546.	47886.	37836.	30647.	13621.	7662.	4904.	3405.	2502.
3.4	3154338.	788584.	350482.	197146.	126174.	87620.	64374.	49287.	38942.	31543.	14019.	7886.	5047.	3505.	2575.
3.5	3243751.	810938.	360417.	202734.	129750.	90104.	66199.	50684.	40046.	32438.	14417.	8109.	5190.	3604.	2648.
3.6	3332972.	833243.	370330.	208311.	133319.	92583.	68020.	52078.	41148.	33330.	14813.	8332.	5333.	3703.	2721.
3.7	3422001.	855500.	380222.	213875.	136880.	95056.	69837.	53469.	42247.	34220.	15209.	8555.	5475.	3802.	2793.
3.8	3510838.	877710.	390093.	219427.	140434.	97523.	71650.	54857.	43344.	35108.	15604.	8777.	5617.	3901.	2866.
3.9	3599483.	899871.	399943.	224968.	143979.	99986.	73459.	56242.	44438.	35995.	15998.	8999.	5759.	3999.	2938.
4.0	3687936.	921984.	409771.	230496.	147517.	102443.	75264.	57624.	45530.	36879.	16391.	9220.	5901.	4098.	3011.
4.1	3776197.	944049.	419363.	236012.	151048.	104894.	77065.	59003.	46620.	37762.	16783.	9440.	6042.	4196.	3083.
4.2	3864265.	966066.	429363.	241517.	154571.	107341.	78863.	60379.	47707.	38643.	17175.	9661.	6183.	4294.	3155.
4.3	3952142.	988036.	439127.	247009.	158086.	109782.	80656.	61752.	48792.	39521.	17565.	9880.	6323.	4391.	3226.
4.4	4039827.	1009957.	448870.	252489.	161593.	112217.	82445.	63122.	49874.	40398.	17955.	10100.	6464.	4489.	3298.
4.5	4127319.	1031830.	458591.	257957.	165093.	114648.	84231.	64489.	50955.	41273.	18344.	10318.	6604.	4586.	3369.
4.6	4214619.	1053655.	468291.	263414.	168585.	117073.	86013.	65853.	52032.	42146.	18732.	10537.	6743.	4683.	3441.
4.7	4301728.	1075432.	477970.	268858.	172069.	119492.	87790.	67214.	53108.	43017.	19119.	10754.	6883.	4780.	3512.
4.8	4388644.	1097161.	487627.	274290.	175546.	121907.	89564.	68573.	54181.	43886.	19505.	10972.	7022.	4876.	3583.
4.9	4475368.	1118842.	497263.	279710.	179015.	124316.	91334.	69928.	55251.	44754.	19891.	11188.	7161.	4973.	3658.
5.0	4561900.	1140475.	506878.	285119.	182476.	126719.	93100.	71280.	56320.	45619.	20275.	11405.	7299.	5069.	3724.
5.1	4648240.	1162060.	516471.	290515.	185930.	129118.	94862.	72629.	57386.	46482.	20659.	11621.	7437.	5165.	3794.
5.2	4734388.	1183597.	526043.	295899.	189376.	131511.	96620.	73975.	58449.	47344.	21042.	11836.	7575.	5260.	3865.
5.3	4820344.	1205086.	535594.	301271.	192314.	133898.	98374.	75318.	59510.	48203.	21424.	12051.	7713.	5356.	3935.
5.4	4906107.	1226527.	545123.	306632.	196244.	136281.	100125.	76658.	60569.	49061.	21805.	12265.	7850.	5451.	4005.
5.5	4991679.	1247920.	554631.	311980.	199667.	138658.	101871.	77995.	61626.	49917.	22185.	12479.	7987.	5546.	4075.
5.6	5077059.	1269265.	564118.	317316.	203082.	141029.	103613.	79329.	62680.	50771.	22565.	12693.	8123.	5641.	4145.
5.7	5162246.	1290562.	573583.	322640.	206490.	143396.	105352.	80660.	63731.	51622.	22943.	12906.	8260.	5736.	4214.
5.8	5247241.	1311810.	583027.	327953.	209890.	145757.	107087.	81988.	64781.	52472.	23321.	13118.	8396.	5830.	4283.
5.9	5332045.	1333011.	592449.	333253.	213282.	148112.	108817.	83313.	65828.	53320.	23698.	13330.	8531.	5924.	4353.
6.0	5416656.	1354164.	601851.	338541.	216666.	150463.	110544.	84635.	66872.	54167.	24074.	13542.	8667.	6019.	4422.

List A at 1.1 percent at 5,000 pieces. Repeats will be plus or minus .30.

List B at 1.4 percent is .3 above List A, or just a shade more than the .25 mark, indicating a marginal difference.

List C at 1.7 percent is .6 above List A. This means List C shows a significantly better response than List A but it's response is marginal compared with List B.

Had we mailed 10,000 pieces and received the *same* percentage responses, the table for List A at 1.1 percent and 10,000 pieces shows a variance of ±20%.

Both List B at 1.4 (or +3 compared with .2) and List C at 1.7 (+6 compared with .2) show better response levels than List A. In addition List C at +6 compared with List B at +3 indicates that List C is significantly better than List B and much better than List A.

Table 10.1 also can be used to determine the permissible error from a current mailing, which can be taken into account on future mailings. If we mailed 25,000 pieces of our customer file and received a 2.7 percent response. What will the next 25,000 similarly selected pieces do with the same offer?

By locating 2.7 on the table and moving right we find the quantity 25,000 (25,231 exactly) under the .20 column. This means we will hit 2.7 ± .20 or between 2.5 percent and 2.9 percent. This provides very comforting news on what to expect. If, however, we reduced the future mailing to 5,000, and then read the table for 2.7, we find the nearest figure is under .40. The range can be statistically valid within 2.3 percent to 3.1 percent, which is a much greater spread then if 25,000 pieces were mailed.

These figures, particularly the plus-or-minus ranges within statistical probability, explain why five samples of the same size, drawn from the same universe can test out at five different response levels. (For example, if five samples of 5,000 of the hypothetical customer file above, were mailed, the five responses might come in at 2.4, 2.6, 2.7, 2.9, or 3.0. Their average (for the entire 25,000 would then show between 2.5 percent and 2.9 percent—in this case at 2.7 percent).

CHAPTER 11

The Mathematics of Direct Response

There are two major segments in this book given over primarily to the mathematics of direct response. Chapters 9 and 10 provide every answer to "who, what, when, where, and how" to test, and include all of the basic mathematics required to give you full understanding not only of what to do, but also what not do do.

This chapter will discuss mathematics not directly concerned with testing. Here you will find data on index numbers and predictions, what makes up the back-end costs of a direct-mail operation, and further information on understanding terms such as order margin, R.O.P., R.O.I, and a few high hard ones like incremental evaluation. I suggest you first skim through this chapter and then reread those sections that pertain to your operation.

WHY PERCENTS COUNT IN DIRECT-MAIL RESPONSE

Direct Mail involves very large differences in very small numbers derived from very large universes. A difference of one-tenth of one percent (from 1/10 to 2/10 for example) in response can be the difference between profit and loss. In no other economic activity that I know of is a difference of one-tenth of 1 percent significant. (This underlies the entire argument for keeping postal rises in modest bounds.) At each increase some offers can no longer succeed. At each postal increase the "order margin" (the sum left after all costs except promotion are subtracted from the selling price) needed for profit in the mails must increase. Increases in prior years have killed offers with $5 or $10 of order margin, and are already threatening offers with order margins higher than this. Each rise in cost forces some marginal component out of the mails.

Knowing the "order margin" of a given offer, and then knowing the cost of promotion it is a simple matter to divide one into the other to determine the number of responses required for breakeven.

How to Record Responses by Source in Eight Steps

To record responses by source it is necessary to first code each variant. For example, if the same package with the same copy and the same offer is mailed on the same day to ten different lists, the variable measured through response is the relative responsiveness of the lists. (This same method is used to test one offer against another, one package against another, or one premium against another.)

- *Step 1*—Code the segment or variable to be measured by response.
- *Step 2*—Provide some method to capture these codes.
- *Step 3*—Record the number of responses and the number of dollars for each code on a daily basis.
- *Step 4*—Cumulate the number of responses and number of dollars on a running daily basis.
- *Step 5*—Calculate the half life (This turns out to be a relatively short period providing an important management tool based on partial response.)
- *Step 6*—At the end of the offer calculate the total response, total dollars, and the net effect (plus or minus) achieved for each keyed promotion.
- *Step 7*—Create a data bank of successful lists that can be accumulated and mailed in quantity at some subsequent period.
- *Step 8*—Determine which variation, such as which list or lists to continue with an increased order, which variation to retest with a slight variation to improve the breed, and which variation to eliminate from future consideration.

These steps or variations of them are to be taken in every form of direct response.

The same basic steps are required to measure the effectiveness of prospecting through space advertisements. The space has a given cost. The order margin (or the gross profit on average for a group of simultaneously offered products) is known. A given number of responses (and perhaps a given number of catalog requests in addition to sales) are required to pay the costs of promotion and the costs of goods sold. The result is either a profit or a loss for each individual insert in each individual medium. (The variant here, if the "copy" is standardized, is the medium, in this case a newspaper or a magazine advertisement.)

A number of quite complex statistical procedures are employed in the direct-mail field in an attempt to improve the response rate. However, the calculation of breakeven and the steps involved in measuring, recording, and analyzing response are simple mathematics and you should start there.

HOW TO CREATE INDEX NUMBERS
FOR COMPARING PERFORMANCES

To provide a single set of numbers to review for a whole series of keys, an index number can be created. While any criteria can be used to create this number, it is usual practice to make one hundred the breakeven on the cost of promotion. Then each key can be compared with any other key by noting its relation to the index. This method is helpful in comparing two different campaigns when the percentage of response or the total dollars per thousand catalogs may be misleading. Here is an example of the validity of the index number:

	Pieces	Cost/ M	Total cost	Sales/ M	Total sales	Percent of response	(Index)
Campaign 1	25,000	$420	$10,500	2,150	$53,750	2.1%	(209)
Campaign 2	25,000	$460	$11,500	2,250	$56,250	2.2%	(181)

On the surface, Campaign 2 looks better than Campaign 1 because an expenditure of $40 more per thousand catalogs increases the response rate for Campaign 2 by one sale at an average of $100 over Campaign 1. What the table above omits is a way to equate the two in the number of dollars of profit per thousand catalogs mailed. This can be done by specifying the number of dollars. It can be most easily placed on a scale by using the index number.

An index number is also very useful for interim reports where the operator wishes to see how well each key is doing. Index numbers at the end of one, two, or three months of response can be compared directly with indexes obtained in comparable timeframes on previous mailings.

The index is equally useful on reviewing space keys. Here 100 equals amortization by gross profit on sales of the cost of the insertion. Use of an index number also can be helpful in analysis of performance by each item on each page of a catalog.

After first providing weighting for extra value for the covers, center spread, and the order form, the total for these special areas is subtracted from the total cost of the catalog. The balance is then divided by the number of pages to get the value or "100 Index" for each page. This sum must be covered by gross profit dollars from sales before a page can be said to produce a profit.

From these data an index based on 100 for breakeven compared with the cost of promotion can be created for each estimated segment of a page, for example, 1/2, 1/4, 1/8, 1/3, 2/3, 3/4.

The 100 Index for the smaller segments can be by simple division such as a $\frac{1}{2}$ page has a 100 Index at half the cost of a full page. As smaller space usually bears a higher price per inch than larger space, a simple weighting can be added to the actual arithmetic proportion. The concept establishes an index of 100 which equates each unit equally on the basis of cost.

HOW TO ANALYZE RESPONSE BY AGE OF LAST ORDER

Mailing by cells based purely on the time of the last purchase or the time since the receipt of an unconverted inquiry, produces, in almost every case, a descending array of penetration. Where the response does not follow a simple progression based on age of the last order, that is a signal to research and find out the reason for the aberration. Here is a typical response structure:

Latest purchase by buyer	Response to today's catalog mailing (percent)
Last 3 months	3.3%
4 to 6 months	2.8
7 months to 1 year	2.3
13 to 18 months	2.0
19 to 24 months	1.7
2 years to 3 years	1.3
Over 3 years	0.7

Receipt of catalog requests	Conversion to customer status (percent)
Last 3 months	1.9%
Last 6 months	1.7
7 months to 1 year	1.4
13 to 18 months	1.0
19 to 24 months	0.7
Over 2 years	0.5

If the cost of mailing and the average order determine that the breakeven response needed to justify continuation is 1.5, then in the table above only customers who have not purchased in the last three years fall below the line. (It is probable that customers who have not purchased in the last three years and a few months will be close to the line while those customers who have made purchases in the last four or five years will no longer justify additional catalog mailings. Similarly each aged segment of inquiries should be renewed. Note that those received seven to twelve months ago are not marginal. This should indicate that all inquiries one year old or more should get a "one last chance" offer. (Such an offer almost always gives a lift to response, and allows the mailer to identify those nonresponse customers or inquiries that now should be dropped.) If the seven- to twelve-month cell is large enough the result in the previous table would indicate a need to split these by number of months on the file to determine when in the seven- to twelve-month period continued catalog conversions can be justified.

The results in the table are based on a program of mailing catalogs six times per year to all responsive cells, both customer and catalog requests. This means some catalog inquiries, if not converted earlier, would have received four or five additional catalog mailings following the initial catalog sent to service the request when received.

Determining Profitable Cut-off Points

This type of analysis is available to every mailer and every catalog operator. If the mailer has a number of different offers to make to his or her customer file, each one will have a different cut-off point for profitability. For example, if a response rate of 2.0 percent to a catalog mailing is required to justify a special offer, then this table indicates only customers who have bought in the last eighteen months are eligible for such a special offer, and only those catalog inquiries received in the last three months should be tried to see if any level here will pay out.

If an analysis is made on the basis of gross profit per cell (rather than percentage response) data can be provided to establish which cells need to be mailed at the predicted profit ratios to hit a predetermined overall gross profit on the mailing. Leaving off lower cells still profitable by themselves but not profitable enough based on the predetermined cutoff will provide sound data for quantities to mail.

Data like those shown in the table on the following page provide answers to profitability. If the desired profitability totals $30,000, then only the top three cells, totalling 50,000 names should be mailed. If the desired profit is $40,000, the next two cells with 33,000 additional names should be added. If we use the cost of the mailing as investment, the return on investment decreases, cell by cell, as follows:

Last 3 months	$13,800 profit on $6,000 cost	= 230%
4 to 6 months	$10,100 profit on $5,600 cost	= 180%
7 months to 1 yr	$16,900 profit on $8,400 cost	= 130%
13 to 18 months	$ 6,800 profit on $6,800 cost	= 100%
19 to 24 months	$ 4,500 profit on $6,400 cost	= 70%
2 to 3 years	$ 3,400 profit on $11,200 cost	= 30%
Over 3 years		Loss

The figures above are "indexed"—that is, 100 percent equals amortization of the cost of promotion through the order margin on sales. Note that only those customers who last purchased prior to eighteen months show an index of 100 percent or better. If a decision were reached to mail only those cells with the profitability of producing 130 percent or better, only customers who purchased in the prior year would qualify.

First Sale vs Second Sale

The hardest sale to make in direct mail, and this is true of catalog mail operations as well, is the second sale. When you mail your customer file you are mailing not to cold prospects but to individuals who have recently purchased from you. Although it is understandable that customer files will produce much higher response rates than cold prospect files they rarely produce response rates of more than 4 or 5 percent, which are highly profitable. But note if the mailing is made to first-time buyers, only 4 percent become multiple buyers. If these same customers are mailed to five more times, the total cumulative penetration—those buying for the second time or more—rarely exceeds 20 to 25 percent. This means,

Array of responses by age of last purchase

A	B	C	D	E	E-C	F	
Latest response by catalog buyers	Quantity	Response rate	Total cost of mailing @ $400/M	Total sales (at $100 average)		Gross margin GP40	Gross profit
Last 3 months	15,000	3.3%	$ 6,000	$49,500		$19.800	$13,800
4 to 6 months	14,000	2.8%	5,600	39,200		15.700	10,100
7 months to 1 yr	21,000	2.3%	8,400	48,300		19.300	10,900
13 to 18 months	17,000	2.0%	6,800	34,000		13.600	6,800
19 to 24 months	16,000	1.7%	6,400	27,200		10.800	4,500
2 to 3 years	28,000	1.3%	11,200	36,400		14.600	3,400
Over 3 years	41,000	0.7%	16,400	28,700		11.500	– 4,900

after one year, 75 to 80 percent of first-time buyers are still only one-time buyers after repeated promotion.

Perhaps most catalog operators are willing to do more to induce a prospect to become a first-time buyer than they are willing to do to induce that first-time buyer to become a multiple buyer. Once the value of a customer is approximated, it is usually clear that it would be better to provide comparable or even greater inducements to obtain a second sale.

As it happens, there is a distinct differential in production of second orders depending on individual mediums such as individual newspapers, magazines, and just as certainly from individual mailing lists.

If we have a situation where $1.50 of sales for every $1.00 spent on promotion produces breakeven we can have a series of responses by key which run:

Response rate	Result per order
1.7	+4.70
1.7	+4.70
1.6	+2.50
1.6	+2.50
1.5 Breakeven	0
1.5 Breakeven	0
1.4	−2.50
1.4	−2.50
1.3	−6.00
1.3	−6.00
1.2	−10.00
0.9	−20.00
0.9	−20.00
0.6	−60.00
0.6	−60.00

If we use a figure like $100 per order, at 1.5 we are looking at fifteen orders averaging $100 each. This covers all promotional costs, plus product costs and all other costs of running the business including the cost of money. Those segments or keys that come in above 1.5 are showing a profit on the initial promotion. Those at 1.5 are at breakeven; those below 1.5 show a cost to buy the fourteen, thirteen, twelve, or nine new orders. On this basis it seems that each of two or more keys that show the same initial percentage are equal. This is a good first way to look at results. But it is far from the total picture. If we look at production of second orders by individual key it will be quickly evident that what starts out as equal does not necessarily remain equal.

Let's add second-order conversions to those initial pairs and then take another look:

Response	Initial profit	Proportion second sales (percent)	Profit on second sales	Initial and second sales
1.7	+4.50	5%	2.00	$ 6.50
	+4.50	10%	4.00	8.50
	+4.50	20%	8.00	12.50
1.5	—	5%	2.00	2.00
	—	10%	4.00	4.00
	—		8.00	8.00
1.3	−6.00	5%	2.00	−4.00
	−6.00	10%	4.00	−2.00
	−6.00	20%	8.00	+2.00

These figures indicate an initial response of 1.3 with a 20 percent repeat factor is equal to a 1.5 initial response factor with a 5 percent repeat factor. Note that a 10 percent repeat factor over a given period does not amortize the cost to buy an order initially brought in at 1.3, when 1.5 is breakeven.

How to Allocate Your Promotional Dollars

When there are two or more generic types of media used (direct mail and space advertising, for example) a second set of figures is required to determine where the operation should place most of its promotion—that second set consists of the proportion of second (or multiple) sales which are made when the two methods are compared. For example: Buying 1,000 new customers from space ads costs $7.50 each and buying 1,000 new customers from direct mail costs $8.25 each. On this basis it looks as though more dollars should go to space.

However, multiple sales may paint a different picture. One thousand new customers from space ads at a cost of $7,500 deliver one hundred second sales in the first six months at $80 each, with a gross profit of $16 each. Therefore, $7,500 less $1,600 equals $5,900 at the end of six months, or a cost to buy of $5.90 each.

One thousand new customers from direct mail at a cost of $8,250 deliver 200 second sales in the first six months at $95 each, with a gross profit of $20 each. Therefore, $8,250 less $4,000 equals $4,250 at the end of six months, or a cost to buy of $4.25 each. What started out as an extra cost to buy of 11 percent, after checking add sales for the next six months, shows a substantially lower cost.

Why Multiple Buyers Are Your Profit Margin

A mail-order operation is a form of retailing. With the exception of car dealers and perhaps some appliance and furniture stores, no retail operation makes a profit on a single transaction. Bob Kahn, the editor of *Retailing Today* stipulates that "too much time is spent trying to operate specialty and other types of stores on the theory of making a profit on a transaction. Such retailers make a profit *only* on a customer. A supermarket needs customers who come back fifty to seventy times a year. A department or discount store needs customers who come back ten to fifteen times a year. A women's specialty store needs customers who come back five to ten times a year, and men's stores needs customers who come back four to eight times a year." While Editor Kahn did not carry this thought beyond conventional retailing, he would well understand that a mail order operation needs to build multiple business (multibuyers) who buy frequently by mail. The only purpose of direct response is to create customers, not one-time buyers.

What is the difference in value between a one-time customer, and one who will buy a second time? Since a customer cannot buy a third time until he or she has bought a second time, and since one-time and two-time customers are given comparable promotion efforts, it appears that a second-time customer is worth more than twice as much as a one-time only customer. If this is true, then the mail order operator should spend more care, time, attention, and inducements to convert one-time customers to multicustomer status. It is strange how rare such a stance is deliberately taken by successful mail-order companies.

How to Buy an Early Second Sale

A few operators understand the mathematics completely here and they expend extra efforts, with increasingly valuable premiums, in an effort to *buy that precious second sale in the early months* after receiving the first order from the customer. As noted in the section on response by age in the file, the longer customers are on the file without a sale, the lower the response will be. There is a mathematical need to reach the new customer early and often and with inducements to buy rather than to mail all age cells alike. When a cell of first-time buyers shows a response to the first offer or catalog of 3 or 4 percent, a mailing only a few weeks later, will pull a response in the 2.0 to 2.8 percent from that same cell. That may well be more than they will do when aged six months. Any first time buyer sent six, eight, or ten subsequent offers in the next year without buying should be placed on a schedule to receive only one, two, or three offers in the second year. Those one-time only buyers should be expired completely, probably sometime in the third year, when results from cold prospecting show more profitable results.

Following is an example that clearly shows these differences.

Assume a cell contains 1,000 *new customers*. The typical program will be something like Example A below with six mailings via catalogs spread out over close to two years.

A	3.9% first mailing in 3 months	2.5% second mailing in 6 months	2.0% third mailing in 9 months	1.6% fourth mailing in 12 months	1.2% fifth mailing in 16 months	0.9% sixth mailing in 20 months	Total
Converted to multiple customer	39	24	19	15	11	8	119 = 12%

Now compare that total with the more efficient use of what some advertisers call "action time" which means promotions at the most propitious times—which in direct mail means early, not late.

	First mailing in 4 weeks	Second mailing in 6 weeks	Third mailing in 8 weeks	Fourth mailing in 12 weeks	Fifth mailing in 16 weeks	Sixth mailing in 20 weeks	Total
Converted to multiple customer	48	37	31	28	23	19	176 = 18%

Note that the same number of mailings are made in each case to the balances left after each mailing but through quick action timing the conversion is *50* percent more efficient than with conventional handling. In addition, each of these multibuyers are on the file for an average of seventy weeks longer than if converted by the slower means. And their increased orders over this period are probably equal to another 50 percent gain for the mailer.

Converting Catalog Requests into First-Time Buyers

The even faster decline in conversion of catalog inquiries should induce catalog operators to adjust their mailing schedules here to speed up whatever conversion is likely.* (Few do!) The immediate conversion upon sending a catalog for the first time produces the greatest percentage conversion to be obtained by far. The next mailing then does better than the following but as the months go by between such conversion mailings, the balance of the catalog inquiries tends quickly to produce smaller and smaller conversion percentages.

The differences for conversion of catalog requests into first-time buyers are even more striking than for conversion of one time buyers to multiple buyers. The figures in the table on the following page are for a cell of 1,000 new catalog requests.

Here, by mailing the same number of times, but over a "hurry-up" period of only sixteen weeks instead of close to two years, conversion to first-time buyers is virtually double. In addition, each of these first-time buyers will be on the customer file about seventy five weeks longer than if conversion was done by a slower method. The increased value over that seventy five-week period is probably equal to doubling again the differential to be gained by mailing on an "action-time" program designed to get the most from every catalog request received. When you look at figures like these you wonder why all these who induce catalog requests do not use "Action Time."

CATALOG REQUEST CONVERSIONS

Well run catalog operations usually include careful attention to the production of inquiries for catalogs. Care must be taken that inquiries are not set up like multiple-choice questions where curiosity seekers can tick any choice they want. Such inquiries often are not worth the paper they are printed on and end up costing the company relatively large sums to fulfill such requests. This author has had, on several occasions, the dubious pleasure of pointing out that continued mailing of catalogs to names secured in this way is a good way to pour money down the drain.

Inquiries secured through catalog mailings and offers in space ads that *invite* those who seek more information to write in individually for a catalog are golden. This also may be true for catalog requests obtained from small space ads specifically

---

*Bill Fitzgerald, the mastermind of Hanover House has stated: "We are getting $4 back on a book when it is mailed back the same day. If you don't send back a catalog in a week's time, you're wasting your time sending one."

Conversion rates – based on length of time between mailings

A	1.9% First mailing in 3 months	1.5% Second mailing in 6 months	1.2% Third mailing in 9 months	1.0% Fourth mailing in 12 months	0.7% Fifth mailing in 36 months	0.5% Sixth mailing in 20 months	Total
Conversion from requests to first-time buyers (conventional schedule)	20	15	12	10	7	5	67 = 7%

B	3.5% First mailing in 2 weeks	3.1% Second mailing in 4 weeks	2.5% Third mailing in 6 weeks	2.0% Fourth mailing in 8 weeks	1.5% Fifth mailing in 12 weeks	1.0% Sixth mailing in 16 weeks	Total
Conversion from requests to first-time buyers (action timing schedule)	35	30	24	19	14	10	132 = 13%

aimed at inducing such requests, particularly when they are "qualified." To qualify an inquiry the requestor pays a small sum, usually $1.00 or $2.00 which usually will be credit against a first order. (Qualification by requesting 25¢ or 50¢ may be useful for some classifications, particularly where the average order is under $20, but even here care must be taken to test the relative value of each type of catalog inquiry.)

Catalog inquiries add another dimension to the analysis of the relative value of a given source of orders. Normally solid, valid catalog inquiries will outpull any other cell of names, even new first-time customers. It is not unusual for such inquiries to convert to first time customers at a rate of 10, 15 or even 20 percent. Thus a key that appears marginal in initial orders may be remarkably productive when conversions of catalog inquiries are factored in.

Where Requests Begin

Requests for catalogs come from a number of different types of promotion. The request may be the result of a "pass-along" copy of the request form sent by a current customer to a friend of the prospect. The request can be produced as part of the response to a space ad where nonbuyers and buyers alike are invited to send in for a catalog. Such requests can be from a buyer but most of them will be prospects that are interested in seeing all the products in the catalog rather than one, two, or a few items in the ad. There also are catalog requests produced by small space ads whose entire thrust is to sell the catalog.

Determining Costs for Catalog Requests

It is only fair that the costs to attract each catalog request should be subtracted from the ostensible profit to be made on conversion into first-time buyers. Where the entire effort has been to induce such requests, the figure to use for each inquiry, whether the figure is converted to a sale or not, is the cost of the ad divided by the number of traceable requests. (Nontraceable requests can be allocated in proportion to response, or simply lumped together as a separate keyed group and identified as unallocated.)

Differential Costing of Requests

1. Those received from friends of customers—no assessment.
2. Those received through "white-mail"—first class letters sent by prospects—no assessment.

3. Those induced through various forms of catalog promotions—cost of the ad divided by the number of catalog requests. (On TV requests, take particular care—the costs per response can very quickly get out of line.)

4. Those received along with orders from a space or catalog promotion— no assessment—but to provide a fair analysis of the results of the promotions, credit needs to be given to the promotional cost for the value of such requests as measured later by conversion to sales. More on this follows.

Friend-of-a-Friend Inquiries

One form of "catalog inquiry" is especially important. This is the name and address of a person that is sent in at the request of the company that believes the person would appreciate receiving a copy of the catalog. Often called "friend-of-a-friend," if such leads are handled properly they show a high conversion to customer status. The secret to achieving high conversion here is simple: If you just mail out catalogs to friend-of-a-friend names the response rate will be somewhat like that received from cold canvassing any list. That destroys the reason for requesting the friend's name in the first place. The right way to do this is to tie the two names together by noting to the recipient, Mrs. Y, that her friend, Mrs. X, suggested the catalog be mailed. This can be done mainly in a word processor or a simple form letter. If the quantity of recipients is small the very least one should do is inscribe the two names on the form with a colorful felt pen.

Variance in Response Analysis

The value of inquiries varies depending on source but if all inquiries are reasonably qualified that variance may turn out to be rather modest. In other words, a homogenized value can be established for each inquiry on the basis of the average proportion of conversion by all inquiries to first-time buyers. It is not unusual for such inquiries to have a gross-margin value of several dollars each. *The variances then will be in the proportion of inquiries to sales by key—both in space ads and by direct mail.*

If we assume, for purposes of demonstration, that each inquiry has a gross-margin value of $5 and that on the average the value of each order is equal to half the sales amount then the initial figures for breakeven should take this into account. Let us now add in the value of $\frac{1}{2}$ inquiry to the figures shown in the following table.

Response by key	Gross margin per order	Value of inquiry	Total from initial sale
1.7	+ $4.50	$2.50	+ $7.00
1.6	+ 2.00	2.50	+ 4.50
1.5	0	2.50	+ 2.50
1.4	− 2.00	2.50	+ .50
1.3	− 4.50	2.50	− 2.00
1.2	− 10.00	2.50	− 7.50

Value of Inquiry Production

The average increment from catalog inquiry conversion alone adds more to the bottom line than the gross margin represented by obtaining one more or one less order than required in the example above for breakeven. However, this average is useful only for statistical purposes. The actual proportion of inquiries per order per key needs to be assessed, and the range can be rather dramatic as some keys deliver $\frac{1}{2}$ inquiry per order while others deliver two inquiries for every order. Note what this does to the evaluation of particular keys in the following table:

Key number	Response by key	Gross margin per order	Number of inquiries per order	X $5.00 per inquiry	Total for initial sale
101	1.7	+ 4.50	0.5	2.50	+ 7.00
110	1.7	+ 4.50	2.0	10.00	+ 14.00
115	1.6	+ 2.00	0.5	2.50	+ 4.50
107	1.6	+ 2.00	2.0	10.00	+ 12.00
109	1.5	0	0.5	2.50	+ 2.50
122	1.5	0	2.0	10.00	+ 10.00
106	1.4	− 2.00	0.5	2.50	+ .50
118	1.4	− 2.00	2.0	10.00	+ 8.00
114	1.3	− 4.50	0.5	2.50	− 2.00
123	1.3	− 4.50	2.0	10.00	+ 5.50
117	1.2	− 10.00	0.5	2.50	− 7.50
125	1.2	− 10.00	2.0	10.00	0

The great impact inquiries that are properly handled can have on the value of one key against another is clear: In this example a key that fails by three out of fifteen orders (or 20 percent) to hit breakeven, but which delivers two inquiries for every order, is just as good as a key that hits breakeven but produces few inquiries.

The value of a name (inquirer or customer) for rental purposes is a major factor in the conversion process. While each name used, is worth only pennies per use, a name that is rented ten, fifteen, or twenty times per year can multiply those pennies into quarters and half-dollars, and on rare lists, into $1 or more per name. For our purposes we will omit this added revenue since it adds equally or almost equally to every name added to the catalog lists.

How Establishing a Norm Can Help You Evaluate Responses

We have discussed the major ways that a single key can vary in bottom-line profit—namely initial response, inquiry production, conversion of inquiries to first time sales, and conversion of 1st time sales (from any source) to multiple buyer status.

An operator who rents additional names or purchases additional comparable space in a given publication on the basis of response alone is going to be beaten to the broader utilization of list sources and space sources by the operator who arms himself in addition with information on inquiry production and conversion to 2nd time buyers.

Perhaps the easiest way to include such data in the process of deciding which list segments to continue, which space units to schedule, and which catalog request ads to run, is to first establish a norm from your own records of the four factors listed in the previous section.

Once a norm has been established, each test can be evaluated against that norm, and dollar values per order can be calculated for production above and below the norm.

For example here is a weighting used by a catalog operator in the gift mail order business:

- Norm = $40 order margin
  a. 3/4 of one catalog inquiry per order
  b. Conversion of 10 percent of catalog inquiries to first-time order
  c. $8\frac{1}{2}$ percent conversion of first-time orders within six months to second purchase

- For every percent less than 130 percent of promotion cost reduce order by $.40.

Table 11.1

How weighing of results affects evaluation of promotional sources

List keys	Base	Percent of prom cost	Variation	Inquiries	Variation	Percent of conversion of inquiries	To first orders	Percent conversion to second order	Variation	Total
U	$40	130%	0	3/4	0	10%	0	8½%	0	$40.00
V	$40	120%	−4.00	2.0	+$6.25	10%	0	12½%	+$2.00	$44.25
W	$40	135%	+1.50	1.5	+$3.75	15%	$2.00	20%	+$5.50	$52.75
X	$40	140%	+3.00	2.0	+$6.25	20%	$4.00	3%	−$2.50	$48.75
Y	$40	120%	−3.00	1/4	−$2.50	6%	$2.00	1%	−$3.75	$26.75
Z	$40	150%	+6.00	1.5	+$3.75	18%	$3.20	22%	+$6.50	$59.45

Note that in these few examples two keys (V + Y) with identical ratings for capture of promotional cost end up with weighted values 65 percent apart. This much is certain: Once a catalog operator begins to purchase promotional continuations on the basis of a weighted scale for auxilliary production, he or she will never again be able to return to the more halcyon and more simplistic days of just considering looking at response rates.

- For every percent more than 130 percent of promotion cost increase order by $.30. (This calculation takes into consideration the average size of the order and the response rate)

- For every 1/4 of a catalog inquiry per order less than 3/4 reduce order by $1.25.

- For every 1/4 of a catalog inquiry per order above 3/4 increase order by $1.25.

- For every percent of catalog conversion to sale less than *10 percent* reduce order by $0.50.

- For every percent of catalog conversion to sale more than *10 percent* increase order by $0.40.

- For every percent below $8\frac{1}{2}$ percent of conversion to second order reduce order by $.50.

- For every percent above $8\frac{1}{2}$ percent of conversion to second order increase order by $.50.

Using this weighting we can compare a group of keys, as shown in Table 11.1.

HOW TO EVALUATE AN INCREMENTAL COST

To measure the effectiveness of an incremental cost, it is necessary to first measure net contribution without the added cost and net contribution after the added cost. Then you must determine if the differential produces a higher or lower R.O.I. In effect, the calculation determines whether or not the added cost is worthwhile compared with other variable uses for money.

If the initial mailing costs $375 and produces twenty-five orders, does it pay to expend $50 more to obtain thirty orders? The correct answer is, it depends on such factors as the average size of the order, the average value of the premium (if there is one), and the value of money. The following table shows the experience of one mailer's costs:

	Regular package	Enhanced package	Incremental data
Cost per M	$375	$425	
No. of Sales per M pieces Mailed	25 (at $70 ea)	30 (at $70 ea)	
Total Sales per M (in Dollars)	+$1,750	+$2,100	+$350
Cost of Total Sales per M	−1,000 (at $40 ea)	−1,200 (at $40 ea)	−200

	Regular package	Enhanced package	Incremental data
Difference—Contribution	+750	+900	+150
Premium Cost	−125 (at $5 ea)	−150 (at $5 ea)	−25
Advertising Cost	−375	−425	−50
Total of Advertising Cost	−500	−575	−75
Net Result (Contribution Less Advertising Cost)	+$250	+$350	+75/per M

A review of the three columns shows that an expenditure of an extra $50/M on the package results in an extra $75/M, which is an R.O.I. of 150 percent. If the figures had shown a net contribution of $250, for either package (with a negative R.O.I.), the decision may well have been to utilize the *more* expensive package because for the same number of names it produced 20 percent more new customers. This shows that incremental calculations based only on initial sales without consideration for catalog inquiries or repeat sales may provide a misleading picture.

Variable Catalog Costs Are Incremental in Nature

It may seem unbelievable that these costs are incremental in nature—until variable costs of individual mailing lists are considered. Mailing lists make up from one-tenth to one-third of the total cost of mailing a catalog or package. Thus it stands to reason that a homogenized cost-in-the mail will hurt lower-cost lists and benefit higher-cost lists. This is particularly apparent when a mailing program for a catalog includes both mail order response files *and* compiled files. The following table shows what happens to breakeven as the only variable, the list, rises in cost per M.

Fixed cost of identical mailings (dollars)	Mailing list rental (dollars) per 1000 names	Total cost in mail (dollars)	Breakeven at order margin of $30 (dollars)
$250	$ 25	$275	$ 9
250	50	300	10
250	70	320	11
250	100	350	12

The $70/M mail order response list requires one-fourth more sales at an order margin of $30 than the $25/M compiled file does. However the $70/M mail order response list may outpull the compiled file by more than the $45 differential—and thus would be a better buy.

FORECASTING SALES: THREE MAIN PROJECTIONS

A strategic plan for a direct-mail operation, particularly a catalog operation, requires the building and review of three projections:

1. Sales and customer acquisition projection
2. Cash flow projection, or more to the point, alternative cash flow projections
3. Return on investment projection

Sales Projection

Sales projection is used first and foremost in projecting sales as all of the other basic figures flow from it. It is formed from a series of building blocks:

1. Sales in the next year to customers already on the file.
2. Number of new customers to be added in the next year taken from space ads and direct mail advertising.
3. Repeat sales to new customers added in the year.
4. Number of catalog inquiries to be obtained in the next year.
5. Proportion of catalog requests converted to sales in the next year.
6. Repeat sales to newly converted catalog requests in the next year.
7. Estimated average sales to: old customers, new customers, converted catalog requests
8. Estimated fixed costs, back-end costs, and administration
9. Estimated cost to buy a new customer
10. Estimated gross margin on sales during the year

The foregoing set of answers for Year One of a three- or five-year forecast provides the base for the following:

1. Total loss (cash flow drain) on costs incurred through space ads or direct-mail advertising to buy new customers
2. Total added requirement for inventory (partial cash flow drain)

3. Total sales

4. Total costs, including catalogs and space ads, fixed costs, back-end costs, and administration

5. Total gross margin on sales

6. Total projected profit for Year One

7. Total R.O.I.

The estimates for new customers and for converted requests provide input to calculate the projected new customer file quantities, as well as new unconverted catalog inquiries, at the start of Year Two. Several new cells are then created:

1. New one-time customers in Year One

2. New multiple customers in Year One

3. New converted requests in Year One

4. New unconverted requests in Year One

Each of the customer cells on hand at the beginning of the year are now mentally updated by one year which changes the calculation of anticipated sales from old customers in the following year.

In similar fashion each of the four new inputs are provided with estimates for new sales in Year Two (the first full annual year on the file) from historical records. At that point the procedure used for Year One can be used to project estimates for Year Two.

It is good practice to provide figures for the company's best estimate for what is reasonably expected as well as two other sets of figures: one well below the best estimate, and one well above. By going through this arithmetic of low and high figures, certain discrepancies are certain to surface. Such discrepancies, such as number of catalogs, dollars spent for space ads, average size of orders, or total cash drain in a given quarter, usually result in meaningful adjustments to the range of expectation.

Cash Flow Projection

Cash flow is calculated on a quarterly basis, by using historical data on inventory turnaround, promotional expenditures, and payment terms. A calculation is required for each quarter of what bills will be rendered, what cash sales will be received, and what dollars will be expended. If desired, "cash in bank" can be entered at the start of each quarter by utilizing the cash balance (+ or −) at the end of the prior quarter.

Catalog businesses tend to be explosive in growth but not necessarily in profit in the early years. Then, as the business matures, it becomes harder and harder to maintain growth. For example, a 20 percent increase in sales over last years total sales of $800,000 is a far cry from obtaining a 20 percent increase over a prior year that logged $9,800,000.

The figures used for any increases from year to year are dependent in part on where in the profit or loss cycle the business is and where it can reasonably be expected to be in two, three, or five years. Projected increases of sales of 10 percent per year produce a cumulative increase of 100 percent by the seventh year. Projected increases of 15 percent per year come near to doubling in five years.

Great care must be taken with flat sales increases from year to year. Such compounded projections, however, are useful for they almost inevitably show important limitations on such growth, which may and often is, the cash flow needed to produce such increases, or the delving into marginal areas of space ads or direct-mail advertising to reach goals where expectations are too high.

It is a sad but true fact that in the early years of explosive growth, when only the best media and the best lists are used, the opportunity for much faster growth is at hand but fledgling catalog operators do not have the knowledge, heart, or capital to do more. They are at the limit of their resources just as the business begins to grow at a faster pace than they can control. Then when the sales curve cools down a bit and the business matures, there are ample dollars (created by sales or borrowed), but the window for great growth may have either closed or become somewhat smaller.

Return on Investment Projections

A five-year projection for a $5,000,000 catalog operation may require a solid week of analyzing the figures, particularly the low and high estimates, to achieve the best estimate. If all other factors, including the economy, competition, suppliers, and consumer confidence are equal, a projection based on this approach can provide a road map that can be approximated very closely. In fact, many successful direct-response operations set up targets like this for the next year, and then measure their competence against the projected bogey—not the prior year. Slavishly following such a pattern, however, can cause you to miss opportunities. A new large list may surface that tests well but there is only so much money in the budget. For example, a default lot of merchandise may be available for a song but there is no purchase money in the budget.

This is a field in which it is essential to keep alert and flexible at all times. Projections are guides to the future, they are not cast in concrete and can always change.

Guidelines for Premailing Estimates

Mankind is the only animal who attempts to predict the future. All those involved in direct mail, from the inventor that runs three classified ads, to the publisher that mails 50 million pieces, make forecasts, even if only mental forecasts, of what each hopes or expects will happen.

Some forecasts may be nothing more than hunches or dreams but there are guidelines for establishing legitimate forecasts as follows.

1. The records of past promotions offer useful benchmarks.

2. Trend of sales over a period of time—sales may increase, decrease, or remain stable. (This must be on an indexed basis, or dollars of sales per thousand pieces in the mail, as total dollars can be strikingly affected by the total size of one mailing compared with another.)

3. The season of the year may be a plus or minus factor.

4. In a catalog, the positioning of a group of items, say, in the front of a catalog versus the back of the catalog, can have a marked influence on item sales.

5. The proportion of "new" items and items that are advertised as "not available elsewhere" are important to forecasting.

This premailing forecast will determine the size of the mailing and the budget; influence purchasing decisions for inventory; affect the timing of cash flow needs; and determine for a given period what kinds of promotion will be undertaken.

Let us look at the figures in the table on the opposite page for a tool wholesaler who for all practical purposes does all of his selling and prospecting for new accounts with his catalog. This chart shows what happens to customers over a stretch of 5 years.

Before we add in the amount from prospecting for new customers, note that *on average* each customer on file as of the beginning of the year had an anticipated sale of $188, which in this case is close to the average individual sale anticipated of $196. But also note that multiple orders are equivalent to slightly less than 10 percent of the size of the file at the start of the year.

Now let's look at how promotion to obtain new customers affects results. In 1987 our tool wholesaler planned to mail 3 million catalogs. Approximately 350,000 of these were pledged to "old" customer mailings, and these 350,000 catalogs were expected to produce the $924,000 of sales noted above at an average of $2,600 per M. That left 2,650,000 catalogs for prospecting to be dropped at an average rate of 220,000 pieces per month. (This spread is required in many catalog op-

Analysis of one-time customers – by year of acquisition

Year started	Buyers in 1987	Percentage buying in 1987	Average order in 1987 (in dollars)	Buyers in next year	Gross sales
1986	9,000	20%	$230	1,800 × $230 =	$414,000
1985	12,000	12%	200	1,440 × 200 =	288,000
1984	8,000	8%	180	640 × 180 =	115,000
1983	6,000	6%	150	360 × 150 =	54,000
Prior to 1983	14,000	3%	125	420 × 125 =	53,000
	49,000		$196	4,700	924,000

New customers (who have not bought in a subsequent year)

413

erations to level out the number of orders that can be handled at the catalog order desk per day, week, and month.)

The tool wholesaler anticipated sales of new customers would produce total sales from prospecting of $2,120,000. And such mailings would then produce four new customers per thousand—that is,

$$4 \times 2,650 = 10,700$$

Total projected sales for 1987 were taken from:

From Old customers on hand as of Jan. 1	$ 924,000
From New customers from first-time sales	2,120,000
From Repeat customers (average of six months) from New first-time customers	250,000
	$3,294,000

Over the course of the year, the average new customer will be on the rolls for six months. In that period, 10 percent will buy again during 1985.

Now let us move on to the next year.

The 49,000 one-time customers have been reduced by 4,700 new customers who have purchased in 1987 and are now qualified as current buyers. In addition 10,700 new customers have been added from prospecting, and 1,070 of them have already bought for a second time in 1987. Thus customers who have purchased in 1987 (new as well as multiple) total 15,400.

For 1988, the *customer file* can be expected to produce the following customers:

Year started	Number of customers	Percent buying in 1986			Gross sales
1987 customers	15,400	20% =	3,080 @ $230 =	$ 718,000
1986 customers	7,200	12% =	870 @ 200	174,000
1985 customers	10,600	8% =	850 @ 180	103,000
1984 customers	7,400	6% =	450 @ 150	68,000
1983 customers	5,600	3% =	200 @ 125	25,000
Prior to 1983 customers	13,600	2% =	270 @ 125	34,000
	59,600			1,120,000

In 1988 the mailer decided to increase his prospecting to 4 million. As his oldest customer (for over 5 years now) was expected to produce 2 percent of sales over six mailings, or reasonably close to the .4 expected from prospecting, each customer will be mailed to six times, which with bounce backs and inquiry fulfillment, will total 400,000. That leaves 3,600,000 for prospecting.

At $800/M this produces a total of sales from new customers of approximately $2,880,000. The 3.6 million new catalogs at 4 new sales per M produces 14,400 new customers. These new customers, on average, were available for repromotion for half a year and produce $331,000 of multibuyer sales in 1988.

Total sales projected for 1988 looks like this.

"Old" customers	$1,122,000
New first-time buyers	2,880,000
1986 multibuyers	331,000
	$4,333,000

This is an increase of $1,039,000 over 1987, which on a percentage basis, is an increase of 32 percent.

This mailer, based on 1987 and 1988 forecasts, purchased: 10,700 new customers in 1987 and 14,400 new customers in 1988.

Let us examine what these new customers have "cost" the company to buy.

In 1987 the cost in the mail for the catalog was $330/M. The average gross margin on $800 was produced by four sales for each 1,000 catalogs and totaled $36\frac{1}{2}$ percent:

Cost in the mail	$330
Sales	$800
Margin	$36\frac{1}{2}$%
Gross margin	$292
Loss per 1,000 catalogs	$38
Cost per new customer	$38 ÷ 4 = $9.50 each

In 1988 the cost in the mail for the catalog escalated to $360/M but gross margin increased to 39.8 percent.

Cost in the mail	$360
Sales	$800
Margin	39.8%
Gross margin	$318
Sales and margin	$42
Cost per new customer	$42 ÷ 4 = $10.50 each

To put these two figures in perspective, in 1987 the company estimated it would expend 10,700 × $9.50 or some $100,000 purchasing new customers. In

1988, the 14,400 at $10.50 each will cost about $50,000 more. It should be noted that as the cost to buy a new customer can be decreased, a catalog operator can afford to increase his or her purchase of new customers. The fact that 20 percent of all new buyers for this operator can be expected within one year to buy $230 is emphasized. That is equivalent to stating each one will buy $46 of product. The gross profit, say 40 percent, on $46 equals $18, so the $9.50 or $10.25 cost to buy will be amortized by new sales in approximately six months.

Growth versus Profit

There is an interesting tug of war that takes place as catalog operators get their numbers in order. One end cries, "I want to grow" as opposed to the other end crying, "I want to make a greater profit." As long as there is a cost to buy a new customer these cries will resound. Profit for the future involves growing now. Growth may reduce profits now but given the numbers, a catalog operator can choose almost exactly how many new customers he or she wants to buy in any given period, and if his or her costs are low he or she can build profits very swiftly indeed.

To make a greater profit, a catalog operator with a well established customer file that can be relied on to be mailed profitably time after time, can change the profit ratio dramatically by cutting down or eliminating prospecting mailings that produce new customers but only at an out-of-pocket cost. Some operators looking to sell their operations make drastic reductions in such prospecting costs for a year or two knowing full well this is a gilt-edged way to make the short term profit and the current balance sheet look much better.

Other methods also can be used to add new customers. The next most common method is through direct-mail advertising in space ads. Mathematics hold here as well. The cost of space is equivalent to the cost of the catalog. Sales are logged, and the gross margin earned from the sales is compared with the cost of space. The cost to buy a new customer from space ads is then determined by dividing the number of sales by gross margin into the shortfall. For example:

Space cost	$1,000
Sales	$2,100
Average sale	100
Number of sales	21
Gross margin	39%
Total gross margin	39% of $2,100 of Sales = $819
Shortfall	Space cost ($1000) less gross margin (819) = $181
Cost to buy sales	Shortfall ($181) divided by number of sales (21) = $9

EFFECT OF PRICE ON RESPONSE

The offer, particularly the price within the offer, has a major effect on the number of responses a given direct-mail effort will produce. As a corollary to this rule, the same product priced at different levels, will tend to bring in the same dollars per thousand pieces mailed. That is, a mail order unit priced at $10 that brings in thirty orders or $300/M will produce at $20 about fifteen orders per thousand or again $300/M. This "iron rule" of dollars is operative almost irrespective of the offer, except on very costly items where the price may dry up orders altogether. Seminars priced at $495 for three days very rarely average out as high as one-tenth of 1 percent (one order per thousand). The same basic market may produce three orders per thousand (0.3 percent) for a one day seminar priced at $150; while a one day seminar priced at $85 will have little trouble obtaining responses at the rate of 6 per 1,000 (0.6 percent) in most fields. It is difficult in prospecting for new or unused lists to produce more than $500 per thousand pieces in the mail. The range is usually between $250/M and about $650/M, or on a per-piece basis, a return of from 25¢ or 65¢ for every piece or catalog sent out *prospecting* for new customers.

One mailer with a $100 per year newsletter in the real estate field was convinced to try a series of price tests, ranging from $36 per year to $180 per year. Response above the current $100 price proved there was a great deal of price resistance. At $36 and $49, the same number of dollars per thousand pieces mailed was received, and this was greater than for offers at $76 and $99. At $36, the total number of new customers was 40 percent greater than at $49. The provision of more customers for future conversion from the lower-priced offer completely changed the approach of this mailer. Here is an example:

	@ 2.5 Starts/M pieces mailed	Number of subscribers
Cost to buy 1,000 $100 subscribers	− $14,000	
Cost to service 1,000 $100 subscribers	− 7,500	
	$21,500	1,000
Conversion to second year (26%)	+ $26,000	260
Cost to service 260 subscribers	− 1,950	
Conversion to third year (50%)	+ $13,000	130
Cost to service 130 subscribers	− 975	
Gross profit on 1,000 customers after 3 years	$ 4,600 = $4.60 per start	
Cost to buy 1,000 $36 subscribers	− $ 1,500	
Cost to service 1,000 $36 subscribers	− 7,500	
	− $ 9,000	1,000

	@ 2.5 Starts/M pieces mailed	Number of subscribers
Conversion to second year (57%)	+ $20,500	570
Cost to service 570 subscribers	− 4,400	
Conversion to third year (84%)	+ $17,000	473
Cost to service 473 subscribers	− 3,600	
Gross profit on 1,000 customers after 3 years	$20,500 = $20.50 per start	

This $20.50 per start figure is almost $4\frac{1}{2}$ times more than at $100, and the total subscriber file for the future is over $3\frac{1}{2}$ times as great.

DETERMINING (GROSS) ORDER MARGIN

Much is written in the direct-response field about the number of times a given item must be marked up to be profitable in direct mail. A surprising proportion of such advice is downright dangerous. In a recent speech before the DMA a selfstyled pundit declared a four time multiple was minimal: for smaller priced items six or seven times were required.

Successful direct-response operations require sufficient order margin, not mark-up, to be profitable. Given sufficient orders per thousand pieces mailed, it is possible to sell items in the mail at $99 with an order margin as low as $25 or $30. The most successful watch offer ever made in America, which established a direct-mail house as the largest retailer of watches for two years, was priced on that basis.

Most catalog operators have an average gross margin on their product line of between 34 and 60 percent. At 50 percent, the cost of goods sold covers all attendant costs of handling the variants of orders and is half the retail sales price. If the average order size is $40, the order margin the operator is working with to cover all promotion costs and profits as well is just $20.

As a class, catalog operators fear the effects of raising the average order margin on the list of items in a catalog. There is a feeling that the consumer is going to be able, through comparison shopping at stores and with other catalogs, to discover that prices have risen slightly. One of the largest sellers of bandaids, aspirins, nonaspirin pain relievers, and first aid kits to business came into the market a number of years ago with an order margin of 25 percent. Catalog sales for this same seller today stand at 41 percent—a price probably above the cost for the same goods at retail discount drug stores. The business, once barely marginal, is highly profitable today.

A split test of two or three sets of prices for a catalog is relatively expensive although there are printers who can make price changes on fair-sized segments of a major run at a cost most operators can afford. Usually such tests indicate very little, if any, price sensitivity unless the split test is mailed only to the house list segments where some basic prices have been repeatedly drummed into the consciousness of those on the lists. (If you split-price test, base your results on what your market of prospects lets you know!)

Gross margin is another basic factor in the mathematics of direct response. For each million dollars of gross sales, an increase of 1 percent produces $10,000 more for the bottom line.

It is good practice to include a group of desirable items in a catalog that are so unusual and unique that comparison shopping is not possible. These goods should bear higher-than-usual order margins to make up for those items that must be offered at market prices.

In the book trade it is customary to include a deluxe edition that carries a distinctively higher price and a distinctively higher-than-usual order margin. Often such deluxe editions provide 30 to 50 percent of the gross profit registered by the title. This, or a similar practice, in multiple-offer catalogs can do much to help "up" the average size of the order, and with it, the average order margin on the whole. (The watch campaign mentioned earlier, added for the first time four diamond-studded watches to the line in the second year. Profits from the sale of the diamond watches alone covered most of the costs of promotion.)

However, even without special items or deluxe editions, the catalog operator should be aware that a very small increase, such as 1 or 2 percent overall, will be absorbed by the market without peril to the volume or the number of sales or the number of customers. For every catalog that prices itself out of business by margins that are considered too high by the market, fifty or one hundred fledgling operators fail because their overall order margin is too small.

ORDER SIZE DIFFERENCES

Each form of direct response produces a different average order size as well as a different range of order sizes. Actually, each separate test produces a different *average* order size as well as a different *range* of orders by size.

Almost all direct-response operators are aware of and use the average order size (Total Sales ÷ Total No. of Sales). It is a prime component of all breakeven analyses baseed on response rates because that response rate, times the average order size for a given effort or key, equals gross sales per thousand pieces mailed. But only minimal attention is given to the range of order size, with one exception: cold canvassing for fundraising. A chance $100 or $200 donation can throw off a projection of total dollars per thousand pieces mailed based on dollars. Without first eliminating these welcome "donations" a projection is bound to be hopelessly optimistic.

When the variance of order size for a given list or medium is large, the probability of breaking even on continuations diminishes. When the variance of order size range is narrow and the test is above breakeven, chances are increased that continuations will also be at breakeven or better. When differences occur not only in the range of order size, but also in the average size of orders, which is what is usually found in direct response, then the conditional profit assigned to a continuation is likely to fluctuate also.

A catalog offering to cold prospects hundreds or even thousands of different items at prices ranging from a few dollars to possibly several hundreds of dollars, will ordinarily produce an average order for a given media which tends to hover within a few dollars of a given figure, depending on the catalog mix and the market served. Once established, this average size of orders (total $ sales divided by total number of orders) is usually remarkably stable. Note, however, this concerns only prospecting. Continuing offers to customers will, in time, also tend to jell around a fixed sum, but each mailing may produce distinct differences. When these differences are traced, they are usually found to be based on what would otherwise be thought of as an unusual range of order.

VARIABLE VERSUS FIXED COSTS

The concept of variable versus fixed costs is applied by statisticians to direct-mail activities in different ways. Perhaps the easiest way to split these costs into the two streams is on the basis of promotion costs versus all other costs. By splitting costs this way, promotion costs, which can be increased or decreased at will, are considered variable costs while all the costs that determine the order margin on a given effort are considered fixed costs per unit. If a fixed order margin is calculated, taking into consideration all costs including those that result from sales, a fixed cost structure per unit will be set.

It is possible to somewhat affect by scale and thus create a new fixed cost per unit by increasing mailings. In the same rationale, if a program starts with a given projected order margin and the program fails, the actual fixed cost per unit, including abandonment, may increase substantially—and over the number of units sold may increase enormously. This emphasizes a great need to know and understand the figures for both promotion and all other or fixed costs.

We have seen that promotional cost is a variable cost—that is, by increasing the promotion, the proportion of variable cost to total costs rises. However, we must recognize that promotional cost is the largest cost of doing business through direct response. If fixed costs for "all other costs" including cost of goods sold is, say, $11, and the sales price is $29.95, that leaves an order margin of $18.95. To breakeven on this offer a mailer could spend $19.00 in promotion cost per unit, or in this case, 170 percent of the nonpromotion cost. This example shows that at breakeven, promotional cost will be 64 percent of expenditures while product and all other costs will be 36 percent.

HOW TO LOOK AT DIRECT-RESPONSE SELLING COSTS

Throughout this book there are numerous examples in which the total cost of selling through direct response totals 30 to 60 percent of sales.

In past years, most business-to-business marketers have been extremely reluctant to commit adequate resources for direct marketing because they insisted on equating the cost of the entire direct-response process with advertising. And advertising could not possibly be 30, 40, or 50 percent of total sales!

As more and more business-to-business marketers have discovered, the advantages of direct mail, particularly where the costs to place a salesperson in the field have become too expensive, this reluctance to "pay" the costs of direct mail have somewhat abated.

This has occurred in part because more and more marketers recognize that direct response is *not* advertising. Direct response is neither concerned with nor involved with cost per thousand ads, but rather with the cost for *each* inquiry, catalog request, donation, subscription, or order received. Direct-response practitioners use mass media such as radio, TV, Cable TV, magazines, and newspapers when the costs per thousand may be as low as $2, $3, or $4 per thousand. But at the same time they are eagerly looking at likely opportunities to obtain cost-efficient responses at 50 and 100, or even 200 times such costs.

Almost any business marketer with a sales force in the field would be delighted with a total selling cost of no more than 35 percent. For direct marketers, the catalogs and brochures sent by mail to prospects are the sales force. These are the selling tools, and their costs can be compared with discounts given to brokers, wholesalers, retailers, as well as compared with the salaries, commissions, and travel costs paid to the sales force. On this basis, the costs of direct-response selling are comparatively low. And what is more this method plus the phone are doing what the sales force no longer can afford to do, which is market parts, supplies, and low-priced products on a one-to-one basis.

Further Analysis

This section focuses on the fact that it can be very misleading to read results based on response or sales volume alone. Cost per order is an important fact to know, but it is only one part of tracking to determine profitability per dollars spent for promotion. The mathematical data in this section carry important variants based on the lifetime value of a given block of original orders received from a given promotional effort, and also trace second and subsequent sales, catalog request conversions, and so on.

The same type of data are required for each aspect of the entire promotional scheme, which inevitably must affect profitability. These include:

- The use of money in inventory form in
  incremental promotion costs
  handling of bad debts
  handling of credit, collections, C.O.D.s

- Using testing procedure as a way of life to
  check the lifetime of the current offer
  investigate possibilities with new offers
  possibly new calved-off catalogs
  make certain the "tested" data bank of media is still profitable

- Disposal of excess inventory through the
  use as premiums
  company store promotions
  retail sales
  dumping via spot buys
  trashing

An example of this is the offer of credit terms on an expensive item purchased through mail order (space ads or direct mail). Credit can increase the number of orders received per $1,000 spent for promotion and thus reduce the cost per order. However, this increase must consider the following factors:

1. Bad debt overall as a percentage of gross sales, and the charge for bad debt per order.
2. Carrying cost of money per order.
3. Administration cost of the credit procedure per order.

4. Cost of extra returns per order (if any).

5. Cost of extra refurbishing of extra returns (if any).

Credit cards are a way of life in America, and no catalog operator would even dream of competing today without offering this form of credit. However, the initial pains of handling a flow of credit card sales has proven distressing to almost every operator who has been going along comfortably with a cash-only policy. Until additional resources and personal phone work can result in some sort of electronic transmission of both authorizations and deposits, chances are credit card orders are costly both in wear and tear, and in the commission paid for the use of credit.

PROFITS AS A PERCENT OF SALES VERSUS RETURN ON INVESTMENT

At the end of a given campaign the profit on sales will be the same whether the bills for all costs are paid in advance, upon receipt, or net thirty, sixty, or ninety days. But there is a remarkable difference in the return on the invested dollar if expenditures for that campaign can be deferred as long as no harm comes to either the company's reputation or credit standing.

In direct-response marketing one-half of all orders that will be received come in with surprising rapidity—after a few days for first class mail to a few weeks for solo direct mail, to at most, a few months for the most laggard of catalog sales. Thus the investment in promotion and inventory is quickly recovered; in many instances fast enough for the gross profit on sales to be used to pay part of the overall costs of inventory and promotion.

Where a mailing buys new customers at no profit, but no loss, the entire advanced sum is returned and can be used over and over again. This ability to reinvest sales dollars into continuing campaigns produces a far different type of R.O.I. than advancing the entire sum of the reinvestments at one time would. This is one of the unusual advantages of the direct-response-business which encourages entrepreneurs to start small and grow rapidly. This is one aspect of direct marketing that is not at all understood by the "bean-counter" type of mentality.

In this field, moderate profits used over and over again during the year, produce inordinately high returns on investment—three, four, five, or six times the return if all payments were made in advance. In conventional business, a sum of, say, $50,000 might be necessary to launch a small operation. In direct response, an initial $5,000 can be invested to revolve six or seven times in the course of a year, with total mailings increasing with each turn. Insiders know or understand this intuitively. Outsiders find this way of doing business very difficult to grasp.

R.O.I. is undoubtedly one of the important measures of business success: If you think like a bookkeeper, you will never approach success in direct response. To achieve a high R.O.I. in direct response, you must think like a marketer and seek every legitimate means to improve the growth factor, called R.O.I.

HOW TO MEASURE RETURN ON PROMOTION

Return on Promotion (R.O.P.) measures the cost to buy the customers above the cost of promotion which is then treated as an investment. Then the return on this investment is measured by the difference between: (1) The gross profit or contribution that accrues to a cell of orders as a result of all subsequent transactions and, (2) the cost to buy that group or cell of orders.

For example, if the cost to buy is $10 (−$10 per new customer) and subsequently the cell of customers provides an average gross profit of $25, the profit is $15, which on a $10 investment equals 150 percent. The formulation for this is:

$$\text{R.O.P.} = \frac{\text{contribution (\$25)} - \text{cost per order (\$10)}}{\text{cost per order (10)}} \times 100 = 150\%$$

Where there is considerable variation in the performance of individual "starts," as on a continuity plan or a club plan, the R.O.P. is a convenient way to measure activity at any point in the history of any group of customers. A single R.O.P. for all cells on the books long enough for significance is usually used as a benchmark for how well the mathematics are working out overall.

You do not have to be a club plan operator or continuity program operator to grasp the advantages of the R.O.P. concept. If a change, say, in a premium is to be made which will increase or decrease the initial cost, R.O.P. will provide the answer as to how much larger or how much smaller the response rate needs to be to equal the prior standard. For example: Standard is $375/M in the mail with a $5 premium and an R.O.P. of .67 based on 25 order per thousand (at a cost of $15 each).

$$\text{R.O.P.} = \frac{\$30/\text{contribution} - \$5 \text{ premium} - \$15 \text{ cost of order}}{\$15 \text{ cost of order}} = .67\%$$

How many additional orders must be received to equal this standard if the premium is increased to $8?

$$R.O.P. = \frac{30 - 8 - \text{new CPO}}{\text{CPO}} + \text{solving for CPO} = \$13.25$$

In this case, the new cost per order, $13.25, divided into $375, equals the cost of promotion per thousand of 28.3 times. Thus to equal the Standard, ($25 as noted above) response must increase by 3.3 orders or by over 13 percent.

On the other hand, if the premium can be reduced to $2.50, what will this do to the number of responses per thousand mailed to equal the R.O.P. of the Standard?

$$R.O.P. = \frac{30 - 2.50 - \text{new CPO}}{\text{CPO}} + \text{solving for CPO} = \$15.75$$

Dividing $15.75 into $375 = 23.8 orders. Thus reducing the premium by $2.50 reduces the required response rate by 1.2 orders per thousand, or in comparison with the Standard of 25 by just 5 percent.

When the initial investment, say, the cost per thousand in the mail *varies*, the analysis for R.O.P. must be made on the incremental investment. If the incremental R.O.P. is plus, this measures an increase in contribution. If the incremental R.O.P. is a negative amount, this measures a decrease in contribution.

If the cost of promotion increases, say, from $375 to $425 per thousand, with the same response rate for the same offer, the incremental R.O.P. will be a negative amount. But what is the result if raising the cost of promotion is accompanied by an increase in orders per thousand mailed? The following table shows why incremental R.O.P. is essential to such an evaluation:

	Example A	Example B	Incremental difference between A and B
Cost per thousand	$ 375	$ 425	
Number of sales @ $70 ea.	25	28	
Sales per thousand	+1,750	+1,960	+$210
Cost of sales at $40 ea.	−1,000	−1,120	−120
Difference (contribution)	+750	+840	+90
Premium	−125	−140	−15

	Example A	Example B	Incremental difference between A and B
Advertising cost	−375	−425	−50
Total advertising cost	−500	−565	−65
Net (Contribution—Less advertising cost)	250	275	+25
R.O.P.—including premium	.50	.49	.38
R.O.P.—advertising only	.66	.65	.50

This example shows that the higher-priced package on an extra expenditure of $50 for promotion resulted in an incremental increase of $25 per thousand in the net return. There is an additional contribution to overhead from the extra expense. In a million-piece mailing that differential would translate into an extra $25,000 of net profit. The differential here however, is quite a fragile one: If response drops to 27 per thousand from 28 per thousand, the incremental R.O.P. drops to zero, which shows that the addition of $50 of advertising cost is a dead loss.

Given the preceding table, most managements would opt to pay the increased increment to net the extra $25 per thousand if, and only if, several lists and continuations indicated that the anticipated number of orders would hit 28/M or above. Where the margin between profit and loss on an incremental basis is so slim, a good deal of judgment is required before authorizing a sizable rollout. While there may be a good reason to increase investment up to the point where incremental R.O.P. is zero or close to zero, the cut-off point is usually substantially higher—25 to 30 percent or more—in order to reflect risk, cost of money, and the ability to use the same funds to better advantage in other investments.

The same kind of thinking (increasing increments to gain extra net) is also used in selected mediums in space ads or selected lists for direct mail. The R.O.P. is bound to drop if multiple insertions or multiple usages are close together but the gross profit from the opportunity offer may outweigh this. Where the value of a new name from each source is known over a given period of time, an R.O.P. can be prepared that will come close to maximizing the return for the total sum invested in promotion. This R.O.P. will allocate available cash flow by type of media, media within each medium, and if enough data are known, the time or times each market segment is to be promoted.

The proliferation of retail stores by catalog operators is based in good part on two forms of analysis: R.O.I. and R.O.P. (ROP, obviously), provides a measure to compare promotional sums expended in direct-response media versus promotional sums expended to produce retail traffic in stores. A treatise is waiting to be written on this growing market phenomenon.

HOW TO ANALYZE FRONT-END PERFORMANCE

Most discussions of direct mail concerns *Front End*—the number of dollars spent per thousand on promotion and the response that promotion has obtained. Front-end performance relates to the analysis of initial results to a mailing. Its counterpart, back-end analysis, covers the entire process that takes place after an initial response has been achieved.

Five Aspects of Promotion Costs

To assess front-end performance, you must first know the total cost attributable to a given promotion. Promotion costs include five specific parts:

1. Cost of the package, catalog, or mailing. This includes all printing and plates, purchase of outside envelopes or wraps, provision of order forms, business reply envelopes or cards.

2. Cost of inducements or premiums. Costs here need to be allocated on the basis of quantities *used* based on response. (This is usually done after the fact.) Costs of carrying and inventorying premiums, and the loss on disposed surplus are legitimate costs to be added here.

3. Cost of list rentals. Total cost per thousand including all selection charges, less any discount negotiated for quantity or merge–purge use are all part of the costs for list rental. The merge–purge cost must then be added despite the fact that merge–purge and zip code correction may well save valuable dollars otherwise wasted. If carrier route coding is provided this also is a cost, which is, however, offset by lower postal charges.

4. Cost of fulfillment. All costs involved in putting the pieces in the mail stream are accounted for. As a bare minimum this includes addressing, sorting, bagging, and tieing and taking the mail to the post office for certification and mailing. It also can include folding, nesting, inserting, stapling, tabbing, coding, and all other operations necessary for getting the pieces ready to mail. (Some operations such as gluing, sealing, die-cutting, personalizing, and so on, may be accomplished at this stage, if required, or at the printing plant. The importance is not when a given operation is conducted but rather making certain all costs are accounted for.)

5. Postage. Costs include per piece on the mail, by type, and on an average for the entire mailing.

These costs of promotion do not include any provision for the cost of preparation of the mailing or for the creative efforts involved. Cost of promotion starts with camera-ready copy and includes all costs from that point to the deposit of the pieces in the mail stream. (For a discussion on why it is preferable *not* to include creative costs and mechanical production costs in the costs of production, see the section on Think Like a Marketer—not Like a Bookkeeper on page 345.)

Once all the costs are assembled, and the number of pieces mailed have been certified by the USPS, it is a simple matter to determine the cost per thousand (CPM).

$$\text{CPM} = \frac{\text{Total costs}}{\text{Number of pieces mailed}} \times 1,000$$

or perhaps a simpler way is:

$$\frac{\text{Total costs}}{\text{Number of thousands of pieces mailed}}$$

If total costs are $25,000 and total mailings are 60,000 pieces, then

$$\text{CPM} = \frac{\$25,000}{60,000} \times 1,000 = \$41\text{o}$$

or

$$\frac{\$25,000}{60} = \$416$$

This concept can also be utilized to get a rough idea of the CPM for space advertising. Here CPM is calculated by dividing the total costs (space plus costs of the insert or plate) by the circulation of the magazine:

$$\frac{\text{CPM for a given space}}{\text{as described}} = \frac{\text{Space change + other costs}}{\text{Circulation of the medium}} \times 1,000$$

The equation above can also be calculated in a simpler way:

$$\frac{\text{Cost}}{\text{Number of thousands of circulation}}$$

THE IMPORTANCE OF BACK-END COSTS

Most mailers have little or no difficulty figuring out the apparent profit or loss per order on a mailing based on the differential between the selling price, plus any attendant service charges, and the cost of merchandise, plus delivery, handling, and drop shipping. This differential can be referenced by multiplying the order margin by the response rate and dividing that amount by the cost per thousand pieces in the mail.

Rarely do mailers figure in back-end costs which include:

- Processing
- Credit checking
- Cost of collection
- Cost of returns (including cost of refurbishment)
- Cost of bad debt
- Cost of money tied up in inventory

Orders refused for credit must be subtracted; orders returned not only affect the response index, but add on extra costs of handling. Sales can only be net after deducting credit rejects and returns. Return costs include an administrative return service charge, possibly a lost drop shipment charge, plus the cost of shipping out and shipping back. Then time must be spent to open and inspect the return and to take necessary steps to repair breakage and replace missing items. All of this must be in the calculation of the return cost per net sale.

Bad debts require the establishment of reserve funds, which means the funds used to cover bad debts must be subtracted from the cost per net sale. Last, but not necessarily least, is the cost of money. Money tied up in inventory could be put to work and gain interest elsewhere. This is a cost in which interest is lost for the period the inventory is carried until that inventory is sold and paid for. The greater the inventory in relation to sales, and the fewer turns per year of the inventory, the higher the total cost of money. This can be expressed as an approximate cost of money per net sale.

The mathematics of direct mail splits all costs into two parts: (1) cost of promotion, which includes inducements or premiums and their attendant costs including the cost to carry and inventory them and, (2) "everything else," which includes processing, credit checking, cost of collection, cost of returns, cost of bad debts, and cost of money. Each of these buried costs must be translated for all costs into a single cost figure per net sale, and figures for all costs or a single figure including all costs sometimes expressed as a percentage of gross sales must be included in the everything else cost category along with the cost of goods sold. Only when these back-end costs are included in the calculation can the real or true order margin be established.

BACK END-TRACKING OF ALL COSTS

This book is mainly concerned with marketing and the ways to improve front-end performance. The consulting firm of R. Kestenbaum & Company has written a brief treatise on direct marketing profitability analysis which is so comprehensive in its coverage of all costs, and particularly "all other costs" that it is reproduced for your information.

*HOW TO MEASURE THE PROFITABILITY OF DIRECT MAIL**

Contribution

To improve your insight into the profitablity of direct-marketing programs, it is necessary to know how much money is available to cover selling cost and profit. This brings us to the concept of *contribution* of circularization cost (Promotion Cost) and profit.

Simply stated, contribution is the amount remaining after all costs of merchandise, operations, administration, and overhead are subtracted from net sales. Note that circularization costs are not included when determining contribution.

Because the calculation of contribution forms the basis of the more elaborate measures of success, its determination must be careful and thorough.

First, the determination of contribution should be all encompassing. Every category of cost should be included. A form should be developed to serve as a checklist that assures all potential cost centers are considered.

Second, cost estimates obtained should be *compared* with other financial records to be sure that estimates are reasonable. To facilitate this validation, and to permit statement of costs or groups of costs as a percentage of revenue, it is preferable to base contribution on *net sales* after returns.

Third, if contribution is based on net sales, it is necessary to take account of the fact that

*By R. Kestnbaum & Company

certain costs are incurred in connection with each order or each shipment, but *must be borne only by those units that stay sold* and that are not returned.

Fourth, a major effort should be made to determine the *frequency* with which each kind of cost occurs.

Figure 11-1 shows the first page of a form we use to collect revenue and costs related to an average order. You may find it helpful when thinking about your own programs. Each organization should identify revenue sources and costs in a way that is meaningful to its business and that reflects the way it does its accounting. In that manner, periodic accounting reports should be available to use in validating revenue and cost assumptions. It is also useful many times to group costs into those which are *fixed* or *semi-fixed* versus those which *vary* directly with transactions or sales volume.

Figure 11.1

DIRECT MARKETING PROFITABLITY ANALYSIS
PART 1: COST AND RATE ASSUMPTIONS

Client: _____
Project: _____
Date: _____

A1 Selling price, cash $_____.___
A2 Selling price, charge $_____.___
A3 Installment terms: number of payments   _____
A4 Installment terms: amount of payment $_____.___
A5 Total installment price $_____.___
A6 Shipping and handling charge $_____.___
A7 Additional price of option or accessory $_____.___

B1 Merchandise cost $_____.___
B2 Cost of premium, free with purchase $_____.___
B3 Cost of option or accessory $_____.___
B4 Cost of premium, free for examination $_____.___
B5 Average inventory value $_____.___

C1 Drop shipment and delivery $_____.___
C2 Order processing and first invoice $_____.___
C3 EDP handling $_____.___
C4 Order card postage $_____.___
C5 Cost of second and later invoices $_____.___

D1 Return handling $_____.___
D2 Return refurbishing $_____.___
D3 Postage refund on returns and exchanges $_____.___

By R. Kestnbaum & Company

Figure 11.2 shows the second page of this form, which is used to record key frequencies and those costs which are determined as percentages of revenue rather than as per unit expense.

To determine frequencies of such factors as cash versus charge orders, periodic samplings can be made.

When these cost and rate assumptions are processed by a computer, we obtain the analysis that appears in Figure 11.3. The elements to note about this report are:
Column 1 shows the average base cost of each line item.
Column 2 shows the frequency with which each line item occurs.
Column 3 is the product of the first two columns.
Column 4 shows the final cost per net sale. Items on lines 160 through 380 are factored up to recognize that the net units remaining sold must bear the cost of all transactions processed and of all returns, exchanges, and other losses.

This determination of contribution focuses finally on a single number shown here on line 400 in column 4, the amount of money available in each typical sale to pay for the circularization cost, and after that cost is paid for, to yield a profit.

Breakeven is calculated very simply. If a mailing or a catalog is sent out at a cost of $250 per thousand pieces mailed and the average order produces a contribution of $35.57, the breakeven is $250 ÷ $35.57 or seven units. This is equivalent to a response of 7/10 of 1 percent. As the circularization or selling cost per thousand changes, so does the breakeven, so that if the cost to contact a thousand people drops to $185, the breakeven point drops to 5.2 units per thousand or 5/10 of 1 percent.

Contribution may be viewed as a pie that can only be divided into two parts, selling cost and pretax profit.

At the breakeven point, the entire pie is eaten by selling cost. Nothing remains for profit.

If we want to set a pretax profit target of 17 percent of sales, in this example 17 percent of $107.22 or $18.23, then only $17.34 of each order may be applied to recovery of selling cost.

Required net response to achieve each targeted profit is readily calculated by dividing the circularization cost per thousand by the remaining funds available to apply to that cost.

It follows that as the contribution per order grows, fewer orders are required to reach breakeven. Since direct marketers have found that they can obtain two, three, or four orders per thousand for a wide range of products, there is growing attraction to merchandising "big ticket," or more expensive, products that yield lucrative profits at low-response levels. With the growing affluence of buyers in all countries in which direct marketers are active, it is probable that the interest in selling more expensive products will continue to grow rapidly.

Figure 11.2

	(1) % Frequency rate	(2) % Discount/ uncollect	(3) Month's payment delayed	(4) % Credit check	(5) Credit check cost	(6) % Credit reject
E1 Cash with order	_._				$_._	_
E2 Net 30 days	_._	_._	_	_._	$_._	_
F1 Charge to Amex	_._	_._	_	_._	$_._	_
F2 Charge to Carte Blanche	_._	_._	_	_._	$_._	_
F3 Charge to Diners Club	_._	_._	_	_._	$_._	_
F4 Charge to BankAmericard	_._	_._	_	_._	$_._	_
F5 Charge to Master Card	_._	_._	_	_._	$_._	_
F6 Charge to other cards	_._	_._	_		$_._	_
F7 Total charge cards	_._					
G1 Installment record kept	_._	_._	_	_._	$_._	_
G2 Installment record sold	_._	_._	_		$_._	_
G3 Sales tax	_._	_._	_	_._	$_._	_
H1 Purchase with option or accessory	_._					
H2 Lost in shipment						
H3 Returned goods	_._					
H4 Exchanges	_._					
H5 Goods lost in return shipment	_._					
H6 Interest paid	_._					
I1 Corporate overhead						
I2 Departmental overhead	_._					
I3 Selling cost target	_._					
I4 Pretax profit target	_._					
I5 Return on investment target	_._					

Figure 11.3

DIRECT MARKETING PROFITABILITY ANALYSIS
PART 2: AVERAGE CONTRIBUTION PER ORDER

CLIENT   : Any Company
PROJECT: $100 Item
DATE   : April 18, 19XX

Line number		1 Base cost	2 Factor (%)	3 Weighted cost (per unit)	4 Net cost (per unit)
10	Selling price	$100.00	80.0	$ 80.00	$ 80.00
20	Installment price	107.40	20.0	21.48	21.48
30	Shipping and handling	2.50	70.0	1.75	1.75
40	Additional options and accessories	19.95	20.0	3.99	3.99
50	Total average selling price			107.22	107.22
60					
70	Merchandise cost	45.00	100.0	45.00	45.00
80	Premium for purchase	0.50	100.0	0.50	0.50
90	Options or accessories	7.50	20.0	1.50	1.50
100	Credit card discount	5.58	20.0	1.12	1.12
110	Receivables discount	0.00	0.0	0.00	0.00
120	Sales tax not collected	4.29	1.0	0.04	0.04
130	Bad debt	107.22	2.0	2.10	2.10
140	Subtotal			50.26	50.26
150					

No.	Description		RATE %		
160	Drop shipment and delivery	2.40	100.0	2.40	2.67
170	Premium for examination	0.00	100.0	0.00	0.00
180	Incoming order postage	0.15	100.0	0.15	0.17
190	Order processing and first invoice	3.00	100.0	3.00	3.33
200	EDP handling	0.40	100.0	0.40	0.44
210	Credit check	0.78	100.0	0.78	0.87
220	Return handling	0.50	10.0	0.05	0.06
230	Return refurbishing	2.00	11.0	0.22	0.24
240	Shipping exchanges	2.50	1.0	0.03	0.03
250	Postage refund, return, and exchange	2.50	11.0	0.28	0.31
260	Goods lost in shipment	47.00	0.5	0.24	0.26
270	Monthly statement cost	2.40	20.0	0.48	0.53
280	Subtotal			8.02	8.91
290					
300	Total direct costs	—	RATE %	58.28	59.17
310					
320	Cost of money—receivables	0.06	12.0	0.01	0.01
330	Cost of money—product inventory	0.00	12.0	0.00	0.00
340	Overhead—departmental	103.99	7.0	7.28	7.28
350	Overhead—corporate	103.99	5.0	5.20	5.20
360	Subtotal			12.49	12.49
370					
380	Total cost			70.76	71.65
390					
400	Contribution to selling cost and profit		33.2%	36.46	35.57

By R. Kestnbaum & Company

TESTING BY MEANS OF MARKET RESEARCH

A good deal of research is conducted by direct mail and telephone. This research is affected by the same concerns as those that apply to testing of mailing lists. Important questions to answer in the conduct of market research are:

1. Is the proper universe being surveyed?

2. Is the sample drawn from that universe a fair one?

3. Are the proper questions being asked?

4. Has the questionnaire been properly tested before it was rolled out?

5. Are the answers quantifiable, meaningful, and statistically reliable?

6. Is the market being researched subject to meaningful answers by phone or mail research techniques?

7. Is the response level achieved acceptable? (Is there, for example, a decided skew among those who do not, cannot, or will not answer?)

FOCUS GROUPS

One growing field of research within the direct-response field is *focus groups*. This type of research offers the feelings, opinions, guesses, hunches of respondents, "soft" data (not data which is or can be quantifiable). Focus group research can assist in the process of deciding on a given product or process but it cannot provide the final decision.

Customer Knowledge

Where research *for* direct response (not research *by* direct response) is sought, it must be carefully delineated. It is particularly important that the objective is subject to meaningful answers—one of the requisites listed earlier.

For twenty years this author's office has held open the following offer to any market research firm or direct mail advertising agency: We will supply five packages for the same product, all of which have accurate response data. If the agency can array them in sequential order by response—not percentages—simply place them in order we will pay the agreed-upon cost of the research. If however the research fails to provide the correct array of information, the research will not be billable. No research firm, ad agency, creative writer, or creative direct-mail agency has ever been willing to do this on these terms. Their reluctance is well-founded because what people tell you they will do is a far cry from what actually happens when you research the market by testing one offer against another.

Not too long ago a major insurance company asked 1,000 of its known mail order insurance buyers if they would buy insurance by mail. Over 70 percent said "no." Rodale Press, a major direct mailer questioned a sizable portion of their own book buyers, each of whom had been sent at least thirty-two other Rodale mailings after buying a book. Most of them could not, unaided, even recall the name! AT&T, prior to the breakup of the system, held four focus group interviews with forty well known direct-mail brokers, list managers, writers, and mail order house operators. They were asked their opinion of the value of the AT&T classified telephone customer file. (These have since been assigned to individual operating companies.) The consensus of this industry cross-section was, "Ho hum, so what, there are classified lists available." It happens that the phone companies, including AT&T, have the most current, deliverable, and most useful basic data on households and nonhouseholds in the country. Once these data come on the market, every segment of every list in America over three or six months old will find it either desirable or necessary to use this great resource. In a recent review of these classified I estimated the saving to the list-using universe for access to these data would be in the nature of $350,000,000! So much for the "ho hum" answer.

Suspect Data

Most data derived from individual surveys on matters such as income, readership, and years of education are suspect. We all have a human desire to look better than we are. Questionnaires bring out this desire in spades. Given a bingo card to check off at no charge, the typical response is to check off twenty, thirty, or all choices. Why not? It is all free, and maybe some of the data sent in will be interesting. Those long questionnaires that are part of warrantees permit the product owner to analyze responses. Some answers are accurate and precise; others are marked simply because they are printed on the form.

Copy research on different offers, appeals, and approaches, particularly if you need to winnow three or four likely prospects for mail testing from a host of possibilities, can be helpful. But if you use such research to determine the first, second, and third best responses, you are wasting your money. For the same relatively few thousand dollars that research will cost, you can conduct a grid test in which the customers can tell you with their dollars exactly what you should do next. No market research can ever hope to match the fundamental research you conduct with every mailing, insertion, and direct response commercial.

This is particularly true of research that attempts to predict the relationship between price and response. Not too long ago a customer had an overstock of tape recorders and his "research" among friends and neighbors indicated the best discount price was $29.75. Split tests were made at $29.75, $39.75, $49.75, and $69.75. The client insisted they were not worth that much. However, he sold more at $39.75, made more money at $69.75, and produced the lowest number of sales per M mailed at $29.75! Research done "over the backyard fence" is a waste of time. When *Readers Digest Condensed Books* came on the market, the "price" offer was split evenly on the first book for 1¢, 5¢, 10¢, 25¢, 50¢, and $1.00. One of these price "offers" outpulled any of the others by over 100 percent. Yet bets were placed in advance all along this 100 to 1 "price" spectrum by knowledgeable direct-mail people working on the project. You cannot decide the best price point—only the market can do that by voting based on its pocketbook.

Directed Research

The comments in the preceding sections do not imply that direct response should override all other methods of research. One form that should be used by almost all of us is to periodically survey our customers to find out what they think of our products, services, personnel, and abilities to service their needs. A lot of surprises lurk in this type of research, and you should be prepared to find out what customers think and do something about it.

One major use of market research, as it refers to a direct-response file, is to identify and clarify the customers: who they are, demographically; where they live, geographically; how they live, psychographically. Research can help define the number of families or businesses that make up the logical, reachable, available universe, and provide significant data on how best to appeal to such a universe.

One of the best forms of internal research is to read on a regular basis either all, or as much as possible, incoming white mail, particularly complaint mail. In a marriage, two hopes, two needs, two illusions, and two realities merge. Something like that goes on between a business and its customers. What you believe your customers are thinking may not jibe with what they prove when they request, grouse, and gripe about issues you weren't aware of. The rule is simple: Always read, listen, and learn.

Periodically it is wise to review where you and your business stand when compared with your closest competitors. What is your position today? What was it yesterday? What would you like it to be tomorrow? Keep a folder on each individual company that keeps you on your toes because of its advanced thinking (or copying)—and drop into this folder every bit of information you can obtain on their sales, products, profit, marketing, sales force, money, markets, and mailings. Review this folder every three to six months and place your candid opinion of your status at the time of that review into the folder. Over a few years you will find these folders quite revealing.

Directed surveys can provide all kinds of insights and give you much food for thought. You may wish to review the demographics of your customer base by age, income, proportion of working women, and proportion of working women with children. You may wish to get some idea of how they might feel about new products. Is there a difference between one-time buyers and multibuyers? You may wish to compare your "image" with your customers in the last survey you took. Some surveys can be conducted by enclosing a return card or envelope in outgoing shipments. Some can be conducted to carefully segmented cells of your customer file. The more you know about your customers, the better you can run the mail order business that depends on them. You must always keep in mind that a customer file is not monolithic. That file contains people who love you, people who are dead, people who will never buy from you again, people who will gladly pass your catalogs to friends, people who haven't looked at any one of your last nine catalogs, people who are one-time buyers, and people who buy something from almost every catalog you mail out. These customers are different, and you need to know how they differ.

Most studies of postings to a catalog of sales of product by page, area, and mark-up are principally designed to determine whether to keep a product or product line in the catalog, or in the product mix, and if so at what level of promotion. Try looking at the figures in a new way to see if there are pointers, from the sales figures, to new offers, new products, possibly a calved-off catalog. One clothing retailer found sweaters deserved a catalog of its own. Sears now sends out more specialized catalogs (but probably not yet more pages, although that will come) than copies of its general merchandise catalog. A sophisticated tool vendor found a new market that demanded a new approach to craftspeople who worked at home instead of inside or outside business. Look for the pointers to the future. If you look you are almost certain to see some flashes of inspiration.

Keep in Touch

Don't get out of touch with the field. This means you should use directed research as well as unstructured research. At trade shows, be sure you get out and visit the booths and listen to what your customers, as some of them are certainly there, are saying, asking, and complaining about. Read customer correspondence regularly so you are aware of what your staff is doing from the other side of the fence. You should also make an occasional follow-up call on major customers to see where you stand, and where you can be more helpful. In the book, *In Search of Excellence*, the key points are that top companies are those that care about the customer and have learned to "keep in touch."

Regression Analysis

Some forms of statistical research, such as regression analysis, are given high visibility. This author is reluctant to give much space and attention to one of the great buzz words of our industry, namely regression analysis. The reason for this is that of the 790,000 holders of third class bulk mailing permits, not over a few hundred will ever use regression analysis to attempt to improve their results in their entire careers. These few hundred major mailers already know about this form of research and have already formulated their own policies as to whether or not to incorporate it into their test procedures.

There are some amazingly extensive customer lists in America; Sears Roebuck & Company now can address over 65 million. At least one file will, in time, have over 100 million customers, and *Readers Digest* has two files each with an estimated count of 25 million or more each. Donnelley, Polk, Data Base America and Metromail each can reach 75 million or more households, and there are three or four lists primarily from driver license records with counts of over 100 million adults. Such lists can profit from almost any data that can enhance response but they are the exceptions. The average list of customers in America is probably in the 10,000 to 20,000 range. One recent research study placed the midpoint for this range at 14,000.

By using a regression analysis program, an owner of a major customer file can structure a model and then test results by segment against the model, to "cream" off all segments irrespective of age, frequency, dollars, item and source. This will produce response above a given desired cut-off point—very desirable but not in the cards for most of us. But keep-in-touch research is something all of us should be doing, all the time.

For those statistically inclined, let me state here what regression analysis is—and does. Regression analysis establishes the intereaction between a dependent variable (number of orders per thousand catalogs mailed, for example) with independent variables such as recency, frequency, dollars, items, method of payment, and source, including inquiries, bouncebacks, friends-of-friends. Visualize half a dozen "cells" for recency, three or four for frequency, maybe eight or ten for dollars (highest, cumulative, quarterly time buckets) ten or twelve for classification by item, four or five for method of payment, and a dozen or so for source. What weighting is to be given to each cell, and which combination will produce the highest response, and the lowest?

What a multiple regression is utilized for is to analyze as much individual descriptive information as is available (for both respondents and nonrespondents) to see if there are any statistically significant patterns. Where respondents are compared with nonrespondents what is hoped for are statistically significant differences that can be utilized to improve the selection process.

The regression analysis report, which may or may not bear out some personal predilection can, if the sample is large enough produce a pattern in the form of a diamond (shown here), in which the top 1 percent (or 5 or 10 percent) calls for a given cluster of independent variable cells, while the bottom 1 percent (or 5 or 10 percent) will call for an entirely different mix within the independent factors available.

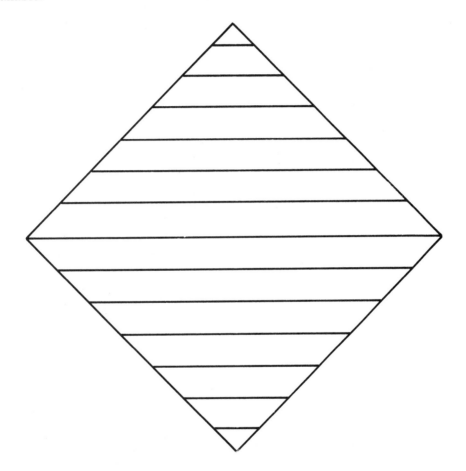

In effect (but not in actuality) the computer looks at each independent variable, and suppresses all the others. Visualize a pot of variables. The computer allows one to pop up, and analyzes it, pushes it down, and allows another to pop up—keeping track all the time how one factor, two factors, three factors, number of factors affect the valuable dependent variable—the number of sales per M.

CHAPTER 12

Special Mathematical and Computer-Based Direct-Response Techniques

PART I DIRECT-MAIL MARKETING METHODS

PENETRATION ANALYSIS: PROFILING CUSTOMER FILES

Almost all statistical techniques used to measure results first and then use data for improved selection are based on the share of the market examined for each cell. The key is to find cells in which the market penetration is well above average, and do more with them. In the same vein, with cells where the penetration is well below average, do less or nothing. This is an extension of the first rule of direct mail which is to learn which results pay and do more, and which results do not pay and do less or nothing.

Penetration analysis can be conducted for consumer customer files as well as for business mail order files.

Penetration Analysis of Business Lists: Three Main Variables

The first and major variable affecting response for business lists is classification. The second variable is size which is often also a major factor. The third variable is the study of geography. Classification is determined by SIC Code. Size is equated best by the number of employees. Geographic penetration is usually measured by states. In effect, penetration analysis of a business list is an ideal way to "profile" the customer file.

In good part, analysis of business mail order lists usually begins and ends with counts of customers. (In research parlance this is called "bean counting.") If we inspect counts of customers for a given business mailer we may find:

Number of customers	SIC code	Classification	Universe
125	20XX	Food manufacturing	19,000
70	29XX	Petroleum and related industries	2,150
90	2079	Plastics	15,000
218	35XX	Machinery manufacturing	75,000

Looking at the number of customers, it appears that Machinery Manufacture is almost as important as the other three classifications put together, but note what happens when the ratio (the penetration) is calculated for each of these four classifications against the universe of firms in each:

Food manufacturing	125 out of 19,000	or 1/150
Petroleum and related industries	70 out of 2,150	or 1/30
Plastics	90 out of 15,000	or 1/165
Machinery manufacturing	218 out of 75,000	or 1/345

A different pattern emerges immediately. Penetration in Petroleum and Related Industries is over *ten* times as great as in Machinery Manufacturing, five times as great as in Food Manufacturing.

When penetration is taken down to the three-digit level, say, in Food Manufacturing, it appears that while establishments are all equal when counted, some classifications of establishments are far more important in response than others.

Customer analysis by 3-digit SIC for customer penetration in the food manufacturing field

Number of customers	SIC code	Classification	Universe	Penetration ratio
10	201X	Meats	3,600	1/360
23	202X	Dairy products	2,300	1/100

Customer analysis by 3-digit SIC for penetration in the food manufacturing field

Number of customers	SIC code	Classification	Universe	Penetration ratio
18	203X	Canned and frozen foods	2,400	1/133
9	204X	Flour and feeds	2,500	1/277
3	205X	Breadstuffs	800	1/270
2	206X	Sugars and sweets	1,200	1/600
16	207X	Oils and fats	700	1/40
29	208X	Beverages	2,800	1/95
15	209X	Food specialties	2,700	1/180
125	2,000	Food manufacturing	19,000	1/150

When these are arrayed, they show a variance of 1/40 to 1/600.

207X	1/40
208X	1/95
202X	1/100
203X	1/133
All Food	1/150
209X	1/180
205X	1/270
204X	1/277
201X	1/360
206X	1/600

The most telling data show up when the penetration analysis is taken to four digits.

It may appear that penetration within Machinery Manufacturing would not be affected much by one type of machinery against another, but on the following page is a fairly typical penetration pattern. It is not unusual to uncover pockets of potential that are two, five, or even ten times better than the average penetration of a given customer file.

How the SIC Classification System Works in Penetration Analysis

The SIC classification system has been with us for over twenty five years now. The current codes were unchanged between 1972 and 1987 and they have only been given a cosmetic change by the U.S. Department of Commerce for

Customer Analysis by 4-digit SIC for penetration in the machinery manufacturing field

Number of customers	SIC code	Classification	Universe	Penetration rate
15	3531	Construction machinery manufacturers	1,110	1/75
13	3541	Machine tools	1,910	1/150
4	3551	Food products Machine manufacturers	1,080	1/270
9	3565	Industrial pattern manufacturers	1,290	1/145
55	3573	Electronic computer gear manufacturers	2,560	1/45
7	3585	Air conditioning manufacturers	1,080	1/155

1987. Classification is the single most important aspect of a business mail order customer file, yet only a few mailers take any pains to capture this basic fact about each buyer.

The first need is to add SIC numbers to an existing file. SIC numbers can be added to business files either manually or by machine (computer matching).

If the file is on tape, those compilers with complete coded business files can match 40 to 50 percent of the outside customer file during an update or scheduled cycle, and thus add SICs. When the file is small, say, under 3,000, it is practical to engage a compiler to compare the customer list with printed records to post SICs clerically. Where the sampling method is used, it is best to isolate the 1,500 largest accounts, plus a cross-section sample of 1,500 accounts from the rest of the customers, and compare penetration by SIC between the two groups. It is important to determine, if possible, the difference in penetration by classification between major and minor customers.

To look up SICs clerically for a file on tape the customer records must be sorted into Alpha-Geo order first (alpha by company name, within alpha by city, within alpha by state-) and then printed on three-by-five cards with a sequence number on each card replicating that same identification number on the tape. (Once the SIC is posted to the card, the only data that need to be converted for an application run are the four- or five-digit sequence numbers and the four-digit SIC number.) Trained clerks with a good understanding of the SIC system will be able to augment the SIC records found in large credit files with SICs "forced" by name for schools, libraries, colleges, churches, governments, and other institutions.

Several companies with access to a tape copy of the entire universe of businesses, institutions, and offices of professionals make computer matching with outside files of customers available in zip code sequence. At the time a match is made, the following data can be transferred from the master file to the records to be tagged: SIC, telephone number, size of city, number of employees (in part), and classified advertising code. To improve the breed after a machine match, clerical review by that wonderful computer, the human mind, is required.

Size as a Penetration Factor

Where the size of an establishment is a determinent of penetration or of size of order, machine matching can provide some guidance when the data are analyzed by size groupings of numbers of employees. The usual employee ranges utilized are under 10; 10 to 24; 25 to 50; 51 to 100; 100 to 250; and over 250.

Geographic Considerations

Ideally, geographic variation needs to be checked by a single controlled mailing in which the number of pieces mailed to each state are available, along with the responses per state, so that percentage of response or penetration is measured by state.

A count of the customer file by state can be run against the business universe or the manufacturing-only universe, or the wholesale-only universe (depending on the market at hand) by state to see what skew, if any, is introduced by geography. In general, for business lists it is far more important to classify the kind of business than to be concerned with geographic location. A missing state may mean nothing more than the fact that no mailings have been made into the area.

Number of employees for manufacturers is available on most compiled files; employee strength for other major classifications are not complete. Where employee strength is available, it is advisable to include two, three, or four ranges in the analysis of penetration. If there is a distinctive pattern for both SIC and number of employees, and lists for prospecting can be rented by those characteristics, that adds additional assurance that the prospect lists have been properly selected. If the customer file is fairly large, say, 30,000 or 40,000 or more, a merge–purge of the new prospect names against the customer file may be in order. A modest percentage of pieces withheld from mailing because of duplication, which can be eliminated by a business list merge–purge, will more than pay for itself.

Some business customer files show a preponderance of orders from large customers. Where this can be logically expected, the penetration analysis should be made against a file of big business. Such an analysis quite often provides the essence of a business plan for future penetration for the next five years. For such larger businesses there are a number of lists available with data on number of employees, sales volume, SIC, and geography. Most major trade journals, as a means to sell an audience to their advertisers, cover firms with fifty employees or more; others only cover those with one hundred employees or more. One ideal list for this purpose is the Standard & Poors Register of Big Business, available from S&P or from its list manager, Ed Burnett.

For those mailers intent on reaching *smaller firms*, the fact that 90 percent or more of all establishments have less than ten employees and about 80 percent have less than four employees means that disregarding the number of employees within desired classifications does not seriously impair reaching the desired market. The proportion of small businesses provided can come very close to 100 percent if the computer is programmed to omit all establishments (a few hundred thousand) with twenty or more employees.

CUSTOMER PROFILING FOR CONSUMER LISTS

For a long time direct marketers talked about consumer customer profiling, but what they were really doing was reporting the action—not the profile of those acting. It was well agreed that the more one knew, the better the marketing would be but little was done to discover the profile. Hardly any company was accumulating individual profile data but worse than this, there was no way to apply profiles even if they were creatable.

Matching through Overlays

Until recently there was no economic way for a modest or small consumer mail order merchant to profile his or her list. Costs to tag a small list by a run against one of the mass-compiled files were exorbitant. Today the concept of list enhancement by overlaying one list upon another is almost commonplace, and there are half a dozen firms willing and able, usually on a once-per-month basis, to combine the files of several small mailers and run this against a file of 75 million odd-coded families. Minimum charges are modest enough that a customer file of 10,000 or 20,000 can now be tagged and profiled.

For the most part the data available include individual family income (by far the most important fact to mailers) as well as type of dwelling; car ownership; length of residency, and median data, which can be affixed to as small a geographical unit as a carrier route; for age of head of household; median for highest level of education reached; median value of home; and an index of limited value for number of children under eighteen years of age per family. Some consumer lists now have precise ages both of adults and of their children.

Little of this useful information is very helpful in selecting *new mail order buyer lists*, which have no comparable "handle" or tag to select on. Basically, only two groups can afford to mail those segments in demographically compiled files that match a pattern found by consumer profiling. They are mass marketers who need vast numbers, and smaller marketers who wish to take every logical name in a confined area.

Clustering as a Profiling Consideration

A number of services, through clustering zip codes of about thirty to fifty perceived general characteristics, offer to improve response. There is no doubt that this clustering has a beneficial effect but where mail-responsive lists, which eliminate from 50 to 68 percent of families that do not and probably will not buy by mail, outpull compiled files by a factor of two to one, no type of clustering is going to close this gap.

Penetration by Zip Code

It is rather fascinating that many of those services that swear by clustering must determine which zip codes show the greatest penetration. In some cases this is done by measuring a response to a major mailing or zip code by zip code. At that point the zip codes are arrayed by penetration and that array is used to rent names from rented lists. (More and more firms are willing to run a zip code selection tape against their rentable records to select only those zip codes believed to be best for the mailer.) Clustering, after having an array like this, would seem to be a step backward.

The major argument against zip code clustering, however, is the lack of homogeneity in zip code cells that average 6,000 to 11,000 families. A measure across a much smaller cell is needed. There are two measures available, of which one is almost universally available and the other (*enumeration districts*) is almost universally out of reach. The first of these two measures, and for 99 percent of mailers the most important, is the development of carrier-route demographic coding. Carrier routes are remarkably homogenous bits of real estate averaging 350 families each. In the average urban zip code with 7,000 families there are, on average, twenty carrier routes. When clustering attempts to utilize enumeration districts or subblocks, the data may be valid, but few lists, if any, can be tapped this way. Compilers of major consumer files, however, are now able to cluster down to enumeration districts and subblocks—as well as by carrier routes.

A Specialized Use of Zip Code Analysis

There is one simple penetration analysis that should be used by every school, every college, every giver of seminars, every large retailer, every retail mall, and every other activity in which patrons are drawn from a relatively limited local radius. This analysis only requires a *count* of customers by five-digit zip codes. This can then be compared with the number of households in each zip code to determine the ratio (the penetration) of customers.

Nonprofit membership operations (symphonies, ballet, theater, dance) can *all* profit by determining penetration by zip code in their area. (Few of them have learned to do this and continue to mail to areas.) Fundraisers who wish to make a mark on their fundraising activities for membership and seat sale operations can easily double response with this tried-and-true method. The net result of this targeted marketing is higher total response from smaller total mailings.

One major college was mailing 300,000 pieces by three-digit zip codes in and near its campus. The ratio of students to this universe was 1 in 400. By comparing the enrollment by zip code, and selecting only those zip codes with the highest penetration, a ratio of one student for every ninety households was selected. The same 300,000 mailing, this time targeted to the most fruitful zip codes, resulted in a response rate almost four times as great to a comparable offer of a course catalog. Costs per response dropped from $24 to $6 each!

Penetration by Carrier Routes

Where a customer penetration analysis for a local institution has been provided by zip code and has shown marked improvement, up to several hundred percent, the next analytic step is to look "inside" zip codes to penetration by carrier routes. Where there is some concentration within carrier routes, such a study is valid. Usually the concentration is sparse, and improvements, above using the best zip codes, will be far less than those obtained from simply selecting zip codes with the highest penetration. However, the modest improvement made by carrier-route penetration may still be very significant.

How to Analyze Carrier Routes

Carrier routes may be analyzed by type, zip code, city, or even individually. The number of households for an individual carrier route (about 350) makes individual analysis too pointilistic in most cases for the trouble involved. However when a customer file is carrier-route coded, the fact that records are found in some routes and not in others may be significant in the choice of routes to mail to. On a simpler basis some mailers choose only those carrier routes where one or more correct records have been established. The types of carrier routes and their quantities are:

City delivery	135,000 (This can be further broken down by size of city.)
Rural routes	75,000
Post office boxes	144,000
Highway contractors	8,000

Mailers are discovering some interesting response data based on carrier routes. Perhaps the one of most importance is that of a mailing split into three streams (qualified for carrier-route discount, qualified for five-digit discount, and residue) those which can be mailed qualified for carrier-route discount seem to produce more than the other two segments. This may be because the delivery is better.

A more direct route to the mailbox is used since carrier-route qualified mail is delivered directly to the carrier for his or her sortation and delivery, bypassing many postal handlings of nonqualified mail. In time, nine-digit coded mail will likely prove more productive than mail not so qualified, due to better delivery.

If selection can be made in any of twenty carrier routes within a zip code rather than to take either the entire zip code, haphazardly or dropping it entirely, then selection can be improved. Along with improved selection, response also can be improved. The main concern then becomes how difficult is it to select by carrier routes. It is not very difficult because a list from multiple inputs can be carrier-route coded for $2/M or less. The real concern then becomes how carrier-route "selection" (not coding) can be accomplished. If the desired file is one of the mass-compiled business or consumer files that make output available by carrier routes, all that needs to be placed on the order is the series of codes for the routes or provision of a tape with these routes encoded.

For a mail order list or a group of lists that have been merged and are unduplicated, an encoded tape can be used to split the file into two parts; those that match the encoded carrier route tape and those that do not. Mailing of both lists, separately coded, will determine the differential, if any. If the differential is 10 percent or more, which is usually the result, the mailer is in a position to offer to pay for all records from a mail order list pulled by his or her selection of carrier routes. This is not a perfect solution but at least it is worth investigating.

A few major statistically based services bypass carrier routes because they change, and rely instead on the more immutable subblocks and enumeration districts redefined in each decennial census. Their argument is that if carrier route cells of 350 families are better than census tract cells of 1,000 or zip code cells averaging 4,000 then would not cells of 140 be better than cells of 350? Although this seems logical you must consider that only about twenty lists today are coded to the block group, and the cost to code is initiating a cooperative venture to split costs among a few dozen more. A few censuses ago only four services in America coded lists to identify the geographic limits of each of approximately 400,000 districts: Donnelley, Metromail, Data Base America, and Polk. The cost then was so great that these services performed the process cooperatively and each now has its own coded file. There is little likelihood that this "better way" will topple carrier route from its destiny as the one best way to go.

Carrier routes do not change for mailers except for twice a year when a new CRIS (Carrier Route Coding) tape is issued. The routes analyzed are correct for now, and they are reasonably comparable with those of last year. The CRIS tapes are the last word on carrier route makeup according to the USPS, and those mailers who use handwritten flyers before they are issued in the new tape to change their codes, run the risk of increasing their undeliverable rate.

The nine-digit zip code, with over twenty million segments, will never develop any marketwise data for a file that has one-fourth as many block faces as the country has families. Nine-digit zip code may slowly make its way through very large businesses with very large and repetitive first class volumes but it is not going to add an overlay that will help mailers market better. Will it be tried? Absolutely but my advice to all but the largest mailers is do not invest in the programs until you are certain there is a cost-benefit for you, not just for the postal service.

THE TWO-STEP PROMOTION PROCESS AND HOW IT WORKS

Perhaps without pointing it out we have covered a special form of the two-step promotion process in the analysis on conversion of a catalog request to a first-time buyer and the mathematics of getting a first-time buyer to become a multiple customer. The term *two-step* as a promotion process however, is usually used to describe the process of having respondents identify their interest in a proposition by requesting some information promised in the offer. This can be anything from a piece of literature to a booklet or a full-fledged business proposition. The initial response is referred to as a "lead," and there are two separate sets of costs and two separate rates of return to consider.

The first cost is the cost to "buy" the lead. Irrespective of the number of "leads" developed by a given space ad or mailing, there is a cost per lead which involves the total cost of the particular promotion divided by the number of responses or leads obtained. However, leads are not sales. There must then be a conversion process in which the leads obtained are first serviced with the initial fulfillment package and then promoted. Since the cost to obtain a sale is the only true measure of success or failure, every cost, including the cost of the lead, the cost of fulfillment, the cost of promotion, and the cost of collection must be accounted for. Leads that are unqualified but very low in initial cost may in reality be very expensive indeed. For example, bingo card requests can be very misleading in this regard. A magazine may deliver a host of such requests, in connection with an ad which may turn out to be primarily from curiosity seekers. You add bingo card requests to your regular list for multiple solicitations at your own risk. It is *not* unusual for such requests to fail even on a first mailing.

Qualifying catalog requests by obtaining a token payment is usually satisfactory. However, low-cost and small wares catalogs, even qualified by a payment of 25¢ or 50¢ may not convert successfully. Qualified by a $1.00 payment, such requests are well worth having. (A problem with this approach may be the cost to buy the request in the first place.)

Catalog requests received from keyed space advertisements for a product or group of products in the catalog itself are typically golden. Conversion is almost always several times the response rate to prospect lists. Often such conversion is higher than almost any other source second only to a bounce-back catalog placed in the outgoing package conveying an order to a customer. (That "bounceback" is a must; response to bounce back offers is remarkably high.)

The simplistic two-step process first involves delivery of the requested information, a reproduction of an ad, a copy of a poster, a copy of a survey, or a booklet on a given subject. If the process stops here, it should be considered advertising, not direct marketing.

In the world of promotion, delivery of the requested data is simply the first step in a selling process in which the recipient is repeatedly requested to send in his or her order. Just as in a renewal service for a magazine subscription, there may be an entire series of mailings, each of which offers a bit more and promises a bit more in an attempt to convert. If the potential sale is large enough, at some point the lead may be followed by a phone call.

Once a sale is recorded there may be a need for several mailings in order to obtain the balance due on the sale. This emphasizes that the *cost* of such an operation must include not only the original cost of the inquiry but also all costs of subsequent efforts to get a conversion and complete the transaction through receipt of the full or final payment.

Costing must reflect the *total cost-per-paid order*. The value of the initial request for data will not be known until the conversion process is complete. Thus high initial response but low conversion may easily be less cost effective than a modest initial response and better conversion. For example, take a look at the following figures:

	Number of inquiries	Cost of inquiry	Total cost	Conversion Percentage	Conversion Number	Conversion cost per M	Total cost per M	Cost-per-paid order
A	1,000	$4.50	$4,500	6%	60	$3,000	$7,500	$128
B	1,000	$9.30	$9,300	12%	120	$2,500	$11,800	$98

On first glance, it would seem that A, which produces initial requests at less than half the cost of B will be well ahead. But after the conversion process (in this case, a set of six mailings) the differential per paid order is over 25 percent in favor of B. Note one thing more in particular. The very modest cost to buy inquiries escalates into a rather impressive cost-per-paid order.

LEAD PROCESSING PROCEDURES

This section is not a review of the methodology of lead processing. Rather it is a brief discussion of how the list business is involved in the two-step process of servicing leads. Lists are used to produce leads; the production of leads produces lists.

Most leads are of individuals who have identified themselves as interested in a given offer. The indentification is in the form of a request for literature, a directory, or a booklet. The same basic methodology is used by many mailers to generate requests for mail order catalogs. For example, not long ago, a major manufacturer of peripheral computer equipment offered its new personal-computing catalog in space ads and by direct mail. From the requests it built a list for a new catalog. The responses initially serviced by delivery of the requested catalog were retained for future use.

All lead processing incorporates at least two reports for management—one at each end of the process. If sales are involved, there is always a sales report. At the start of the process, in order to get a base by source there is an effort-key report. Most keying of lead advertising is done with a few digits or characters. The program that edits the data and produces the effort-key report can easily use a transposition table to identify the following:

1. Type of media
2. Medium within that media
3. Offer
4. Insert (or mailing) date
5. Fulfillment package
6. Date of the fulfillment

The effort-key report provides a cost per inquiry, such as phone versus mail, by individual key. With the keyed lead as a base, further reports are produced on the cost per forwarded lead, the cost per sale, and the percentage of response (if this is measurable).

Consumer versus Business Leads

Generation of consumer leads encompasses such efforts as leads for encyclopedia sales, home repair sales, solar energy units, family insurance, personal loans, children's photographs and portraits, and self improvement books. The person who influences the response if there is one, is a member of the family. The product or service purchased is for the benefit of the individual or the family and is paid for by the individual, not by his or her employer. Two-step consumer leads can range from a $300 set of books up to a multi-thousand dollar contract, say for home repair.

Generation for business leads differs from consumer leads in that the product or service is for the benefit of the establishment and is paid for from company funds. Such leads are usually for items with high price tags. Many a $100,000 to $300,000 computer installation has resulted from providing proper sales attention to some person at a business who has "raised his or her hand" to show his or her interest in a given product line. Because of the higher cost of some offers, conversions of business leads often require presentations to several executives involved in the decision process. The size of the ultimate sale and the order margin represented by such a sale make each business lead, which can be qualified, a very valuable piece of information. Most of what follows deals primarily with business leads.

Some of the most sophisticated mailers in the country control production of leads on a planned basis to fit the market and to fit the sales force available to serve that market. These companies work by numbers. They first determine how many leads they want per salesperson per week. They then determine the response rate. The mail flow is set to produce, within given limits, exactly the number of leads derived. For example, if there are one hundred salespeople to be provided with six leads per week for forty nine weeks, that calls for production of 30,000 leads. (In quantities like this, the lead will, out of necessity, have to be a "loose" lead, not a "tight" lead in which almost every name is a logical prospect to buy.) If the response rate is 2 percent (twenty leads per 1000 pieces in the mail) this calls for rental or use of 1.5 million names. Mailings can be made weekly or biweekly, and a flow can be maintained for the field.

The system of producing leads to serve a widespread sales force works well overall but only if the sales force is distributed where the market is. In many sales organizations, distribution is by city area. For example, a branch in Keokuk, Iowa may have one salesperson, while a branch in Cincinnati, Ohio may have two salespeople. There may be six salespeople in a metropolitan New York branch. This skew in sales force distribution almost inevitably leads to an attempt to skew the mailing to match. There have been many campaigns in which 1,000 mailings have been allocated per month, per salesperson, whereby in smaller towns every logical prospect gets mailed to twelve times in the course of a year and responses in such areas go from very little to nil. If at all possible, the mailings for leads should follow the market.

Servicing Leads

In many lead programs, the value of the sale makes it imperative that each lead be serviced not only once, but several times. In effect, multiple mailings to acquire leads result in a string of mailings—something like a string of firecrackers where each one is timed to provide some sales impetus after a given programmed interval. The handling of such intermittent mailings, in which one group is getting Letter 2, while another is getting Letter 3, requires highly efficient computer control. To control multiple mailings, it is mandatory that lead mailings be controlled through a central point.

Lead production and the Great Name Drain go hand in hand at many companies. Companies will spend thousands of dollars in advertising to get leads, and then take two or three weeks to answer them, or manage some way not to answer them at all. If each lead has cost $5 to $10, this is not only a name drain but a good sized financial loss as well.

Probably the major sin in the lead business, and another form of the Great Name Drain, is to fail to remail leads that did not result in immediate sales. A lead that may have cost $15 may represent a possible prospect for a $2,000 sale with an order or gross margin of 40 percent. That lead may be mailed only once at a cost of, say, $2.00. With an order margin of $800 and a cost for remailing of, say, $1/unit, any remailing that can produce one or more sales per 1,000 remailed pieces can be very valuable. If the second mailing produces five orders per 1,000, then the balance should be mailed and mailed again until it is no longer economical.

Qualifying and Reviewing Leads

Leads should be profiled and qualified almost in the same way that a customer list should be profiled. For a business list this means reviewing:

1. SIC by two-digit at least or four-digit if the numbers warrant
2. Size of company
3. Geographic location
4. Availability of a telephone number, especially if requested

What is ultimately required is a review of the profile of two lots of leads that will permit the comparison of the demographic pattern of those who have purchased with the pattern of those that have shown interest but have not purchased.

When a two-step promotion process fails completely or fails to reach its promised return, the reason is almost invariably that the second step has been poorly handled. The follow-up to the typical request for information is a single packet of material, and if there is no response, the mailer gives up. This can be true irrespective of the cost to buy the inquiry in the first place. Those who use the two-step process *must* know how much they can afford to pay to convert the inquirer into a customer. Once this sum is known, then every effort should be made, as long as conversions stay at that cost or less, to convert the requests into sales. This means an entire campaign must be initiated, with results checked after each effort, much like what is done to renew a lapsed or lapsing subscriber. (For paid-for subscriptions the sum available is straightforward—it is any conversion which costs less than the cost to buy a new subscriber.) (On page 398 there is an important rule for another form of two-step: conversion of catalog inquiries, which in essence, says mail right away, then again promptly, then again soon. It is important on all two-step processes to follow-up the receipt of the inquiry immediately, and then start the balance of the campaign in motion right behind the first mailing.)

Lead Handling Suicide

A large number of catalog operations and other businesses obtaining requests and inquiries for later conversion now opt to hold requests until enough requests have been assembled to make a batch mailing at lower postal rates possible. This is a form of marketing suicide. The rapidity with which an inquiry or request tends to age, from high conversion potential at the outset to low and costly conversion months later, is a clarion call to handle *all* inquiries as quickly as possible—the same or next day if at all possible. Those who wait save pennies per piece and lose thousands of dollars in salable converted customers.

RESEARCH WHAT OTHERS DO

If you are contemplating a two-step promotion process, it is advisable to find out how other processes work by investigating different types of offers. Record the date of your request and the date of the initial fulfillment, and then keep and count the number of additional conversion attempts made. Some like Troybill, Warner Electric, and several agent solicitations utilize a series. Some will not even answer; others answer only once and then stop. Those that do not answer deserve the fate they get, which is *nothing*. Those that answer only once usually do not stay around long. With just a whiff of mathematics, winners can be sifted from losers.

TWELVE STEPS TO A THOROUGH INQUIRY FOLLOW-UP SYSTEM

The steps listed here cover only the handling of the requests: These steps omit all the creative effort required to determine sales strategy, copy, media, development of the essential fulfillment package, questionnaires, distribution forms, and letters and follow-up promotion and premiums. They only hint at the computer requirements to capture and control the data flow on a programmed basis. Few companies will be able to do all that is indicated in this list mainly because of cost. But those companies working for high-priced sales will find this an ideal way to wring out every last order. These steps provide some indication of the importance of follow-up as the one way to make the initial purchase of the leads worthwhile.

1. Capture data for computerized control, including key data by media and medium.

2. Fulfill the initial request within 48 hours of receipt of the phone or mail request.

3. Forward those requests that specifically stipulate they wish to have a sales representative call to make an appointment to field representatives, and sales management.

4. After waiting the proper time for delivery of fulfillment package, call all respondents who asked only for literature and qualify those who can be convinced to see a salesperson.

5. Forward additional qualified leads, with all data gleaned from qualification calls, to sales representatives and sales management. (Transmittal to the sales force should be through multiple-part forms that require feedback in a given period of time.)

6. After a given time period, send questionnaires to recipients who have requested individual attention in order to see if the assigned sales representatives have made the call. (If the representative has not, the call reverts back to the district and should be immediately assigned to another sales representative.)

7. Mail to those who have requested a sales call, as well as those who have not, a newsletter with a business response card (BRC) on a periodic schedule. Add free gifts or premiums as additional inducements on later invitations.

8. Forward those new requests flushed out by "servicing" inquiries with repeated mailings to field representatives.

9. Ascertain conversions through:

   a. responses to questionnaires

   b. matching sales against the inquiry file

10. Analyze individual mediums for prospective continuations based on:

    a. cost per response

    b. cost per conversion

11. Analyze sales production by salesperson

12. Continue mailings to literature requesters until cost to buy new salescall requests exceeds the predetermined maximum cost.

TRIAL OFFERS

The *trial offer* is a special form of the *two-step* promotion process. Like the two-step process the bottom line is determined by the relationship between the cost to buy (the "start") and the conversion. However, in trial offers the conversion is not to a sale but to a fullterm commitment for a subscription.

Cost per trial is determined by dividing the cost of each promotion by the number of starts. All costs, including costs of each effort to obtain conversion must be totaled to obtain the total cost of each order for each key. The number of efforts will tend to continue as long as the conversion response is profitable. The final cost per order will be an average cost based on the number of conversion promotions. These total costs should include telemarketing costs, costs of premiums, costs of free goods or longer terms—anything and everything expended to induce a conversion.

The Mathematics of Continuity Plans

The initial mathematics of solo mail, even catalog mailings, is straightforward: The number of sales per 1,000 pieces times the order margin is checked against the total promotion cost.

The mathematics of a continuity or club plan are much more complicated because profitability can only be measured on an ongoing basis. While the initial order in solo mail is extremely significant, in continuity programs data based on the initial order only can be mildly indicative at best, and in most cases such initial data can be disturbingly misleading.

The breakeven on a book sold through solo mail may come on the initial order or shortly thereafter. The breakeven on a typical book continuation or club plan may not be reached until the average "starter" purchases three, four, or five more selections. In practice, after a given new start has received and paid for the second and third shipment, several clubs then "load up" the buyer with a bulk shipment of the remaining volumes in the series. (By FTC rules, "load-up" shipments after a minimum completion order, must be spelled out in advance to the customer.) The buyer, who may have contracted to buy one book a month is then still obligated to pay unless he or she cancels, but may usually at his or her option, arrange to make monthly or bimonthly payments rather than one lump-sum payment. (The mailer, of course, hopes for and sometimes attempts to obtain the total balance due in one payment.)

Those mailers who use bulk shipments have found that returns and cancels from this abrupt shift in deliveries are ordinarily very modest and easily accommodated within the projected return on investment. Some invoices for "load ups" will not be paid and will have to be written off as a bad debt.

The management of a continuity program is also straightforward. Given a product that fits into the continuity formula of periodic delivery of a new unit against periodic payments from the buyer, the computer control of where in the series that buyer is, is also relatively simple.

What is not simple is the positioning of the continuity offer in the first place, which has a great deal to do with which lists, list segments, and other mediums when space advertising is used, will be productive. Among the questions to be answered by split tests are:

1. What price line should be established for each unit?
2. How generous should the initial offer be?
3. What part of the initial offer can be "free" goods?
4. What periodic interval should be offered?
5. Is the offer open-minded, or will only a fixed number of items be offered?

Analyzing a Continuity Program: Four Main Areas

The analysis of a continuity program involves four interrelated sets of information:

1. Information on media and promotion usage:
   a. Media
       medium
       description

    b. Offer
        with premium
        without premium

    c. Key

2. Information on promotional costs pertaining to initial enrollment

    a. Advertising production cost

    b. Media cost

    c. Premium cost (if any)

    d. Postage and handling

    e. Returns and allowances

3. Information on production of initial orders from promotion

    a. Gross number of orders per 1,000 pieces

    b. Gross number of orders per $1,000 of expenditures

4. Information on membership activity

    a. Length of active membership (number of cycles)

    b. Percent never canceled

    c. Percent canceled and reinstated

The analysis of a continuity program requires facts as to:

- Cost of the product
- Cost of a single unit of delivery
- Cost of bulk deliveries
- Cost of returns—single units
- Cost of returns—bulk lots
- Provision for bad debt
- Percent cancelled and not reinstated
- Gross sales never cancelled
- Gross sales cancelled and reinstated
- Net sales per member
- Bad debt per member
- Postage and handling

- Net income (loss) per start
- Net income (loss) per active member

As the table listing cost factors indicates, profit and loss for a continuity program, *after the conclusion of the program,* consists of accounting for costs—both direct costs created by sales and promotion costs that created these sales—compared with net sales. This is a "dodo bird" approach—looking at the program once all the evidence is in. The art in forecasting in this field is to project what is likely to happen when the program is just beginning. Typically, three projections, high, medium, and low, are analyzed. When even the high projection predicts a loss, it may be time to go back to the drawing board, or it may simply indicate that the given key is not a likely prospect for a continuation. When the projection on the low side indicates that profit is reasonably certain, that is similar to discerning from half life on a solo mailing that the key is a bona fide success early in the game.

Two Key Attrition Rates to Consider

The mathematics of a continuity program is concerned primarily with *attrition rates*. This term describes the rate and type of cancellations. There are two attrition rates to consider. The first measures the percentage of starters who pay for each shipment on time and continue with the program. The second measures what happens to all those who for one reason or another fall behind in payments and are temporarily suspended from receiving further shipments. As some of these starters pay up, the proportion of starters receiving each shipment gradually increases.

If a forecast is made based on only the first pattern, total sales will be understated. A forecast based on the results of combining totals for the first and second patterns will predict total sales but will not provide data as to when such sales will be made.

In the direct-mail business, forecasting sales and payments on the basis of early performance data from individual starting groups by effort-key is critical. Even more than for conventional solo direct mail or catalog sales, the decision to reinvest in media for a continuity offer depends on reading such early results correctly. Sales in a continuity program accumulate over the economic life of both kinds of starters, and that life can extend over many, many months or even several years. In these programs it is essential that the seller take into account the cost of money or the loss of opportunity cost incurred in carrying out the program over a protracted time.

NEGATIVE OPTION CLUBS

From the viewpoint of acquiring new members, negative option clubs and continuity programs are very close relatives. Both are used successfully for the sale of books and records; both use the same media, both result in a "starter" group, which was the result of a specific promotional effort. However, once the new member is acquired, the operation is radically different from a fulfillment point of view.

Negative option clubs must ask their members or subscribers for each cycle to respond and notify the seller of whether they wish to receive the next coming selection, or if they prefer to receive an alternate selection from a list provided, or if they do not want to receive any product at all.

The term *negative option* means that if the member takes no action, the shipment of the month or cycle is sent and billed automatically. (The FTC places stringent rules on the timeframes required to permit the member an opportunity to opt for no shipment, but poor mail delivery, delays, oversights, vacations, and other more pressing problems all work in favor of the publisher.)

The fulfillment systems for a negative option club are much more complicated than for a typical continuity plan or club. Each cycle must be announced, each response must be captured within the cycle life, each cycle must have a fixed cut-off date beyond which requests from members are treated as nonresponses: Each cycle triggers the issuance of labels for the automatic selection as well as for the far less numerous individual alternate requests. The payments for each cycle and one cycle on top of another provide a remarkable explosion of cells based on status. (From a forecast point of view, the seller must be able to forecast from acceptance rates—that of the featured negative option selection each cycle, as well as that of the alternate selections.) Despite this substantial difference in operation between continuity plans and the specialized continuity of sales reflected by a negative option plan, the economics of both are quite similar. In each, new members are acquired at a loss. In each, only through additional paid sales, can this cost of acquisition be amortized. In each, the measure of profitability is the relationship between the cost to acquire a new member and total yield in dollars over the economic life or *lifetime value* of that member. Like all other forms of direct response, profit ultimately comes down to this relationship.

HOW TO ORGANIZE DEALERIZED MARKETS

Some years ago, the cost of the average personal sales call on business and industrial firms was estimated at about $10. Today the cost of the average industrial personal sales call is over $200 and rising. Most companies paying these costs are now being forced to find some way to make every personal sales call worth this staggering expenditure. The best method used by leaders who sell to businesses has been to use direct mail. Direct mail usually has just one function—to elicit a response by mail that can be followed up by mail or by personal solicitation.

These companies buy a lead or inquiry from a live prospect for the item they are selling for a fraction of the cost of sending a salesperson out on a cold call. Direct mail, at 35¢ or so per unit, flushes out that small proportion of the total market most ready to buy and most ready to listen to the sales story on the given product. Salespeople, being human, eminently prefer to call on those interested and ready to buy. Direct mail, if properly used, gets these businesspeople to raise their hands and say, "Call on me. I'm interested. I have some need for what you have to sell."

Where a company distributes products and services for business through a dealer organization, such lead-building direct mail can be a potent force in getting more business for dealers—more business which not only makes the dealer more money but also serves to tie him or her closer to the parent company.*

Six Steps to Build Dealerized Leads in Direct Mail

The planning and creation of dealerized lead building direct mail is an art that involves such factors as:

1. How much of the story to tell by mail. If you tell too much your prospect may believe he or she has all the data necessary to make a decision—and decide not to ask for more information.

2. How qualified a lead is. If you wish only prospects who are ready for a demonstration, or specifically request they mark a box inviting a salesperson to call, you can dramatically reduce the number of leads per 1,000 pieces mailed.

3. Use of premiums as inducements to respond. If you make the premium too valuable, the prospect may feel there is something wrong with the product; if you do the opposite he or she may feel you are underrating his or her importance. Well selected business-connected premiums will produce good leads at lower cost than nonpremium offers. We all like something for nothing. But poorly selected premiums will add little but cost.

4. Dramatized offers. The use of sweepstakes, for example, has far from run its course in business mail. A well conceived, well promoted sweepstake can substantially increase valid leads at relatively modest additional cost.

*Consumers, of course, can be "dealerized" as well to reach local markets for a gas station, phone company, cable TV, and so on.

5. Creative copy, color, and graphics. The appearance of the mail salesperson and what that mail salesperson says affects results.

6. Timing. Except for a mid-summer lull, and the crush of mail and work at Christmas time, timing for most products and services is relatively insignificant in dealerized lead producing mailings to business.

Three Basic Premises for a Successful Mailing

To mail to businesses successfully and economically for and with dealers, there are three basic requisites:

1. Access to a universe consisting of all, or almost all classifications of business on one zip coded master file.

2. A realistic appraisal of what parts of the universe can be considered valid markets for the given product or service by classification, size, and area.

3. Computer competence to select, organize, and produce those customized mailing segments that embrace the desired business markets in dealerized sequence.

Since 1 and 3 above are the concern of your supplier, let us start with 2, where your knowledge and hopefully that of your list counsel permit you to identify two markets: the prime market, and peripheral markets.

It is advisable to be somewhat hesitant about both. What looks like the market in today's world is almost certainly only part of the market. What looks like the right list segments may turn out, in testing, to be somewhat less than that. There is one ideal way to find out—test. Response to a fair-sized test, carefully controlled by classification, size, and area, may well disclose immediately what is important and what is not.

It is also most advisable, irrespective of product or service, to "profile" your customer list to find out what kind of businesses (by SIC) you are selling to, and what penetration you already have reached within each of the major areas of sales. A knowledgeable list counsel can help you here by analyzing your customers by SIC against known universes—segmented universes, if need be, by size. You may, for example, have 5 percent of customers in food manufacturing plants, and 3 percent in chemical plants and believe food is your better category. But there are close to three times as many plants in all classes of foods as there are in all classes of chemicals so your penetration ratio is much more impressive, overall, in the latter.

From social security payments we know that the total number of employers plus self employed in the United States total close to 15 million. This breaks down as follows:

Farm operators and owners*	2,500,000
Institutions	1,500,000
Professional, self-employed	1,500,000
Business entities	4,500,000
Business at home	4,500,000

To provide something close to universal coverage, Data Base America and D&B make an unduplicated list available consisting of 8,000,000 business enterprises.

The use of a file of 4,700 classified phone directories provides a unified source for the balance of business not covered, or not properly covered by one of the major credit rating companies as well as complete coverage of all entities with phones in every professional class and virtually every institutional class (such as associations, churches, social service, clubs, fraternal orders, and labor).

After sorting this file of over 14,000,000 SIC records to remove duplication (to provide one address per phone number) it is filed in straight zip code sequence with the following coded information:

- SIC
- 5th Digit SIC—Over 3,400 additional classes heretofore buried in what SIC calls "N.E.C." or "not elsewhere classified." For example, 8,000 business machine retailers now have a pseudo-SIC, and can be selected out of a catch-all which formerly included over thirty other miscellaneous business-oriented retail classifications.
- Number of Employees
- County code

*Through the unique facilities of *Farm Journal,* the country's number 1 agricultural magazine, a list, called "Farmail" is available of virtually every farm owner and farm operator in the United States. This unique list includes individual data for each farmer as to total number of acres, cultivated acres, estimated dollars of gross farm income, and for over 1,000,000 records includes data on livestock and crop as well. This file can be dealerized and dealers can select which size farms and in which areas, to mail to. A number of major agricultural mailers use this file for dealerized sales of tractors, agricultural implements, seeds, fertilizers, pesticides, and agricultural chemicals. This list, dealerized or not, is available through list brokers.

- Branch/home office (where indicated)
- Corporation (where indicated)
- Zip code—three-digit and five-digit

From such a file we have available counts by SIC, rating, and state to provide initial data on the scope of market coverage.

Thirteen Steps to Establishing a Business Mail Campaign for Producing Dealerized Leads

Let us trace through the steps that need to be taken in establishing a business mail campaign to parts of this list to produce mail leads for a dealer organization. The following list presumes that the mail itself is to be imprinted for each dealer and that each participating dealer pays, at least in part, for the mail he or she opts to use.

1. We provide a deck of cards, per the marketing requirements of the customer—either a county deck (approximately 3,050) or a zip code deck (956 if three-digit zip code, many, many thousands if five-digit zip.)

2. The company (we hope!) sorts the cards into applicable markets covered by individual dealers, branches, distributors or sales territories. We suggest these be placed in sealed envelopes with a number assigned to each such lot. (Where the company elects to duck this job, the compiler will take it on—but it is best for this to be a user responsibility.)

3. We gang punch into each lot (and carefully verify) the assigned code for each dealer or assigned territory. (For split areas, carrier routes or AB splits are utilized to guard against duplication.)

4. The list segments—by SIC (classification), size (rating), and area (zip and/or county) required or desired for review, evaluation and *local* selection are selected off the master file.

5. Through relatively simple computer programming, the assigned dealer or territory codes are tagged on every record of the selected file.

6. This file is now sorted by dealer number and by zip code (or by county by zip code if so desired) which places the company-owned file in dealer sequence.

7. At this point, one of two "availability" books can be printed.

The most usual is a count program, showing the total selected universe by area (zip, city, or county as desired) by classification. Thus, dealer No. 21 might show in county A 573 records, split into twelve SIC classifications, one-half of which, perhaps, have 20 or more employees.

The second type of availability is both a listing of the actual records, plus a count. In this case, Dealer No. 21 would get 573 lines of address data, each with SIC, employee strength, county code, and zip code. Where desired, these data can be ordered within county, or zip area, or for the dealer territory as a whole, in SIC sequence or alphabetic sequence. The elected sequence depends on the use to which the data is to be put.

If the dealer is likely to opt by size rather than by area, or by classification rather than by size, the print out can be designed to make this relatively simple. Where we know the dealer will opt on an individual record basis (or a cut-off basis—all here, or all in this SIC, or all within a given county) we produce the "availability" listing with sequence numbers to expedite getting back to and using the selected records on the main file. (It is possible for dealers to add to records at this point, but the cost makes it quite unfavorable.)

8. The dealer then exercises his or her first option to participate at all, and if so, to what extent, and for what records. (We have learned the hard way to provide three copies of such files for opting—one to the dealer, one to the customer for control, and one at our control center for solving those who lose or misplace the original set.)

9. It is necessary to establish and maintain, hard and fast, a cut-off point for initial participation. (There are always some stragglers—and these cost more—and either they or the company must be prepared to pay tail-end costs.)

10. At the close of the cut-off period, we have all dealers in hand who have opted and their options. We now split the working file into two parts: the records to be run, and those selected, but not opted for run.

At this point, we can provide a count program to the customer both of opted records and unopted records. The unopted file can be used to reoffer to the dealers, or as often happens, to offer new territory to dealers who have already opted to pay for one area.

11. The labels (one, two, three, four sets as desired) are then run from the opted file in dealer, zip sequence—with sheet ejection, or space-skip between dealers. This provides stopping points on a continuous four-across form for the series of dealer imprint plates that can print in tandem with the application of the labels to the pieces or envelopes. At this point, if the dealers have been working from an availability count only, a copy of the list, for each dealer, in any given order, can be printed for each dealer for his own control and follow-up. (Obviously, a tape, in dealer order, can be provided for those who opt for direct addressing.)

12. Here come the tailenders—and again a firm cut-off point beyond NINO. These are now tagged to the unopted file and the desired records selected and printed in dealer order with sheet ejection or space skip between dealers.

13. If the program extends over a period of more than six months, it may prove practical to provide one or two updates to the company file prior to running the next set of labels. In this case, the original set of labels is produced with a unique identifying code or match code and all post office changes and kills are reflected in the opted company master file prior to running another set (or sets) of labels. (The telephone number, in reverse, is ideal for this use.)

As a general rule, this type of program is not set up unless the client and his or her dealers opt to mail a minimum of three times to the selected list segments. Four or six times per year is fairly typical.

In general, price overall per unit, on a several hundred thousand list that uses a well printed selfmailer with a return card, can be in the 22¢ to 24¢ per unit range. Smaller programs run somewhat higher, but unit costs utilizing multiple copy labels can be kept well within average prices paid for conventional business mailings.

A dealerized program, without requirement of dealer cost participation can be much simpler than the program outlined here. Any company can obtain approximate counts for a given pull by SIC, size and area, and order the labels, and mail and arrange to have all leads filter through headquarters to the dealer operation. Some programs mail for the dealer 1,000 names (or 1,000 names per salesperson) per period and bill the dealer or not. Such programs work well in large cities but not as well in smaller towns. Occasionally, a dealer initiates a local program with such success that the home office makes it available to the entire force.

To summarize, here are some of the variables that can be built into such dealer campaigns.

1. Overall company mailing for benefit of dealers with no participation in costs by dealers and no sorting by dealer or imprinting for dealers.
   a. Simple selection of list data, and purchase of 1, 2, or 3 sets of labels.
   b. Establishment of a set-up file for the company's use exclusively; provision for updating and cleaning; running of labels periodically at a lower cost.
2. Dealer participation—dealer option.
   a. Dealers provided availabilities of names and opt to mail all, part, or none.
   b. Dealers provided copies of names solicited or not.
   c. Dealers given option to edit records or not.

d. Dealers given option to join after cut-off or not.

e. Data delivered in zip code order, zip-county order, zip-SIC order, or zip-county-SIC-rating order as desired.

f. Data prepared for dealer—imprinting or not.

g. Reports to home office on opted and nonopted segments.

3. Data selected from universe of all business, professional and institutional names.

a. By SIC classification—over 1000 4-Digit SICs; over 3400 additional 5 digit classified headings.

b. By size number of employee ranges

c. By area (state, metro area, county, three-digit zip, five-digit zip)

4. Number of mailings—from one to a regular monthly campaign.

5. Cleaning and updating—from multiple sets of labels, with no updating, to regular changes in company file as master file changes as reflected on quarterly cycle.

6. Area of coverage—system can handle change in territorial alignment (on zip/county and carrier route within zip codes) such as adding new dealers, combining two territories.

From this list of variables, we can add the variations that such programs are likely to cost: Here are some benchmarks.

For a set-up file irrespective of quantity, classification, rating, or area	$60 to $100/M for 1-year use
Run charge	
all records	$8/M
selected records	$12/M
minimum run charge	$100
second set	$5/M
For a set-up file, sorted into dealer sequence	$60 to $80/M for 1-year use
Run charge	
all records	$8/M
selected records	$12/M
minimum charge	$100
second set	$5/M
Dealer copy	$5/M

For a fully dealerized program	
Programming and systems	$2500
Set up file and provide availability run	$20/M
Two sets of labels dealerized	
by option, records	
utilized only	$30/M
Additional sets	$5/M
Copy for dealers	$5/M

NEW WAYS OF WORKING WITH ZIP CODES

Zip Code Mapping

A number of companies can now provide zip code maps of areas, and then provide colors for each zip code on a computer screen. The color display can be controlled by any set of variables the user wishes. Almost all such uses start with a list. Some typical uses are:

- Population density for aid in retail store location
- Customer penetration for aid in retail store location
- Branch penetration comparisons
- Establishment of reasonable visual market potentials and quotas
- Location of all zip codes with a store of chain X
- Location of all zip codes with stores of both chains X and Y
- Number of outlets of a given classification per 1,000 population
- Location of students for a school or college
- Location of zips with dealers available for service and repair

The AMA now produces a new service for physicians called Market Area Profile (MAP) which is designed to help doctors decide where to establish their practices. This service lists and then maps all physicians and hospitals within a given radius of any point in the United States. The reports list physicians by address, specialties, age, and type of professional proficiency. The hospitals are listed by address with a detailed description of each as well as a profile of admissions, occupancy statistics, patient census, and profile of the medical staff. In addition each report provides a demographic profile of the area. A young obstetrician using this service for example can note the number of women of child-bearing age and locate areas where an older obstetrician may be preparing to retire.

Centroid Marketing

A *centroid* is the midpoint of a zip code as defined by its longitude and latitude. Once centroids have been calculated for each zip code, the distance between one centroid and any other centroid is a basic mathematical calculation based on the differences in longitude and latitude. Thus all zip codes within X miles of a given centroid on a map can be located in seconds so that primary and peripheral markets for any operation in a given zip code can be closely defined from a distance point of view.

By adding in population by zip code, families with an income level over $25,000 by zip code, or customers by zip code, counts can be provided for "rings" of zips around a given centroid. Such counts can of course be utilized for "dealerized" programs.

With a program that can identify all dealers of a given company by location, an inquirer can be directed to the closest dealer or dealers. The computer only needs to know the centroid to determine which name or names to provide.

(Note—mapping is now being done from specific points (of latitude and longitude) which can be anywhere within a zip code. Mileage maps can easily be plotted—and with the use of carrier routes or sub-blocks, mileage maps around a given point need not embrace total zip codes.)

PART II DIRECT-RESPONSE MEDIA (OTHER THAN DIRECT MAIL)

CLASSIFIED ADS FOR DIRECT RESPONSE

Perhaps the one method in direct response with the smallest downside risk is through the placement of ads in classified columns of magazines. Although copying what others are doing is anathema in direct mail, it is a logical way to start when beginning classified advertising. Carefully study those offers that are found repeatedly over and over again in magazines or Sunday newspapers. (Sunday newspapers have higher circulations, better readership, and longer lives than daily editions.) Make certain your offer is as good as, or better than, your competition.

The first rule to remember when placing an ad is that payment is based on a per-line or a per-word count. Every word must work, and work hard. Because the space is small and the copy so limited, classified advertising cannot be used successfully for products or service sales where the price rises much above $7.50. Small space ads, including classifieds, can however be used very successfully to develop inquiries as well as requests for booklets, information, samples, and catalogs.

The first word or phrase is critical. If you do not connect with the reader's need as he or she scans a column, the ad will fail. The address should be a street address, not a box number. Every ad must be keyed and every response must be logged. This method of advertising involves great detail and continuous record-keeping.

As in list testing, a single insertion tells very little—nothing more than what has happened to that ad in that issue of that publication. A given offer should be run in a minimum of three magazines simultaneously, and where the multiple rate is attractive, each ad should be run in each book three times. Just as responses to lists vary, so responses to classifieds vary by publication.

Success breeds success, which means classified advertising works best when there is a good-sized volume of classifieds and the publication has been able to develop a following by classification.

Classifieds are a good place to test copy for catalog and booklet requests. Classifieds are also a good way to get interested dealers and agents to write for more information.

THE MATHEMATICS OF RESPONSE ADVERTISING ON RADIO OR TV

All forms of response promotion are measured initially by the cost to acquire an order (CPO). The CPO based on radio advertising is calculated by dividing the total cost of the air time by the number of responses (leads, requests, or orders) generated and adding the cost of the answering service.

An expenditure of $500 on spot radio which generated 125 responses means each response cost $4. If an answering service is used and their charge is $1.25 for each response logged, the acquisition cost would be $5.25 per response. (As with direct mail or space ad purchases, the expenses of creating and producing commercials and the attendant follow-up and fulfillment costs are kept separate from the basic promotion cost which is used to calculate the CPO. These other costs must be taken into account when the program is finished.)

Cost per order covers only the promotion cost. It must be low enough to provide a reasonable R.O.I. as well as a rational margin for the costs connected with refused or returned CODs, pay up of any residual billing, and the cost of money for inventory and handling as well as for radio continuity. There also are factors beyond control, such as unusual weather, a local strike, or some local news that might alter conventional listening habits.

Direct mail and radio or TV both require copy and development of an offer. Both can seek a direct response. But the two media are widely divergent when it comes to the media buy. Mailing lists in general are relatively stable, but the cost of radio time varies by the length of the spot as well as by the time of day, the day itself, the time of year, and particularly by the market. Buying time for direct response must consider all of these variations. It is best to use an agency or time-buying service experienced in buying time for direct-response advertising.

In what some early viewers of TV may consider deja vu, a small group of entrepreneurs, selling business advice, are now successfully advertising one-half hour and one-hour educational programs on cable networks in the very early hours of the morning as a form of direct-response TV advertising.

There are very few people either involved with or not involved with television who believe that any hour program, at any time, could be commercially productive. But such is the power of TV. The propensity of a fair share of Americans staying up after midnight has also increased such off-time advertising.

Perhaps the leader in TV programming selling business advice is a well known business evangelist whose kits include a book on how to obtain low-cost loans from governments. His programs produce sales of kits at $350, books at $75 as well as inquiries for additional information on how to use the resources of government for personal aggrandizement. This unique evangelist is a powerful speaker who also offers free seminars to generate additional sales and inquiries for his growing customer database. The building of his audiences, city by city, is a finetuned combination of space advertising, positioning on local talk-radio and talk-TV shows, the local mailing of his growing file of inquirers and customers, plus the addition of selected real estate-oriented and opportunity-oriented mailing lists. Here the proportion of those who are mesmerized by the message to buy kits and books then and there, which is direct response *at the source,* is sufficient to provide a profit.

The bottom line for this type of operation is almost exactly like that of a direct-mail or space ad campaign. The total sales, less returns and cancellations, must cover all other costs (costs of travel, support staff, data processing, and order handling) plus the rather high cost of promotion before any profit is produced within each city. In fact each appearance (usually two or more per city) is like unto a separate "key" for a more conventional direct response-placement.

It should come as no surprise that each form of promotion is a key within a key as there is a need to know the cost to "buy" an attendant at each seminar, by each "effort" using each medium. Thus we are back to "effort-key" reporting, with multiple efforts being cumulated for each city just as much as multiple keys for a major mailing are cumulated for an overall reconciliation.

SPACE ADVERTISING

Most of what this book has to say about the analysis of space advertising is covered in two major sections titled Rules for Testing and Mathematics, in which results can be read for an ad that is substituted for the package placed in the mail for prospecting. A special section on how to time space ads in relation to variance in response starts on page 478. A special use of space ads, which is of great interest for mail responsiveness, is classified advertising, described on page 473.

Cooperative Catalog Request Programs

There is a number of programs appearing in nationwide mail media, magazines, newspapers, and credit card stuffers, which on a per-inquiry or per-order basis are providing dozens of catalog operations with requests through a variation of the bingo card offer. The respondents are shown a page of twenty to thirty "covers" of relatively well known catalogs, and are invited to send in requests, usually, for free copies of catalogs that interest them. The average number of catalogs requested is in the four to five range. The costs are quite modest, and the numbers can be quite alluring. As noted earlier, the easier it is to respond, the lower the level of value of that response. These requests are presold to the respondents at 25¢ to 50¢ each, which is very low by catalog operation standards. But the proof comes with the conversion to customer status. No one can predict in this field; the only way to find out if the offer will be successful is to buy a block of names and test with a conversion offer.

Magazine Split Runs

When a magazine can provide split runs of two, four, eight, or sixteen even separations of its circulation, a single meaningful test can include headline tests, offer tests, and premium tests. All splits are not equal. An AB split (or an ABCD split) provides a true representative sampling of the publication of both the subscriber and news stand. Unlike the split test, a 50/50 split simply means that half of the magazines delivered will carry ad "A," while the other half will carry ad "B." But there is no attempt to randomize each of the halves, so the test is flawed. Even worse but nevertheless used because it is inexpensive, is a regional or geographic split. One of the added problems such a test raises is the need to compare percentage response based on the actual circulation of the magazine. Comparison of counts by code provides the basic answer for Nth number or AB splits. The actual number of pieces delivered will vary depending upon region, in which case a simple count may be misleading. Magazine split runs serve in the same way as grids for testing more than one variable at the same time.

Space in the Catalogs of Others

A number of catalogs now accept advertising from direct mailers. (This, in some ways is an outgrowth of the move by suppliers to catalog operators of advertising allowances and preprinted sections for special accommodation in the catalogs of their customers.) This provides an opportunity to do spot promotion to lists of known mail order buyers.

Advertising from direct mailers has inevitably led to cooperative catalogs in which the costs are shared by a number of mailers. Some of these are mailed; others are given out on airlines. One co-op features short-form identical-size catalogs from six different business-to-business mailers in which each participant provides one-sixth of the list universe from his or her customer file for the mailout.

Perhaps the bellwether in this field is Bloomingdales, which in 1985, carried national advertising in its catalog for the first time. This shows that the emphasis is on national advertisers rather than in the mail order merchants, and the principal classifications displayed in catalogs are liquor, automobiles, perfumes, and cigarettes. It is not likely that space ads in the catalogs of others are economical for the advertiser or for the creator of the catalog. Like excess editorial matter, they do not improve the response rate.

Space Advertising Versus Direct Mail

Paul Bringe, who until his death a few years ago, wrote one of the most provocative newsletters on direct mail as a promotion piece for his copy service, once stated:

Generally you can multiply results by 12 when sending mail to the same people who have been exposed to your space ad. . . . This does not necessarily mean the mail will be successful, even if the space ad was. Figure your order per thousand circulation from the ad, multiply by 12 for mail results per thousand and you still may not have a going proposition. Cautious testing is the only way to be sure.

(True to his calling, Bringe wrote the above using one-syllable words 75 percent of the time.)

The Bringe ratio, described above, will vary depending upon product and market and underlines the fact that direct mail will, from any publication list, provide far greater response than any space ad can produce.

Catalog Request Promotion in Space Advertising by Size

Some advertisers believe that all space promotion used to obtain requests for catalogs should be done through small units. This can be the right answer if the catalog operation is well known. In fact the rule seems to be the better known the name the smaller the space needs to be to get requests at a satisfactory cost. The reverse seems to be true if the name is not too well known. In that case large space is required to provide a correct ambience to offer a catalog to those interested enough to mail a request. Later as the name gets better known in the media, tests can be run of reduced-size ads.

If your catalog specialty is covered by a column in the newspaper or magazine, use a small one- or two-column ad placed right next to the text. If there is a column running on a subject somewhat related to the specialty covered by the catalog, test a small space insertion adjacent to the text for whatever improvement such location will bring.

Timing of Space Advertising

As direct-mail catalogs can be used to sell such disparate products as garden supplies, computers, bathing suits, fishing gear, calendars, school supplies, and so on there can be no one set month or months that are best for advertising all of them.

If data are available for a year for dailies, weeklies, Sunday supplements, and monthlies by date (this means date of issue, not necessarily the cover date) it is highly desirable to produce an index (100 percent being recovery through order margin on sales of the cost of space) for *each* insertion arrayed by kind and date. (Profit or loss per order can be substituted for an index because the index only denotes whether the result was plus or minus and by how much.)

In addition, if space ads are used to generate some worthwhile catalog requests along with sales the average gross profit of such requests that can be converted on the first conversion effort should be calculated and factored in. (Monthly magazines are much more likely, per $1,000 of space advertising, to produce catalog inquiries than are weeklies or dailies.)

The following table, for example, shows median indexes for groups of monthly magazines based on production of new customers only, compared with those indexes adjusted for the value of catalog requests received at the same time from the same sources:

Date	Index Percent of new customer production	Index Percent of new customer production and value of catalog inquiries
Jan.	93%	105%
Feb.	84	108
March	120	128
April	95	115
May	78	89
June	116	119
July	115	125
Aug.	108	133
Sept.	125	143
Oct.	135	155
Nov.	240	242
Dec.	212	234

Note that the addition of credit for catalog inquiries changes the months of January, February, and April from minus (under 100 percent) to plus. Note also that July and August, rather sluggish months here for customer production, are quite productive when catalog request conversions are factored in. The progression from May through December is also noteworthy. Once index figures are produced in this manner it is essential that expenditures by month be compared with the index or profit per order as shown in the table on page 48.

Note that the expenditures in the table follow the conventional wisdom that June, July, and August are months to cut back. Production here indicates just the reverse. Expenditures and production are in close correlation in October. The bulge in November offers all kinds of opportunity if there are sufficient space media reaching the types of markets desired.

Production of customers from space as well as direct-mail solicitation can be

Expenditure for space compared with historical index–by month

	Index including catalog request conversion (Percentage)	Expenditures Monthly space for advertising	
		Dollars	Percent of average month
Jan.	105%	$ 41,000	150%
Feb.	108	28,000	95
March	128	35,000	120
April	115	26,000	90
May	89	14,000	48
June	119	12,000	41
July	125	20,000	69
Aug.	133	21,000	72
Sept.	143	39,000	134
Oct	155	43,000	148
Nov.	242	49,000	169
Dec.	174	26,000	90
		354,000	

Median percentage = 127   Average monthly expenditures = $29,250

Table 12.1

Variation by month and by quarter in production of catalog requests— from space ads and from catalogs.

Month	Weeklies and Dailies			Monthlies			Catalog Mailings		
	Requests	Expenditures (thousands of dollars)	Requests per $M expended	Requests	Expenditures (thousands of dollars)	Requests per $M expended	Requests	Expenditures (thousands of dollars)	Requests per $M expended
Jan.	1,100	$25	44 ⎫	7,400	$41	180 ⎫	6,050	$55	110 ⎫
Feb.	900	18	50 ⎬ = 41	6,100	28	220 ⎬ = 180	6,045	39	155 ⎬ = 123
March	550	20	28 ⎭	4,700	35	160 ⎭	2,835	27	105 ⎭
April	220	14	15 ⎫	1,080	26	45 ⎫	2,420	48	50 ⎫
May	190	10	19 ⎬ = 13	3,210	14	90 ⎬ = 65	1,830	41	45 ⎬ = 54
June	60	8	7 ⎭	700	12	60 ⎭	810	12	68 ⎭
July	410	13	31 ⎫	1,340	20	67 ⎫	1,232	22	56 ⎫
Aug.	405	17	24 ⎬ = 27	1,170	21	56 ⎬ = 56	1,680	40	42 ⎬ = 45
Sept.	610	23	26 ⎭	1,800	39	46 ⎭	2,090	55	38 ⎭
Oct.	610	29	23 ⎫	1,650	43	38 ⎫	3,075	75	47 ⎫
Nov.	620	36	17 ⎬ = 20	1,280	49	26 ⎬ = 24	2,640	110	24 ⎬ = 27
Dec.	300	14	21 ⎭	185	26	27 ⎭	315	21	15 ⎭

The seasonal averages are also indicative:

Requests per $M Expended

Quarterly	Weeklies	Monthlies	Catalogs
First quarter	41	187	123
Second quarter	13	65	54
Third quarter	27	56	45
Fourth quarter	20	24	27

481

increased substantially if results are reviewed by type of space and by week and month.

Most catalog operators simply tabulate new catalog requests by week or month, with occasional breakdowns by source key. That offers useful data of a homogenized form. It is far better to isolate each key for both new customers and inquiry production, and factor in the relation per $1,000 expended.

If such data are then combined by week or month by major source, as shown in Table 12–1 the variation in the production of such requests, by source, will in time provide a pattern of opportunity. The table indicates that it is far easier to induce catalog requests, along with orders, in the first months of the year than at any later time. This well may signal the operator to use more space early in the year to induce a higher production of useful and profitable catalog requests.

Increasing Response with Support Advertising

There is no doubt that a direct-mail campaign augmented by a schedule of TV or radio spots and designed to increase efficiency in obtaining direct responses will do better than direct mail only. The question is, does it pay? Exploring this unusual alliance establishes a few guidelines: Support advertising, which must be coordinated within the requisite timeframe, should only be used when the appeal is close to universal, where direct-mail coverage can be reasonably matched to the coverage of the station or stations used, and the schedule employed is intense enough to make a difference. (Radio and TV spot campaigns apparently have a "critical mass" syndrome. Too few spots placed sporadically apparently do not work well, and if the cost limits the schedule to a choice between a few choice spots or quite a few secondary spots, the latter is almost always more successful.)

Radio or TV support advertising draws attention to the primary medium, either space ads or direct mail. One practitioner aptly noted it is like a marching band announcing the coming of the circus. This form of advertising carries messages by an electronic media and does not try to give all the details of the offer, nor does it seek any action other than to ask the listener or viewer to be on the alert for the special offer coming soon in the local newspapers or to the mailbox.

How to Measure the Effect of Support Advertising

To measure the effect of support advertising, it is necessary to designate matched pairs of markets sufficiently removed from each other so that the only variable is support advertising in one, with no support in the other. The pair must be similar in size, region, current economic conditions, and essential market coverage, and cost per rating point by the selection stations. (The radio or TV commercial is a variable here, but by using three sets of paired markets, a reasonably fair test can be constructed to see if support advertising pays. In the example below, support advertising raises the cost per response by about 3 percent but increases total response dramatically by 86 percent. This greater percentage may make the support pattern preferable.)

	Market A (support $)	Market B (nonsupport)
Direct mail	$15,000	$15,000
Electronic medium	$13,500	0
Total promotion cost	$28,500	$15,000
Total responses	2,050	1,100
Cost per response	$13.90	$13.60

Coupon and Sample Mailings to Households

Almost all *national* couponing and a good part of market-by-market sampling are conducted by very large list owners or list compilers. The three lists usually tapped are: a phone/car registrant list, an augmented driver's license file, or an area wide occupant file. It is very rare for a local fulfillment house to get involved in this field.

The largest distributor delivering coupons by mail is the extremely successful Carol Wright organization which delivers coupons eight or nine times per year to 30 to 40 million families by name. A typical Carol Wright envelope will contain fifteen to twenty-five redeemable coupons, plus a few Donnelley-sponsored low-cost product offerings, and over recent time, a long questionnaire on brand and product usage. Data obtained here are tagged onto the Donnelley household file to provide a psychographic overlay to the demographics already on the file.

Two other major distributors of co-op mail, Advo and Harte Hanks, are also important in coupon delivery to homes. Their "marriage mail" cooperatives and shoppers are distributed to the large occupant lists, without the name of the individual householder, which each compiles and owns.

Local coupon books offering discounts at local retail and service establishments are usually small entrepreneurial affairs with distribution in the 10,000 to 20,000 range. The list is usually a stratified file of households by name, selected primarily for income, and perhaps single-family dwellings. "Welcome Wagon" type mailings to newcomers to an area are, in effect, local discount-coupon books mailings. Some firms have extended this service into multiple markets, even multiple states. The list used for this is some form of "new connect" to gas, or electric, or phone service in the area. It is interesting to note that Donnelley entered this field with a magazine called *New Connections* by using data on new connects from local phone companies. The phone companies (without ever disclosing the names to Donnelley) mailed out the books on a contractual basis within ten days of access to service. But Donnelley found, as many before them have, that the rigors of lining up suppliers with their discounts and coupons for the constant trickle of newcomers did not do enough for either the suppliers or for Donnelley, and Donnelley retired from the fray. It must be conceded they had a unique list! These same data began arriving in bits and pieces on the market in 1985 from individual phone companies. Phone companies are now starting co-op mailings to their current customer files. Such mailings are remarkably deliverable when compared to mailings over lists supplied by such major compilers as Donnelley, Polk, Data Base America, or Metromail.

CHAPTER 13

How to Use
Merge–Purge

WHY MERGE–PURGE?

There is one major advantage and a number of secondary advantages to a successful merge–purge operation. The main advantage is that by reducing or eliminating duplicates, the mailer can save money by reducing the number of pieces mailed. (And by arranging to pay for 85 percent of all the names given or for net names only, the initial rental cost of the list is reduced.) Secondary advantages include:

- Internal duplicates (within a given list) can be identified, removed, and their cost can be deducted.

- Recipients are not turned off by receiving two, three, or four identical pieces in the same mail.

- Multiple duplicates can be isolated and, under given conditions, mailed separately at some later date.

- By maintaining stat tabs of usage of a given list, say a magazine file from the prior year, those names already circulated once, even though a year ago, can be suppressed for the new mailing.

- By combining lists, enough names may be involved to justify adding carrier-route presort codes as part of the operation.

- By combining lists through merge–purge more mail will result that will qualify for postal discounts, carrier-route presort, five-digit zip code, three-digit zip code, and less, at the highest rate for what the USPS refers to as "residual."

- There are forms of "enhancement" that can be done at reasonable cost for one large merged unduplicated list, which are almost certain to prove uneconomical if done for each list individually. These enhancements, which can be read out list by list, as well as for the merged list as a whole, include:

  a. Adding of phone numbers
  b. Verifying of zip code numbers
  c. Verifying addresses and providing change of addresses
  d. Adding consumer demographic data (sex, age, income, car ownership)
  e. Identification of apartment numbers
  f. Adding business demographic data (SIC, number of employees, city size)
  g. Coding for zip codes, for 9 digit zip, for carrier routes

- There are also forms of "suppression" that can be performed at reasonable costs for one merged unduplicated list, which are almost certain to prove uneconomical if done for each list individually. These suppressions, which also can be read out list by list as well as for the merged list as a whole, include:

  a. Omission of mail preference names—those names that request through DMA that they receive no mail. This omission may save the cost of answering their letters if they complain to various federal authorities. (At the same time, if desired, those who request to be put on lists can be added.)
  b. Omission of bad payers and doubtful credit risks.
  c. Omission of change of addresses from known recent movers.

Types of Merge–Purge

There are two basis types of merge–purge: those involving households—that is, consumer names and addresses and those involving nonhouseholds—that is, covering businesses, institutions, and offices of professionals. This may involve home offices of businesses, branches, divisions, sales offices, conglomerates, executives by name, titles, functions, internal departments and more.

In addition, all merge–purge operations can be broken down into two functional types: unduplicated (conventional merge/purge) and creation of a data bank.

What works well enough for simple three-line "home" addresses of consumers is not at all good enough for the more complicated problems involved in a "business" list merge–purge. This is also true when it comes to the construction of a database.

Types of Duplication

Merge–purge, if done correctly, identifies three kinds of duplications:

1. Internal duplications (those found within the same list).
   a. Within the customer file
   b. Within a given prospect file
2. Duplication with the customer file (when the customer file is made one of the inputs, arrangements can be made with some list owners to credit charges for all names that duplicate the customer's own file).
3. Interduplication (those found between two or more of the new inputs used). All such records are multidupes.

HOW TO USE MERGE–PURGE RECORDS TO PREDICT FUTURE MAILING SUCCESSES

While it is uneconomic to mail duplicates unnecessarily, the duplication that exists among lists of a given concept and the basic customer file does have a very important economic plus if you are willing to study it.

The higher the duplication, the more likely the balance of a prospect list will produce a profit. Similarly, the lower the duplication, the lower the likelihood of success.

Two Levels of Duplication to Consider

Do not simply file and forget your merge–purge matrixes. Study them. Look for and record the following *two* duplication levels on your list usage cards:

Level 1—Duplication with your customer file This becomes more and more significant as your customer file grows. With a file of 100,000 or more it may be more significant as a predictor than total duplication.

Level 2—Total duplication This takes into account duplication found between prospect lists as well as between the prospect lists and your customer list.

How to Deal with "Near Misses"

Any fair sized schedule of list tests will produce a few winners, a group of "dogs" you will never even wish to test again, and a few "near misses" or marginal tests that almost, but not quite, measure up to the desired profit standards.

You have three options for near misses:

1. Forget them.
2. Go back for a second try—where the odds are you will pay for another test which will miss again.
3. Determine some way to improve the breed.

The practicality of using the predictability of duplication makes comparison possible, *before mailing* of whatever list segmentation is available: hot lines, sales-by-dollar ranges, giftees, credit card buyers, recent removals, multiple buyers and so on.

Using this type of prediction, which does not necessarily provide perfect correlation with success, you can with some certainty identify keys and even complete lists that should not be mailed. Even if you pay rental costs for these lists and do not mail, you are well ahead on the bottom line. The more you work with these valuable prediction measures the higher the proportion of successful tests will be.

It is good practice to pull out former reports on merge–purge which, unfortunately, too few in direct mail even look at, and see if there is a correlation between duplication with the customer file and response to the mailing made. (The reports *must* be of the allocation type, and not those that provide priorities to given lists.) It is likely that at a given percentage, say, 3, 5, 7, or 10 percent that such a proportion of duplication is virtually a guarantee of success for the mailing. Similarly, those lists that measure under 1 percent or under one-half of one percent duplication probably show up rather poorly on the mailings.

Once a successful correlation model showing duplication vs. mailing success can be developed for a particular offer, it makes rational "go–no go" decisions possible based on a set of historical facts. This can and should lead to a substantial increase in entering lists into a merge–purge by segments to use the duplication data to help evaluate each segment. If the list owner is made aware of the test nature of such segmentation, with its promise of a rollout on segments that work, he or she may answer positively to a petition for a negotiated price to have a crack at substantial future rentals.

DETERMINING HOW MUCH TIME YOU NEED FOR A SUCCESSFUL MERGE–PURGE

All too often mailers fail to provide enough time for their merge–purge service to do a complete and thorough job. In this case some late inputs never get in and the service must rush and cut back on the reviews necessary for control. Thus the job is often shortchanged.

In a merge–purge operation, the basic process starts when all inputs have been received, dumped, reviewed, and reformatted, and all questions concerning input such as location of name, title, coding, and so on have been satisfactorily answered. It is not uncommon for four, or five, or more weeks to go by in this fashion. (Our firm recently combined data from thirty separate insurance companies. It took almost $2\frac{1}{2}$ months to obtain the last two tapes.) *Suggestion:* Draw a PERT time diagram in reverse starting with your mail drop. For a business merge–purge, allocate three to four weeks; to obtain lists allocate five to six weeks. Order your lists at least two months prior to the date you would like to mail. For consumer mail order merge–purges, allow two to three weeks for processing and four to six weeks for list acquisition. For best results, have all the tapes with tape layouts, a tape dump, and a count, shipped to your own office so you know which laggards to get after. If you have the tapes delivered to your service bureau, that permits the service to review each one long before the last one arrives, which will save time in the long run. But make certain the service gives you daily reports on the receipt of each list, along with some idea of the count for each list received. You do not wish to find out when it's too late, that List A, scheduled for 60,000 homes has come in at 6,000 homes.

It rarely pays to go through the merge–purge process for a list that arrives after the cut-off date. Either cancel or mail the list separately.

Your merge–purge specialist is entitled to extra recompense if he or she adds carrier routes, splits out multibuyers, or prepares the mailing tapes or labels for a three-tier mailing. These costs should be spelled out beforehand, however, so there are no surprises. Occasionally, some records will come in late or so badly organized that extra time and care must be taken. You will need to have faith in the integrity of your merge–purge house, which wishes to work with you in the future.

HOW TO CHECK THE RESULTS OF A MERGE–PURGE

You should always check the results of a merge–purge. You should look for the following criteria in a merge–purge review:

1. A good sampling of all of the matched pairs resulting in the killing of one or more records identified as dupes.

2. If your customer file is sacrosanct, proof that every (unduplicated) name in your customer file has survived.

3. A fair-sized block perhaps, a small state or four or five contiguous fair-sized three-digit zip areas, to see what duplication you can spot, including dupes which show up in two different zip codes, in other words, data you would have preferred be left out.

Some care must be taken in your review. What instructions did you give your service—to overkill (leaving as few dupes as humanly possible), or underkill (leaving as many even questionable dupes as necessary to ensure mailing the largest number of good records)? If done correctly, and to your order, you should be able to recognize that your instructions have been followed.

You may find some odd abberation such as a record or two that should not have survived but somehow did. (Remember your eyes, and the eagle eyes of clerical workers who update files by hand, represent by far the best computer in the world, far better at making value judgments than any machine, no matter who has programmed it.) Look at the percentage of names that are suspect, and see if you are down to 1 percent or one-half of 1 percent or less which may be the limit you can expect with the files you have provided.

You should be rigorous in your review but aware of the fallibility of machines (and human beings) in getting out the very last possible bit of duplication involved. It *never* pays to try and attain perfection.

HOW TO CHOOSE A MERGE–PURGE SERVICE

When it comes to consumer names, your choice of merge–purge services is wide. It is still best to work with a firm that has a proven track record in this field, has handled multimillion name merges, has no difficulty in providing you with input data and output data by source code. Be sure of one thing: Do not attempt to teach a new service how to do merge–purge!

On the surface your options might appear just as broad for business merge–purge but unless the firm you select has spent the requisite time to wrestle with the complexities of four- and five-line business merge–purge it is likely you will pay for something that cannot be delivered. The main thrust of this chapter has been to explain why business merge–purge is an entirely different animal from consumer merge–purge, and it must be handled differently. As a starting point you might find out which service firms are large business mailers, particularly large business magazine and directory publishers, prefer for their merge–purge efforts. Your service certainly can provide a list of current customers whom you can and *should* check. Your service certainly also can provide you with samples of duplicate identification, and a copy of their standard merge–purge report.

Your service may be able to show you how it is possible insofar as data bank building is concerned, (D&B versus S&P for example) to have the same name, phone number, address, executives, and even the same titles, but two different zip codes. When this happens, some firms simply forget it as it is too costly to solve even though every other name may be a definite duplicate, but one that will not show in a list in zip code order. The correct procedure is to rip out both, check the zip code, and reinsert the right block of names.

WHEN IT PAYS AND DOES NOT PAY TO MERGE–PURGE

When measuring response to a direct-mail effort, experts will unequivocally state there are only two kinds of lists, those that work and those that don't. The same is true of merge–purge. There are some uses of multiple lists where it does not pay to consider merge–purge.

Typically, a program involving ten, fifteen, or twenty tests of 5,000 names each falls into this category. With names spread at random over 35,000 different zip codes and 400,000 census enumeration districts, the probability of duplication is remarkably small—something under $\frac{1}{2}$ percent unless the data are skewed to sample only one area or one state. Such tests can be kept unduplicated even more certainly by selecting samples based on fourth- and fifth-digits of the zip code.

Where a customer file of, say, 80,000 names is to be mailed, and two test lots of 5,000 each of competitive files are planned, the duplication may be as high as 2 to 3 percent of the 80,000. The cost to avoid this may be uneconomical.

If less than 50,000 names are encompassed by a merge–purge, unless it is a dense business grouping, it is likely the cost to do the job will be more than the saving. Even if it is not, the loss in time and effort will probably not justify the effort.

Some uses of multiple lists where it is essential that merge–purge be performed occur when:

1. A mailer uses a minimum of 100,000 names beyond his or her house list from a number of lists, and the lists are compatible from a psychographic profile. Since upwards of 20,000 of the rented names are likely to be duplicates, the savings are easy to calculate.

2. A mailer is mailing a single competitive file along with his or her house list which is at least 25 percent or more as large as the house list. (This is a case where the duplication factor is almost certain to exceed 5 percent.) The house list in this case must consist of 75,000 or more names to justify the effort.

3. A mailer wishes to mail several hundred thousand names, omitting the customer file. (For example, a magazine that wishes to offer a half-price offer to new subscribers only.)

4. A mailer wishes to identify multiple "hits" and mail the unique records first, and then follow up with selections from the multiple file.

5. A mailer, even in a small area, say a TV station seeking donors, must use many small, even minuscule lists, with known high duplication. Merge–purge here still pays out handsomely even including the higher cost for small list segments.

A few rules to remember when using merge–purge are:

1. The higher the cost of the package in the mail, the lower the percentage of duplication required to be economic.

2. Catalog operators, with higher than average costs in the mail, both consumer- as well as business-oriented, should use merge–purge even at breakeven. The result of multiple catalogs in a single mail is detrimental to response.

3. When in doubt, check with your list broker, who knows a good deal about the makeup of the lists you have chosen. However, be sure not to rent two lists under different descriptions, which cover essentially the same audience. Such duplicate costs often show up in merge–purges involving compiled names or similar magazine files.

Merge–Purge Costs to Consider

Costs of merge–purge include:

1. Handling and reformatting of input. The more inputs you have, the higher the cost will be.

2. The merge-identification and merge–purge run or runs. This ordinarily bears a minimum charge against a cost per thousand records handled. Note this is records handled, not records actually used. A merge–purge con-

sisting of 1,200,000 records may result in a mailing of only 900,000. The merge–purge operation applies to the 1,200,000 handled.

3. The production of the output—keyed labels or tapes in zip code sequence, with counts by source, both in and out, as well as multiple hits, providing for a payment record based on usage to list suppliers.

The merge–purge operation, depending on inputs and size, will run from approximately $3.50 to $10.00/M records *inputted* for a consumer mailing, and from $8.50 to $15.00/M for a business mailing. As an example, we will use midpoints of $6.75/M for consumer, $11.75/M for business and assume a 20 percent reduction in count. The cost per M mailed rises to $8.10/M for consumers and $14.10/M for business.

If the package in the mail costs	Breakeven will be at a saving of	
	Consumer	**Business**
$200/M	4.0%	5.9%
250/M	3.2	4.7
300/M	2.7	3.9
350/M	2.3	3.4
400/M	2.0	2.9
500/M	1.6	2.4

It should be noted how small a percentage of duplication needs to be identified to pay off in direct mail. It is not unusual to find 10, 15, or 20 percent duplication in merge–purges. Saving, say, 10 percent of a $500 package, or $50/M, is like picking up gold coins in the street.

The true cost of a list that undergoes merge–purge is the total price you pay for the rental divided by the number of names that are mailed. If a $50/M list shows a 25 percent duplication, the cost *in the mail* is not $50/M, but $50 divided by 75 percent, or $66.67/M.

If the owner of the $50/M list in the example agrees to a 15 percent net name agreement, in which you pay for 85 percent of the names irrespective of how many you mail, the cost *in the mail* is reduced. But the list in this example still costs more than the initial rental price. The figures here are:

$$\$50 \text{ at } 85\% = \$42.50 \div 75\% = \$56.67/M$$

MERGE–PURGE TECHNIQUES FOR THE BUSINESS MAILER*

The merge–purge of business names and addresses (with four or more lines of information) is *substantially* more difficult to handle than identifying duplication among three-line consumer names and addresses. Since the processes of unduplicating and merging several lists for a single mailing, and unduplicating and matching records to create a database, *are two separate and distinct functions,* each requires decidedly different handling and criteria to perform its function efficiently.

For a single mailing, it is often acceptable to unduplicate lists in such a way that the program will net out to a minimal number of residual duplicates, though this is often accomplished at the expense of losing good, effective names through "overkilling."

Such a technique is unacceptable when it comes to building a database. A database, by definition, requires *all records* to be retained and identified. The need here is to create effective control of all data, so that information available in a record coming from one source file can be matched to records coming from other source files. In this way, demographic data and other pertinent information can be applied to the resultant records forming an information base that has real meaning for the future.

In the best of all possible worlds, the creation of such a database would proceed in an orderly and logical manner. Unfortunately for computer programmers, much source information arrives in a very "undisciplined" manner, and this is especially true of business files. It is, for example, not unusual to receive data with no demographic information whatsoever, or with demographic data put together in such a way that it is not identified in a usable form.

Here is a partial listing of the problems too often encountered by programmers:

1. Individuals' names are often intermixed with company names. Fields are often switched in random fashion.

2. Sometimes there are no individual names at all.

3. Sometimes there's a title in the name field either with or without an accompanying name.

4. Sometimes the company record is associated with the division; other times not.

5. Sometimes only the division, instead of the company, is given.

Paul A. Goldner, President PAGEX Systems, Inc.

6. Sometimes all that is given is a job function. (Response lists in particular, provide all kinds of combinations of undisciplined information. Even purchase order numbers and related instructions can be found in the "name" or "company" fields.)

Such undisciplined data require extensive, and often expensive, research to resolve. Sometimes the needed information is not even "findable."

Consumer Merge–Purge Techniques for Business Files Spell Trouble!

Just as every mailing and every list is different—so, too, is every merge–purge. At least it should be! Unfortunately, many mailers use only one data processing shop, and most shops (no matter what their ads promise!) are only able to apply *consumer* merge–purge techniques to the business merge–purge function. (This is all well and good if you don't mind costly duplication, and the elimination of many good records that such single-pass matching on the individual name invariably brings!)

Let's take a closer look at merge–purge variants.

Most consumers use a single "version" of their address, and a single zip code—no matter how often they fill out a form. The name, however, may change dramatically from initials and abbreviations, to fully spelled-out first names and even "Mr. and Mrs." combinations. Women, in particular, will often interchange their own first name with that of their husband. The last name, however, remains pretty uniform—except for spelling errors.

Business, on the other hand, makes life much more complicated. Most businesses have multiple trade names, numerous variations on each, divisions or pseudodivisions and abbreviations galore.

Business *response* lists, created by direct response, or stemming from industrial catalog sales operations, are particularly prone to variation and undisciplined data capture. Such lists are the result of an order processing function. The order processing function is purely and simply to accomplish the following:

- Record the order
- Record the sale
- Handle the payment
- Process the lines of the order through

This function, quite properly, is concerned with getting the goods to the customer, and recording the transaction. There is no particular concern over the fact that a designated "name field" ends up reading, "Please refer to purchase order number 1234" or "Direct all deliveries to Receiving Department."

When such phrases do show up, the average merge–purge program begins to "stutter" in such a way that it is almost impossible to use the records.

The typical consumer merge–purge "package," offered by the majority of data processing shops, cannot handle undisciplined data effectively. Consumer merge–purge programs *match by individual name on a single pass*, leaving in costly duplication, and killing many good, unique records of vital importance to a business file. Such consumer programs never "look" at the company or divisional field and only occasionally "look" at the individual address. All work only within a zip code. The result is that anyone with the same name or a similar last name, sometimes with or without the same first initial, will be "killed." (Figure 13.1)

The "Killing" of Corporate America

When it comes to the executive staff within a firm, complications abound. Corporate America is first and foremost a family affair—even among the largest companies in the country—and family-oriented enterprises are badly mangled by the typical consumer merge–purge program.

The General Tires of this world are populated by a whole passel of O'Neill's; the Jonathan Logans are populated by a multitude of divisions. Within each division there are many Schwartz's—and so it goes throughout the world of business. In fact, 44 percent of this country's largest companies have two or more operative executives with the same last name.

Corporate America is reminiscent of that famous refrain from a Gilbert and Sullivan operetta, ". . . all his sisters and his cousins, and his aunts (and he's got them by the dozens)." Therefore, to be effective, a merge–purge program for a business file must take into consideration the *full name* of the individual, his suffix, junior, senior, and so on, his or her title, and, in many cases, his or her initial or middle name as well.

It is not uncommon to find that the chairperson of the board, or chief operating officer is Robert *A.* Jones, while his son, who is the president or the sales manager, or the treasurer, or holds some other important position, is Robert *B.* Jones, or Robert A. Jones, *Jr.*, or even Robert A. Jones, *III*.

It may be that the wife of Robert A. Jones is also working there. She's the corporate secretary, and she's Mrs. Robert A. Jones, so the sex code, if available, is another important piece of information if the merge–purge is to do an effective job of identification.

No consumer merge–purge need be concerned with these niceties and details because the end product of a consumer merge–purge $99\frac{2}{3}$ percent of the time is to get one piece of mail to a residence. In fact, most consumer merge–purge

Figure 13.1

SCF
[Sectional Center Facility]

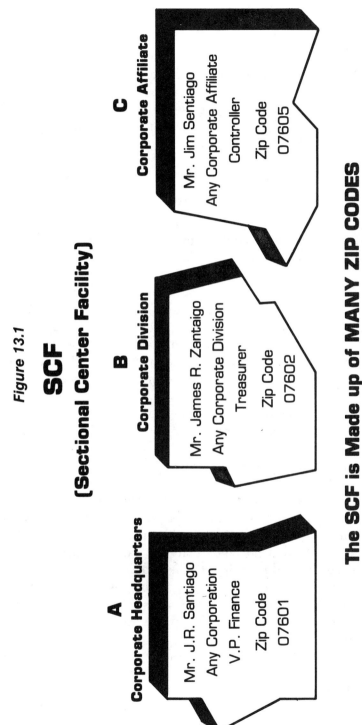

A
Corporate Headquarters

Mr. J.R. Santiago
Any Corporation
V.P. Finance

Zip Code
07601

B
Corporate Division

Mr. James R. Zantaigo
Any Corporate Division
Treasurer

Zip Code
07602

C
Corporate Affiliate

Mr. Jim Sentiago
Any Corporate Affiliate
Controller

Zip Code
07605

The SCF is Made up of MANY MANY ZIP CODES

How Many of These CORPORATE LOCATIONS are
IDENTIFIED as DUPLICATES on Your HOUSE LISTS and
OUTSIDE LISTS Used in Your **"MERGE-PURGE?"**

packages are not designed to handle multiple dwellings where two or more people with the same last name may be found. Such programs get one piece of mail to that name, at that building, and lose one or more records. The response rates of consumer-type mailings are usually such that it is more economical to overkill, and make sure that no more than one piece gets to a prospect.

With a business merge–purge, the process is quite often precisely the opposite, because it is extremely important that:

1. An enterprise not be lost.
2. The various functional capabilities that exist within a firm not be lost.
3. Pieces of mail can be directed to different functions within the company, and, therefore, to different people within the company in order to get proper coverage and response.

It is vitally important when matching on a business list, therefore, that the reach that exists within a corporation be taken into consideration, and that all the various aspects of a given corporate enterprise be properly identified. The rules for matching on individual name are now significantly altered because once within the enterprise, it becomes extremely important to know who's who, and what's what, within that company. Only in this way can a dupe or a nondupe be properly identified.

Why not ask your data processing service how they handle duplication factors for the following business list problem areas?

Business Titles

Many business lists contain three-line addresses or records with a title slugged in, (or both)—even when they are supposed to be "individual name" lists. As it is often crucial to mail to a specific title certain titles must be retained, unless a match to the specific executive who holds that title can be made. Thus it is necessary to unduplicate all titled records with their variations, and then identify the title of the executive, which is often buried in the name field, in order to unduplicate effectively within a particular company. As titles can assume so many variations, dictionaries of possible titles and key words are required.

Multiple Zip Codes

The corporate enterprise quite often exists in multiple zip codes. This shows up in a variety of ways:

(1) It is not uncommon for a corporation to have a box number in one zip

Figure 13.2

In NEW YORK CITY There
are THREE **SCF** Designations

100   101   102

Every OFFICE BUILDING Not Just the EMPIRE STATE BUILDING
and the WORLD TRADE CENTER Have Their OWN ZIP CODES

A GOOD **"MERGE-PURGE"** System Should
Be ABLE to HANDLE This

code, and a delivery address in another, or (2) to have more than one zip code within a town, or (3) even have a zip code that is unique unto itself. (Virtually every bank of significance in the country has its own zip code today.)

In the borough of Manhattan, one of the five boroughs of New York City, even an SCF, is no longer sufficient for a matching process, because there are now three SCFs existing there: 100, 101, 102. 101 and 102 serve nonhouseholds exclusively by being reserved for individual buildings, individual corporations, or business entities that get sufficient mail to justify a unique five-digit zip code (Figure 13.2).

The result of this unique aberration is that virtually every building of significance in New York City has two legitimate zip codes, and where there are two such codes they will not be in the same SCF. Similar unique problems exist in other major metropolitan areas such as Los Angeles, Washington, D.C., Houston, Wilmington, Chicago, Boston, and others.

No computer program that treats only *one* zip code at a time can possibly catch such business duplication. Even a program that stretches out to handle an entire SCF will not suffice. A program must be designed to handle a combined matching operation, not in multiple zip codes, but rather in *multiple SCFs*.

Multiple Facilities

A further refinement well beyond the capacity of conventional consumer merge–purge programs concerns multiple facilities. Many key executives in businesses operate out of more than one facility. Typical industrial directories and business magazine lists show the same branch or plant manager by name at two or three branches or plants often hundreds of miles apart. Certainly, within the same town, this is repeated over and over again. Almost invariably, the various divisions of a corporation will contain the same financial head.

If these divisions are not cross-referenced, numerous mailings to financial executives will be needlessly duplicated. This cross-reference is necessary outside of the zip code and even outside of the particular plant location because the financial individual at these addresses can be the same even when the sales, marketing, or advertising people, for instance, may be different.

Local Addresses

The local address of a particular company can pose another difficult problem in unduplicating records of corporate America. Addresses range from shopping centers and plazas, to "vanity-type" addresses, such as "#1 ABC Corporate Row." Some companies use no local address whatsoever, indicating, as it were, that they are big enough to own the town! Addresses such as "Corner of Court and Center," or "Broad and Market" abound (and raise havoc with zip code programs). Similar obtuse addresses can be found in almost any large business list.

Another complicating factor is box number versus local address. Many companies maintain multiple boxes for different purposes, as well as "regular" delivery addresses of great variety—a problem that needs to be handled in a very careful manner.

No standardized zip coding program can adequately handle the array of multiple zip codes existing today for corporations. Corner addresses, vanity-type addresses, and other "nonlegitimate" addresses also are not handled adequately. Not infrequently, a particular corporation will make its own arrangement with the local postmaster, which is not reported to Washington much less reported to any of the companies that supply zip coding systems. Variation in address is rampant, and very complex programs are required to decide when to, and when not to use address as a "matching" factor among companies, or among various portions of the same company.

Corporate Names—Find the "Correct" One

Variations in spelling create another group of problems for the merge–purge specialist when matching on corporation name. For example: 3M Company versus Minnesota and Manufacturing, IBM versus International Business Machines, GE versus General Electric, and plus all of the above abbreviations, permutations, and combinations that clerks can devise.

Is G.E. Large Turbine Division any different than General Electric Corporation? Is the absence or presence of the word "GE" in that particular title necessary at all?

Great care must be taken with methods used to match company division combinations, as well as other variations of company names. Chances are that your own company—small or large—has a number of corporations and trade names that it uses for various purposes. Thus an effective merge–purge program dealing with business lists requires attention to all of the components of the address and all of the components of the data supplied, including telephone number, local address, as well as all data given for branches and divisions.

Last but not least, the individual name field must be examined. Quite often the only way to pull two records together that are obviously duplicated is to examine the individual name. After examining the company name and determining that it is a likely duplication, the next step is to go back and examine the company address. Then a decision must be made as to whether or not the data are duplicated. If there is an identical individual name or telephone number at an identical address, it is not unreasonable to conclude that a duplication exists even if the company name is totally different. This linkage can then allow the system to pull other records together that are less identical. Here's an example. "Joe's Bar and Grill" and "Grace's Catering Service." The substance of this business record is a husband and wife who are running a two-person business. In reality, it is a single establishment, and deserves only one piece of mail. Is there anything similar about the two names? No. Are there two people? Yes. Are they part of the same enterprise? Absolutely. Should they be netted out for a data base or a merge–purge? Yes, there is no doubt about it.

These decisions must be made in a very careful manner because the mailer does not want to mail to the wrong name or the wrong address. So, when a merge identifies "Floral Arrangements" that is also advertised under "Funeral Parlors," the mailer wishes to make sure that the mail to "Floral Arrangements" gets to these people under the proper company name. If this is not done, the mailing piece appears to be erroneous and is likely to be offensive to the company receiving it.

A New Merge–Purge Technique: Chaining

Once all the problems surrounding a business merge–purge are discussed and analyzed, it becomes obvious that a single pass through a system cannot do even an adequate job.

Further, once all the records for a company have finally been "joined" together, the job of blending (tagging) such data as SIC code, number of employees, sales, and so on, must still be accomplished. Data coming in from various sources may or may not be compatible—quite often it is different—which means that complex algorithms must be evolved to decide which data are usable, and from which sources. The integrity of each record must be retained so selection can accurately be based on the *specifics* of particular records.

To answer these problems, **PAGEX** Systems, Inc. has created a merge–purge process called *chaining* (Figure 13.3), which can handle the variations in business files. In the chaining process all records within a corporation can be linked, and all multiple records for a division, and in turn, for an individual can be linked. This is done without "dropping" any records. Chaining matches *but does not remove or change* the original input records fed into the merge–purge. The file retains all of the records it began with but they are now linked together in a logical way.

Chaining gives us the ability to select characteristics that pertain to the individual desired record. If we have an individual who is vice president of his or her present company, *and* president of a division, we can select either record

Figure 13.3

SAMPLES OF THE "CHAINING" PROCESS BY PAGEX SYSTEMS, INC.

ORIGINAL FILE INPUT UNDISCIPLINED DATA

NAME	COMPANY/DIVISION	ADDRESS	CITY	ST	ZIP
PO BOX 829	BLAUSER WELL SERVICE INC	507 2ND ST	MARIETTA	OH	44750
MAIL LOCATION 569	UNIV RADIOLOGY FUND OF CINN	RADIOLOGY BUS OFFICE	CINCINNATI	OH	45267
BEDFORDTOWNSHIP 79 R	ECHOING HILLS VILLAGE INC	ATTN COMPUTER DP MGR	WARSAW	OH	43844
THE DUPPS CO		JOHN DUPPS JR VP	GERMANTOWN	OH	45327

(based upon the particular offer to be mailed) and address this executive with the correct title, and most importantly, at the company name and address that "makes sense."

Here is a brief example of chaining-style decision making: After identifying all of the components, the chaining process decides:

1. Is this a corporate entity?

2. Within the corporate entity, is this a divisional entity, a branch entity, or a related component business? (Figure 13.4).

3. Are the following individual records in fact the *same* individual, even though the names may be slightly different, the company names may be totally different, the location the same, although the addresses may be different, and so on? (See Figure 13.5)

Because chaining matches, but does not alter the original information, the final analysis shows that which is mailed is targeted directly and expressly to the original record as given (whether it came from a directory, subscriber list, or mail order respondent list). As all records are selected and addressed based on *original criteria*, even if an individual has been combined into a nonrelated grouping, when we select the SIC or other criteria, it will be selected *only if appropriate* and printed as originally indicated. It is deliverable because the address and information remain unaltered.

Chaining permits two records that have a similar names and/or addresses to be identified as two *unique* records where they otherwise may have been dupe-eliminated (overkilled) by the machine. For instance, if there are two Robert Jones at 342 Madison Avenue, each of them, *when selected for their particular characteristics*, will be individually mailed to at a particular firm, at this particular address. (Figure 13.6) No mistake is made. The mortician's mailing isn't sent to the florist or visa versa. Each record retains its individual identity although both have been "related" by the machine.

The chaining process of merge–purge is a *multiple path process*. This process cannot be accomplished in one pass. The matching and merging process checks individual names, identifies likely duplicates, and sets up a "file" that contains all these names, on a chained or net name basis. This is a two-step process in that first company matches are identified, and then the individual name matches are identified. In most cases doing this means separate passes, separate sorts, and dealing with the file in various sequences that enhance the likelihood, in the final end product, of proper matching.

It is extremely important to identify those business records that contain no

Figure 13.4

DUPLICATE SAMPLE

NAME	COMPANY/DIVISION	ADDRESS	CITY	ST	ZIP
ROY WEISENBORN	ELLICOTT DRUG CO	BOX 1129	BUFFALO	NY	14240
MR ROY WEISBORN MGR	ELLICOTT DRUG CO	1650 WALDEN AVE BX 1129	BUFFALO	NY	14225
JOSEPH F ACARDLE MD MGR	HENS AND KELLY INC	PO BOX 1355	BUFFALO	NY	14240
J F MCARDLE MERCH MGR	HENS AND KELLEY INC	478 MAIN ST	BUFFALO	NY	14202
L J SAMMARTIN	KENTUCKY CTRL LIFE INS CO	KINCAID TOWERS	LEXINGTON	KY	40507
LARRY SMMMARTIN	KENTUCKY CENTRAL LIFE	KINCID OWERS	LEXINGTON	KY	40508
MR ROBERT FERGUSON VP M	AMERICAN SIGN MARKETING	P O BOX 247	FLORENCE SE	KY	41042
ROBERT GERGUSSEN S M MGR	AMER SIGN ADVERTISING SER	7430 INDUSTRIAL RD BX 24	FLORENCE	KY	41042

505

Figure 13.5

"CHAINING" BY EXECUTIVE NAME

NAME	COMPANY/DIVISION	ADDRESS	CITY	ST	ZIP
JULIUS CASALI	STANDARD MOTOR FREIGHT INC	2700 SMALLMAN ST	PITTSBURGH	PA	15222
MARTIN H POLLOCK	STANDARD MOTOR FREIGHT INC	2700 SMALLMAN ST	PITTSBURGH	PA	15222
PETER J SARDANO	PEERLESS TRANSPORT CORP	2700 SMALLMAN ST	PITTSBURGH	PA	15222
PETER J SARDANO	STANDARD MOTOR FRIEGHT INC	2700 SMALLMAN ST	PITTSBURGH	PA	15222
PETER SARDANO	BROWN BROTHERS BULK TRANSPORT	2701 RAILROAD ST	PITTSBURGH	PA	15222
MARTIN W SNOW	PEERLESS TRANSPORT CORP	2700 SMALLMAN ST	PITTSBURGH	PA	15222
MARTIN W SNOW	STANDARD MOTOR FREIGHT INC	2700 SMALLMAN ST	PITTSBURGH	PA	15222
MARTIN SNOW	BROWN BROTHERS BULK TRANSPORT	2701 RAILROAD ST	PITTSBURGH	PA	15222
JASMES YEARSLEY	PEERLESS TRANSPORT CORP	2700 SMALLMAN ST	PITTSBURGH	PA	15222

NAME	COMPANY/DIVISION	ADDRESS	CITY	ST	ZIP
RUTH PARSONS	FERRELL REALTY CO	SUITE 12 WACHOVIA BLDG	WINSTON-SALEM	NC	27101
J C SMITH	FERRELL REALTY CO	SUITE 12 WACHOVIA BLDG	WINSTON-SALEM	NC	27101
J C SMITH	COLONY PLACE APARTMENTS	WACHOVIA BLDG	WINSTON-SALEM	NC	27101
J C SMITH	MOUNTAIN LODGE APARTMENTS	3905 BETHANIA RD	WINSTON-SALEM	NC	27106
E V FERRELL JR	FERRELL REALTY CO	SUITE 12 WACHOVIA BLDG	WINSTON-SALEM	NC	27101
E V FERRELL JR	COLONY PLACE APARTMENTS	WACHOVIA BLDG	WINSTON-SALEM	NC	27101
E V FERRELL JR	MOUNTAIN LODGE APARTMENTS	3905 BETHANIA RD	WINSTON-SALEM	NC	27106
ZACK RAYNOLDS	MOUNTAIN LODGE APARTMENTS	3905 BETHANIA RD	WINSTON-SALEM	NC	27106

Figure 13.6

"CHAINING" BY COMPANY NAME

NAME	COMPANY/DIVISION	ADDRESS	CITY	ST	ZIP
C CASTAGNA	SMITH BARNEY REAL ESTATE CO	1345 AVE OF THE AMERICAS	NEW YORK CITY	NY	10105
	SMITH BARNEY HARS UPHM	1345 AVE OF THE AMERICAS	N Y	NY	10019
	SBHU HOLDINGS INC	1345 AVE OF THE AMERICAS	NEW YORK	NY	10019
	SMITH BARNEY HARRIS UPAM	1345 AVE OF THE AMERICAS	NEW CITY	NY	10105
MARK FRANZAK	CARRO SPANBOCK LONDIN	1345 AVE OF AMERICAS	N Y C	NY	10009
ELAINE ACKERMAN	CARRO SPANBOCH LONDIN FASS	1345 AVE OF THE AMER	MANHATTAN	NY	10015
ELAINE ACKERMAN	CARRO SPANBOCK, ET AL.	1345 AVE. OF THE AMER.	NEW YORK	NY	10125
C E WAGER	WHITIAKER GEN MED CORP	8741 LANDMARK RD	RICHMOND	VA	23261
D REISENWITZ	PHIPPS AND BIRD CO	P O BOX 27324	RICHMAND	VA	23261
MR JERRY BISHOP	WHITTAKER GENERAL MED CORP	8741 LANDMARK RD	RICH	VA	23228
LIN H CARNEAL	WHITTAKER GEN MED CO	8741 LANDMARK RD	RICHMD	VA	23261
AL GREBE	WHITTAKER GEN MEDICAL L	BOX 27452 8741 LANDMARK	RICHMND	VA	23261
A GREBE	PHIPPS & BIRD INC	8741 LANDMARK RD	RICHMOND	VA	23261

individual name, but may contain a title such as "Attn: Purchasing Manager," "Chief Librarian," and so on.

These titled records must be separated and handled as an entity unto themselves. Records must be examined to determine the variations in such titles. This is required to develop a uniformity of title variations and abbreviations used so that the matching nets out only one record per company per title, within that universe. It then becomes important—in consultation with the client—to determine which titles, if any, to retain.

Create a Custom Program

A separate decision, in consultation with the client, must be made concerning the use of titles, where a record for an individual exists for that particular company. If titles are to be supplied along with individual names, and the client says, "No matter what, I want a record that reads 'Attn: Purchasing Manager,'" a decision must be made as to what must be done with a record of an individual by name, whose title says he or she is the purchasing manager. Matching individuals versus matching title records becomes a complex step unto itself which results in a combined file, under highly specialized rules, that suits that particular client's requirements and particular product offer.

After this step is completed and after a net file is built, almost any selection the client requires can be made. Various mailings can be targeted for various computer letters and they may be segmented by type of individual mailed to, or selection can be made for flights of mailings, based on function or the number of people within a corporation that appear on the resultant output file.

This becomes an important consideration when mailing in depth to a particular corporation. It is a known fact that if too many pieces of a similar type of mail hit the mailroom of a major corporation these multiple pieces may never be delivered. Sophisticated mailers, knowing this, use chaining to identify X number of names per company to go out as a flight. The balance of records are reserved to be mailed at a later date on a second, third, or fourth flight. The result is greater effectiveness of the mailing piece.

The chaining process of identifying the individuals within a company, divisions within a company, and various functional capabilities becomes important, too, when disseminating information to a sales force, or planning a telemarketing campaign. Depending on the needs of the particular company, a custom program is sometimes required for analysis, statistical data, and counts that extend beyond the reach of the ordinary merge–purge capability. Because of the segmented, multiple-pass requirements of the chaining process, the type of analytic data available are far more comprehensive than the grids of net-name-by-source that come out of a typical consumer merge–purge package.

Merge–purge can be custom-tailored to a particular client need although this can result in an almost infinite amount of work to be done depending on the degree of perfection demanded by the client. A one-time mailing, never to be looked at or used again, can be tailored down to a lower-cost base than a database created for perpetual use. It is, therefore, of critical importance that the chaining process be performed for a knowledgeable, actively involved buyer who is interested in quality, knows the market, and is willing to take the time and trouble to examine the input, output, and level of duplication found, as well as be involved in the quality control that is so often missing in the list label merge–purge function as it exists today in direct marketing.

Recently one of the major industrial publishers in America used a well known consumer merge–purge house to service a 1,500,000-name mailing from over eighty separate business list sources. When the data were examined, the client said, "This is not good enough." The supplier admitted, "This is the best we can do." The entire job was done all over again from the original records by the chaining process, which more than satisfied the client's needs.

Be a Knowledgeable Buyer . . .

It is a known fact that perfection cannot be achieved—particularly in an area of business list merge/purge. There is an axiom that says there is a geometric progression in cost to try to reach the unattainable 100 percent perfection level. 99 percent will cost geometrically more than 98 percent, which will cost geometrically more than 97 percent, and so on. Therefore, the concept of "good enough" is a very important one. But "good enough" in a business merge/purge is a much different animal than "good enough" in a consumer merge/purge. The two must not be confused.

Price—You Get What You Pay For

The knowledgeable buyer must determine whether or not his business merge/purge is being done with a consumer package, at consumer package prices—or whether it is being done in a manner that will give him an adequately unduped file—without overkill—*and* a successful mailing. When the costs of today's business mailings are examined, the few extra dollars per thousand expended on a *good* merge/purge program pale into insignificance when examining the resulting product of an inadequate program. As much as 15 percent or 20 percent variation can exist between that which "is done" and that which, sadly, "should have been done."

That 15 percent or 20 percent is the result of two types of errors. The first is duplication in the file which cannot be seen on cursory examination—because such dupes will be in separate Zip Codes—or in a sequence that is not easily discernable. The second will be good records missing due to overkill—which is usually not seen at all.

Clients who use business merge/purge should be careful to guard against this vast variation between what they should get, and what—for the most part—they do get. To do this they should:

1. Request and *review* matched pairs of records that are identified as duplicates that have been dropped. This may, by itself, be eye-opening.

2. Request *and carefully examine* a solid chunk of net output stretching over several 3-digit SCF areas (not an Nth number sample which, of course, will be clean of all duplicates) to see what proportion of duplication has been left. Preferably, this listing should be in alphabetic sequence to "pull together" multiple Zip Code problems.

Human nature, unfortunately, dictates that quality suffers when quality control and inspection are not performed. The wise buyer will conduct these two tests. If more clients did—the type of business merge/purge available today would be immeasurably improved.

TWO SPECIALIZED MERGE–PURGE OPERATIONS

The Department of Defense and Priority Merge–Purge Allocation

Each year the Department of Defense rents lists of every available junior and senior high school student and selected college entrant students for its recruitment mailings for the armed forces. To obtain the best price for the government, each of the half dozen or so vendors supplies a tape copy and a sealed bid price. The Department of Defense has its merge–purge contractor give initial *priority* to every name provided by the lowest bidder. The second lowest bidder gets credit for, and is paid for, those names on the list that were not on the lowest bidder's list. The third lowest bidder is paid a higher price for only those names that are not already available and paid for from the first two lists. This process is repeated up to the highest bidder who is paid only for those records that are not already supplied on any of the other bidders lists. The prices and quantities supplied by each vendor at the end of the process are then available to all the vendors, which undoubtedly makes for some interesting pricing debates. Note that the use "priority" favors one list over another; the allocation system on the other hand, gives equal weight to each record; where one name is supplied by three lists, the allocation methods gives $1/3$ credit to each.

Credit Approval

The surge of financial offers by banks, stock brokers, and insurance companies has brought forth a number which needs to be mailed only to those consumers who have been pre-screened for credit. The process is complicated and time consuming and must be entrusted to a qualified data processing house. If you desire multiple inputs the first step is to go through a merge–purge process. The unique records to be screened must be reformatted with the match code required by each of the credit bureaus involved. Each of these match code extracts is appended to each originating record.

In some cases, the only records the mailer can or will use are those that are accepted or approved. In others, the mailer may elect to mail a short-form offer to prescreened prospects and a long-form offer to prospects that have lower credit limits with no adverse qualifications.

The next step is to match the returned match codes against the tape of the original records and pull only those records that can or will be mailed.

There is usually a strong temptation to bypass the merge–purge operation by using one of the major files of compiled households by name, rather than a group of selected mail order buyers and magazine subscribers. This saves time and initially, it saves the modest cost of a merge–purge. However, as the cost or credit checking will run three to five times or more the cost of the merge–purge even in large quantities, such a use will normally turn out to be more costly in the long run. Carefully selected response lists provide two or more times the response of a stratified list, and if dollar differentials are in the picture, the response list will show a higher average size.

One of the major questions to ask when considering types of mailing is whether or not the credit approval step can be cost justified. If it cannot be justified what type of substitute offer or offers can be made? (The answer may be, "Credit Approved Lists." These lists, unchecked against other files are now coming onto the market at rather high prices per 1000 names. At least two of the five major U.S. Credit Bureaus offered direct access in 1987 to their files of multi-millions of credit checked names. In time such files will almost certainly be offered with mail order respondent overlays.)

CHAPTER 14

Database versus Data Bank: A Look at What They Can Do for the List User

The terms *database* and *data bank* tend to be used interchangeably but are best defined by the relation of the data to the user. Data that belong exclusively to one company or institution are stored on a data*base*. In general, all data on the base are generated by the owner, and all added transactions as well as data added to records already on the base, come from information supplied by the owner. Overlays added to the major information on the database of United States census data, zip codes, carrier routes, telephone numbers, originate with outside vendors, and the application of them may be by outside services. A database is not usually available for outside rental or sale; it incorporates the single most important set of records for its owner—namely the customer or subscriber file.

A data *bank*, on the other hand, encompasses multiple sources, often both compiled- and response-oriented, and generally rental is available of a large number of records already pre-merge–purged and unduplicated. Data banks for rental almost always already have been overlayed to produce appropriate United States census data, zip codes, carrier routes, and telephone numbers. Although some are proprietary and include the proprietor's customer records, it is more usual for a data bank to include only outside sources. (A number of multiple magazine publishers make an unduplicated merge–purged list of subscribers and recipients available, which in effect, is a hybrid of a database for internal use and a data bank for outside use.)

BUSINESS DATA BANKS

Public Data Banks

A public data bank, for all practical purposes, is a merge–purged list composed of multiple inputs from multiple owners. Public data banks are available for business establishments as well as business executives. Public data banks for establishments have the following characteristics:

- Are produced and marketed by one company.

- Usually involve large numbers of records, up to the entire universe available.

- Are available for rental.

- Are available for multiple use on a one-year contractual basis.

- Contain source data (either indicated or obvious).

- Usually marketed through multiple layers of distribution, including both national and regional franchisers, wholesalers, brokers, and compilers.

In the consumer field, the files of telephone registrants, automotive registrants, driver licenses, and voters' registrations, provide data banks of more than 75 million households.

Some Historical Background

The history of business data banks has revolved around the data published by D&B as augmented by address and phone data from classified telephone directories. In 1956–57, aided by *The Wall Street Journal*, Creative Mail, a major Mail Fulfillment Source, placed all D&B rated and/or listed business establishments and their SICs (approximately 3 million) on 3 by 5 cards, and then looked up local addresses from the classifieds. The list was updated every eighteen months. In 1958, Leo Gans of National Business Lists (NBL) keystroked the three million D&B records onto punchcards and added the addresses and phone numbers by the same method to the cards from the phone books. The cards were interpreted, duplicated, and then sorted into three files of three million each by alphabetic, geographic, and SIC listings. In 1960 a sale of the entire file by the Burnett organization would have meant shipment of nineteen tons of cards! This led to conversion to tape.

In 1970, Ed Burnett and Dave Florence, formerly New York area representatives for NBL, started a rival file at Direct Media (DM). This was purchased a few years later by CCX which then sold the file to Market Data Retrieval (MDR). In 1984 MDR purchased NBL, its major competitor. In 1986 Dun & Bradstreet purchased MDR. In that year, Ed Burnett Consultants, Inc. launched Data Base America as an effective alternative to D&B, followed shortly by a restructured file from Compilers Plus.

The Major Business *Establishment* Data Banks and What They Offer

There have been two important new recent developments in this field. The first is the entry into the list field, for the first time, of a few of the telephone companies. Mountain Bell and four of the five states of Ameritech (Illinois, Ohio, Indiana, Wisconsin) now provide access to current records, including the exceedingly valuable "new connects" on a current basis. Several other former Bell entities are now studying how best to market their list data. In late 1987, Chesapeake and Potomac Telephone Company appointed Ed Burnett Consultants as its list manager. Unlike lists based essentially on conversions of telephone books after they are published, the phone companies, obviously, can provide current data on all listed establishments. And while phone conversion files can only be updated once a year as the new phone books for an area are published, the phone company computerized billing files are never more than a few days behind any changes, or adds, or disconnects.

The second important development has been to confirm or verify data on these business files from secondary or tertiary sources to improve deliverability by mail, and offer higher proportion of connect phones for telemarketing. Two of the lists (D&B, and Data Base America) are making tremendous efforts in this regard. Both (as Fig. 14.1 shows) now offer over 6 million records either confirmed or verified through added source data.

Some fifteen years ago Vined Gupta, who owns American Business Lists, began to compile records from the classifieds by classification. But unlike earlier compilers who over the years continued to compile ten, fifteen, or twenty major classifications, Gupta persevered in his determination to extract all data, and by 1986 was able to provide to the list field the first complete file consisting of virtually every record in every yellow pages phone book. What is more, his updating capacity is more current by a number of months than was ever achieved by MDR or NBL.

It is perhaps of some interest to note that telephone books particularly in larger cities take six to eight months to canvas; it then takes two to three months to print; those using them can take up to two months to get a current copy, at which time it takes as much as six months or so to convert the data and get it into the updated file. And then that data stays on file, untouched for a year, until the

Figure 14.1

	D & B	Data Base America	ABL	Compilers plus
Total number of unduplicated records	7,000,000	8,300,000	7,400,000	7,400,000
Number of phones	All	All	All	All
Second source confirmation	7,000,000 (est)	6,100,000	-0-	2,000,000
Confirmed phone numbers	2,500,000 (est)	4,500,000	-0-	Unknown
Executive 1 per company	7,500,000	3,000,000	-0-	1,400,000
Sales volume	Yes	No	No	No
Number of SIC classifications	2,600	4,400	3,000 (est)	3,000
Brand names	No	Yes	Yes	Yes
Suppression of establishments in bankruptcy, or with liens	No	Yes	No	No
NCOA cleaned	Yes	Yes	No	No
BPA approved	Yes	No	Yes	No
Selection of multi-sourced establishment records	Yes	Yes	No	No

next directory is obtained. American Business Lists in its directory frankly notes that "the telephone directories are 5 to 10 percent out of data on the day they're printed."

Interestingly enough D&B guarantees that not one record in their D&B National Business file is generated from a classified phone record. And almost all are confirmed before use by a second source. Much of this confirmation is now by phone. The D&B file is unique in its coverage of sales volumes for most establishments, and its strength is in reporting the number of employees for almost all establishments, plus its listing of a top executive for most establishments.

Data Base America, alone among the major files, compares its records with some 20 million open "accounts receivable records" in over 9.0 million establishments. It is this source that provides Data Base America with a means to suppress those establishments in bankruptcy or with business liens against them. The high watermark for failures in America was 1986, with over 61,000 publicly reported, which is almost one percent of all establishments. This file with each update shows increases (now 3 million) in number of establishments with number of employees (virtually total coverage of all establishments with twenty or more).

Compilers Plus has added to its basic coverage a file produced through phone calls by a major insurance company, which gives access to some 1,400,000 executives confirmed by phone.

Both D&B and Data Base America have placed on the market a new aspect of business listings, namely the "cottage industry"—people running businesses from their homes. D&B ostensibly uncovers a good part of those 750,000 names it offers from credit requests. Data Base America provides a list of over one million records extracted from millions of names of businesses listed in alphabetic telephone directories, and then unduplicated by phone number and by merge–purge against Data Base America. Two true unduplicated supplements to Data Base America are then created—the cottage industry per se, and a host of business listings in alphabetics of businesses and institutions not available anywhere else— with their phone numbers.

Business *Executive* Data Banks

D&B led the way into business executive data banks and was followed by S&P, by compiling the top executives of large companies on a research basis. D&B now publishes records of 550,000 executives at over 100,000 home offices, while S&P offers records of 240,000 executives at the top 45,000 companies. It is estimated each of these publishers spends $10 or more per company to provide current printed data.

The start of large business executive data banks came about with the advent of sufficient computer power to merge and unduplicate large files of recipients of magazines. Virtually all multiple publishers now provide such an unduplicated list, among them are McGraw-Hill, CMP, Hayden, Industrial, Thomas, Penton, Technical, and Gralla.

The need of seminar operators that required greater penetration of executive names than available from magazine publishers fueled the creation of a number of large composites of executives, several of which now range from 7 million to 10 million individual names. The two best known are the Mal Dunn Associates (MDA) file and the American Registry file (now managed by D&B). MDA, as the list manager for all McGraw-Hill properties, starts with an unduplicated file of magazine respondents (approximately 2 million), adds in S&P data and a large number of other magazine files as well as mail order buyer lists. Barring McGraw-Hill, D&B builds up to 10 million records from publishers and mail order buyers.

Based on size of company and classification, not every name in the MDA file or in the American Registry file can be considered equal. But they do offer unique, unduplicated coverage of executives. A comparable file, now totaling 5,000,000 executives including those at the 400,000 largest companies is available through Data Base America.

Another file, now publicly available for the first time, is a former cooperative data bank, (originally for member list owners only), now offered by List Technology. This list fuses together 50 lists primarily comprised of high-tech industries. Clearance to use any of these lists, is based mainly on good taste.

Private Data Banks

In addition to these large data banks accessible to the public, there are a number of major companies that have built or had built for them, private data banks for one company's use only. The first of these, looking much like MDA and American Registry data banks do, was conceived, funded, and is now used by the AMA. In time this led to the creation of a comparable bank for Penton Learning, the major competitor of seminar giving to the AMA. Above and beyond seminars, private data banks covering a large part of the commercial market are on file for AT&T, Merrill Lynch, and IBM. There also is a good number of Fortune 1,000 companies that have copies of D&B or Data Base America data on their own computers. Thus it is not surprising to find all D&B data online for public access through the Lockhead "Dialog" system.

Some publicly accessible business data banks are small in comparison with the huge files discussed above, but each small data bank has its place. *Disclosure* is a list of all publicly owned companies that must submit annual reports and 10K quarterly reports to the SEC. This list, which consists of only 8,000 companies and 50,000 executives, is accessible through computer terminals and is updated *daily*. So far this is the only known data bank that is updated with such currency today.

Direct Media has produced a data bank built exclusively from the customer lists of a group of mail order business companies. The file is periodically matched against a classified data bank to provide each participant with access to the unduplicated business universe.

One of the most advantageous selling points of these large data banks of executives is that they have been unduplicated. They have been merge–purged and reduced to a file, ostensibly, of unique records. The higher price usually assessed for these names is in part justified by the fact that there is no need to pay for a merge–purge. The only problem with this argument is that almost all major users pull names from these data banks and then place them along with their customer file, in a final merge–purge. For these names the mailer may, in effect, be paying twice for the same service. The data bank managers who do get a fee above the list costs (if rented directly) do not harp on the fact that each user pays this extra fee, so the merge–purge, if that is at least part of the reason for the addition, is paid for not only once but over and over again.

CONSUMER DATA BANKS

Some Historical Background

In the early 1950s, Donnelley and the predecessor to Metromail were converting all consumers with registered phone numbers to tape. In the 1970s and early 1980s, Donnelley was the lone compiler of all such names. Since then, Donnelley has sold a copy of the telephone data to Metromail. Metromail in turn has sold to Polk the phone names in those eight, nine, ten, or so states that did not furnish Polk with car registrations. Then Polk, which has annually compiled lists of forty or fifty states accessible by car registrations, sold a copy of the car registration data to Donnelley. In addition, Polk canvasses over 1,200 localities house-to-house to build a separate data bank of 26 million households by occupation. This file includes Detroit, which is the home base of Polk, but does not include New York, Chicago, Los Angeles, Philadelphia, or Cleveland because the costs of canvassing a major city and the R.O.I. make the task uneconomic.

The major compilers of name data have each expanded on conventional demographic data to include special information such as the names and ages of children, the exact date of birth (mainly taken from driver license files), access to two or more adults in a given household, and last but not least, the addition of "known mail order buyers." This expansion has increased available information of the 75 million households now on file.

In the 1960s, files of drivers' licenses began to surface with data available from seventeen states. The files of drivers' licenses now total over 130 million adult names. These data provide age and date of birth data; some even provide size and weight data. But the data, as published, must be updated against a telephone or car registration file as drivers' licenses are untouched for three to five years. Some sporadic records from voter's registrations from time to time are added to these files. Changes of addresses are secured from notices of moves given to magazines, for the most part, and insurance companies in addition to USPS file cleanings to improve deliverability. For the most part, these compiled records are not as deliverable as the compiled car and phone lists, which in themselves leave much to be desired.

Occupant Lists: All-Encompassing List Coverage

Only one type of list in America provides coverage of all households. It is called an *occupant* list and consists of addresses of householders only, without names of the home owners. When mailed, these addresses are usually addressed to "occupant" or "resident."

Occupant files are owned by about 150 companies, each of which has a state or group of states or an area of local coverage. Two firms, Advo and Harte Hanks, have coverage of a majority of the country, but each local segment may or may not be as complete as that compiled by a competing local operator. These files, if they encompass 90 percent or more of the households in a specified area, can be and almost universally are updated by the USPS for a fee. Provided the data are delivered to them on cards (usually interpreted punched cards), the USPS inserts cards for each missing address and returns the cards, carrier route by carrier route, in *carrier-walk route*. This is the order in which the mailcarrier walks his or her route. Mail sent to the postal carrier in his or her walk route does not need to be cased or can be easily placed with other mail. Full coverage of an area for a local grocery supermarket or a department store, through an occupant file in walking order, gets even better delivery than first class mail because the great majority of it is delivered on the *specific* day required, usually a Thursday for weekend sales.

Checking counts for political divisions such as state, county, metro area, city, or SCF on two occupant lists gives an idea of how thorough such coverage can be. If both lists have been updated recently by the USPS, the two counts will be essentially the same. Substantial differences may be a result of different geographical parameters, or one list may be much more thorough than the other. It pays to find out. While the USPS now provides attractive discounts for carrier-route sorting, no additional discount has ever been established for occupant mailers who deliver billions of pieces of third class mail to the USPS not only sorted by route but also sorted to the walk order determined by each individual carrier.

SPECIAL DATA BANKS

Beyond the better known major data banks for the AMA and Penton, and the more or less individually developed data banks used by IBM, Xerox, Merrill Lynch, and Armco, there are a large number of other esoteric data banks. Here is a sampling:

Company	Classification of data bank
Camel cigarettes	Smokers
Wholesale beauty aids	Beauty shops, including those without business phones and at-home addresses
General Electric	Restaurants by type and size
Olin Mills	Families with children in school
Kodak	People who use film or are expected to
Pan American	Frequent flyers
American Airlines	Frequent flyers based on the route segments they fly
Emery	Customers and prospects qualified by cargo use
Black Box	Counters on how often ten classifications of product are discussed by prospects or purchased by customers
Sears	Over 200 cells based on what has been bought, when, and at what prices from 400 million catalogs per year

A number of retailers have children's clubs with exact date of birth and send birthday reminders to their customers. For example, Cook Chocolate does this for its buyers of chocolates for Christmas gifts. Banks and stock brokers are finally recognizing holders of multiple accounts. Macy's knows who has a deposit account and what each customer buys. Many mail order companies keep lists of gift givers and the recipients called "giftees".

The Burnett organization provides as part of its S&P's coverage, all top executives at the first Fortune 500 and the second Fortune 500 industrial giants, as well as the Fortune 300, which covers the top executives of the top fifty companies as delineated by the editors of Fortune in the five fields of banking, construction, wholesaling, insurance, and utilities.

HOW DATABASES SHOULD WORK—IDEALLY

There are about as many definitions of what is meant by the word *database* as there are marketers writing about them. To students in computer courses, a database is an on-line real-time disk-oriented group of interrelated files that react to a transaction affecting one or more files. To a software house, a database is a program that controls the workings of interactive, online, real-time files. To marketers, a true "direct-marketing database" would be a set of files providing online, real-time, data on the following:

- Customers
- Inventory
- Inquiries and requests
- Prospects and suspects
- Agencies, dealers, wholesalers, and branches
- Order files
- Catalog items
- Promotion uses and responses

On such a set of interrelated files, if a mailing is made to a customer, it shows on the promotional file and on the customer file. When a purchase is made this affects the order file, customer file, inventory file, and response file. With maximums and minimums set on the inventory file as well as location and on-order status, that order may trigger a new order for inventory, or move inventory from backup to picking-bin status. The order automatically increases accounts receivable, creates a bill with an audit trail, updates the sales tax due, and updates the catalog item sales file.

Although this procedure has not yet been used to its fullest extent, all the parts are in place and many catalog and direct-mail operations have a large part of this interaction working now.

Four Conditions for Successful Database Management

A direct mailer who adds recency, frequency, and dollars to his or her customer file has created a database if it satisfies the following conditions:

1. It is owned exclusively by one firm.
2. It is dynamic—it is and can change.
3. It is online in real-time so individual records can be reviewed, changed, or updated at will.
4. The owner uses the derived data to improve customer sales and customer responsiveness.

Of these four points, the most important is the last. There is no reason to build RFU$ISM into a database system if the analytic data produced from this are not used as a tool to manage the customer file. Many firms become enamored with the mechanics of the database and forget the reason for building it. The operative word here is *management*. The interrelationship of the data elements is designed to help operators make more intelligent decisions.

John Stevenson, President of the Consulting Company "Experts in Direct Marketing" notes:

> *"The feedback in direct response is a continuous stream of facts and certainties. They come out of the real world from real people, and real markets, and are about real products and services. In this feedback every single step of the process becomes a variable that can be individually identified and therefore measured. And the relationships among variables can be observed. There is far more to the direct-marketing process and in the feedback than sales alone."*

The more study given these variables the clearer it becomes that different variables produce different effects in terms of the bottom line. As noted in the chapters on testing, the one factor which has the greatest influence on response is the list or the market. Direct marketers have an absolutely indispensable need to get their *best* message to the *right* persons at the *right* time.

How Database Management Operates

The database of customers provides a means for a mailer to locate, reach, and have a dialogue with each cell of customers on the file. With database management, an operator can more often reach his or her prime customers, shorten intervals between catalog request conversion mailings, identify segments of customers who should not be mailed to more than once or twice a year, and at the same time identify cells of customers that should be mailed to twelve times per year.

Once prime customers have been identified, steps can be taken to make extra efforts to locate and promote others. If, for example, there is no way to determine which sources provide customers who buy more than once, prospecting is relegated to renting only those names that produce the highest number of initial sales per thousand. The fact that of two lists one can bring in first-time customers, of which 30 percent will buy again in the following year, while the other will bring in only 10 percent repeat buyers will never come to light.

Every name on the database comes from a source or through an offer. Every inquiry and request has its own history. The source may have been space ads, direct mail, premium offers, card decks, or responses to a general advertisement.

Each of these inquiries "voted" to respond. This history tells what each inquirer did, what was bought, how much was spent, how often they purchased, and how and when the purchases were paid. This history of promotion and response indicates the value of each separate cell on the file.

Once the history of promotion and response is recorded continuously, the cells of customers and inquiries based on the RFU$ISM function will tend to cluster in one of three layers:

1. Cells that correlate to a high degree with response

2. Cells that correlate to a lesser degree with response

3. Cells that always appear to be highly correlated to nonresponse

In all probability, at the first analysis, the main objective will be to isolate those cells and those segments that show either a zero correlation with response or a correlation so low that it is obvious mailing them is a losing proposition.

The mathematics involved in the analysis of a large database can get quite esoteric. There are a number of professionals who provide regression analysis and they can help when needed. (And if the problem is brought inside the house, there are now several research programs which can be run on the PC.)

Many mailers today treat all customers and all inquiries, irrespective of age or source, in exactly the same manner: If the plan calls for two, three, or four catalogs per year, each customer and each inquiry receives two, three, or four catalogs, irrespective of response. It is not uncommon to find catalog requests that are two or more years old, in which ten or fifteen offers have been mailed at a cost of $5 to $10 to no avail and that still receive the same annual promotion as multicustomers who buy each and every year.

DATABASES—HOW THEY REALLY WORK

A database in direct marketing terms is:

1. A comprehensive collection of *interrelated data,* including sales as well as nonsales, that reflect transactions on the customer and inquiry files.

2. Designed to serve *multiple applications* and report to *multiple receivers.*

3. A system that allows prompt and accurate *retrieval of data,* and manipulation of that data.

Historically, list files contain only a single type of information, while a database contains many types of data which are linked together and interact. List files usually derive information from a single source, and support a limited number of applications. The database, which derives information from multiple sources, is designed to support and report on multiple applications. List files usually can be accessed only by a single method in batch mode, which is rather cumbersome and provides almost no means to get quick answers to marketing questions. The database is designed for multiple access by a number of different departments at will. Once independent files are brought together in a database their value to the corporation increases enormously. *The customer database becomes the one most valuable asset to a direct-mail company or division.*

Typically a direct-mail reporting system will have several *individual* streams. First, may be counts by segment within the customer file. Second, may be item data, inventory-oriented, with reports on sales, returns, and so on by item. Third, may be a cash reporting system based on invoices and the resultant accounts receivable data. None of these data streams "talks" or interacts with each other even though item sales affect fulfillment, the customer file, the accounts receivable ledger, and inventory. If there is a catalog involved, the item count, along with revenue and gross margin, will influence product selection as well as product or group of products emphasis. *In this standard pattern, reporting may be specified as being "item" driven.*

Shifting Gears: From "Item" to "Customer" Emphasis

In database management (Figure 14.2), the emphasis changes dramatically from "item" to the "customer." The historical record of the customer is important, not only what is bought but also who buys what, when, how often, and at what influence on the profitability of the company.

The fundamental database application consists of customer segmentation. This segmentation, based on the size of the list, and therefore the size of the cells, usually starts with some combination of recency, frequency, and dollars. If the file extends through $2\frac{1}{2}$ years, breaking the customer file down by quarters provide eleven cells to start with. If this is split between one-time customer and multiple customers that multiplies the eleven age cells to twenty-two age-by-frequency cells. If only three levels of dollar purchase are to be checked, that increases the twenty-two age-by-frequency segments to sixty-six age-by-frequency-by-dollar-sales cells. Using this example, imagine the number of cells Sears or J.C. Penney can review, after including ten to twenty item classifications plus five or ten different sources, and possibly five different methods of payment, plus length of payment period and credit rating. All those considerations indicate that a better method needs to be developed to act as a guide to the history of purchases.

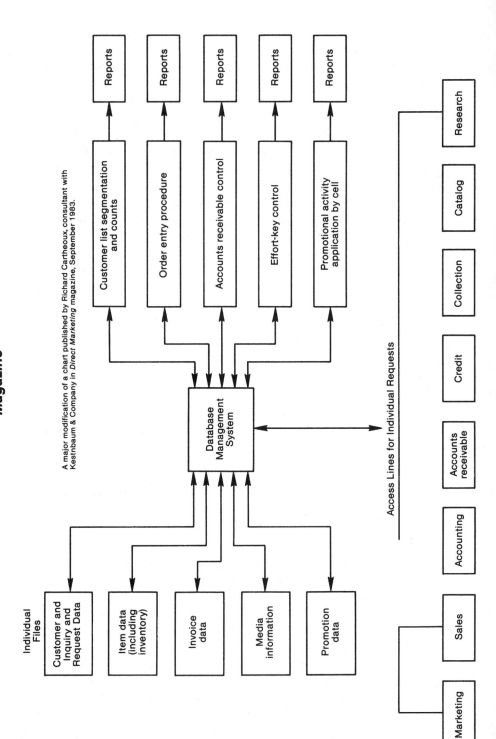

Figure 14.2

A major modification of a recent chart published by Richard Cartheoux, consultant, formerly with Kestnbaum & Company in *Direct Marketing Magazine*

A major modification of a chart published by Richard Cartheoux, consultant with Kestnbaum & Company in *Direct Marketing* magazine, September 1983.

Individual Files

Customer and Inquiry and Request Data

Item data (including inventory)

Invoice data

Media information

Promotion data

Database Management System

Customer list segmentation and counts

Order entry procedure

Accounts receivable control

Effort-key control

Promotional activity application by cell

Reports

Reports

Reports

Reports

Reports

Access Lines for Individual Requests

Marketing

Sales

Accounting

Accounts receivable

Credit

Collection

Catalog

Research

How Small List Owners Can Determine Response by Age of Last Sale

List owners with small customer files, say under 150,000, (which is the greatest proportion of lists owned by all direct marketers by far) should not despair. A selection by age of last sale *alone* will provide a series of progressive steps where the later the buy, the higher the response, and with that higher response the greater the number of dollars per 1,000 catalogs in the mail. To do this, select segments that are large enough to provide sufficient *responses* for statistical validity. On tests, that number can be set with some confidence at fifty. For segment analysis it is best to construct splits so that one hundred or more responses can be realized from mailings to the average segment.

Before discussing predictable modeling for larger files, it is useful to discuss what is workable for the more modest customer files most operators must work with. Data are presented below for the customer files only. Keyed prospect mailings accompany these schedules.

Example 1:

File of 25,000 Customers—3 years or less
plus 14,000 inquiries and catalog requests

	Response level (percentage)	Breakeven—Sales of $820/M $ per M catalogs mailed
Most recent 5,000 customers	4.5%	$2,200
Next most recent 5,000 customers	4.1	1,850
Third most recent 5,000 customers	3.4	1,630
Fourth most recent 5,000 customers	3.2	1,550
Fifth most recent 5,000 customers	1.7	870
Most recent 4,000 inquiries	2.1	1,050
Next most recent 4,000 inquiries	1.4	740
Balance of inquiries	1.1	340

On the next mailing these data would indicate that the final fifth of customers on the list and the next most recent 4,000 inquiries should be split into two halves to see if parts of each group are worthy of continuation mailings. The balance of inquiries have almost certainly outlived their usefulness. Any good prospect list is likely to now produce more response and dollars than the $340/M reported here.

Example 2:

File of 109,000 Customers—4 years or less
plus 41,000 inquiries, catalog requests, friends of customers

	Number	Response level (percentage)	(Breakeven—Sales of $950) $ per M catalogs mailed
Last 3-month Buyers			
Over $50	3,900	4.1%	2,950
Under $50	3,500	3.8	2,240
Next 3-Month Buyers			
Over $50	3,700	3.6	2,770
Under $50	3,100	3.6	1,880
Next 6-Month Buyers			
Over $50	7,400	2.9	2,450
Under $50	5,900	2.7	1,580
Second-Year Buyers			
Over $50	16,800	2.6	2,210
Under 50	11,900	2.4	1,480
Third-Year Buyers			
Over $50	16,400	2.1	1,450
Under 50	14,500	1.6	990
Fourth-Year Buyers			
Over 50	7,400	1.6	1,140
Under 50	8,600	1.1	765
Last 3-Month Inquiries	7,300	3.1	1,590
Next 3-Month Inquiries	6,200	2.4	1,240
Next 6-Month Inquiries	7,500	1.5	890
Next Year's Inquiries	13,500	1.1	640
Prior	5,200	0.7	455

It is worth noting that even fourth-year buyers, if purchases are initially over $50, produce a modest profit over the cost of promotion (this is not true for the under $50 group). There is strong indication here that earlier approaches to the inquiry list would create a greater conversion proportion.

These sample records indicate that even modest files should be split. (Researching for facts should be a rule for *every* mailing.) The key factor to look at is age of the buyer. The longer time has elapsed since the last sale, the lower the penetration that can be expected.

An assumption made on this table is that the customer file is being mailed

X times per year as it should. Those records, which on one mailing, appear to be below the line should be isolated but not thrown away. As an expire file, they may do well enough at certain times of the year to deserve a mailing or two. In addition those records that are about to expire should be sent a "last chance" offer before name removal. This quite often moves part of an aging, inactive file into a last bit of productivity. In addition there may be special buyers, other multibuyers, or large single buyers in a file to be expired. Some experimentation, primarily by phone, should be done before these names are removed along with those names hopelessly below the line.

DATABASE SELECTION OPTIONS

Perhaps the most important computer algorithm in database management is NINO (Not In–Not Out). What is not put on the file in a codable way can never be pulled out or selected for use. Database selection options, depending on NINO, can include some or all of the following:

File source who owns or maintains the file.

List profile essence of the data on the file (businesses, executives, consumers, buyers, inquirers).

Prefix title proper salutation for doctors, reverends, captains, and so on.

List source source of the individual list (or lists) from which the individual record comes.

Employee size exact number of employees at a given location, or for a company as a whole, or ranges of same.

Title select access to the entire gamut of business titles found in the database.

Field of interest or function a vice president may be in sales, finance, production, or research.

Recency date of the last sales or inquiry transaction by a given customer.

SIC and industry group two-digit, three-digit, four-digit, or fifth-character SIC coding.

Multibuyer selection of those who have purchased two or more times.

Cell count access to count data by different segmentation; also on a one-for-ten basis, the number of records in a given cross-section for research purposes.

Record selects by fifth-digit zip code, Nth Name, or first letter of last name.

Add titles option to add titles where title is not available; also ability to add extra records for given establishment.

Max per record limits the number of names selected from a given firm to a predetermined maximum.

Flights means of isolating multiple prospects at one location and arranging to mail a few each day in separate "flights" and thus reduce a glut of identical third class mail pieces at the company mail receiving room.

Split outputs capacity to split out any key, segment, and list source for individualized attention, and then tag and count the data sets for mailing in one string for postal savings.

Credit Status and Number of Promotions Update

In addition to purchase data and conventional marketing information a database also provides the credit status of each customer. It is efficient to have the update program record each time a given customer is promoted since the last purchase as a means to increase or decrease mailings based on results. Building a customer database should more than pay its way in improved selectivity alone.

HOW TO CREATE A DATABASE MANAGEMENT SYSTEM

Simply creating a database does not launch a company into database management. You must first create a database management system. This means capturing all the desired information on a computer large enough to handle the system needs, organizing that data for use, arranging methodology for updating and maintaining it, and establishing channels to readily retrieve and manipulate the data for marketing use. Sad but true, this is a very complex, difficult, time consuming, and expensive task. It is not for the faint of heart! The data collection needs highly disciplined keying standards which must incorporate name data, address data, background data, and all interactions between the data and the business.

Establish a Detailed Company Order–Entry Manual

To obtain name and address data, a set of rules, which are to be followed rigorously, must be set up. These rules determine what is to be done with prefixes, titles, initials, and suffixes such as MD, CLU, LV, JR., III. It is important to exercise firm discipline in this regard if correspondence is not to read "Dear Inc."

or "Dear MD Mr. Smith Jr." Rules should also specify what is to be picked up, in what order, and in what way. The person entering the data should not have to make decisions; they should all have been made for her or him in the company order-entry manual.

Among the topics the company manual on *order entry* should cover are complete instructions of what to do *if* the

- Item description does not match the item number
- Price is wrong
- Shipping and handling charges have not been added
- Source key is not given
- Zip code appears to be wrong for the area
- Credit card numbers are missing or incomplete
- Required phone number is omitted
- Signature is missing
- Sales tax has been omitted or misstated
- Order is less than the minimum or over a given size
- Check is missing, unsigned, or postdated
- Color ordered is not available
- Item must be backordered
- Several line items will not be shipped at one time
- Address is a post office box number for a package shipment
- Order matches a deadbeat or "do not promote" record

Specialized software programs must either be created or purchased and modified to capture, organize, and retrieve the data. Computer people who know their way around a system as complicated as this must be on hand through the entire development period, which may run from six months to a year.

Attend to Billing and Shipping Details

There is a host of billing and shipping details that must be considered. Saving both "shipped to" and "billed to" data is mandatory because not many buyers are actually located at their "billed to" addresses. Zip codes must be verified and data probably requires carrier-route coding. It may be necessary to differentiate by type of address whether the record is a household, a business, an academic establishment, a library, government, or hospital. It is important to be able to run all executives against a gender file, and end up with a system which is both flexible and responsive to a special request, is user-friendly and customer-oriented, and is in the control of those who wish to use it.

Other Key Strategies to Consider

Database management strategy involves waste reduction activities, as well as changes of address, and perhaps, running against bad debt files to eliminate poor prospects and bad risks.

This embraces marketing strategy—the what to do with what is available to make more money for the company.

Implementation of a longterm-oriented marketing plan is another important strategy. The best program in the world will do no good for its creator if it is not implemented.

Finally, database marketing puts extra emphasis on the back end—what happens when a phone call comes in on the WATS line, what happens when a request comes in for information, what happens when a new order hits the order desk. Everything that has already occurred can be reduced to rubble if the fulfillment is not in place to match the marketing. Database management is more than data on a computer—it is a system for controlling laborpower to see that the system works; it provides raw data that must be shaped into a marketing program. These data must be targeting, planned, created, and implemented. Last, but not least, the fulfillment must match the marketing needs created.

HOW TO USE A MODELING APPROACH FOR A GIVEN OFFER

Where a list is growing, and simplistic cell structure is no longer practical, a modeling approach is indicated. Models can encompass any and all facts about groups to provide a basis for future prediction. Models can actually be developed that can find a specific type of buyer. It is very difficult to define cells effectively for such a specific application. Models do provide weighted predictive numbers which reduce the need to worry about whether individual small cells provide statistical reliability. The modeling approach involves the following steps:

1. Definition of the offer, including breakeven requirements.
2. Offer a test large enough, say, 750 to 1,000 responses, to provide data for predictive modeling.

3. Predictive model development and application of weighted values to the customer file.

4. Selection of customers for rollout to include all above line and some at breakeven and below, to confirm the predictive capability.

Modeling for an offer can provide four types of information:

1. Is the offer generally viable?

2. If viable, is the predictable success sufficient to warrant a continuation?

3. From split-test results, what is the best form of the offer?

4. To which cells on the data bank should the offer be circulated?

HOW TO DETERMINE THE LIFETIME VALUE OF A CUSTOMER

As noted elsewhere one of the most elusive figures in direct marketing is the long term or "lifetime" value of a customer.

Lifetime value of a new customer is the present value of all future contributions to overhead and profit to be expected from a customer. Without some appreciation of the lifetime value of a new customer, proper decisions cannot be made on such important decisions as:

1. How much can be expended to buy a new customer.

2. How much can be expended to reactivate a customer.

3. What cash flow restraints are involved in customer acquisition and reactivation.

4. What effect does new customer acquisition have on growth and profit.

5. What return on investment is available over a period of time and how does this compare with other investment opportunities.

6. What the value of the customer file is today and where this will be tomorrow.

Bridging the Gap between Growth and Profit with List Development

The "war" between growth and profit arises because virtually all first-time customers are created at a cost, which must then be amortized from subsequent purchases over a given period of time. Thus the greater the number of new customers created, the greater the loss of money caused by such creation.

Each new name added increases the total sales that can be anticipated from a larger base. Thus *new* customers *now* create an additional value to be realized in the future. To quantify this *future* gain *now* a sum can be assigned for *"list development."*

When this value is factored in for most mail order operations with multiple customer mailings, longterm-oriented decisions usually lead to lower short-term profits (usually losses) but significantly larger profits in the longterm.

It is fairly simple to work out the mathematics involved in a single mailing per season. Complication sets in when there are multiple mailings to the customer file per season. This is now an increasingly common practice as most mailers are successfully learning to mail more often to the better segments of their customer files. Tests conducted through offers are no longer completely germane because one mailing on the heels of another "robs" some of the response that may have come into the prior mailing.

A test must be designed which will measure the incremental effect of additional circulation. Here extracting known segments based on predictive modeling can be used successfully for matched test panels in which one segment tests A, one tests A and B, one tests A, B, and C, and one tests A–C. Such a test is based on an entire season. The balance of the file is then mailed, say, only A, and the results are analyzed for sales as well as for contribution to overhead.

As direct marketing at the catalog level is becoming more and more an ongoing process, the database, which links together all of the interrelated factors involving marketing, becomes more and more important in the planning, execution, and evaluation of marketing. Database marketing, using predictive weighting is long-term not short-term oriented; it makes careful targeting of each effort possible, even when one effort is plied against another. It offers a way to measure results in hard dollars and cents. By quantifying all aspects of both longterm and shortterm marketing, it provides a way to build a direct-mail business on a solid mathematical base.

One master builder of databases for customers puts it this way, "Knowledge is power, the power to define, the power to identify, the power to predict, the power to sell, the power to fill a need." Databases define, identify, and provide the facts for realistic predictions and sales.

OVERLAY SOURCES FOR DATA TRANSFER

Any time two files are merge–purged to obtain a single file of unique records, a transfer of data from one base to the other (on the matched records) can be made. Every merge–purge run carries this possibility. Most merge–purges, however, do not result in data transfer except for the identification (if desired) of those records that appear on more than one list.

Seven Types of *Consumer* Overlays

Consumer overlays, in which data are added to records (not only the suppression of records for pandering names, or bad pay names, or unwanted zips or wrong addresses) can be split into several groups:

1. Stratigraphic files from Donnelley, Polk, Data Base America, or Metromail to add: ·
   Individual income
   Median age (by carrier route)
   Median education (by carrier route)
   Median value of home (by carrier route)
   Type of dwelling
   Length of residency
   Number, make, model, year, and value of car
   Phone number

2. Driver license data from Executive Services, CCI, Lead Marketing, Demographic Systems, as well as Donnelley, Polk, Data Base America, and Metromail to add:
   Other adults in household
   Age of each adult
   Names of husbands and wives
   Exact date of birth

3. Composite of children's mail order and store distribution lists primarily from Demographic Systems to add:
   Names of children
   Sex of children
   Exact date of birth of children

4. Mail order and Questionnaire Responses components added to files by Donnelley, Executive Services, Metromail, Data Base America, Polk to add:
   Mail order responsiveness and psychographic interests to segments of compiled files

5. Lifestyle questionnaire respondents from Lifestyle Selector, Donnelley, Blair, Data Bank America, Polk, Behavior Bank to add:

Hobbies

Interests

Ownerships of products

(Donnelley is matching all psychographic data from its questionnaires to its household data bank. Polk is adding outside mail order data to its data bank. Life Style Selector is incorporating all Polk data into its data bank so as to encompass data on 50 million additional families. Data Bank America is adding a Life Style Selector to its growing coverage.)

6. Canvass for city directories by Polk to add:

Occupation

Retired persons

Size of family

Number of children

7. Cluster analysis programs by Prism, Claritas, Donnelley and others to select:

Geographic areas by approximate lifestyle affinity

Donnelley uses thirty-nine clusters. These are quite comparable to the cluster descriptions used by others. Every zip code, census tract, sub-block group, and carrier route is "fitted" into one of the following thirty-nine cluster descriptions, by their apparent "demographic characteristics."

Donnelley's Demographic Characteristics

Cluster code	Demographic characteristics
S 01	Highest SESI, highest income, prime real estate areas, highly educated, professionally employed, low mobility, homeowners, children in private schools
S 02	Very high income, new homes and condominiums, prime real estate areas, highly mobile, well educated, professionally employed, homeowners, families with children
S 03	High income, high home values, new homes, highly mobile, younger, well educated, professionally employed, homeowners, married couples, high incidence of children, larger families
S 04	High income, high home values, well educated, professionally employed, married couples, larger families, highest incidence of teenagers, homeowners, homes built in the 1960s
S 05	High income, high home values, well educated, professionally employed, low mobility, homeowners, homes built in the 1950s and 1960s

Cluster code	Demographic characteristics
S 06	Highest incidence of children, large families, new homes, highly mobile, younger, married couples, above-average income and education, homeowners
S 07	Apartments and condominiums, high rent, above-average income, well educated, professionally employed, mobile, singles, few children, urban areas
S 08	Above-average income, above-average education, older, fewer children, white-collar workers
S 09	Above-average income, average education, households with two or more workers, homes built in the 1960s and 1970s
S 10	Well educated, average income, professionally employed, younger, mobile, apartment dwellers, above-average rents
S 11	Above-average income, average education, families with children, high incidence of teenagers, homeowners, homes built in the 1960s, small towns
S 12	Highly mobile, young, working couples, young children, new homes, above-average income and education, white-collar workers
S 13	Older, fewer children, above-average income, average education, white-collar workers, homeowners, homes built in the 1950s, very low mobility, small towns
S 14	Retirees, comdominiums and apartments, few children, above-average income and education, professionally employed, high home values and rents, urban areas
S 15	Older, very low mobility, fewer children, above-average income and education, white collar workers, old housing, urban areas
S 16	Working couples, very low mobility, above-average income, average education, homeowners, homes built in the 1950s, urban areas
S 17	Very young, below-average income, well educated, professionally employed, highly mobile, singles, few children, apartment dwellers, high rent areas
S 18	High incidence of children, larger families, above-average income, average education, working couples, homeowners
S 19	High incidence of children, larger families, above-average income, average education, younger, married couples, homeowners, homes built in the 1960s and 1970s, primarily rural areas
S 20	Areas with high proportion of group quarters population, subdivisions available including college dormitories, homes for the aged, mental hospitals and prisons
S 21	Average income and education, blue-collar workers, families with children, homeowners, lower home values, rural areas
S 22	Below-average income and education, older, fewer children, single family homes, primarily in the South
S 23	Below-average income, average education, low mobility, married couples, old homes, farm areas, north central region
S 24	Highly mobile, young, few children, low income, average education, ethnic mix, singles, apartments, urban areas

Cluster code	Demographic characteristics
S 25	Younger, mobile, fewer children, below-average income, average education, apartment dwellers
S 26	Older, mobile, fewer children, below-average income, average education, mobile homes, retirees, higher vacancy rates, primarily rural areas
S 27	Average income and education, single family homes, lower home values, homes built in the 1950s and 1960s
S 28	Below-average income, less educated, younger, mobile, high incidence of children, mobile homes, primarily rural areas
S 29	Older, low mobility, high proportion of foreign languages, average income, below-average education, old homes and apartments, urban areas, northeast region
S 30	Low-income, poorly educated, higher vacancy rates, families with one worker, farms, rural areas
S 31	Older, fewer children, low income, less educated, low mobility, retirees, old single family homes
S 32	Old, few children, low income, below-average education, one-person households, retirees
S 33	Below-average income, less educated, blue-collar workers, manufacturing plants, homes built in the 1950s and 1960s, very low mobility, low home values
S 34	Old, below-average income, average education, blue-collar workers, low mobility, rural areas
S 35	Old housing, low income, average education, younger, mobile, fewer children, apartment dwellers, small towns
S 36	Average income, less educated, blue-collar workers, Hispanic, families with children
S 37	Average income, below-average education, blue-collar workers, manufacturing areas, high unemployment, primarily in the north central regions
S 38	Old, lowest incidence of children, very low income, less educated, apartment dwellers, one-person households, retirees, urban areas
S 39	Older, very low mobility, very old housing, below-average income and education, blue-collar workers, manufacturing areas

Business Overlays

Data are added to records available from D&B as well as from Data Bank America through their files held at CCX and at Pagex: Data that can be transferred from the master file of D&B include:

- Four-digit SIC
- Number of employees (on most records)
- Sales volume (on high proportion of records)

- Key executive (on most records)
- County code
- Metropolitan area code
- Telephone number

Overlay data available from the 8 million establishment Data Bank America file available through CCX and Pagex include:

- Four- and five-digit SIC
- Multiple SICs
- Number of employees (on part of the records)
- County code
- Metropolitan area code
- Carrier-route code
- Advertising code
- City size code
- Telephone number
- New businesses
- Change of address
- Suppression of companies with liens or in bankruptcy

Selected Data Bank America data compiled by the Burnett organization is the main component of the "Focus Master" system run regularly at CCX.

Telephone Data Banks

Teleprospectors and telemarketers were appalled after the breakup of the Bell system in May of 1985, at the 50 cent charge imposed for interstate directory assistance calls in excess of two per month. (In October, 1985 this was increased to 60¢!)

This charge created a great deal of exploration to find ways of bypassing the costly directory assistance operation necessary to obtain "direct access" on an electronic basis to the database resident, on disc, or tape at the local telephone companies.

Substantial interest in providing telephone listing information through direct access has been shown by the twenty-two individual Bell operating companies, and the seven regions into which they have been formed under the divestiture agreement. Several have already offered what they call "Direct Customer Access."

The local phone companies can offer only local phone appending—that is, Illinois Bell can provide numbers for Illinois, but if numbers are desired for Pennsylvania, that would necessitate ordering from Pennsylvania Bell. The problems of creating a nationwide service, because of politics, the governmental climate, variances in recordkeeping, and computer capabilities of the operating companies is enormous. The advantage of obtaining access to telephone data banks is that the phone numbers will be current. The average error on phone numbers from lists compiled from printed phone directories is at least 15 percent.

There are several extant files of *all listed* phone numbers, both alphabetic and yellow pages. Although not as correct as numbers that may be available by direct access, telephone numbers for the country as a whole can be tapped.

Companies with listed *alphabetic* phones include, Donnelley, Data Base America, Polk, Metromail, MED (a subsidiary of Metromail), and CCX, which serves as a phone append processor.

At least five companies have rather complete *business* phone numbers for the country: D&B, R.L. Polk, American Business Lists, Data Base America, and Compilers Plus. (Survey Sampling has a complete file of telephone numbers attached to yellow page headings without company or establishment names.) American Business Lists, unique among business list compilers, makes its names available "on line" for access via phone lines to remote terminals and PCs. This availability may be modified by a recent settlement between Southwest Bell, the copyright owner, and American Business Lists.

The only current nationwide list of customers with phone numbers in the country is owned by AT&T long lines, which is the "court of last resort" for long distance calls that cannot be accessed by any other service. In 1985, AT&T began billing for its portion of service in test areas, a prelude to billing all or part of its large customer file nationwide. Whether AT&T will be a player or not in phone number appending has not yet been determined.

Ethnicity

Ethnicity is another selection factor made possible by overlays, in this case by means of a surname match overlay. Catholic, Jewish, and Spanish-speaking or Spanish-sounding consumers are readily identifiable. Irish and Italian Catholics are rather well defined, and other ethnic language groups are available even though the numbers of those with a high proportion of certainty tend to be rather small. Black families cannot be identified by matching last names. Demographically, the proportion of Black households in each United States census geographical area is given by the United States Bureau of the Census. When this figure is 60, 70, or 80 percent Black, such areas are considered ethnically Black.

CHAPTER 15

The How To's
of Marketing
for Catalog Operations

WHY CATALOG SALES ARE INCREASING

Catalog sales, from all reports, are growing faster than over-the-counter purchases. It is likely when all retailing is included the growth is restricted to specific categories within specific classifications because direct response has very little to do with retail sales of gasoline, staple foods, most drugs, most flowers, virtually all hardware, building and garden supplies, most clothing, most apparel, most textiles, virtually all furniture, and virtually all automobiles. Similarly direct response has no part of the greatest proportion of variety store merchandise and stationery store supplies, nor appliances, nor the vast proportion of liquor, sporting goods, bicycles, arts and crafts, greeting cards, fuel and ice and coal, news dealer sales, opticians goods, pet shop sales, and typewriters, all of which are basically sold over the counter.

Catalog distribution and catalog sales are increasing. The reasons for this increase are listed below:

- Specialized coverage
- Available twenty-four hours a day
- Better and more complete product information
- More complete selection (the catalog can offer thousands more items than the retail store that enters the market can stock and sell over the counter)

- Fully stipulated money-back guarantee
- Toll free "800" number for immediate ordering
- Cashless shopping by credit card or personal check
- Considered purchase—not impulse shopping
- Reference value of the catalog for product information and for returns and allowances

A number of major catalog operators are now selling page space in their books to other advertisers. Some believe this is a new phenomenon. It is not. Catalogs have included the ads of others for fifty years. Usually such hybrids have a short life. The dollars paid for a space ad do not equate with the dollars an extra hardworking catalog page can produce.

A catalog is a "specialty store on paper," designed to be a place where people want to shop. It is an advertising medium that features a group of associated items for sale on a direct-response basis. It has one purpose: To induce those to whom it is sent to peruse its pages and buy items it presents by direct response, either by mail or by phone.

In 1980 a careful sampling for the USPS by a University of Michigan task force disclosed that 2,717,000,000 of the then 22 billion direct-mail pieces with advertising were in the form of catalogs of twenty pages or more.

In 1979 catalogs were 3.3 percent of all nonhousehold created mail. Of this quantity 2,224,000,000 went to households (or close to 30 per household) and 493,000,000 went to nonhouseholds (or close to 60 per establishment).

The University of Michigan analysis showed that receipt of catalogs by class of nonhousehold was as follows.

Business	310,500,000
Government	12,800,000
Schools	169,400,000
Nonprofit Organizations	2,300,000
Hospitals and medical services	5,700,000
Foreign governments	2,500,000

Some idea of the value of the school market in America is indicated by the vast number of catalogs they receive: over 1000 per year per school and per school district. Hospitals and medical services receive over one hundred catalogs per year. Business establishments as a whole, including offices of professionals, receive about fifty catalogs per year.

It is estimated that *some* 80,000 of 5,200,000 business establishments (1.5 percent) use catalogs in their promotional efforts. The figures for originators of catalogs by major classification are as follows.

	Catalog operators	Universe of firms
Mail order companies	11,500	13,500
Department stores	10,500	58,000
Home delivery sales operations	15,000	59,000
Manufacturers other than printers and publishers	15,000	300,000
Publishers	15,000	30,000
Mail service companies	6,000	7,000
Printers	5,000	46,000
Other businesses	3,500	4,700,000

A few predictions seem reasonably safe in this turbulent field.

1. Catalog volume will increase. One major study predicts that the volume printed in 1990 will double the 1979 total of 2700 million.
2. Specialty catalogs will grow in number, but the number of operators will be reduced by combination, attrition, and acquisition.
3. Retail catalogs will continue their strong growth.
4. Catalog showrooms, which became prominent in the 1970s, will grow in the 1980s, but at a much lower rate.
5. Catalogs produced by big business will increase in number as well as volume. The larger the firm, the larger the number of mailings and the greater the volume.

By 1986, that 22 billion of pieces of mail with advertising in 1980 had increased to some 45 billion and if, as seems likely, catalogs increased at a proportional rate then the total number of catalogs now in the mailstream is on the order of 5 billion. In 1980 one company alone, Sears, Roebuck & Co., produced 10 percent (300 million pieces!) of all the catalogs received in U.S. homes. Over half of these were specialty catalogs, the balance was the big general catalog. In that year the total number of pages were still greater for the general catalog than for the specialty catalogs. If that has not since shifted, it is clear as numbers mount, and new specialty catalogs are produced, that Sears specialty catalogs will not only outnumber its general catalogs, but the total number of pages will be greater as well.

ONE CATALOG SUCCESS STORY: SEARS, ROEBUCK & CO.

One-fifth of Sears's huge volume comes from catalog sales (over 90 percent of which are phoned in, which boggles the minds of most mail-minded merchandisers). Catalogs display and sell merchandise. The phone is the personal link in the sales chain.

The Sears catalog operation employs 350 people, with a budget of over $250 million. Each year, 9500 new catalog pages are produced (most are now for specialized segmented catalogs). Over 155,000 tons of paper are consumed yearly. Split-run ad tests run into hundreds per year.

Single-item testing is done by using selected cells (based on recency, frequency, dollars, item source, and method of payment in the credit buyers file of 25 million names).

Sears operates 850 retail stores, 375 of which are full-line and 475 condensed or incomplete, with a restricted number of departments. Of forty-nine separate selling divisions in Sears, the catalog sales division is the largest.

Sears does a huge business in specialty catalogs, offering a much broader assortment than any general-merchandise store could possibly handle. Among these specialty catalogs (seventeen in all) are:

40-page western-style clothing

80-page big and tall men

44-page floor covering

144-page power and hand tools

However it is now evident that the Sears specialty catalogs will have to be improved in content and coverage if Sears is to continue its dominance in the catalog market. For individual specialized catalog operators are providing even more spirited offerings today than Sears.

The essence of the Sears story was spelled out in a few simple points by J.B. Kelley, former vice president of catalog sales and the person in charge of a program producing 1 million catalogs every business day! His first point is based on a comment by the marketing specialist, Bob Stone:

> *It is not the awesome size of Sears' catalog operation that makes it unique, but the emphasis on catalogs as a marketing force instead of an advertising or promotional effort. Each of Sears' seventeen specialty catalogs support the retailer's philosophy that catalog circulation and retail stores should support one another.*

Kelley goes on to make these other points:

- Catalog sales set the pattern for the geographic location of new stores, both full-line and restricted. The best customers of a new retail store are catalog customers. Stores tend to be located where catalog sales indicate sufficient penetration.

- The catalogs supplement the assortment of merchandise, which can be carried economically within the walls of a retail store.

- A family that receives a Sears catalog is twice as likely to shop in a Sears retail store as a family that has not qualified to receive one, and such a family will spend twice as much at Sears.

- Catalogs help develop more credit customers for Sears. Credit enhances customers use of Sears, and the convenience of personal shopping or ordering by phone and paying later picks up extra business. One-third of the households in America have a Sears credit card.

- Catalogs are the forerunners of merchandise directions. Millions of dollars of business is transacted through the catalog in the very items and lines that Sears is offering on a test basis.

It is no accident that Sears has opened business machine stores in five test markets (self-standing, or not associated with main stores and not in shopping centers). These stores stock and sell small business computers (including the new IBM home computers), software, copying machines, calculators, typewriters, word processors, and dictation equipment. Hundreds of Sears stores are projected.

It would be surprising if Sears did not have on the drawing board two catalogs in this field, one for electronic gadgets for the home and a second for office and business equipment. The pattern for the latter may have been set by the gourmet food catalog now mailed for gift purposes to 350,000 businesses.

Sears, perhaps better than any other retailer in America, is aware of the great recent changes in society, including the following:

1. The rise in the cost of energy.
2. The changing attitude about women's place in the workforce. (Sears stores are now open 80 hours a week to serve the needs this creates.)
3. Shifts in population and the mobility of the American people.
4. The shift away from shopping as a pleasant leisure-time family activity and the gravitation of business toward marketers that make shopping increasingly convenient.

It should be no surprise to find that Sears is experimenting with electronic catalogs. The initial experiment uses the Pioneer system laser disc, which is not compatible with the RCA discs Sears sells. The complete catalog on discs with stop action, played through a home TV, is serving 1000 test customers near six selected stores.

MARKETING—THE FRONT END

Product Selection

It is becoming increasingly evident that direct-response marketing can be effective in the sale of a tremendous range of products and services. At one time high-priced merchandise was considered beyond the effective range of direct mail. There now seems to be no limit to the high end. Interestingly enough the price barrier has now shifted to the low end where low-priced items with an order margin of less than $10 may not be viable by direct response.

Conventional wisdom stipulated that products for sale through direct marketing had to be unusual or unique, yet Americans buy such ordinary products as vitamins, candy, screws and bolts, even aspirin tables, Tylenol, antacids, and bandaids by mail. Business-to-business marketers move stationery, books, copier paper, scotch tape, and envelopes through mailed catalogs and telemarketing.

Not all direct-response advertising is required to make an immediate sale. The function given direct marketing may be to generate inquiries or requests that can be followed up by mail, phone, or personal solicitation. This increases markedly the scope of products and services that can be marketed by direct-response means.

Products for sale by direct marketing means do require a reasonably definable group of prospects of sufficient number than can be reached economically enough to justify the effort and cost of the promotion. Products do occasionally define the market (by attracting from some larger universe those with a particular interest). But for the most part, the available market universe defines where and whether a product or group of products can be marketed.

This peculiar affinity between market (lifestyles, requirements, needs) and product to offer results in product choice being basically an art, and one not easily learned or acquired. Many a successful direct-response business has been built initially on only one product or proposition which on its surface (ant farms, nuts and bolts, first aid kits, orchids, spreadsheets, folding boats) appeared to be highly suspect. The selector of product often is not the individual who can run a business. Many who run direct-marketing operations do not have that "special sense" for product. Few recognize that product selection is as much an art as is the creation of the offer, package, timing, and selection of the list.

Price Considerations

Determining Gross Margin

Pricing of a catalog is a delicate art in which the operator seeks to aggrandize the greatest return in three ways: (1) increased response, (2) increased size of order, and (3) increased average gross margin.

The chief aspect of these three increases, which is controlled by the operator, is price and therefore the gross margin on each item. (Customers then determine the average gross margin for the catalog by what they buy and in what numbers or proportions.) Thus with some foreknowledge of how customers respond, even the average gross margin is controlled by the operator.

If anything, the average catalog operator in the market only a short time is too timid about his or her prices (and thus the gross margins) he or she should obtain. If this were a perfect world with perfect competition and perfect knowledge by all parties, then and only then, would everyone provide the same competitive price on each item. But this is not a perfect world and customers and prospects are not aware of small differences in price, or if they are aware they act as though they are not because of their desire for a given item at a given time. (Economists call this "place economy"; in direct mail it might better be called "availability economy" because "place" has little or no part in the decision process.)

On a catalog grossing $1,000,000 in sales, an increase in gross margin of 1 percent adds $10,000 to the bottom line. An increase of 2 percent adds $20,000. There are very few specialty catalogs in the United States where an increase overall of 1 or 2 percent will impact upon sales.

One of the best ways to raise the average margin is to include several attractive products unique in the field, and thus not susceptible to any form of price comparison, at much higher than average mark ups.

Note the following:

	Current price	Current margin (percent)	Profit per item	New price	Margin increase (percent)	Dollar profit	Increase (percent) in profit
A	$18.95	41%	$ 7.78	$19.37	1.0%	$0.42	5.4%
B	27.50	39	10.73	28.50	1.0	1.00	9.3
C	65.00	45	28.25	67.50	.7	2.50	8.8

A relatively minuscule increase—1 percent or less—results in an increase in profit per item many times that. In B and C above, profit per item increases by 9 percent.

One of the more fascinating factors of a well run catalog operation is that there is an apparent synergy among margin and size of order and response rate. Thus it is not unusual to find that based on better analysis a new edition of a catalog with new products at slightly higher margins will also produce higher average orders (hence greater profit per order) as well as higher response (hence lower cost to buy a new customer).

The rule here is don't be afraid to get a reasonable margin. A catalog operation is a retail store—sales are made of one line at a time—not a wholesale operation where sales are made in bulk. Catalogs must be priced at or near retail margins to be profitable. Minor increases happen to produce notable increases on the bottom line.

How do you start? Collect every catalog in your chosen field of specialization. Note the surprisingly different prices for comparable items in catalogs which ostensibly compete with each other. Calculate the mark ups of say twenty bell-weather items to see how others exercise the art of pricing and then make certain your pricing provides a "living wage" for all the work entailed in running your large store on "paper."

What to Include When Estimating Catalog Operation Costs

When it comes to estimating the cost of a catalog operation, it is essential to include every item that affects total cost. Such items can be grouped under the following classifications:

1. Preparation
     Counseling and creative
     Art
     Photos
     Typography
     Pasteup

2. Printing
     Catalog
     Covers (if separate)
     Bound-in order form
     Outside envelope (if required)

3. Mailing Lists
   Customer files
   Outside files
   Merge–purge
   Carrier-route coding
   Label or tape production (bag tags, USPS certification)

4. Fulfillment
   Addressing
   Sort, bag and tie, mail and certify
   Postage (by type)

5. Back end
   Merchandise
   Premiums (if any)
   Storage
   Order entry and picking and packing
   Merchandise return and refurbishing
   Supervisory labor administration
   Heat, light, telephone
   Customer service
   Shipping and handling
   Cost of money (carrying cost of inventory and losses)

THE IMPORTANCE OF A CLEAR ORDER FORM

This text makes no effort to cover the infinities of the preparation and production of packages, letters, space ads, and catalogs. But there is part of every response effort which deserves a few words because of the importance of its effect on that response—that is the order form.

A good rule in writing copy is to write and lay out the order form either first or immediately after deciding on the headline. The best copy and offer can be ruined by a poor order form. Coupon ads calling for a written response have been run in reverse—white type on a black background—in magazines. Many order forms leave almost no room to squeeze in the name and address. Some leave off the address they are to be mailed to. Some provide costs for postage and handling in six-point type for which a magnifying glass is needed. Be sure! Don't be sorry! Study a group of order forms run time after time by major firms and see how careful they are to make the order form clear and concise and user friendly as far as ease of use is concerned.

PACKAGING DETAILS

How Many Pages Should the Catalog Contain?

The best catalog for a specialty operation includes every or almost every important item that fits the needs of those who are interested in that specialty, with one proviso—the "store" so designed is a profitable venture. There is a desire as the catalog matures to increase coverage of items and increase pages. The best rule here is to increase the coverage and pages in relatively small increments. Even adding eight or twelve pages can be quite a chore. Jumping from sixteen to forty-eight pages is a tremendous effort. If your present catalog is twenty-four pages, try thirty-six pages and see if the R.O.I. pays for the extra effort and the extra cost before you add twelve pages more.

How Large Should the Catalog Be?

Most catalogs today have a trim size of 7×10 inches or $8\frac{1}{2} \times 11$ inches. The larger size tends to have a longer life than smaller trim sizes and it usually produces more customers per thousand catalogs mailed.

The smaller sized page offers greater "bulk" in hand for the same amount of paper and roughly the same cost. This may be an advantage. (The actual space available on a sixty-four-page $5\frac{1}{2} \times 8\frac{1}{2}$ inch "half-page" catalog is a little less than a thirty-two-page $8\frac{1}{2} \times 11$ inch catalog because there is more margin space.) For some product lines the need for larger space for photos and descriptions makes the larger catalog preferable.

The half-page catalog seems to do nicely for low-cost items, jewelry, some apparel, and some tools. If your catalog is to be a new venture, it is wise to collect copies of all catalogs currently in the field. The Direct Marketing Association at both its New York and Chicago offices has a good selection of current catalogs, and so may your list broker.

What about Catalog Production and Packaging Practices?

A recent survey by the DMA on catalog practices found that one-third of catalog operators design from three to twenty-four catalog types, 23 percent design two types while 45 percent are content to design only one type. Approximately two-thirds of catalog operators, whose sales spread rather evenly from $250,000 to over $10,000,000, sold to the consumer market, and one-third sold to the nonhousehold (business) market.

Only 40 percent of catalog operators are able to adhere strictly to preset schedules. This may be influenced by the fact that 80 percent of all production requirements are obtained "out of house."

Forty percent of catalogs feature a specific product on the cover. About 30 percent use an illustrative or "mood-selling" cover, and the other 30 percent alternate between mood and product selling. Only one-third of all catalogs use an outer wrapping.

When Does It Pay to Have a "Stripped-Down" Catalog?

Almost every producer of a sixty-eight-page catalog costing, say, $400 to $425 in the mail, while looking at the variability in sales by item, has at one time or another had an inclination to produce a stripped-down catalog with only the best sellers. The net result is a lower-cost catalog with, say, one-fifth the number of items, and every item is a proven profit-maker. Sounds like a winner—with one exception. It just doesn't work! A full-scale catalog may be able to buy a new customer at a cost of $10 or $5, or at breakeven against the cost of promotion. A stripped-down catalog mailed to the same markets will produce orders, but at a cost of six to ten *times* the cost of the full catalog. What is involved here is the affect on the buyer and his or her *perceived value* of the offer. When tests are made of using a stripped-down catalog (costs less?) instead of a full catalog as a bounce back, the full catalog always wins hands down. The rule is—think about it but decide not to use it!

Because weight and size are important criteria for insertion of stuffers in billing mailings by others, the mini- or microcatalog may well have some place in the insert market and several major mailers are now experimenting with their microcatalogs sized 3 inch by 5 inch to be inserted at some negotiated price differential, in card decks. It is likely only some of these will prove to be cost efficient.

Should Solo Offers Be Used as Entry Type Mailings Instead of More Costly Catalogs?

Probably the best overall answer to this question is given by your mailbox. You may receive from catalog houses one or two solo mailings, single product mailings, or minicatalogs in the course of a year compared with perhaps dozens of full-fledged catalogs sent to your home or business searching for a first order. The reason is not hard to find! The cost of a solo offer in the mail is almost always so little less than a full catalog mailing that it just does not pay.

It certainly seems to make sense to design a low-priced piece which will create enough first-time buyers to be economic and send all new buyers the catalog.

But in practice, this just does not happen. It does have relevance in space ads. It is fairly common to see a catalog operator feature one item in modest space ads, and run and rerun this in many catalogs many times over. Such ads produce new customers who are more likely to be responsive to catalog offers than cold prospects on known adequate lists. The secret is to buy these new one-time one-product customers at a low enough cost to justify their purchase in the first place. There are some operators who get high enough sales of single products through magazines to show a modest profit on each order as well as conversion to first-time catalog buyer status at a favorable rate.

Similarly, space ads that only seek a request for a catalog can be productive if the cost of each request is modest enough while the conversion to first-time buyer status is healthy enough.

Returns and Their Importance

It is sound practice to run returns against sales by item to get a true picture of sales. Hardly any action in direct mail can impact the value of a given item in a catalog as much as excessive returns can. Viewing returns in general or as one lumped figure buries this impact. In any catalog there are usually only a few items that seem to get out of line as to the costs involved in handling the returns, issuing the credits, refurbishing the items (where possible) and adjusting the inventory.

Offering Quantity Prices

It is relatively rare to see a line in a catalog that reads something like, "Ask us for our Low Low Quantity Prices." Yet, a given mailer may prospect to dozens of different market segments with hundreds of thousands or even millions of catalogs. Only a very small proportion of these customers, even in the business field, may have a need for quantities, but that small proportion may be a few hundred or even a few thousand prospects for one or more items in quantity. It hardly costs anything to find out!

ESTABLISHING A MINIMUM ORDER SIZE

Because of the costs of even the smallest selection by computer, minimums are a way of life for everyone renting a mailing list. However some firms that have no difficulty in establishing a $250 or $300 minimum charge for rental of a test quantity of their customer file cannot bring themselves to establish a minimum order size for their catalog offer to prospects. These executives, some of them running relatively large catalog mail order operations, believe a minimum order will work against them. What is really working against them are two facts caused by a plethora of small orders:

1. As high as 50 percent of all orders deliver no more than 10 or 12 percent of total volume.
2. The average order size—a main determinant of profit for direct response— is arbitrarily lower than it could or should be.

One major business mailer with no minimum order but with an average order from new customers of $75 and an average order size overall of $140 receives 100,000 orders a year, half of them under $50 and half of that half are under $25. The 25,000 orders under $25 average less than $15. By establishing a $25 minimum (that can be broken for special accounts) the average value of the small order group would increase by $10 or more and add $6 or more in gross margin per order. The loss of orders under such a stipulation in today's world would be close to nil. The addition, over $150,000 of gross margin, would add a nice proportion to the bottom line.

DETERMINING HOW OFTEN CATALOGS SHOULD BE MAILED

There are very few "retail stores on paper" that do not have at least two normal seasons, so the minimum times a catalog should be mailed is twice a year. To determine whether this should be three, four, or six times a year requires a split test. As a catalog customer file usually delivers a sizable number of orders per thousand catalogs mailed, it is likely that mailing cells of 3,000 catalogs will provide a useful indication here. This calls for mailing to one group twice a year, another group three times, a third group four times, a fourth group six times. At the end of the period (about fifteen or sixteen months), the following data are collected for each of the four groups:

1. Total sales
2. Total costs (including the costs of each mailing)
3. Total profit

Philosophically, you are trying to measure the sales you have lost by not being in touch with your customers often enough compared with the possibility that by mailing too often the next catalog will "steal" too many sales from the previous catalog and thus decrease profitability.

If you are in any doubt about whether you are mailing your catalog often enough, it is odds on that the right answer is you are *not*. By any stretch of the imagination you do not have exclusive "ownership" of the names in your file, and each time a competitive catalog, which may not even be in your field, is received in place of yours, you may have suffered the loss of some sales you might have had. Up to four times a year, the amount of "stealing" one catalog does to its predecessor is quite minor. Tests may indicate that this is also true for six-time mailings.

What to Keep Track of on Previous Orders

There is much information to be learned from each catalog mailing if you key every cell. This calls for identifying at the very least the following cells on the basis of last order or inquiry along with the original source code:

- Most recent 3-month customers
- Most recent 6-month customers
- Most recent 12-month customers
- Most recent 18-month customers
- Most recent $2\frac{1}{2}$-year customers
- Most recent 3-year customers
- Most recent over-3-year customers

- Most recent 3-month catalog requests
- Most recent 6-month catalog requests
- Most recent 9-month catalog requests
- Most recent 12-month catalog requests
- Most recent 18-month catalog requests
- Most recent over-18-month catalog requests

By coding each cell, you can determine at which point in time it pays to drop catalog requestors who, over a given period, have been given X number of chances to buy from this and prior catalogs. That point is determined easily when outside lists produce higher response than the oldest records on the file.

There will be a definite progression of decending response as you dip deeper into the aging segments of your file. Here, for example, is a typical array with most current as 100 percent for one mailing to a consumer catalog customer list:

- 3-month buyers <u>100</u>
- 6-month buyers 90
- 12-month buyers 82
- 18-month buyers 69
- 30-month buyers 58
- 3-month catalog requests <u>100</u>
- 6-month catalog requests 84
- 9-month catalog requests 75
- 12-month catalog requests 64
- over-12-month requests 51

When to Mail by Segment

Most catalog operations mail to every customer irrespective of how old and irrespective of the size of his or her last order, as well as all inquiries, again irrespective of how long they have been in the file and irrespective of how many offers they have already received.

There is *no rule* that says you must mail to each segment the same number of times per year. Mailing on aging groups of catalog requests, the final 60 or 70 percent of those who originally came in two, three, or four years ago, is almost always a losing proposition. The problem is that many operators make the mistake of homogenizing new inquiries with old, and on average obtain an adequate conversion rate. But such homogenization forever buries the fact that the current inquiries may be converting at 10 percent, while the oldest part of the aging group may be at 1 percent or less. Mailing an increasing number of aging requests undifferentiated by age over and over again inevitably reduces the value and validity of those much more valuable current inquiries being added between each catalog mailing.

Even the very oldest inquiries may deserve one mailing per year. This can be determined first by mailing a test sample rather than the whole block which is suspect because of age. A "last chance" offer is usually quite productive.

THREE STEPS FOR SECURING THE SOURCE CODE OF EVERY ORDER

Securing the source code of every order is one of the more difficult problems in running a direct-response operation, particularly for a business-to-business catalog. A sizable proportion of orders comes in on company purchase orders; some come in without coding on catalog order forms; telephone orders are placed by a purchasing department at the request of some department without any documentation other than the item number, price, and where to buy it. It is not unusual for traceable source codes to be no more than 25 or 30 percent of all orders received which leaves a sizable doubt as to how to allocate the balance. One thing is certain: Every step possible should be taken to find out and capture the source code of every order.

To accomplish this, the following steps, should be taken:

1. On phone orders, the communicators should be carefully trained to request help from the customer to obtain the source code from either the address label or the order form. At the very least, the description, price and page number will almost always provide identification of the catalog issue.

2. Special effort should be made on the order form itself to have the customer refer to or transmit the code. A small note stating "so we may serve you better, please . . . " is always helpful.

3. By having the addressing done by a printer or fulfillment shop with dual ink-jet capacity, the source code can be economically printed next to the address as well as on the order form. (This can be done on line where the order form is gathered in after match coding with the address label, as one signature.) Moreover, this same system permits printing an individualized message on the face of the catalog. For prospects this might point out the pages with special products or special discounts. For a customer mailing, the message can tie in with some product purchased previously and include suggestions and page numbers for related products.

In companies where telemarketing is provided for selected, direct-mail, produced accounts (on the basis of size of order, consistency of ordering over a period, or identification as one of America's giants) it is fairly typical for the source code of the initial order to be replaced by a code for the telecommunicator assigned. It is far better practice to maintain the initial code and cumulate all sales over given periods by both mail and phone, for that source. Only in this way can the lifetime worth of the source be evaluated realistically. Telephone sales can be maintained separately so the telecommunicator gets adequate credit and compensation.

MAKING THE MOST OF BOUNCE BACKS

In direct-response terms a *bounce back* is a printed offer by the mail house delivered in the package just shipped out in response to an order by the customer.

Where this order has originated from a catalog or a mailing piece, the ideal bounce back (surprising to some) is a copy of the same piece from which the order was generated. The bounce back needs to be individually source coded. At the same time the initial source code needs to be on the piece as well. Computer control will then be necessary to provide a report covering bounce backs as a media source, as well as how bounce-back response affects each source code.

No mailers who open their packages to inserts by noncompetitive mailers fail to include their own bounce backs, plus, if available, new and special offers (also separately coded). But this is not true of all those operators who either have not or will not make package inserts available. Some short-sightedly believe they cannot afford the extra cost to print and include a duplicate of a catalog already sent and reviewed. This is short-sighted because the bounce back can be one of the most productive "mailings" made to the customer file at no expense for postage. In addition it is the "hot" part of their hot-line buyers—the very buyers most likely to buy again if given the chance.

If there were such a thing as overuse of a catalog file, it would seem that bounce backs would show this by being only modestly profitable or even marginal. To the contrary, bounce backs, to customers who have just purchased, normally produce a higher response than any other mailing made to the customer list. The advice to make quick new offers prior to shipping the merchandise to new first-time customers is a concomitant of this happy finding that the best customers on your file for your next or current offer are those who just sent you an order. (This is why package inserts tend to work for offers of outside vendors which go along with the bounce backs of the operator shipping the merchandise.)

Those who include a catalog as a bounce back, and do not separately code it, both as a bounce back and for the initial key which produced the customer in the first place, are losing their proof of the validity of using the catalog as a bounce back, and at the same time are probably losing control of the source of the customer for tracking purposes.

HOW TO USE CREDIT CARD SALES TO YOUR ADVANTAGE

Credit cards provide four advantages for direct-response operators:

1. They increase total response.
2. They provide a higher average size sale.
3. They provide almost immediate prepayment.
4. They add a bit more "creditability" to the offerings in the catalog.

A small number of operators refuse to use credit cards for two reasons. The second reason is often more relevant than the first.

1. The charge extracted for the service by the credit card company.
2. The bother of handling a small proportion of sales in a different manner than usual.

Automatic Credit Card Authorization

Where the number of credit card transactions is onerous, from a clerical viewpoint, some form of automatic credit card authorization should be explored. Instead of calling in each number and each sum and waiting for authorization, transactions can be transmitted in bulk through phone lines, in which the computer automatically dials the bank. The computer transmits data for all credit card orders that require authorization, and then waits for the bank to return a transmission of authorization. Approved orders have their authorization code posted and are then released for picking and shipping. Declined orders are placed on hold for clerical review and handling by customer service. The systems available can enter deposits at the time of authorization, or can see they are entered at the time of shipment. As a final step, a credit card register is produced detailing each transaction.

How Credit Cards Provide Add-On Sales

There is some question as to whether or not WATS lines pay. But there can be no question about offering credit card sales in direct response. Credit cards do not cost you any money; they simply provide add-on sales unlikely to come in any other way. The proportion of credit card sales (upwards of 15 percent for the majority of mailers) means the overall cost to provide this form of short-term consumer credit is negligible.

If 15 percent of sales come in on credit cards, and the fee is 4 percent, then overall the cost on sales is six-tenths of 1 percent. If the order margin of a given mailer on an average sale of $50 is $20, then the addition of credit cards will reduce that figure by 12¢. If we assume that breakeven is reached at fifteen orders, this means the increase at breakeven will be 15 × 12¢ or $1.80. With an order margin of $20, credit cards need only increase response by one-tenth of an order ($2.00) to cover the cost base for using credit cards. On a 10,000 mailing that would be an increase from 150 orders to 151. Normally credit cards *add* 8 to 10 percent of sales which might never have been received otherwise.

If for some reason, it is necessary to have only one credit card, then select American Express. Better by far is to offer the two "T&E" (travel and entertainment) cards: American Express and Diner's Club and Carte Blanche, as well as the two so-called "bank" cards, VISA and MasterCard.

Customers differ, thus it should be no surprise to find that customers who charge on one card are different from those who charge on another. In most cases the first-time customer charging on the American Express card is a better mail order customer (more likely to become a multiple buyer) than a customer using a Diner's Card. Either of the T&E card customers is usually more valuable as a mail order customer than those who charge on one of the "bank" cards. (This hierarchy continues down through business checks, personal checks, cash, and money orders.) Some mailers who have offered only the bank cards believe they have not gained anything from it. If so, it may be for other reasons, including the reluctance of inadequately trained phone clerks to process credit card orders. One business catalog operator prefers CODs with their attendant risk to credit cards, even though both means of payment are acceptable. The apparent saving here, if any, is dissipated by the friction the payment causes when the package arrives.

Credit cards go hand in hand with WATS lines and telephone orders. Without them the growth in WATS lines would be creeping, not exploding. Credit card orders usually result in fewer returns, and larger orders. (Having an opportunity to talk to the customer over the phone can lead to add-on sales, but even without this, credit card orders usually are larger than orders sent with checks through the mails.) Thus credit cards result in larger dollar volume and more *not less* gross profit.

There is another advantage to credit cards that relatively few mailers latch onto. That is credit card sales can be offered to delinquent accounts. New profitable sales to customers ordinarily "never to be sold to again" tend to help reestablish the friendlier relation that existed before, and for some, this regeneration is helpful also in resolving any problem on the delinquency.

A catalog should not leave your home office without listing all accepted credit cards.

A Look at Who the Credit Card Holders Are

The Federal Reserve Bulletin published some revealing 1983 figures on who owns travel cards.

Type of card	Median household income
Travel and entertainment	$40,000
Gas	31,000
Bank	30,000
Retail	26,000
All households with and without cards	19,400

Direct-mail operators find that people who charge on T&E cards are better mail order customers than those who charge on bank cards. The fact that T&E cardholders, on average, have median income one-third larger than holders of bank cards might go a long way toward explaining why.

Approximately 63 percent of American households now have some form of credit cards, about the same proportion as in 1977. The discontinuance of gas credit cards by oil companies, and the countrywide introduction of a differential at the pump for cash payments has caused households with gas credit cards to drop from 34 percent in 1977 to 28 percent. In this same period, VISA and Mastercard cardholders through vigorous marketing, have increased from 38 to 42 percent. T&E cards are now held by 10 percent of families, or close to 9 million of the more affluent among us. (But the fact that a customer pays through his or her American Express card is not of itself a guarantee of affluence. Half of all holders have family incomes of under $40,000, a good portion of these probably have incomes under $20,000 per year.)

MAILING/SHIPPING DETAILS

How to Provide a Super Quick Delivery

Mail order companies take a number of different routes to provide super quick delivery. Among them are:

1. Establishment of a "fast track" for orders requesting or requiring quick delivery. Rush telephone orders on credit cards can bypass the usual order–entry procedure and enter the picking area a day or two ahead of conventional orders. The same can be done, if there is a swift way to check credit of the orderer, for orders phoned in by regular accounts that expect to be billed.

2. Tagging fast-track orders with a color code so there is no delay in the warehouse or shipping operation. A few innovative mailers have begun to offer guaranteed overnight delivery for a surcharge. By negotiation with the overnight delivery services, a price for this service can be arranged which some customers will pay.

The higher the value of the purchase, the greater the interest there will be in this form of "instant gratification." This service extends the delivery season at major holidays. Such a service should not be offered if the mailer is not prepared, through expeditious handling, to implement it and make it work.

How to Handle Orders from Customers
Located Out of the Continental United States

It is usual for a business-to-business mail order house to receive from one-half of 1 percent to $1\frac{1}{2}$ percent of its gross volume from United States customers located outside the continental limits in Alaska, Hawaii, and Puerto Rico. Some business-to-consumer operations do even more business in these 3 remote areas of the country.

The only problem is that shipping to these points can be very costly, and charges based on conventional UPS, USPS, Federal Express, or DMH charges are not always reasonable. There are two ways to handle shipping costs on these types of orders:

1. Specify on the order form that shipping costs must be researched and billed separately. All orders received must then be acknowledged with the specific shipping charges before the order can be considered "in house."

2. From historical data on size and weight costs, calculate an "adder" for such shipping and handling, and be prepared to nurse the financial wounds caused by those few unusual charges per year that do not fit the pattern.

A possible solution to the entire problem is to stop mailing catalogs to these areas completely but very few operators who have found response here above the average for the rest of the states are willing to give up the business they attract from the three outside territories.

Customer Mailings to Bill-to and Ship-to Addresses

In the business marketplace (and to a modest extent in the sales of goods by mail to consumers) both bill-to and ship-to addresses are provided and captured. Some operators mail only to one or the other. Some operators mail new offerings to both.

Given an adequate computer operation there is no problem in selecting out both addresses and testing whether dual mailing adds sales at a profit, or brings in so small an amount of added sales as to be uneconomic. For the great majority of concerns the right answer is to mail to both. A high price has been paid to obtain every name on the file and there may be individuals at both addresses willing to buy again. (Keying the two kinds of addresses should be done in any case, after unduplicating and saving only one address where both are in the same five-digit zip code.)

PERSONALIZED CATALOGS

Once the printing press was married to a computer, it took only a short gestation period to produce personalized catalogs. The computer was first used as a high-speed typewriter in the production of match-fill and fully computerized letters. Then came computer addressed pieces, quickly followed by adding individualized lines of copy next to each address. About the same time, printers found they could personalize a message as well as address a form, and this opened the door to personalized wraparounds, leaving the rest of the catalog untouched.

That left personalizing the entire catalog and we now are set to see a few personalized inserts making each individual catalog different from all (or almost all) others. The major web printers are already asking marketers to imagine finding their names printed within any advertisement in a magazine they subscribe to. Within reach is complete computer production of each page, with personalizations on every page (if desired). This is now well within the technical competence of the computer-driven printer. Like the early computer letter, it is likely at first to be a bit much but those who have RFU$ISM data as well as promotional history on their file will be able to suggest Bs to go with As already purchased; initiate family product buying; make each prompt relevant to the individual customer; and in effect create, on the fly, separate individualized catalogs (different strokes for different folks). If customers, after receiving five, ten, or fifteen catalogs, have shown no interest in 30 percent of product offerings, these can be suppressed or supplemented by other offers. Once this occurs, almost every current rule for catalog creation is going to have to be restudied.

Even now, major web operators can stop the press on long runs and replace the black plate on five-color printing at modest cost. Since the black plate comes with prices and code numbers, this opens the door to split tests of price levels. (In 28 years, the Burnett office had only seen two or three true price level tests across an entire catalog, because the cost, up to now, has been too great.) It is relatively simple to provide a 100 percent efficient code structure for each mailing test by providing a *unique code on every item* not just a change of code on the order form. Will this be done for each 5,000 or 10,000 list? Not likely. But when each list on a continuation runs into 25,000, 50,000, or 100,000, it becomes quite likely.

CATALOG GLUT: HOW TO HOLD YOUR OWN AMONG THE EXCESS

Much heat is generated from consumer catalog operators that there are now too many catalogs, and too few known mail order buyers from catalogs. The estimated 5 billion catalogs per year are split between business and consumer (perhaps 500 million and 4.500 million). Then, on average, each of the 87 million households (on a homogenized basis) is receiving fifty catalogs, or one catalog per week per household. If these catalogs are, for the most part, restricted to the one-third of the population that are the most likely mail order buyers, this "glut" turns out to be three catalogs per week for such mail-responsive homes. As consumer catalogs tend to peak in the months of October, November, and January, three catalogs can easily jump to an average of six, or one per day. There are always a few hundred thousand avid mail order buyers from catalogs who are on multiple hot lines and therefore receive an inordinate number of these "stores by mail."

Those operators who blame their problems on "catalog glut" are looking at the wrong end of the horse. Catalogs provide an ideal way to serve specialized markets. Their format provides an opportunity to test multiple new products with each issue. All of the infinities of direct mail: copy, art, layout, page size, color, premiums, offers, and charge cards are available. The mathematics of customer purchase and customer retention are available at least to any operator who wishes to know this business. Although space ads do not usually generate new customers at the same cost as canvassing with the catalog itself, space ads plus catalog inquiry productions can and are being used to locate new mail order buyers effectively. Glut is not the problem. Improper marketing knowledge and improper control and management are.

In a recent study of a *Better Homes and Garden's* consumer panel, 92 percent of consumers reported that catalogs were welcome despite the fact that less than half the respondents indicated they had ordered or requested catalogs to be sent to them. Of those who bought an item by mail and then received that company's catalog, about 70 percent recalled buying additional items.

A second sale penetration made in this way would bring great color (green) to the coffers of any mail order company, but the figures do emphasize why catalog operators send one catalog after another to current customers.

A remarkably high proportion of catalogs now originate with local department stores or general merchandise retailers. These catalogs seek more to create store traffic than to make the sales through mail or phone from the printed page. However, their appearance is much like the catalogs sent by out-of-town department stores seeking mail order customers. In major retail markets, local retail store catalogs often delivered as self-standing inserts in the local newspaper, can be 30 or 40 percent of all catalogs received. A nationwide catalog competing with conventional mass retailers is going to be buffeted by this growing trend. There is, however, no catalog glut for the specialty catalog operator.

CATALOG BACK-END THINKING: THREE KEY AREAS OF CONCERN

This section on *Catalog Operations* is concerned with back-end processing of orders, capture of data, and the use of that data to improve results. We will discuss the problems of the back end, including complaint mail, but for the most part this section deals with the kind of reports a catalog operator needs to run the business both for customer analysis as well as item–product and catalog analysis.

In direct response, everything that leads up to the order is considered front end. The back end is everything else, including inventory control, order entry, purchasing, picking, packing, buying, drop shipping, returns, complaints, updating, and reports. It is likely that as many direct-response firms fail for poor handling of that "everything else" as from inadequate marketing and control on the front end.

Back end thinking is divided into three parts:

1. *Operational Activities* that take place once an order or a request is secured.
2. *Customer-oriented activity and reports* originated through further marketing after first being placed on file.
3. *Product-oriented reporting,* including item sales analysis, as well as page-for-page catalog analysis.

Let's look at each of these parts a bit more closely.

Operational Activities

Back-end thinking, much like front-end thinking consists of both art and science. The art is incorporated in the selection of products. This seems to be innate with some, and cannot be easily taught or learned. The science is in the mathematical control and analysis of all of the costs, all of the marketing and all of the product data developed. The rounded catalog operator must be proficient in all these areas.

Obtaining Half Life on Catalog Sales

If there ever was a business in which the need for good information early on is paramount, that business is running a catalog operation. The time between catalogs is so short that the next catalog must be put to bed before all but the very first indications are in from the catalog just put in the mail.

Catalogs and current space ads, like every other form of direct response, each have their half life—the time when half of all of the orders that will ultimately be obtained are in. This half life can be pegged to a given day or two after a specified number of days or weeks from the receipt of the first order.

Results from one catalog mailing may not be available to influence the product mix, price lines, or gross margin to be used in the next mailing, but with the use of half life, the essential juice can be squeezed from the early results to help make valid and useful decisions about the next catalog after the one now on the drawing board.

Half life is affected by the number of catalogs you send out as people may be inclined to toss out your old catalog when your new one arrives. You must keep in mind that half life is usually quite different for consumer catalogs mailed out prior to holiday periods than at other seasons. It is best to obtain your own specific half life for each of your own catalogs for each season.

Half-life figures are a statistical gift of immeasurable value. Be sure you obtain these figures for every effort key and for every item within each catalog you mail.

How to Handle Complaint Mail

Complaint mail, which might better be called informational mail, is a fact of life in the direct-mail industry. People who complain are just the people a mailer needs to hear from, and the mailer should heed what these very special people are saying about services, products, mailings, and prices.

The best advice is don't overreact and don't feel it is necessary to change mailing plans. *The Wall Street Journal,* as this book was written, continues to withhold its valuable subscriber base from the rental market because a few recipients wrote and complained that their names were being used for outside direct-mail offers. Believing that these few recipients represented numerous others, and not desirous of upsetting its basic business, *The Wall Street Journal* gave up an estimated $4,000,000 of rental income per year. (The income could easily have been preserved by giving each recipient the option to suppress the use of his or her name for rental use.)*

Complaints can be legitimate gripes or crackpot excuses. But it is important to answer each one. Where the gripe is not under the mailer's control, this should be explained. For example, misspelling of names may come from rented lists. When someone sends in proof of duplicate pieces, this is a valid complaint. The pieces should be analyzed and the limitations of computer matching explained. (You also might like to review your own merge–purge reports.)

People who take the trouble to complain are *reaching out to help* your

*In January 1988, the WSJ returned its subscriber file to the rental market!

business. They are seeking some individual response not a cold form letter, or worse, no answer at all. Handled properly, complainers (unless chronic) can become among the best customers and best supporters of a mail order company.

So don't panic. Do react individually to each complainant, and seek to convert those who complain into supporters.

How to Tie in Marketing Costs with Accounting Data

A natural antipathy exists between bookkeeping and accounting and the marketing function. The former tries to keep everything shipshape, with every item of cost accounted for and attached to the proper program or account. Marketers tend to develop their own ways to record and analyze results, which may not be anything like the hard and fast outline used by bookkeepers. Bookkeepers are not bookkeepers unless they make every trial balance and every P&L statement balance. Most marketers are content to have rational costs per order, total sales, and supposed total costs leaving a balance for profit. The glitch may be that marketers, unlike good bookkeepers, will miss some costs. For example, recently, a catalog house calculated profits on a large mailing wave but failed to include a fairly heavy cost for zip code correlation and merge–purge.

With the proliferation of modest priced computers into almost every stage of business, and with their capacity to handle all aspects of both costs and sales, there is no longer any good reason why both areas cannot be furnished with current and complete data. In addition, once the proper prethinking about needs is done, computers can bring together and compare results for different programs, catalogs, and media within each major program. In this way, once the figures are accepted, there will be no surprises, missed data, or conflicting reports for management to reconcile.

An inventory report needs to show inventory position by item, and the latest purchase order data by item, including the anticipated arrival date for out-of-stock items. This may also show "max and mins"—the maximum number to have in inventory at any time and the minimum number to have in inventory; the latter serving as a trigger to reorder the item.

Some picking systems have room for current stock only; the inventory must show how much is in live stock and how much is in the hold area of storage as well as the movement in bulk to live stock and then out individually from live stock to the customer.

One particularly valuable report, which is often omitted, is a customer service report showing complaints by source *and* item. Reviewed weekly, such a report can provide valuable information on problems, trends, and customer awareness.

A concomitant of this report is one on returns, with careful study to see if the problems are service-connected, product-connected, or delivery-connected in nature. It is a good idea to check these reports involving customer service to see if standards set for turnaround time on orders, response time on written orders, the ratio between orders and customer contact, and the unit cost for the fulfillment services are within company or usual DM standards.

When entering new customer data, steps need to be taken to minimize error and maximize deliverability. Interestingly enough minor typing errors in alphabetic data (name, city, street name) rarely affect deliverability, but an error in the street address may hurt. Any error, particularly in the zip code, will result in a nondeliverable piece. Zip code checks are a requisite. At the very least an edit should be run to see that the zip code falls within the range for the state. Given a table for the first letter of each locality for each zip code makes certain the zip code and the locality match. If a table is generated and maintained that contains the city, state, and zip code for each zip code, there is no need to permit incorrect mailing by zip code.

Customer-Oriented Marketing and Reports

Customer-oriented marketing and reports describe all activities that affect a name or record once it is added to the customer file. From an analytic point of view, what we are seeking is a record of further purchase behavior by a group of customers entered at a given time under a given key—those that become first-time customers through a given advertisement or offer. This involves having access to records by service key and acquisition date so as to measure contribution to overhead, amortization of the cost to buy, and profitability.

To track in this manner, it is important that a system be established and maintained, in which the initial key and the initial date are retained for each name throughout its life on the file. One of the typical errors that many direct mailers commit is to drop the initial code and replace it in subsequent mailings with a key about age of the record (latest three or six months or latest year). This produces data about the validity of the importance of recency but effectively seals off any data about how customers from different initial keys have performed. (Even here there is some hope as data processors, through hard experience, have learned to keep copies of initial records. If these can be found, it is possible through careful merge identification, to add the individual codes back on a majority of the affected records. This solves one problem—it answers the question as to performance by key—but leaves unsolved how to make these data part of an ongoing system.)

What You Can Learn from Tracking by Key

What can come out of a tracking by key?

1. The relative value of each media used (direct mail, daily newspapers, weekly newspapers, Sunday supplements, weekly magazines, monthly magazines, bounce backs, friend of a friend).

2. The relative value of each medium within a given media (List A versus List B, daily newspaper A versus daily newspaper B).

3. The lifetime value of a customer by media, and by medium within media.

4. The average multiple order.

5. The proportion of first-time orderers who will buy in a given period.

6. The period in time required to amortize, through further sales, the initial cost to buy a customer.

7. The total volume of the business after a given period and a given set of efforts.

8. The value of a given lot of catalog requests.

9. The number of new customers the company can afford to buy at a given period of time.

10. What can be done to increase profits, at the expense of growth? What can be done to increase growth at the expense of profits?

11. Determination of which cells should be promoted more often, less, or not more than once a year.

Consider two companies, one of which can track and thus has solid data on which to base current and future plans, and the other which simply knows initial response to the offers. Which one is more likely to succeed in the increasingly competitive life we lead? A good way to start a catalog control operation is to check into the type of reports a direct-response operator needs.

First among the information an operator needs is sales—number of orders; number of dollars broken down perhaps by orders received over the phone versus those received in the mail, and then perhaps further categorized by cash, credit, or hold for credit checking or release. Next might be a report on sales by items, with a separate runup of backorders and drop shipments.

To compare one catalog mailing with another, it is necessary to know the following:

- Cost per M in the mail
- Average gross margin
- Total quantity mailed
- Total dollars of sales
- Match being made of comparable segments
  Customers against customers
  Prospects against prospects
  Evaluation of differential due to attempts to
  compare results from two different seasons

From these comparisons the one basic statistic can be constructed which permits a realistic comparison between the two mailings—profit per M catalogs mailed. The following example of two mailings to the same customers shows this:

	A	B	C = A × B Total	D	E = B × D	F	G = E × F Total	H =	I =
	Cost per M	Total mailed	mail cost	Sales per M	Total sales	Average gross margin	gross margin	Less promotion	Profit per M
Mailing 1	$400	250,000	$100,000	$2,500	$625,000	38%	$238,000	$138,000	$552
Mailing 2	$410	325,000	$133,000	$2,200	$715,000	41%	$293,000	$160,000	$493

Note the interplay between the number of dollars of sales per M pieces mailed and the average gross margin. It is not until the final calculation that it is clear that Mailing 1 produced 12 percent more profit (per M pieces mailed) than Mailing 2.

To evaluate a current mailout, the basic figures needed are:

1. Total dollars of sales
2. Total number of orders
3. Average size of order (usually by groupings of product line)
4. Average sales per dollars of promotional cost (or per M catalogs used)
5. Average gross margin
6. Profit per M catalogs and total

It may also be desirable to compute total dollar sales and total profits on a per M pages basis. This provides a rough means to compare two catalogs of different numbers of pages.

Product-Oriented Reporting

The primary rule of direct mail is to learn what improves the bottom line and do more. At the same time you should learn what does not work and do less. In the catalog field this requires systematic and continuous analysis of a number of different factors, including products, pricing, space allocation, and space positioning.

While all direct-mail success is based on the mathematics of the cost to buy a customer and the lifetime value of that customer, catalogs in particular require detailed mathematical control. A catalog is an entire store full of items in print and every part of every page can only be measured efficiently if basic controls are in force. A review of each item and its associated control numbers is required to determine which items to:

1. Continue in the next edition
2. Drop from the next edition
3. Give more space to
4. Give less space to
5. Move closer to the front of the book and which to move further back

What You Need for Item Analysis

For item analysis the following data are usually necessary:

1. An array in descending order of items by sales and total profit.
2. An array of natural groupings of product lines by sales and total profit. (This second array may disclose a need to bolster one group or another; it may also provide information that rather than a few scattered items, an entire group should be retired.)
3. An analysis of the relation between size of space and dollars of sales and dollars of profit. This calls for placing all or a good part of the following information in a computer:
   a. Item number
   b. Item name

c. Item description

d. Page number

e. Proportion of page (space allocation)

f. Price of item

g. Sales

h. Gross margin (This takes into account merchandise cost, cost of returns, order processing and fulfillment costs as well as credit and collection costs)

i. Gross profit

j. Allocated cost of the space

k. History of previous catalogs in which item has been included

l. Cost per order (average)

m. Merchandise class (items need to be grouped into a number of relevant classifications)

n. Special product features (male/female, country of origin, domestic, exclusivity, personalized, set, part of)

The ratio between allocated cost and gross profit reflects the profit made on the item. An item occupying one-half of a page will bear an allocated cost twice that of an item occupying one-quarter of a page.

If desired, the dollars of sales and the gross profit per item can be figured per 1,000 catalogs mailed and divided by the size of the page the item occupies. Thus a quarter page will in this way be multiplied by four, a half-page by two, providing a rough rule of thumb to measure on this index the success of each item as though the space allocated were a full page. (*Note:* Simply multiplying the space by two or four does not indicate what the item *would* have done if a full page had been used.)

Price points. Analysis here can determine total sales first for each group of products irrespective of classification grouped within a given range. Such a review may indicate a need to add more items to spread the distribution by price. The average size of sale may indicate a need to add more costly items; the number of orders per M catalogs may indicate a need to review new items of lower cost. The most important understanding is the need to have the facts so a responsible decision can be made.

In a catalog that has items ranging from a few dollars to $99, the price points might be under $10, $10 to $20, $21 to $35, $36 to $50, $51 to $75, $76 to $99. A tabulation by sales will show the distribution by price groups. Ideally this will be a tepee or bell shape. Where sales deviate from the fitted line this is an indication of at least a need for some tinkering of that price group.

Each page can be studied individually—as well as each 2-page spread. Once the computer figures are available at the close of a catalog's life, there should be posted on a control copy, marked "not to be removed on pain of death" each of the following bits of information for each item . . . no. of sales, no. of dollars, gross profit percentage, total gross profit, proportion of page, allocated cost per item, and balance left in inventory.

With a bit of programming all of this data, by page number, can be printed on a set of pressure sensitive labels (preferably colored) which can then be pasted next to each item.

After posting all details for each item on each page, post the total of dollars and items and total profit grossed at the top of each page; in the gutter of each spread post the same totals for combinations of the two facing pages.

One way to estimate the extra value, and therefore the extra expectation of results, of the four covers; the inside spread, where a book normally falls open; and the items on the order form is to check the premium that major magazines and some catalogs charge for such preferential areas as compared with the regular page rate.

On the page-by-page results, arrayed in descending order, calculate the average page on an arithmetic basis and draw two ruled lines atop and below the median range in the array. These will prove useful when making comparisons by page.

Breakeven for each page in the catalog, other than covers and order form, is determined by dividing the total number of pages including covers, into the total number of dollars spent for the catalog. These costs must include preparation of the catalog (typography, art, photos, pasteup, printing, mailing list rental, addressing and mailing, and postage.) If catalogs are used as bounce backs, these must also be included. The breakeven sum for each page provides a benchmark against which to compare the gross profit earned per page. Typical comparisons cover:

- Blocks of five or ten products arrayed in descending order on basis of sales
- Classifications of product groups, arrayed in percent of sales or in catalog order
- Price point groups
- Blocks of five or ten pages arrayed in descending order
- Pages by one color, two color, or four color
- Spreads arrayed in descending order

(It is usual to place better items up front in a catalog and to give them added space. Thus the first five or ten pages set the tone for the entire catalog. There is a need, however, for excitement and surprise so product types and prices should be intermixed throughout the catalog to entice the recipient to go through the printed "store" "aisle by aisle.")

The main management control figures needed are:

- percent of sales by the indicated group
- profit per group
- percent total profit by group

On items that have been in previous catalogs it is important to note whether sales, on a comparable space and location basis, are remaining steady, increasing, or decreasing. A product that has done better and is now nearing "only average" value may have outlived its usefulness for inclusion in the next catalog. A very simplistic but useful listing is:

Page (by number)	General description	Sales in dollars	Percent of total sales	Rank
2	Home tools	21,000	2.5%	16
3	Home tools	48,000	5.7	2
4	Shop tools	39,000	4.8	9
5	Shop tools	43,000	5.2	7

Merchandise decisions are motivated primarily by 3 rankings:

- largest dollar sales
- largest unit sales
- greatest gross profit.

In every catalog there are some items that produce the greatest number of dollars. Some items with lower-price points become stars when measured by unit sales. There also are usually a few items that are only fair in total dollars or unit sales but have margins that are so good they keep on getting selected for the next catalog. An array of each by item makes selection for the next catalog that much easier.

CHAPTER 16

How to Use Telecommunications in Direct-Mail Operations

HOW TELEMARKETING AND TELEPROSPECTING DIFFER

Telemarketing and teleprospecting with the aid of the phone companies has tended to grow a bit like Topsy. Few users of the telephone use this channel of distribution in accordance with a strategic plan. Everyone uses the telephone as a marketing tool so it is overly simple to add telephoning to the mix. But unless the telemarketing objectives are defined along with the strategy, tactics, and resources to reach those objectives, the costs may prove remarkably high and the results difficult to determine.

Two branches of telephone service should be clearly differentiated at this point:

Telemarketing is the service of talking to those who already, in some fashion, have come to you.

- Customers or donors, recipients or subscribers
- Inquirers
- Requesters
- White mail
- Qualified prospects (at the very least)

Teleprospecting (comparable in function to direct mail-prospecting or prospecting for a sale through some form of space or electronic medium) is a service that attempts to get some response from a cold prospect to an offer made orally. (A large part of what is written about telemarketing is really concerned with teleprospecting. But the great majority of telecommunication by business is inbound with those calling for information or service not outbound by the establishment attempting to increase sales or penetration or knowledge.)

In 1985 there were 500 known entities providing service to marketers by telephone. Dozens of these had staffs of 200 or more telecommunicators at a given location, and probably 1500 others making efforts to join them. (One company alone has half a dozen telecommunications centers each with 250 to 300 operators.) (It is of some interest to compare these numbers with the numbers of addressing and mailing shops in the United States—some 6500.)

Telephone Marketing

A general rule of thumb, which should be tested for any specific operation, is that a telephone follow-up to a direct mailing will generate an incremental response from $2\frac{1}{2}$ to 6 times the response achieved by mail alone. It may be, however, that new mailings to continuations will be more cost effective because the phone cost per order may easily be six to eight times the cost of the mail response. A simple AB test with one segment mailed only, the other mailed and then phoned, with all costs and results captured will provide data on one list. For a reasonable confidence level it is better by far to test three lists in this way to eliminate any bias (to phone or to mail) which may be inherent in one list.

There are several mail-phone combinations, each of which has its adherents. Each requires proper evaluation.

1. Mail then phone
2. Mail then phone then mail
3. Mail 1, mail 2 then phone
4. Phone then mail
5. Phone then mail then phone

Customer Massaging via Phone

The cost of telephoning a customer file provides (or it should) almost instantaneous awareness of the vast differences among cells within the same file. *Emer-*

gents are customers who can be counted on to buy with some regularity and become even more loyal buyers if contacted by phone. Those slipping through the cracks but of more than average value, can be "brought back to life"; important companies (mainly by size) can be identified and sent on to phone specialists to change them from first-time-only customers to something well beyond that. Those customers with special patterns of buying can be spotted, and their needs anticipated before some competitor gets the same idea. The problem usually is not deciding which group to go after but rather establishing a priority so that *outgoing* calls produce the best results for the house.

The Importance of Prescreening Prospects

Although all direct-response efforts attempt to limit recipients to those most likely to respond profitably, the urgency for selectivity for phone access is heightened by the high cost of each completed call. If two-thirds of a given group either are not good prospects or do not have the wherewithal even if good prospects, it is extremely important to screen them out before the calling begins. If this cannot be done because of lack of data, the first calling should be directed toward identifying those segments worth continued effort.

TELEMARKETING VERSUS DIRECT MAIL

Although mail has been used to sell merchandise for at least a century, the WATS line for merchandising has been part of the marketing mix only since the early 1970s. Yet in that period the dollars spent for telemarketing, about $12,000,000,000 is already more than all the dollars spent for all forms of direct mail advertising. There is no doubt that use of the phone will continue to grow and outstrip direct mail as we know it today. This is so because of a number of factors: the increasing costs of other forms of communication; the increased technology aimed at marrying the telephone and the computer; the increasing use of credit cards; and the increasing preference of the American public to place vocal interactive orders over written form through the mail. (This should not be misconstrued as stating there are more telephone impressions than mail impressions. The average telephone call runs about $1.50, or at least four to six times the cost of the average mailing piece. So until phone dollars exceed mail dollars by a factor of four, five, or six, the greatest number of impressions will belong to mail.)

Few direct-mail specialists have any idea of the overwhelming proliferation of telephone usage. There are, for example, over 275,000 in-bound WATS lines in America, paid for by about 200,000 companies and institutions. About 80,000 of these, by individual request, are listed in two "800 directories"—one for consumers, a second for commercial use—offering free long distance calling for virtually every classification found in the yellow pages of a major local classified directory. (The other 200,000 lines are for internal or private use and their owners do not wish to make these lines available to the public.)

The AT&T WATS lines now produce over 5.5 billion calls per year, which at an average systemwide cost of $2.00 each represents billing by AT&T of $10,000,000,000. That, on a homogenized basis, represents $100 in WATS billing per year for every household and every business in the country.

Perhaps the most surprising statistic about WATS is the number of free calls made per day for information about WATS numbers—300,000 per day, 100 million per year! There are many shoppers, (AT&T research indicates it may be as high as 65 percent) who will not make a sales or request call if they must pay the phone charge.

Hardly a catalog (of the over 5 billion now printed) is placed in the market without prominent space being given to the availability of a free call via WATS lines. More often than not, this availability is repeated at the foot of every page.

There are many, many times more establishments using the phone for some type of direct response (inbound or out) than are using the mails. All mail users of every kind, many of them (clubs, local associations, churches, for example) with no response need total no more than 1 million. Telephones are a way of life in about 6.5 million businesses, not including another 1 million institutions and another 1 million offices of professionals as well as for approximately 2 million farmers, and a growing minimum of 5, 6, or 7 million business operations of some sort operated out of the home. Taking orders or placing requests or orders by phone is a form of telemarketing that is big—and getting bigger.

As the use of the phone in direct marketing increases, the number and size of the telephone services (both inbound and outbound) are growing. Most direct-response companies that also have retail stores will also have more people operating phones rather than counters.

TOLL-FREE NUMBERS: HOW EFFECTIVE ARE THEY IN DIRECT-MAIL RESPONSE?

One of the ongoing arguments in the direct-response catalog marketplace is whether or not an "800" service is cost effective.

Most operators added "800" services because of what they perceived as competitive pressure. Most of those who would like to discontinue the cost for budgetary reasons are afraid their customers will desert them in favor of a competitor's toll-free line. It is sad but true that most who have 800 numbers have never tested its cost effectiveness to find out for certain if increased phone sales in fact do more than offset the extra cost of the calls. The higher the proportion of sales recorded by phone the more reluctant the operator is to tinker with an attempt that drops free calls via WATS.

How a Split Test Can Help Determine the Success of a WATS Line

The only way to get a line on the value of an 800 service is to make a substantial split test in which half the catalogs for prospecting carry the 800 number and half do not. The two halves can be compared quite adequately in this way, but a decision not in favor of using a WATS line may still be considered a very risky undertaking. In addition, the multiple customer, the mainstay of a catalog operation, may be more conditioned to use free calling than the newest customer added to the rolls.

Split testing has convinced a handful of operators that they can function without WATS lines. Why some operators can or cannot function is not quite clear. The more powerful and secure the customer franchise, the less an 800 service apparently can offer. Those catalogs with a solid customer base and products exclusive to them may find WATS lines offer little in the way of a lift in response. On the other hand, those catalogs selling convenience goods often bought on impulse will probably find a WATS line measurably increases orders. Those operators building up a catalog operation almost always opt for a WATS operation. WATS lines are almost always used for high-ticket goods because the extra cost of the call (believed to be up to ten times the cost of handling a mail order) is a small percent of the sale. Low-ticket item operations, as a rule, shun the use of WATS lines.

In the business world, WATS lines are used by almost every catalog operation. Business orders tend to be technical and there is a greater need to discuss features, sizes, and uses. For this reason free calls for advice on a WATS line seem almost mandatory. There have been consumer catalog operations that have tried WATS lines and decided not to continue. It is hard to locate a business mailer who has ever given up his or her WATS line.

AT&T, by giving away 1,300,000 copies or more of its 800 directories each year, is betting that WATS-line usage will continue to grow. That appears to be a safe bet. We will have more WATS lines in the future and more catalog operations will find they cannot afford to be without them.

Telephone orders are usually larger than orders received through the mails, and in conjunction with credit and payment, they usually increase total sales by a significant amount. The phone provides a means for selling more products while the patron is on the line—something that cannot be done with a written order.

It is hardly known or even noticed that most WATS lines (but not the most prominent utilization) are for private or intercompany transactions such as sales, repair, or production use, and are not available to the general public. But the public is increasingly being served in new and different ways by WATS lines. I.T.T. has a WATS line expressly for information about the company that any financial consultant can call to get solid business facts and not sales pitches. Catalogers have learned the wisdom of repeating the WATS number on every other page of the catalog as well as placing the number prominently on the cover. Every electronic direct-response ad features the WATS numbers; many TV commercials show WATS-line operators at work taking orders or giving information.

Fully 20 percent of ads in *Fortune* and *Business Week* and 15 percent in *Time* and *Newsweek* promote an 800 toll-free line. One specialized service available on 800 lines is a dealer locater service in which the caller is directed to the nearest dealer for advertised brands such as Ford, Panasonic, Smith Corona, Sony, General Electric, and Pitney Bowes. (This is another marriage of the phone to a computer in which all dealer locations, plotted and mapped by longitude and latitude, are retrievable within any given zip code.)

A few major companies have latched onto the 800 service to handle and, in most cases, defuse, customer complaints. Every Proctor & Gamble (P&G) package since 1981 has carried 800 numbers to provide an easy way for the customer to register a complaint. General Electric has found that an open line to customers is a source of new product ideas and advertising suggestions as well as an opportunity for customers to air their views to a sympathetic listener. Other makers of household products, including General Motors, offer a similar service. Chrysler opens a "900" number during its annual stockholders meeting, and for $.50 for the first minute and $.35 for each successive minute, a faraway stockholder can listen in on what is taking place.

Telecommunication Services

There are five main categories of telecommunication service as well as subcategories of each service:

1. Selling
   a. Order fulfillment
   b. Direct sales

    c. Pledge production and follow-up

    d. Reactivation of customers

    e. Cross selling as well as upselling and substituting

    f. Combination (mail plus phone)

2. Lead generation and qualifying

    a. Production

    b. Qualification

    c. Catalog requests

3. Information gathering and public relations

    a. Research (both positive and negative)

    b. Voting

    c. Company and product data

4. Improving cash flow

    a. Collections

    b. Renewals

    c. Purchasing control and follow-up

5. Customer service

    a. Dealer location operation

    b. Help on hot lines

    c. Product inquiries

COLD CALLS: THE HEART OF TELEPROSPECTING

There are growing numbers of special situations—and more developing every month—where teleprospecting (calling on a cold canvas basis) is proving to be cost efficient even at the high cost of connected calls. These situations also are producing a backlash which a surfeit of calls can produce. Most of these situations entail obtaining an appointment or house call for a personal sales call follow-up. Almost of necessity, this situation dictates that the size of the order (and thus the size of the commensurate sales commission) be large enough to justify the phone call and the personal visit. Among the products and services sold in this way are stocks and bonds, solar heating installation, home repairs, roofing and siding, security systems, power systems, insurance, real estate transfer, and business computers.

Who Uses Teleprospecting?

There are growing numbers of products and services that use teleprospecting to make the sale then and there on the phone: business directories, advertising in directories, cleaning chemicals, magazine subscriptions, refrigerator insurance, office supplies, and calling on prospects who have received a recent mail offer.

There is no end of variations in the use of this remarkable and interactive channel. One west coast company featuring tools (with several imitators) first mails to obtain a list of buyers, and then never mails again. Every customer is turned over to a high-powered phone operation to sell additional tools through carefully worded prompts. Another company, selling chemicals, first calls logical prospects (hotels, motels, hospitals) to qualify them by size and to elicit the name of the person who controls the purchase decision. This person is then mailed a sample and the phone crew goes to work on these qualified prospects only. There is a company that calls on specific types of manufacturers to purchase waste that can be salvaged at a profit. Co-op owners are researched by phone as to whether they would like to sell their apartments. Telephone calls are important reinforcements to remind prospects of their planned attendance at a seminar or a restaurant meeting, where they will be regaled with remote sales pitches and pitches by eager sales reps. A few very smart catalog operations that send out loaners or demonstration units as part of their sales operation also have shrewd telecommunicators who offer discounts to have the user buy the loaner instead of returning it in exchange for a new unit. Software transmitted over phone lines is often sold by phone, along with the modem for making the transfer possible. No insurance salesperson worthy of hire by a major company exists without making a requisite number of cold calls every day. Cold calls are the essence of teleprospecting.

Sales Effectiveness of Cold Calls

There is an old saw in marketing that arrays direct sales media in order of "sales effectiveness" as follows.

1. Direct sales calls (in person)
2. Telephone calls
3. Personalized letters
4. Nonpersonalized direct mail

This order may not always hold true for all markets. There are markets that are too dispersed or too small to justify the cost of face-to-face sales. There are some products and services where the extra cost to personalize the mailing is not cost effective. There are two-step programs where it would be suicidal to use the phone first, and there are two-step programs where using the phone first is more effective in the long run than direct mail. There are mailings where a title address outpulls mailings to a name. The order of sales effectiveness truly depends on the nature of the market.

HOW TO SUCCESSFULLY MANAGE A TELEPHONE MARKETING SERVICE TO SUPPLEMENT YOUR MAILING OPERATIONS

Like any other medium of communications, the use of the telephone requires careful planning to meet carefully planned goals. This planning requires an analysis of how the telephone fits in with the company's products and services, as well as how telemarketing and teleprospecting fit into the marketing structure, including distribution channels, advertising mix, the place of direct response and the competitive climate. The use of the telephone for outbound marketing requires the ability to segregate and select the customer base by cell. All telephone work in process must be reviewed to integrate that which is being done with that which can or should be done. Any such study will, of necessity, help determine whether telecommunications are to be provided inside the company only, or outside the company only, or partly inside and partly outside the company.

In-House or Outside Service?

For most catalog operations, a WATS system operated in house by trained full-time employees is preferred over the use of an outside service. Only in this way can the catalog operation serve its customers and their various needs in the most helpful and sympathetic way possible. Perhaps only in this way can upselling be done satisfactorily for the good of both the customer and the catalog supplier. In general, the transactions are so specialized and so lengthy that no outside service can do them justice.

The case for using an outside service for certain kinds of telephonic help is, however, a strong one. Seasonal peaks and valleys may require continuous review and change. Space for expansion may not be available. Volume may not justify or require specialized equipment such as automatic call distributors and computer analysis. Key-effort reports may prove to be challenging. The number of credit card transactions may necessitate special handling. The number of screens and stations may be too few. The need for special training for short periods may be a problem, as may a requirement for special handling of receipt and transmission of orders.

KEEPING TRACK OF TELECOMMUNICATIONS PRODUCTION

With reports available by phone or by operator by connected minute, the phone is perhaps the most accountable medium available to marketers. By means of individually recorded calls stipulating time of call as well as elapsed time, benchmarks can be established for production. When the individual records are combined by hour and by day parts comparisons can be made between communicators. From compilations of such daily reports, a master tally can be derived that will aid in evaluating list source as well as affording a benchmark for the operation as a whole.

Telephone experts project that a well trained and supervised telecommunicator can reach 7,000 to 10,000 outside consumer contacts, or handle 10,000 to 20,000 incoming calls per year. That last figure can be checked with a little arithmetic. If the average inbound WATS line costs $.37 or so per connected minute, and the average call runs $5\frac{1}{2}$ minutes, then in a seven hour day (at eight calls per hour) an operator can take fifty-five different calls (but not that many different callers because of callbacks). If fifty different persons per day are reached that equals 250 calls per week and in a forty-nine-week year that totals 12,250 calls.

If we use 12,250 inbound calls per communicator as a benchmark, the cost for one person to operate that phone must include salary, fringe benefits, and space, plus a minimum of $25,000 for the phone rental, not an inconsiderable sum to play around with. In business it is rare to think of providing a machine service that *rents* for $25,000 per year to every sales clerk but that sum is to be expected for handling sales over a WATS line—a high-volume high-cost labor process.

A phone communicator can speak with about forty business decision makers in eight hours. An average salesperson may be able to speak face to face with no more than four or five customers a day. When sales volumes produced by phone operators are carefully monitored and compared with sales volumes produced by salespeople it is not unusual for the top phone sales personnel to outproduce middling personal sales reps. IBM, noted for its blue-suited face-to-face sales force, has one sales division that sells and services almost entirely by telephone. The geographical area covered is too wide and too dispersed to be covered effectively any other way. Every maker of business machines has augmented its personal sales force with telephone representatives and mailings in order to reach small, marginal, and hard-to-reach accounts too costly to reach through utilization of personal sales representatives.

THREE MAIN COMPILED TELEPHONE NUMBER LISTS
AND WHAT THEY OFFER

In the list world you rent × number of names, print × number of pieces, and mail × number of pieces (less a small percentage for spoilage in addressing and in sorting). In teleprospecting to rental lists (with or without a prior mailing) the control of names is handled quite a bit differently because the right to call the names available for mailing may be withheld by the list owner. Few lists come with phone numbers so cost, time, and loss factors are incurred when phone numbers have to be tagged on. Finally, the completion rate (the proportion of numbers finally reached after a given number of trials) reduces the net number. Rarely can 1,000 names produce 400 connected calls.

Telephone tagging now has a success rate of about 50 percent on consumer names. Clerical- or phone company-assisted lookups for the balance are usually too costly to be used in direct marketing.

There are three large compiled lists available which include telephone numbers. They are:

1. All connected and listed consumer phones (approximately 57 million)
2. All connected nonconsumer phones (approximately 8.5 million in business institutions and offices of professionals)
3. All major executives of major companies (approximately 750,000)

Consumers with phone numbers are selected by income, make and model and value of cars, length of residence, type and value of home, geographical area, as well as by median information for age, education, and number of children. In addition, through overlays some of these selections are also available for known mail order buyers.

Businesses are available by classification, size, and geographic area. Business executives are available through discrete data on sales, number of employees, stock market listing, import, export, or even rank—for example, the Fortune 500, 1000, 1300, or 2000 largest companies. These lists can be made available on tape that then can be used for production of mailings as well as calling, or the list can be in hard-copy form, either sheet listings or 3 by 5 telephone calling cards. The business data can be sorted by primary SIC, or by primary plus secondary SIC, or alphabetic. Geographically these business data can be provided by state, city, three-digit zip code or five-digit zip code, or county or carrier route.

There are machines on the market and in the hands of telephone service bureaus that can make calls automatically, either from a tape fed to them or sequentially. The latter will make calls to listed as well as unlisted numbers. The use of such machines must be handled with great care. Some of the newer models do the dialing automatically and then connect the call to a personal operator.

COPING WITH TELEPHONE'S "BLACK HOLES": UNLISTED NUMBERS

The total number of households in America based on 1985 data reported by the USPS is 87 million. Of these, 85 million (or all but $2\frac{1}{2}$ percent have TV sets and 83 million have phones in their homes. However, the total file of households with telephone numbers listed in all the alphabetic phone books of the country is only 57 million and 5 million of these households do not list street address data, so delivery is suspect.

The figures above indicate that 30 percent of all telephone lines (26 million out of 83 million) cannot be reached through registered telephone listings. These "missing" phone number records consist of unpublished numbers (nonpubs) or unlisted numbers, which predominate. Ten major metropolitan areas have unlisted phones totaling from 40 to 46 percent of all telephone numbers! Five of these areas with the highest percentage of unlisted telephone numbers are in one state, California. The following table shows the percentages of unlisted numbers in these ten major metropolitan areas.

Metropolitan area	Percent of unlisted telephone numbers
Las Vegas, Nevada	46.4%
Jersey City, New Jersey	45.0
Los Angeles–Long Beach, California	42.5
Chicago, Illinois	40.9
Sacramento, California	40.7
Flint, Michigan	40.6
Fresno, California	40.2
San Jose, California	40.0
San Francisco–Oakland, California	39.5
Tucson, Arizona	39.4

A sizable proportion of these unlisted phones show up as long distance customers on the files of AT&T long lines as well as eight or ten competitors offering long distance phone service. Households with unlisted phone numbers must make up a sizable proportion of the 20 million households that are added to the listed phone households when households owning registered automobiles are added. The same holds true for a fair share of individuals added to major household files that are originally from driver license files.

Who Has Unlisted Numbers?

From a research point of view, having one-third of a nation's phone numbers unavailable for selling is not acceptable, particularly as those households with unlisted or unpublished numbers are an important and unique segment of the population which is different from those households with phone numbers in some significant demographic dimensions.* For example, phone numbers for people under 34-years of age can be broken down as:

Listed 29%

Unlisted 63%

This means that well over half of all households headed by an adult under thirty-four years old with phones cannot be reached through published listings.

Phone numbers for people aged fifty-five and older are broken down as follows:

Listed 49%

Unlisted 15%

A random calling of a cross-section of homes with published phone numbers will reach 50 percent more households headed by an adult fifty-five years old or more than those under thirty-four years of age.

Finally, phone numbers for unemployed/retired people (including students) can be broken down as follows:

Listed 34%

Unlisted 19%

Random calls of listed phone numbers are almost twice as likely to reach unemployed people than random calls to unlisted households are.

*(Data from *Journal of Advertising Research*, Copyright, 1982).

Research to Include Unlisted Numbers

Survey Sampling Inc. of Westport, Connecticut, compiles every phone number in every classified phone directory along with its yellow pages heading. This unusual list of phone numbers only is used as a suppress file and run against samples taken from randomly selected phone numbers to remove the 10 percent or more business-connected phones. Each random-digit number released on an order, after checking for every working block of numbers in every exchange, is then tagged to guard against reuse for research purposes for a period of one year. The system also removes all duplicate phone listings from multiple phone books as well as providing the part of the current live listings of the 18 percent or more American families that move each year.

The Classified Phone List as a Business Research Tool

The classified phone list by itself can also be sampled for business research. Perhaps the most impressive fact about this file is that it originally consists of over 26 million key-stroked phone numbers from over 4,700 directories. The list nets down to 8,800,000 unduplicated phone numbers, which after mentally removing those establishments with two different phone numbers, indicates the total of *all* unduplicated business establishments with phones to be approximately 8.5 million. In this instance, business includes institutions as well as offices of professionals.

As there are phone numbers on name and address files compiled from the same classifieds a way exists, through matching phone numbers, to add names and addresses to samples taken from the phone-only list. Both lists can be sorted by phone number to encompass multiple listings within a given phone book. The phone-only list, by denoting records by phone book, can identify records where the same phone number is listed and therefore promoted in more than one book.

Access to Phone Company Data Bases

As predicted a few years ago, when the twenty-two local operating companies of the AT&T empire were split off and assembled under seven regional umbrellas, current phone data (deliverable for direct mail, with current phone numbers for teleprospecting and telemarketing) is coming on the market, but in bits and pieces. At least three regions now accept billing stuffers, but with diffidence; at least three of the regions now rent names, primarily "new connects"—perhaps the most valuable phone names extant—while at least five companies and parts of two or three regions now offer local area on-line access to directory assistance for the purpose of obtaining current phone numbers. Costs of this on-line access appear to run, when access and monthly charges are included, in the \$.12 to \$.20 per number range, lower than charges by some outside services utilizing phone data usually a year or more older than the up-to-the-day records available at each phone company. (AT&T in 1985 was holding to its \$.50 per call rate which many phone users contend is too high.) Ed Burnett Consultants in late 1987 made available phone number matching through Chesapeake and Potomac Telephone Company.

SEVEN KEY LEVELS OF TELEPHONE COMPANY BUSINESS LISTS

Information on what the coming of current telephone registrant data will do to the list business as we know it today has been discussed earlier. This section gives an idea of the wealth of list data each major phone company controls. There are seven levels of such data: One or two companies will opt to offer only the first level, others will offer the first and second levels, and still others, which appear to be the majority, seem intent on offering all seven levels of data available. Even now, several telephone companies are experimenting by offering advertising stuffers in their billing envelopes. Most, by regulation, are making raw data available for directory publishers. Five of the seven regions in which the former Bell system is split have offices in New York, and are working on various kinds of countrywide projects, mainly in publishing. Hence, list work is just a matter of time for the telephone companies.

Here are the seven levels of data they have to offer.

Level 1—A copy on tape of the current list held by the phone company. These data approach on average one year old and are more current than the master files of both consumers and classifieds converted from the printed phone books today.

Level 2—An updating of each phone book as it becomes available.

Level 3—A weekly or monthly updating of all changes, adds, or kills.

Level 4—Levels 1, 2, or 3 enhanced with unique data available only from the phone companies including:

Number of lines

WATS lines inbound

WATS lines outbound

Advertising by dollar ranges

Telephone usage by dollar ranges

Primary SIC

Level 5—Addition of the names of executives on business lists based on one executive taken from 8 million accounts.

Level 6—Updating of Levels 4 and 5 on a weekly or monthly basis.

Level 7—Provision of business listings in alphabetics not published in classifieds. (These data have never been made available before.)

Telephone data in time will be the main source of all updating of lists, both household and nonhousehold. They will provide a continuous, guaranteed flow of new businesses and new offices of professionals on a weekly or semiweekly basis. They will offer every classified and every classification, extending selectability by five-digit classification from 2,500 headings now available to over 26,000 headings, of which 6,000 will be selectable by a fifth and sixth character added to the four-digit SIC. This will increase the counts by five-digit SIC (or similar code) from 11 million records to over 14 million.

Much socio-economic research will be transformed by the advent of correct phone data. For example, telephone data based on extrapolations from comparison of one phone book to another, is today's standard of measuring the mobility of our highly mobile civilization. Image how different this will be when mobility can be measured on an ongoing basis down to subblock groups or carrier routes on a daily basis, not by a computer fourteen to eighteen months after the fact.

AT&T Consumer List

Most telephone marketers believe, despite IBM's move into the long distance field through its minority interest in MCI, that AT&T will end up being the long distance phone company of choice by 80 percent of consumers. The seven smaller phone companies, plus MCI and Sprint, will split the 20 percent balance. But as AT&T is the "source of last resort" when others fail, and as calls for long distance information logically go to AT&T, as do AT&T charge phones, and most long distance calls outside the home are more than likely to go through AT&T, these same telephone marketers expect AT&T, which is beginning to bill some customers for long distance directly and not just through cooperating phone companies, to in time have garnered all or almost all of the 83 million phone numbers on its customer files, plus upward of 10 million businesses, institutions, and offices of professionals. This will provide the only source, so far as is now known, of virtually all household phones (as well as nonhousehold phones) in the United States, including unlisted numbers and nonpublished numbers, as well as numbers extant from the major and minor telephone companies representing 20 percent or so of homes not originally serviced by the Bell system. AT&T will use its own billing stuffers to sell AT&T products to its vast customer file. Further, such bills may be open to stuffers provided by outsiders. In line with what the local phone companies are doing (and the direct-response fraternity is lobbying for) AT&T

may find it possible to provide a nationwide online access to directory and phone number assistance.

Richard Halliburton, the author of *Royal Road to Romance* expostulated on first seeing the Grand Canyon, "Golly! What a Gully!" Golly! What a List! And what a jolt this will be to the list business if this file is made available to marketers.

It is certain telephone company data will through "new connects" provide the best basis for consumer changes for the foreseeable future.

HOW TO LOCATE NEW BUSINESSES THROUGH TELEPHONE DATA

There are two channels to locate new business today. First, it is a simple matter to produce those records new to classifieds this year. This will produce a file of over 1 million records by four-digit SIC and with telephone numbers. The timing, however, may be a problem. Second, a list of close to half a million records per year can be copied from records in county clerks' offices in major cities, and such data are usually available before a new classified phone book is published.

On the horizon, with the first "new business" lists breaking in 1985 and 1986, then sweeping through the country in 1988, will be access to the remarkable data available at the telephone companies.

To put the value of these data in perspective, compare telephone data now online with the way classified data now come to the market.

Canvassing a major city phone book market takes six to seven months to canvass. It then takes three months to print the phone book. It then takes a compiler about two months to obtain a copy of the new directory, and two more months to convert (computerize and integrate) into the file. Then that data, the most recently published data remains untouched for a year.

What the Telephone Company Offers

The telephone company, which is the source of lists, offers:

1. Up-to-the-minute data on every name and address on the file.
2. Every "new connect" on its system on a daily, weekly, or monthly basis.
3. The names of individual executives at the firm.
4. Data on number of lines and billing ranges for each registered phone.
5. Some data on connected WATS lines both inbound and outbound.

From the list above, we are most interested in the availability of new connects by far the best source for new businesses in America. As there are 1 million new businesses started in America every year, there is a great deal of interest in getting to them as soon as they "come on line." The phone companies, if they so opted, could also provide names of companies that have increased their telephone lines or service in any given period.

What New Business Lists Should Provide

Sources that are tapped to produce usable business lists should provide:

1. Coverage of every major prospect with whatever depth of management executives is required.
2. Coverage, if desired, of every other logical prospect with minimum executive coverage, if desired.
3. Ability to segment by company size.
4. Ability to segment by geographic areas; to "dealerize" by area, if desired.
5. Ability to follow up by personal sales or by telephone, if desired.
6. Ability to add essential demographic and psychographic data to the file.

ELECTRONIC CLASSIFIEDS

Phone companies are precluded by a Department of Justice ruling until 1990 or later from providing classified phone information online in the form of electronic classifieds. In the interim, several phone companies are making directory assistance for phone numbers available through electronic as well as mail access. When Electronic Classifieds come in the year 199$\times$ Mr. or Mrs. Householder will sit at a terminal or TV set connected to the phone with a small keyboard and type in "Restaurants." The terminal will immediately display the question, "What kind?" with a list of twenty-one classifications. They may choose "French," and the machine will ask "What price range?" and list eight or ten ranges. They select $15 to $20 (or more likely $30 to $40 in 199$\times$!). The terminal then asks, "What location?" The couple keys in "Manhattan between 34th Street and 59th Street." This answer is not accurate enough for the program which gently reminds, "East (1) or West (2)?" After the selection is made, the terminal displays nine French restaurants with phone numbers on the east side of Manhattan. One of these restaurants even lists its "Specialité de Maison"—Lobster fra Diavola at $36!

Most Americans would be surprised to learn in a few more years that France plans to stop publication of the phone books, both alphabetic and classified, once the new low-cost terminals are distributed to all households and all non-households in the country. Should that happen in the United States, many users will be very unhappy over the loss of a directory they have used all of their lives. With electronic access to constantly and continuously updated online current phone data, users of the terminals will no longer need to look through phone books or make a call to Information for directory service.

Electronic Yellow Pages

Electronic yellow pages may be closer to becoming a reality than we now realize. D&B and S&P have their huge business databases on line through "Dialog." Data by SIC classification and area (and number of employees in the case of D&B) can be accessed by Dialog subscribers through their own terminals. It is reported use is increasing with each passing quarter of a year. American Business Lists has its 11 million SIC records (about 75 million unduplicated establishment addresses) on line for computer access, and claims several thousand customers have purchased "electronic classified data" from this source through their PCs. Data Base America has a copy of its master file resident at CCX. Over 120 customers with dedicated terminals (and an increasing number of PCs replacing inadequate "dumb" terminals) can place orders online for this file, obtain virtually instantaneous counts while connected online, and the means are available (but the costs are yet "out of line") to send the ordered data over leased lines to label printers in the offices of those ordering the data. The Burnett organization, with the aid of its computer facility, Pagex, makes available instantaneous counts on line for its copy of Data Base America. Every order desk at CCX, at American Business Lists, at Ed Burnett Consultants is equipped with a terminal providing instant counts for thousands of separate business classifications.

The Phone as a Research Tool

If seminar creators wish to get an idea of the validity of a new seminar they "test" by offering the seminar through the mails, which usually calls for a mailing of 10, 15, or 20 thousand pieces. (Response to a $350 seminar is normally in the one-tenth of 1 percent range so that a mailing of 2,000, 3,000, or 5,000 is not significant.) Seminar creators can use the phone and call prospective customers, or have a well trained outside service make as few as 200 sales calls and get a good feeling of whether the subject being offered will prove worthy of a mailing campaign or not.

One important advantage of phone research (or phone selling which partakes of research) is the collection of negative information such as reasons for not buying a product. These data are not available through conventional mailings. Phone research provides significantly greater, more believable, and more candid data than does a conventional mail survey. Through a carefully crafted phone research program, candid, unrehearsed, and unprompted data can be elicited to avoid having to give away the offer or suffering any other consequences.

If research is conducted properly, executives will answer questions on the phone that they might not answer in writing. Their comments may be far more pithy and more useful than a few banal words written in a space asking for additional comments. Success is dependent on the art of communication used by the researcher.

The phone can be used, at least in part, to test prices, product combinations and product features. The data available through phone research (as opposed to offering products for sale by phone) are somewhat like that from a focus group "soft data"—opinions, feelings, and not "statistical" response data. These can be very useful and should not be overlooked.

TELEPHONE PREFERENCE SERVICE

The DMA has instituted a new consumer service that is modeled after DMA's fifteen-year old "Mail Preference Service." It is designed to help consumers reduce the number of telephone sales calls received in the home.

Consumers who wish to avail themselves of this name–phone removal service can write to Telephone Preference Service, Direct Marketing Association, 6 East 43rd Street, New York, N.Y. 10017. The name, address, and phone number must be included with their request for removal. As with the mail preference service, tapes containing the names of these consumers are circulated quarterly to companies participating in the service. This is a fledgling service, originated in 1985, and it will take some time for it to result in a reduction of unwanted, unsolicited phone calls. (The financial industry in particular might find any help it can get to reduce calls on annoyed consumers worthwhile.)

CHAPTER 17

Response Is the Name of the Game (Direct Mail Is Just One of the Players!)

To the surprise of many, direct mail is not the primary method of prospecting for direct response. Match book covers with offers are several times as numerous. The number of self-standing advertising supplements that fall to the floor from each bulging Sunday newspaper exceed direct mail advertisements by over 60 percent. No one really has any count as to the size of the audience reached by direct-response advertisers on TV and radio, but it is without doubt larger than direct mail. All direct-mail advertising combined reaches each household about 400 times per year, or roughly one time per day. In the five or six hours each television family spends before a TV set each day, many more than three response offers are viewed per day.

If you are a user of direct mail, and have not yet looked into the fabulous array of response-oriented vehicles made available by some of the brightest merchandising brains in America, you may well be missing a good part of the *response* you are looking for.

This section discusses direct mail-(space) advertising only insofar as space ads can be enhanced by a response vehicle that replaces, or in most cases, transforms the conventional coupon. No effort has been made to discuss use of TV or radio for response or the coming revolutions in Pay TV, CATV, ultra-high frequency, electronic transmission, or two-way response systems. Discussion is limited to the following forms of advertising, most of which are in printed form:

- Package inserts
- Stuffer inserts
- Printed media inserts
- Hand-delivered inserts and samples
- Cooperative mailings
- Specialized response media

These forms provide a multitude of variations, possibilities, sources, and opportunities, and as you run through them you may wish to consider the following questions in order to zero in on which form is best for your needs.

1. What can be handled? (Offers or samples?)

2. To whom can they be directed? (Businesses or consumers? Groups or individuals?)

3. What movement takes place? (Consumer moves to product or offer? Or offer or product moves to consumer?)

4. How does offer movement take place? (Hand delivered or mailed?)

5. What is the source of the media? (Sponsored and used by one firm? Or commercially available and not sponsored?)

6. What kind of payment can be arranged? (Per M, per inquiry, per sale?)

PACKAGE INSERTS: IT PAYS TO USE THEM!

Why use a package insert? There is only one answer—because it pays. In many cases it pays handsomely. Don't shy away from using an insert because a list or a category has been marginal. Package inserts offer immediate, guaranteed mail order buyers with no wasted circulation, the understood endorsement by the mailer of your product to his or her loyal customer, and delivery to names that are more current than the next update.

The most current "list" available from a major direct-response company is the customer, either first-time or multiple, who is just getting delivery of his or her purchase. The names of these "new" buyers are so recent they are not even on hot lines available for rental.

Renting the right to insert a noncompetitive product or service offer into packages is an important form of alternative media. For some mailers, package inserts are so successful that they often find that this form of co-operative, per dollar spent, will outpull solo mail.

A number of direct-response mailers with relatively weak offers (from a mail order response point of view, occasionally not much more than catalog pages or reproductions) can produce a profit by placing selected package inserts, yet lose out on all solo mail tests. (This is probably an indictment of the presentation not a slur on solo mail.)

Continuations in very successful package insert programs can prove somewhat frustrating. Although in most cases, a test of a list with a known balance can lead to a continuation, the fact that a mailer is permitted to test the placement of his or her inserts in a package program does *not* automatically mean that mailer can immediately arrange for a continuation. Some package programs are actually offered on a reservation basis, and a test for one of these packages only qualifies the mailer to continue when some other mailer drops out. There is a "catch-22" to this offer because no mailer is going to opt for a large continuation without at first testing the response the program produces. The program always allows for tests, however, so the pipeline of offers is kept full.

There are two costs to a package insert program—the printing of the piece and the rental cost of the insertion in the package. Package inserts run from about $45/M to $65/M and the response is normally measured in a few tenths of a percent. Programs will vary from a limit of four outside pieces to eight outside pieces, with six the usual number plus a bounce back from the merchant sending the package. Typically, because of the low percentage of response, a minimum test is required of 25,000 pieces.

The Risk: No Guarantee of Success

Package inserts are a "blind" commodity—that is, the mailer has no guarantee, other than the reputation of the program owner, that his or her pieces have all been received and inserted. The bill from the program shows only quantity, date started, and date completed. Placing a key on 25,000 pieces for program A will permit tracking of response to that key but it will in no way guarantee what proportion of the pieces were actually inserted. There is only one way to get a good handle on what has gone on, and that is to number each response form serially, which printers can do at very low cost, and use, say, 0025001 to 0050000 as a key for a given test, and then record the serial number of each response. If there is an unusually large gaps between order numbers, at least there are some data to work with. The fact the pieces are numbered serially, which should be noted on the rental placement, alerts the people responsible for inserting the pieces that this particular list needs to be given above-average care.

Advantages of Package Inserts

Package inserts have some advantages that relatively few mailers are aware of. First, a test schedule for 100,000 inserts, 50,000 in four or five package programs and 25,000 each for two co-ops, will normally cost less than a solo direct-mail program requiring the mailing of 30,000 to 40,000 pieces to a number of lists. Thus package inserts provide a reasonably low-cost way to make split tests of offers and formats. Then, as exposure is limited to those who receive a package, exposure of new offers to competitors is slight. Second, as no competitive offers are accepted, competition is preempted from using packages carrying a given insert. As noted above, some mail-response businesses that cannot succeed through direct mail are built through the use of package inserts.

TYPES OF PACKAGE INSERTS TO CHOOSE FROM

Can selections of classifications be made by product line, customer income, value or product, sex, or other categories? The answer is Yes, except that the range is somewhat less than for direct mail. The types of inserts available today (package, stuffer, hand-delivered, printed media), probably total 1,000. Those available include a high proportion of the big merchandisers by mail, the ones who really make direct mail pay, and their open-to-buy is well up in the hundreds of millions.

Inserts may be in the form of stuffers, folders, wallet flap envelopes, catalogs, return cards, or mailing pieces. Many mailing packages, unlike billing stuffers, can accept (for a fee) full-fledged mailing pieces.

Insert Classification by Sex

Is your market *male* oriented? Then you will perhaps find your markets in the following product lines:

- Automotive
- Architectural plans
- Fishing and hunting
- Hobbies
- Scientific gear
- Sports equipment

- TV and electronics
- Tools
- Toys (perhaps model sport cars)
- Work clothes

Is your market *female* oriented? Your markets may include the following product lines:

- Apparel
- Birth announcements
- Bridal items
- Cooking
- Cosmetics
- Decorative accessories
- Fabrics
- Fashion
- Housewares
- Needlework
- Panty hose
- Personalized labels
- Roach traps
- Stationery
- Teens
- Wigs

Gift and General Merchandise Inserts

There is a golden treasury for you in gift and general merchandise products, including credit checked buyers of:

- Art
- Goods offered by discount houses (like Unity, Nationwide)
- Films

- Gadgets (like Spencer and Sunset House)
- Gift merchandise (the names here read like a "Who's Who in Direct Mail")
- General merchandise (Aldens, Fingerhut, Foster Trent, Grace Holmes, Hanover)
- Nursery Goods
- Records (with selection for nostalgia, pop, classical, stereo, tape, disc)

Health Inserts for the Elderly

If your "package" lies in the age and health field, you can test inserts in:

- Health goods
- Magnifying glasses
- Reducing aids
- Trusses
- Vitamins

Business-Oriented Inserts

You may wish to reach groups or business or work-oriented recipients that will open cartons carrying your insert along with:

- Advertising specialty
- Bookkeeping supplies
- Church supplies
- Club plans
- Office supplies
- Uniforms

Specialized Inserts

These classifications above do not include some fascinating peripheral specialized opportunities in packages carrying inserts such as:

- Aquarium supplies
- Astrological charts

- Dolls
- Educational toys
- Religious goods

There are a few more variables to contend with in what is one of the fastest growing mazes in the response world. Most of these involve the restrictions placed on your inserts by the mail order merchandiser who opens his or her packages on his or her own terms.

MAILING RESTRICTIONS OFTEN IMPOSED ON INSERTS

Just as in any list usage (here you are using the newest names as fast as the merchandiser mailing the package is) your insert must be "cleared" by the mailer. Over and above the acceptance of the offer, the mailer usually establishes some or most of the following conditions:

1. Size
2. Weight
3. Number of pages
4. Minimum quantity
5. Limited number of inserts per package
6. Noncompetitive with other inserts
7. Noncompetitive with own offer
8. Time
9. Insertion, which can be loose (better), or in an enclosure as a large envelope.

There are some additional problems caused by restrictions on inserts which are basically inherent in any operation you do not control. The main problem is time because, say, a package insert test may require several weeks or months to run its course. During this period your pieces can get lost or mislaid. (Keying is an absolute must as is rigorous daily posting so you can track each insert.)

A second problem occurs if the merchandiser accepts too many inserts. Your response and that of your inadvertent fellow co-operative "mailers" may suffer. In this instance you must move your keyed materials to someone else's plant, which offers another chance for printed materials to go astray. (Although this may add a few grey hairs to your production control, the golden dollars at the end of the line are much more important.)

Note that a package insert provides almost as great a range for format, color, art, size, ingenuity, and creativity as direct mail itself and is limited only by the conditions laid down by each individual shipper of packages to his or her own customers.

STUFFERS

There is an entire series of inserts available where the conditions of use are quite a bit more rigorous primarily due to limitations in size and weight.

Where Stuffers Are Found

A number of major mail order firms now insert merchandise and service stuffers along with their bills and statements. These categories include such disparate operations as:

- Credit cards
- Horticulture
- Magazine renewal series
- Record buyers
- Stereo or tape buyers
- Utility bills
- Charge card customers

There are intriguing variants to the list alone. For example, one specialist works primarily with 400 major retail stores and chains and places millions upon millions of stuffers in the outgoing charge account statement mailings. In the magazine field one can now select from renewal efforts for *Ladies Home Journal, American Home, Photoplay, Sport, TV-Radio Mirror, True Story, Mobile Home,* and even a few industrial type publications with more selections to come. The promoter of the International Winter Sports and Ski Show permits stuffers in the mailings sent with free tickets to entice trade show attendance. A major producer of signs for small business will accept stuffers in its customer mailings asking for refill orders.

The criteria for stuffers include:

1. Size
2. Weight of stock
3. Machine-insertable by given equipment
4. Quantity requirement (often full use of given medium rather than conventional minimum quantity)
5. Limited number of inserts
6. Noncompetitive
7. Time

PRINTED MEDIA INSERTS

There is a small number of magazines, catalogs, and books that will accept inserts. These inserts can be either "bound in " or "loose." As they are appearing in a print medium they can be augmented with printed advertising (by demand in some cases) or not. With rare exceptions the use of such an insert means paying for the complete print run, which may be a far cry from actual selling circulation.

Magazine Inserts

In magazines you can select one or more of the following classifications. Others are certain to follow.

- Boating
- Business opportunity
- Drag racing
- Fraternal orders
- Farming
- Home
- Gardening
- Handyman

- Opportunity
- Ranching

Catalog Inserts

Catalog inserts, like magazine inserts is a field only developing now. Inserts can be placed in catalogs for:

- Automotive products
- Bargain goods
- Coin buyers
- Cosmetics and beauty aids
- Low-cost gifts
- Mail order merchandise
- Record clubs
- Stereo clubs
- Teen offers
- Vitamins

Book Inserts

Inserts (bound in or loose) also can be placed in books. One representative of major general publishers of paperbacks offers over 1,000 titles totalling over 100 million printed copies in generalized fields such as:

- Health
- Parents
- Self improvement
- Science fiction
- Youth market
- Reprints
- Novels
- Biographies
- History

One interesting problem with this esoteric but productive field is the length of time it takes to get cards ready for books; books ready for binding; packages ready for distribution; pipelines established through distributor to wholesaler to dealer filled with products for 60,000 outlets; and finally sales over a period of several months or longer to consumers. Think in terms of six months to a year before you get results!

Bind-in Cards

Bind-in cards, in association with a full-page advertisement, are an effective way to increase response from space ads seeking a direct response. Like everything else in direct response, the only way to find out is to try. But most who do, when seeking an order, find response is increased from four to six times, while response when seeking an inquiry or request (as for a catalog) is increased from four to eight times.

The bind-in order card is best used with a very soft offer such as "bill me later" as used by book clubs and record clubs to get starters for a negative option continuity program.

It is important to make the bind-in card as easy to tear out as possible without affecting the rest of the magazine. Diamond shaped cutouts along the perforation help in this regard.

NEWSPAPER PREPRINTS

The total number of pieces of newspaper preprints used for prospecting for new response customers is greater than all direct-mail carrying advertising. In the fields in which it shines such as lower-priced products, home fads, new home introductions, there is no doubt its volume exceeds direct mail many times over.

These inserts are unlike usual space advertising in that they generally include a coupon; some provide a vehicle for easy response such as a BRE or return envelope. In effect they are direct-response ads conveyed to homes through newspapers rather than through the mails.

Preprints can be solo efforts for one company or one product or they can be cooperative ventures wherein each participant is given his or her own coupon. One thing is certain by this time: If there is a medium there will be some bright advertising-minded person making a cooperative venture of or from it.

These preprints are a powerful way to reach large numbers of prospects at a far lower cost than through the mails. As such their volume has been increasing every year despite the angry wails from newspaper publishers, associations about the postage charge for third class mail. From 1970 to 1980, preprints increased by 400 percent from 7.1 billion to 27.3 billion. In 1985, this had increased to over 35 billion pieces. On one recent Sunday the *New York Times* carried thirteen stuffers with over 156 pages advertising over 2,000 items and including eighty-one coupons! Preprints were so profitable that the product managers at the *Times* complained because they could not get an opportunity for preprints for their own literary properties!

The half life of a Sunday preprint is remarkably short—three or four days at most—so the preprint provides a quick reading of results. The preprint offers most of the infinite variables available to direct mail in general, including color, size, pictures, drama, and cooperative splitting of the costs of printing and inserting. As a free-standing piece, the preprint can be retained for future action even after the newspaper has been discarded.

Newspapers tend to charge per insert and do not charge extra for using color. Thus preprints can offer color and extra pages usually at little more than the extra cost of printing.

Testing Considerations for Preprints

In testing preprints, it is important to recognize that each newspaper reaches a different market. The selection of papers to use requires some selectivity so that the market delivered by the newspaper matches, as closely as possible, the demographic and psychographic profile of the expected buyers of the product being offered. In addition, a study should be made of who is using these stuffers, when, and how often. Individual markets vary rather widely. Repeat insertions in the same newspaper of the same offer are a good indication of the value of that market for preprint use.

Cost Factors

The cost of preprint space varies widely, as does the CPM when the circulation is taken into account. Cost for printing preprints is primarily a matter of value. When testing a preprint program, it is essential to measure response against a rollout cost rather than the actual cost including test quantities. This is the only way the program can be evaluated properly.

The direct-response operater must not become infatuated with the huge numbers available locally for preprints nor overly impressed with the low CPM (although this is rising as newspapers find that they can charge more). In particular, the operator should not suffer any delusions about great expectations. A solo mailing that produces seven, eight, or less per thousand pieces may, when converted to a self-standing stuffer, produce no more than one order for every 20,000 circulation.

The correct approach is to key every insertion, research all the sources, and test—beginning with the very best papers first, and then working down. There are two good reasons for this: If the proposition does not pay out with the best buys available, it will not work with secondary journals, and if the best buys are not tried and the program fails, there will always be some doubt as to whether the fault lies with a weak offer or the choice of markets (newspapers).

COOPERATIVE MAILING INSERTS

A co-op describes any form of advertising in which two or more disparate advertisers reach a specific audience. There are newspaper insert co-ops, bank and utility billing co-ops, shopper co-ops, package inserts, cardvertiser deck or card-pack co-ops, direct mail (marriage mail) co-ops and even new catalog co-ops, even Magalogs, a cross between a magazine and a catalog. (Although not included under this banner, straight-run advertising in newspapers, magazines, and sponsorship of major TV shows are all forms of cooperative advertising.)

Types of Co-ops Available

Different types of available co-ops can be distinguished primarily by:

1. Market covered
2. Physical makeup
3. Periodicity (if any)
4. Proportion of control of printing and production

Interest here lies in those co-ops that are mailed in which a participant can obtain access to a market for a fee rather than bearing the entire cost of solo mailing. The major co-op in America is the Carol Wright Organization which conveys twenty to twenty-five offers and coupons to 30 million or 40 million households eight or nine times per year. This organization uses the Donnelley DQII file, which is the telephone/car registrant file compiled by Donnelley and overlaid with significant demographic data. Advo and Harte Hanks, with their millions upon millions of occupant addresses, also are well into the consumer couponing field. One recent addition to these multimillion co-ops has been the insertion by the owners of a demographic survey, which when answered, provides a new list of mail order respondents, and another list of self-styled owners of selected products, computers, for example. These data are then tagged to the mailing file to correlate mail order response with useful demographic data. (Most nationwide questionnares are funded in good part by major tobacco companies eager to build up their files of known smokers.)

There is no shortage of direct mailed cooperatives. There are library, computer, "new baby," scientific, and medical doctor co-ops, along with a few hundred different business co-ops. However, in the educational field, there is a proliferation for schools at various levels as well as appeals to college youngsters in almost every guise known to the promotional advertising person. For some student co-ops, the list is simply a list of schools and places to post offers that say "take one." For most, mailing lists are used to reach the students at home or at school. Successful college co-ops have one unusual twist: They contain twice as many offers and materials to read as those student co-ops that do not do as well. Students believe that more is better. Most participants in co-op advertising (almost everything except solo mail) are convinced that the smaller the number of competing offers, the better they will do.

Solo Mailing Versus Co-op Mailings

Most mail is solo mail—that is, a mailing making one offer from one company to one business or one household. It is "from me to you." What can be inferred from this is that solo mail, dollar for dollar, produces more than co-ops. If it did not, all smart mailers would make mostly co-op their mailings. (Some do!)

Co-ops, particularly catalog co-ops, tend to suffer somewhat from the fact that each mailer would actually prefer a somewhat different audience. In co-op mailings, the audience, in effect, picks or elicits the offer. In solo mail the offer, by affinity, determines the audience the mailer wishes to reach.

Large co-ops, until quite recently, were often sold "off the rate card" and "after the close" of the cycle. In other words, a good deal of "hondling" goes on. It is not uncommon to strike a deal at half price with the understanding that any subsequent uses will be at the rate card price. A true story that demonstrates this fact is that of a film processor who wished to get his offer in a large multi-million wave of coupons but the co-op owner stood firm on price. Finally, probably in a fit of desperation, the owner told his would-be client, knowing there was no alternative, that if his pieces were at the shipping dock by 5:00 PM that night he would accept the client's price. The client instructed the owner to look out the window—the trucks were fired up and ready to go!

Some major direct-mail practitioners provide a number of ways to participate as co-op advertisers in their promotional activities. This includes package inserts (riding along with merchandise shipped daily), catalog ride alongs (where noncompetitive offers are placed in the catalog or its carrier envelope) conventional mailing ride-alongs (where noncompetitive offers are stuffed into the same envelope), and card deck mailings. (Some are originated by one mailer with multiple products. Such decks can accept outside cards or not, whichever the mailer decides.)

Mailing co-ops tend to be a bit ephemeral. They start big and then fade out, or the sponsor or entrepreneur doesn't do well enough to continue or start anew. If you test a co-op, it is a good idea to find out in advance if your offer is successful what the odds are that there will be a comparable vehicle for you to use for your continuation.

Ride-Alongs

Some mailers, to cut down on their own costs in the mail, offer to include noncompeting offers in the package they are mailing out to their own prospects for new customers. This is a specialized form of co-op called a *ride-along*.

Although not as universal as package inserts, ride-alongs are available for a surprising range of opportunities from novelty items for magic to personnel forms: from free film offers to magazine solicitation: from records and books to vitamins.

Billing stuffer programs are a form of ride-alongs, but the essence of the true ride-along is that the creator is seeking a new customer and therefore competing with those other offers he or she chooses to permit to accompany his or her pieces. The measurement is simple: By mailing twenty, thirty, or 50,000 pieces with ride-alongs and the same number without, the operator can determine quickly whether the reduction in response due to the co-op competition, is less in dollars than the payments made by the ride-along to reduce total postal charges. Where a ride-along is offered over and over again, the trade-off ostensibly is in favor of the sponsor. Usually he or she attempts to have others pay for the total cost of the postage.

Cardvertisers

Perhaps the most successful co-ops (although this may be disputed) are the so-called postcard mailers, loose or bound-in cards, called cardvertisers (card decks) produced primarily by trade magazine publishers. Some idea of the sales value of this new industrial marketing medium might be gleaned from the fact that the second largest industrial publisher in the world insists that each of its over thirty magazines produce a minimum of two such mailers per year. This very successful advertising format has been used by medical publishers as well as mailers seeking to reach business opportunity lists, investors, teachers, and advertising executives. It is likely that the early development of this media is in some measure traceable to the continuing success of the three major publications competing for one-ninth page ads for new processes, parts, and equipment, each of which now augments more conventional advertising with cardvertisers.

Cardvertisers have provided mailers, primarily business-to-business mailers, with one of the most responsive media yet dreamed up. Providing the desire is to get an inquiry or request or make the sale of a low-cost item, cardvertisers, dollar for dollar will outpull almost any other form of advertising.

Loose packs are to be preferred to bound-in cards; if two color is available, it should always be used. If four color is available, eschew it unless it is essential for display of the item being offered.

There are problems with cardvertisers in that it is *too easy* to get a response. Card decks consist of a pack of preprinted business reply cards which are returned directly to the advertiser (but printed in a gang run by the promoter). All recipients have to do to indicate some interest is flick the cards they favor into an out box or drop them in the mail. Therefore, those that do direct a card in your direction (for you to postage pay) may not be qualified prospects. But the numbers are striking and the method is one that any business mailer (and a good number of consumer catalog operators) should try. The key to success with this medium is tied into the cost to convert. Be certain to monitor the back-end conversion very carefully.

To save recipients even the modest task of writing their names and addresses on cards, some ingenious card-deck publishers are now including six preprinted return labels on pressure-sensitive stock. All the recipient of the deck needs to do is peel off a label, affix it to the desired card, and send it off through the mails. (This is like the character who won the "laziest man" contest by requesting he be turned over so the prize could be placed in his pocket.)

Most card packs are printed five-up then guillotined into single cards so that knowledgeable users can easily, and at very little extra cost, make a five-way split test of copy, headlines, offers, premiums, and so on, on almost any deck. Very few practitioners take advantage of this elegant way to learn more from every key.

The list of these cardvertisers (over 400 are available) ranges through the entire gamut of trade publishing from air conditioning to vending machines: from food service to utilities. Executive groups are selectable for purchasing, data processing, training, electronics, education, designers, and over twenty different approaches to metalworking alone, including finishing, equipment, maintenance, engineering, automation, and materials handling.

If your product is sold to businesses, this is probably one of the most efficient media to use to obtain requests and inquiries from logical, identifiable, and interested prospects.

The latest format designed to get even higher productivity of sales than is usual for a card in a card deck, is a "microcatalog" printed on very thin paper and folded down to the conventional 3 by 5 inches of the card deck. These miniature catalogs can be four, six, eight, twelve, or sixteen pages filled with multiple products. Most card-deck publishers charge double for the piece, plus an adder for the difficulty of insertion into the plastic wrap. Most microcatalogs feature an offer for the major catalog. The addition of merchandise is designed to offset part of the costs to buy such catalog requests. It is a method well worth exploring if the pages are "strong" enough in their selling and telling mode.

Mail Cooperatives

When those of us in direct mail think of cooperatives, we usually are visualizing direct-mail cooperatives in which several different offers or pieces are inserted in the same envelope. (It follows that a solo mailer who adds a stuffer for another offer or includes another piece is creating a cooperative of his or her own). As we will see, although this covers most cooperative response efforts, it is far from all the cooperatives available.

Within the general framework of a set of pieces inserted in an envelope, an editorial attempt can be made inside or on the envelope, to encompass all participants under one umbrella. The envelope also may direct attention to only the mailer's offer and leave the other pieces to shift for themselves. (One cooperative even offers an endorsement of your product for an extra fee per thousand!) A number of magazines, recognizing the value of their specialized lists to mailers, have created mail co-ops, including new parents, craftsmen, children, and selected hobby fields.

Other envelope co-ops, some completely controlled and printed by one entity, others from the same mailers offering package inserts, go to markets such as

- Birth announcements
- Business opportunity
- Catalog buyers
- Churches

- Cosmetics
- Credit card buyers
- Education
- Film
- Gasoline stations
- Gifts
- Industrial
- Insurance
- Institutions
- Libraries
- Mail order (female and male)
- Medical
- New mothers
- Occult
- Opportunity seekers
- Puzzles
- Data processing seminars
- Senior citizens
- Sign buyers
- Teachers
- Vitamins

In addition there are co-ops made to the specifications of mail order buyers, for example the "Big List" which can be drawn from 20 million buyers. If you wish to reach organizations interested in products for fundraising, or scientists in nuclear engineering, or parents with children of a given age, or maintenance engineers in plants, there is a cooperative inviting you to join in. It is likely that if you wish to reach only consumers in only one of a few major markets, you can find a local cooperative to ride along with.

Your cooperative does not need to be mailed. You can have samples or direct response offers handdelivered through the growing network of private door-to-door delivery services. These localized services can give saturation coverage of an advertiser's marketing area by delivering his or her material in a plastic bag which is hung on the doorknob of each residence by a uniformed carrier who today usually is a homemaker with about 400 homes to cover in her immediate area.

If market selection by area is too broadly based, perhaps you would like to enter a cooperative which is handdelivered to medical people only, churches only, college students or high school students only, military only, or prenatals only. Perhaps, you would like to send your sample of offers only to homes with known purchasing habits. A company named Compusamp interviews approximately 5 million people by mail or telephone about their brand and product usage, and then sends them a preselected package of competitive products. Your offer may even be inserted in a package that the recipient pays to receive.

You may wish to have samples or pieces given out by hand at supermarkets or chain drug stores, or to given classes of viewers at motion picture theatres. If so, sign up for a cooperative. You also may have a product for sampling that requires refrigeration. These products now can be delivered by your friendly milkman. Gift packs to babies, new mothers, patients at hospitals, new arrivals in a neighborhood, *and* boy scouts at camp are sometimes mailed but the better part are given out by hand.

In the college market if there isn't a media exactly to your liking, some young entrepreneur just may tailor-make one for you. You can mail to college men or women by name of resident address; or reach mail order teens; a campus rep will give away your precious material at the time of school registration or at the gates of the stadium. A package also can be left in the dormitories or "take-ones" can be stapled together on bulletin boards. Further, you can buy a cooperative to go in the college press, or tag along with campus reps appointed to get subscriptions for news magazines.

There now are complete mediums (other than cardvertisers) established exclusively for response advertising with a requirement (for success) that the offer feature coupons, "cents-off," premiums, contests, or sweepstakes to invite participation. Some are almost complete magazines of response ads. Others are miniature mailers. One creator of a free-standing stuffer format, with slit ends called a "flag waver" has obtained a patent and obtains royalties from unsuspecting advertisers who attempt to emulate his attention-getting response-inducing devices.

SPECIALIZED RESPONSE MEDIA

You might ask at this point, how specialized can you get? For starters let's try the unbiquitous match book covers printed and used by the billions. Most of these carry advertisements, and a fair proportion now carry response advertising.

Inserts and ads for homemakers now go into millions of egg cartons each week. You can buy a response ad on board stiffeners for shirts or on the cards attached to fake handkerchiefs placed in suits just cleaned or pressed. Response ads can be bought for the reverse side of trolleycar or bus transfers or as a pad of stapled on "take one" cards to a car card, or they can be distributed in "take one" boxes to banks or restaurants or terminals or colleges. If you have a grocery product, you can buy an insert in grocery store bags inserted at the time of production or printed on the outside, or a piece can be inserted at the check-out counter.

There is now a slip with five or six different offers inserted into millions of packs of cigarettes—and other products will follow. One sports publisher, for example, offers its books to sports fans who open an Aqua Velva package insert.

This all boils down to: *response* is the name of the game. All these forms are designed to provide alternative media to standard direct mail.

Sample Size for Alternative Media

The size of the sample required for reliable tests of *solo direct mail* is covered in detail in the section on "Rules for Direct Mail Tests."

The size of samples required for *other forms of direct response*, while partaking of the same need to receive fifty or more responses per key have their own special requirements.

- *Self-standing stuffers* (for a solo product). At least 100,000 in five or more locations.

- *Classified advertising* (for a solo product). At least insertions for two- or three-time runs in at least three separate magazines.

- *Space* (for a solo product). If tests indicate that one geographic edition of a nationwide magazine or newspaper serves as a useful bellweather, by all means use this edition as a guide. To find such a bellweather will require testing with modest space in at least half a dozen publications.

- *Radio and TV spots*. At least a flight of twelve per station in a limited time (one to two weeks). There is almost no useful response data generated by a continuous series of one commercial in a number of markets.

- *Package inserts*. A minimum of 20,000 per program (50,000 per program is better). The ideal way to measure whether or not your pieces have been inserted is to number every piece serially and record response by key and serial number. If you print 100,000 pieces, receive orders from 40,000 in the middle, and nothing from the balance, you at least have a chance to find out what happened to the other 60,000.

- *Billing stuffers*. A minimum of 50,000 per program. If the program cannot generate large numbers for continuations, it is probably best not to program your test dollars on such.

- *Cardvertisers* (card packs, advertising card decks). Here the limitation is the universe covered by the publisher or packager. Less than 20,000 pieces, unless highly specialized, are probably not worth the effort, 50,000 to 100,000 pieces provide a better gauge.

- *Bound-in reply cards*. Most users find these cards (plus a requisite full page ad) will increase coupon response (without the card) for orders by four to six times; inquiries can run up to eight times more. The print run of the medium determines the need.

- *Paperback books*. Blow-in cards, like self-standing stuffers, tend to fall out and cry "look at me" when the book is opened. They can require a print run of 500,000, 1 million or 1.5 million. The problem is that it usually takes a full year, sometimes more, to get an idea of whether or not a given insert in paperbacks has been profitable or not. Where profitable, there may be no comparable titles to try.

CHAPTER 18

"Neither Rain nor Snow . . . " A Look at Modern U.S. Mailing Practices

HOW THE U.S. MAIL AFFECTS MAIL VOLUME AND DELIVERY OF DIRECT MAIL

Advertising Volume

Approximately 30 percent of all mail generated by nonhouseholds includes advertising. Over 85 percent of this advertising mail is delivered through third class mail so third class volume is a good indication of the health of direct-mail advertising.

Third class mail is by permit. In 1984 there were 509,000 for-profit permit holders and 280,000 approved nonprofit permit holders. (In 1980 these two figures were 314,000 and 293,000 respectively). These two groups can be further broken down by whether the entry of their pieces into the mail stream is by lower-cost carrier-route presort, or by regular bulk third class mail.

The USPS fiscal year 1986 (through September 30, 1986) split third class volume into the following three categories:

(in billions of pieces)

1. *Total third class mail 55.0*

2. *For-profit mailings*
   Total 44.0
   25.0   Carrier-route presort
   19.0   Regular third class bulk

Figure 18.1

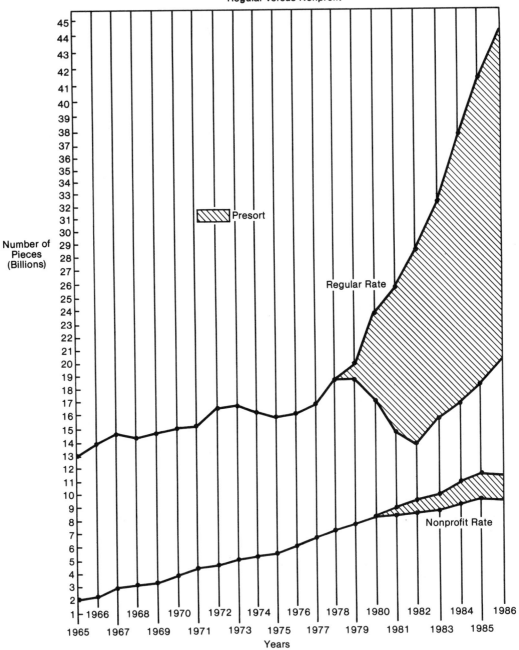

Third Class Bulk Rate Mail
Regular versus Nonprofit

Number of
Pieces
(Billions)

Presort

Regular Rate

Nonprofit Rate

Years

3. *Nonprofit mailings*
   Total 11.0
       2.0   Carrier-route presort
       9.0   Regular third class bulk

Direct Mail is far from the major means of prospecting for new direct-response customers. Self-standing stuffers now total over 50 million per year, or almost twice as many impressions as all direct mail with advertising for prospecting put together! This figure does not include direct-response TV ads, radio ads, magazine ads, newspaper ads, car card ads, "take one" boxes, and ads on products, in products, in packages, on packages, and even on match books.

How Direct Mail Has Grown

Perhaps the simplest way to show the growth of direct mail is to show a twenty-five-year chart of third class mail volume because as third class mail has grown so has the volume of advertising matter in the mail stream. Figure 18.1 shows that at the left hand edge of the figure in 1965, all third class mail for both profit and nonprofit groups combined was fifteen billion pieces. In the seven years between 1969 through 1975, a period in which rates doubled, there was no increase in third class volume for profit mail. In fact, measured against the number of pieces of mail per family or per $1,000,000 of gross national product, third class bulk for profit mail actually declined. It is also true that between 1973 and 1975 actual volume declined about 5 percent per year. Figure 18.1 shows that without the attractive discounts offered for carrier route presort, in which the mailer pays to prepare the mail so it goes directly to the carrier, bypassing all intermediate handlings, third class volume might have topped out a few years ago at about 36 billion pieces.

In the past several years, the volume of for-profit carrier route presort has been greater than all other third class for-profit mail. In 1985, for the first time, the slow continuing climb of non-profit third class volume was only made possible by the majority of the increase coming from the relatively belated use of the presort discount.

It is likely that direct mail volumes are at, or very near, their peak and a plateau instead of increased growth can be expected in the last years of the 1980s. A decline seems imminent in the 1990s because postal costs have increased over the last quarter of this century at a compounded annual rate of 9 percent and there are no indications this will not continue. New and higher rates will be established in early 1988.

U.S. Postal Service volume—by selected classifications
1972 through 1986 (in billions of pieces of mail)

	1972	1974	1976	1978	1980	1982	1984	1986
Total mail volume	87.2	90.1	90.1	97.0	106.3	114.0	131.5	140.1
variance		(+2.9)	(-0-)	(+6.9)	(+9.3)	(+7.7)	(+17.5)	(+8.6)
Total first class								
volume	50.3	52.9	52.5	56.0	60.3	62.2	68.4	76.2
variance		(+2.6)	(−0.4)	(+3.5)	(+4.3)	(+1.9)	(+6.2)	(+7.8)
Total third class								
volume	21.9	22.5	22.5	26.3	30.4	36.7	48.2	55.0
variance		(+0.6)	(-0-)	(+3.8)	(+4.1)	(+6.3)	(+11.5)	(+6.8)
Carrier route presort				2.9	7.1	14.8	23.0	26.1
variance					(+4.2)	(+7.0)	(+8.2)	(+3.1)
Percentage of mail								
with advertising	24%	25%	26%	27%	28%	29%	30%	31%
Volume of mail with								
advertising	20.9	22.5	23.4	26.2	29.8	33.1	39.9	44.6
Proportion of third								
class mail	77%	78%	79%	80%	82%	84%	86%	88%
Proportion of first								
class mail	23%	22%	21%	20%	18%	16%	14%	12%

(*Note*—Total volume of advertising is roughly 2/3rds for prospecting, and 1/3 for customer support. Only those records used for prospecting involve rentals or purchases of mailing lists.)

Third Class Is Continuing to Increase but at Decreasing Rates

In 1986 all third class mail increased by 2.9 billion from 52.2 billion to 55.1 billion, an increase of 5.5 percent.

Buried in the 1986 increase was a net decrease of approximately 100 million pieces of third class nonprofit mail (from 11.0 billion to 10.9 billion)—the first decline in nonprofit mail volume in America in twenty-one years. During this time nonprofit mail increased about 400 million pieces per year in a straight-line progression. The drop in nonprofit mail is likely to presage a cessation of increases in for-profit third class mail with the rate increase now slated for the first quarter of 1988. (There can be no rate increase in 1987 due to the prescribed length of the procedure for setting rates.)

The total increases, per year, of third class mail over the last few fiscal years have been:

Years	Quantity	Increase (percentage)
1984 over 1983	7.5 billion	15.0%
1985 over 1984	3.9 billion	7.9
1986 over 1985	2.9 billion	5.5

Increases in first class mail have been declining over the last three fiscal years, but no where near the decline of third class mail increases over the same period as the following table shows.

Increases in billions of pieces (per year by class)		
	First class	*Third class*
1984 over 1983	4.2%	7.5%
1985 over 1984	4.0	3.9
1986 over 1985	3.7	2.9

This table may cause postal watchers to question the conventional wisdom that third class volume generates increased first class volume. There may be some correlation as the figures indicate, but there certainly is no one-to-one or two-to-one direct relationship. It is likely if third class volume increase drops first to 2 billion, and then abruptly to 1 billion or less (with the 1988 rate increase) that first class volume will still be increasing by 2 or 3 billion pieces per year.

Third class volume, as a proportion of all domestic mail volume, has for the last three years been quite consistent—37.1 percent in 1984, 37.5 percent in 1985, and 37.6 percent in 1986. If first class outpaces third class, as it may do over the next few years, then we have seen the peak of third class as a proportion of the total mail flow in America. If third class rate increases in 1988 are drastic, the proportion of third class mail is destined to be further reduced.

Four Major Mail Flows

There are four major mail flows:
- Non Households to Non Households

- Non Households to Households

- Households to Non Households

- Households to Households

```
Nonhouseholds ──────→ 28% to          Nonhouseholds
         ↓                                9% to
       57%                                  ↑
        to
Households ──────→ 6% to              Households
```

About 85 percent (perhaps even more with the continuing increase in carrier-route coded mail) of the total mail flow originates with nonhouseholds. Two-thirds of carrier-route coded mail is delivered to households; one-third is delivered to nonhouseholds.

The current volume (based on the fiscal year 1986) of U.S. mail in pieces is 147.3 billion. Nonhousehold *originated* mail is almost six times larger than mail originated by households.

"Aunt Minnie" mail, the mail you and I write to friends or family, is only 6 percent of the total mail flow. Almost half of this mail consists of Christmas cards mailed in the month of December. The 9 percent mail flow traveling from households to nonhouseholds is primarily in the form of payments.

The percentages of each of these flows, encompassing a total volume (in fiscal 1986) of 147.3 billion pieces, is shown in the following box:

Contents of mail sent by nonhouseholds			
	Overall	**To households**	**To nonhouseholds**
Membership identification and credit cards	0.3	0.3	0.3
Correspondence, form letters, and cards	13.1	11.4	24.5
Communications (includes magazines, newspapers, newsletters)	7.7	3.3	11.3
Advertising and merchandise	44.0	56.9	18.1

Perhaps surprising in this area is the remarkable proportion of business-to-business correspondence. Half of all the mail received by nonhouseholds from other nonhouseholds (other than bills, orders, payments and receipts) consists of business letters. This turns out to be a greater volume of correspondence than all correspondence exchanged among households. "Aunt Minnie" is very important to the USPS, but business-to-business correspondence is more important.

Basic Facts on Mail Produced by Nonhouseholds

1. Nonhousehold mail flow by class of mail:

Class	To households (percentage) by class	To nonhouseholds (percentage) by class
First class	60%	40%
Second class	93	7
Third class	91	9
Fourth class	59	41

2. Postage paid by nonhouseholds

Type of postage	Percent
Stamped	12%
Metered	40
Penalty (count)	2
Permit	46

3. Type of addressing of nonhousehold originated mail:

Type of addressing	Percent
Hand addressed	2.5%
Computer and mechanically printed	97.5

4. Contents of mail sent by nonhouseholds (totals over 100 percent:)

	Overall (percentage)	To households (percentage)	To nonhouseholds (percentage)
Bills, orders, payments, receipts, notices, and checks	29.2%	25.5%	48.5%
Legal and financial documents	5.2	5.1	7.0
Enclosed return envelopes and labels	7.7	9.8	4.6

Pieces of Mail Received by Households and Nonhouseholds

In the 1830s the average number of letters received by each person per year was only three in the United Kingdom, according to a report in *Scientific American*. By 1882 that figure had risen to thirty-five per year. The figures for other major countries in that year per person were: Spain, five; Italy, seven; France, sixteen; Germany, seventeen; and the United States, twenty-one. By 1985 the average per capita in the United States was over 375 pieces of mail per year, the average per household was over 1,000 letters per year.

Although there are some problems with the USPS, size is certainly not one of them. The mail handled by the New York post office is greater than the total volume of mail in Germany; the mail handled by the Chicago post office is greater than the total volume in Japan. With over 800,000 employees and 35,000 local offices, the USPS handles over half of the world's total mail flow.

Most business establishments in the United States are small. Almost 80 percent employ less than ten employees. The following table shows the size of nonhousehold establishments in the United States—by number of employees:

6,700,000 nonhousehold establishments have 10 or less employees	78.8%
1,500,000 nonhousehold establishments have 11 to 49 employees	17.6
200,000 nonhousehold establishments have 50 to 100 employees	2.4
100,000 nonhousehold establishments have over 100 employees	1.2
	100.0

Nonhouseholds receive approximately one-third of all mail delivered in America, or about 44 billion pieces.

The average business address *receives* five times as much mail as does a household address. The average bigger-business establishment *receives* twenty times as much mail as the average household.

Since approximately one quarter of all mail received by nonhouseholds contains advertising matter, the average nonhousehold receives twenty-five pieces of advertising mail per week, or five pieces per day. (Larger firms receive an average of four times as much.) The average household receives about one piece of direct-mail advertising per day, or five per week, 250 pieces per year. (Some households receive several times this amount.)

Perhaps a reasonable estimate (there are no sound figures available) would use 15 percent of the vast recent increase in mail volume to be business-to-business. In 1980, when the total mail volume was 106.3 billion, the average number of pieces of mail received per business (nonhousehold) establishment per year was 5,400. In that same year the average number of pieces of mail per household was 750.

If fifteen percent of the 34 billion pieces of mail added to the mail flow between 1980 and 1986 are allocated to the 8.5 million businesses, the average establishment would receive about 400 additional pieces of mail, or a total of 5,800 per year. The 34 billions added to the household mail flow, if homogenized over the 87 million mailable households, added some 250 pieces per family per year, or a current total of some 1000 pieces. A good part of this increase may well be that proliferation of catalogs which so many in direct mail are concerned about.

SIZE OF THE MAILING LIST MARKET AND SALES CREATED BY DIRECT MAIL

We have a few "givens" here:

1. The total mail flow in 1986 was 140.1 billion pieces.

2. In 1980, according to an authoritative study made by the University of Michigan for the USPS, advertising matter was included in 27 percent of nonhousehold mail.

3. In 1980 the total of this advertising mail was 22 billion pieces.

4. The estimated number of prospect mailings (all with advertising) totalled 14 billion pieces. (Of these 2 to $2\frac{1}{2}$ billion were business-to-business mailings, from compiled, mail order, and circulation list files.)

5. In 1980, four out of five (80 percent) of all advertising mail was third class, the balance was first class.

6. Between 1980 and 1986 the total third class mail flow has increased by 24 billion pieces.

7. In that same period carrier-route pre-sorted third class bulk mail increased by 23.5 billion pieces.

To adjust 1980 advertising to 1986 requires a bit of educated guesswork along the following lines:

1. Of the vast increase in carrier-route coded third class mail, an estimated 70 percent included advertising. Seventy percent of 23.5 billion equals 16.5 billion.

2. Seventy-five percent of this increase was in all probability for prospecting, 25 percent for customer support. (The proportion in 1980 was 64/36.) This breaks the 16.5 billion into two parts, 12.4 and 4.1 billion respectively.

3. Of the increase in first class mail probably one-third included advertising. Thirty-three percent of 16 billion equals 5.3 billion. If we use the same prospect/customer proportion as for third class carrier-route presort the two segments total 4.0 billion and 1.3 billion respectively.

If we now add these educated estimates we get:

	1980	Increase in carrier-route mail	Increase in first class mail	Total
Prospect mail	14.0 billion +	12.4 billion	+ 4 billion =	30.4 billion
Customer support mail	8.0 billion +	4.1 billion	+ 1.3 billion =	13.6 billion
The total of advertising mail in 1986 was				44.0 billion

The total of advertising mail in 1986 was 44.0 billion.

We now can allocate the 30.4 billion of *prospect* mail with advertising (omitting those modest rentals for noncustomer mailings not carrying advertising) as was done for 1980 (see the following table).

Size of the list market 1986 compared with 1980

	(in billions) pieces		(in millions) dollars		Average price per/M	
	1980	1986	1980	1986	1980	1986
Business compiled names	1.5	3.3	45	115	$30	$35
Consumer compiled names	2.8	7.0	55	175	$20	$25
Occupant or resident addresses	5.0	11.3	25	80	$ 5	$ 6.80
Response names	4.0	8.8	140	355	$35	$40
Totals	13.3	30.4	265	725	$20	$23

In the six-year span shown in the table above mail pieces for prospecting advertising increased 120 percent, while dollar volume increased 175 percent. The difference measures the increased costs to rent mailing lists. Customer mailings in the same period increased from 8 billion to 13.6 billion, or some 70 percent.

If the rule-of-thumb estimate, accepted by most in the field, that total direct-mail expenditure (for both prospecting and customer mailings) in 1983–84 was approximately $12,000,000,000, then the mailing list proportion of this was about one-twenty fourth, or 4 percent. Let's see if we can corroborate this another way:

Type of mail with advertising	1984 volume
Prospecting with advertising	24.7 billion
Customer mailings with advertising	11.6 billion
	36.3 billion pieces

Approximately 36.3 billion pieces for $12,000,000,000 works out to an average cost in the mail of about $331. If customer mailings (including multiple catalogs) average out at, say, $400/M for 11.6 billion pieces, that would consume 4.6 billion dollars, leaving 7.4 billion dollars for the 24.7 billions of pieces for prospecting which would then average $300/M.

It is this author's belief that the $12,000,000,000 is somewhat inflated. (It was certainly inflated when used as the benchmark for 1983.) The $400/M figure for customer mailings "feels" about right, considering all the types of mailings done. Prospecting, including the 9.9 billion or so occupant mailings (48 percent of all prospecting is through occupant mail) probably averages out closer to $260/M than $300 so this part of the total volume spent for advertising mail is probably closer to $6.4 billion than $7.4 billion, making the total for all advertising mail $11 billion, and not $12 billion.

By fiscal year 1986, the number of pieces with advertising increased to 44 billions (30.4 billion for prospection, 13.6 billion for customer support). If we use the same figures for cost of mailing of packages in the mail for 1986 as for 1984; the total number of dollars spent for direct mail advertising promotion in 1986 was 44 × 331/M or $14.5 billions.

Now that we have a grasp of the number of pieces with advertising mailed in 1986, we are in a reasonably good position to realistically estimate the total volume of sales racked up exclusively by direct mail.

This calls for another educated guess to establish a likely range within which such sales fell in 1986. The following table provides a reasonable projection of that range:

	Cost in the mail (per M)			Sales in millions of dollars ($M × no. of pieces)		
	Low	**Middle**	**High**	**Low**	**Middle**	**High**
Prospecting mail 30,400,000/M at average sales per M of	$350	$400	$450	$10,640	$12,160	$13,680
Customer mail 13,600,000/M at average sales per M of	$2,000	$2,700	$3,500	$27,200	$36,720	$47,600
Total				$37,840	$48,880	$61,280

The figures in the table above stipulate on the basis of sales per M that sales created by direct mail in 1986 were between $38,000,000,000 and $61,000,000,000, with the half way mark at $49,000,000,000. Note that using 44 billion pieces (the total of all advertising mail) the average thousand pieces in the mail produced $1110, or $1.10 for every piece of advertising placed in the mailstream. If you happen to see some estimates 50 percent or 100 percent higher than $49,000,000,000 for sales created exclusively by direct mail, consider what this means in number of dollars per M pieces mailed.

NEED TO IMPROVE THIRD CLASS DELIVERY THROUGH USPS

For many years the old United States post office and the current independent and semi-autonomous United States Postal Service gave lip service to business mail, particularly to third class bulk mail, which makes up the majority of advertising mail originated by the 500,000 for-profit business mailers with third class permits. It has taken many years for postal officials to recognize that if it were not for the growth in this mail, the cost of a first class stamp would be double its current price.

Despite that realization, third class bulk mail, particularly those parts of it represented by large pieces (flats) and heavier items, such as catalogs, is receiving relatively poor delivery through the USPS.

How to Handle Address Corrections

There are several factors to look into where address correction by the United States Postal Service is concerned:

1. For prospect lists. It is not too well understood that nondeliverables have virtually nothing to do with response. A list that is 10 percent undeliverable and produces 1.0 percent in response, would, if all names were deliverable, show a response of 1.1 percent. Prospect lists either work, are marginal, or fail. Continuations are made on the basis of tests and a dirty list that works is preferable to a list 100 percent deliverable that fails to hit breakeven.

The rule for prospect lists is: Do not pay for address correction. If for some reason you need to know the level of deliverability, make arrangements with the list owner to have him or her honor results of a modest test of a few thousand pieces marked "return requested" and mail the balance without. What you want from this is for the list owner to pay you for nondeliverability over his guarantee for the entire lot mailed, based on the results of the test.

2. For the customer file. The cost of address correction was increased in 1986 to 30¢ per unit. That means it will cost $300 per M pieces returned. Address correction brings back two types of information. The first and most useful is a change of address, which happily, is now mainly computerized and is much more legible than in the recent past. These are bona fide changes that can and should be made on the customer file. (Note—such mail is *not* forwarded. The USPS has now made the cost of forwarding prohibitive.)

The second type of return is usually stamped "undeliverable as addressed," which would seem to indicate that particular customer is gone forever. This is not necessarily so. Remailing the "undeliverable as addressed" names again by third class bulk mail will quickly confirm that approximately only half will be returned the second time. The general belief is that those that "stick" the second time have been delivered and the address is correct. Before killing those pieces returned twice as nondeliverable by the Postal Service, each name should be mailed first class with a little plea, "Please tell us where you are!"

By the time this three-step cleaning process is complete, including the cost to correct the returns, the average cost to correct those returned will be over $1.00 per unit, which immediately raises the question: What is the worth of each name? There are some customer files that will not justify expending $1 or more per return to obtain the best possible cleaning. Some consideration should then be given to a single "Return Requested" pass, which leads to making the reported changes but simply killing those "undeliverable as addressed."

For large aging lists, the costs to refurbish are much too expensive. There are overlays available that can refurbish at least part of such aging lists.

List Cleaning and Third Class Bulk Mail

When rates are discussed, the only figures usually referred to are those for one ounce first class piece and a third class bulk piece weighing up to the maximum number of ounces allowable on a per-piece basis without surcharge. Lost in the welter of costs for presorted first and third mail is the cost for return of a piece of undeliverable mail and the cost of servicing a BRE (business return envelope) or BRC (business reply card).

In 1986 the USPS raised the cost of a business reply card or envelope to 37¢ and 45¢ respectively (with a deposit account, minimum of $160, then fees reduce to 21¢ and 29¢ respectively). Since these are the responses, either requests or orders, sought by the mailers, this cost will have to be borne by the list user and the differential absorbed in some way. An example may help explain the cost factors involved.

If a list of 100,000 names is mailed "return requested" and 8 percent are returned, 3 percent with change of addresses, 5 percent undeliverable as addressed the following costs will be incurred.

Cost of 8,000 returns at 30¢ each	= $2,400
Key stroking of 3,000 change-of-address records at 30¢/each	= $900
Remailing of 5,000 undeliverables by third class bulk mail at $350/M	= $1,750
Cost of 2,500 second-time returns at 30¢ each	= $750
Key stroking of 2,500 kills at 10¢ each	= $250
Merge of 2 sets of returns for update	= $100
	$6,150
	or 77
	per
	record
	handled

The cost to run the update is omitted here. That cost, probably $500 or so, must be borne when an update, with all inputs, is required prior to the next mailing. The cost for 8,000 returns here averages out at over 77¢ for each name or record.

How the NCOA System for Change of Address May Save Mailers Money and Time

The NCOA (National Change of Address) will in time be a vast improvement over the former system of address correction where change of address information is now maintained at about 190 computer-forwarding system sites on over 86,000 carrier-route discs. The data were used to produce the yellow mail forwarding labels now seen on some returned mail.

Address correction information is filed at each local post office or zip code area, and the greatest part of this information is already computerized. Thus data exist for a national "CHADs" (or change of address file). The logistics to bring together all the data has already been solved, as has the program for updating the tape. The NCOA system is designed to eliminate nixies before the mailing and eliminate the need for forwarding. Mailers are already seeing modest savings on production, postage costs, and more timely delivery. Another potential feature of NCOA will be address enhancement as well, in time, by the provision of apartment numbers, to addresses when they are missing.

When you consider that an estimated 15 percent of all third class mail is never delivered, the savings that could be realized through an NCOA system are very significant. For example, in fiscal year 1984, third class mailers paid $4.7 billion in postage for 48 billion pieces. Thus over $700,000,000 of postage were wasted, plus a minimum of another $1,500,000,000 in lists, paper, printing, envelopes and inserting costs not to mention the waste in the post office at about 150 percent of the cost of regular mail to handle up to 7,200,000,000 pieces "undeliverable as addressed."

As of late 1987, the USPS had appointed 17 large fulfillment agencies from over one hundred applicants, to utilize the NCOA tapes. A number of problems has arisen. The matching required is so detailed that, for example, Ed Morrison cannot be matched with E. Morrison. (This is done for the protection of privacy as if all mail required the same handling as a stock certificate or a check.) Over 10 percent of the names in the country are not yet computerized and will not be until 1990. The file is almost useless for four-line business list correction. The cost of adding nine-digit zip code is mandatory. Postal watchers are reasonably certain there will have to be some "give" if this program is to succeed. It is likely that a "nixie" file will be created in time so that the file will have some use in reducing undeliverables from large multilist merge–purges before mailing. The number of accepted contractors is likely to increase. The matching rules will in all likelihood be somewhat relaxed as the list is used.

Alternate methodology will come to the fore. Major list owners, such as Donnelley, Polk, and Metromail are already promoting their own change of address services based on running their large files initially against the NCOA as well as adding their own change of address sources.

Although some see the NCOA as a highly profitable operation, the proliferation of availabilities, plus the need by the initial contractors to recoup the hundreds of thousands of dollars involved in preparation not to forget the $100,000 first year fee imposed by the USPS are more likely to see a true cat and dog rate war in which profits, if any, will prove to be ephemeral.

Why Missing Apartment Numbers Can Slow Down or Prevent Deliveries

One of the major reasons for nondelivery in metropolitan areas is the lack of apartment numbers on virtually all compiled name lists. The USPS and all of the

Direct Mail Associations continuously advertise the necessity of including apartment numbers but minimal attention is given to this at best. New sources promise to make at least a dent in solving this problem.

The first is the "Change of Address" list created by the USPS which will in a few years include apartment numbers on the majority of changes affecting apartment house dwellers. The second is the entrance of phone company lists into the rental market as in all cases the address for delivery of the phone bill includes the apartment number.

The USPS has had, now has, and will continue to have great difficulty in delivering mail to people living in apartment houses. This means that lists including people living in multiple dwellings are going to have higher nondeliverable rates than those that do not. There are some postmasters in cities, particularly in the southwest, which despite all warnings by the USPS, have issued edicts that no mail for apartment houses are to be delivered to the address unless they carry apartment numbers.

Apartment numbers are slowly being added to lists. Major mailers (magazines, department stores, banks, utility companies, insurance companies) with the avid help of the postal service are leading in this endeavor. The changes-of-address provided by the USPS almost always include apartment numbers.

There is one type of mailing list that always includes apartment numbers. This is the "occupant" or "resident" list which is a list of households without names of the residents. The USPS offers a service for a fee to correct any occupant file in a given area that encompasses 90 percent of the households, and which is delivered to the USPS on cards (usually IBM punched and interpreted cards) in carrier-route order. The USPS fills in any blanks, and then returns each pack of cards by current carrier route, in carrier-walk order. By doing this the USPS provides missing characters or numbers for each multiple dwelling within each carrier's route. This specialized service makes it possible (virtually mandatory) for occupant or resident lists to be delivered to the postal service in just the way the postal worker chooses to walk his or her route.

Where apartment numbers are made part of the address, the postal service should be able to deliver the piece. There is a directive in the postal service which stipulates that where the number of pieces of the same mail, say, a flyer from a department store or a chain store, equals or exceeds the number of apartments (mail box slots) one piece is to be placed in each box, and any extra pieces are to be inserted into the mailbox beginning with the first box. The only difficulty here is that each post office tends to interpret USPS rules a bit differently.

If a mailer wishes to get some idea of the size and scope of this problem, and uses a compiled name list that can identify multiple dwellings, test mail for return requests equal sized segments of single-family dwellings and multiple dwellings. This may lead to suppressing multiple dwelling records until the USPS can provide a better measure of deliverability.

Even when the USPS gets its CHADs list in full operation, the industry will continue to use a few specialized lists to improve deliverability and the bottom line.

The first requisite is a merge–purge operation of some size for which the mailer can then opt to use:

1. One of several large change-of-address files compiled primarily from current changes reported to magazine publishers.

2. One of two or three credit prescreening programs that indicate people with poor payment histories with mail order companies offering sales on credit. One segment of such files identifies known rip-off artists who have "hit" many other mailers.

3. Screening on the basis of either credit worthiness or income, or both for some offers.

4. The DMA mail preference file of people who have asked to be removed from mail order lists.

RETHINKING THE USE OF ZIP CODES

Zip Code Area Size Variations

There are approximately 36,000 zip code areas that encompass the 87 million households in America, or 2,400 consumer mail delivery points per zip code on average.

Zip code areas do, however, vary in size from a few dozen families, say, on some island with its own zip code and therefore its own post office, to many of the big city zip codes that range up to 20,000 families and over. In the state of Ohio, the distribution of families reachable by mail by zip code is shown in Table 18-1.

The majority of zip codes in a large state like Ohio include less than 500 households. One third of all zip codes (actually 75 percent of all zip codes except those with less than 500 households) are between 1,000 households and 13,700. They embrace 70 percent of the mailable households by name in the state. All zip codes with over 15,000 households each total only slightly over 3 percent of all 2021 zip codes in Ohio. But these 3 percent of zip codes embrace one-quarter

Table 18.1

Analysis by zip code size—number and percentage of households

Number of households	Number of zip codes	Percentage	Number of households	Percentage
0–500	1,111	55.0	76,968	1.6
500–1000	163	8.1	117,640	2.6
1001–2499	290	14.3	475,900	10.3
2500–4999	156	7.7	555,310	12.1
5000–7499	84	4.1	527,042	11.4
7500–9999	67	3.3	582,499	12.6
10000–12499	54	2.6	608,855	13.2
12500–14999	34	1.6	463,281	10.1
15000–15999	12	.6	184,732	4.0
16000–16999	8	.4	132,133	2.8
17000–17999	8	.4	140,255	3.1
18000–18999	7	.4	129,630	2.8
19000–19999	6	.3	115,840	2.5
20000–20999	6	.3	122,367	2.7
21000–21999	3	.2	64,292	1.4
22000–22999	2	.1	45,039	1.0
23000–23999	5	.2	118,079	2.6
24000–24999	0		0	
25000–25999	0		0	
26000–26999	1	.1	26,100	.6
27000–27999	1	.1	27,139	.6
28000–28999	0		0	
29000–29999	0		0	
30000–30999	2	.1	61,534	1.3
31000–31999	1	.1	31,568	.7
Total	2,021	100	4,606,203	100

of the households. The average zip code in Ohio has 2,280 households which is virtually identical with the average for the country.

How Response Is Affected by Zip Codes

The art of testing consists of the analysis of the data and the use of that analysis. Zip code analysis, the determination of what response has been achieved (what penetration) by zip code, only makes sense when there are enough responses or penetration points to study. A retailer with 10,000 customers spread through one hundred zip codes, or a school or college with its 2,500 part-time students spread over fifty zip codes can do a very efficient job of determining penetration by zip code. But where the response level (or the penetration of customers) drops down to a few per zip code, little can be gleaned as to what such zip codes will do unless there are other nearby zip codes with far higher penetrations after the same amount of promotion, which points up how better to spend the next promotional dollars.

Where response within zip code area is so small as to be unreliable for analysis some means are used to encompass larger sectors of geography such as SCFs, counties, cities, states, or clusters of zip codes as sponsored by Acorn or Prism which have their own groupings of all zip codes in some forty "types."

In direct-mail response analysis, no matter what geographic sector is being measured, it is imperative that the number of pieces mailed to each sector be known. They need not be and invariably are not the same to each sector being measured. This is true because the response level is measured as a ratio (percentage) of response. Thus if sector A gets five times as many pieces as sector B, but A and B respond similarly, it is evident that B has done better, and therefore, will do potentially better on a continuation.

Dealing with Incorrect Zip Codes

Let us start with a given that *any* piece mailed to the wrong zip code by third class bulk mail will end up as a nixie. It is the *rare* list on the market that has very few zip code errors. In preparation for merge–purge, the experts in that service almost always first make a "zip correction" run. (Some mailers rather misguidedly try to "save" the $1 to $2 per thousand that is usually charged for this service.) A zip correction run isolates wrong zip codes that cannot be zipped and corrects those that can. Typically, on major mail order customer files, this results in about 2 percent that cannot be zipped and about 2 percent that can be corrected. Where the average package in the mail is in the $300.00/M range, that means a savings of $12/M. Note that merge–purges are working in the consumer field with most of the best known mail order buyer lists in America.

The average list available in the market probably has a zip code error of 5 percent or more. It is probable any list you own has a zip code error factor of this size. If nine-digit zip code becomes the order of the day, this error factor will be increased immensely.

The USPS Zip + 4 Program and Its Impact on Third Class Mail Handling

Zip + 4 is designed primarily to reduce the costs of casing mail. Mail now reaches the average letter carrier in about fourteen streams. The carriers for

160,000 established routes in and near major cities, plus 200,000 or more pseudoroutes in outlying areas, spend from one-third to one-half of each day placing mail in vertical cubbyholes in large cases in the walk order they will use as mail carriers to deliver the mail on foot, to each of 350 delivery points (households and/or offices).

This job requires memorization of the location of every delivery point in the route, the capacity to review each piece expertly and quickly, and almost on sight toss each piece into the correct one of over one hundred similar cubbyholes. Only a trained letter carrier knows the streets and buildings on his or her route, as well as the end points of each street covered by his or her route. Sortation by a substitute carrier involves a long learning curve. The 10 percent of routes that change each year due to demographic changes in neighborhoods, differential volumes, and local exigencies simply add to the labor-intensive costs involved.

The question facing list owners is: "Can automation reduce this great drain of inside time and labor manpower? The USPS says it can through the development of the nine-digit zip code.

Zip + 4 has been voluntary since its inception, but should the USPS find as it has been that the system is failing all but the favored few, it can impose conditions that will in effect make nine-digit zip codes mandatory—something postal watchers have warned of for some years. The five-digit zip code was voluntary at first also, but to qualify for third class bulk rates every piece must be zip coded and sorted by zip code. This is a form of mandatory action forced by rates and conditions of use.

From Voluntary to Mandatory: Some Problems to Expect

If the nine-digit zip code becomes mandatory every envelope, invoice, letterhead, and reply device must be reprinted. Every computer program must be changed, every computer list must be revised, and all makeup of the mails must be made to conform. Business lists in particular will be battered since the current nine-digit code structure codes no more than 80 percent of the average business list. Many business establishments are offered multiple four-digit add-ons, a boon to the company and a nightmare to those seeking to code or unduplicate lists. Even at 90 percent conversion by tape to tape, costs to add "+4s" to consumer lists are no bargain, because the missing 10 percent must be laboriously and slowly reviewed by clerical labor. (Smaller lists that cannot be computer coded, if given to the post office in volume, would choke the USPS until the year 2000. Recognizing this the USPS quickly rescinded its offer to code all lists at no charge and will accept lists only on sheets in a given format. For the same reason a free "phone in" service had to be quickly scotched.)

On its surface the nine-digit concept with immutable block faces that will not change (even though carrier routes do) is a magnificent concept. The coding structure on tape however is available only to very large operators. There are over 22 million separate bits to describe 87 million households and 8.5 million non-households—close to one record for every four individual local addresses. The idea that this will provide a marketing bonanza is patently false. There will be no demographic data available for such finite units.

Let us see what might be made possible by the universal application of the nine-digit zip code. (This means the fourteen streams of mail now descending on each carrier each day will be reduced to no more than three or possibly four and that the mail will be delivered to each carrier in segment and sector—that is, full nine-digit order. Since each segment and each sector code delineates a given location or string of locations on a given block face, such mail can be easily cased by sector within segment by any clerk who can read the numbers. Although mail cased in this way will not be in walk order, it will, for the greatest part, be within the given carrier route. Once the mail is placed in the sector slots, the carrier can, in minimum time, reassemble those sectors belonging to his or her route into his or her desired walk order. For large buildings (and floors within buildings) with their own nine-digit zip code, all nine-digit coded mail will come together as one sector. The savings to the postal service under this plan are expected to be a reduction of half the current cost of casing—a savings of some \$1.700,000,000 or 6 percent of the total cost (\$30,000,000,000) to deliver the mail at current breakeven.

That is the vision of the USPS and the main reason for the commitment to Zip + 4. Without it, the USPS is convinced future savings through automation will not be possible. But visions, no matter how pretty, are not necessarily realities. It is essential to look at where the system is now, and what will be required over a period of years to convert the USPS vision into an operational reality.

As long as any substantial part of the mail flows to the carrier "without the numbers" the carrier will still be required to identify and case the mail as he or she does now. Therefore there is a vast need, in time, if the system is to succeed in saving years of labor for every piece to be sorted to segment and sector order. If this sortation is by the postal service this means all such pieces will be bar coded. If industry does part of the job, their sortation might well be without use of bar codes.

This need affects three constituencies rather drastically:

1. It changes the manner in which the USPS handles the mail.
2. It impinges upon the work-sharing activities of outside suppliers preparing mail for the USPS.

3. It requires new thinking on the subject of discounts for mail processing, which in turn relates to postal rates for mailers.

It is easy to delineate some of the changes involved and how they will affect each of the three constituencies: the USPS, the service houses, and the mailers. But there are too many unknowns at this time to do more than sketch in some possible scenarios.

Nonhousehold originated mail whether delivered to households or nonhouseholds originates at every establishment in the United States—some 9 million (plus probably 5 million to 7 million homes utilized for commercial purposes). This mail includes the 61 billion pieces of mail prepared in extremely large lots by the 4,000 largest mailers, of which only 120 establishments handle 42 billion pieces, down to the bill sent out by the local druggist or tailor. Nonhouseholds originate over 83 percent of all mail. This mail includes the most homogeneous mail (first class presort from banks, insurance companies, utilities, department stores) as well as the most nonhomogeneous, including carrier-route presorted, carrier walk-order presorted, fourth class packages, third class single pieces, first class miscellany, second class magazines, express mail, and foreign mail.

The nine-digit zip code (with incentives) has been with us for over five years. During that period the USPS has induced the mailers of some 8 billion of 75 billion pieces of first class mail to add +4 codes to their pieces. At the present time that leaves a mere 125 billion outgoing (other than return mail) pieces yet to be coded. In that endeavor, the USPS, with or without the help of industry, must contend with the following problems among others:

1. Reading and coding of handwritten mail.

2. Extending nine-digit service to third class mail and to second class mail.

3. Handling or rehandling of mail presorted to the post office in walk order.

4. Handling of flats, packages, odd shapes.

5. Phasing out of carrier-route presort as presently prepared.

6. Incorporating apartment numbers into coding and identification procedures.

7. Establishing an army of two-line optical readers able to add four digits to correctly addressed five-digit mail.

8. Establishing a means to move millions of tons of mail presented at any of 36,000 post offices to some 250 locations where two-line optical readers can provide nine-digit bar coding.

For some time there has been apprehension that the imposition of the nine-digit zip code was destined to kill-off the very successful carrier-route presort program. What is really envisioned for the short term is a combination of the nine-digit zip code and the carrier-route code so that mail sorted will be in nine-digit order *within* carrier routes for easier casing and handling. In time, carrier-route mail will disappear. In time third class mail by nine-digit code will be handled much as first class mail with zip-plus-four is to be handled. And the net result, a good number of years from now, will be the death of third class mail. There is a heavy cloud hanging over this dream that involves adding nine-digit bar codes to *all* mail (with the possible exception of occupant mail already sorted within carrier route to carrier walk order). To add nine-digit bar codes to all mail, the USPS is planning to establish readers for all mail flows, at some 250 localities, and move the thousands of tons of mail first to these "reading and writing" locations. The history of the USPS, when large new changes are instituted, is not very sanguine, for example the disastrous bulk centers, the errors in nine-digit zip code imposition, and the false start with the NCOA file to which many can testify.

Reviewing the list of problems the nine-digit zip code is going to incur makes it clear that the vision of the USPS is some time away—probably closer to ten years away than 5 years away. In this ten-year timeframe there are bound to be serious dislocations in the way the USPS will utilize work-sharing on the part of industry; and the vast change in the handling of the mail will also affect discounts for mail preparation as well as rates for the coming changes in classifications.

To induce industry now to process mail for even easier handling than down to the carrier routes (via carrier route presort) the USPS along with the Postal Rate Commission should find it expedient to provide discounts for mail presented in sector within segment within carrier route. Such mail will be ready to simply pick up and place in the sector/segment bins within a given route in the route case of a given carrier. (To get to sector within segment such mail will of necessity be nine-digit zip coded. As it happens the addresses for such mail *can* be presorted by computer without going through the bar coding step. Whether the USPS will accept mail prepared in this way for the established sector/segment sortation remains to be seen. So does the size of the discount.) The concept is now being tested.

What might discounts look like in the early 1990s? Hopefully there will be a hierarchy of subclasses of mail providing increasing but modest discounts for five-digit mail, carrier-route sorted mail, possibly barcoded mail, and mail sorted to segment and sector.

In the interim the USPS will make multiline readers available in all major locations now able to read almost any printed address, and bar code the piece for automatic sortation. The USPS is working toward retrofitting all single-line optical readers now but may decide to move to the newer more accurate multiline readers just around the corner. In any case the readers will be able to bar code the mail for nine digits from an address and a five-digit zip code. (Note there is no need to provide nine digits to such machines.)

WHAT THE NEAR TERM FUTURE SEEMS TO HOLD FOR THE DIFFERENT U.S. MAIL CLASSES

First Class Mail

First class mail may become eroded by "electronic funds transfer." The majority of the 11 percent of all mail from households to nonhouseholds consists of checks for payment of rent, utilities, mortgages, bank loans, and car payments. It is conceivable in time to find five or six billion pieces of this 15 billion single-piece mail supplanted by phone calls or instructions over computers to banks. On the other side, social security payments and railroad retirement payments now flow en masse to banks from the U.S. government through electronic means. It seems reasonable to project that electronic transfer will erode first class mail, but rather slowly, and that first class mail, which increased by some 4 billions of pieces in each of fiscal years 1984, 1985, and 1986 will continue to increase modestly despite this invasion.

There is another modest cloud on the horizon for first class mail and that is the development of computer-based electronic communication systems as a substitute for hard-copy transmission through the USPS. Some of this is at hand now, and other uses are well along in the planning stage. The "Big Four" automobile makers are about to implement a policy which would require suppliers to join an electronic network and eliminate the mountains of paperwork now moving through the mails. (It will also reduce the lag time in the ordering procedure by seven to ten days.) The U.S. grocery industry already has an electronic document transmission system linking manufacturers with supermarket chains. Other big businesses in chemicals and metal handling are exploring possibilities. While impressive, these business inroads are hardly likely to dent total first class volume.

Second Class Mail

Second class mail volume is particularly vulnerable in large cities where joint delivery by hand for publishers, bypassing the USPS, is economic. With each price increase in second class rates, another piece of volume is siphoned off. The recent move to change second class red tag service and force second class mailings through the bulk centers has hurt delivery and increased the pressure to find alternative delivery carriers. But the bulk of second class volume is not likely to leave the single universal service available.

Third Class Mail

Third class volume faces the specter of a heavy-handed increase in 1988. At least two of the current panel of nine governors of the postal service are on record as believing third class for-profit rates should be raised to dampen the volumes of mail the USPS is handling. Non-profit organizations, which still enjoy a modest differential in rates in relation to for-profit mailers, now face a drastic percentage increase if Congress reduces or eliminates entirely the payment by the public treasury for "revenue forgone," the difference between actual rate and attributable cost.

All efforts and discounts offered so far by the USPS to induce use of zip-plus-four have been addressed to first class mailers. While most postal watchers expect discounts in time to induce third class mailers to add zip-plus-four codes, it is not likely that this will even start for several more years. It will take that period of time for the postal service to install the requisite 2-line bar code readers to expedite first class zip-plus-four mail. There seems to be very little interest, as yet, in inducing industry through work-sharing, to deliver mail sorted down to sector and segment within current carrier routes.

The chances are that third class mail will peak at something under 60 billion pieces by 1990 or before. 1986 volume was 55 billion.

Alpha-Numeric Sorting

There are some champions in the USPS who believe the wave of the future is in processing of mail alphanumercially. This methodology, being tested in 1985 and 1986, if implemented, would eliminate the carrier route as a set piece of postal geography, bowlderize geographically-oriented targeted marketing and possibly jeopardize the carrier-route discount rate incentive.

Believed to have been last killed in 1984, this rather odd abortion seems to be hydra-headed, and is once again being tested by the USPS.

Alternative Forms of Delivery

House-to-house distribution has been with us probably before Benjamin Franklin organized the first U.S. Postal Service, fueled mainly in the early years by a need to distribute political messages, tracts, and information for voters, locally.

With each increase in the cost to deliver a third class piece of mail there has been a resurgence in handdelivery as opposed to mail. Most national magazines with concentrations in major cities, usually in cooperation with other publishers, now are being delivered in part by local house-to-house operators. In the early 1970s an entire chain of these operators reaching areas that could be serviced on foot was in place. The development and rapid growth of mail presorted to carrier route initially impeded the growth of alternate forms and then, as volumes grew, caused many of these services to retire from the market. As of 1986 there are mainly pockets of opportunity left in well heeled suburbs that can be effectively delivered by homemakers working part time.

Recently the Magazine Publishers Association (MPA) provided a list of its members to one alternate delivery service for an offer of hand delivery which features logos of major publisher clients, including Time Inc. and Meredith. The senior vice president of MPA, Robert Farley, stipulated MPA "would do the same for any other alternate delivery service . . . as postal rates rise and rise, we want the postal service to know there are alternative (ways to deliver magazines.)"

There are now twenty-two firms that handdeliver mailings in the country, all now loosely connected as one network. This is a one-price service, rendered on one bill for comparable services provided by any or all of the twenty-two firms. Meredith today places approximately 5 percent of its total circulation (500,000 of close to 20 million per month) in the hands of alternate services. Time Inc. reports it is now using hand delivery for slightly over $1\frac{1}{2}$ percent of its huge volume (220,000 out of over 13 million units) per month. The corporate production manager is on record as stating that if second class rates were to increase drastically, Time Inc. would place 60 percent of its total circulation with alternate sources. "We've put ourselves in the position where we are poised to take off."

It is of some interest to note that the major cooperative form of advertising to reach prospects at their residences is called "marriage mail," in which multiple offers are enclosed or nested in a printed carrier. At one time it was believed such pieces would be diverted locally to house-to-house delivery, but that has not happened, although much house-to-house delivery is made of two or more advertisers in a plastic bag hung on front doorknobs. (By law, only the USPS may place pieces of *any* kind of mail in your mailbox.)

Fourth Class Mail

Fourth class mail has been reduced by the superb service of UPS and Federal to an auxilliary service for small mailers. The cries of the past that package delivery outfits would only offer profitable areas, and take the cream off the top of parcel post has been thoroughly scotched as both UPS and Federal offer service countrywide. The major courier services also offer service to every hamlet, and they and UPS indicate what the USPS could have done with small package handling had the source providing traceability, service, and accountability. Future cost increases here will simply provide a ceiling for price increases by USPS. It would be nice to be able to hope this could be turned around but that is asking too much.

Special Mailing Services

Express Mail. This high-priced overnight service does well in some areas but the courier services, particularly Federal Express, have captured the majority of the market, and, if anything, the gap between them and Express Mail is widening.

Electronic mail. The USPS Board of Governors has stopped the USPS advent in the E-Com field and have stipulated it be sold. So far as is known, there have been no realistic offers to date for this failed service. A substitute Wire-Laser-1st class mail operation called Tecom will start operation in the fall of 1987.

Meanwhile, major long distance phone companies, and one or two of the courier services have pioneered in providing electronic transmission of hard copy as well as the establishment of electronic mail box connections with owners of a personal computer. While not ruled out of electronic mail by that, the USPS has no active service to offer other than a modest link-up for international transmission in competition with the major wire services.

CHAPTER 19

How to Cope with List Problems and Abuses

LIST PROTECTION

As we move into the information age, it is becoming more and more evident that mailing lists are more than names and addresses. They also are repositories of information and there is a need to protect lists, at least as much for the information they contain, as for the name and address data that make them mailable. List protection is a major concern throughout the industry.

As the capacities of computers have grown to match and identify and tag data from one list to another, the problem of list security has become much more complex. In the past it was sufficient to seed a list and add seeds for each order for adequate protection. Today the use of decoys or seeds, although adequate to detect unauthorized use, is quite inadequate to guard against other misuses of a list. (Seeds, decoys, dummies are names inserted into a list or into a list order to positively identify the list. Only mailings provided by approved users should reach addresses of such seeds. When an unapproved mailing arrives at one or two of these "dummy" addresses it is a signal that shows mischief is afoot.)

HOW TO PROTECT YOURSELF FROM LIST THEFT

It is probable that the one problem list owners fear most is the least likely one to occur. That is theft of their list. In my experience, which now spans over

180,000 list orders for close to 3 billion names, I have been involved in only three known cases of outright thievery, and something less than six possible thefts. The most dramatic incident was the appearance of a young man at my office with a reel of names which ostensibly showed dollars of interest reported to the IRS. I could not get rid of him quickly enough, and left the word "Leavenworth," ringing around in his head.

That incident, unique though it was, points up the true danger spot in list transmission, which is not by the mailers, but rather by those at your own data processing center where your list is maintained and run. Converting 100,000 cheshire labels is a long, tedious, and costly affair. But someone in your own computer center, or the outside center you use, can very easily conceal a tape reel with 200,000 records under a suit coat. The type of control exercised at your data center is all important.

It should be of some comfort to know that the new copyright laws are remarkably strict and enforceable, and outright theft, partly because of this, is a minor problem in the list area.

Protection can be obtained by:

1. Limiting access to the list.
2. Screening the users.
3. Restricting utilization to a controlled service bureau wherever the possibility of trouble may be foreseen. (In such a case, the mailer is given permission to use the list only if the list owner does the mailing.)
4. "Salting," by adding dummy names or seeds which can come only from the given list and thus be able to monitor whether the approved package, and only that approved package, was mailed, and whether an unauthorized use of the list (perhaps a second use) has been made.

HOW TO USE DUMMY OR SEED NAMES TO MONITOR YOUR LIST

In creating seeds, it is important to make them so unique and so undeniable that they will serve as precise proof of unauthorized use. Thus it is not enough to change a middle initial (the mailer may remove *all* middle initials), nor are add-ons to the address (as Room 19) certain to survive. The best seeds are well garbled second names (Syzmuth for Smith, Rollimer for Miller) or constructs. It should be noted that replacing all first line names with "resident" or "occupant" will remove any change made to seed data by changing the name.

One or two major list compilers, working from phone books, have created dummy companies with legitimate addresses, with a listing in the phone book along with an assigned telephone number. Any other compiler using that phone book would have no way to know this is a dummy name created essentially for competitive list surveillance.

In dummying a list, it is almost useless to utilize names of employees only in the city or state of origin. It is too easy to skip that state. Seeds must cover a number of different areas. Ideally, there should be one or two seeds for each thousand names but this is rarely accomplished. On large lists, one seed in every 5,000 is probably closer to the mark.

Most standard seeding systems break down, or lose their effectiveness for list rental purposes. In the average list, a 5,000 or 10,000 test sample much more often than not, will get shipped without one seed. To solve this problem, mailers and their service bureaus have turned to seeds "implanted" at the time of rental. Where these are the same basic seeds, and the machine is told to add five or ten names to a test at random, the first four names on a California test may be addresses in Connecticut, North Carolina, Ohio, and Oklahoma. It does not take a mailing genius to recognize these are "dummy" names. Despite this, in the majority of cases such names are mailed, and the owner does get back a proof of use. When possible the seeds added to the file should be within the area covered. It is good practice to date stamp seeds, or code them by the job number so that the date of initial use will be determined easily. Dating can either be the Julian system or a pair of characters to identify month and year.

At the service bureau, a few rules will help:

1. Each use of the list should be logged out and logged in by date and individual and reason for the use.
2. Shred all carbons and sheet lists that are not in use or are not to be used. (Many a stockholder's list in years gone by came on the market because a copy was "filed" in the trash pile.)
3. Erase tapes and discs when the data are no longer needed.
4. Do not produce lists in mailable form when, say, the name and the zip code are all the data required.

If protection is desired, it is not enough to simply seed the list and establish some procedures. Every use of the list (both for the client as well as for rental uses) must be logged, and the sections from each seed checked against the control. All suspicious utilizations should be investigated promptly.

Monitoring through Mail Seeds

Monitoring of mail can provide information on:

1. How long it takes given pieces of mail to arrive (third class bulk mail takes an *average* of eleven days, individual pieces will take from a few days up to twenty-five days. Time monitoring provides some idea of when to anticipate response).
2. Whether or not an unauthorized use has been made of your list.

On response lists it is usual to obtain a "clearance" to mail from the owner, based on approval of a given package. It is this package, and this package only, that is "cleared." Monitoring can determine whether the package mailed conforms or not. In addition, any other use can be proven. Proof in the form of at least two seeds is usually sufficient evidence of unauthorized use.

The DMA offers a network of experienced mailers for mail monitoring. Private services are also available on a fee basis. (One customer in high dudgeon berated D&B for including a mail drop in its Million Dollar Directory. He had actually attempted to make a personal call on this paper entity!)

It is always good practice to include your own name on the list you rent. This can be accomplished very easily by typing up a pressure-sensitive label addressed to yourself, and using it to cover up one of the labels. You must cover up a label in the same zip code because a piece of third class mail misdirected by zip code is not deliverable. You should do this continuously as one more effective monitor on your own mailings.

On your customer mailings, you can insert not only your own address but that of friends, relatives, and associates, widely spread, who have been alerted to watch for and return any mail specially seeded for this purpose.

Watch for Attempts to Remove the Seed Names on a List

Another possibility is the deliberate attempt to remove seeds placed in the list by the list owner as a means of identifying when and by whom his or her list is being used. There is no excuse for this exercise which can only be undertaken with some ulterior motive. (Occasionally computer-oriented types like to play games; whatever is inserted into a list as a dummy, decoy, or seed by one computer expert can usually be spotted by another. One list that arrived at this author's computer bureau came with the challenging phrase, "You will never be able to locate the seeds." That was a challenge we could not overlook. We found the seeds for that company, including an illustrious trucking company in their home city called the "Gans & Hoffa Transportation Company." For the segments for outside use, (they really had faith!) all the trust companies were spelled *Mis*trust. We simply sent them a list of their seeds and left them in.)

UNAUTHORIZED MAILING PIECE SUBSTITUTIONS

This involves substitution of a new or different mailing piece from the one given clearance to mail by the list owner. This practice, which was fairly rife twenty-five years ago, has virtually disappeared. Any mailer who "substitutes," marks himself or herself for all time as a sly character, and word of such activity spreads rapidly in an industry where there are very few secrets.

A recent incident illuminates this point. The list owner had specified that the mailer could mail for his newsletter, but not for a highly competitive technical seminar. Mailing dummies for the seminar surfaced. Cut and dried case! Almost! The list owner had sold a copy of his list to a third party without setting any controls. The third party sold a copy to the mailer. The use by the mailer was perfectly legitimate and he had used the specified updated list for his newsletter only as agreed.

Some mailers use data from outside lists as input to their own files. Some send out rented lists with address correction requested and incorporate the corrected records into their house files.

Some look up phone numbers for outside lists and then others phone the household (without authorization) or pick up the name as a proven list name and not a seed.

FIVE WAYS IN WHICH COMPUTER-LIST HANDLING CAN BE ABUSED

In good part, the nagging problems of possible list misuse have been created by the technological advances made in the ability to match and identify mailing list segments and mailing list duplicate records. If it were not for this capacity to identify, match, suppress, and transfer information from one file to another we would not have:

- Merge–Purge—to identify and remove duplicates (nor would we have any problems with the use of duplicates).

- Overlays—to add demographic and psychographic data to customer files (nor would we have any worry about data transfer).

- Zip Correction—to identify and handle unzippable and incorrect zips (nor would we have purloined zip data).
- CHADs—to use change of address data to correct mailing lists before mailing (nor have access to change data after mailing).
- Prior List Suppress—to improve response rates and at the same time raise all kinds of questions regarding payment for lists and list data.

How Merge–Purge Identifies Multiple Buyers

When the merge–purge of outside lists identifies a multibuyer several possibilities exist:

1. The client mails to only one of the duplicates. If an agreement with list owners for a specific percentage, say, 85 percent, has been reached, mailing a second time to the multibuyers is specifically proscribed. However if full payment is made for all names, then the multibuyers may be mailed as often as they show. A two-time multibuyer can thus be mailed a second time, a three-time multibuyer can be mailed twice more. It is understood that the unique names have already been mailed once.
2. The client, with or without permission of or payment to the owner(s), mails the duplicate names from the same mailing, but sometime after the first mailing.
3. The client, without the permission of or payment to the owner(s) mails a second offer to the duplicates.
4. The client orders his or her merge–purge house to extract all multibuyers from two or more lists, and after mailing them a second time adds them to his or her house list.

Merge–purges identify three forms of duplications:

1. Internal duplicates in a rented list.
2. Duplication between a rented list and the customer files.
3. Interduplication between two or more rental lists.

Internal duplicates cause no conniption; the mailer normally makes a claim based on the merge–purge report, and takes a credit for the unwanted names provided. This is almost always honored by the list owner or his or her manager.

Duplication between the house list and an outside rented mail order or subscriber list provides a bit of knowledge not heretofore known that these particular buyers buy by mail from more than one source, and they buy (based on the list source) a given class of product or editorial matter or service as well as the product or service of the house list. That such knowledge can be tagged onto the house list, without authorization, and without the knowledge of the owner of the outside list is one of the concerns of the list community.

Some mailers include in a merge–purge with mail order buyers a large stratified list of householders to permit the transfer of the desired response characteristics to the latter, and in effect create a mail order list out of a compiled file. They then use the names that match from the stratified list for several mailings, in effect depriving the owner of the psychographics of the fee due him or her for multiple use of his or her proprietary information. Every so often a merge–purge (usually of compiled names, or if response-oriented, from financial or fundraising lists) discloses the fact that two list inputs are really one list with two different names. The various descriptions of affluents as "wealthy Americans," "Affluent America," "Families with Incomes of $50,000 Plus," do not indicate by their names that only one list is being described. It is likely this type of nomenclature will be with us as long as there are lists and as long as list purveyors exercise their ingenuity as copywriters.

The same segment of the same list provided by only one source can be obtained from a host of entities in the list field, brokers, list managers, list compilers, list wholesalers. Many of these will be supplying mailing labels or tapes as though they themselves are the producers of the file.

This can lead to a higher proportion of duplication, even identical duplication, than is desirable. Once it is understood that there are no more than:

> Three companies originating lists embracing all or most telephone homes
>
> Three companies originating lists of most businesses in the United States
>
> Three companies compiling lists of college students
>
> Five or six companies compiling lists of driver license files
>
> Three companies with access to all available car registrations

It becomes a rather simple task to learn the source of any such set of desired names. If there are no more than 25,000 architectural services in the United States, buying architectural services from two or three sources offering 22,000 to 26,000 can add only minutely to the first list, at a very high cost for such an addition. If the list supplier will not tell you the list source, there is a simple rule: Find another supplier.

How Merge–Purge Reports Can Be Abused

Reports of merge–purges are designed to show credit, by list source, for every "unique" record provided, as well as for records found on more than one list. On a strict allocation basis, each list gets equal credit for its share of duplicate records. By any form of prioritizing, in which only the first list gets credit for a record found on multiple lists, a decided skew is created. Since it is from purge counts that list owners are paid, it is essential that the methodology used be carefully detailed, explained, and most of all examined.

How Overlays Permit Tagging of Data

Once a match between the outside list source or sources and the house list is determined, it is a relatively simple computerized matter to tag any significant data, already carefully denoted in fixed fields, to the house file. Among the data that might be transferred this way are:

Psychographic
  Name or code designating the matching list or lists
  Average order size, as ordered for the merge–purge
  Recency of the last order, as ordered for the merge–purge
  Method of payment even to the type of card used
  Whether the buyer ordered by mail or phone. (About the only data that will not ordinarily be present is the earlier buying history of the buyer.)

Demographic
  Business
  Phone number
  SIC
  Size data
  Name of an executive (if given)
  Code for advertising
  Consumer
    Length of residence
    Make, number, year, and value of cars
    Type of household
    Name of occupant (if different)
    Sex of individual
    Age
    Education
    Number of children under 12; under 18
    Exact dates of birth of names furnished

Where a list with demographics is overlaid against the house list with the intent of adding one or more demographic factors to the house list, all of the demographics can be transferred to the house list as easily as one or some, and there is a danger that some factors not under consideration can be added without the list owner being notified.

Often a demographic file is part of an overlay involving several files. For example, a compiled list of those above a given income may be used as a screen against a group of mail-responsive lists to ensure mail receptivity as well as the desired discretionary income. In this instance, all the data on the demographic file that matches can transfer along with the income ranges.

A client rents a list of families with children, and the list arrives with the names, ages, and dates of birth of each child. In the merge–purge, 10 percent of these names match his house file, which has no birth dates. Does he have the right to add this unique proprietary familial data to his house file?

Every merge–purge and every overlay provides an opportunity for such tagging. The control must lie with the mailer; the service bureau cannot be placed in the position of being a police officer guarding list usage. It is understood the service bureau has too much to lose if it does not live up to the letter of the law.

More and more tagging is being authorized, and the mailer in most cases is working out payment not only for the service of matching but also for the access to add data to embellish his or her file. This is a common practice when a customer file is matched against a large compiled file for just this purpose. Where telephone numbers are transferred, it is understood that the buyer of the telephone names has the right to call them if desired. However where phone numbers are picked off without authorization, no use can be made of the data on a legitimate basis.

How Zip Code Correction Procedures Can Lead to Abuses

Zip code correction provides another opportunity for some unauthorized dealing. A typical zip code correction of a group of merged mail order buyer lists will ordinarily identify about 2 percent or more with wrong zip codes, and another 2 percent that are not zippable by machine methods (no local address, corner of X and Y, such and such a building and the like). A disreputable mailer can:

1. Pull off all the records where the zip code has been corrected and add these to a house list.

2. Pull off all the unzipped records, and put them through a clerical zipping procedure to salvage a fair part of them and add the salvaged records to the house file.

How Change-of-Address Files Can Be Misused

The ubiquitous ability of the computer to identify records that meet a given set of conditions and to set them aside for future use is one of the two major concerns of the USPS as it moves to produce a countrywide change-of-address file. This file is designed for only one purpose: To correct those records on a list about to be mailed where a change of address has been affected over a given period of time. But in passing a tape which has data detailing:

Address was _____
Address is _____

for millions of names, the list will (in essence) split into three streams:

1. Those names in which the "address was" data on the USPS tape matches the to-be-mailed tape, and these records will be changed to "Address now is," which are then deliverable as changed.
2. Those names in which the "address now is" data on the USPS tape matches the to-be-mailed tape. These records can legitimately be tagged with the fact the USPS stipulates they are deliverable as addressed.
3. The balance of the "address now is" records on the USPS tape that do not match the customer or the house file. These names can be in jeopardy as all that is required is to split them off and mark them as good deliverable names. This is not the intent of the USPS but the possibility exists, and work is now going on to ensure that only the correct use will be made of this file.

Some mailers use data from outside lists as input to their own files. Some send out rented lists with address correction requested and incorporate the corrected records into their house files.

Some look up phone numbers for outside lists and then others phone the household (without authorization) or pick up the name as a proven list name and not a seed.

Improving Response Rates and Lowering
List Payments with Prior Name Suppress

This technique is used by more and more mailers to improve response rates. It entails maintaining match codes of names mailed today to suppress a file against a subsequent mailing. Although the intent is to use the names from a list as a suppress against the continuation of that list, in practice, where merge–purge is involved, the entire lot originally mailed tends to be used as a suppress against the totality of the next lot.

Where a mailer uses hot lines only of a given list, the match codes of each flight for six or more months are combined to make certain the same name, which can reappear on a good list over and over, does not survive.

There are stories of mailers saving match codes for one, two, even three years and using all such names as a suppress file against a current flight. (For years and years list specialists have proclaimed correctly that the list is the least expensive part of a mailing. "Prior name suppress" is tending to change that. If a list rents for $65/M and only 50 percent of the names survive the prior suppress, the net effect is for the list (if all names are paid for) to cost $130/M. It is for this reason that those using prior suppress attempt to reduce payment to net names mailed.

How Prior Name Suppress Works

A list supplier can suppress previous usage by tagging, by job number and user, each record used, say, on a test. If a list test is ordered by fifth-digit zip code, by simply skipping that digit a continuation can be free of any duplication of the test quantity.

In the early days of the computer, the method used to guarantee unduplication was simple: The initial file was split into two reels, one was addressed and mailed, the other held. The proliferation of tapes was one problem, and the fact that the week the balance tape was scratched would be the very day an order for the balance would arrive.

For some uses, a copy of the names mailed to or a list is kept and when a new order arises, the copy of the list is run against the main file as a suppress tape while a sample is selected from the unduplicated balance.

Many major mailers elect to monitor reuse and continuations to eliminate and thus not pay for, names that are duplicates of those utilized in a prior mailing, even one a year ago. To this end, the computer service bureau is ordered to keep a copy of the names used or a match code extract of the names that can serve as a suppress file, but unlike concentrated orange juice, cannot be "reconstituted" and remailed. There is no good excuse for the first option; there can be good reasons for the extract. But for the most part this practice is neither mentioned nor discussed by the mailer. Owners of new mailing lists learn about this practice only when they receive a computer report of such inadvertent duplication and a check for unduplicated names only. (It is a far better practice to note on the initial purchase order that duplication uncovered on continuations will not be paid for.)

When to Expect Duplications

A question that often surfaces is, "How can such duplication arise?" That question might better be stated, "How often can a list owner supply names for a continuation which do not contain duplicates of those already supplied?" A company orders $100+ buyers in March from a given list owner and then, with good results, orders all $50+ buyers. Unless the owner can suppress only those $100 buyers first provided, some $50 buyers may also be $100 buyers. At best only a few hundred list owners can reasonably guarantee to omit previous usage.

Sometimes a mailer, using all names supplied by all list owners as his or her suppress, can claim as a duplication a new name on a continuation that matches either his or her house list or a list used prior. It is best to spell out what is allowable and what is not. Owners of important lists have, for example, been able to enforce payment for names that match the house list. The rationale here is that the reason to use the outside list is the very fact that it contains a noticeable (though small) proportion of names that *do* match the house list.

Mailers are searching for ways to control and/or suppress abuses. Some, in their search, create abuses of their own. One company in its terms of use specifically "permits" the use of a nonmailable match code from a rented list as a prior name suppress against future duplicates found to be coming in for a subsequent mailing. The rational intention is not to mail names a second time on the same offer. What it specifies as a fair use of its data becomes an unfair means to reduce payments to owners of other lists. Prior list suppress should apply legitimately only to future use of continuations of the *same* list where the list user does not wish to pay that same list owner twice for the use of the same name.

What Types of Codes May Be Retained

In its guidelines, the Mailing List Users and Suppliers Association specifically stipulates that only nonmailable match codes may be retained, and may be used "to suppress names and addresses found in the rental list data in later mailings of the same offer only *against the same list* made by the mailer who paid for the original rental."

The utilization of Prism, Acorn and ComSelect to select some zip codes and omit others (as a suppress file) on a geographical basis raises some difficult net-net negotiation problems. What names should a mailer pay for if half are knocked out not by any inadequacy in the records but rather by a proprietary zip code selection that has nothing to do with the list owner?

These "problem" areas point out the need for much more careful contractual relations between list owners and list users where computer matching comes into play. What can and what cannot be done needs to be spelled out, and the merge–purge houses need to be made aware by their customers of just what has been contracted for, and make certain that no more than that is done with the records under their control.

The rules in the direct mail community indicate that there is a small set of practices to which all agree concerning one-time rental versus sales, the right of the renter to all mail responses (this is not yet so clear for telephone responses) and reasonable payment terms.

Other rules cover relatively uncommon usage or unacceptable usage (from one side or the other) that must be negotiated on an above-board, all-facts-on-the-table basis between the list owner (or his or her agent) and the mailer (or his or her agent). In the long run, this means that negotiations will be required to determine the outcomes of the following questions.

- If an activity is unspecified, is it permitted unless prohibited?
- Under what terms can names on one list be added to another?
- Under what terms may data on one list be appended to another?
- Who owns the enhanced list after data have been added to it?
- Under what terms may names rented be refused, returned, or not paid for?
- Who owns outside names cleared by address correction procedures?
- Under what terms and in what times may owners utilize prior list suppress?
- What are the terms of a net name or a net-net name agreement?
- Under what terms may a renter refer to a rented list usage?
- Can a list be used twice, when one use is a preannouncement of the other, with payment for just one?

TELEMARKETING: ETHICAL QUESTIONS TO CONSIDER

Telemarketing offers a whole new set of ethical conundrums. If a telemarketer rents a list from one source, then pays an outside source to append phone numbers, who owns the records with phone numbers? Does a telemarketer have the right to call a rented response name without asking for approval? Is the list owner entitled to compensation for this further use? Does the list owner have a proprietary right to the information obtained on a phone call to his or her list?

What needs to be done about the practice of calling on the recipients of the list by phone, usually after mailing, to increase response dramatically, without prior permission and no extra payment?

DEALING WITH NAME PRIVACY

There is a good deal of brouhaha on the subject of the commercial use of mailing lists obtained from governmental sources. Some thirteen states have placed either a total embargo on lists of auto registrations or restricted their use to mailings connected with auto use only. Interestingly enough two states which removed auto registrations from the list market some years back have since returned them for access by mailers. Voting registrations are normally local which means that no national list has ever evolved from this source. Some major areas, such as New York City, will permit their use for mailing for political purposes only. There is a concerted effort today to obtain voter registration lists in states in which drivers registration data are being withheld. Drivers registrations are a major source of mailing data on adults in households. Close to half the states now prohibit commercial use of these data. A fairly substantial part of such data that are available includes the exact date of birth.

In the legislatures of the fifty states at any time there are a number of proposed laws designed to inhibit or prohibit the use of given public records for mailing list use. A good number of them pertain to data available on connection or viewing habits of cable TV subscribers. So far all efforts that would seriously impair the mailing list business have been beaten back by strenuous efforts by mailers and by the trade associations that represent them.

Availability of list data from the Federal Government is protected by privacy statutes, and by officials who interpret such statutes as denying all public use; on the other hand such data come under the purview of the so-called "Sunshine" act which attempts to make as much Federal data as possible available to any interested users. While this is a Ying and Yang conflict, those opting to withhold (because it is a far safer stance) have been dominant. A few years ago my office contracted to build a minority business file for the United States Department of Commerce. This file, built to increase government purchasing from minority businesses by federal contractors was then withheld from those contractors eager to even find such firms to do business with! By law major contractors must provide 10 percent of their subcontracts to minority businesses but they cannot have access even now to the file built by the U.S. Government! So a private concern has built what must be close to an exact duplicate of all minority owned businesses; has published it in list form; printed it in directory form; and made the data available online for computer terminal access. There are, however, at least two massive federal lists that are and should remain sacrosanct. These are the files of Social Security records, and the records of the IRS.

An outcry of an entirely different kind erupted in 1984 when the IRS, in an attempt to locate people of means who had not even filed income tax reports, went to the list market to rent lists that would indicate a given level of affluence. Every major compiler refused to rent names for this purpose for two basic reasons: (1) such use constituted a direct invasion of the privacy of individuals and families singled out, and (2) the fact lists could be used for such a purpose would provide ammunition to those attempting to stifle the use of mailing lists altogether. A small wholesaler did provide the desired test data to the IRS which publicly declared the only use to be made of the data was to identify people who possibly should have filed but had not.

In addition to the voluntary removal by names of the Mail Preference Service, major mailers who rent their customer files (which means most in the country) have found it both expedient and good business to permit those customers who do not want their names rented to register this desire with the mail order house or publisher. Less than one-tenth of 1 percent of those given this opportunity request their names be suppressed.

The direct-mail industry, again led by the DMA, has utilized peer pressure through its ethics committee, to self-police areas where privacy might be invaded. A list manager who made available a list of people who paid bills through money orders was convinced by this means that the file should be removed from the marketplace. A credit card company when offered a substantial sum for its list of those people turned down for credit, came to the conclusion that such data should not be made available. Although these are rather overt examples, the fact the industry is extremely aware of the need to protect privacy has undoubtedly solved many other similar situations.

SALES TAX: A STATE-BY-STATE CONCERN

As this book went to press no state had been able to collect sales taxes on goods sold by mail by a mailing company in a foreign state with no presence or nexus (business establishment) within its borders. However every state legislature has at one time or another tried, and the sales tax issue is today boiling perhaps as never before. In-state retailers are constantly being reminded by in-state tax collectors and their agents that their retail sales are being taxed, while those of mail order companies, some "just across the state line" are not. The mailing fraternity is fighting any such imposition of taxes with tooth and claw. The logistics of tracking, collecting, and accounting for sales taxes in forty-nine different states offers a spectre that mailers fear mightily. It is likely at some time in the future that Congress will be required to legislate on the right to sell across state boundaries, by mail, without incurring the need to charge and collect local sales taxes.

Although sales taxes on mail order sales remain, as yet, troubles to come, sales taxes on direct mail, and particularly sales taxes on mailing lists are a day-to-day reality. In New York all other forms of advertising, radio, TV, magazines, newspapers, and shoppers, are free of sales taxes. But direct-mail advertising produced in New York and distributed in New York is taxable, and all mailing lists, irrespective of where the addresses are located, if delivered in New York state are taxable. The business of list management, which in effect is list merchandising of lists owned by others, is considered a taxable service by New York state which has caused several firms to move to Connecticut or New Jersey, or to move that function out of state. Moving may not be a viable option. New Jersey has rulings comparable to those of New York state. Connecticut is now threatening to match its neighbors. Similar conditions apply in some of the other states. One step a list purveyor must take is to determine the sales tax liability involved in doing list business within his state and probably, soon, in all states.

CHAPTER 20

Rental Practices and Problems

HOW TO MANAGE PAYMENT FOR LISTS

Net Names: The 85 Percent Rule

The first merge–purges were probably done by magazine publishers who did not wish to give their current subscribers the offer being made to attract new subscribers. (The worry was and to some extent still is, that even though obviously not a first-time buyer, the current subscriber would accept the half-price offer as an extension of his or her current subscription commitment. Where this happens today, the publisher almost universally accepts the add-on order.)

Since this need preceded the application of zip code and the use of computers, the work was done by hand. First, the rented lists were run on the envelopes to be utilized for the mail-out. The subscriber file was then run on tinted envelopes to differentiate them. Then all the envelopes were sorted into one geo-alpha file (alphabetic by name, within alphabetic by city, within alphabetic by state.) Where two or more white envelopes matched, one survived. Where a tinted envelope (subscriber) matched a white (rental) envelope, both of them were pulled. Then the tinted envelopes were pulled into a separate file, and the unique, unduplicated white envelopes were utilized for the prospect mailing.

With the advent of the computer, making possible computerized merge–purge, mailers began insisting on discounts for names rented but not mailed. For all practical purposes, the so-called 85 percent rule is the result of a good deal of huffing and puffing over a negotiated price for names delivered but not mailed. It seems the average upscale consumer merge–purge was uncovering a duplication factor of from 10 to 20 percent so 15 percent was selected as the "going" rate to which major list owners would discount their lists for merge–purge purposes, providing a minimum number, 50,000 names or more in the main, was ordered.

The "85 percent" rate means the mailer "wins" if he or she reduces the mailable quantity by 10 percent. The list owner wins if he or she is paid for 85 percent but the mailer can only mail 80 percent. So some negotiations work out to 85 percent initially, with the actual payment to be based on the actual number of names mailed.

Many mailers however have not been content with this "standard" and sought special accommodations from list owners, particularly on large rollouts. By this time, while the 85 percent rule is still in general use, net name agreements are no longer limited to this once accepted standard. Negotiation between the buyer (the list user) and the seller (the list owner) is now more and more common. These negotiations take into account the number of names to be used, the number of times the names will be used, the size of the list, the competition, and reciprocity and exchanges.

What to deduct before applying the 85 percent rule

There is general agreement on the net name allowance that the following items can be deducted from the names shipped before the 85 percent figure is applied:

- Unmailable names as reported by the merge–purge service. (This may be due to lack of a local address or an unzippable address where zip code correction is part of the service.)
- Unordered names—foreign, APOs, and states or areas specifically ordered to be omitted
- Internal duplicates found in the merge–purge within the list
- DMA mail preference "No's"
- Prior name suppress, where agreed to by the list owner

Net-net names are those actually mailed after reduction by merge–purge, prior usage suppress, and screening (for credit or discretionary income total). For example, a first use might be for a merge–purge on an 85 percent basis. The net names (irrespective of the duplication found) will be 85 percent. After the merge–

purge, a screen for income reduces the names entered to 50 percent. The net-net names (those actually mailed) would then be 50 percent.

Where a list must pass a screen (for income or for credit worthiness) the actual number mailed may drop to 50 percent or less. Most list owners, recognizing this is opening markets heretofore closed to them, are moving toward negotiated pricing based on net names mailed.

In virtually all cases where the price for the list used or to be paid for is negotiated, there is a price applied to a "run charge" for those names supplied on tape but never used. A few years ago this fee was a reasonably standard $3/M, more or less an attempt to get back the cost of running the list. This price by most has now been changed to $5 to $9/M, which means a modest profit can be realized even on the names not rented. A few owners charge $15/M which the list community considers exhorbitant.

Net Not Price Pressure

List owners wish to be paid for all the names they provide; list users wish to pay only for the names they use. For the past decade or so the 85 percent rule has been honored. Internal duplicates are subtracted first, as well as unordered states, zips, classifications, or selects.

From this, via "prior name suppress" the user omits payment for those names identified as having been rented and paid for prior—from the given list—or just possibly from lists other than the one in question. In this determination any of the owners house files may also be subject to subtraction. Until recently, that was the end of the reductions. But new wrinkles are being used to reduce the payment due under net–net terms.

The list user may exclude perfectly valid records that do not fit his preconceived best five-digit zip area selections. Or the file can be overlaid by a cluster program such as Acorn or Claritas that reduces the balance of the names to this point by half or more. A credit screen can reduce the balance by 70 or 80 percent.

Some very shrewd major mailers renting very large blocks of names from major lists offer a flat percentage. One company, still mailing, has for years offered to pay for 20 percent of the number of names shipped—irrespective of the number mailed. He still finds lists to mail.

The DMA is working assiduously through its List Leaders and List Council to produce guidelines for the use that may be made of lists, to include a checklist of what is permitted, and what is not. This set of guidelines, with its checklist, will be of considerable help in speeding the negotiation, which, more and more, is becoming the norm in the buyer-user relationship where the data of mailing lists are concerned. (A preliminary set of DMA Guidelines is provided on pages

673 through 677. These are due to be supplanted by the new guidelines in late 1987 or 1988. I suggest you place your name on the list to receive these when issued.

It is for these reasons that a few far-thinking list owners are now offering list rental based on net names mailed. Since the computer can establish, on an allocated basis, exactly what has happened to each list, and list owners are content with count sheets provided by merge–purge suppliers, there is reason to believe that more and more "net–net" offers will prevail.

LIST PRICING ON THE RISE

For many years the average compiled list was priced at $25/M or so, and conventional mail order buyer lists were running at $35/M or so. In recent years, fueled in good part by the inflationary years of the 1970s, list rental prices have all escalated. When Horchow set a price of $100/M for rental of its current buyers, most in the list world were thunderstruck but many mail order buyers, formerly rented at $35 to $50 now bring $75/M or more. Now compiled files are $50/M. One major business list compiler has a price for small quantities which rivals the $100/M list rental of Horchow. Small esoteric lists, which a few years ago would have been content to obtain $100 for 2,600 names, now are priced at $125/M, or over three times as much.

What the list card states, and what the list owner actually receives may be quite different. All compilers publish quantity discounts which for millions of names reduces prices to the $12 to $15/M range. While some mail order buyer list owners are adamant on price, others recognize the market, and for larger quantities or multiple uses will work out "negotiated prices."

Dealing with Tape Returns

Years ago when tape copies of lists were only beginning to move from one computer to another, the fact a $15 or $20 tape reel was involved created a somewhat hysterical attempt to log and control such reels out and in. Excessive charges were threatened if the original tape reel was not returned within a reasonable time. Despite the fact that tape-to-tape copies are now commonplace, there are some list owners who still insist on the return of their tapes.

The basic rationale behind this now irrational request is undoubtedly fear— fear that somehow if the original tape is not returned, data will in some way be misused. In actuality, the receiving computer house could hardly care less. The first step, after receiving a dump and a layout is to reformat the tape. The desired list data are copied from the original tape and placed on a new tape or disc in the format desired by the receiving service bureau. (The data on the original tape are not affected any more than the sound on a record or a tape which is played back removes the original recording.) If a merge–purge is included, the same data may end up on five to ten additional tapes as the data are sorted and run through a dupe elimination, followed by splits for mailing, segmentation for special mailings, and preparation for postal presort. Returning the tape does nothing to add security. In fact, it may get lost in shipping, or be misread upon return and used inadvertently as input for another job.

Although it may seem that controlling a $10 or $20 item would be economical, exactly the reverse is true. There are shipping and handling costs. If the original tape gets mislaid, then the telephone lines begin to sputter between the mailer, broker, manager, originating computer house, and the list owner. Finally, one or two months after the mail date, someone finds the tape and returns it, but leaves off any coding and the computer house must now dump the tape, determine what list it is, and finally go back to its control and mark the case closed, but not before issuing a credit for the billing of the heretofore "lost" tape.

The rule is very simple. Bill a fair price to the customer for the tape reel. Mark it carefully *not returnable* and avoid the administrative headache of trying to control tape copies.

Late Charges for List Payments

As interest rates rose in the 1970s thus increasing the cost of money, more and more mailing list owners and managers added interest charges for list payments running sixty, ninety, or more days overdue. Payment for late charges will increase if conditions for payment are clearly understood at the outset. Simply billing without first announcing the practice will get some to pay, but most will simply not comply and if the user has arranged for payment thirty days following a mail date, which is still two months ahead, then late charges will be totally ignored.

Controlling Disputes between Renters and List Owners

In a market where 34 billion names are rented in a given year through 6 million transactions to a list-using universe, which can number over 1 million mailers, there is certain to be an amount of grit created. Until recently there were no organized means to resolve the various types of problems discussed here. This is a void that is being filled by the various associations that can call upon specialists within their ranks to help two "opponents" come to some reasonable solution.

There does seem to be an iron rule that renters of mailing lists, overall, will find from one-half of 1 percent to $1\frac{1}{2}$ percent of rental billing uncollectible, even with the most strenuous efforts to keep nonpayments to a minimum. There are so many first-time mailers, usually with somewhat great expectations, that such a loss is now understood by most. Even owners who work through reputable list managers find 100 percent collection simply means the list has not been merchandised as widely as it could have been.

One rather interesting dispute that surfaces more at conventions and over drinks is the long time it takes to get collection for mailing lists. There are some list managers who are able to fund their own growth in the field by extending the period after they have been paid by the mailer and the time of their payment, less their commission, to the list owner. Collection in this odd market rarely begins before 60 days go by from delivery of the list. Most list owners of any size will always be carrying a good portion of their list rental receivables in the 90- and 120-day category. Where a mailer uses a broker who gets the list from a list manager who finally pays the list owner, the time for the payment to get to the ultimate beneficiary, the list owner, can be, by ordinary business standards, a long, long time indeed. While some list owners are insisting on payment within thirty days on a contractual basis, the net profit on list rental (in the 55 to 60 percent range) is so attractive that not too much has *yet* been done to place list rentals on a more "businesslike" basis.

However the need for cash flow is causing many major list owners to place much more emphasis on current collection of list rental dollars. In response to this need the Burnett List Marketing Division is paying list owners the sum due sixty days after mail date whether the user or the broker has paid or not.

A fair number of new mailers seem to believe there is no good reason to pay for a list rental unless the list owner withholds action on a subsequent one. Many in the field now run every list order through the credit department to be certain there is no balance due before processing the new order. (A number of compilers now insist upon prepayment of the first order since only a small proportion of mailers of compiled names become repeat customers.)

CLEARING THE MAIL DATE

This really should be treated as two different problems: one for tests and one for large continuations or full runs. It is quite important on the latter to observe the mail date agreed upon. Some owners will not permit use of their names by renters during one or two specific periods of the year when their own offers will be barraging their own customer file. A mail date clearance, properly controlled, leaves a given period (a week or two weeks) before *and* after the mail date in which no competitive offers are permitted on the list being run in some quantity.

This is a favor to the mailer, and an attempt by the owner to provide a better opportunity for a favorable response. Both parties do better—the mailer does somewhat better and the list owner has a better crack at more rental business from the mailer.

Missing a mail date by a day or two is no tragedy; missing it by weeks can create competitive problems for two mailers, the one who mails on time as agreed, and the mailer who, missing his or her own time-window, mails out just when a competitive offer is in the mail.

When a date must be missed it is up to the mailer to notify the list owner of this and request a new date. It is not the prerogative of the mailer to mail when he or she is ready or when he or she feels like it, if he or she has contracted to mail at a given date.

Where modest sized list tests are concerned it is this author's belief that some list owners miss the doughnut for the hole by attempting to monitor the time of such tests. While it is possible that a test may be so close to marginal that a competitive offer over the same list may cause it to fail, the list test is just that— to determine whether or not to continue a given list for a given offer. As such, tests usually are specific enough on an up or down basis whether "protected" against some one offer or not. If there is any doubt and the list is marginal or close, which means it has been close to "cost free," a retest can be utilized.

RESTRICTIONS ON USE OF RESPONSES TO SPECIFIC LISTS

Not only does the list owner have the right to say "yes" or "no" to whether a given offer can be mailed over his list, he also is in a position to impose certain restrictions on the use that is made of names that respond to offers made to his or her lists. Such restrictions are rare but *Modern Maturity* (MM), the 15 million circulation list of the American Association of Retired Persons (AARP), is asking advertisers to sign agreements that they will not rent the names they garner from the MM subscriber file. This contractual relationship has mailers also agreeing not to resolicit such MM respondents with an offer substantially different from the product originally advertised.

CANCELLATIONS: WHAT TO DO

The equity of cancellations depends on time and the activities that have taken place since the order to be cancelled has been created. If there has been no action other than to cut an order and forward it to the list owner or manager, there is usually no charge.

If the order has been selected but not run—that is, it is still in tape form and no labels have yet been produced, it is usual to bill a modest cancellation charge to cover the out-of-pocket costs. This will usually be in the $20 to $50 range.

If the order has been selected and then run, but not as yet shipped, it is usual to charge a run charge for each thousand. This varies depending on list owner or manager but is usually between $4/M to $7.50/M, with a minimum of at least $50.

If the order has been selected, run and shipped, and the mail date is past there are a number of mail order houses or list owners who insist upon full payment. Most compilers are a bit more compassionate and charge a run charge with or without a separate minimum.

The type of cancellation request that creates great ill will and is virtually inexcusable is to have a tape or set of labels returned unused, some months after receipt, with some lame excuse as to why the names were not used or sent back sooner. More and more owners are insisting on full payment with the understanding that the mailer has the right at some future date to a current run of the same size at some discounted price.

If a tape is to be utilized for a merge–purge and fails to reach the computer house in time and is then returned for cancellation, there is usually some discussion as to fault. Some accommodation is almost always reached.

Occasionally a mailer will contract for a two-time or more use of a list, find out on the first mailing that multiple use is not economic, and seek to change the terms. This type of cancellation is normally honored by the list owner . . . as long as the one-time rental price is honored.

THE RIGHT TO CONTINUE RENTING A LIST

Usually any withholding of the right to continue after a test arises out of an unequal exchange, in which one of the two parties has an unsuccessful test while the other does well and wishes to continue to exchange, or to have the right to rent following the exchange. To protect an exchange from being deprived of a worthwhile continuation, it is best to spell out the terms at the time the exchange is arranged. If both parties are granted the "right to continue" at the rental price, this particular problem need not erupt. But if no such agreement is reached in advance, then the right to continue for only one of the two parties might be inferred but the granting of that right is up to the list owner.

Occasionally on a conventional list rental, the right to continue is withheld even though the test was made, as both owner and mailer knew, for the express purpose of determining whether or not to rent a continuation. While some upheld the right of the owner to withhold, the conventional wisdom is that in renting the list, the owner has implied the right to continue.

HOW TO TELL IF A LIST TEST IS "STACKED" OR "LOADED"

List tests are made to determine whether or not to make a continuation of that particular list or of a particular segment of a particular list. Where the continuation falls well below the test result there is often the feeling the small list test has been "stacked" or "loaded" with more responsive names than those furnished for the larger list rollout or continuation.

Where this happens it is best to take two steps before accusing the list owner of "stacking" the deck:

1. Check the tables on pages 386 and 387 to see whether the dropoff is within statistical probability.

2. Reread the section on page 383 on why rollouts almost always are less than those tests that are continued.

LIST PROBLEMS BY RANK

Some 300 companies in a recent list council study ranked six issues facing the list community. Weighting the choices with 10-for-1, 7-for-2, 5-for-3, and 4-3-2 respectively for fourth, fifth, and sixth rank, the figures show:

	Consumer catalogs	All mailers
Rising prices	573	1,510
Net-net arrangements	436	1,026
Restrictive legislation	419	1,499
List misuse	398	1,175
Standards of practice	332	926
List rental agreements	318	811

Even on this scale it is evident that the cost in the mail (rising prices, net-net arrangements, restrictive legislation) is of more concern at this time than the problems of list misuse. This indicates that mailers are able to view list abuses in a realistic manner even when they are reminded of the possibilities in this realm.

STANDARDS OF PRACTICE

The litany of list problems discussed here amply indicates the great amount of heat that surrounds approved and unapproved utilization of mailing lists at this time. It is evident that only a few principles are universally acceptable by users, owners, managers, and brokers, and that almost all other aspects require some form of agreement as to terms between the buyer (the mailer) and the seller (the owner of the list).

The principles that virtually all agree upon can be stated in a few brief statements:

1. The list belongs to the owner and he or she alone determines who can use the list, and what can be mailed to it (or phoned to it).
2. Unless otherwise stated, all approved utilizations are for one-time rental use of the owners data only.
3. All responses that the mailer gets for his or her approved offering mailing belong to him or her.
4. The owner makes no declarations of any kind as to the response to be received or likely to be received by the mailer. The only guarantee, if there is a guarantee, is for a given proportion of deliverability.
5. Compiled data may be purchased or leased for continual use by one mailer for a period of one year upon payment of an agreed upon fee over and above the cost for a one-time rental of the same data.
6. Magnetic tape reels including data for merge–purge or computer addressing are billed by the list owner to the list user and are not to be returned.

There are more uses and prospective uses of mailing lists that do not have universal acceptance than those that do. To help establish a meeting ground between buyer and seller, the DMA has recently published the following set of guidelines for mailing list producers. These guidelines were produced by the DMA in cooperation with the DMA List Council and the DMA's Ethics Committees. They are printed here as a useful checklist for users and owners alike although it is patent that simply listing the areas of possible contention does not provide hard and fast answers.

SUGGESTED GUIDELINES FOR DIRECT MAILERS TO FOLLOW

General

All involved in the transfer, rental, sale or exchange of mailing lists—owners, managers, compilers, brokers and users, and their suppliers and agents—should follow these guidelines.

Accuracy in description of lists

Article #1 All concerned should fairly, objectively, and accurately describe each list, particularly with respect to its content, age of names, selections offered, quantity, source, and owner.

Advertising claims

Article #2 Before and at the time of distributing a list data card or promoting or advertising a list as available for rental, those who promote the list should be prepared to substantiate any claims they make and should avoid any untrue, misleading, deceptive, or fraudulent statements and any references that are disparaging of competitors or of those on the list.

Screening of offers/list usage

Article #3 All involved should establish and agree upon the exact nature of a list's intended usage prior to the transfer or permission to use the list. Samples of all intended mailings should be reviewed by all involved in the rental process, and only approved materials should be used in the mailing, and on an agreed upon date. Lists should not be transferred or used for an offer that is believed to be in violation of any of the DMA Guidelines for Ethical Business Practices.

Protection of lists

Article #4 All those involved with a list should be responsible for the protection of list data and should take appropriate measures to assure against unauthorized access, alteration, or dissemination of list data. Those who have access to such data should agree in advance to use those data only in an authorized manner.

One-time usage

Article #5 Unless agreement to the contrary is first obtained from the list owner, a mailing list transaction permits the use of a list for one time only. Except for respondents to its own mailing, a list user and its agents may not transfer names or information to its own customer files or recontact names derived from a rented or exchanged list, or provide the names for another to make such contact, without prior authorization.

DMA Mail Preference Service/name removal options

Article #6 Every list owner who sells, exchanges, or rents lists should see to it that each individual on the list is informed of those practices, and should offer an option to have the individual's name deleted when rentals or purchases are made.

The list owner should remove names from its lists when requested directly by the individual, and by use of the DMA Mail Preference Service name removal list.

List brokers and managers should take reasonable steps to assure that list owners and compilers follow these list practices.

Purposes of lists/list data

Article #7 Lists should consist only of those data that are pertinent and necessary for marketing and related purposes. Direct marketers should transfer, rent, sell, or exchange lists only for those purposes.

List data/privacy

Article #8 All list owners, brokers, managers, compilers, and users should be protective of the consumer's right to privacy and sensitive to the information collected on lists and subsequently considered for transfer, rental, sale or exchange. Information such as, but not limited to, medical, financial, insurance or court data, and data that may be considered to be personal and intimate in nature by all reasonable standards should not be included on lists that are made available for transfer, rental, sale or exchange when there is a reasonable expectation by the consumer that the information would be kept confidential.

Any advertising or promotion for lists being offered for transfer, rental, sale or exchange should reflect a sensitivity for the individuals on those lists. Promotional methods and language that tend to portray characteristics of those individuals in a disparaging way should be avoided.

Laws, codes, regulations, and guidelines

Article #9 Direct marketers should operate in accordance with all applicable laws, codes, and regulations and with DMA's various guidelines as published from time to time.

Considerations for Mailing List Transactions

Mailing list transactions are controlled by the legal principles affecting contracts. As such, mutual understanding, good faith, clear communication, defined terms, and a meeting of the minds are imperative. To that end, a list of factors to be considered when entering into a mailing list transaction has been developed to assist contracting parties in developing a clear understanding of their respective rights and obligations, as well as to help them avoid the problems that typically ensue as a result of misunderstanding.

The list of factors that follows is not intended to be exhaustive, nor is it intended to dictate the terms of any agreement. Rather, it is presented to raise pertinent questions so that they may be addressed properly and adequately by the parties. The list of factors may be modified from time to time as trends develop in the industry or as technology or list usage changes.

1. Identification of all parties to the transaction

- Has each party to the transaction been identified by proper name and address?
- Are there other parties involved besides the list owner and the list user (for example, list broker, list manager, list compiler, or service bureau)?
- Have these other parties been properly identified?
- Is the scope of authority of these third parties understood?
- Should each of these third parties agree to be bound by the list agreement?

2. What is being transferred?

- Is the agreement intended to be comprehensive?
- Is an unspecified activity prohibited unless permitted?
- Is an unspecified activity permitted unless prohibited?
- Is the transaction an outright sale or assignment of the list?
- Is the transaction an exchange or trade for the use of another's list?
- Is the transaction a rental or one-time permission to use?
- May the list user add information to the rented list before using it (for example, telephone numbers)?
- Does adding information to the rented list change its nature?
- Who owns the enhanced list after information has been added to it?

3. What constitutes use?

- May the user merge–purge the list with other rented lists?

- Is the user permitted to add names that appear on more than one owner's list to its own lists?

- May the user code or tag its own file with information derived from a rented list where the rented list contains names that already appear on the user's list?

- May the user impose its own "qualifications" on a list, return the names that do not "qualify" and receive a refund?

- Does it matter what the qualifier is (for example, names on more than one list, a particular carrier route, certain demographics)?

- Is it all right if the list owner "qualifies" the list prior to rental?

- May the user send "address correction requested" mail and retain the results?

4. What constitutes one-time?

- May the rented list be used a second time in a different medium (for example, telephone)?

- May the user mail to a name on a list one time for each rented list the name appears on?

- Does it matter whether each list owner was paid for the name?

- Does it matter whether multiple mailings to the same name are related (for example, part of a series of mailings)?

- Does it matter what the time period is between mailings?

- May the list user or its service bureau retain names that appear on one or more rented lists for comparison with future rentals?

- May the list user do so to suppress names from future mailings to the same rented list?

- May the user do so for nonlist-specific data?

- Are there any additional purposes for which the rented list may be retained?

5. The method of and basis for payment

- How many names are being rented?
- What are the allowances, if any, for duplicates, for undeliverables, and so on?
- Is there a special request or selection to be satisfied?
- What is the price (for example, dollars per thousand names)?
- Has sales tax, if any, been accounted for?
- Is there a broker or manager involved?
- To whom is payment sent?
- Are commissions spelled out?
- Is there a net name agreement?
- Are the terms clear?
- Is there provision for verification?
- Have duplicates and multibuyers been removed or accounted for?
- Is there a reuse discount?
- Have the payment terms been clearly set forth and agreed upon?

6. What is to be received, where, and when?

- What is the format of the rental (for example, tapes, labels)?
- How much information will physically appear on the tapes or labels (for example, name and address, address only, with Zip + 4)?
- Where and when is the list to be shipped?
- Who is at risk for failure to satisfy this provision?
- Upon whom does loss fall if damaged in transit?
- Upon whom does loss fall if mailing dates cannot be kept?
- Are there any guarantees on deliverability?

7. Approval of the mailing and date

- Does the list owner have the right to approve the mailing?
- Must each phase of a staged or sequenced mailing (for example, catalog followed by gift certificate followed by personalized letter) be approved?

- Has the mailing date been approved?
- Must the list user notify the list owner if the date is to be changed?

8. Impact on others

- Does the user have the right to prohibit the rental of the list for a competitive mailing for a specified time period before and after the user's mailing date?
- Do the parties employ a negative checkoff option or DMA's Mail Preference Service for the protection of those on the list?
- Is the list being used only for a marketing purpose?
- Has the list been seeded?
- May the user refer to the source of the list in any promotion?
- Is it clear that the user becomes an owner of all respondents?

CHAPTER 21

A Look into the Future

POSTAL MATTERS

Rate Increases: Is an End in Sight?

Postal rates have been increasing at 9 percent per year, compounded, for over twenty years. There is nothing to indicate this will not continue. Even the $1,000,000,000 loan taken out by the USPS at the end of 1985 (to forestall a 1986 rate increase on top of the one established in 1985) will not change this.

The reasons for a new rate case are not hard to find. Expenditures based on increased volumes were based on unrealistic expectations. The "revenue foregone" element in which the entire taxpayer body politic pays part of the costs of the USPS is in deep jeopardy. It is this element that makes possible the remaining modest differential for nonprofit as compared to for-profit third class rates, as well as covering the uneconomic costs of keeping multitudes of small post offices open with local services that have nothing to do with moving the mails. If this sum, near $700,000,000 is voted out of existence (by simply not being included in the allocation of dollars) nonprofit rates will rise to the for-profit level, and rates already due for a large jump in 1988, will be increased by another 5 percent or 6 percent to recover from this blow—which means users of the mails will be subsidizing what was once "revenue foregone." And subsidize they will, for no member of Congress will permit the closing of his or her post offices, or the elimination of money orders and other losing services.

Nonprofit mailers, given years to reach parity with for-profit mailers are already in a quickening spiral. And one of the main reasons for the coming 25¢ (at least) first class stamp, plus a hefty increase in third class is due to the fact that the Bureau of the Budget is successfully forcing a transfer in 1988 of several billions of dollars of cost for the unfinanced liability for Postal Service retirees from the Treasury Department to the U.S. Postal Service. In addition, the USPS must absorb a 1987–1988 labor settlement with its 800,000 postal workers.

A 26¢ first class stamp may already be in the offing, along with a 15.5¢ or 16¢ third class bulk rate. By 1990 first class will in all probability be between 33¢ and 35¢, with third class bulk somewhere over half of this.

In recent years, the rates have been set and left alone for a period of three or four years. The new rate is then set to show a profit in the early part of the next span, and work out to break even (or close) until the next rate case. Rates for 1987 were published in February of 1985 and until the USPS Governors elected in late 1985 to borrow one billion dollars, there was every likelihood that rates would be raised again as early as 1986. It now appears that rates will be stabilized until the spring of 1988 which, as this is written, is now just around the corner.

Costs of all other advertising will in all probability increase as much (and maybe more) and the cost of making an individual sales call will likewise increase. Mail, except for start-up operations where the cost to buy a customer will inevitably increase, will not suffer appreciably by comparison.

First Class Mail: A Two-Tier Structure?

Before the end of the 1980s, there will be a two-tier structure for first class mail. Coleman Hoyt, Postal Consultant par excellence, and an esteemed member of the Postmaster's Advisory Committee, recently prophesied

> that first class mail will inevitably be subdivided into two subclasses: mail with low processing cost characteristics (which can be handled via automatic procedures) and mail with high-processing cost characteristics (which requires higher cost manual processing).

Hoyt further predicted that third class mail inevitably will fall into three rate categories or subclasses: carrier-route presorted third class mail regardless of its physical characteristics, machinable third class mail which can be processed along with first class mail in the optical character reader/bar code reader letter mailstream, and nonmachinable third class mail. (In the long run 3rd class as we know it will disappear. Mail will either be machinable, or not irrespective of how it was formerly classified).

The Rise of Private Mail Services

In the next few years, the high labor costs of the USPS will cause USPS management to experiment with the privatization of selected postal functions involving first class mail. This will be the first chink in the monopoly granted the USPS on the carrying of first class mail by the Private Express statutes. If so, a fair portion of the service will be privatized before the end of the century. The balance will remain in government hands as the only way to assure the nation of universal mail service.

Nondeliverable Mailings Will Decrease
with Improved Change-of-Address Lists

Despite the opposition of several mailing list companies to the USPS supplying a CHAD which can supplement their privately created lists, the USPS, had by mid 1987, available a reasonably complete United States list of all current address changes for the mobile U.S. economy. In a matter of some years this list, continuously updated on tape, will be available through enough companies providing overlay services to reduce the current nondeliverable rate from the current 15 percent to something approaching 12 percent. The value for the public using the mails of such a reduction will be a savings of something like $3,500,000,000 worth of direct-mail sales otherwise going down the drain.

Walk-Order Discounts Will Begin

The concept of sortation to carrier route for a discount, was proposed by mailers and their mail processing shops for many years before the USPS agreed to establish in 1978 a separate rate. For almost as long, owners of and mailers utilizing occupant or resident lists have been petitioning for a *special lower rate* for providing sortation not only to the carrier route but to the actual order, house number by house number, in which the carrier walks his or her route. All occupant lists that cover every mailing address in a given territory (usually a large metropolitan area or a state or group of states) when corrected by the USPS on punch cards are returned to the mailing shop in exactly the order each individual carrier desires. These lists, which represent a large portion of rented mailing lists with advertising, are then maintained and mailings addressed from them are delivered to each carrier in his or her walk order. At some point, the importance of this form of list and the "extra mile" its producers take to reduce the cost of handling should qualify it for a realistic discount.

Perhaps this discount will come at the same time that the USPS and Postal Rate Commission opt to offer a discount for nonoccupant mail sorted down to nine-digit sector and segment within a zip code. Once the nine-digit codes as well as the carrier route codes are on the tape used to address the mail (or the labels), computers can easily provide addresses by sector within segment—and even within sector—by segment by even numbers and odd numbers that will closely approximate the way a mail carrier today walks his route. It should be noticed that lists provided to merge-purge houses need not be coded for zip-plus-four, and that there is *no need* for such mail to be bar coded. The solution made possible in this way (if some discount is provided) is, if anything, even a finer sort than can come out of bar code readers.

Two-Line Mailing Readers

In what might be termed a "sudden fit of sanity" (a phrase I am borrowing from a good friend) the USPS, under continuous pressure from Congress is now retrofitting its single line encoders for 2-line reading and coding which will permit the postal service a graceful way to automate a higher proportion of the mail flow. The 2-line readers will be able to read the local address line, as well as the city, state, and zip and provide an electronic means to code mail for carrier route sorting.

Taxation of Interstate Mail

After fending off for years the imposition of the need to collect sales taxes for sales made out of state by a direct-mail concern, it is now reasonable to conclude that one way or the other such collection will become the law of the land, and each direct-mail operator (or each direct-mail operator with a given volume or volume in a state) will perforce become a sales tax collector for each state. The tax will be on sales made in a state irrespective of whether the concern has a local presence (or "nexus") in that state or not.

Copyright Laws for Mailing Lists Will Be Altered

Almost all compiled lists on the market are compiled from sources that are copyrighted. This includes alphabetic and classified telephone books. Prior to 1978 the law was more often disregarded than not and most lawyers, aware of the limited protection afforded by the law, were not interested in taking action on a copyright suit. The passage of a new copyright law in 1978 provided real guidance and clout. Copyright protection was updated by that law to apply to

An original work of authorship fixed in a tangible medium of expression, now known or later developed, and from which the work can be per-

*ceived, reproduced or otherwise communicated, with the aid of machine
or device for a period of more than transitory duration.*

Under this new law, producers of trade directories have won damages from
individuals and organizations copying names. Printed directories are now better
protected under the copyright law than ever before. Lists compiled from such
directories without authorization are in jeopardy. Whether or not an alphabetic
phone book can be protected by copyright is, however, moot. One case decided
in Minnesota, and later appealed decided "no." A case now slowly proceeding in
Kansas City, Missouri involves three uses of classified phone book listings, by a
compiler for lists, for online electronic yellow page access, and for the creation of
directories. This case due for trial late in 1987 may determine the marketing stance
that each phone operating company and region will take in the future as to how
its unique current data are presented to prospective renters and buyers.

Phone companies that wish to make their data available for rental must first
determine which entity in the company (or in each of the seven regions carved
out of the Bell System) "owns" the database and therefore has the right to place
it on the market and profit from its sale and rental. They have two choices: (1)
they can take legal action to enforce their copyright, which means suing each of
the major compilers, both consumer and business, who rely on phone book data
or, (2) they can ignore those copying data from the aging phone books, and simply
enter the list arena with their current and constantly updated data and let the
market decide. So far, with the exception of the Kansas City case, those former
Bell operating companies which have tentatively entered the list arena have elected
the latter option. However, as a possible sign of the times, Southwest Bell, the
initial litigant against the compiler, has now been joined by Bell South, yet another
of the seven sisters carved out of the former AT&T monopoly. (This yellow pages
case has been decided out-of-court in favor of the telephone company.)

CATALOG MARKETING

The number of different catalogs will continue to increase as entrepreneurs
find likely niches to exploit. The total number of catalogs along with total third
class bulk mail in general, will tend to stay about the same.

The total number of families induced to buy by direct mail will be increase
over the next years, due to:

1. Demographics—with the increase in number of families, the changes in
   family formation, and the growing affluence of the baby boomers moving
   to the top of the income ladder.

2. More innovative list building both by the list community and by catalog marketers themselves.

There is not, nor will there ever be a catalog glut. If all consumer catalogs (something like 5.5 billion) are distributed only to the 25 million families with discretionary income, that means the average household of this type will receive 180 catalogs of all types (a substantial minority, possibly 35 percent, from local retail stores). The 120 nonretail catalogs per household averages less than one in three days or only slightly over two per week. (The word glut comes from the fact that the majority of these catalogs arrive in a few months during the fall and many new ones are "me-too" copies of well-established catalog operators.)

More and more retailers will place catalogs in the mail as they watch the growth of chain store operators who augment retail store sales with catalog "store" sales. But more retail catalogs will fall by the wayside than make it to the third year, as retail store managers find direct-mail mathematics far different than retail store markups and markdowns.

One of the true breakthroughs in the near future, from technology already available, will be the printing of individualized pages in catalogs, and ultimately the creation of complete catalogs especially designed for each individual. When the printing press is "driven" by the data available on the database, the individualized catalog can match products and prices with the preferences and tastes of the individual who will find his or her name in the copy or perhaps on every page.

Importance of Counts

At the present time, most count programs are in batch mode. A count report is run one night and called in or transmitted via a terminal the next day. This "appearance" of online counts is already changing to true instantaneous online counts for any selection or segment (or segment within a segment) desired. Rather than waiting twenty-four hours to get a count, the sales representatives of major list marketing operations are now able to provide unduplicated counts, in seconds, while the prospect or customer is on the line or at his or her desk. Such counts are based on the actual records, and not just on extracts pulled periodically. The counts given for a given select are then matched, record-for-record, by the counts on the list when it is delivered. This is beginning to eliminate the countless iterations now required to define major schedules. Companies offering online instant counts and exceedingly fast production once the account is approved and the order placed include CCX—the computer utility in Conway, Arkansas, American Business Lists in Omaha, Nebraska, and Data Base America, both at Ed Burnett Consultants in Englewood, New Jersey, as well as at CCX.

Database Marketing Improvements

Database marketing of information, as well as lists, will grow as more and more information, and more and more data are placed online. D&B & S&P are available online through "Dialog" as is Disclosure, the listing of data on all publicly reporting companies. The D&B list includes data not only for the United States but also for 132 additional countries. There are already online lists of patents, lists of abstracts, lists of forecasts, lists of airline fares, lists of bankruptcies, lists of international hotels with their rates, and lists of securities with much, much more to come.

The coming of the laser disc with its incredible capacity for storage of data on a very small computer will in time expand the utilization of microcomputers and word processors to handle lists of considerable size and increase the number of companies doing some or most of their own list updating in-house.

BIG BUSINESS AS A MAJOR INFLUENCE

Big business is entering the direct response field in increasing numbers. The largest mailer in America, after Sears, Roebuck & Company is now without much doubt AT&T which, following divestment, is advertising both old (regulated services) as well as a number of new (unregulated) products and services with impressive multimillion mailings.

Major companies with large direct-response subsidiaries include American Express, General Mills, Standex, Mobil, Horn & Hardart, CMP, W.R. Grace, Campbell Soup, Quaker Oats, and Pitney Bowes.

In addition, virtually every major manufacturer of office machines, copiers, telephones, and computers is selling parts, supplies, and service through direct mail, which means IBM, Xerox, DEC, Wang, NCR, Burroughs, Control Data, Hewlett Packard, and so on are now all major business mailers.

Some idea of the strength of this movement is given by the number of companies that have built or are in the process of building large countrywide data banks including both customers and prospects. They include more than one division of AT&T, as well as IBM, Xerox, Merrill Lynch, Xerox, J.C. Penney, American Express, American Management Association, Penton Learning, National Foundation of Independent Businesses, MCI, United States Department of Commerce, the US Department of Defense, and many many more.

There is every indication that this is far from a temporary phenomenon. It is creating a number of pressures on the establishments servicing the direct-response field. There is consolidation among list purveyors as compilers, list managers, and list brokers find acquisition the quickest way to grow.* It certainly has helped fuel the almost frantic effort by major advertising agencies to acquire direct-mail agencies to be able to offer a full range of promotional capacities to their major company accounts. On the other side of the foreign coin the growth of multinationals, most of whom are already in direct mail, worldwide, has been an important factor in the merger of foreign agencies into multinational U.S. ad agencies offering direct mail as well as advertising agency expertise.

PROLIFERATION OF LIST MERCHANDISERS

Years ago the three major forms of list professionals (brokers, compilers, and managers) were each for the most part in their own separate spheres. Today, such compartmentizing hardly exists except on paper. Without exception every list broker now wears another hat or has another subsidiary as a list manager. A number of these list broker/managers also are wholesalers of compiled files and appear to be compilers as well. The major five or six true compilers stick very close to their knitting. Only rarely does a D&B salesperson dabble in response names, and the only response names Donnelley, Polk, or Metromail will offer are those in some way tagged onto or tagged by their compiled consumer files. Some compilers who specialize in educational lists tend to offer such specialized lists only. But the host of self-styled list compilers/list consultants (in actuality list merchandisers of lists produced by others—list wholesalers in effect—offer any and all forms of lists available to them.)

This means the list world is now a patchwork quilt with creators (converters of data) copiers, dealers, brokers, wholesalers, consultants, ad agencies, list houses, publishers, list owners, and computer service bureaus all having a hand in the marketplace.

List merchandising is no longer the simple affair of yesteryear when listing with a few brokers was all that was required. Now there are publications, list data banks, magazine files, online electronic data banks, source data for new and changed businesses and households as well as overlays for refurbishing and validation, enhancement and augmentation. To serve this field adequately requires a thorough knowledge of all the players and all of their changing interconnected roles.

---

*R. R. Donnelley, the major printer of catalogs in America, in the summer of 1987 purchased Metromail, one of the four major compilers of consumer names, for $282,000,000. R. R. Donnelley is not to be confused with R. H. Donnelley, owned by Dun & Bradstreet and a major consumer list competitor to Metromail.

PRIVACY

The increasing capacity of a computerized society to invade the privacy of its citizenry caused the United States Congress in 1975 to appoint a Privacy Commission. The report of that commission, which included a study of direct mail, concluded that direct mail sent through the USPS was not a violation of privacy. The recipient could, without any difficulty, toss away a piece without even opening it.

The fact that the industry, through the good efforts of the Direct Marketing Association, has made available a well publicized voluntary means whereby individuals can opt to be removed from commercially available mailing lists had a good deal to do with this decision of the Privacy Commission.

LIST CLEANING AND THIRD CLASS BULK MAIL

In February 1985, the USPS changed both the rules and the costs for third class forwarding, return requests, and address correction procedures. In all cases the costs are now higher than ever before.

For simple address correction requests (with no forwarding) a piece is returned with correction or reason for nondelivery. The fee is 30¢.

To add forwarding to address correction requested the following calculations are used: Mail forwarded + 30¢ per unit (irrespective of weight) for address correction + 2.733 × the single piece rate for mail returned which cannot be forwarded. This adds

$$2,733 \times 22¢ \text{ for a 1 ounce piece} = 60¢!$$
$$2,733 \times 56¢ \text{ for a 3 ounce piece} = \$1.53!$$

Address correction requests for all but 1st class mailers now costs 30¢ per unit.

To obtain forwarding plus address correction for a 3-ounce piece costs $1.53; for a 10-ounce catalog this increases to $3.24 each. Very few third class mailers will find this a worthwhile service at that cost.

If there is a definite need or desire to get the piece back, the lowest cost service through USPS runs 56¢ for a 3-ounce unit. A 10-ounce catalog runs $1.18 and since in the mailing out and the return a large proportion will be damaged, this is not an overly viable option either, as it is likely to be greater than the incremental cost to buy new catalogs.

For reasons of its own, the USPS has priced the alternatives so that only address correction requests will be used by most third class mailers. This means to clean a customer file is a cost which must be borne periodically. (Some mailers who used to send out prospect mail with address correction requests and then incorporate the corrections into their house files may now find the costs for such chicanery rather prohibitive.)

A NOTE ON POSTAL VERIFICATION

There are two verifications to make. The first is to make certain each USPS permit is current and correct. Numbers of nonprofit organizations can run afoul of extra costs when they discover a third class for-profit bulk permit, which looks alright, but does not permit mailing at the nonprofit rate. The second is to verify both pieces the postal service will handle—the outgoing package and the reply form as well. This is particularly important if the format is unusual. Check size, positioning of copy and address, lineup of address (if 90° off the horizontal, the USPS has the right to refuse the pieces), colors and benday areas, classification, and last but far from least the postal sortation requirements. It is good advice to have the mail processing shop handle these verifications; the shop must keep up to date on all postal regulations.

MAIL AND MAILING LISTS

There Will Always Be a Market for Direct Mail

As long as there are books and magazines and newspapers—in other words, as long as human beings read and use the printed word, there will be direct mail. There is nothing in the electronic revolution that can change the need for a one-on-one form of communication in print to individual householders and individual businesses and business executives.

The volume of mail—141 billion pieces in 1986—is destined to level off, probably between 160–165 billion pieces. Business-to-business mail for prospecting is destined to increase modestly over the next few years. Nonprofit mailings in total will be adversely affected by the recent multiple raises and erosion of the differential below for-profit mailings as costs force institutions to attempt to take increasing advantage of carrier-route presort discounts.

Carrier-route coded presort volume, already over 57 percent of all for-profit third class bulk mail, will continue to rise. The Postal Rate Commission, through its charter, will continue to provide attractive discounts for the savings realized by the USPS by the makeup of such mail by the private sector. Part of this increase will be fueled by the growing awareness of nonprofit mailers that only through presort discounts can escalating postal costs for nonprofits be kept in line.

The "collision" between the nine-digit zip code and carrier-route presort program, and it is coming, will not surface until 1990 or later as it will take that long or longer for the USPS to put its nine-digit coding for all mail in some useful shape. In time carrier-route pro-sent, the most successful marketwise program ever instituted by the Postal Service will go the way of the Dodo Bird.

Review of Factors Affecting Direct Mail

The chief factors certain to affect total mail volume, and the type of mail volume, and the distribution of direct mail volume, in America, are:

- *Rising costs of direct mail*—leading to a slowing down, and shortly to a modest decline in total mail marketing.

- *The bi-modal distribution of income in America*—with its extremes of inequality.

- *The importance of two-wage earner families for availability of discretional income.*

- *Increasing age of the American population* (see data on Demographics).

- *The vanishing species*—the so-called "Nuclear Family" for soon the average family in America will consist of three members.

Glossary

ACTIVES Those names on a list that have made a recent purchase.

ADDITIONS Those names added to a list during an update cycle or operation.

ADDRESS The location of a record in a file; also the local address on a mailing list record.

ADDRESS CORRECTION SOURCE A service provided by the USPS to help provide corrected addresses for pieces undeliverable as addressed mailed third class bulk.

ADDRESSING FORMAT The type style, line length, and number of lines utilized for a given name and address.

ADDRESSING MEDIA The means used to add name and address to a mailing piece. The major ones are cheshire labels, pressure-sensitive labels, computer, or ink-jet generated. Names and addresses are also supplied on telephone cards, IBM cards and sheet listings.

AFFINITY GROUP A classification, either demographic or psychographic, which identifies a given record or list source.

AFFLUENTS That portion of householders with 30 percent or more than the cost of living, plus taxes, in America. About 25 million (of 87 million) families qualify.

AGE   A demographic selection factor; also the period since the last transaction for a given record; also for compiled lists, the date of the directory.

AGENT   The broker serves as the "agent" of the mailer; the list manager serves as the "agent" of the list owner.

AGREEMENT LETTER   A letter signed by the mailer agreeing to usage terms established by the list owner.

ALPHABETIC   Data which include alpha characters; filing in alphabetic order.

ALPHANUMERIC   The use of both letters and numbers for coding or identification.

ALTERNATE DELIVERY SYSTEMS   Any means of delivering pieces to households other than the mails. Usually refers to handdelivery in localities of co-op advertising or shoppers.

ALUMNI   Graduates of a given school or college. A major list source for educational fundraising.

ANNUAL LEASE   Provision of a given set of records for unlimited use by one mailer for one year. Cost, for compiled files, is customarily twice the single use rental fee per M.

APARTMENT NUMBERS   The numbers or letters identifying the location of an apartment in a multifamily dwelling.

APARTMENTS (Numbers)   Designation by letters or numerals of dwelling units in multifamily buildings.

AREA CODES   Three-digit codes assigned by the phone company to encompass all phones listed in a given area.

ASSIGNED MAILING DATE   A date for a mailing approved by the list owner to provide "protection" against competitive offers.

ASSOCIATIONS   Rosters of members serve as sources for lists by classification.

ATTENTION LINE   A prefix before an assigned title added to three-line business addresses.

AUDIT BUREAU OF CIRCULATION   Auditing entity for consumer magazine circulation.

AUGMENTATION   To increase the value of a customer file by utilizing an overlay from another source.

AUTOMOTIVE   (See CAR)

AVAILABILITY REPORT   The available records in given classifications in given zip code areas. Usually produced for dealerization programs.

BABY BOOMERS   Large contingent of births between 1946 and 1964. Now entering affluent status.

BACK END   All activities at a direct-response operation once promotion is launched. Back-end performance relates to purchase behavior over a given period of time by respondents.

BALANCE   The remainder of a list or segment left after a test or a test and continuation. "Balances" become the heart of list banks for future mail drops.

BANK CARDS   The two major credit cards held by customers—Master Card and Visa.

BAR CODE   A coding structure printed on a mailing piece which is used for sortation by the USPS.

BATCH PROCESSING   Data processing is either "online in real time" (usually a record at a time,) or in batches in sequential mode. Most list processing is done by batch processing.

BED SIZE   A selection factor for size for hospitals, and nursing homes (Comparable to number of rooms for hotels and motels.)

BEHAVIORAL LISTS   List data elicited through lengthy questionnaires.

BIBLE BELT   A section of southern and southwestern states which are inclined toward Christian fundamentalism.

BILLING STUFFERS   Advertising folders for mail response placed in envelopes along with invoices for Utilities and Department Stores.

BINGO CARD   A prepaid card bound into a magazine listing multiple free offers by advertisers.

BIRTH DATES   A selection factor available on some lists—often called exact date of birth. (occasionally "EDOB".)

BITS PER INCH   The packing of magnetic data per linear inch of magnetic tape. The usual packing is now 1600 BPI, which is being supplanted by the more economical 6250 BPI.

BLACKS   Lists primarily or exclusively of Black consumers or Black-owned bu i-nesses, or Black professionals.

BLOCK GROUP OR SUBBLOCK   A small geographical area within a census tract, defined by the U.S. Census, consisting of a few hundred households.

BOOK CLUBS   Individual members who have made a commitment to buy books. There are two types of clubs—negative option and positive option.

BOOKBUYER DATA BANKS   Merged, unduplicated, names of bookbuyers from multiple publishers, or multiple magazines.

BOOKBUYERS   Lists of mail order buyers of books, usually by subject matter (Also see Book Clubs)

BOUNCE BACK   A subsequent offer by a mail order operator sent to the most recent buyers in the same package with the merchandise just ordered. Catalog operators often supply another copy of the catalog which created the order as the bounce back. (Outside offers are package inserts not bounce backs.)

BPA   (Business Publishers Association) The auditing entity for commercial and business magazine circulation.

BRC   The acronym for a business reply card.

BRE   The acronym for a business reply envelope.

BREAKEVEN   Dollars of response, measured by order margin, are equal to the total cost of promotion. (Breakeven for the business means the order margin must equal promotion plus all other costs.)

BPI   A measure of "packing" of data on a magnetic tape in "bits per inch." Most tapes today are 1600 or 6250 BPIs.

BROADCAST MEDIA   Radio and TV spot advertising used to produce direct response.

BROKER   See List Broker.

BROKER DATA CARD   See List Data Card.

BROKERAGE COMMISSION   A proportion, usually set at 20 percent, paid to the broker by the list owner for rental business placed on a list.

BULK RATE MAIL   Mail prepared to USPS standards to qualify for three third class discount rates—namely, bulk rate, fifth-digit, carrier-route presort.

BUSINESS LIST   A list of establishments or individuals at establishments at business addresses. Includes businesses, institutions, offices of professionals.

BUSINESS LIST—COMPILED RESPONSE   A merged list of business mail order buyers from multiple owners.

BUSINESS MERGE/PURGE   See merge–purge.

BUSINESS OVERLAYS   Addition of demographic data, primarily city size, number of employees, telephone number to a business customer file.

BUYER   An individual or establishment that has ordered and paid for a product or service delivered through the mails.

CANCELLATION   List order cancellations usually result in no charge unless the list has been run prior to cancellation, in which case a run charge is usually assessed. Cancellation of a continuity program or a "til forbid" contract must be in writing. Cancellation of a subscription billed with the delivery of the first issue is usually satisfied by marking and returning the invoice.

CAR OWNER   Next to telephone registrants, the most important register of data concerning households. Car registration data makes selection by number of cars, type, brand, age, and value possible.

CARBON COPIES   Either cheshire labels or sheet listings can be run with two or three copies at the same printing by a computer.

CARDS, 3″ × 5″   Provision of list data on 3 by 5 card stock. Often sorted by sales territories or classification. Usually provided with ten-digit phone numbers for teleprospecting.

CARD DECK OR CARDVERTISER   A direct-mail cooperative advertising medium consisting of a pack of postage paid cards addressed back to each advertiser individually.

CARRIER ROUTE   A geographical area consisting of 350 households as walked by an individual mail carrier. There are 160,000 listed by the USPS plus 240,000 pseudocarrier routes provided by major compilers of consumer lists.

CARRIER-ROUTE CODE   The alphanumeric code provided on a mailing label to identify a given carrier route. The geographical designation for these codes is updated every six months by the USPS which furnishes a CRIS tape (carrier route information system) to be used for carrier-route coding and sorting.

CARRIER-ROUTE-PRESORT   A subclass of third class bulk mail which qualifies for a substantial postal discount.

CASH BUYER   A buyer who sends cash or check along with the order.

CATALOG   The provision of a specialty store with a very broad product line in print. There are now over 5 billion catalogs mailed in the United States or roughly one of every eight pieces mailed by third class bulk mail that carry advertising.

CATALOG   A mailing consisting of twenty-four or more pages offering for sale by mail a specialized group of related products.

CATALOG BUYER   An individual or establishment that has made a purchase from a given catalog.

CATALOG REQUESTS   Individuals who have called in or written in for a copy of the catalog.

CENSUS TRACT A geographical segment of a zip code in metropolitan areas delineated by the U.S. Census Bureau embracing approximately 1,000 households. Major consumer compilers provide demographic profiles for each tract.

CHADS A shorthand term for change of address. The USPS has prepared a CHAD list for the entire country as a service to mailers. (The goal is to reduce the 15 percent of third class mail, which is undeliverable as addressed today.)

CHANGES OF ADDRESS PROCESSING A means to match known movers to a list prior to mailing to provide correct new addresses for such movers.

CHARGE BUYERS Buyers whose credit rating and past history provides them access to mail order merchandise and services on a charge or open credit basis.

CHECK DIGIT An added digit to a group of numbers which calculates to a given proof that the figures are accurate.

CHECKING COPY A copy of a list, usually a sheet listing, used to monitor response to a mailing or phone solicitation.

CHESHIRE OR CHESHIRE LABEL An ungummed, machine-affixable label prepared on a computer or a word processor.

CHESHIRING Affixing of cheshire address labels by a cheshire-affixing machine.

CHIEF EXECUTIVE A title for an executive at a business or institutional establishment.

CHILDREN Families with children make up a substantial portion of all families in America. Data are selectable by age of child, in some lists by actual birth date. One specialized list here is of Newborn Babies.

CIRCULATION LIST The actual recipients of a magazine, book club, house organ, or newsletter. Circulation lists may be selectable by term, length on file, how initial order was received, besides any demographic data pertaining to the classification or type covered. A list of regular recipients (paid, controlled, or qualified) of a publication or periodical.

CITY There are over 12,000 cities in the United States with populations of 2,000 or more. They may be selected by population size and area. Can address officials by name, or by title.

CITY DIRECTORIES Over 1500 cities are canvassed, house to house, on a scheduled basis, to provide individualized data on householders including occupation. One company, R.L. Polk publishes city directory data on 26 million households. Only major source for individuals by occupation at home addresses. Includes apartment numbers and phone numbers.

CLASSIFICATION   While discretionary income is the most important single factor where consumers or households are concerned, the most important single fact about a business record is the kind of business it is—the classification in other words.

CLASSIFIED ADVERTISING   Small space advertising in the classified columns of mediums noted for mail response has been the starting point for many mail order fortunes. There are fifty classifications available, and literally hundreds of magazines and newspapers that offer mail order propositions.

CLASSIFIED DIRECTORIES   There are over 5,000 separate directories of classified (yellow pages) listings covering over 14 million listings for some 8 million unduplicated companies, institutions and offices of professionals. Most such directories are published once a year by the 1600 or so phone companies in the United States.

CLEANING   A term used to describe the updating of a list to remove "undeliverable as addressed" (or aging) data from a file.

CLEARANCE   The appraisal given by a list owner for the mailing of a specific package to his or her list. A necessary step in obtaining the right to rent for all mail order buyer lists.

CLUB PLAN   A method of selling on a continuity basis.

CLUBS   America is a highly social society and as a result has tens of thousands of different kinds of clubs—business, social, educational, military, political, social service, and religious. Clubs with phones denote those that have their own individual meeting place. The majority of clubs in America meet in the homes of the current chairperson. In small-town America, one of every ten full-time homemakers is the president of a local club.

CLUSTERING   Selection of names on basis of similarity of geographic, demographic, or psychographic characteristics. Clustering can be broad-brush by zip codes, or very finite such as member of boards of directors and their next door neighbors. Several proprietary computer programs for cluster selection are on the market.

CODE OR CODING   A means to identify a specific promotional effort.

CODE LINE   A line on an address imprint utilized to identify basic data about the addressee, such as length of service, dollar volume of purchases, recency of purchase, and so on.

CODING, GENERIC   A form of coding (either initially by key, or transmitted later by means of a lookup table) which utilizes a single character to compare results of mail order sales by media, and then by mediums within each media. Generic coding makes it possible for the computer to produce basic report data assembled by source.

COLD LIST   A prospect list as yet untested by the mailer.

COLLATE   A process by machine or by hand, which brings together several individual parts of a mailing or a catalog. A collation may be forty cards into a card deck or twenty coupons into a co-operative, or the assembly of a letter, folder, order form and return envelope into an outer envelope for a solo mailing.

COLLEGE STUDENT   Three firms in America each compile several million college student names each fall. One list is sponsored by *Time* magazine, one by *Newsweek*.

COMMISSION   The sum paid a list broker for arranging the rental of a list or a cardvertiser, also the fee paid an agent or agency for placing electronic direct-response ads.

COMMUNICATION   While internal communication is important, this word in direct-mail terms usually refers to telephonic communication with customers and prospects.

COMPILED LIST   An original list of individuals or establishments taken from printed records. Such list data can be rented for one time use or leased for unlimited use by one mailer. Compiling is the only methodology to obtain complete coverage of a classification. Most major compilations in addition to names and addresses include phone numbers as well.

COMPUTER LETTERS   Letters produced by a computer can be one of three types: match fill letters in which the name and address is computer generated onto a preprinted form letter; individual complete letters; or computer "spectaculars" in which the letter is only one element computer printed. The new laser printers now can produce two full 35-line letters per second.

COMPUTER PERSONALIZATION   As more and more data find their way to more and more lists, the capacity of computer-generated correspondence is increasing exponentially and with it the capacity to personalize more and more mail.

COMPUTER PROGRAM   A set of instructions for a computer.

COMPUTER SERVICE BUREAU   An independent business offering computerized handling of mailing lists.

CONFIDENCE LEVEL   Statistically valid measure of how often, in one hundred attempts, test results can be expected to be within given limits. Confidence level is based not on the number of pieces mailed, but on the number of responses received.

CONSUMER LIST   A list of individuals at household addresses. May be a compiled list, a response list, or a list produced as the result of a local canvas. May also be a list of addresses only for a title addressing to resident or occupant.

CONTINUATION   A mailing to the same list following a successful (or near successful) test. Usually four to ten times larger than the test if the list universe warrants. May be a roll out, which usually means a larger part or the entire balance of a list.

CONTINUITY PROGRAM   An offer consisting of a starter item or set, followed at timely intervals with a series of allied products, particularly books or music.

CONTINUOUS FORMS   Forms, preprinted or plain, with matching pin holes to either side used to produce computer labels, cards, sheet lists, and reports.

CONTRACT   An agreement between an owner or his or her manager and a renter. Most list management agreements are also contractual in nature.

CONTRIBUTORS   Respondents who have made donations to a charitable or fundraising appeal. Often called donors. Selections on some lists include recency, frequency, and size of donation.

CONTROLLED CIRCULATION   Recipients of a magazine free of charge who are qualified to receive it by their classification, lifestyle, or group affiliation.

CONVERSION   The process of converting an inquirer, or a trial offer buyer, or a catalog requester via a sale to regular customer status; also the process of converting list data on hardcopy to some magnetic form.

CONVERSION OF A LIST   Transfer of printed data, almost always by key stroke, to magnetic form for access by a computer. Now also applies to transfer from tape to floppy discs.

CONVERSION RATE   The percentage of responses converted to customer status.

COOPERATIVE   Any form of direct-response advertising involving offers from more than one mailer. Includes billing stuffers, package inserts, cardvertiser decks, split panels, or pages in self-standing stuffers, ride-alongs, and all forms of "marriage mail."

COPIES   Extra copies of a mailing list, either on sheet list or labels, usually carbons if cheshire, but second originals if pressure sensitive. If a sheet list and a set of labels, requires two separate computer runs.

COPY   Five factors cause a change in response: package, offer, timing, list and copy. Direct mail without copy, without words, is tongue-tied and useless.

COST OF MONEY   One of the costs of running any business and often forgotten in the analysis of the costs to run a direct-response operation.

COST PER THOUSAND   The entire promotional cost of a mailing package in the mail. Includes four separate cost inputs: printing, forms, and envelopes; rental of outside mailing lists; postal costs; and fulfillment (all operations to get packages into the mail stream).

COST TO BUY   Like cost per order this pertains to the expenditure for promotion *not* amortized by the order margin of sales.

COUNTS   The number of names available (either on an estimated basis or actual) for a given selection; also basic list counts as given for universes in list catalogs, or as given on a list card for a given list or available online for instant access.

COUNTY   There are some 3050 political units called counties in the United States. Some 500 of them have a population of over 50,000. While many businesses are now oriented to do their marketing on zip code lines, many firms still utilize counties to define branches and territories.

COUPON CLIPPERS   Respondents who make a practice of filling in coupons, bingo cards, or free requests through cardvertisers, but have no intention to buy. By raising qualifications the numbers of these "information hounds" can be reduced or kept under control.

COUPONS   Coupons delivered by direct mail have the highest redemption rate; they also have the highest cost per thousand.

COURIER   Direct mail lists now are shipped either by UPS or by one of the major one-day or two-day courier services, which provide much faster and much surer delivery than parcel post. In addition all courier services provide a receipt and can trace every shipment.

CPI   The short form for cost per inquiry. Usually refers to the first stage of a two-step (or more) selling operation.

CPM   The total cost in the mail of 1,000 pieces. This includes four parts: cost of printing, cost of the list, cost of the postage, and cost of all aspects of fulfillment at the mailing shop. It does not usually include the cost or preparation of the printed pieces.

CPO   This stands for Cost per Order, the amount paid above amortization by order margin of the costs of promotion, divided by the number of orders.

"CREAMING" A LIST   Providing for test purposes the most responsive segments of a list; mailing only to best segments of a list. Utilizing an offer which elicits an unusual proportion of response.

CREDIT CARD BUYERS   Respondents who buy by phone or by mail and charge such purchases to a credit card.

CREDIT CARD REPORTS   Daily logs of credit card transactions provided for authorization and control. (Manual, if under twenty-five per day; usually automated to save clerical time if more numerous.)

CREDIT SALE   A direct-response sale to be paid after delivery. May involve financing the account receivable if time payments are involved.

CREDIT SCREENING   Some "short-form" financial offers can be made to those individuals who pass a given credit screening. Process involved is costly and time consuming. Proportions of high level lists that pass are usually quite modest. Some credit screened lists are now available for list rental.

CRIS TAPE   A USPS coding structure on magnetic tape providing a means to carrier-route code a list for third class presort bulk mailing.

CRITERIA   If there were to be one word to define the most important aspect of lists, it would be "criteria." Criteria distinguish one list from another, one segment from another, one selection from another.

CROSS-SECTION   A statistical selection from a list segment or universe which is accepted as a representative sample. Sampling methods include Nth number, fifth-digit of zip, first letter of last name and randomization.

CRT   In computerese this describes a cathode ray tube on which customer data (usually) can be displayed and individually manipulated. Off premise data processing uses CRTs to obtain access to data on the lists of others.

CULTURAL   A large number of mailers seek cultural lists for books, records, newsletters, opera, theater, ballet, and fundraising. There are cultural-type buyers and cultural-type donors. Some 5 million homes qualify as part of the cultural market.

CUSTOMER PROFILE   The demographic and/or psychographic description of a typical buyer on a direct-response customer file.

CUSTOMERS   For printed data, these are subscribers, or recipients. For charitable and fundraising offers they are known as donors. For products and services sold by direct response they are the buyers.

DATA Any and all information available on a list file, or made available to augment, correct, change, or effect that file.

DATA BANK A file consisting of multiple inputs, merge–purged into an unduplicated file for public access on a rental basis. A few data banks are similarly created but are available for one company use only.

DATABASE A file consisting of all inputs owned or controlled by a single company, including its customers, which can be accessed, retrieved, selected, augmented, and manipulated through multiple channels on line in real time for management of the marketing function.

DATA CAPTURE The act of extracting from each transaction the data required for list building or list updating and preserving such data in magnetic mode.

DATA CARD A printed card providing basic data for rental on a given list. Standardized as to size ($5'' \times 8''$) and also for the most part by the information presented.

DATA ENTRY Conversion of selected data of transactions from hard copy to magnetic form.

DATA OVERLAYS Programatically transferring any item or items or data from one list source to another.

DATE OF COMPILATION When dealing with compilers, it is good practice to ask the source and date of the data. If the compiler cannot or will not answer these questions, find one that can. There are no secrets on this type of list.

DATE STAMP The date of the order or response, essential if a list is to be expired after a given time. It is imperative to keep the initial date stamp on every record and add on date stamps for subsequent transactions. Two digits usually suffice—one for month, (with X and Y for November and December) and one for year. (See Julian Dating.)

"DEADBEAT" LIST Lists of "bad pays" or poor risks which are used as suppress files prior to a major mailing.

DEALERIZATION Allocation of given records in given classifications in given areas to match branch, dealer, or sales representative markets. Lists so "dealerized" are usually utilized several times. (See Availability Report.)

DECOY Also known as a "seed" or dummy. A record unique to only one list inserted as a control to flag what was mailed, at what time, by whom.

DELETIONS All updating of lists involves adds (new records), changes (canape adds or changes in a record already on the file) and "kills" (deletions). Simplistically "changes" are often made in two steps: first a kill of the old record then a changed add (as a replacement).

DELINQUENT   A mail order buyer who has not paid his or her bill.

DELIVERABILITY   The proportion of a list which is deliverable by third class bulk mail. (This varies immensely from 99 percent or more for a list like the AMA list which is updated weekly, to 75 percent or 80 percent for some segments of compiled files which have not been updated in eighteen months or longer.)

DELIVERABILITY GUARANTEE   Most compiled files (and virtually no response files) guarantee to pay postage costs for that portion of mail "undeliverable as addressed" which exceeds a stipulated percentage. This guarantee does not apply to duplicate sets. When undeliverables or "nixies" exceed the "guarantee" a refund is made providing the mailer sends proof in the form of the returned pieces to the owner within the stipulated time frame.

DELIVERY DATE   The date set by the list renter (or his or her agent) for the receipt of a list at a mailing house or a merge–purge house.

DEMOGRAPHICS   The basic demographic selection factors on a list, chief among them for consumers; income, location, age, education, family makeup, length and type of residence and ownership of cars. For nonhouseholds, the chief demographic factors are classification, size, and location.

DENSITY   From a list point of view, how many records are available for a given geographical area. For floppy disc use it is essential to know the name and physical characteristics of the disc and the system under which it will operate.

DIRECT ADDRESSING   A means to address directly to the mailing piece with or without coding and commentary. Now done by creating a mailing tape to run a computer or ink jet. Formerly done through moving the pieces to where the list was maintained primarily on metal plates.

DIRECT-MAIL (OR RESPONSE) ADVERTISING   The process of placing ads in space or on electronic media to elicit a direct response. (*Direct mail* describes *mailing* an offer to a prospect to elicit a direct response.)

DIRECT MARKETING ASSOCIATION (DMA)   One of the chief trade associations serving the direct response field, with emphasis on direct-mail marketing through all four classes of mail. As one of its special interest groups, the DMA has a list council.

DIRECT MARKETING COMPUTER ASSOCIATION (DMCA)   A professional association of computer services both internal and external serving all aspects of computerization in the field of direct marketing. The President for 1986 is Paul A. Gildner, partner of Ed Burnett. In 1987 this organization came under the aegis of the DMA.

DIRECT-RESPONSE LIST   Individuals or establishments that have responded to offers through the mails.

DIRECTORIES   Defined by the American Library Association as "a list of persons or organizations systematically arranged usually in alphabetical or classification order, giving addresses, affiliations, functions and similar data for organizations." In the list world, the major directories are alphabetic and classified (yellow pages) lists of phone registrants. Other directories for list work include industrial directories, trade directories, membership directories, club rosters, and so on.

DISCOUNT   List owners provide a discount of 20 percent to brokers for placing business on their lists. In addition, the management fee, if the list if managed, runs from 10 to 20 percent and is, in effect, a sales discount (so far as the owner is concerned) from the published list price.

DISCRETIONARY INCOME   The U.S. government stipulates that the line delineating affluence is an income 30 percent greater than the local cost of living plus taxes. The sum above this is "discretionary income" available for the better things in life. Much of direct mail to householders is an attempt to tap this fund of discretionary income.

DISC   A means to store list data magnetically for easy retrieval in compact form. Can be a hard disc, a laser disc, or a floppy disc or diskette.

DISPLAY   See CRT.

DMA LIST COUNCIL   A group of DMA members with special interest in mailing lists and the problems of mailing lists generated by computerized technology.

DMA MAIL PREFERENCE SERVICE   See Mail Preference Service.

DOLLARS   A selection factor for the size of purchase or purchases from a direct-response customer file. Can be dollars per item, per quarter, per year, highest dollars, or cumulative dollars where available.

DONOR LIST   Individuals (or establishments) who have made a donation to a charitable or fundraising appeal.

DRIVERS' LICENSES   The major source of exact age data utilized by compilers of consumer data.

DROP (MAIL DROP)   The time and usually the description of a given mailing. Drop day is the day such a mailing is scheduled to be delivered to the postal service. (If test groups are not mailed at the same time, the measurement of half life may be mangled.)

DRY TEST   A mailing made to solicit orders for a product not yet available to determine the likelihood of success through direct mail or direct-mail advertising.

DUAL ADDRESSES   In business lists, the ship-to address may be and often is different from the bill-to address. It is good practice to keep and mail both.

DUAL ADDRESSING   With tandem ink-jet printing, the coding on the label can match the coding on the order form. This increases the proportion of orders that can be traced to a given key quite dramatically.

DUMMY   Another name for a decoy or seed.

DUMP   A printout, character by character, of a few hundred records of a given tape. A dump should accompany any tape delivery along with a description of the file, and a "tape layout."

DUPE   Trade lingo for a duplicate record that has been identified and eliminated. It is good practice to look at the "matched pairs" or "dupes" so identified.

DUPE ELIMINATION   The process through merge–purging, by which duplication is removed from a list or a group of lists.

DUPLICATION FACTOR   The proportion of names and addresses on one list that also are found to be on another list. Merge–purge programs produce reports on internal duplication (intra dupes within the house file), duplication between outside lists and house files, as well as interduplication between two or more outside lists brought in to merge–purge against the house files. The rate of duplication between the house lists and each outside list is a meaningful indicator of the affinity of such outside lists for the product or service being offered.

EDIT CHECKING   A programmatic screen to ensure that the data entered fit given parameters such as zip to be numeric only and five digits.

EDITING RULES   A discipline for entry established as a set of rules so that all data and every field entered are compatible.

EDUCATION   There is a large number of lists in the educational field—schools, colleges, school districts, coaches, as well as educators by over 250 disciplines.

ELASTICITY   Comes from "elasticity of demand" to determine what effect in response a change in price or offer will create. Those markets that show little change are inelastic; those that vary greatly with price are highly elastic.

ENGINEERS   Direct mail, covers all types of engineers: aeronautical, chemical, plastic, metalworking, sanitary, quality control, electronic, safety—over 50 disciplines available through the mails.

ENHANCEMENT   This specifically refers to any increase in selectivity and value that can be added by a mailer from his own records. It is more and more coming to mean any addition to a list to improve its value whether from inside data or through matching with outside lists.

ENUMERATION DISTRICTS   The small geographic areas assigned by the U.S. Census Bureau. For these small areas and subblocks (an average of about 140 families) the census publishes a huge volume of demographic data. Only the very largest lists are coded down to subblocks and enumeration districts, as in the country there are some 400,000.

ENVELOPE   The addressed outer carrier (paper or plastic, or a combination of the two) in which the parts of the mailing are enclosed.

ENVELOPE STUFFERS   Ads placed in the envelopes of others, either other mailers or billing envelopes for utilities or department stores.

ENVELOPES   Envelopes come in all sizes and all colors. The conventional envelope for first class mail is the $4'' \times 9^{1}/_{2}''$ number 10 envelope. Other frequently used sizes are the $6'' \times 9''$, the $9'' \times 12''$, and the Baronial measuring $5'' \times 7''$.

ETHNIC LISTS   List data, selected on the basis of surnames, to indicate ethnicity. List proportions of Black families and Hispanic families are published by the U.S. Census Bureau. Overlays based on surnames are available to ethnicize segments of a customer file.

EXCHANGE   A reciprocal relationship in which one mail order company swaps data, usually on a name-for-name rental basis, with another mail order company; often both are prospecting in the same market.

EXECUTIVES   A good portion of business mailings goes to executives, both at home and at business. Major lists offer up to thirty or forty functional titles for executives. Some lists provide selection by size of company (by employees or sales) provide the stock exchange, besides making possible geographical choice, with or without the phone number.

EXPIRE   A former customer or former member of an organization, or former subscriber, or former continuity buyer; any record which is removed from a live file.

EXTERNAL LIST   Any list other than the house files of a mailer.

EYEBALL A LIST   Visually reviewing the output of a list to check the validity of the data.

FACTOR ANALYSIS   A statistical analytic tool used to determine the selection factors within a list that influence response.

FANFOLD FORMS   Folded, perforated, continuous (blank or preprinted) forms utilized for computer printouts.

FARMERS   China has 800,000,000 living on farms; the United States feeds itself and part of the rest of the world from 2,600,000 farms. Selection is available by size, crop, type, as well as number of livestock, also by type.

FIELD   The location on a tape of given sets of information—such as name, address, city, state, SIC, zip code. May be variable length or fixed. For addressing purposes almost always in "fixed fields" where zip code for example, is always found in the same five positions in a record.

FIFTH-DIGIT ZIP SELECT   Utilizing the fifth number in a zip code as a cross-section selection method.

FILE SEQUENCE   The sequence (alphabetic, zip code, SIC, arranged by volume) in which a list of names is maintained.

FILE TAGGING   Adding data from one file to another; can refer to the unauthorized additions to house files of information owned by others.

FINANCIAL SERVICES   There are over 500,000 establishments providing financial services. Here are found lists of banks, savings and loans, stockbrokers, insurance and real estate firms, and cemetaries.

FIRST CLASS MAIL   It is now estimated that 15 percent or so of all mail with advertising is placed in the mail stream as first class mail. First class mail in the United States in total has grown from 1983 to 1986 by over 12 billion names.

FIRST-TIME BUYER   A mail order patron who has purchased from a given mail under operation for the first (and only) time to date.

FIXED LISTS   Cost per sale including all other costs except promotions.

FLAG   A computerized means to identify data added to a file or the usage of a list segment, by a given mailer.

FLAT CHARGE   A fixed cost for the total of a rental list, usually applies to smaller lists.

FLEXIBLE DISC   See Disc, floppy.

FLIGHT   A given mailing, particularly where multiple drops are to be made on different days to reduce number arriving at one company at one time.

FOREIGN MAIL   Lists of householders and businesses outside the United States.

FORMAT   The location of each item of data on each record of a mailing list.

FORMER BUYER   Record of an individual or establishment showing purchase within a prior period.

FORTUNE 1000   The thousand largest industrial—that is, manufacturing companies in the United States as published by *Fortune* magazine. Almost all have sales volumes per year of over one billion dollars.

FORTUNE 300   Fortune Magazine's selection of the largest fifty companies in six classifications: banking, retailing, wholesaling, insurance, construction, and utilities. Compilers provide up to ten executives by name and title for each of these large companies.

FOUR-LINE ADDRESS   The typical individual name list at-business addresses requires a minimum of four lines: name of individual, name of company, local address, city, state and zip code. Three line lists are usually at-home addresses. Computers can easily split out three-line addresses from records requiring four or more lines.

FOURTH CLASS MAIL   This by another name is parcel post, the USPS service to deliver mail parcels weighing over 16 ounces.

FREE-STANDING INSERT   An advertising insert, either solo or co-operative, inserted in newspapers, usually the Sunday editions, delivered with the newspaper. It is a little known fact that this form of prospecting is now greater by a substantial margin than all direct mail for prospecting.

FREQUENCY   A measure of multiple purchases by a mail order buyer. One of the selection factors when utilizing mail order buyer files.

FRIEND OF A FRIEND   A name supplied on request by a customer of a mail response firm of his or her friend as a likely prospect for the offers of that firm.

FRONT-END RESPONSE   The initial responses generated by a direct-response promotion without consideration of returns, credit, payment, and subsequent purchases.

FULFILLMENT   All activities to get in the mail stream performed after printed pieces and mailing list data are delivered to the mailing service plant; also refers to the physical handling of an order, or an information request, or a premium or a refund. (Should not be confused with subscription fulfillment which requires unique computer programming.)

FUNDRAISING LISTS   Lists which contain individuals who have either demonstrated willingness to contribute or are considered worthy of testing for contributions.

GALLEY LISTING OR SHEETLIST   A printout of list data on sheets, usually in zip or alphabetic order.

GENDERIZATION   A program run to add gender to mailing lists (based on first names where available). Sex is a useful selection factor in the list business.

GEOGRAPHICS   A selection factor based on location, can be state, city, SCF, zip code, telephone area code, enumeration district, or carrier route.

GIFT BUYERS   Mail order buyers of gift merchandise; also buyers who order gifts in some quantity to be shipped to others.

GIFTEES   Lists of individuals sent gifts or magazines in bulk by mail by friends or donors or business firms. Giftees are not truly mail order buyers; rather they are mail order recipients and beneficiaries.

GOVERNMENTS   An often overlooked source of lists. Governments register cars and homes and dogs; bankers and hairdressers, plumbers and veterinarians. Government lists include buyers, subscribers, inquirers. Governments license TV stations, ham operators, and CBs.

GRID TEST   A means to test more than one variable at the same time. This is a particularly useful method to use to test different offers by different packages over a group of prospect lists.

GROUPS   Society is formed of "groups"—that is clubs, associations, memberships, churches, fraternal orders, political groups, religious groups, sporting groups, collector groups, travel groups, and singing groups. Wherever human beings are, there we find groups.

GUARANTEE   There is no "guarantee of results or response" in direct mail. Some compilers offer guarantees of percentages of delivery (usually from 90 to 95 percent) and pay the postage costs on all returned "undeliverable as addressed" that exceed the guaranteed proportion. Almost all direct mail operators have "money back" guarantees in case of dissatisfaction with the merchandise received.

GUMMED LABELS   A form of perforated label requiring dampening to affix. Replaced for all practical purposes by pressure-sensitive labels which can be peeled off and affixed without water.

HALF LIFE A formula for estimating the total response to be expected from a direct-response effort shortly after the first responses are received. Makes valid continuation decisions possible based on statistically valid partial data.

HANDLING CHARGE A fixed charge added per segment for special list requests. Also shows up as part of "shipping and handling" charges for transportation of labels, cards, sheets, or tape.

HARD COPY A printout on a sheet list or galley of all data available on a magnetic source such as a tape, a disc, or a floppy.

HEAD OF FAMILY From telephone or car data, the name and sex of the individual on the registration file.

HEADLINE The primary wording utilized to induce a recipient to read and react.

HEAT TRANSFER A form of label which transfers reverse carbon images on the back of a sheet to mailing pieces by means of heat and pressure. (After use for transfer, the labels, now one-up, can be glued and affixed by machine which provides a second copy of the list.)

HIGH SCHOOL STUDENTS Several compilers provide lists of high school juniors and seniors at their home addresses. The original data, usually printed phone rosters, are not available for all schools or localities.

HIGH-TICKET BUYERS Buyers who have purchased expensive items by mail.

HOME OFFICES For major businesses, the executive or home office location as differentiated from branch offices or plants.

HOME OWNERSHIP Seventy-five percent of American families live in homes they own. Twenty-five percent of American families are renters. Renters have little interest in offers to maintain, upgrade, or improve living quarters.

HOMOGENIZATION The unfortunate and misleading combination of responses from various sources. Often the use of a single "average" response for a mailing made to customers and prospects alike.

HOT LINE The most recent buyers on a list which undergoes periodic updating. (Those who have just purchased by mail are the most likely buyers of other products and services by mail.)

HOUSE LISTS Those list segments controlled or owned by the list owner. Includes customers, inquiries, expires, warrantees, white mail, salespeople's qualified prospects, gift buyers, giftees, trials, and so on.

HOUSEHOLDS   All lists are delivered to households (homes) or to nonhouseholds. Households are selectable on a demographic basis. Householders (consumers) may be selectable on a psychographic basis.

INACTIVE BUYERS   Buyers who have not placed an order or responded during a specified period of time.

INCOME   Perhaps the most important demographic selection factor on consumer files. Major compiled files provide surprisingly accurate individual family incomes up to about $40,000. Incomes can be selected in $1,000 increments; counts are available by income ranges for every zip code.

INDEXING   Creation of a standard, say 100% of recovery of promotion cost, to enable comparison between mailings of different sizes.

INDICIA   The required indication in the area usually reserved for the postage stamp designating the type of mailing.

INDIVIDUAL   Most mailings are made to individuals. However all occupant or resident mail in effect is to an address only. A portion of business mail is addressed to the establishment (by name and address) only, or to a title and not to an "individual."

INFLUENTIALS   In business mail order, those executives who have decision power on what and when to buy. Also those who exercise clout in their business classification or community. In consumer PR mail, those individuals (executives, professionals, educators, clergy; labor, and so on) who make a difference in their localities or work.

INITIAL SOURCE CODE   The code of the effort which brought the name to the customer file for the first time. It is important to maintain this code for the file of the customer if "lifetime" value is to be calculated, and the source evaluated.

INPUT DATA   Original data, usually in hard copy form, to be converted and added to a given file. Also taped lists made ready for a merge–purge, or for a data bank.

INQUIRY (OR REQUEST)   A response in the form of an inquiry for more information or for a copy of a catalog.

INSTALLMENT BUYERS   Mail order buyers who have purchased goods or services on a periodic payment basis.

INSURANCE LISTS   Lists of people who have inquired about or purchased various forms of insurance. Also insurance agents, brokers, adjustors, executives.

INTRALIST DUPLICATE A name and address appearing two or more times in the same list.

INTERLIST DUPLICATE A name and address appearing on two or more lists. (Usually not duplicating the basic customer file.)

INVALID RECORDS Records which when passed against an edit screen are found to be wrong in some significant way. Such records are "bumped" from the file, and then printed out for clerical review.

ITEM In the selection process with a mail order list, denotes the type of goods or service purchased. In input terms, it is a part of a record to be converted.

JOB FUNCTION The descriptive title of an executive at a business address; also a title added to a three-line business address to direct the mailing piece to a given function.

JULIAN DATING A three-digit numerical system for date stamping a transaction by day. January 1 is 001, while December 31 is 365.

KEY CODE A means utilized to identify a given promotional effort so response can be identified and tracked.

KEY CODE–GENERIC A form of hierarchal coding in which promotional vehicles can be analyzed within type of media—newspapers, magazines, Sunday supplements, self-standing stuffers, mailing lists, radio and promotion, TV promotion, takeovers, and so on.

KEY LINE A line of alphanumeric characters designating selected facts about an individual customer record such as length of term, size of purchase, classification, identification number. In magazine updating, it is almost imperative for the key line to be provided to make any change in the record, as for example, a change in address.

KEY PUNCH A means to convert hard copy to machine-readable form by punching holes in either cards or paper tape.

KEY PUNCH/KEY STROKE The clerical means used to convert hard copy data, one character at a time, to magnetic form.

KEYSTONE A measure of mark-up (100% of all costs except promotion). Not recommended for direct mail. (*See* ORDER MARGIN)

KEY STROKE A means to convert hard copy to machine readable form through a typewriter key or similar. A good portion of key stroke conversion today goes directly to some electronic form usually either on a cassette or a tape. When many key-to-tape machines are linked together, the data go directly to disc in the computer complex.

KEY VERIFYING   Having two operators at the data entry stage key punch the same data for 100 percent accuracy.

KILL   To delete a record from a file.

LABEL   A paper form bearing a name and address wh.ch when affixed (usually by machine) to a mailing piece, serves as the mailing address.

LABEL, PEEL-OFF (OR PRESSURE-SENSITIVE)   A self-adhesive label form that can be peeled off its backing form and pressed onto a mailing piece by hand. When the backing sheet of a peel off label is affixed to a mailing piece, the recipient can be invited to peel off the label and affix it as his or her return address to an enclosed order form.

LABELS, GUMMED   Perforated label form on paper stock whicи ...ust be individually separated and moistened before being applied with hand pressure to the mailing piece.

LABELS, ONE UP   Conventional cheshire or pressure-sensitive labels for computer addressing are four-across horizontal. One-up labels are in a vertical strip with centerholes for machine affixing.

LASER LETTERS   Letters printed by the latest high speed computerized imaging method. The new lasers can print two letters side by side, each of thirty-five or forty lines, in one second.

LAST DIGIT ZIP   See Fifth-Digit Zip.

LATE CHARGE   A charge for the cost of money imposed by some list owners for list rentals not paid within a specific period.

LENGTH OF LINE   The computer which has capacity to print 132 characters across a $14^{1}/_{2}''$ sheet has forced discipline here. In four-across chesiring, the longest line can not be more than thirty characters; for five across this limit is twenty-three characters. Capable data processors, utilizing all eight lines available on a $1''$ deep label can provide two full lines, if need be, for the title line.

LENGTH OF RESIDENCE   Major compilers who utilize telephone or car registration data maintain the number of years (up to 16) a given family has been at the same address. This provides another selection factor available from these stratified lists.

LETTERSHOP   A *lettershop* handles all details of printing and mailing letters and stuffers; a *mailing house* essentially handles the preparation and the mailing of bulk quantities of mail.

LIBRARY LISTS There are two major classifications of libraries, private (plus special) and public. Public libraries can be selected by number of purchase dollars available per year for book funds. In the public sector, there are public libraries, high school libraries, and college libraries. In the private sector, there are specialized collections such as science, business, law, medicine, and religion. There are also librarians by name, including members of the Special Libraries Association.

LIFESTYLE SELECTIVITY List professionals seek actual proof of lifestyle habits through lists indicating what people need, what people buy, what people own, what people join, and what people support. Major lists based on consumer surveys provide data on hobbies, ownership, and interests.

LIFETIME VALUE There are two key factors: the first is the cost to buy a customer, and the second is the lifetime value of that customer. It is the lifetime value (and the promotional span) which determines whether or not a given effort key has produced a profit for the operation.

LIFT LETTER A separate piece added to conventional solo mailings asking the reader to consider the offer just once more.

LIST AFFINITY Correlation of a mailing offer to selected mailing list availabilities.

LIST BANK See Bank.

LIST BROKER A service to handle all details to bring the buyer (the list owner) and the seller (the list owner) together.

LIST BUILDING The process of collecting and utilizing list data and transaction data for list purposes.

LIST BULLETIN An announcement of a new list or of a change in a list previously announced.

LIST CARD The conventional 5″ × 8″ card utilized to provide essential data about a given list.

LIST CATALOGS Directories of lists with counts prepared and distributed, usually free, by list managers and list compilers.

LIST CLEANING Another phrase for list updating—the process of correcting a mailing list. "Cleaning" implies the removal of the records "undeliverable as addresssed."

LIST COMPILATION The business of creating lists from printed records. The individual or company making such lists is known as a compiler.

LIST COUNT   The number of names and addresses on a given segment of a mailing list; a count provided before printing of tapes or labels. The universe of names available by segment or classification.

LIST CRITERIA   Those factors on a mailing list that differentiate one segment from another. The criteria can be demographic, psychographic, or physical in nature.

LIST, CUSTOM COMPILED   In prior years, all compiled lists were typed and thus were custom prepared to order; today, virtually all compiled files, with multiple data elements, are precompiled on tape for virtually any selection the user wishes.

LIST DATA BANK   See Data Bank.

LIST ENHANCEMENT   The transfer via overlay of data elements from one list to another; to differentiate from augmentation list enchancement occasionally means the adding of data from inside sources (as an executive to a business file) while augmentation is enhancement from outside sources.

LIST EXCHANGE   See Exchange.

LIST FRANCHISE   Major compilers often provide copies of all or parts of their files on a franchise basis to list wholesalers and mailing shops. Most such contracts are for a short period of years. The list may be paid for on a fee basis or, particularly on large files, on a royalty basis.

LIST KEY   See Code or Key.

LIST MAINTENANCE   The methodology to keep a mailing list current through timely updating of adds, kills, and changes.

LIST MANAGER, IN-HOUSE   Almost all list managers are independents serving multiple lists; some very large list owners, however, opt to manage the list rental activity through full time in-house employees.

LIST MANAGER/LIST MANAGEMENT   While the list broker works for the mailer, the list manager services the list owner as merchandiser of a list, involving all details of promotion, rental, collection, and control.

LIST MONITORING   See Monitoring.

LIST PERFORMANCE   The response logged to a mailed list or list segment.

LIST PROTECTION   Lists are valuable. They are protected by review of mailing and mailer, insertion of list seeds, obtaining of a guarantee of one time use only.

LIST RANKING In building a "bank" of lists for future use, each list is ranked in descending order on the basis of logged response and/or logged dollars of sales.

LIST RENTAL An arrangement in which a mailer obtains the right to mail the list owned by another on a one-time basis at an agreed upon cost per thousand names.

LIST RENTAL HISTORY A report showing tests and continuations by users of a given list. This usage record, exclusive to each broker or to the list manager, is the key to list recommendations. Historical data can be maintained by list, mailer, product or source of business. Repeat usage by mailers by name is perhaps the most important information desired by a knowledgeable direct marketer.

MACHINE-READABLE Imprinted alphanumeric data, including name and address, which can be read and converted to magnetic form by an optical character reader.

MAGALOGUE A mail order catalog that includes paid advertisements, and in some cases brief editorials, making it similar to a magazine format.

MAGNETIC TAPE A means to store names and addresses in magnetic form for sequential processing by a computer. Most tape lists are furnished in fixed field format (the zip code is always in the same five positions on each record), on nine-track 1600 or 6250 BPI (bits per inch) in IBM mode.

MAGNETIC TAPE CHARGE A charge made for the tape reel on which a list is furnished. The reel usually is not returnable for credit.

MAIL ADVERTISING SERVICE ASSOCIATION (MASA) The major trade association of mailing houses responsible for fulfillment in the United States. MASA has some 500 members; there are over 6,000 lettershops and mailing houses in the United States.

MAIL COUNT The amount of mail deposited with the USPS on a given date as reported on the certification form provided by the postal service.

MAIL MONITORING A means to determine how long individual pieces of mail take to reach their destinations; also utilized to verify content and ascertain any unauthorized use.

MAIL PREFERENCE SERVICE A well advertised program of the DMA providing a means to consumers to remove their names from a large number of mailings. This same service provides a means to consumers to add their names to get more mail. As of now two of three opt to add, only one-third to remove.

MAILER   The organization that enters mail in the postal mail stream. For third class mail this includes over 750,000 establishments with permits; the mailing house is also sometimes called by this term.

MAILER'S TECHNICAL ADVISORY COMMITTEE   A group of representatives from virtually all associations involved in any form of mailing and related services that meets periodically with USPS officials to provide pragmatic advice and technical information and recommendations on postal policies.

MAILING HOUSE   A direct-mail service establishment which among other services for the mailer, will affix labels, sort, bag and tie the mail, and deliver it in qualified zip code strings to the USPS for certification. Many mailing houses also provide printing as well as computerized services.

MAILING LIST/USERS AND SUPPLIERS ASSOCIATION   An association founded in 1983 specifically targeted to mailing list uses and abuses.

MAILING PACKAGE   What is mailed with all of its pieces. This is the way the offer is "dressed" when it arrives in the mailbox.

MARGINAL LIST TEST   A test that almost, but not quite qualifies for a continuation.

MARKET   In the list world, each list is a market; all potential buyers that can be reached by mail are the market.

MARKET PENETRATION   The proportion of buyers on a file to the total list or to the total area. For business lists, penetration is usually analyzed by two-digit or four-digit SIC.

MARKUP   A term utilized by retailers to denote percentage added to cost of goods sold. It is not germane in direct-mail calculations. The operative phrase in direct mail is "order margin" which is a discrete number of dollars, not a percentage or proportion of anything.

MARRIAGE MAIL   A form of co-op in which the offers of two or more disparate mailers are combined in the same folder or envelope for delivery to the same household or establishment.

MASTER FILE   A file containing all of the data to be found on subsidiary files.

MATCH CODE   An extract of parts of a name and address which serves to identify a specific record.

MATCHED CITY PAIRS   For testing purposes when individual markets must be utilized, a means to do A in city Y, but not B, while doing A and B in city X with the premise that the two cities are reasonably matched as to size, income spread, and type of lifestyles.

MAXIMUM COST PER ORDER Lifetime value (and time span) of each major cell of customers on a customer file. This helps set a limit to the price to pay for a new customer.

MECHANICAL ADDRESSING SYSTEMS While this is the computer age, a large number of lists is filed on cards or plates and addressing is done by mechanical means. Most such lists are quite small. Card lists can be easily updated by the owning organization.

MEDIA Response is the name of the game, and direct mail is just one of the players. The other major media used for response include space advertising (newspapers and magazines) self-standing stuffers, radio, TV, take-ones, car cards, package inserts, billing inserts, and hand delivery. (With generic coding, each one can be compared, in total, with each other media.)

MEDIAN DEMOGRAPHIC DATA All U.S. Census data are based on medians rather than an individualized basis. Thus a census age is the median for a group of householders. It is important to distinguish between stratified median data and individualized data such as length of residence, ownership of a car, and family income.

MEDIUM The specific part of the media—that is, the individual magazine, newspaper, TV station or mailing list.

MEMBER A person who belongs to a given organization. Direct mail creates some special members such as book club members, discount club members, barter exchange members, and online service members.

MERGE To merge two or more lists into a single list utilizing the same sequential order (without unduplicating between them); the lists are sorted together, usually by zip code.

MERGE–PURGE A process to combine two or more lists and at the same time unduplicate the output files required for third class carrier-route coded mailing. A quite simple step for consumer lists which ordinarily overkill to guarantee very small residential duplication. But the process for business lists is highly technical and difficult.

MILITARY LISTS Lists of those in the military service (or recently released) are quite scarce. Military personnel can be moved on one day's notice so deliverability in and around large military post offices is sometimes problematical.

MINICATALOG A new prospecting device consisting of a fanfolded set of minipages 3″ × 5″ used in cardvertisers, billing stuffers, and package inserts. Also utilized by some mailers as a bounce back.

MINIMUM   A minimum billing applied to list rentals involving a small number of names. May cover an entire small list. Also a minimum billing for given mailing and/or computerized sources.

MINIMUM ORDER REQUIREMENT   A stipulation, irrespective of the quantity utilized, that payment of a given number of dollars will be expected.

MOBILITY RATE   The United States is a nation on the move. Some 20 percent of U.S. families move in a year; 15 percent of businesses die or change names or are absorbed each year, and 15 percent new starts take their place.

MODELING   A process involving use of spreadsheets via a computer which provides reasonable answers to "what if" scenarios. Utilized primarily by magazines balancing the costs and productivity of multiple means to maintain or build circulation.

MODEM   A device that makes it possible to deliver list data in electronic form to a computer any place in America over telephone lines.

MONETARY VALUE   A selection availability on a good proportion of mail order buyer lists as to price range, amount of last order, and cumulative buying history.

MULTIBUYERS   The identification through a merge–purge of all records found on two or more lists.

MULTIFAMILY   See Multiple Dwelling.

MULTIPLE BUYERS   Those who have made more than one purchase from the same mail order firm. (These can be selected on the basis of frequency.)

MULTIPLE DWELLING   A housing unit for three or more families at the same address. For adequate delivery to apartment dwellers it is more and more necessary to include the apartment number in the address. Multidwelling families can be selected or omitted on major compiled files.

MULTIPLE REGRESSION ANALYSIS   A statistical procedure that studies multiple independent variables simultaneously to identify a pattern or patterns that can lead to an increase in response.

MULTIPLE SICs   On major files of large businesses, the primary SIC classification is augmented with up to three more four-digit SICs. Business merge–purges often disclose multiple SIC alignments unavailable on any single list source.

NAME   An entry of an individual by name, on a mailing list.

NAME DRAIN   The loss, mainly by large businesses, of the names and addresses of prospective customers who write to them or visit their stores.

NATIONAL CHANGE OF ADDRESS This is a service for the USPS to provide national data on CHADs (changes of address). In 1987, 15 percent of third class mail was "undeliverable as addressed"—a loss to mail users of over $2,000,000,000.

NEGATIVE OPTION A book club utilizing negative option provides its customers, usually each month, with the opportunity to return a card and refuse a selection; if the card is not returned or not returned in time, the selection is automatically forwarded and billed to the customer.

NEGOTIATED PRICE With the growth of technology, list rental is becoming more and more a form of negotiation based on list data provided against list data actually mailed.

NET NAMES The actual number of names of a given list mailed after a merge–purge. Also, the concept of paying only for such names.

NET-NET NAMES An agreement made by a renter with a list owner to pay only for names that survive given screens including income, credit, house list duplicates, prior list suppress names, zip suppress programs, and so on. The surviving portion can be quite small.

NET UNIQUE NAME FILE The resultant one-per-record unique unduplicated list, one of the chief outputs of a merge–purge operation.

NEW BUSINESSES Lists of businesses just started (or just located as just started). In the United States there are some 1 million new business starts (including institutions and offices of professionals) per year. In the same time an equal number of nonhousehold establishments go out of business, or change their name, or are absorbed by others.

NEW CONNECTS New names added to the connected lines of telephone, gas or electric utilities. At this level, new connects are available monthly, weekly, even daily on what the industry calls "daily addenda." These "new connects" are slowly beginning to surface as list sources for new names.

NEW HOUSEHOLDS Data on new connects by local phone companies are beginning to come on the marketplace. Data new from one telephone book to another are over one year old. A service based on local compiling is usually quite spotty.

NEWSPAPER LISTS List data on engagements, births, deaths, and news-making items and changes published in newspapers.

NINE-DIGIT ZIP CODE A USPS system designed to provide an automated means to utilize an extended zip code to sort mail down to small contiguous areas within a carrier route. It is not faring very well.

NIXIE   A piece of mail returned as "undeliverable as addressed." In direct mail, nixies always precede any responses.

NONPROFIT   Over 250,000 institutions have qualified with the USPS as nonprofit agencies and can mail at the nonprofit rate, a preferential rate which has been eroding of late.

NTH NAME OR INTERVAL   A statistical means to take a given number of names equally selected over the full universe of the list segment being sampled. The Nth number interval is derived by dividing the total names in the list by the sample number desired.

OCCUPANT (RESIDENT) LISTS   Lists compiled from households passed which consist of addresses only. The chief lists used for chain grocery and department store flyers. Includes apartment numbers and it is the only list source covering all 87 million households. Occupant lists are maintained not only in carrier-route order, but in carrier-walk order by carrier route.

OFFER   A description of what it is the mailer wishes the recipient to buy or request.

OFFICES   Compilers of businesses with telephones can provide offices of professionals as well as multiple professionals per office, where desired, brought together by their common telephone number.

ONLINE AVAILABILITY   A linkup system in which an operator at a remote terminal can obtain list information from a data bank or database at another location.

ONE-SHOT MAILING   An offer designed to make the sale in a single transaction.

ONE-TIME BUYER   A single transaction buyer who has not placed an additional order.

ONE-TIME USE   An established trade custom that a list *rented* for a mailing will not be used more than one time.

ONE-YEAR CONTRACT   A form of lease in which the renter is granted unlimited use for one year (for one company use only) of a given set of compiled records. Usually treated as a "sale for one year."

OPPORTUNITY SEEKER   A class of mail order buyers or prospects that seeks a new and different way to make an income. This ranges from people who wish some modest way to work at home, or "at their homes" to expensive franchises.

OPTICAL CHARACTER READER (OCR)   An electronic scanning device that can read characters, either typed with a special OCR font, or computer created, and convert these characters to magnetic form.

"OR CURRENT RESIDENT"   A line added via computer to a three-line consumer list in an attempt to obtain greater deliverability and readership in case of a change in residential personnel.

ORDER ENTRY PROCEDURE   The process of capturing the name, address, item, dollars, and key for a transaction, and connecting it to electronic data which then triggers creation of a picking document, a billing document, and usually the effect of that transaction upon inventory and inventory control.

ORDER FORM   Key to good direct mail. What the customer is to fill in per your direction

ORDER MARGIN   The sum represented by the differential between all costs (except promotion) and the selling price (after returns.)

OUTSIDE LIST MANAGER   See List Manager.

OVERLAYS   The authorized use of a list to add information and data, through match identification, by tagging to another list. The transfer can be demographics, or a telephone number, or a job function, even psychographic data on buying habits.

OWNERS   The owners of mail order response lists are the operators of mail response companies. They "own" the customer and inquiry lists that they offer on the list rental market. All such proprietary lists must be "cleared" by such owners or their agents to be rented for one-time mailing by others.

PACKAGE   The mailing piece as placed in the mailstream; can be a package to fulfill a request for information.

PACKAGE INSERTS   Mail response offers by outside operators placed in current packages being sent to most recent customers of a given mail order firm.

PACKAGE TEST   A test of two or more packages, one of which should be the current "standard" to determine which package to mail on any continuation.

PAID CIRCULATION   Subscribers to a magazine who pay for the privilege of receiving the publication.

PANDERING LIST   List of individuals who have reported receipt of sexually offensive literature to the USPS to insure that the same mailer cannot, except by facing criminal charges, mail similar matter to them again.

PANEL   A group of people of similar interests used for research purposes. (See also Focus Research.)

PASS-ALONG EFFECT   Mailings to businesses may benefit from this effect as executives tend to forward particulary interesting mail to their associates. Business catalog mailers seek to harness this effect by printing a group of germane titles on the cover as a suggested routing for such pass-along readership.

PASSING A FILE   The process of reading a file sequentially by computer to select and/or copy specific data.

PAYMENT, METHOD OF   A record or tag showing how a customer paid for a purchase (by check or credit card or money order). Available as a selection factor on a number of response lists.

PAYMENT RATE   The percentage of respondents who buy on credit or take a trial on credit and who then pay.

PEEL-OFF LABELS   See Labels.

PENETRATION   The relationship between the number of names on a segment of a customer file and the universe available for that segment expressed as a percentage or ratio—that is, 2 percent or 1 in 50.

PENETRATION ANALYSIS   A study made of the "share of market" held by a given mailer within various universes by classification or other demographic characteristics. For business mailers, the chief means to ascertain which markets by SIC and number of employees are most successfully penetrated in order to prospect more efficiently.

PERIODICAL   Lists of recipients of printed material mailed to them on a regular or periodical cycle; primarily magazines and newsletters.

PERIPHERAL   Peripheral list thinking is the creation of a variant kind of audience from that specified. For example: To the parents of College Student or High School Student X; titling to Mrs. X from a list of doctors by name and address at home; addressing a child by name, to attract the eye of the parent; inviting the new neighbors to view a new car at a given address.

PERSONALIZATION   A means to add the name of the individual to a mailing piece; or the use of a computer to input data about the psychographics of the customer being addressed. The wave of the future will see entire catalogs printed and selectively bound to match personal data identification.

PIECE RATE   Third class mail breaks into two main streams, third class bulk (for discounts) and third class piece rate. For the price of a first class stamp, a piece weighing up to $3\frac{1}{2}$ ounces may be placed in the mail stream without any prior sortation. This charge is currently over 40 percent greater than the unit charge for third class bulk mail.

PHONE LIST   See Telephone List.

POLITICAL LISTS   There are two main forms of political lists, voter registration files mailed primarily during political campaigns, and fundraising files of donors to political causes of different hues.

POSITIVE OPTION   A book club on positive option mails mainly offers of new selections to its membership and solicits orders as a catalog mailer might. There is no obligation to buy.

POSTAGE REFUND   A sum returned to a mailer by an owner or manager for nondeliverables exceeding a stipulated guarantee.

PRECLEARANCE   The act of getting clearance on a rental before sending in the order.

PROJECTED ROLLOUT RESPONSE   Based on test results, the response anticipated from a large continuation or program.

PREMIUM (PREMIUM BUYER)   An addition of a gift to an offer to induce greater responses. Usually a buyer who responds may keep the premium, which raises the cost per completed sale, even if the product ordered is subsequently returned or cancelled.

PRESORT   The USPS offers discounts for those who prepare the mail for direct delivery to post offices or to carriers at post offices. While little known, over half of all for-profit third class bulk mail is now mailed at carrier-route presort discount rates.

PRICE LINING   Price lining in retail parlance means choosing either even dollars or selected endings in cents ($11.95) to obtain best sales results. In direct mail parlance price lining means testing a group of prices through a grid test to permit the buying public to select for the operator the one price producing the most bottom-line profit.

PRINTOUT   A copy on a sheet listing of a list, or of some selected data on a list such as matched pairs indicating duplication from a merge–purge, or an array of largest buyers or donors.

PRIORITY   For a continuation, arranging the tested lists and list segments in descending order on the basis of number of responses, or number of dollars of sales per thousand pieces mailed. For political mail, a special next day delivery service offered by the USPS.

PRIOR LIST SUPPRESS   Utilization of prior data to remove matching data from a new run and thus reduce the payment for the list data as used.

PROFESSIONALS   Every professional with a telephone listing is available from major business compilers. There are some thirty classifications from architects to veterinarians. A fair-sized number can be reached at home addresses. A new list on the market based on a classified list of doctors (MDs) with phones has verified addresses and phone numbers of over 100,000 of some 190,000 physicians in private practice.

PROFESSIONALS, OFFICES OF   See Offices.

PROMOTIONAL LIST   See Cost in the Mail.

PROSPECT LIST   A list owned by others used to obtain new customers, subscribers, donors, or requesters.

PROSPECTING   Mailings made to lists, usually untried, owned by others.

PROTECTED MAILING DATE   A time, usually one or two weeks prior and one or two weeks after the protected mail date for a large quantity of names, in which the list owner guarantees no competitive offer will be given access to the list.

PSEUDOCARRIER ROUTES   The USPS Carrier Route (CRIS) Tape lists millions of bits of data to delineate 160,000 individual carrier routes. Major consumer compilers break up the areas not serviced by individual carriers into 240,000 extra pseudocarrier routes for marketing penetration selection or omission.

PSEUDO SICs   The United States Department of Commerce Standard Industrial Classification utilizes some 1000 four-digit designations. By adding a fifth character to this, major compilers now provide 4,600 SIC classifications with greater specificity. When the phone companies provide all of their classified listings, the number of different classifications for selection can total over 8,500. A six-digit SIC system is now under construction by the joint efforts of Dun & Bradstreet and Data Base America. This expanded classification will be published under the aegis of the DMA in 1988.

PSYCHOGRAPHICS   The lifestyle characteristics or qualities of individuals on a list which indicate living styles; purchase, reading and hobby habits; opinions, mores, and social roles. The affinity of such psychographics are matched as closely as possible to a specific offer.

PUBLISHER'S LETTER   See Lift Letter.

PULL   Usually refers to the proportion of response by mail or phone to a given promotional activity.

PURGE   The act of identifying and eliminating duplicate or undesirable names from a mailing list or from a file of names.

PYRAMIDING   See Continuation.

QUALIFICATION SORTATION   Third class bulk mail sorted to meet USPS qualification for three different mail streams.

QUALIFIED LEADS   Names and addresses of individuals who have taken a positive action to indicate genuine interest in a given type of offer.

QUANTITY PRICING   Pricing, usually by compilers, offering price breaks for varying list quantities rented over a period of a year.

QUOTE, QUOTATION   A price transmitted to a prospective mailer before running of a list order requiring special processing.

RATE OF RESPONSE   See Response Rate.

RECENCY   The group of names on a file with the most recent purchase or activity.

RECORD   A name and address entry on a file.

RECORD LAYOUT   A description covering the entire record length to denote where on a tape each part (or field) of the record appears such as name, local address, city, state, zip, and other relevant data.

RECORD LENGTH   The number of characters occupied by each record on a file.

REFORMATTING   Changing a computerized tape list to a different tape layout.

REFUND   For a list, return of part of payment due to shortage in count, or excessive nondeliverables (over the guarantee). For a product sold by mail, a complete (usually) return of the purchase price if an item is returned in good condition. Refunds of style merchandise normally run 10 percent or more, and their costs are built into the cost per completed sale.

REGISTRATION LIST   See Telephone, Car, Driver's License, Voters Lists. Some business lists are constructed from state or local political division registration data.

REGRESSION ANALYSIS   A statistical means to improve the predictability of response based on an analysis of multiple stratified relationships within a file.

RENTAL   An agreement to utilize a list for one-time mailing.

REPEAT BUYER   See Multiple Buyer.

REPEAT MAILING   Mailing of the same or very similar packages to a list for the second time.

RESIDENT LIST   See Occupant List.

RESPONSE RATE   The percentage of responses received from a given promotional effort.

RESTRICTIONS   Limitations on rental use placed on a list by its owner or manager.

RETAILING   In the business field there are over 2 million retailers with telephones and several hundred thousand without. They are selectable by over eighty different specialized product lines. Catalogs are a special form of retailing in which the specialty store and its product line is brought to the home of the consumer rather than the consumer physically going to and entering the store.

RETURN CARD   A postage paid business return card (BRC).

RETURN OF LISTS   Lists are printed to order. There is no way they can be utilized by the owner. When list orders are cancelled after being run, negotiation for a run charge is required.

RETURN ON INVESTMENT (R.O.I.)   In direct response, the return on investment is one of the main ways to measure the effectiveness and profitability of any given promotional effort. Since response starts very quickly, dollars from an effort often permit multiple use of a given investment as the charges against that investment are being paid off, providing a particularly attractive "return" on the original dollars put to risk.

RETURN POSTAGE GUARANTEED   Third class bulk mail so marked, if undeliverable, will be returned, for a fee.

RF$USISM   Acronym covering major selection availabilities on major direct mail sold customer files: R = recency; F = frequency; $US = dollars (highest, periodic, total); I = item or service purchased; S = source of initial order (not subsequent mailings by age on file); M = Method of payment. Large operations like Sears, Roebuck and Co. utilize over 160 "cells" based on this acronym.

RIDE-ALONG   A form of co-op mailing in which outside offers are accepted to accompany the cold-prospecting mailing the ride-along provides.

ROLLOUT   A continuation mailing after a successful test made to a full list or to a substantially larger portion of a list.

ROYALTY   See List Royalty.

RUN CHARGE   A charge by a list owner for names produced for a renter but not used. On a list order negotiated for an 85 percent payment, irrespective of the names utilized, the fee per thousand for the run charge, determined by the list owner, is billed for the balance or for 15 percent in this instance.

SALES TAX   Current attempts by many state governments to impose a tax on goods sold via mail in their jurisdictions.

SALTING—VIA SEEDS, DUMMIES OR DECOYS   Names with special characteristics added to a list for protection and identification purposes.

SAMPLE MAILING PIECE   Owners or managers of mail response lists for protection of their lists, require presentation of a sample of what is to be mailed for review and clearance or rejection. Rough copy occasionally is acceptable.

SAMPLE SIZE   See Test Sample.

SCF   Sectional Center Facility: the first three digits of the zip code.

SCIENTISTS   Just as there are different classifications of engineers available in list form, so there are lists of scientists available by their field of specialization from bio-chemists to physicists, from data system operators to geologists. Most such data comes from rosters of associations or from magazines.

SCRATCHING   The term used to describe "wiping out" or erasing data from a magnetic tape.

SCREEN   The use of an outside list (based on credit, income, deliverability, zip code selection) to suppress records on a list to be mailed.

SEASONALITY   Selection of time of year; also influence of timing (seasonality) on response rates.

SECOND CLASS   Second class mail in the postal rate system covers periodicals.

SECTIONAL CENTER FACILITY   The first three digits of zip code. Some 900 have been assigned by the USPS.

SEED   A dummy or decoy name inserted into a list.

SEGMENT   A portion of a list or file selected on the basis of a special set of characteristics.

SEGMENTATION   The process of segregating or selecting specific records from a list with specific criteria.

SELECTION   The process of obtaining from a list, file, or databank only those records with desired criteria. Often one select is within another, as $50 buyers, female, who have purchased in the last six months.

SELECTION CHARGE   A fee above the basic cost of the list for a given selection.

SELECTION CRITERIA   The options for segmenting a list open to a mailer.

SELF-MAILER   All mail can be divided into three types: envelope mail, "flats," (large pieces requiring hand rather than machine handling) and "self-mailers" cards (on card stock) or folded pieces of paper placed in the mail stream without an outside carrier. The majority of catalogs are mailed without an envelope as "self-mailers," or "flats."

SELF-STANDING STUFFERS   Promotional printed pieces delivered as part of a daily or Sunday newspaper.

SENIOR CITIZENS   Lists of older individuals past a specific age. Lists are available for over-50, 55, 60, 65 year olds.

SEQUENCE   See List Sequence.

SERVICE BUREAU   See Computer Service Bureau.

SET-UP CHARGE   A flat charge assessed on some lists in addition to the cost per thousand.

SEX   This is now a significant selection factor in business lists as well as on consumer files. Female lists in business include over 30,000 top female executives in big business, over 300,000 working women subscribe to a magazine, over 1,500,000 owners of individual Keough investment plans.

SHIPPING TIME   The approximate number of days required for production of a list order.

SIC   Standard Industrial Classification, a system to provide a pigeonhole for every type of business, institution, and office of a professional.

SIC COUNT   A count of the number of records available by two, three, four, or five-digit classification.

SIGNIFICANT DIFFERENCE   In mathematical terms, a difference between tests of two or more variables, which is sufficient to indicate that similar mailings will produce the same or similar differentiation. The significant difference varies with the confidence level desired. Most direct-mail penetration utilizes a 95 percent confidence level wherein 95 times out of 100 the results found in the test will come close to duplicating on a retest or combination. It is fair to state that most mailers do not understand this term or its significance.

SINGLE-FAMILY HOUSEHOLD   Private homes, housing only one household, as distinct from multiple-family residences.

SINGLES   One or single-person households. Also refers to lists of unmarried adults usually for social linking.

SORTING   A computerized process to change the given sequence of a list to a different sequence or to interfile two or more lists.

SOURCE CODE   A key or code identifier on a list or list segment.

SPACE One of the major producers of new mail order buyers is mail order advertising in newspapers, magazines, and self-standing stuffers. Space ads, electronic media, and direct mail are the major media utilized for prospecting for new customers.

SPACE BUYER The media buyer (usually at an advertising agency) who places print mail order advertising.

SPACE SOLD RECORDS Any record on a house file (customers, inquirers, catalog requests) which has been generated through advertising space placed in printed publications.

SPECIFIC LIST SOURCE Original source material for a compiled file.

SPECIFIER An elusive list desideration, particularly at larger businesses, the name of the individual who can specify or purchase a product or service. In many cases the specifier is not the individual who enters the order.

SPANISH LISTS Hispanics may in a few years exceed Blacks as the major ethnic minority in America. Lists based on surname selects are available to reach this market.

SPECIFIC ORDER DECOY A seed or dummy inserted in the output of a list order for that order only. The specific seed, which identifies the order, is usually in addition to list protection decoys in the same list.

SPLIT RUN Printing of two or more variants of a promotional ad run on an Nth or AB split through the entire edition; use of geographical segments of a publication for testing of variants.

SPLIT TEST A mailing in which two or more variants are tested simultaneously. (See also Grid Testing.)

SRDS Standard Rate & Data Service, which prints a *Rates and Data* book covering basic information on over 20,000 mailing lists.

STANDARD INDUSTRIAL CLASSIFICATION A U.S. Dept. of Commerce assigned four-digit number by function and product for every U.S. business, institution, and office of a professional. There are over 1000 such codes. A few major business list compilers can provide additional 4,600 fifth-digit classifications for more precise target marketing.

STANDARD METROPOLITAN STATISTICAL AREA (SMSA) Major compilers provide estimated proportions of a national list based on metropolitan area coverage.

STATE COUNT Publication of list counts for each state. Usually as part of a list card.

STATEMENT STUFFER See Billing Stuffer.

STORAGE   A data processing term indicating the volume of name and address and attached data which can be stored for future use on a given computer or system.

STRATIFICATION   The capacity to offer demographic segmentation on a list; the adding of such demographics to a customer file.

STUDENT LISTS   A number of compilers provide lists of students. For college students, both home and school addresses are available. For high school students, home addresses for juniors and seniors are available.

STUFFER   A short form for self-standing stuffer, a form of promotion piece delivered with daily and Sunday newspapers.

SUBBLOCK   Along with enumeration districts, the smallest geographical segment of the country for which the U.S. Census Bureau provides demographic data.

SUBSCRIBER   A recipient of a magazine who has paid for the privilege.

SUPPRESS FILES   Files entered into a merge–purge for the express purpose of removing any record that matches before mailing.

SUPPRESSION   Utilization of data on one or more files to remove any duplication of specific names that the mailer wishes to be removed before mailing.

SUPPRESSION OF PREVIOUS USAGE   This can be accomplished by using the previous usage or stat tab match codes of the records used as a suppress file. Unduplication can also be assured through fifth digit pulls, first digit of name pulls, or actual tagging of each prior record used.

SUPPRESSION OF SUBSCRIBERS   The use of the subscriber file to suppress its current readers from rental lists prior to mailing.

SURNAME SELECTION   For ethnic selection, the surname is a reasonable method for selection of such easily identifiable groups as Irish, Italian (and hence Catholic), Jews and Spanish (actually Spanish-sounding names). Specialists have extended this type of coding to more esoteric groups such as German, English, Scotch, and Scandinavian.

SUSPECT   A somewhat qualified cold prospect, one more likely to order than the cold prospect. In some two-step operations, a name given the initial inquirer when only one in X can be expected to convert.

SWEEPSTAKES LISTS (SWEEPS)   Responses, the majority of them nonbuyers, to a sweepstakes offer.

SYNDICATION   A mailing for a specialized offer prepared by a company having inventory or access to inventory which is mailed to its customer list by a company having nothing to do with the product except the use of its name to increase response. Oil company and utility and bank card stuffers are good examples. Some syndicated offers are so powerful that they can be successful as solo mailings.

TAGGING   The process of tagging information to a list. Can be the transfer of data or control information for usage and unduplication.

TAPE   Refers to magnetic tape, the principal means of recording, storing and retrieving data for computerized mailing list operations.

TAPE CONVERSION   Converting hard copy data to magnetic tape.

TAPE DENSITY   The number of bits of data packed into one inch of magnetic tape (BPI). The usual densities today are 1600 BPI and 6250 BPI.

TAPE DUMP   A printout, character by character, of a few hundred records of a tape sent along with the tape and its layout as a checking copy.

TAPE FORMAT (OR LAYOUT)   The location of each field, character by character, of each record on a list on tape.

TAPE REEL   The medium on which data for computer addressing or merge-purging is handled.

TARGET MARKET   The ideal audience for a mailing effort. Usually defined in psychographic and demographic terms.

TEASER   A bit of introductory copy, usually on the outside envelope, to induce the recipient to open the envelope and find out more.

TELEMARKETING   The use of the telephone to increase sales to customers, inquiries, catalog requestors. Phoning to prospects who already have a relationship to the caller.

TELEPHONE HOUSEHOLD   A household with a listed phone number. (Random access calling can ring unlisted and nonpublished numbers).

TELEPHONE HOUSEHOLDS   Those households with phones listed in alphabetic phone books (now some 57 million).

TELEPHONE LIST   A list of consumers (usually) or establishments compiled with phone numbers from published phone directories.

TELEPHONE PREFERENCE SERVICE   A program instituted in 1985 by the DMA to provide consumers a means to have their names removed from the calling lists of teleprospectors.

TELEPHONE USE RESTRICTION   A large number of owners of mail order lists will not permit their customers to be called by strangers by phone.

TELEPROSPECTING   Cold canvassing of telephone households or telephone nonhouseholds by personal phone calls. (Not to be confused with telemarketing which pertains to calls made to customers or inquirers.)

TELEPROSPECTING LIST   A list of prospects with phones used for telephonic (cold calling) prospecting.

TEST CAMPAIGN   Mailings of test pieces to a number of outside lists to establish a bank for continuation mailings; must not be to only one list which is a "continuous series of one experiment."

TEST QUANTITY   A test mailing of a sufficiently large number of names from a list to enable the mailer to evaluate the responsiveness of the list. The test quantity must satisfy three conditions. It must be a reasonably random sample of the universe, it must be large enough to provide breakeven response for the mailer, and it must provide enough response for statistical validity. Most mailers require fifty to one-hundred responses. *Note:* The size of the test quantity has *nothing* to do with the size of the list.

THIRD CLASS MAIL   Over 85 percent of mail carrying advertising or promotional material utilizes third class postage which costs considerably less than first class.

THIRD CLASS PERMITS   There are now over 750,000 establishments with permit numbers entitling them to mail via third class bulk mail. Some 250,000 are for nonprofits; 500,000 and more are issued to for-profit establishments. This is roughly 1 of every 10 establishments in the United States!

THIRD CLASS PRE-SORT   See Presort.

THIRD PARTY ENDORSEMENT   A mailing made for the joint benefit of an outside mailer and a company over the company's customer file, with the express imprimatur of the company. (Example: Brittanica mailing the Farm Journal list with an offer ostensibly from the publication to its subscribers.)

THREE-DIGIT ZIP   The first three digits of a five-digit zip code denoting a given SCF (sectional center facility) of the USPS.

THREE-LINE ADDRESS   For consumer mail, a conventional home or household address of an individual; for business mail, the name and address of an establishment, without the name of an individual.

TIME BUYER   The media buyer (usually at a specialized agency for direct response electronic media) who "buys" time periods and spots for direct response radio or video promotion.

TIME ZONE SEQUENCING   Providing lists with phones for telemarketing or teleprospecting by time zones for most productive calling.

TIMING   See Seasonality.

TITLE ADDRESSING   Utilizing the title or function at a business, or adding a title to a business address rather than addressing to a specific person by name.

TOKEN   In direct-mail sweepstakes packages, a paper piece to be punched out and placed in one of two slots, usually "yes" or "no." It is a means to get involvement on the part of the prospect.

TOWN MARKERS   Asterisks printed on mailing labels at the end of geographical areas by the computer, usually one for each town, two for each five-digit zip code, three for each three-digit zip code sectional center facility.

TRACK RECORD   What a given list or list segment has done for given mailers in the past.

TRADE SHOW REGISTRANTS   Registrants published by the Trade Show Operations; those registrants who stopped at a given booth and signed up to receive additional information or a sales call; those individuals or executives assigned by their companies to operate the booth or booths.

TRIALS   Individuals who ordered a short-term subscription to a magazine or newsletter, or continuity program. In list rental parlance, trials are not equal to those that convert to customer status.

TRUNCATION   Dropping the end of words or names to fit an address line into thirty characters for four-across cheshire addressing.

TURNOVER RATE   The number of times within a year that a list is or can be rented.

TYPE AND SCAN   A computerized data entry system that utilizes data typed by typewriter with a special font that is then optically scanned to magnetic tape.

TWO-STEP   See Inquiries.

UNCOLLECTIBLES   See Bad Debt.

UNDELIVERABLES   A nixie—a piece returned as not being deliverable.

UNIQUE ZIP CODE   A five-digit zip code assigned by the USPS to a company or organization to expedite delivery of its large volume of incoming letter mail. With the advent of zip + 4 a large number of businesses and institutions will have their own unique zip code.

UNIVERSE   The total names and addresses in a given list or segment.

UPDATING   The process of maintaining and keeping a file current, usually on a scheduled basis.

UPS   The initials of the United Parcel Service, a major supplier of small package delivery (with tracing capabilities) of mailing list tapes and labels.

UPSCALE LIST   A generic description of a list of affluents. Can be mail-responsive or compiled.

U.S. BUSINESS UNIVERSE   A database containing the names and addresses of virtually every business, institution, and office of a professional in the United States. The known total is 9.0 million. Some 8.8 million are available through commercially available sources.

USAGE HISTORY   A listing of utilization by mailers or managers or brokers of a given list.

UTILITIES   One of the major groupings of business lists. Often included with mining, contracting, manufacturing, and transportation as part of the "industrial complex" of America. (This does not include wholesaling, retailing, finance, or services.)

VALIDATION MAILING   A second modest mailing to confirm initial test results prior to making a large continuation or rollout.

VARIABLE LENGTH RECORD   A means of packing characters on a name and address record so as to eliminate blank spaces. For most rental work such lists must then be reformatted to fixed fields, in which each field whether filled or unfilled occupies the same numerical positions on a tape.

VARIABLES (CRITERIA)   Identifiable and selectable characteristics that can be tested for mailing purposes.

VENDORS   Suppliers of any facet of direct-response advertising. Includes lists, creative, printing, marketing, computerization, merge–purge, fulfillment.

VOLUME DISCOUNT   A scheduled discount for volume buyers of a given compiled list.

VOTERS REGISTRATION LISTS   Lists utilized to add multiple family members as well as age data to compiled consumer files.

WALLET FLAP ENVELOPE   A special BRE that utilizes the inside of a large flap to serve as the order form.

WARRANTEE LISTS   Buyers who mail in warrantee cards identifying the particular product and its type, with or without additional demographic data.

WATS   The initials stand for Wide Area Telephone Service. Almost all direct mail operators selling to consumers as well as to businesses provide WATS for free inbound telephone communication for their customers. Many also buy area coverage for outbound WATS.

WEIGHTING For evaluation of customer lists, a means to apply values to the RF$UISM data for each cell. (For large lists this is better done by a computer regression analysis.) For merge–purge, a means to apply a form of mathematical analysis to each component for unduplicating.

WHITE MAIL Mail that comes in from customers without a purchase order form or other identification. It can include complaints, commendations, names of friends, "hate" mail, orders, checks, even cash. A very important part of every direct-mail operation.

WHOLESALER (OR RE-SELLER) A merchandiser of lists compiled or owned by others, usually working with compiled lists mainly covering a local area. Differentiated from a broker by type of list and coverage.

WINDOW ENVELOPE An envelope produced with one or more openings, usually glassine covered, through which the address of a direct-mail piece shows along with some color or teaser copy, if there are two areas. The window envelope is preferred for computer-addressed personalized mail which can be folded to show the address and thus not need a separate addressing on the envelope.

WORD PROCESSOR A typewriter with a memory utilized to produce individualized letters; also useful in updating of smaller mailing lists.

WORKING WOMEN A relatively new selection factor for mailers. Lists may be compiled (as women executives of S & P major companies) or mail order responsive (as paid subscribers to *Working Women* magazine).

YIELD The count anticipated from a computer inquiry; the responses received from a promotional effort, the mailable totals from a merge-purge.

YUPPIES A term describing young upwardly mobile professional people.

ZIP CODE One of 36,000 areas in the country denoted by a five-digit numerical code.

ZIP CODE COUNT The number of names in each zip code on a given mailing list.

ZIP CODE OMISSION The use of a zip code suppress file to eliminate all records from a mailing in given zips.

ZIP + 4 CODE The designation by the USPS for the nine-digit zip coding structure.

ZIP STRING Compilers can provide multiple selections merged into one zip code string to avoid minimums. In the SIC system, each record can be individually coded and counted so response can be calculated.

Index